CONTENTS

SCOTLAND

Aberdeen, Banff & Moray 307
Argyll & Bute 311
Ayrshire & Arran 315
Borders......................................318
Dumfries & Galloway 321
Dunbartonshire 325
Dundee & Angus 326
Edinburgh & Lothians 327
Fife 334

Glasgow & District 336
Highlands (North)....................339
Highlands (Mid) 340
Highlands (South) 341
Lanarkshire..............................346
Perth & Kinross........................347
Stirling & The Trossachs 351
Scottish Islands 353

WALES

Anglesey & Gwynedd 359
North Wales 362
Carmarthenshire 368
Ceredigion 369

Pembrokeshire 370
Powys.......................................373
South Wales 377

REPUBLIC OF IRELAND......380

Special Welcome Supplements

Non-Smoking 381
Special Diets 384
Disabled 386

ENGLAND and WALES Counties

NORTH WALES
1. Denbighshire
2. Flintshire
3. Wrexham

SOUTH WALES
4. Swansea
5. Neath and Port Talbot
6. Bridgend
7. Rhondda Cynon Taff
8. Merthyr Tydfil
9. Vale of Glamorgan
10. Cardiff
11. Caerphilly
12. Blaenau Gwent
13. Torfaen
14. Newport
15. Monmouthshire

©MAPS IN MINUTES™ 2003

Please mention Bed & Breakfast Stops when enquiring

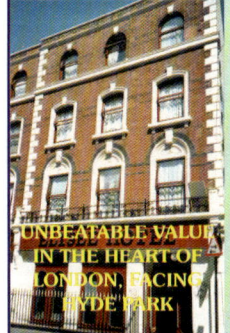

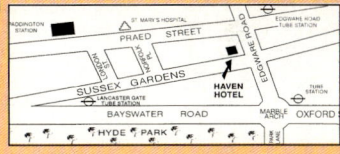

8

Tranquil welcoming atmosphere on attractive arable farm. Set well back off A1 giving quiet, peaceful seclusion yet within easy reach of the RSPB, the Shuttleworth Collection, the Greensand Ridge Walk, Grafham Water and Woburn Abbey. Cambridge 22 miles, London 50 miles.

All rooms have tea/coffee making facilities, most have bathroom en suite and two are on the ground floor.
There is a separate guests' sitting room with TV. Family room.
Dogs welcome by arrangement. No smoking. Most guests return!

Prices from £30 per person per night.

Mrs M. Codd, Highfield Farm, Tempsford Road, Sandy, Bedfordshire SG19 2AQ
Tel: 01767 682332; Fax: 01767 692503
e-mail: margaret@highfield-farm.co.uk

GUESTACCOM "GOOD ROOM" AWARD.
BEST ETC B&B REGIONAL WINNER FOR EASTERN COUNTIES.

Netherton Hotel

96 St Leonards Road, Windsor SL4 3DA
Tel: 01753 855508 • Fax: 01753 621267

This recently refurbished hotel offers a comfortable and friendly atmosphere. All rooms are en suite, with colour TV, direct-dial telephone, and tea/coffee making facilities. Also available are hairdryers and ironing facilities. There is a TV lounge for guests' use. Full English breakfast. We have a private car park and are easy to find. Children welcome.

- Walking distance to Windsor Castle, town centre, train stations and Legoland is only one mile away.
- Central London can be reached in 35 minutes by train.
- M4 only two miles, Heathrow seven miles.

e-mail: netherton@btconnect.com

Mitchell's of Chester Guest House

28 Hough Green, Chester CH4 8JQ

Tel: 01244 679004
Fax: 01244 659567
e-mail: mitoches@dialstart.net
www.mitchellsofchester.com

This elegantly restored Victorian family home is set on the south side of Chester, on a bus route to the city centre. Guest bedrooms have been furnished in period style, with fully equipped shower room and toilet, central heating, TV, refreshment tray and other thoughtful extras. An extensive breakfast menu is served in the elegant dining room, and the guest lounge overlooks the well-maintained garden.

The historic city of Chester is ideally placed for touring Wales and the many attractions of the North West of England.

A homely, friendly, peaceful and comfortable country retreat just over the Welsh border, ideally situated for exploring the historic City of Chester under seven miles away. Easy access to all routes (five minutes from the A55) makes this an ideal base for touring North Wales, West Cheshire and North Shropshire.

Beryl and John, previous winners of a Prince of Wales' Award, will offer you warm hospitality and invite you into their home, which has recently been renovated and furnished to a high standard. A double room and a twin room are available, overlooking open countryside. Tea/coffee making facilities, TV, shared private bathroom with bath and shower, central heating, off-road parking, pleasant gardens. There are two pubs within the village offering excellent cuisine. Non-smoking.

Bed and Full English Breakfast from £20 per person, with reductions for weekly stays. Please send or telephone for our brochure.

Green Cottage
The Green, Higher Kinnerton, Chester CH4 9BZ
Tel & Fax: 01244 660137
★★★ **Guest House**

ROCKLANDS

"Rocklands" is situated overlooking part of Cornwall's superb coastline and enjoys uninterrupted sea views. The Lizard is well known for its lovely picturesque scenery, coastal walks and enchanting coves and beaches, as well as the famous Serpentine Stone which is quarried and sold locally. Open Easter to October. Generations of the Hill family have been catering for visitors on the Lizard since the 1850s. Three bedrooms with sea views, two en suite, tea/coffee making facilities and electric heaters; sittingroom with TV and video; sun lounge; diningroom with separate tables. Children and well trained pets welcome.

Bed and Breakfast £23pppn, en suite £25pppn; reductions for children under 10 years.

Mrs D. J. Hill, "Rocklands", The Lizard, Near Helston TR12 7NX • Tel: 01326 290339

Rosemullion Hotel

Gyllyngvase Hill, Falmouth, Cornwall TR11 4DF
Tel: 01326 314690 • Fax: 01326 210098

AA

Built as a gentleman's residence in the latter part of the 19th century, Rosemullion Hotel offers you a holiday that is every bit as distinctive as its Tudor appearance. Rosemullion is a house of great character and charm, appealing strongly to the discerning guest. The emphasis is very much on that rarest of commodities in today's world - *peace*. *That is why we do not cater for children and do not have a bar of our own.*

A family-owned hotel continually being refurbished and updated to first-class accommodation. Fully centrally heated with 13 bedrooms, some with glorious views over the bay. Large parking area. Non-Smoking.

Room & Breakfast £23.50 to £27.50 per person incl. of VAT.

e-mail: gail@rosemullionhotel.demon.co.uk • website: www.SmoothHound.co.uk/hotels/rosemullion.html

The Copse is situated in peaceful, unspoilt countryside midway between Plymouth and Looe. The beaches and the golf course at Whitsand Bay are two miles away. We offer en suite rooms with colour television and drinks-making facilities. The Copse is an ideal base for touring Cornwall and South Devon, and visiting the Eden Project. Non-smoking. Regret, no pets.

Mrs S.M. Hoskin, The Copse, St Winnolls, Polbathic, Torpoint PL11 3DX Tel: 01503 230205

£18 to £22 per person per night

Publisher's Note

While every effort is made to ensure accuracy, we regret that FHG Publications cannot accept responsibility for errors, omissions or misrepresentations in our entries or any consequences thereof. Prices in particular should be checked because we go to press early. We will follow up complaints but cannot act as arbiters or agents for either party.

Ambleside Lodge

Heart of the English Lake District. *This elegant Lakeland home, dating from the 19th century, has been sympathetically converted and now offers a high standard of accommodation. All bedrooms are en suite, with colour TV, tea/coffee making facilities and delightful views. The Premier suites and king-size four-poster rooms with jacuzzi spa baths offer relaxation and indulgence. Leisure facilities available at a private club just 5 minutes' drive away include swimming pool, sauna, steam room, squash, gym and beauty salon.*

www.ambleside-lodge.com

AMBLESIDE LODGE, ROTHAY ROAD, AMBLESIDE, CUMBRIA LA22 0EJ
015394 31681 • Fax: 015394 34547 • e-mail: enquiries@ambleside-lodge.com

---

Cherry Trees GUEST HOUSE
16 Eskin Street, Keswick CA12 4DQ

Comfortable, warm and spacious Victorian guesthouse. Situated within easy access of town centre, lake and fells. Tastefully furnished with king-sized beds!! All double and twin rooms en suite, single room has private facilities. All have colour TV, clock/ radio, hairdryer, tea/coffee making facilities and direct dial telephones. Excellent freshly prepared food and home made jams and marmalades. Packed lunches. Secure cycle store. Non-smoking. B&B from £23 - £28.   **Tel: 017687 71048**

e-mail: cherry.trees@virgin.net • website: www.cherrytrees-keswick.co.uk

---

Craigburn Farmhouse
Catlowdy, Longtown, Carlisle CA6 5QP
Tel: 01228 577214 • Fax: 01228 577014

A warm welcome awaits you at our family-run guest house. The house has been tastefully modernised, all six bedrooms having central heating, en suite, colour TV and tea/coffee making facilities. Our small farmhouse restaurant serves traditional roast Carvery dinners on Saturday evening and Sunday lunchtimes, with homemade sweets our speciality. A selection of wines is available and we also keep a small well-stocked bar. Ideal stopover to and from Scotland and Northern Ireland. We look forward to meeting you.

e-mail: louiselawson@hotmail.com
website: www.craigburnfarmhouse.co.uk

The Dower House

Lovely old house, quiet and peaceful, stands on an elevation overlooking Lake Windermere, with one of the most beautiful views in all Lakeland. Its setting within the 100-acre Wray Castle estate (National Trust), with direct access to the Lake, makes it an ideal base for walking and touring. Hawkshead and Ambleside are about ten minutes' drive and have numerous old inns and restaurants. Ample car parking; prefer dogs to sleep in the car. Children over five years welcome.

Wray Castle, Ambleside
Cumbria LA22 0JA
Tel: 015394 33211

Bed and Breakfast from £28.00
Optional Evening Meal from £14.50
Open all year round

The Ferndale Hotel

Lake Road, Ambleside, Cumbria LA22 0DB
Tel: 015394 32207
e-mail: info@ferndalehotel.com
website: www.ferndalehotel.com

The Ferndale Hotel is a small, family-run Hotel where you will find a warm, friendly welcome and personal attention at all times. Offering excellent accommodation with good home cooked English or Vegetarian breakfast. Our 10 attractive bedrooms have all been individually decorated and furnished, each with full en suite facilities, colour television and tea/coffee making tray. Full central heating throughout, several rooms having views of the fells, and including ground floor bedrooms. The Ferndale is open all year round with a car park, is licensed, offers packed lunches, hair dryer, clothes/boot drying and ironing facilities. A wide choice of places to dine, within minutes' walking distance, ranging from excellent pub food to superb restaurants of many varied cuisines will complete your day.

Bed and Breakfast £24.00 - £26.00 pppn. Weekly £155 - £165 pp. **Please phone for brochure.**

Holly-Wood Guesthouse

ETC ◆◆◆◆

Holly Road, Windermere, Cumbria LA23 2AF • Telephone 015394 42219

Holly-Wood is a beautiful Victorian house offering clean comfortable accommodation in a quiet position. A perfect location for your visit to the Lake District and within reach of the Dales and Morecambe Bay. Traditional or vegetarian breakfast.
Cosy residents' lounge. Bus and station transfer. En suite and budget rooms available, with central heating, tea/coffee making facilities, television and hairdryer. Low season and short break reductions. Bed & Breakfast from £18.50 to £29 per person.

No Smoking • No Pets
www.hollywoodaccommodation.co.uk

Langdale

Victorian town house, quietly situated, yet close to town, park, lake and fells. All rooms furnished to a very high standard, having quality en suite facilities, central heating, colour TV, tea/coffee making facilities throughout. Family, double or twin available. Enjoy a good home cooked English or vegetarian breakfast or our popular Continental breakfast. We have a non-smoking policy throughout the house.
We will ensure your stay is a pleasant one.
Bed and Breakfast from £21; Theatre Breaks.
Special three nights midweek/weekend breaks November to March.

Mrs S. Park, Langdale, 14 Leonard Street, Keswick CA12 4EL
Tel: 017687 73977 • www.langdaleguesthouse.co.uk

Rothay House is an attractive modern detached guest house set in pleasant gardens with views of the surrounding fells. All bedrooms are comfortable and well furnished with en suite facilities, colour TV, tea and coffee trays. Robin and Margaret combine 20 years quality hotel experience with a friendly atmosphere in clean attractive surroundings. The house is within easy walking distance of the village centre. Ambleside has a variety of interesting shops and restaurants and makes an ideal base for walking, touring or enjoying sailing, watersports and angling on Lake Windermere. Car not essential, but ample parking. Open all year. Children welcome; sorry, no pets. Strictly non-smoking. *Bed and Breakfast from £25 to £30; Winter Weekend Breaks available.*

ROTHAY HOUSE

Rothay Road, Ambleside,
Cumbria LA22 0EE
Tel/Fax: 015394 32434
e-mail: email@rothay-house.com
website: www.rothay-house.com

Stone Cottage

A charming cottage in the quiet village of Clifton, one mile from the Georgian market town of Ashbourne.

Each bedroom is furnished to a high standard with all rooms en suite, all with four-poster bed. TV and coffee making facilities.

A warm welcome is assured and a hearty breakfast in this delightful cottage. There is a large garden to relax in.

Ideal for visiting Chatsworth House, Haddon Hall, Dovedale, Carsington Waters and the theme park of Alton Towers.

B&B from £21 per person. Good country pubs nearby serving evening meals.

Enquiries to: *Mrs A. M. Whittle, Stone Cottage, Green Lane, Clifton, Ashbourne, Derbyshire DE6 2BL • Telephone: 01335 343377 Fax: 01335 347117 • E-mail: info@stone-cottage.fsnet.co.uk*

Our Bed & Breakfast accommodation is set in the heart of rural England in the beautiful undulating limestone landscape of the Peak District National Park. The farm is situated on our family farm, where the sheep and cattle are nurtured in easy harmony with the abundant wildlife and wild flowers. In the spring and summer months you can enjoy watching the new lambs and calves gambolling in the fields with their mothers and listen to the skylarks' song rising above the unspoilt countryside. It is set within a few miles of the nationally renowned beauty of the Manifold Valley and Dovedale. The bedrooms are comfortable, well-equipped and spacious; all have washbasins and tea/coffee facilities, and are en suite or have private bathrooms. Despite the peaceful rural location we are within easy reach of Alton Towers theme park as well as Chatsworth and the historic pottery works of Stoke-on-Trent. Nearby, the charming local market towns of Ashbourne, Leek and Buxton move at a gentler pace. From £27 pppn with reduced rates for children.

Details from Mrs M.A. Richardson, Throwley Hall Farm, Ilam, Near Ashbourne, Derbyshire DE6 2BB Tel: 01538 308202/308243 • e-mail: throwley@talk21.com OR throwley@btinternet.com website: www.throwleyhallfarm.co.uk

---

Ye Olde Cheshire Cheese Inn

How Lane, Castleton, Hope Valley S33 8WJ Telephone: 01433 620330 • Fax: 01433 621847 website: www.peakland.com/cheshirecheese • e-mail: kslack@btconnect.com

This delightful 17th century free house is situated in the heart of the Peak District and is an ideal base for walkers and climbers; other local attractions include cycling, swimming, gliding, horse riding and fishing. All bedrooms are en suite with colour TV and tea/coffee making facilities. A "Village Fayre" menu is available all day, all dishes home cooked in the traditional manner; there is also a selection of daily specials. Large car park. Full Fire Certificate. B&B from £25.00. All credit cards accepted.

SPECIAL GOLF PACKAGES ARRANGED

Cannon Croft
Tel & Fax: 01433 650005

Cannonfields, Hathersage, Hope Valley S32 1AG www.cannoncroft.fsbusiness.co.uk

Enjoy panoramic views from the conservatory of our Gold Award-winning B&B. Famous for our breakfasts – try the Sundancer eggs and whisky porridge for example. Flower arranger's garden with sun terrace. Recently refurbished en suite rooms have TV, hospitality tray, hairdryer and many extras. Non-smoking establishment. Private off-road parking and bike storage.

"There are no strangers here, just friends who have not yet met"

Holiday Which? Recommended 2003.

Double/twin en suite from £25pppn (based on 2 sharing).

Sandra & Mike Oates look forward to meeting you

Brambles

Set in beautiful, tranquil countryside, Brambles is a pretty, thatched cottage offering every comfort, superb views and a friendly welcome. There is a choice of en suite, twin, double or single rooms, all very comfortable and with colour TV and tea/coffee making facilities. Pretty garden available for relaxing in. Full English or Continental breakfast served. Evening meals available by prior arrangement. There are many interesting places to visit and wonderful walks for enthusiasts. B&B from £20 to £28 per person.

Woolcombe, Melbury Bubb, Dorchester DT2 0NJ • Tel: 01935 83672

Ferndown Guest House

A friendly welcome awaits you at Ferndown Guest House. A welcoming place to stay,it is family-run by Mark and Jean. Situated just two minutes' walk to the seafront and five minutes into town, it is the ideal place to stay in Weymouth. All rooms have washbasins, colour TV and tea and coffee making facilities. Some en suite rooms available. Visitors are welcome to use the lounge with colour TV. Open from April to October. Bed and Breakfast from £18.00.

Mark and Jean Mitchell, 47 Walpole Street, Weymouth DT4 7HQ (01305 775228) e-mail: jeanmitchel@amserve.com

Hemsworth Manor Farm
Witchampton, Wimborne BH21 5BN

Our lovely old Manor Farmhouse which is mentioned in the Domesday Book, is situated in an exceptionally peaceful location, yet is only half-an-hour's drive from Salisbury, Dorchester, Poole, Bournemouth and the New Forest. Hemsworth is a working family farm of nearly 800 acres, providing some lovely walks. The farm is mainly arable, but is also home to sheep, horses, ponies and various domestic pets. We have three fully equipped en suite bedrooms, all with colour TV. Separate lounge for guests' use. There are excellent pubs locally. Brochure available.

Tel: 01258 840216 • • Fax: 01258 841278

Kingfishers

Come to Kingfishers and relax on your large sunny balcony overlooking the river and gardens. Set in beautiful surroundings on the banks of the River Char, Kingfishers offers a secluded setting yet is only a short stroll to the beach and village amenities.
2 Miles Lyme Regis • Adjoining National Trust Land • South Coast Path • Free Access • Ample Parking • Home Cooked Food including clotted cream teas available throughout the day.
Ann & Andy Gorfin, Kingfishers, Newlands Bridge, Charmouth, Dorset DT6 6QZ. Tel: 01297 560232 E-mail: anniegorfin@msn.com

This country house with its friendly and homely atmosphere welcomes you to the heart of Hardy's Wessex. Central for touring the many places of interest that Dorset has to offer, including Corfe Castle, Lyme Regis, Dorchester, Weymouth, Lulworth Cove, etc. Lovely country walks and many local attractions. Two double rooms, one single, en suite or separate bathroom. TV lounge, dining room. Large garden. Open all year. Central heating. Car essential, ample parking. Bed and Breakfast from £18. Take A35 from Dorchester, we are the last house at the western edge of the village.

Nethercroft

Mrs V.A. Bradbeer, Nethercroft, Winterbourne Abbas, Dorchester DT2 9LU (01305 889337)
e-mail: v.bradbeer@ukonline.co.uk

The Old Rectory
Winterbourne Steepleton, Dorchester DT2 9LG

Built in 1850 on one acre of land situated in a quiet hamlet. The grounds have croquet lawns, putting green, children's swing. The outstanding natural surroundings offer country walks giving superb views of the valley. The four guest rooms are all individually furnished to a high standard, each with en suite facilities. No smoking. Breakfast is a delight, enjoyed in the Garden Room with views of the beautiful courtyard; special diets. Local pubs and a large selection of restaurants in Dorchester and Weymouth are available. Many activities for all can be enjoyed in Thomas Hardy country. French spoken. Open all year except Christmas. Bed and Breakfast from £28 per person. Brochure.

Tel: 01305 889468 • Fax: 01305 889737 • e-mail: trees@eurobell.co.uk • www.trees.eurobell.co.uk

---

SOUTHERNHAY HOTEL
42 Alum Chine Rd, Westbourne, Bournemouth BH4 8DX
Tel & Fax: 01202 761251
enquiries@southernhayhotel.co.uk
www.southernhayhotel.co.uk
ETC ◆◆◆

The Southernhay Hotel provides warm, friendly, high standard accommodation with a large car park. All rooms have colour TV, tea/coffee making facilities, hairdryer and radio alarm clock. The hotel is ideally situated at the head of Alum Chine (a wooded ravine) leading down to the sea and miles of safe sandy beaches.

The Bournemouth International Centre, cinemas, theatres, restaurants, clubs and pubs are all within easy reach; minutes by car or the frequent bus service. Seven bedrooms, five en suite. Open all year. Details from Tom and Lynn Derby.

Bed and Breakfast from £20 to £30 per adult per night.

Stocks Farm is a family-run farm and nursery situated in peaceful countryside just one-and-half miles from the lovely country town of Wimborne Minster, off the B3078. Surrounded by lovely Dorset countryside and pretty villages; coastline, beaches and New Forest within easy reach.

Bed and Breakfast accommodation consists of one double en suite bedroom and one twin bedroom with private bathroom, both on ground level. Disabled guests are very welcome. Tea and coffee making facilities in both rooms. All accommodation is non-smoking. Situated in secluded garden with patio for guests to enjoy breakfast outside. Local pubs and restaurants offer varied menus. Bed and Breakfast from £20 per person per night.

Stocks Farm
Tel & Fax: 01202 888697
Mrs King, Stocks Farm, Furzehill, Wimborne BH21 4HT

The Gables

**10 South View, Middlestone Moor, Spennymoor,
Co Durham DL16 7DF**

The Gables is a spacious Victorian detached house, 10 minutes from the A1(M) access and only 7 miles from medieval Durham city. Ideal touring base for all the North East. We offer 5 en suite rooms, 3 on the ground floor. All rooms have colour TV, hospitality tray, toiletries, hairdryer and radio alarm. Breakfast is a choice of seasonal fresh fruit and yoghurt, cereals and toast, traditional English or Continental breakfast. We have private off-road parking. Dogs welcome by arrangement. Room rates from £32 single and £26pppn double/twin. For travel directions and cancellation policy please see web page.

The Gables is strictly non-smoking.

Tel: 01388 817544 • Fax: 01388 812533
e-mail: thegablesghouse@aol.com • www.guesthousedurham.co.uk

A large, quiet farmhouse set in 350 acres, built on the site of monastery between the Malverns and Cotswolds, half a mile M5-M50 junction. Six en suite bedrooms with colour TV and tea making facilities. Centrally heated. Open all year except Christmas. Large lounge with open fire and colour TV. Spacious diningroom. Licensed bar. Good home cooked food in large quantities, home produced where possible. Children's own TV room, games room and playroom. Tennis lawn. Play area and lawn. Cot and high chair available. Laundry facilities. Ideally situated for touring with numerous places to visit. Swimming, tennis, sauna, golf within three miles. Coarse fishing available on the farm.

Bed and Breakfast from £19 to £21. Reduced rates for children and Senior Citizens.

**Mrs Bernadette Williams, Abbots Court, Church End, Twyning, Tewkesbury GL20 6DA
Tel & Fax: 01684 292515 • e-mail: bernie@abbotscourt.fsbusiness.co.uk**

Aston House, Broadwell, Moreton-In-Marsh GL56 0TJ

ASTON HOUSE is in the peaceful village of Broadwell, one-and-a-half miles from Stow-on-the-Wold, four miles from Moreton-in-Marsh. It is centrally situated for all the Cotswold villages, while Blenheim Palace, Warwick Castle, Oxford, Stratford-upon-Avon, Cheltenham, Cirencester and Gloucester are within easy reach. Accommodation comprises a twin-bedded and a double/twin room, both en suite on the first floor, and a double room with private bathroom on the ground floor. All rooms have tea/coffee making facilities, radio, colour TV, hairdryer, electric blankets for the colder nights and fans for the hot weather. Bedtime drinks and biscuits are provided. Open from March to October. No smoking. Car essential, parking. Pub within walking distance. PC and internet access available. Bed and good English breakfast from £25 to £27 per person daily; weekly from £175 per person.

Tel: 01451 830475 • e-mail: fja@netcomuk.co.uk • www.netcomuk.co.uk/~nmfa/aston_house.html
RAC ◆◆◆◆ **Warm Welcome Award, Sparkling Diamond Award** • **ETC** ◆◆◆◆ **Silver Award**

★ Traditional Cotswold Country Inn
★ Donnington Ales ★ Home-cooked food
★ Children welcome
★ Small parties catered for
★ On site parking ★ Beer garden
★ Situated on the beautiful Donnington Way
★ En suite B&B from £30pppn

The Golden Ball Inn
Steve and Maureen Heath

**LOWER SWELL, NEAR STOW-ON-THE WOLD,
CHELTENHAM, GLOUCS GL54 1LF
TEL: 01451 830247**

Hunters Lodge

**Dr Brown's Road,
Minchinhampton Common, Near Stroud GL6 9BT
Tel: 01453 883588; Fax: 01453 731449
E-mail: hunterslodge@hotmail.com**

Premier Collection

HUNTERS LODGE is a beautiful stone-built Cotswold country house set in a large secluded garden adjoining 600 acres of National Trust common land at Minchinhampton. The accommodation comprises - one double room en suite; two twin/double-bedded rooms both with private bathrooms. All have tea/coffee making facilities, central heating, dressing gowns and colour TV and are furnished and decorated to a high standard. Private lounge with TV and a delightful new conservatory. Car essential, ample parking space. Ideal centre for touring the Cotswolds, Bath, Cheltenham, Cirencester, with many delightful pubs and hotels in the area for meals. You are sure of a warm welcome, comfort, and help in planning excursions to local places of interest.

Bed and Breakfast from £25-£27pp; single £35. Non-smoking. Children over 10 years only. Sorry, no dogs. SAE please, or telephone.

Tel & Fax: 01452 840224

Quality all ground floor accommodation. "Kilmorie" is Grade II Listed (c1848) within conservation area in a lovely part of Gloucestershire. Double, twin, family or single bedrooms, all having tea tray, colour TV, radio, mostly en suite. Very comfortable guests' lounge, traditional home cooking is served in the separate diningroom overlooking large garden. Perhaps walk waymarked farmland footpaths which start here. Children may "help" with our child's pony, and hens. Rural yet perfectly situated to visit Cotswolds, Royal Forest of Dean, Wye Valley and Malvern Hills. Children over five years welcome. No smoking, please. Ample parking.

*Bed, full English Breakfast and Evening Dinner from £29;
Bed and Breakfast from £20.*

**S.J. Barnfield, "Kilmorie Smallholding", Gloucester Road, Corse, Staunton, Gloucester GL19 3RQ
e-mail: sheila-barnfield@supanet.com**

POOL FARM

Bath Road, Wick, Bristol BS30 5RL

Tel: 0117 937 2284

Welcome to our 350 year old Grade II Listed farmhouse on a working farm. On A420 between Bath and Bristol and a few miles from Exit 18 of M4, we are on the edge of the village, overlooking fields, but within easy reach of pub, shops and golf club. We offer traditional Bed and Breakast in one family and one twin room with tea/coffee facilities and TV; guest lounge. Central heating. Ample parking. Open all year except Christmas. Terms from £20.

South Hill Farmhouse

**Fosseway, Stow-on-the-Wold,
Gloucestershire GL54 1JU
Tel: 01451 831 888 • Fax: 01451 832 255**

Friendly B&B in the heart of the Cotswolds

*Siân and Mark Cassie welcome you to
South Hill Farmhouse.*

The house is a Listed Cotswold stone farmhouse (no longer a working farm) situated on the ancient Roman Fosse Way on the outskirts of Stow-on-the-Wold. There is ample parking for guests, and it is only 10 minutes' walk to the pubs, restaurants and shops of Stow-on-the-Wold.

*2004 prices: •Single £38 •Double/Twin £52•Family (3) £66
per room per night including generous breakfast.*

Non-smoking house

**e-mail: info@southhill.co.uk
website: www.southhill.co.uk**

Bolden's Wood
Fiddling Lane, Stowting, Near Ashford, Kent TN25 6AP

Between Ashford/Folkestone. Friendly atmosphere – modern accommodation (one double/twin, two singles) on our Smallholding, set in unspoilt countryside. No smoking throughout. Log-burning stove in TV lounge. Full English breakfast. Country pubs (meals) nearby. Children love the old-fashioned farmyard, free range chickens, friendly sheep and... Llamas, Alpacas and Rheas. Treat yourself to a Llama-led Picnic Trek to our private secluded woodland and downland and enjoy watching the bird life, rabbits, foxes, badgers and occasionally deer. You could round off your trip by booking a short sightseeing or fishing trip on our Folkestone fishing boat! Easy access to Channel Tunnel and Ferry Ports. Bed and Breakfast £23.00 per person.

E-mail: StayoverNight@aol.com
Website: www.countrypicnics.com

Tel & Fax: 01303 812011

- en suite facilities and TV in all rooms
- TV lounge, tea/coffee making facilities, telephone, ironing facilities & hairdryer
- licensed bar and themed restaurant
- special diets catered for
- non-smoking facilities • parking
- credit cards accepted • children welcome

Malvern Hotel, Eastern Esplanade, Cliftonville, Margate CT9 2HL
Tel & Fax: 01843 290192
e-mail: themalvern@aol.com • website: www.malvern-hotel.co.uk

Penny Farthing
GUEST HOUSE

109 Maison Dieu Road, Dover CT16 1RT
Tel: 01304 205563
Fax: 01304 204439

Close to docks and town centre, the A2, the A20 and only ten minutes from the Channel Tunnel.

Impressive Victorian house with spacious en suite accommodation offering extra facilities. Choice of breakfast, early starters catered for. Penny Farthing is an excellent base for touring Kent and ideal for the one night ferry client or the cruise passenger. Our house is non-smoking.

e-mail: pennyfarthingdover@btinternet.com • website: www.pennyfarthingdover.com

FHG
Visit the FHG website
www.holidayguides.com
for details of the wide choice of accommodation featured in the full range of FHG titles

Broadwater HOTEL

356 Marine Road,
East Promenade,
Morecambe
LA4 5AQ
01524 411333

Mrs R. Holdsworth

THE BROADWATER is a small friendly hotel, situated on the select East Promenade with glorious views of Morecambe Bay and Lakeland Mountains. Only five minutes' walk from the town centre, shops and amusements. We offer every comfort and the very best of foods, both varied and plentiful, with choice of menu. All rooms en suite with heating, colour TV and tea making facilities.

A perfect base for touring, the Broadwater is only 45 minutes' drive away from Blackpool, Yorkshire Dales and Lake District, and 10 minutes from the historic city of Lancaster. Open all year. Dinner available.

Bed and Breakfast from £18.

Sunnyside & Holmsdale Hotel
25-27 High Street, North Shore, Blackpool FY1 2BN

Two minutes from North Station, five minutes from Promenade, all shows and amenities. Colour TV lounge. Full central heating. No smoking. Children welcome; cots available. Reductions for children sharing. Senior Citizens' reductions May and June, always welcome.

Special diets catered for, good food and warm friendly atmosphere awaits you. Bed and Breakfast from £18. Morning tea available. Overnight guests welcome when available. Small parties catered for.

Elsie and Ron Platt
Tel: 01253 623781
e-mail: elsieandron@amserve.net

THE EXETER GUEST HOUSE
Wakerley, Oakham, Rutland LE15 8PA
Tel: 01572 747817 • Fax: 01572 747339
website: www.ExeterGuestHouse.co.uk

Welcome back to Rutland and welcome also to this homely, family-run Bed & Breakfast. Set in the picturesque Welland Valley with both Wakerley Woods and Rockingham Forest harbouring a host of interesting walks for ramblers. Burghley House, Rockingham Castle and Kirby Hall are nearby, as is Rutland Water, Europe's largest man-made lake which offers excellent fishing, sailing and bird watching. Easy access to Stamford, Peterborough, Corby and Leicester. A newly-renovated and extended annexe provides attractive accommodation. All 7 bedrooms have en suite facilities, colour television, tea/coffee-makers and underfloor heating. Children welcome. Cots available. Parking. Garden area. A wholesome, wide ranging, Continental breakfast is included. *This is a quiet and well-run hostelry ideal for a break that is just that little bit different.*

Publisher's Note

While every effort is made to ensure accuracy, we regret that FHG Publications cannot accept responsibility for errors, omissions or misrepresentations in our entries or any consequences thereof. Prices in particular should be checked because we go to press early. We will follow up complaints but cannot act as arbiters or agents for either party.

Westbrook Bed & Breakfast House

At Westbrook House we offer carefully designed, thoughtfully equipped, quality en suite accommodation in a tranquil village location, between superb beaches and the Lincolnshire Wolds. Breakfasts and optional evening meals are served in the conservatory overlooking the patio garden, and feature "Tastes of Lincolnshire". There is a galleried TV/sitting area with tourist information. Ideal base for local market towns, countryside, walking, cycling etc (bikes available). B&B from £20.

Discover the "Real Lincolnshire".

Open all year • Central heating • On site parking

Tel: 01507 450624 for colour brochure • WESTBROOK HOUSE, GAYTON LE MARSH, ALFORD LN13 0NW
e-mail: westbrook_house@hotmail.com • www.bestbookwestbrook.co.uk

---

Mrs S. Evans, Willow Farm,
Thorpe Fendykes, Wainfleet,
Skegness PE24 4QH
Tel: 01754 830316
Email: willowfarmhols@aol.com
Website: www.willowfarmholidays.co.uk

In the heart of the Lincolnshire Fens, Willow Farm is a working smallholding with free range hens, goats, horses and ponies. Situated in a peaceful hamlet with abundant wildlife, ideal for a quiet retreat – yet only 15 minutes from the Skegness coast, shops, amusements and beaches.

Bed and Breakfast is provided in comfortable en suite rooms from £17 per person per night, reductions for children (suppers and sandwiches can be provided in the evening on request). Rooms have tea and coffee making facilities and a colour TV and are accessible to disabled guests. Friendly hosts! Ring for brochure.

Beeston Hills Lodge ~ Sheringham

Bed and Breakfast seaside holiday accommodation. Our Edwardian lodge which is marvellously located next to the Norfolk Coastal Path, cliffs and ocean, obtains good views of the sea and green. Beeston Hills Lodge is one of the highest dwellings here, located opposite the putting green and the sea and set back from the road so there is no passing traffic. The house is equipped with a four-poster, king-size bed, an old piano, satellite system, home cinema with giant screen TV in lounge, video player and several colour TVs with boosted feeds to the bedrooms, and DVD. One shower and separate bathroom with shower. Garden with garden furniture. Car parking for two cars. Ten to twenty minutes' drive from the golf course and cinema. The Lodge can accommodate up to eight people in four bedrooms (cot available if required), with sea views. Children, Senior Citizens and well behaved pets welcome. Terms from £20 pppn. Non-smoking. Creative writing courses available, as the owner, a writer and poet, has recently reached the finals of an International Writing competition. *Please contact for further details.*

Tel: 01263 825333 • 0788 7751760 (mobile) • Fax: 001 775 542 2519
e-mail: enquiries@bhlodge.co.uk • website: www.bhlodge.co.uk/lodge.htm

---

Malthouse Farmhouse, Malthouse Lane, Ludham, Norfolk NR29 5QL

The farmhouse dates back to 1700 and has retained lots of its period features. It is situated in quiet countryside on the edge of Ludham village in the heart of the Norfolk Broads, where country walks and cycle rides start at the gate. We are 5 minutes' walk from Womack Water and boat hire; within easy reach of the coast; 15 minutes' drive to Yarmouth races.

B&B accommodation comprises one double bedroom (making yours a completely exclusive stay) with private bathroom/shower; use of the barn room for TV viewing, use of garden, tea-making facilities.

• Full farmhouse or vegetarian breakfast • Evening meals available from village pub 5 minutes' walk • B&B £30.00 to £35.00pppn.

Tel: 01692 678747 • Brochure on request

4B&B STRENNETH

Country Bed and Breakfast

Airfield Road, Fersfield, Diss, Norfolk IP22 2BP

STRENNETH is a well-established, family-run business, situated in unspoiled countryside just a short drive from Bressingham Gardens, Snetterton Motor Racing Circuit and the picturesque market town of Diss. Offering first-class accommodation, the original 17th Century building has been carefully renovated to a high standard with a wealth of exposed oak beams and a newer single storey courtyard wing. There is ample off-road parking and plenty of nice walks nearby. All seven bedrooms, including a Four-Poster and an Executive, are tastefully arranged with period furniture and distinctive beds. Each having remote colour television, hospitality trays, central heating and full en suite facilities. The establishment is smoke-free and the guest lounge has a log fire on cold winter evenings. There is an extensive breakfast menu using local produce. Ideal touring base. Pets most welcome at no extra charge. Outside kennels with runs if required. Bed and Breakfast from £25.00.

Telephone: 01379 688182 • Fax: 01379 688260
E-mail: pdavey@strenneth.co.uk • Website: www.strenneth.co.uk

---

Overlooking the Venetian Waterways and Seafront

Swiss Cottage Hotel

- Close to racecourse, golf, tennis, bowling greens, shows etc
- Good base for Norfolk Broads attractions
- Single, twin and double rooms, most en suite
- All rooms with colour TV, radio/alarm and tea/coffee making
- Rooms with superb sea views available.
- Full English breakfast with fresh local produce
- Private car park • Spacious residents' lounge with colour TV
- Open all year

Swiss Cottage Hotel, 31 North Drive, Great Yarmouth NR30 4EW
Tel: 01493 855742 • Mobile: 07734 980289

ENJOY A HOLIDAY in our comfortable 17th century farmhouse with oak beams and inglenook fireplaces. Four-poster bed now available. Peaceful surroundings, large garden containing ancient circular dovecote. Dairy Farm is a working farm situated in a beautiful Northamptonshire village just off the A14, within easy reach of many places of interest or ideal for a restful holiday. Good farmhouse food and friendly atmosphere. Open all year, except Christmas. Bed and Breakfast from £25 to £35 (children under 10 half price); Evening Meal £16.

Mrs A. Clarke, Dairy Farm, Cranford St Andrew, Kettering NN14 4AQ
Telephone: 01536 330273

South Hazelrigg is situated between the market town of Wooler and the coastal village of Belford, approx. 10 minutes off the A1 road, ideally placed for trips to the beach, Farne Islands, Holy Island, the Cheviot Hills and the many castles. Rooms are spacious and comfortable with hospitality trays and colour TV. Breakfast is served in the elegant dining room and the local village inns provide an extensive menu. Local activities include birdwatching, fishing, horse riding and golf, Bamburgh being the most scenic English course.

Sheila Dodds, South Hazelrigg, Chatton, Alnwick NE66 5RZ

e-mail: sed@hazelrigg.fsnet.co.uk
www.farmhousebandb.co.uk

01668 215216 • mobile: 07710 346076

Silver SILVER AWARD

Struthers Farm
Catton, Allendale, Hexham NE47 9LP

Struthers Farm offers a warm welcome in the heart of England, with many splendid local walks from the farm itself. Panoramic views. Situated in an area of outstanding beauty. Double/twin rooms, en suite bathrooms, central heating. Good farmhouse cooking. Ample safe parking. Come and share our home and enjoy beautiful countryside. Near Hadrians Wall (½ hour's drive). Children welcome, pets by prior arrangement. Open all year. Bed and Breakfast from £22; Optional Evening Meal from £12.

Contact Mrs Ruby Keenleyside

01434 683580

Westlea

We invite you to relax in the warm, friendly atmosphere of "Westlea" situated at the side of the Aln Estuary. We have an established reputation for providing a high standard of care and hospitality. Guests start the day with a hearty breakfast of numerous choices and in the evening a varied and appetising four-course traditional meal is prepared using local produce. All bedrooms are bright, comfortable and en suite with colour TVs, hot drinks facilities. Large visitors' lounge and diningroom overlooking the estuary. Ideal for exploring castles, Farne Islands, Holy Island, Hadrian's Wall. Fishing, golf, pony trekking, etc within easy reach. Bed and Breakfast from £22; Bed, Breakfast and Evening Meal from £34. Numerous Hospitality awards.

Private parking Two bedrooms on ground floor ETC ◆◆◆

Janice and Norman Edwards, Westlea, 29 Riverside Road, Alnmouth, Northumberland NE66 2SD • Tel: 01665 830730

Lovely 17th century farmhouse in peaceful village amidst the beautiful hills of South Shropshire, an area of outstanding natural beauty. The house is full of character and the rooms, which are all heated, are comfortable and spacious with en suite or private bathroom and beverage making facilities. Colour TV lounge. We are a working farm, centrally situated for visiting Ironbridge, Shrewsbury and Ludlow, each being easily reached within half-an-hour. Visitors' touring and walking information available. No smoking. Bed and full English Breakfast from £20pp. Weekly rate £135pp.

Mrs Mary Jones, Acton Scott Farm, Acton Scott, Church Stretton SY6 6QN • Tel: 01694 781260

Fax: 0870-129 4591 • e-mail: bandb@actonscottfarm.co.uk • www.actonscottfarm.co.uk

Visiting Shropshire?

Why not enjoy the warm welcome and home-from-home atmosphere at Oakfields, which is in a quiet, idyllic setting located in the picturesque village of Myddle made famous by Gough's "History of Myddle" written in 1700.

All ground floor bedrooms, each tastefully decorated and equipped with colour TV, tea-making facilities, washbasin, hairdryer and shaver point; cot and high chair also available.

Guests' TV lounge. Central heating throughout. Large and pleasant garden for guests to enjoy.

15 minutes from Shrewsbury and Hawkstone Park and convenient for Ironbridge, Wales, Chester, etc. Golf and riding nearby. Extensive car park. Non-smoking.

Bed and Breakfast from £20 pppn.

Nearest main road A528, also straight road from A5.

Mrs Gwen Frost, Oakfields, Baschurch Road, Myddle, Shrewsbury SY4 3RX (01939 290823)

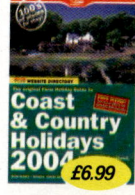

FHG Holiday and Accommodation guides 2004

Each year FHG Publications produce a large range of attractive holiday accommodation guides for all kinds of holiday opportunities throughout Britain. They are great value for money and are available in most bookshops and larger newsagents at the following prices.

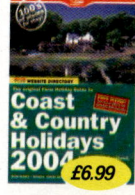
Coast & Country Holidays 2004 £6.99

Britain's Best Holidays 2004 £4.99

Bed & Breakfast Stops 2004 £6.50

Golf Guide 2004 £9.99

Country Inns & Pubs of Britain 2004 £6.99

Short Break Holidays in Britain 2004 £6.99

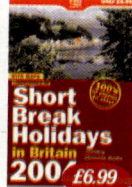

Country Hotels of Britain 2004 £6.99

Pets Welcome! 2004 £7.99

Guide to Caravan & Camping Holidays 2004 £4.99

Pets Welcome! 2004 £7.99

Self-Catering Holidays in Britain 2004 £6.99

Children Welcome! 2004 £6.99

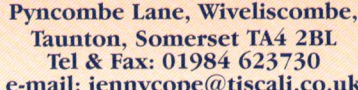

THATCHED COUNTRY COTTAGE & GARDEN B&B

An old thatched country cottage halfway between Taunton and Honiton, set in the idyllic Blackdown Hills, a designated Area of Outstanding Natural Beauty. Picturesque countryside with plenty of flowers and wildlife. Central for north/south coasts of Somerset, Dorset and Devon. Double/single and family suite with own facilities, TV, tea/coffee. Conservatory/Garden Room. Evening Meals also available. Open all year.

Mrs Pam Parry, Pear Tree Cottage, Stapley, Churchstanton, Taunton TA3 7QA
Tel & Fax: 01823 601224
e-mail: colvin.parry@virgin.net
www.SmoothHound.co.uk/hotels/thatch.html OR **www.best-hotel.com/peartreecottage**

See also advertisement in main section.

Deep in the heart of Somerset, this comfortable Bed & Breakfast awaits you. We guarantee you a peaceful stay with excellent rural views and good food. The accommodation available is a double room with a single bed, and a twin room. There is a comfortable lounge with a TV and tea/coffee making facilities. Ample parking. Sorry, no pets. Bed and Breakfast from £20.00; children half price. We look forward to hearing from you on **01458 850905**

Mr & Mrs T. Norton, Watercress Cottage, Jarmany Hill, Barton St David, Somerton, Somerset TA11 6DA

Imposing country house in Exmoor National Park on the wooded slopes of West Porlock commanding exceptional sea views of Porlock Bay and countryside. Set in five acres of beautiful woodland gardens unique for its variety and size of unusual trees and shrubs and offering a haven of rural tranquillity. The house has large spacious rooms with fine and beautiful furnishings throughout. Two double, two twin and one family bedrooms, all with en suite or private bathrooms, TV, tea/coffee making facilities, radio-alarm clock and shaver point. Licensed. Non-smoking. Private car park. Bed and Breakfast from £27.50 to £30.00 per person. Credit Cards accepted. Sorry, no pets.

West Porlock House
01643 862880

Margery and Henry Dyer, West Porlock House, West Porlock, Near Minehead TA24 8NX

Offley Grove Farm, Adbaston, Eccleshall, Staffs ST20 0QB
Tel/Fax: 01785 280205

You'll consider this a good find! Quality accommodation and excellent breakfasts. Small traditional mixed farm surrounded by beautiful countryside. The house is tastefully furnished and provides all home comforts. Whether you are planning to book here for a break in your journey, stay for a weekend or take your holidays here, you will find something to suit all tastes among the many local attractions. Situated on the Staffordshire/ Shropshire borders we are convenient for Alton Towers, Stoke-on-Trent, Ironbridge, etc. Reductions for children. Play area for children. Open all year. Bed and Breakfast all en suite from £24pp. Many guests return. Self-catering cottages available.

Brochure on request.
e-mail: accomm@offleygrovefarm.freeserve.co.uk
website: www.offleygrovefarm.co.uk

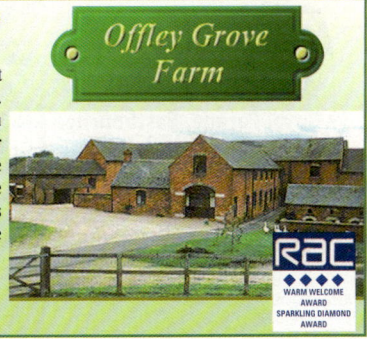

Offley Grove Farm

RAC
WARM WELCOME AWARD
SPARKLING DIAMOND AWARD

MAON HOTEL

26 Upper Rock Gardens, Brighton BN2 1QE

This is a completely non-smoking Grade II Listed building run by proprietors who are waiting with a warm and friendly welcome. No children. Established over 25 years. Our standard of food has been highly recommended by many guests who return year after year. Two minutes from the sea and within easy reach of conference and main town centres. All nine bedrooms are furnished to a high standard and have colour TV, radio alarm clock, hospitality tray and hairdryer and most are en suite. A lounge with colour TV is available for guests' convenience. Diningroom. Full central heating. Access to rooms at all times. Terms from £30. Brochure on request with SAE.

Tel: 01273 694400

e-mail: MAONHOTEL@aol.com

ST OMER HOTEL

a family-run, non-smoking hotel in a prominent seafront position, with panoramic views of the sea, beach and promenade.

- Comfortable guest lounge and sun lounge
- Elegant dining room serving fine English cuisine
- Comfortable bedrooms, all en suite, with colour TV, clock radio and tea/coffee making facilities

Tel: 01323 722152 • Fax: 01323 723400
e-mail: stomerhotel@hotmail.com
website: www.st-omer.co.uk
13 ROYAL PARADE, EASTBOURNE BN22 7AR

"Meadowhills"

Stedham, Midhurst, West Sussex GU29 0PT
Tel: 01730 812609 or Mobile: 07776 262147

Built in 1908 this small, comfortable, country estate is set in its own grounds of 25 acres with magnificent views over the South Downs.

Activities include Fishing Rights • Walkers' Paradise • Riding Stables nearby • 20 miles to South Coast • Golf • Polo • Leisure Centres • Horse Racing at Fontwell and Goodwood.

Places of interest include Uppark • The Weald & Downland Open Air Museum • Petworth House and other National Trust Properties • Chichester Festival Theatre.

Call or write for further information and tariff • www.meadowhills.co.uk

---

THE SQUIRRELS Henfield, Albourne Road, Woodmancote BN5 9BH

The Squirrels is a country house with lovely large garden set in a secluded area convenient for south coast and downland touring. Brighton and Gatwick 20 minutes. Good food at pub five minutes' walk. One family, one double, one twin and one single rooms, all with colour TV, washbasin, central heating and tea/coffee making facilities. Ample parking space. A warm welcome awaits you. Open all year. Directions: from London take M25, M23, A23 towards Brighton, then B2118 to Albourne. Turn right onto B2116 Albourne/Henfield Road – Squirrels is approx. one-and-a-half miles on left. Bed and Breakfast £20.

Tel: 01273 492761

The Globe Hotel

54 Birmingham Road
Alcester
Warwickshire
B49 5EG

Tel & Fax:
01789 763287

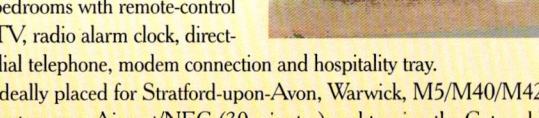

A warm and friendly hotel in the historic market town of Alcester (7 miles from Stratford-upon-Avon).

Stylish and spacious en suite bedrooms with remote-control TV, radio alarm clock, direct-dial telephone, modem connection and hospitality tray. Ideally placed for Stratford-upon-Avon, Warwick, M5/M40/M42 motorways, Airport/NEC (30 minutes) and touring the Cotswolds. Rooms from £35 to £65. Totally refurbished in 2000.

Green Haven Guest House

A cosy and prettily refurbished Guest House, centrally heated with colour TV, courtesy trays and many thoughtful extras. Within easy walking distance of the Town Centre, and easily accessible to historic Warwick and the beautiful Cotswolds. Our bedrooms are all en suite and comprise two family rooms, doubles and twins, with extra large showers and plenty of hot water. Our competitive rates include a delicious English, vegetarian/vegan or Continental breakfast. Private parking. Non-smoking.

Susan & Derek Learmount, Green Haven Guest House, 217 Evesham Road, Stratford-upon-Avon CV37 9AS
Tel: 01789 297874 • Fax: 01789 550487

e-mail: susanlearmount@green-haven.co.uk
website: www.green-haven.co.uk

Holly Tree Cottage
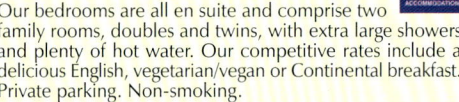
Birmingham Road, Pathlow, Stratford-upon-Avon CV37 0ES
Tel & Fax: 01789 204461

Period cottage dating from 17th Century, with antiques, paintings, collection of porcelain, fresh flowers, tasteful furnishings and friendly atmosphere. Picturesque gardens, orchard, paddock and pasture with wildlife and extensive views over open countryside. Situated 3 miles north of Stratford-upon-Avon towards Henley-in-Arden on A3400. Rooms have television, radio/alarm, hospitality trays and hairdryers. Breakfasts are a speciality. Pubs and restaurants nearby. Ideally located for Theatre, Shakespeare Country, Heart of England, Cotswolds, Warwick Castle, Blenheim Palace and National Trust Properties. Well situated for National Exhibition Centre, Birmingham and National Agricultural Centre, Stoneleigh. Children welcome, pets by arrangement. Non-smoking. Bed and Breakfast from £27 per person.

e-mail: john@hollytree-cottage.co.uk • website: www.hollytree-cottage.co.uk

◆ ◆ Linhill ◆ ◆

35 Evesham Place, Stratford-upon-Avon CV37 6HT
Tel: 01789 292879 • Fax: 01789 299691
• E-mail: linhill@bigwig.net • Web: linhillguesthouse.co.uk

Linhill is a comfortable Victorian Guest House run by a friendly young family. It is situated only five minutes' walk from Stratford's town centre with its wide choice of fine restaurants and world famous Royal Shakespeare Theatre. Every bedroom at Linhill has central heating, colour TV, tea/coffee making facilities and washbasin. En suite facilities are also available, as are packed lunches and evening meals. Bicycle hire and babysitting facilities if desired. Leave the children with us and re-discover the delight of a candlelit dinner in one of Stratford's inviting restaurants. Bed and Breakfast from £20 to £35; Evening Meal from £7 to £10. **Private house sleeps 5 available.**

Manor Farm, Burcombe, Salisbury SP2 0EJ

An attractive stone-built farmhouse with a lovely walled garden, set in a quiet village amid downland and water meadows, five miles west of Salisbury. The two bedrooms are very comfortable with en suite facilities, TV, tea trays and clock-radios. Large lounge and access to garden. This is an ideal location for Salisbury, Wilton and Stonehenge and easy access to many places of historic interest and gardens. For those seeking peace this is an idyllic place to stay with various walks and the local pub only a five minute stroll. Children welcome. Bed and Breakfast from £23 to £24.

01722 742177 • Fax: 01722 744600 • e-mail: s.a.combes@talk21.com

---

16th-18th century part black and white cottage-style country house situated in the River Teme Valley, four miles from Worcester and Malvern. Croft House is central for visiting numerous attractions in Worcester, Hereford, Severn Valley and surrounding countryside. There is fishing close by and an 18-hole golf course opposite. Facilities include three en suite rooms (two double, one family) and two double rooms with washbasins, hospitality trays; TV in all bedrooms. Double glazing, central heating, residential licence and home-cooked dinners. There is a TV lounge for guests' use. A cot and baby listening service are provided.

B&B from £23 to £33 single, £41 to £56 double. Festive Christmas and New Year Breaks available.

Ann and Brian Porter, Croft Guest House, Bransford, Worcester WR6 5JD
Tel: 01886 832227 • Fax: 01886 830037

The Old Coach House Bed & Breakfast

208 Wells Road, Malvern Wells WR14 4HD • 01684 564382
e-mail: info@coachhousemalvern.co.uk • www.coachhousemalvern.co.uk

Welcome to The Old Coach House, situated on the eastern slopes of the Malvern Hills, with easy access from the A449. Convenient for touring the area by car and only a short walk from The Three Counties Showground.
All bedrooms have en suite shower and WC, colour TV, hairdryer, clock radio, and hospitality tray. Hearty English Breakfast is prepared with local produce whenever possible.

Dave and Janet Vale look forward to welcoming you to The Old Coach House where you will be made to feel completely at home.

The Red Gate

32 Avenue Road, Great Malvern WR14 3BJ
Tel/Fax: 01684 565013

Come, relax and be pampered in a centrally heated, beautifully restored Victorian hotel. Situated on a tree-lined road near to Great Malvern railway station, town centre and hills. Parking on the premises. Renowned for friendly informal atmosphere, "It's like coming home". Seven individually decorated bedrooms with en suite facilities, all non-smoking with colour TV and tea/coffee facilities. There is a breakfast menu to suit all tastes. Vegetarians welcome. Residential licence. Enjoy a good book from a wide selection in the attractive lounge. On better days, relax on the veranda or sit in the south-walled garden and forget your cares. Bed & Breakfast from £42.

Guestaccomm
Which? Hotel Guide

e-mail: enquiries@the-red-gate.co.uk • website: www.the-red-gate.co.uk

THE SEACOURT HOTEL

76 SOUTH MARINE DRIVE, BRIDLINGTON YO15 3NS
e-mail: seacourt.hotel@tiscali.co.uk

Standing quietly in a prime position overlooking the beautiful South Bay, with panoramic views of the Old Harbour, town and Flamborough Head, this former large Edwardian house has been refurbished and transformed into a delightful, small hotel of distinction. Luxuriously appointed to a very high standard making it a perfect base to explore the area. The 12 standard and de luxe bedrooms, some with stunning sea views, are all en suite, with colour TV, direct-dial telephones, hospitality trays, toiletries and central heating. Annabel's Restaurant, situated within the hotel, specialises in seafood and offers a wide choice of menu. Bar meals are also available.

Attractions include: miles of safe beaches • 18 hole golf course • bowling green • leisure centre • bars • cabaret theatre • cinema • Sewerby Hall & Gardens • Heritage Coast • Bempton Bird Sanctuary and much more.

Tel: 01262 400872   **...we look forward to seeing you!**

Excellent friendly service awaits you at the

South Dene Hotel

A warm and friendly family-run hotel situated on Bridlington's South Side, just 150 yards from The Royal Spa and approximately 5 minutes' walk to the central shops. Our B&B at £20 is excellent value with a quality breakfast provided. Short breaks/weekend stays are most welcome.
Major credit cards accepted. **Colour brochure available on request.**

94 HORSFORTH AVENUE • BRIDLINGTON YO15 3DF
◆ **Tel: (01262) 674436** ◆

Astley House
123 Clifton, York YO30 6BL
Tel: 01904 634745 • Fax: 01904 621327 • mobile 07830 109215
e-mail: astleyhousehotel@aol.com • www.astleyhouseyork.co.uk

Elegant Victorian house, family-run, within walking distance of the city centre. Beautiful en suite accommodation, some four-posters; all with colour TV and tea/coffee facilities.  Traditional English or lighter breakfasts are freshly cooked and served in a relaxed atmosphere. Evening meals available. Car parking. Discounted rates available throughout the year.

The family-run guest house is situated in the centre of Darley, a quiet village in unspoilt Nidderdale. All rooms en suite and centrally heated with tea/coffee making facilities and views across the Dales. Full English breakfast served between 7am and 9am in the dining room; a TV lounge/conservatory is available for your relaxation. Off street parking. Central for visits to Harrogate, York, Skipton and Ripon, or just enjoying drives through the Dales and Moors where you will take in dramatic hillsides, green hills, picturesque villages, castles and abbeys. Children welcome. B&B from £20pppn double, £22pp twin room and £30 single room, reductions for three nights or more. Yorkshire in Bloom Winner.

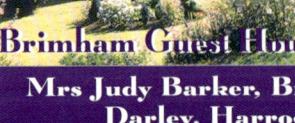

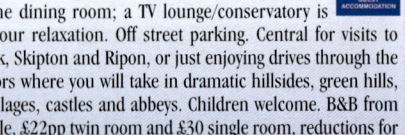

Mrs Judy Barker, Brimham Guest House, Silverdale Close, Darley, Harrogate HG3 2PQ • 01423 780948

Mount Grace Farm

A warm welcome awaits you on working farm surrounded by beautiful open countryside with magnificent views. Ideal location for touring or exploring the many walks in the area. Luxury en suite bedrooms with tea/coffee facilities. Spacious guests' lounge with colour TV. Garden. Enjoy delicious, generous helpings of farmhouse fayre cooked in our Aga. Children from 12 years plus. No smoking. No pets. Bed and Breakfast from £28. Open all year except Christmas.

Joyce Ashbridge, Mount Grace Farm, Cold Kirby, Thirsk YO7 2HL
Tel: 01845 597389 • Fax: 01845 597872
e-mail: joyce@mountgracefarm.com website: www.mountgracefarm.com

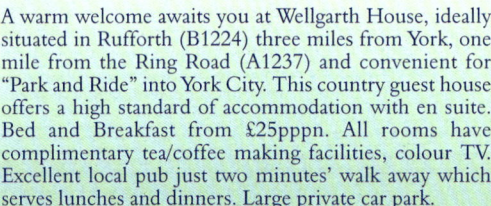

Exclusive to non-smokers, welcoming Yorkshire house of character at the foot of the moors, National Park "Heartbeat" country. Three-and-a-half-miles from Whitby. Magnificent scenery, moors, dales, picturesque harbours, cliffs, beaches, scenic railways, superb walking - its all here! Highly commended, beautifully appointed rooms with private facilities, many extras. Guest lounge; breakfast room with views over Esk Valley. Enjoy the large south-facing terrace and landscaped gardens. Extensive traditional and vegetarian breakfast choice. Local inns and restaurants - two within a short walk. Parking available, also public transport.

B&B double £22-£24, single £21-£26 minimum stay 2 nights. Regret, no pets or children.
Mrs Pat Beale, Ryedale House, Coach Road, Sleights, Near Whitby YO22 5EQ
Tel & Fax: 01947 810534

Wellgarth House
Wetherby Road, Rufforth, York YO23 3QB
Tel: 01904 738592 • mobile: 07711 252577

A warm welcome awaits you at Wellgarth House, ideally situated in Rufforth (B1224) three miles from York, one mile from the Ring Road (A1237) and convenient for "Park and Ride" into York City. This country guest house offers a high standard of accommodation with en suite. Bed and Breakfast from £25pppn. All rooms have complimentary tea/coffee making facilities, colour TV. Excellent local pub just two minutes' walk away which serves lunches and dinners. Large private car park.

Browson Bank Farmhouse Accommodation

A newly converted granary set in 300 acres of farmland. The accommodation consists of three very tastefully furnished double/twin rooms all en suite, tea and coffee making facilities, colour TV and central heating. A large, comfortable lounge is available to relax in. Full English breakfast served. Situated six miles West of Scotch Corner (A1). Ideal location to explore the scenic countryside of Teesdale and the Yorkshire Dales and close to the scenic towns of Barnard Castle and Richmond. Terms from £20.00 per night.

Browson Bank Farmhouse, Browson Bank, Dalton, Richmond DL11 7HE
Tel: (01325) 718504 or (01325) 718246

SCOTLAND
Counties

SHETLAND
ISLANDS

WESTERN
ISLES

HIGHLAND

MORAY

ABERDEENSHIRE

ABERDEEN
CITY

PERTH
AND KINROSS

ANGUS

ARGYLL
AND BUTE

DUNDEE
CITY

STIRLING

FIFE

9

2

6

8

1

5

7

11

E. LOTHIAN

3

4

10

12

NORTH
AYRSHIRE

S. LANARKSHIRE

BORDERS

EAST
AYRSHIRE

SOUTH
AYRSHIRE

DUMFRIES
AND GALLOWAY

1. **Inverclyde**
2. **West Dunbartonshire**
3. **Renfrewshire**
4. **East Renfrewshire**
5. **City of Glasgow**
6. **East Dunbartonshire**
7. **North Lanarkshire**
8. **Falkirk**
9. **Clackmannanshire**
10. **West Lothian**
11. **City of Edinburgh**
12. **Midlothian**

©MAPS IN MINUTES™ 2003

Built in 1760 as a coaching inn for Invercauld Estate, the Inver Hotel has over the centuries established an enviable reputation for warm Scottish hospitality in what nowadays are distinctly elegant surroundings. All attractively furnished bedrooms are fully equipped with en suite facilities, tea/coffee hospitality tray, colour TV (incl Sky satellite – 8 individual channels) and enjoy outstanding views over the surrounding countryside. Family-owned and run, The Inver Hotel is famed for its outstanding cuisine served in the spacious lounge with its open hearth fire. There is a cosy, warm atmosphere in the public bar where visitors can 'meet the locals'. The beer garden with its picturesque outlook over the surrounding mountains has a wealth of colour during the summer months and here visitors can enjoy a drink or meal 'al fresco'. Activities include golfing, fishing, deer-stalking, pony-trekking, hill-walking, climbing and ski-ing.
Rates from: £25 per person double/twin B&B, £35 per person single B&B.

Inver Hotel

Crathie, By Balmoral, Aberdeenshire AB35 5UL
Tel: 013397 42345 • Fax: 013397 42009
E-mail: enquiries@theinver.co.uk • web: www.theinverhotel.co.uk

Scottish TOURIST BOARD ★★★ HOTEL

---

78 Market Street, Macduff, Aberdeenshire, AB44 1LL,
Tel/Fax: 01261 832229

enquiries@knoweshotel.co.uk
www.knoweshotel.co.uk

The Knowes Hotel & Restaurant

- *Renowned for our food prepared from fresh local produce*
- *Panoramic sea views over the Moray Firth Coast*
- *Dinner parties, weddings and functions*
- *8 bedrooms*
- *Table booking is advised at weekends to avoid disappointment*
- *Free Parking available*

Come along and experience the cuisine, the views and the ambience we are well known for. Lorenzo and Kimberly look forward to welcoming you to The Knowes

---

Lyn-Leven GUEST HOUSE

Lyn-Leven, a superior award-winning licensed guest house overlooking Loch Leven, with every comfort, in the beautiful Highlands of Scotland, is situated one mile from historic Glencoe village. Four double, two twin and two family bedrooms, all rooms en suite; sittingroom and diningroom. Central heating. Excellent and varied home cooking served daily. Children welcome at reduced rates. An ideal location for touring. Fishing, walking and climbing in the vicinity. The house, open all year, is suitable for disabled guests. Car not essential but private car park provided. Bed and Breakfast from £22. Dinner, Bed and Breakfast from £200 to £220 per person per week. Credit and debit cards accepted.

Scottish TOURIST BOARD GUEST HOUSE **AA ◆◆◆◆** **RAC ◆◆◆◆** Guest Accommodation

Mr and Mrs J.A. MacLeod, Lyn-Leven, Ballachulish, Argyll PA39 4JW
Tel: 01855 811392 • Fax: 01855 811600 • www.LynLeven.co.uk

Palace Hotel

GEORGE STREET, OBAN, ARGYLL PA34 5SB
01631 562294 • www.thepalacehotel.activehotels.com

A small family hotel offering personal supervision situated on Oban's sea front with wonderful views over the Bay, to the Mull Hills beyond. All rooms en suite, with colour TV, tea/coffee making facilities, several non-smoking. The Palace is an ideal base for a real Highland holiday. By boat you can visit the islands of Kerrera, Coll, Tiree, Lismore, Mull and Iona, and by road Glencoe, Ben Nevis and Inveraray. Fishing, golf, horse riding, sailing, tennis and bowls all nearby. Children and pets welcome. Reductions for children. Please write or telephone for brochure. Competitive rates.

Welcome to Dunduff Farm where a warm, friendly atmosphere awaits you. Situated just south of Ayr at the coastal village of Dunure, this family-run beef and sheep unit of 600 acres is only 15 minutes from the shore providing good walks and sea fishing and enjoying close proximity to Dunure Castle and Park. Accommodation is of a high standard yet homely and comfortable. Bedrooms have washbasins, radio alarm, tea/coffee making facilities, central heating, TV, hair dryer and en suite facilities (the twin room has private bathroom). There is also a small farm cottage available sleeping two/four people. Bed and Breakfast from £25 per person; weekly rate £170. Cottage from £250 per week. Colour brochure available.
Mrs Agnes Gemmell

Dunduff Farm, Dunure, Ayr KA7 4LH
01292 500225 • www.gemmelldunduff.co.uk

BAILEY MILL COURTYARD

Bailey Mill, Newcastleton, Roxburghshire TD9 0TR
Tel: 016977 48617 • Fax: 016977 48074
E-mail: pam@baileymill.fsnet.co.uk

A warm welcome awaits you from Pam and Ian on this small farm holiday complex, nestling on the Roxburghshire/ Cumbrian border. The rural self-contained apartments create a courtyard setting or enjoy Bed and Breakfast or Full Board riding holidays in the farmhouse. Colour TV ; heating (oil), electricity and linen included in the rent. On site sauna, toning table, jacuzzi, games room, laundry, babysitting, fully licensed bar and meals. Enjoy walking or trekking through surrounding forests. Eight horses and six mountain bikes available. Central touring area for Lake District, Hadrian's Wall and Scotland. Forest trekking and lessons in outdoor school. Colour brochure available.

www.holidaycottagescumbria.co.uk
Self catering £88 – £498 weekly • B&B from £20 per person

ETC ★★/★★★
Self Catering

'Shalem'
March Street, Peebles EH45 8EP
Tel & Fax: 01721 721047

'Shalem' is centrally situated in the beautiful Scottish Borders town of Peebles. Peebles is an ideal location for day trips to historic homes, gardens, abbeys or castles, and boasts lovely forest and hill walks, cycling, fishing in the River Tweed and golf. You are assured of a warm, friendly welcome with excellent accommodation. The family room has en suite shower room and the double room has a private bathroom (not en suite). Both rooms have tea/coffee making facilities and colour TV. Dogs welcome by arrangement; reduced rates for children sharing. Family room £25pppn, double room £22pppn, single in double room £23-£25.

FHG   # Publisher's Note

While every effort is made to ensure accuracy, we regret that FHG Publications cannot accept responsibility for errors, omissions or misrepresentations in our entries or any consequences thereof. Prices in particular should be checked because we go to press early. We will follow up complaints but cannot act as arbiters or agents for either party.

Bridge House is a licensed guesthouse owned and run by Russell & Danyella Pearce, providing a warm and friendly home from home, which guests can return to again and again. Stay here on a B&B basis or opt to have one of the wonderful evening meals cooked by Russell, a fully qualified chef who sources only the finest local produce. Start to relax and enjoy the views the moment you arrive.

A traditional freshly cooked breakfast or a lighter option of croissants and Danish pastries is available. Everything about Bridge House speaks of quality, from the interior decoration to the comfortable and sumptuously furnished rooms, all en suite with tea/coffee making facilities and TV. There is a large family room with a king-sized bed and two single beds and the Master Bedroom boasts a traditional four-poster bed along with beautiful views from the large bay window. Twin rooms also available. Come and see for yourself, why it has been called a jewel in Scotland's crown.

❖ Bridge House ❖

Well Road, Moffat DG10 9JT
Telephone: 01683 220558
E-mail: bridgehousemoffat@tiscali.co.uk

THE QUEEN'S ARMS HOTEL
22 MAIN STREET,
ISLE OF WHITHORN
WIGTOWNSHIRE DG8 8LF
TEL: 01988 500 369

A warm and friendly welcome awaits you in this family-run hotel situated in a beautiful conservation village with working harbour. The Isle of Whithorn, situated on the most southerly tip of the Machars Peninsula, is ideally placed for walking, fishing, and golfing, and makes an ideal base for touring some of the most spectacular scenery in South-West Scotland. Comfortable homely rooms (all en suite), delicious home-cooked meals in a well-presented dining room and two bars serving traditional, locally brewed cask ale. Should you wish to stay longer we can offer well-equipped, self-catering holiday cottages, most with sea views.

"Why stay in expensive hotels when you can enjoy superior comfort and 4-star service in our luxurious Galloway home?"

Full breakfast menu with an excellent choice of attractively presented fresh Scottish produce. Quiet lounge, superb conservatory dining room, delightful gardens and a peaceful setting. Four double/twin rooms en suite all with TV, tea/coffee making facilities, hairdryer, iron etc.

Highly recommended for that really special break

Rowallan House
Corsbie Road, Newton Stewart
DG8 6JB
Tel: 01671 402520

**Rates: Single from £30 pppn,
double/twin from £27.50 pppn.
Short break £162. Open Jan – Dec.**

e-mail: enquiries@rowallan.co.uk
website: www.rowallan.co.uk

Scottish
TOURIST BOARD
★★★★
B&B

Albion House
49 Ernespie Road, Castle Douglas, Kirkcudbrightshire DG7 1LD

A warm Galloway welcome awaits you at Albion House, which was built around 1860. Well-positioned on the outskirts of town within an acre of private grounds yet only a few minutes' walk to all amenities. We have a variety of rooms/suites with individual decor providing a high standard of accommodation. Castle Douglas is an ideal location to experience all that Galloway has to offer - stunning scenery, historic buildings, gardens, fishing, golfing and interesting walks. Cycling is now very popular and Castle Douglas has its own cycle hire business.

*Bed and Breakfast from £23 to £27 sharing twin/double.
Dinner by prior arrangement.*

Tel/Fax: 01556 502360
e-mail: pikoe007@aol.com

Scottish
TOURIST BOARD
★★★★
B&B

Heathbank House
Tel: 01479 831234

Drumuillie Road, Boat of Garten, Inverness-shire PH24 3BD

With a friendly welcome, Heathbank House is the perfect base for your short break or longer stay in an unhurried and relaxed atmosphere. The house, which is non-smoking throughout, has six en suite rooms, two with four-poster beds. Five course dinner menus change daily and are served in a Charles Rennie Mackintosh style dining room.

Heathbank House is well situated for traditional and modern outdoor pursuits, cycling, walking, climbing, golf, fishing, bird watching, etc. If you prefer, just take a tour and admire the scenery.

E-mail: enquiries@heathbankhotel.co.uk
Web: www.heathbankhotel.co.uk

Heathmount Hotel
Kingsmills Road, Inverness IV2 3JU
Tel: 01463 235877 • Fax: 01463 715749
e-mail: heathmount@cali.co.uk
www.heathmountinn.com

Situated in the Crown area of Inverness this friendly Highland Inn is only a 5 minute walk from the town centre, Inverness Castle, bus and railway station. All rooms have private bathroom, TV, hairdryer, trouser press and direct dial telephone, and there are two four-poster suites. The extensive à la carte menus offer local fish, game and traditional Scottish dishes. Busy bars with real ales and a large range of malt whiskies. The surrounding area abounds with places of interest for the visitor, including boat trips on nearby Loch Ness and dolphin watching on the Moray Firth.

Rates from £60pppn single, £40pppn double/twin, £45pppn Four-Poster (including breakfast).

Braeburn B&B

Hosts: John & Julie Mackin

Stunning views over Loch Linnhe and the Ardgour Hills. A warm welcome awaits you in this spacious, family-run house with panoramic views of the surrounding area; Ben Nevis only four miles away. Situated in its own private grounds with ample off-road parking and storage for bikes and skiing equipment. 3 miles from the town centre; local hotels and bars serving good food and drink all within walking distance. Ideally situated for touring the West Highlands of Scotland. Relax in our comfortable residents' lounge or on our sunny patio. Enjoy a hearty breakfast to set you up for the day.

En suite rooms ✤ Colour TV ✤ Hospitality tray ✤ Hairdryer
Prices range from £22.50 to £25 per person. Open all year

Badabrie, Fort William PH33 7LX • 01397 772047
e-mail: mackinjj@hotmail.com
website: www.accommodation-fort-william.com

The Braes Guest House is a family-run guest house set in one and a half acres of secluded grounds with magnificent views of The Grey Corries. This is an ideal base to relax or tour some of the very best scenery in Scotland. We cater for all outdoor activities with purpose-built drying rooms and pick-up and drop-off facilities available by prior arrangement. Five double en suite rooms, one twin with private bathroom and one single en suite room. Pets welcome. A non-smoking establishment. Credit/debit cards accepted.

We hope that you arrive as a guest and leave as a friend.

Mr M. Jenkinson, The Braes Guest House, Tirindrish, Spean Bridge PH34 4EU • 01397 712437 • Fax: 01397 712108
e-mail: enquiry@thebraes.co.uk • website: www.thebraes.co.uk

Moray Park House

Tel: 01463 233528

1 Moray Park, Island Bank Road, Inverness IV2 4SX

Moray Park is a lovely old house overlooking Cavell Gardens and the River Ness, and just a few minutes from the main shopping streets.

The Mathieson Family purchased Moray Park House in August 2003 and have carried out refurbishment during the winter. Seven rooms have en suite facilities and one a private bathroom. All are freshly decorated and all but two have river views. One large ground floor room is designed for use by disabled people, with extra space and suitable en suite facilities. There is a car park for residents.

Moray Park House is ideally positioned for access to the lovely Island Bank Walk, the Eden Court Theatre, the Castle, city parks and numerous restaurants, all of which are within a few minutes' walk. Bed and Breakfast rates vary from £20 to £50.

e-mail: MorayParkHouse@aol.com • website: www.MorayParkHotel.co.uk

---

Ben Sheann Hotel Main Street, Strathyre FK18 8NA

Set in a friendly village amidst the beautiful scenery of the Trossachs (Scotland's newest National Park), this Victorian hotel offers accommodation in 10 comfortable bedrooms, all with TV, tea-making and central heating. Amenities include a public bar, lounge bar and dining room; SKY TV and pool table; residents' lounge; entertainment at weekends, quiz nights etc. Bar lunches and evening meals available. Small weddings and functions catered for. Ideal for touring - one hour from Glasgow, Edinburgh & Perth. Golf, walking, fishing, canoeing and shooting in the area. B&B from £20.

Tel & Fax: 01877 384609 • www.bensheannhotel.co.uk • e-mail: colin@bensheannhotel.co.uk

---

Merlindale is a luxurious Georgian house situated close to the town centre. All bedrooms are en suite (two with sunken bathrooms) and have tea/coffee making facilities. We have a jacuzzi available plus garden, ample parking and satellite television. We also have a Scottish library for the use of our guests. Cordon Bleu cooking is our speciality. A warm welcome awaits you in this non-smoking house.

Terms from: £40 Bed and Breakfast single, £27.50 double/twin. Dinner £20. Open February to December.

Mr & Mrs Clifford, Merlindale, Perth Road, Crieff PH7 3EQ • 01764 655205 • Fax: 01764 655205

Riverview House

Leny Road, Callander FK17 8AL
Tel: 01877 330635 • Fax: 01877 339386

Excellent value-for-money accommodation in the Trossachs area which forms the most beautiful part of Scotland's first National Park. Ideal centre for walking and cycling holidays, with cycle storage available. In the guest house all rooms are en suite, with TV and tea-making. Private parking. Also available self-catering stone cottages, sleep 3 or 4. Sorry, no smoking and no pets. Call Drew or Kathleen Little for details.

e-mail: auldtoll@aol.com
website: www.nationalparkscotland.co.uk

B&B from £21.
Low season and long stay discounts available.
Self-catering cottages from £225 per week
(STB 4 Stars).

NOTE

All the information in this guide is given in good faith in the belief that it is correct. However, the publishers cannot guarantee the facts given in these pages, neither are they responsible for changes in ownership or facilities that may take place after the date of going to press. Readers should always satisfy themselves that the facilities they require are available and that the terms, if quoted, still apply.

Helen and Chris welcome you to the Gumfreston Hotel, a fine Victorian house in a quiet residential street.

There are 9 en suite bedrooms, all non-smoking, with tea/coffee facilities, colour TV, radio and central heating. A tasty English breakfast will start your day, and an excellent menu of home-cooked dishes is available with varied starters, main courses and desserts. Vegetarian and children's meals also catered for. Smoking is permitted in the bar. Attended parking only 30 yards away.

**GUMFRESTON HOTEL,
CULVER PARK, TENBY SA70 7ED
TEL/FAX: 01834 842871
e-mail: gumf@supanet.com**

Tenby has four beautiful safe, sandy beaches; other leisure activities include golf, bowling, tennis, horse riding, sailing, surfing, sea and river fishing, and walking.

**Tel: 01437 532990
Twmpath Guest House,
Maenclochog, Pembs SA66 7RL**

Twmpath GUEST HOUSE

TWMPATH GUEST HOUSE has a Tourist Board **THREE STAR** rating and a Welcome Host **GOLD** Award. It offers home comforts, with full facilities for families, elderly and disabled guests. Set in the heart of the Pembrokeshire countryside, ideal for cyclists and walkers. Luxury rooms with full en suite facilities and cuisine of a high standard, combined with a warm, friendly, family atmosphere. We will ensure that your visit to Pembrokeshire is a memorable one. Twmpath Guest House overlooks the picturesque Preseli Mountains, just 20 minutes away from Haverfordwest and Fishguard.

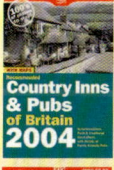   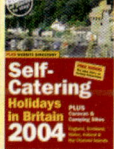
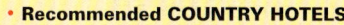
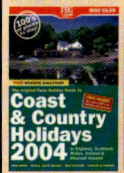 
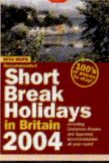 

UPPER GENFFORDD FARM
GUESTHOUSE

Selected 16th century farmhouse, suitable for disabled guests. Set in 200 acres where guests are allowed to walk freely, with footpaths to the mountains. In the Brecon Beacons National Park, Upper Genffordd Farm is an ideal base for exploring the Black Mountains, Wye Valley and the Brecon Beacons, an area of outstanding beauty, rich in historical and archaeological interest, with Roman camps and Norman castles. Picturesque mountain roads will lead you to reservoirs, the Gower coast with its lovely sandy beaches and Llangorse Lake – well known for all kinds of water sports. Livestock markets and open markets, leisure centres, pony trekking centres all within a few miles.

The charming Guest House accommodation includes one double and one twin-bedded room, both with en suite facilities. They are beautifully decorated and furnished, including tea/coffee making facilities, central heating, colour TV and hairdryer. The cosy lounge has a wealth of personal bric-a-brac, maps and paintings. Very much a home from home, with colour TV and books. Guests are made welcome with home-made cakes and tea on arrival. The local pub and restaurant is nearby and Hay-on-Wye, 'The Town of Books', is a short distance away.

Bed & Breakfast from £20 to £25 per person.

MRS PROSSER, UPPER GENFFORDD FARM GUESTHOUSE, TALGARTH, BRECON LD3 0EN
TELEPHONE: 01874 711360
WEBSITE: www.SmoothHound.co.uk/hotels/uppergenffordd.html

Awarded Plaque of Recommendation from the Welsh Tourist Board
Nominated "Landlady of the Year" 1999   Winner of FHG Diploma

---

Visit the FHG website
www.holidayguides.com
for details of the wide choice of accommodation featured in the full range of FHG titles

---

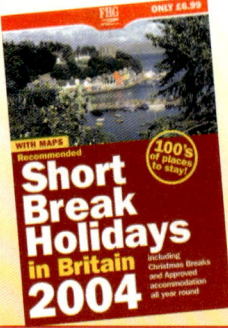

Recommended
Short Break Holidays in Britain 2004

Specifically designed to cater for the most rapidly growing sector of the holiday market in the UK. Illustrated details of hotels offering special "Bargain Breaks" throughout the year.

Available from bookshops and larger newsagents for £6.99

FHG PUBLICATIONS LTD
Abbey Mill Business Centre, Seedhill, Paisley, Scotland PA1 1TJ
www.holidayguides.com

Foreword

When people are considering booking a holiday, we have found that there are three factors which are crucial in helping them make their final decision. As most of us would expect, price is important – but as value for money, rather than low-price. Location also matters, not only for where we want to go on any particular holiday, but also for where the likely holiday property actually is. Thirdly, and perhaps most importantly, the type of facilities available. With the entries in *Bed and Breakfast Stops 2004* as in previous years, we have tried to avoid flowery description and lavish praise and instead have concentrated on hard facts, such as the location of the property, what kind of facilities are offered – bedrooms, bathrooms etc – and at least an indication of price. We hope that all of our advertisers provide friendly service – we ask them to vouch for this when we confirm their entry – and if they have official approval or other gradings from tourism authorities, or AA and RAC etc., we would certainly make this clear. In the end, however, only the paying guest can make the best judgement and so we welcome very warmly any comments which you may wish to send us about any of our entries. You will find full contact details with all the entries in the main sections of the guide, and there is a Special Welcome supplement at the back of the book for those who prefer non-smoking accommodation, or who require special diets or facilities for the disabled.

Anne Cuthbertson, Editor

Other FHG Publications

Recommended Country Hotels of Britain
Recommended Country Inns & Pubs of Britain
Recommended Short Break Holidays in Britain
Pets Welcome!
The Golf Guide: Where to Play/Where to Stay
Self-Catering Holidays in Britain
Britain's Best Holidays
Guide to Caravan and Camping Holidays
The Original Farm Holiday Guide to Coast & Country Holidays
Children Welcome! Family Holiday and Days Out Guide

ISBN 185055 356 4
© IPC Media Ltd 2004

Cover photographs:
Lower Slaughter, Gloucestershire: supplied by Photobank
Cover design: Focus Network
No part of this publication may be reproduced by any means or
transmitted without the permission of the Publishers.

Maps: ©MAPS IN MINUTES™ 2003. ©Crown Copyright, Ordnance Survey
Northern Ireland 2003 Permit No.NI 1675

Typeset by FHG Publications Ltd, Paisley.

Printed and bound in Great Britain by William Clowes, Beccles, Suffolk

Distribution. Book Trade: NBN Plymbridge, Plymbridge House, Estover Road, Plymouth PL6 7PY
Tel: 01752 202300; Fax: 01752 202333
News Trade: Market Force (UK) Ltd, 5th Floor Low Rise, King's Reach Tower,
Stamford Street, London SE1 9LS
Tel: 0207 633 3450; Fax: 0207 633 3572

Published by FHG Publications Ltd., Abbey Mill Business Centre,
Seedhill, Paisley PA1 ITJ (Tel: 0141-887 0428; Fax: 0141-889 7204).
e-mail: fhg@ipcmedia.com

US ISBN 1-58843-360-9
Distributed in the United States by
Hunter Publishing Inc., 130 Campus Drive, Edison, N.J. 08818, USA

Bed & Breakfast Stops is an FHG publication, published by
IPC Country & Leisure Media Ltd, part of IPC Media Group of Companies.

Bed & Breakfast Stops 2004

Value for money accommodation in England, Scotland, Wales & Ireland

FHG Publications, part of IPC Country & Leisure Media Ltd

FHG Diploma Winners 2003

Each year we award a small number of diplomas to holiday proprietors whose services have been specially commended by our readers. The following were our FHG Diploma Winners for 2003.

England

DERBYSHIRE

Mr Tatlow
Ashfield Farm, Calwich
Near Ashbourne
Derbyshire DE6 2EB

DEVON

Mrs Tucker
Lower Luxton Farm, Upottery
Near Honiton
Devon EX14 9PB

◆

Royal Oak
Dunsford Near Exeter
Devon EX6 7DA

GLOUCESTERSHIRE

Mrs Keyte
The Limes, Evesham Road
Stow-on-the-Wold
Gloucestershire GL54 1EN

HAMPSHIRE

Mrs Ellis, Efford Cottage,
Everton, Lymington,
Hampshire SO41 0JD

◆

R. Law
Whitley Ridge Hotel
Beauly Road, Brockenhurst
Hampshire SO42 7QL

HEREFORDSHIRE

Mrs Brown
Ye Hostelrie, Goodrich
Near Ross on Wye
Herefordshire HR9 6HX

NORTH YORKSHIRE

Charles & Gill Richardson
The Coppice, 9 Studley Road
Harrogate
North Yorkshire HG1 5JU

◆

Mr & Mrs Hewitt
Harmony Country Lodge
Limestone Road, Burniston,
Scarborough
North Yorkshire YO13 0DG

Wales

POWYS

Linda Williams
The Old Vicarage
Erwood, Builth Wells
Powys LD2 3SZ

Scotland

ABERDEEN, BANFF & MORAY

Mr Ian Ednie
Spey Bay Hotel
Spey Bay
Fochabers
Moray IV32 7PJ

PERTH & KINROSS

Dunalastair Hotel
Kinloch Rannoch
By Pitlochry
Perthshire PH16 5PW

HELP IMPROVE BRITISH TOURISM STANDARDS

As recommendations are submitted from readers of the FULL RANGE of FHG titles the winners shown above may not necessarily appear in this guide.

THE FHG DIPLOMA

HELP IMPROVE
BRITISH TOURIST STANDARDS

You are choosing holiday accommodation from our very popular FHG Publications.
Whether it be a hotel, guest house, farmhouse or self-catering accommodation, we think you will find it hospitable, comfortable and clean, and your host and hostess friendly and helpful.

Why not write and tell us about it?

As a recognition of the generally well-run and excellent holiday accommodation reviewed in our publications, we at FHG Publications Ltd. present a diploma to proprietors who receive the highest recommendation from their guests who are also readers of our Guides. If you care to write to us praising the holiday you have booked through FHG Publications Ltd. – whether this be board, self-catering accommodation, a sporting or a caravan holiday, what you say will be evaluated and the proprietors who reach our final list will be contacted.

The winning proprietor will receive an attractive framed diploma to display on his premises as recognition of a high standard of comfort, amenity and hospitality. FHG Publications Ltd. offer this diploma as a contribution towards the improvement of standards in tourist accommodation in Britain. Help your excellent host or hostess to win it!

FHG DIPLOMA

We nominate

Because

Name ....

Address..

....

Telephone No..

Ratings You Can Trust

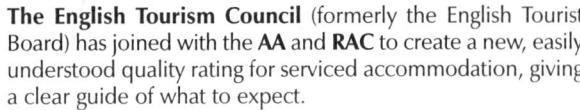

The English Tourism Council (formerly the English Tourist Board) has joined with the **AA** and **RAC** to create a new, easily understood quality rating for serviced accommodation, giving a clear guide of what to expect.

HOTELS are given a rating from One to Five **Stars** – the more Stars, the higher the quality and the greater the range of facilities and level of services provided.

GUEST ACCOMMODATION, which includes guest houses, bed and breakfasts, inns and farmhouses, is rated from One to Five **Diamonds**. Progressively higher levels of quality and customer care must be provided for each one of the One to Five Diamond ratings.

HOLIDAY PARKS, TOURING PARKS and CAMPING PARKS are now also assessed using **Stars**. Standards of quality range from a One Star (acceptable) to a Five Star (exceptional) park.

Look out also for the new **SELF-CATERING** Star ratings. The more **Stars** (from One to Five) awarded to an establishment, the higher the levels of quality you can expect. Establishments at higher rating levels also have to meet some additional requirements for facilities.

SCOTLAND

Star Quality Grades will reflect the most important aspects of a visit, such as the warmth of welcome, efficiency and friendliness of service, the quality of the food and the cleanliness and condition of the furnishings, fittings and decor.

THE MORE STARS,
THE HIGHER THE STANDARDS.

The description, such as Hotel, Guest House, Bed and Breakfast, Lodge, Holiday Park, Self-catering etc tells you the type of property and style of operation.

WALES

Places which score highly will have an especially welcoming atmosphere and pleasing ambience, high levels of comfort and guest care, and attractive surroundings enhanced by thoughtful design and attention to detail

STAR QUALITY GUIDE FOR

HOTELS, GUEST HOUSES AND FARMHOUSES

SELF-CATERING ACCOMMODATION
(Cottages, Apartments, Houses)

CARAVAN HOLIDAY HOME PARKS
(Holiday Parks, Touring Parks, Camping Parks)

★★★★★ *Exceptional quality*
★★★★ *Excellent quality*
★★★ *Very good quality*
★★ *Good quality*
★ *Fair to good quality*

In England, Scotland and Wales, all graded properties are inspected annually by Tourist Authority trained Assessors.

FHG Readers' Offer Vouchers

On the following pages are a selection of Readers' Offer
Vouchers for attractions throughout the country,
giving reduced rate entry or similar discounts.

MUSEUM OF
CHILDHOOD
MEMORIES

If you are planning a family day out and don't want to leave your pet behind, then check out the attractions listed below which allow pets (in most cases they must be kept on leads).

Bucks Goat Centre, Layby Farm, Stoke Mandeville, Aylesbury, Buckinghamshire HP22 5XJ
Tel: 01296 612983
e-mail: bucksgoat@ccn.go-free.co.uk
website: www.bucksgoatcentre.co.uk
The most comprehensive collection of goat breeds in Britain; other animals, shops and cafe.
Dogs must be kept on leads.

Buckinghamshire Railway Centre, Quainton Road Station, Quainton, Aylesbury, Buckinghamshire HP22 4BY
Tel: 01296 655720
website: www.bucksrailcentre.org.uk
A working steam railway centre. Steam train rides, minature railway rides, large collection of historic, preserved steam locomotives, carriages and wagons.

Launceston Steam Railway, St Thomas Hill, Launceston, Cornwall PL15 8DA
Tel: 01566 775665
Victorian locomotives haul from Launceston (buffet, museum, workshops, souvenirs, books) to Newmills (picnic, play area, riverside walk).
Dogs on lead at all times. They are charged 50p but get a ticket!

The China Clay Museum, Wheal Martyn, St Austell, Cornwall PL26 8XG
Tel: 01726 850362
e-mail: info@wheal-martyn.com
website: www.wheal-martyn.com
Industrial museum of the china clay industry. Historic trail with working water wheels; nature trail.
Dogs on leads welcome.

Peak Cavern, Castleton, Hope Valley, Derbyshire S33 8WS
Tel: 01433 620285
e-mail: info@peakcavern.co.uk
website: www.devilsarse.co.uk
Guided tours of this vast limestone cave, whose entrance is so large it once contained a village and rope works.
Dogs must be kept on lead in the cave.

The Milky Way Adventure Park, Downland Farm, Clovelly, Bideford, Devon EX39 5RY
Tel: 01237 431255
e-mail: info@themilkyway.co.uk
website: www.themilkyway.co.uk
The largest all-weather facilities in North Devon including the Time Warp, a huge indoor play area, archery, birds of prey and other live shows.
Dogs must be kept on leads and not taken to live shows.

Beamish, The North of England Open Air Museum, Beamish, Durham DH9 0RG
Tel: 0191 370 4000
e-mail: museum@beamish.org.uk
website: www.beamish.org.uk
An open-air museum illustrating life in the 1800s and 1900s, set in 200 acres of beautiful countryside.
Dogs (except Guide Dogs) not allowed in refreshment areas or period buildings but are very welcome elsewhere at Beamish. Must be kept on a lead at all times.

Hever Castle and Gardens, Edenbridge, Kent TN8 7NG
Tel: 01732 865224
e-mail: mail@hevercastle.co.uk
website: www.hevercastle.co.uk
Thirteenth century castle, childhood home of Anne Boleyn set in award-winning gardens with Italian, Rose and Tudor gardens, topiary, lake, yew and water maze. Two licensed self-service restaurants. Gift, book and garden shops.
Dogs must be kept on lead at all times.

Forde Abbey Gardens, Chard, Somerset TA20 4LU
Tel: 01460 221290
e-mail: forde.abbey@virgin.net
website: www.fordeabbey.co.uk
30 acres of one of the top ten gardens in England surround the 12th century former abbey.
Dogs on short leads please.

Bowhill House and Country Park, Bowhill, Selkirk, Scottish Borders TD7 5ET
Tel: 01750 22204
e-mail: bht@buccleuch.com
Home of the Duke & Duchess of Buccleuch, with outstanding collections of art, silverware and porcelain.
Dogs must be kept on lead and stick to main tracks.

Bo'ness & Kinneil Railway, The Station, Bo'ness, West Lothian EH51 9AQ
Tel: 01506 822298
website: www.srps.org.uk
A living museum of steam and diesel locomotives, carriages and historic buildings.
Pets welcome on lead (not restaurant or museum).

**visit the FHG website
www.holidayguides.com**

A 65-minute journey into the lost world of the English narrow gauge light railway. Features historic steam locomotives from many countries.

PETS MUST BE KEPT UNDER CONTROL AND NOT ALLOWED ON TRACKS

Open: Sundays and Bank Holiday weekends 16 March to 29 October. Additional days in summer.

Directions: On A4146 towards Hemel Hempstead, close to roundabout junction with A505.

FHG PUBLICATIONS, ABBEY MILL BUSINESS CENTRE, PAISLEY PA1 1TJ

Be a giant in a magical miniature world of make-believe depicting rural England in the 1930s. "A little piece of history that is forever England."

Open: 10am to 5pm daily mid February to end October.

Directions: Junction 16 M25, Junction 2 M40.

FHG PUBLICATIONS, ABBEY MILL BUSINESS CENTRE, PAISLEY PA1 1TJ

A working steam railway centre. Steam train rides, miniature railway rides, large collection of historic preserved steam locomotives, carriages and wagons.

Open: Sundays and Bank Holidays April to October, plus Wednesdays in June, July and August 10.30am to 5.30pm.

Directions: off A41 Aylesbury to Bicester Road, 6 miles north west of Aylesbury.

FHG PUBLICATIONS, ABBEY MILL BUSINESS CENTRE, PAISLEY PA1 1TJ

Farm animals, 18th century watermill and farmhouse, farm artifacts, caravan and camping, children's play area. Restaurant and gift shop.

Open: all year 9.30am to 5pm.

Directions: signposted off both A47 and A1.

FHG PUBLICATIONS, ABBEY MILL BUSINESS CENTRE, PAISLEY PA1 1TJ

Cornwall's only Donkey Sanctuary set in 14 acres overlooking the beautiful Tamar Valley. Donkey rides, rabbit warren, goat hill, children's playgrounds, cafe and picnic area.

Open: Easter to end of October and February half-term - daily from 10am to 5.30pm. November to March open weekends. Closed January.

Directions: Just off A390 between Callington and Gunnislake at St Ann's Chapel.

FHG PUBLICATIONS, ABBEY MILL BUSINESS CENTRE, PAISLEY PA1 1TJ

A collection of cars from film and TV, including Chitty Chitty Bang Bang, James Bond's Aston Martin, Del Boy's van, Fab1 and many more.

PETS MUST BE KEPT ON LEAD

Open: Daily 10am-5pm. Closed February half term. Weekends only in December.

Directions: In centre of Keswick close to car park.

World's finest steamboat collection and premier all-weather attraction. Swallows and Amazons exhibition, model boat pond, tea shop, souvenir shop. Free guided tours. Model boat exhibition.

Open: 10am to 5pm 3rd weekend in March to last weekend October.

Directions: on A592 half-a-mile north of Bowness-on-Windermere.

Large range of natural water-worn caverns featuring mining equipment, stalactites and stalagmites, and fine deposits of Blue-John stone, Britain's rarest semi-precious stone.

DOGS MUST BE KEPT ON LEAD

Open: 9.30am to 5.30pm.

Directions: Situated 2 miles west of Castleton; follow brown tourist signs.

A superb family day out in the atmosphere of a bygone era. Explore the recreated period street and fascinating exhibitions. Unlimited tram rides are free with entry. Play areas, shops, tea rooms, pub, restaurant and lots more.

Open: daily April to October 10 am to 5.30pm, weekends in winter.

Directions: Eight miles from M1 Junction 28, follow brown and white signs for "Tramway Museum".

An underground wonderland of stalactites, stalagmites, rocks, minerals and fossils. Home of the unique Blue John stone – see the largest single piece ever found. Suitable for all ages.

Open: Opens 10am. Enquire for last tour of day and closed days.

Directions: Half-a-mile west of Castleton on A6187 (old A625)

Coldharbour Mill Museum

Coldharbour Mill, Uffculme, Cullompton, Devon EX15 3EE

Tel: 01884 840960 • e-mail: info@coldharbourmill.org.uk
website: www.coldharbourmill.org.uk

READERS' OFFER 2004

TWO adult tickets for the price of ONE

valid during 2004

The Big Sheep

Bideford, Devon EX39 5AP

Tel: 01237 472366

READERS' OFFER 2004

Admit one child FREE with each paying adult

valid during 2004

The Gnome Reserve & Wild Flower Garden

West Putford, Near Bradworthy, Devon EX22 7XE

Tel: 01409 241435 • e-mail: info@gnomereserve.co.uk
website: www.gnomereserve.co.uk

READERS' OFFER 2004

One FREE child with full paying adult

Valid during 2004

Killhope Lead Mining Museum

Cowshill, Upper Weardale, Co. Durham DL13 1AR

Tel: 01388 537505

e-mail: killhope@durham.gov.uk • website: www.durham.gov.uk/killhope

READERS' OFFER 2004

One child FREE with full-paying adult (not valid for Park Level Mine)

valid April to October 2004

BARLEYLANDS FARM

Barleylands Road, Billericay, Essex CM11 2UD

Tel: 01268 290229 • e-mail: info@barleylands.co.uk
website: www.barleylands.co.uk

READERS' OFFER 2004

FREE adult ticket when accompanied by one child

Valid 1st March to 31st October. Not special event days

A picturesque 200-year old woollen mill with machinery that spins yarn and weaves cloth.
Mill machinery, restaurant, exhibition gallery, shop and gardens in a waterside setting.

Open: February to December daily 10.30am to 5pm.

Directions: Two miles from Junction 27 M5; follow signs to Willand (B3181) then brown tourist signs to Working Woollen Mill.

"England for Excellence" award-winning rural attraction combining traditional rural crafts with hilarious novelties such as sheep racing and duck trialling, Indoor adventure zone for adults and children.

Open: daily, 10am to 6pm April - Oct Phone for Winter opening times and details.

Directions: on A39 North Devon link road, two miles west of Bideford Bridge.

Visit 1000+ gnomes and pixies in two acre beech wood. Gnome hats are loaned free of charge - so the gnomes think you are one of them - don't forget your camera! Also 2-acre wild flower garden with 250 labelled species.

Open: Daily 10am to 6pm 21st March to 31st October.

Directions: Between Bideford and Bude; follow brown tourist signs from A39/A388/A386.

Britain's best preserved lead mining site – and a great day out for all the family, with lots to see and do. Underground Experience – Park Level Mine now open.

Open: April 1st to September 30th 10.30am to 5pm daily. Weekends and half term in October

Directions: Alongside A689, midway between Stanhope and Alston in the heart of the North Pennines.

Craft Village with animals, museum, blacksmith, glassblowing, miniature railway (Sundays and August), craft shops, tea room and licensed restaurant.

DOGS MUST BE KEPT ON LEAD

Open: Craft Village open all year. Farm open 1st March to 31st October.

Directions: M25, A127 towards Southend. Take A176 junction off A127, 3rd exit Wash Road, 2nd left Barleylands Road.

On three floors of a Listed Victorian warehouse telling 200 years of inland waterway history. • Historic boats • Boat trips available (Easter to October) • Painted boat gallery • Blacksmith • Archive film • Hands-on displays *"A great day out"*

Open: every day 10am to 5pm (excluding Christmas Day).

Directions: Junction 11A or 12 off M5 – follow brown signs for Historic Docks. Railway and bus station - 15 minute walk. Free coach parking.

Discover the fascinating history of cider making. There is a programme of temporary exhibitions and events plus free samples of Hereford cider brandy.

Open: April to Oct 10am to 5.30pm (daily) Nov to Dec 11am to 3pm (daily) Jan to Mar 11am to 3pm (Tues to Sun)
Directions: situated west of Hereford off the A438 Hereford to Brecon road.

The museum of everyday life in Roman Britain. An award-winning museum with re-created Roman rooms, hands-on discovery areas, and some of the best mosaics outside the Mediterranean.

Open: Monday to Saturday 10am-5.30pm Sunday 2pm-5.30pm.

Directions: St Albans.

Kent's award-winning open air museum is home to a collection of historic buildings which house interactive exhibitions on life over the last 150 years.

Open: Seven days a week from March to November. 10am to 5.30pm.

Directions: Junction 6 off M20, follow signs to Aylesford.

We are a working farm, with lots of animals to see and touch. Enjoy a walk round the Nature Trail or refreshments in the tearoom. Lots of activities during school holidays.

Open: Summer: daily 10.30am to 5pm Winter: weekends only 10.30am to 4pm.
Directions: Junction 35 off M6, take B6254 towards Kirkby Lonsdale, then follow the brown signs.

FHG READERS' OFFER 2004

DONINGTON GRAND PRIX COLLECTION
DONINGTON PARK
Castle Donington, Near Derby, Leics DE74 2RP
Tel: 01332 811027 • e-mail: enquiries@doningtoncollection.co.uk
website: www.doningtoncollection.com

One child FREE with each full-paying adult

valid until 01/01/05

NOT TO BE USED IN CONJUNCTION WITH ANY OTHER OFFER

FHG READERS' OFFER 2004

Snibston Discovery Park
Ashby Road, Coalville, Leicestershire LE67 3LN
Tel: 01530 278444• Fax: 01530 813301
e-mail: snibston@leics.gov.uk • website: www.leics.gov.uk/museums

One FREE child with every full paying adult

valid until June 2004

NOT TO BE USED IN CONJUNCTION WITH ANY OTHER OFFER

FHG READERS' OFFER 2004

Skegness Natureland Seal Sanctuary
North Parade, Skegness, Lincolnshire PE25 1DB
Tel: 01754 764345
e-mail: natureland@fsbdial.co.uk • website: www.skegnessnatureland.co.uk

Free entry for one child when accompanied by full-paying adult.

Valid during 2004

NOT TO BE USED IN CONJUNCTION WITH ANY OTHER OFFER

FHG READERS' OFFER 2004

Museum in Docklands
No. 1 Warehouse, West India Quay, Hertsmere Road, London E14 4AL
Tel: 0870 4443855 • Fax: 0870 4443858
e-mail: info@museumindocklands.org.uk

TWO adult tickets for price of ONE. Children go FREE

valid from 01/08/04 to 31/12/04

NOT TO BE USED IN CONJUNCTION WITH ANY OTHER OFFER

FHG READERS' OFFER 2004

PLEASURELAND
Marine Drive, Southport, Merseyside PR8 1RX
Tel: 08702 200204 • Fax: 01704 537936
e-mail: mail@pleasurelandltd.freeserve.co.uk• website: www.pleasureland.uk.com

3 for 2, if two all day wristbands purchased, third provided FREE
• offer not valid on Bank Holiday Weekends

valid from March to November 2004

NOT TO BE USED IN CONJUNCTION WITH ANY OTHER OFFER

The world's largest collection of Grand Prix racing cars – over 130 exhibits within five halls, including McLaren Formula One cars.

Open: Daily 10am to 5pm (last admission 4pm). Closed Christmas/New Year.

Directions: 2 miles from M1 (J23a/24) and M42/A42; to north-west via A50.

FHG PUBLICATIONS, ABBEY MILL BUSINESS CENTRE, PAISLEY PA1 1TJ

Located in 100 acres of landscaped grounds, Snibston is a unique mixture, with historic mine buildings, outdoor science play areas, wildlife habitats and an exhibition hall housing five hands-on galleries. Cafe and gift shop. Plus new for 2003 - Toy Box (gallery for under 5s & 8s).

Open: Seven days a week 10am to 5pm.

Directions: Junction 22 from M1, Junction 13 from M42. Follow Brown Heritage signs.

FHG PUBLICATIONS, ABBEY MILL BUSINESS CENTRE, PAISLEY PA1 1TJ

Well known for rescuing and rehabilitating orphaned and injured seal pups found washed ashore on Lincolnshire beaches. Also: penguins, aquarium, pets' corner, reptiles, Floral Palace (tropical birds and butterflies etc).

Open: Daily from 10am. Closed Christmas/Boxing/New Year's Days.

Directions: At the north end of Skegness seafront.

FHG PUBLICATIONS, ABBEY MILL BUSINESS CENTRE, PAISLEY PA1 1TJ

The Museum In Docklands unlocks the history of London's river, port and people in a nineteenth century warehouse, originally used to house imports of exotic spices, rum and cotton. It now holds a wealth of objects from whale bones to WWII gas masks.

Open: open 7 days 10am to 6pm.

Directions: furthest warehouse along quayside from West India Quay DLR over footbridge from Canary Wharf shopping centre.

FHG PUBLICATIONS, ABBEY MILL BUSINESS CENTRE, PAISLEY PA1 1TJ

Over 100 rides and attractions, including the Traumatizer - the UK's tallest, fastest suspended looping coaster and the Lucozade Space Shot. New for 2003 - Abdullah's Dilemma

Open: March to November, times vary.

FHG PUBLICATIONS, ABBEY MILL BUSINESS CENTRE, PAISLEY PA1 1TJ

Lions, snow leopards, chimpanzees, otters, reptiles, aquarium and lots more, set amidst landscaped gardens. Gift shop, cafe and picnic areas.

Open: all year round from 10am

Directions: on the coast 16 miles north of Liverpool; follow the brown and white tourist signs

---

It's time you came-n-saurus for a monster day out set in over 100 acres of parkland. Enjoy the adventure play areas, dinosaur trail, secret animal garden and lots more.

Open: Please call for specific opening times or see our website.

Directions: Nine miles from Norwich, follow the brown signs to Weston Park from the A47 or A1067

The collections of local eccentric Eric St John-Foti (Mr Norfolk Punch himself!) on view (over 80) and the Magical Dickens Experience. Two amazing attractions for the price of one. Somewhere totally different, unique and interesting.

Open: 11am to 5pm (last entry 4pm) Open all year.

Directions: one mile from town centre on the A1122 Downham/Wisbech Road.

Beautiful walled garden with famous collections of herbs and herbaceous plants, including Roman Garden, National Thyme and Marjoram Collections. Nursery and Gift shop.

Open: From Easter to the end of October 10am to 5pm daily.

Directions: Six miles north of Hexham off B6318 next to Chesters Roman Fort.

A collection of 65 aircraft and cockpit sections from across the history of aviation. Extensive aero engine and artefact displays.

Open: Daily from 10am (closed Christmas period).

Directions: Follow brown and white signs from A1, A46, A17 and A1133.

Journey with us through 300 years of Crime and Punishment on this unique atmospheric site. Witness a real trial in the authentic Victorian courtroom. Prisoners and gaolers act as guides as you become part of history.

Open: Tuesday to Sunday 10am to 5pm peak season 10am to 4pm off-peak.

Directions: from Nottingham city centre follow the brown tourist signs.

Travel back in time to the dark and dangerous world of intrigue and adventure of Medieval England's most endearing outlaw - Robin Hood. Story boards, exhibitions and a film show all add interest to the story.

Open: 10am -6pm, last admission 4.30pm.

Directions: Follow the brown and white tourist information signs whilst heading towards the city centre.

A modern working farm with displays indoors and outdoors designed to help visitors listen, feel and learn whilst having fun. Daily baby animal holding sessions plus a large indoor play barn.

Open: Daily 10am to 5pm.

Directions: 12 miles from Nottingham on A614 or follow Robin Hood signs from J27 of M1.

Historic manor house and farm with traditional animals. Work in the Victorian kitchen every afternoon.

Open: April to 2nd December: Tuesday to Friday 10.30am to 5.30pm. Saturday and Sunday 12-5.30pm.

Directions: Just off A40 Oxford to Cheltenham road at Witney.

The Avon Valley Railway offers a whole new experience for some, and a nostalgic memory for others. Steam trains operate every Sunday Easter to October, plus Bank Holidays and Christmas.

PETS MUST BE KEPT ON LEADS AND OFF TRAIN SEATS

Open: Steam trains operate every Sunday Easter to October plus Bank Holidays and Christmas

Directions: On the A431 midway between Bristol and Bath at Bitton

The world's largest helicopter collection - over 70 exhibits, includes two royal helicopters, Russian Gunship and Vietnam veterans plus many award-winning exhibits. Cafe, shop. Flights.

PETS MUST BE KEPT UNDER CONTROL

Open: Wednesday to Sunday 10am to 5.30pm. Daily during school Easter and Summer (open till 6.30pm) holidays and Bank Holiday Mondays. (10am to 4.30pm November to March)

Directions: Junction 21 off M5 then follow the propellor signs.

Lots of baby animals. FREE pony rides, face painting, green trail, 'pat-a-pet', indoor children's soft play area; gift shop, tearoom, pets' paddocks

DOGS MUST BE KEPT ON LEADS

Open: March to October 10.30am to 6pm

Directions: Follow brown tourist signs off A12 and other roads

---

With over forty rides, shows and attractions set in fifty acres of parkland - you'll have everything you need for a brilliant day out. The mixture of old favourites and exciting new introductions are an unbeatable combination.

Open: From 10am. Closing time varies depending on season.

Directions: Off A12 between Great Yarmouth and Lowestoft.

A plant lover's paradise with outstanding themed gardens and extensive Museum of Natural History. Conservatory gardens contain a large and varied collection of the world's flora. Sussex History Trail. Dinosaur Museum and park. Rides and amusements.

Open: Open daily, except Christmas Day and Boxing Day.

Directions: Signposted off A26 and A259.

The past is brought to life at the top attraction in the South East 2002 (England for Excellence Awards). Step back in time and wonder through over 30 shop and room settings.

PETS NOT ALLOWED IN CHILDREN'S PLAY AREA

Open: 9.30am to 6pm (last admission 4.45pm, one hour earlier in winter).

Directions: Just off A21 in Battle High Street opposite the Abbey.

Wilderness Wood is a unique family-run working woodland in the Sussex High Weald. Explore trails and footpaths, enjoy local cakes and ices, try the adventure playground. Many special events and activities. Parties catered for.

Open: daily 10am to 5.30pm or dusk if earlier.

Directions: On the south side of the A272 in the village of Hadlow Down. Signposted with a brown tourist sign.

FHG PUBLICATIONS, ABBEY MILL BUSINESS CENTRE, PAISLEY PA1 1TJ

Europe's largest indoor family funfair, with exciting rides like the New Rollercoaster, Disco Dodgems and Swashbuckling Pirate Ship. There's something for everyone whatever the weather!

Open: Daily except Christmas Day. Mon - Wed & Fri - Sat 10am to 8pm, Thurs 10am - 9pm, Sun 11am to 6pm. (Open from 12 noon Monday to Friday during term time).

Directions: Signposted from the A1.

FHG PUBLICATIONS, ABBEY MILL BUSINESS CENTRE, PAISLEY PA1 1TJ

---

100 acres of parkland, home to hundreds of duck, geese, swans and flamingos. Discovery centre, cafe, gift shop; play area.

Open: Every day except Christmas Day

Directions: Signposted from A19, A195, A1231 and A182.

FHG PUBLICATIONS, ABBEY MILL BUSINESS CENTRE, PAISLEY PA1 1TJ

Wander through a lush landscape of exotic foliage where a myriad of multi-coloured butterflies sip nectar from tropical blossoms. Stroll past bubbling streams and splashing waterfalls; view insects and spiders all safely behind glass.

Open: 10am to 6pm summer, 10am to dusk winter.

FHG PUBLICATIONS, ABBEY MILL BUSINESS CENTRE, PAISLEY PA1 1TJ

Lovely rural farm with 50 breeds of rabbit, and several breeds of poultry, pig, sheep, goat, horses and ponies. Iron Age Roundhouse. Cafe, craft shop, events throughout holidays, famous pig races, nature trail, indoor and outdoor play.

Open: 10.30am to 6pm in season, weekends 10am to 4pm in winter.

Directions: Near Stonehenge, just off the A303 at the intersection with A338 Salisbury/Swindon Road.

FHG PUBLICATIONS, ABBEY MILL BUSINESS CENTRE, PAISLEY PA1 1TJ

The Deep is the world's only submarium. Here you can discover the story of the world's oceans on a dramatic journey from the beginning of time and into the future.
You can also explore the wonders of the oceans, from the tropical lagoon to the icy waters of Antarctica.

Open: daily 10am to 6pm
(last entry at 5pm).
Closed Christmas Eve and Christmas Day
Directions: from the North take A1/M, M62/A63. From the South take A1/M, A15/A63 follow signs to Hull city centre, then local signs to The Deep.

Steam trains operate over a 4½ mile line from Bolton Abbey Station to Embsay Station. Many family events including Thomas the Tank Engine take place during major Bank Holidays.

Open: steam trains run every Sunday throughout the year and up to 7 days a week in summer.
10.30am to 4.30pm

Directions: Embsay Station signposted from the A59 Skipton by-pass; Bolton Abbey Station signposted from the A59 at Bolton Abbey.

A fascinating display of railway carriages and a wide range of railway items telling the story of rail travel over the years.

ALL PETS MUST BE KEPT ON LEADS

Open: Daily 11am to 4.30pm

Directions: Approximately one mile from Keighley on A629 Halifax road. Follow brown tourist signs

---

The Colour Museum is unique. Dedicated to the history, development and technology of colour, it is the ONLY museum of its kind in Europe. A truly colourful experience for both kids and adults, it's fun, it's informative and it's well worth a visit.

Open: Tuesday to Saturday 10am to 4pm
(last admission 3.30pm).
Directions: just off Westgate on B6144 from the city centre to Haworth.

A fantastic day out for all at the lively and interactive, award-winning Thackray Museum. Experience life as it was in the Victorian slums, discover how medicine has changed our lives and the incredible lotions and potions once offered as cures.
Try an empathy belly and explore the interactive bodyworks gallery.

Open: daily 10am till 5pm, closed 24th - 26th and 31st December and 1st January.

Directions: from M621 follow signs for York (A64) then follow brown tourist signs. From the north, take A58 towards city and then follow brown tourist signs.

FHG READERS' OFFER 2004

The Grassic Gibbon Centre
Arbuthnott, Laurencekirk, Aberdeenshire AB30 1PB
Tel: 01561 361668 • e-mail: lgginfo@grassicgibbon.com
website: www.grassicgibbon.com

Valid during 2004 (not groups)

TWO for the price of ONE entry to exhibition (based on full adult rate only)

NOT TO BE USED IN CONJUNCTION WITH ANY OTHER OFFER

FHG READERS' OFFER 2004

Oban Rare Breeds Farm Park
Glencruitten, Oban, Argyll PA34 4QB
Tel: 01631 770608
e-mail: info@obanrarebreeds.com • website: www.obanrarebreeds.com

valid during 2004

20% DISCOUNT on all admissions

NOT TO BE USED IN CONJUNCTION WITH ANY OTHER OFFER

FHG READERS' OFFER 2004

Dunaskin Heritage Centre
Waterside, Patna, Ayrshire KA6 7JF
Tel: 01292 531144
e-mail: dunaskin@btconnect.com • website: www.dunaskin.org.uk

valid from 1st May to 31st October 2004

TWO for the price of ONE

NOT TO BE USED IN CONJUNCTION WITH ANY OTHER OFFER

FHG READERS' OFFER 2004

Kelburn Castle & Country Centre
Fairlie, Near Largs, Ayrshire KA29 0BE
Tel: 01475 568685 • e-mail: info@kelburncountrycentre.com
website: www.kelburncountrycentre.com

Valid until October 2004

One child FREE for each full paying adult

NOT TO BE USED IN CONJUNCTION WITH ANY OTHER OFFER

FHG READERS' OFFER 2004

Scottish Maritime Museum
Harbourside, Irvine KA12 8QE
Tel: 01294 278283 • e-mail: smm@tildesley.fsbusiness.co.uk
website: www.scottishmaritimemuseum.org • Fax: 01294 313211

Valid from January to December 2004

TWO for the price of ONE

NOT TO BE USED IN CONJUNCTION WITH ANY OTHER OFFER

Visitor centre dedicated to the much-loved Scottish writer Lewis Grassic Gibbon. Exhibition, cafe, gift shop. Outdoor children's play area. Disabled access throughout.

Open: Daily April to October 10am to 4.30pm. Groups by appointment including evenings.

Directions: On the B967, accessible and signposted from both A90 and A92.

Rare breeds of farm animals, pets' corner, conservation groups, tea room, woodland walk in beautiful location

Open: 10am to 6pm mid-March to end October

Directions: two-and-a-half miles from Oban along Glencruitten road

Set in the rolling hills of Ayrshire, Europe's best preserved ironworks. Guided tours, audio-visuals, walks with electronic wands. Restaurant/coffee shop.

Open: April to October daily 10am to 5pm.

Directions: A713 Ayr to Castle Douglas road, 12 miles from Ayr, 3 miles from Dalmellington.

The historic home of the Earls of Glasgow. Waterfalls, gardens, famous Glen, unusual trees. Riding school, stockade, play areas, exhibitions, shop, cafe and The Secret Forest.

PETS MUST BE KEPT ON LEAD

Open: daily 10am to 6pm Easter to October.

Directions: On A78 between Largs and Fairlie, 45 mins drive from Glasgow.

Scotland's seafaring heritage is among the world's richest and you can relive the heyday of Scottish shipping at the Maritime Museum.

Open: all year except Christmas and New Year Holidays. 10am - 5pm

Directions: Situated on Irvine harbourside and only a 10 minute walk from Irvine train station.

An innovative museum exploring the history and environment of West Lothian on a 20-acre site packed full of things to see and do, indoors and out.

Open: Daily (except Christmas and New Year) 10am to 5pm.

Directions: 15 miles from Edinburgh, follow "Heritage Centre" signs from A899.

On show is a large collection, from 1899, of cars, bicycles, motor cycles and commercials. There is also a large collection of period advertising, posters and enamel signs.

Open: Daily April to October 11am to 4pm; November to March: Sundays 1pm to 3pm or by special appointment.

Directions: Off A198 near Aberlady. Two miles from A1.

World famous attraction at Loch Ness. Centre includes shopping complex, coffee shop, restaurants, hotel and boat cruises throughout the summer. Don't miss the Highlands most popular tourist attraction.

Open: all year - times vary.

Directions: 14 miles south of Inverness on the A82 main road.

Award-winning attraction with unique 'Heather Story' exhibition, gallery, giftshop, large garden centre selling 300 different heathers, antique shop, children's play area and famous Clootie Dumpling restaurant.

Open: All year except Christmas Day.

Directions: Just off A95 between Aviemore and Grantown-on-Spey.

Highland croft open to visitors for "hands-on" experience with over 30 different breeds of farm animals "stroke the goats and scratch the pigs". Farm information centre and old farm implements. For all ages, cloud or shine!

Open: July and August 10am to 5pm.

Directions: On A835 15 miles north of Ullapool

Great day out for all the family. Wild Water Coaster*, Microworld exhibition, Forest Trails, Viewing Tower, Climbing Wall*, Tree Top Trail, Steam powered Sawmill*, Clydesdale Horse*. Shop, restaurant and snackbar.
(* Easter to October)

DOGS MUST BE KEPT ON LEADS

Open: Daily (except Christmas Day and attractions marked*).

Directions: 23 miles south of Inverness at Carrbridge, just off the A9.

A beautifully restored cotton mill village close to the Falls of Clyde. Explore the fascinating history of the village, try the 'New Millennium Experience', a magical ride which takes you back in time to discover what life used to be like.

Open: 11am to 5pm daily. Closed Christmas Day and New Year's Day.

Colourful gardens, imaginative woodland play areas and tumbling waterfalls. The Estate combines history with adventure in a fun day out for all the family, where your dog can run freely. Step back in time and uncover its secrets.

Open: Daily 10.30am to 5pm

Directions: Off A8 west of Langbank, 20 minutes west of Glasgow Airport.

A 60-minute ride along the shores of beautiful Padarn Lake behind a quaint historic steam engine. Magnificent views of the mountains from lakeside picnic spots.

DOGS MUST BE KEPT ON LEAD AT ALL TIMES ON TRAIN

Open: Most days Easter to October. Free timetable leaflet on request.

Directions: Just off A4086 Caernarfon to Capel Curig road at Llanberis; follow 'Country Park' signs.

Nine rooms in a Georgian house filled with items illustrating the happier times of family life over the past 150 years. Joyful nostalgia unlimited.

Open:
March to end October

Directions:
opposite Beaumaris Castle

Walk through the Rabbit Hole to the colourful scenes of Lewis Carroll's classic story set in beautiful life-size displays. Recorded commentaries and transcripts available in several languages.

Open: All year 10am to 5pm but closed Sundays in winter and Christmas/Boxing Day/New Year's Day.

Directions: situated just off the main street, 250 yards from coach and rail stations.

A unique theme attraction presenting the history and culture of the Celts. Audio-visual exhibition, displays of Welsh and Celtic history, soft play area, tea room and gift shop. Events throughout the year.

Open: 10am to 6pm daily (last admission to exhibitions 4.40pm)

Directions: in restored mansion just south of clock tower in town centre; car park just off Aberystwyth road

---

Journey through the lanes of cycle history and see bicycles from Boneshakers and Penny Farthings up to modern Raleigh cycles. Over 250 machines on display

PETS MUST BE KEPT ON LEADS

Open: 1st March to 1st November daily 10am onwards.

Directions: Brown signs to car park. Town centre attraction.

Make a pit stop whatever the weather! Join an ex-miner on a tour of discovery, ride the cage to pit bottom and take a thrilling ride back to the surface. Multi-media presentations, period village street, children's adventure play area, restaurant and gift shop. Disabled access with assistance.

Open: Open daily 10am to 6pm (last tour 4.30pm). Closed Mondays October to Easter, also Dec 25th to 1st Jan inclusive.

Directions: Exit Junction 32 M4, signposted from A470 Pontypridd. Trehafod is located between Pontypridd and Porth.

 **FHG**

Visit the FHG website
www.holidayguides.com
for details of the wide choice of accommodation
featured in the full range of FHG titles

ENGLAND

LONDON (CENTRAL & GREATER)

KEW GARDENS

Mrs L. Gray, 1 Chelwood Gardens, Kew TW9 4JG (020 8876 8733). Situated in quiet cul-de-sac, private newly renovated luxury bed and breakfast accommodation in friendly family home. Seven minutes' walk to underground station with easy access by bus or tube to all parts of London, museums, theatres, shopping, etc. Convenient for Twickenham, Wembley, Heathrow Airport, M3 and M4, Hampton Court, Kew Gardens, Public Records Office, Wimbledon, Windsor Castle, Chessington World of Adventure and River Thameside walks. Comfortable, friendly house with TV, central heating, tea and coffee facilities. Varied selection of English pubs and restaurants nearby. Unrestricted street parking. Regret no pets. We welcome tourists and business people looking for an economical alternative to hotel life in relaxed informal surroundings. Open all year.
e-mail: mrsljgray@aol.com

KING'S CROSS

MacDonald Hotel, 45-46 Argyle Square, King's Cross, London WC1H 8AL (020 7837 3552; Fax: 020 7278 9885). Located in central London, just a short walk from Kings Cross and St Pancras main line stations with direct access to Heathrow, Gatwick and Luton airports. With competitive prices, accommodation is provided in a clean and friendly atmosphere. A variety of rooms are available from single to family/quad rooms with both shared and en suite facilities. All rooms are centrally heated, have colour TV, tea/coffee making facilities and wash-hand basins. English breakfast is served between 7am and 9am. Please contact us for further information, our latest rates and for any offers available, or visit our website.
e-mail: enquiries@macdonaldhotel.com
website: www.macdonaldhotel.com

See also Colour Display Advertisement

LONDON

Holiday Hosts Accommodation Service (0208 540 7942; Fax: 0208 540 2827). Holiday Hosts (London) Ltd have 17 years experience in providing excellent private home accommodation in central/south/west areas of London, near to public transport for easy access to all London attractions, also Eurostar/airports/main line train stations. Prices start from £16 to £45 per person per night. Budget/Standard/Superior. Visit our website for further information.
www.holidayhosts.free-online.co.uk
e-mail: holiday.hosts@btinternet.com

LONDON

Mrs B. Merchant, 562 Caledonian Road, Holloway, London N7 9SD (020 7607 0930). Comfortable well furnished rooms in small private home, full central heating. Two double and one single rooms, all non-smoking. Extra single beds for double rooms available. Eight bus routes; one minute for Trafalgar Square, Westminster, St Paul's. Piccadilly Line underground few minutes' walk. Direct Piccadilly and Heathrow. One-and-a-half miles King's Cross, Euston and St Pancras Main Line Stations. Four and a half miles Piccadilly, three miles London Zoo and Hampstead Heath. Two minutes A1. King's Cross for Gatwick. Central for all tourist attractions. Full English Breakfast. Terms: £20.00 per person per night. Children over 10 years. Minimum stay two nights. Unrestricted street parking. SAE, please.

LONDON

Colliers Hotel, 97 Warwick Way, London SW1V 1QL (020 7834 6931; Fax: 020 7828 7111). A clean, budget-priced, family-run hotel, centrally located in Victoria. Ideal for easy connections to London's major tourist spots. A few minutes' walk from Victoria train, underground and coach stations. Friendly multi-lingual staff. Double, twin, family and single rooms available. Children welcome but sorry, no pets. Terms from £28 single. Reductions for children.

THE ELYSEE HOTEL
25/26 CRAVEN TERRACE, LONDON W2 3EL
Tel: 020 7402 7633 Fax: 020 7402 4193
E-mail: information@elyseehotel-london.co.uk
Website: www.elyseehotel-london.co.uk

Unbeatable value in the *HEART OF LONDON: FACING HYDE PARK.* Near London's famous tourist and shopping areas. Rooms with attached bath/shower and toilets, lifts to all floors. Tea/coffee making facilities, hairdryer, Sky and cable TV; security safes. Rates include Continental breakfast. Three minutes from Lancaster Gate Underground, and six minutes from Paddington Station for Heathrow Express.

Single £50.00; Twin/Double £55.00 (for room); Family (3 persons) £75.00; Family (5 persons) £95.00

See also Colour Advertisement

See also Colour Display Advertisement

LONDON

Hotel Columbus, 141 Sussex Gardens, Hyde Park, London W2 2RX (020 7262 0974; Fax: 020 7262 6785). This charming Bed & Breakfast hotel is the ideal choice for individuals and families who seek both value for money and a quality B&B in the "heart of London". Situated in an elegant tree-lined avenue close to Hyde Park and Oxford Street it was a former residence of the aristocracy and has now been converted to provide modern, comfortable accommodation. All rooms now have en suite shower and w.c., telephone, TV, etc. Look no further for London's best B&B!
e-mail: hotelcolumbus@compuserve.com
website: www.delmerehotels.com

See also Colour Display Advertisement

LONDON

Charlie's House Hotel, 63 Anson Road, London N7 0AR (020 7607 8375; Fax: 020 7697 8019). Single, double, triple and family rooms available. All room en suite, with central heating and TV. Nearest Tube station Tufnell Park.

See also Colour Display Advertisement

LONDON

The Blair Victoria Hotel, 78-84 Warwick Way, Victoria, London SWIV IRZ (020 7828 8603; Fax: 020 7976 6536). 48 en suite rooms with colour TV, tea/coffee facilities, direct-dial telephone, hairdryer. Reception Lounge and Garden Room. Some rooms have patios and balconies or direct access to the walled garden. Short walk to the walled garden. Short walk to Victoria coach and rail stations and major tourist attractions. Terms from £35 single, £55 double.
e-mail: sales@blairvictoria.com
website: www.blairvictoria.com

BA London Eye • *London* • *0870 5000 600*
website: www.londoneye.com
The world's highest observation wheel offers unrivalled views over London and beyond on its 30-minute slow-moving flight.

Lincoln House Hotel
London W1

33 Gloucester Place, London W1U 8HY
Tel: 020-7486 7630 (3 lines), Fax: 020-7486 0166

LONDON
Tourist Board and
Convention Bureau

Built in the days of King George III, this hotel offers Georgian charms and character. En suite rooms with modern comforts. Competitively priced. Located in the heart of London's West End, next to Oxford Street and most famous shopping attractions, close to Theatreland. Ideal for business and leisure.

The Lincoln House Hotel is recommended by British and European consumer associations and motoring organisations. It is also commended by many world distinguished guide books for its good value and very competitive tariff.

e-mail: reservations@lincoln-house-hotel.co.uk
website: www.lincoln-house-hotel.co.uk

"Georgian Hotel With Modern Comfort" **WHICH?**

For reservations call free 0500-007 208

See also Colour Display Advertisement

LONDON

Hanover Hotel, 30/32 St Georges Drive, Victoria, London SW1V 4BN (020 7834 0367/7617; Fax: 020 7976 5587). Welcome to the Hanover Hotel, offering comfortable, budget accommodation in Central London. The hotel is conveniently situated, close to Victoria Underground, railway and coach stations. British Airways Terminal and Gatwick Express are both at Victoria. London's top tourist attractions such as Buckingham Palace and the Houses of Parliament are all within walking distance.
e-mail: reservations@hanoverhotel.uk.com
website: www.hanoverhotel.uk.com

See also Colour Display Advertisement

LONDON

Mr S. Mehra, Haven Hotel, 6-8 Sussex Gardens, Paddington, London W2 1UL (020 7723 5481/2195; Fax: 020 7706 4568). Very centrally situated Bed and Breakfast. First hotel in Sussex Gardens from Edgware Road. Reasonable rates. Parking available. Nearest underground stations: Edgware Road, Paddington, Marble Arch and Lancaster Gate. Major shops and attractions all nearby.

QUEENS HOTEL

33 Anson Road, Tufnell Park, London N7
Telephone: 0207-607 4725
Fax: 0207-697 9725
E-mail: queens@stavrouhotels.co.uk • Website: www.stavrouhotels.co.uk

The Queens Hotel is a large double-fronted Victorian building standing in its own grounds five minutes' walk from Tufnell Park Station. Quietly situated with ample car parking spaces; 15 minutes to West End and close to London Zoo, Hampstead and Highgate. Two miles from Kings Cross and St Pancras Stations. Many rooms en suite.

Singles from £25-£34 - Double/Twins from £30-£54
Triples and Family Rooms from £18 per person.

All prices include full English Breakfast plus VAT.
Children half price. Discounts on longer stays.

LONDON

Hazelwood House, 865 Finchley Road, Golders Green, London NW11 8LX (020 8458 8884). Enjoy luxury in a friendly atmosphere at our SRAC listed establishment. Whether on holiday or business, this hotel is famous for its "home from home" atmosphere in London's exclusive district of Golders Green. Private forecourt parking for five/six cars. Children over ten years, animals accepted. Single room with breakfast from £28 per night, double room with breakfast from £38 per night. Longer stays by arrangement.

See also Colour Display Advertisement

LONDON

Europa House Hotel, 151 Sussex Gardens, Hyde Park, London W2 2RY (020 7723 7343; Fax: 020 7224 9331). Europa House is a small, privately owned hotel which aims to give personal service of the highest standard. Full central heating, all rooms en suite. Within easy reach of the West End. Situated close to Paddington Station. Double and twins; singles. Family rooms available. Special rates for children under 10 years. Full English breakfast. Terms available on request. **ETC** ♦♦
e-mail: europahouse@enterprise.net
website: www.europahousehotel.com
www.europahousehotel.org.uk
www.euopahousehotel.net

ENGLAND

See also Colour Display Advertisement

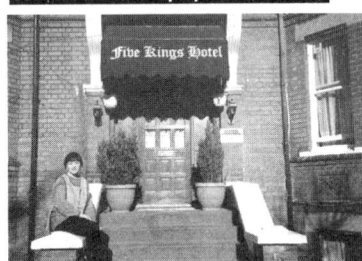

LONDON

Five Kings Hotel, 59 Anson Road, Tufnell Park, London N7 0AR (020 7607 3996; Fax: 020 7609 5554). Five Kings is a family-run hotel and member of the English Tourism Council with Two Diamonds awarded. 16 rooms, seven en suite. All rooms have colour TV. Situated in a quiet area yet only 15 minutes to Central London. Oxford Street, Leicester Square, Camden Lock, London Zoo, all accessible to Northern Line underground station, only 3–5 minutes away. Kings Cross and St Pancras Stations are only two miles away. No parking restriction in Anson Road. Single £24-£30, Double/Twin £36-£46, Family 1x3 £50-£54, Family 1x4 £60-£66. En suite: £46 Twin, £40 Double, £30 Single, Triple Family £50-£56. All prices include English breakfast and VAT. **ETC ◆◆** Also STUDIO FLATS available for monthly lets. Excellent condition. All mod cons. From £150 per week incl.

LONDON

Compton Guest House, 65 Compton Road, Wimbledon SW19 7QA (Fax & Tel: 020 8947 4488 and Tel: 020 8879 3245). Situated approximately six minutes from Wimbledon station and within easy reach of Wimbledon Tennis Courts, Wimbledon Common, Golf and squash clubs. Easy access to the West End and central London, and close to many first class restaurants, theatre and cinema. All rooms are comfortably furnished with washbasin, colour TV, shaver light points, central heating and tea/coffee making facilities. We have room service, and if you decide to have breakfast it is served in the rooms for your own comfort and privacy. Hairdryers and irons available, free of charge, on request. Please contact **Mrs A Haq** for details of competitive prices.

BEDFORDSHIRE

LUTON
Mr and Mrs Wicks, 19 Wigmore Lane, Stopsley, Luton LU2 8AA (01582 423419). Bed and Breakfast accommodation situated just 10 minutes from Luton Airport, just off the M1 Junction 10 and close to the A505. Near town centre and railway stations (Town Centre and Parkway); 25 minutes' train journey to Central London. Large bungalow with double rooms; tea/coffee making equipment and colour TV. Overnight parking available. Close to local pubs, restaurants and shops. Children welcome. A warm welcome awaits.

SANDY
Mrs Anne Franklin, Village Farm, Thorncote Green, Sandy SG19 1PU (01767 627345). Village Farm is a family-run working farm, mixed arable with a flock of 1000 free range laying hens, plus turkeys and geese for Christmas trade. Accommodation comprises one double bedroom, two twin/family rooms, both en suite. Full farmhouse breakfast plus beverages in room. Thorncote Green is a picturesque hamlet within easy reach of many interesting places:- Shuttleworth Collection, Swiss Gardens, RSPB headquarters, Greensand Ridge walk, Woburn Abbey, Wimpole Hall and Cambridge. Bed and Breakfast from £25 per person per night. **ETC** ◆◆◆

See also Colour Display Advertisement

SANDY
Mrs M. Codd, Highfield Farm, Tempsford, Sandy SG19 2AQ (01767 682332; Fax: 01767 692503). Tranquil welcoming atmosphere on attractive arable farm. Set well back off A1 giving quiet, peaceful seclusion yet within easy reach of the RSPB, the Shuttleworth Collection, the Greensand Ridge Walk, Grafham Water and Woburn Abbey. Cambridge 22 miles, London 50 miles. All rooms have tea/coffee making facilities, most have bathroom en suite and two are on the ground floor. There is a separate guests' sitting room with TV. Family room. Dogs welcome by arrangement. No smoking. Most guests return! Prices from £30 per person per night. **ETC** ◆◆◆◆ *SILVER AWARD, GUESTACCOM "GOOD ROOM" AWARD. BEST ETC B&B REGIONAL WINNER FOR EASTERN COUNTIES.*
e-mail: margaret@highfield-farm.co.uk

BERKSHIRE

ASCOT

Nick Chambers, Lyndrick Guest House, The Avenue, Ascot SL5 8LS (01344 883520; Fax: 01344 891243). A large Victorian house in tree lined avenue. A warm welcome is assured with friendly help and advice on places to visit. Well equipped bedrooms with colour TV, radio alarm, hairdryer and tea/coffee making facilities. Enjoy a delicious breakfast in pleasant conservatory overlooking the garden. Ideal base for various tourist attractions. Windsor four miles. Close to Ascot Racecourse. Wentworth, Sunningdale, Swinley, Mill Ride, Berkshire Golf Clubs all nearby. Easy access by train to London - ideal for day trips. Heathrow Airport 25 minutes. Double from £60, single from £45.
e-mail: mail@lyndrick.com

READING (Three Mile Cross)

Mrs M.S. Erdwin, Orchard House, Church Lane, Three Mile Cross, Reading RG7 1HD (01189 884457). Orchard House is well situated close to M4 Motorway, Heathrow 30 minutes away, Gatwick 45 minutes; Oxford 30 miles and London 35 miles (just 29 minutes by train); five minutes' from Arborfield Garrison. Wealth of holiday interest to suit all tastes in the area. Ideal halt for that long journey to Cornwall or Wales. Accommodation all year round in this modern, large, homely house close to the Chilterns and Berkshire Downs. Babysitting can be arranged. English or Continental Breakfast; Evening Drink/Meal/Light Supper available; Packed Lunches on request. Pets permitted at extra charge. Close to Thames, Kennet and Avon Canal/River for coarse fishing. Also close to M3, Reading Rock Festival, and the new Reading football/rugby stadium. We accept guests returning/arriving very late. Ideal for WOMAD festival or on route to Dover, Portsmouth and Newhaven. Tourist Board registered. Terms from £19 for Bed and Breakfast (we accept euros). Taxi service at moderate rates. SAE, please.

WINDSOR

Clarence Hotel, 9 Clarence Road, Windsor SL4 5AE (01753 864436; Fax: 01753 857060). Town centre location. Licensed bar and steam room. High quality accommodation at guest house prices. All rooms have en suite bathrooms, TV, tea/coffee making facilities, radio alarms and hairdryers. Heathrow Airport 25 minutes by car. Convenient for Legoland. **AA/RAC** ◆◆◆

WINDSOR

Mr Robert Sousa, Netherton Hotel, 96 St Leonards Road, Windsor SL4 3DA (01753 855508; Fax: 01753 621267). This recently refurbished hotel offers a comfortable and friendly atmosphere. All rooms are en suite, with colour TV, direct-dial telephone, and tea/coffee making facilities. Also available are hairdryers and ironing facilities. There is a TV lounge for guests' use. Full English breakfast. We have a private car park and are easy to find. Walking distance to Windsor Castle, town centre, train stations and Legoland is only one mile away. Central London can be reached in 35 minutes by train. M4 only two miles, Heathrow seven miles. Children welcome. **ETC/AA/RAC** ◆◆◆
e-mail: netherton@btconnect.com

BUCKINGHAMSHIRE

QUAINTON

Mrs H. Howard, Woodlands Farmhouse, Quainton, Aylesbury HP22 4DE (01296 770225). Woodlands Farmhouse is set in the heart of this quiet and peaceful part of central Buckinghamshire. The recently converted stables provide well equipped and comfortable en suite accommodation. Each unit has its own private entrance to give you maximum flexibility and privacy during your stay. Full English breakfast is provided in the main 17th century farmhouse. Woodlands is well placed for visiting Oxford and Milton Keynes (both 30 minutes) as well as the local attractions of Waddesdon Manor, Quainton Steam Railway and Silverstone. Bed and Breakfast from £30 per person. Vegetarian and organic food available. Children and well behaved pets welcome. Open all year. **ETC ◆◆◆◆**

CAMBRIDGESHIRE

CAMBRIDGE

Paul and Alison Tweddell, Dykelands Guest House, 157 Mowbray Road, Cambridge CB1 7SP (01223 244300; Fax: 01223 566746). Enjoy your visit to Cambridge by staying at our lovely detached guesthouse. Ideally located for city centre and for touring the secrets of the Cambridgeshire countryside. Easy access from M11 Junction 11, but only one-and-a-half miles from the city centre, on a direct bus route. Near Addenbrookes Hospital. All bedrooms have colour TV, clock radio, tea/coffee making facilities; heating and double glazing; seven en suite; ground floor rooms available. Bed and full English Breakfast from £32 singles to £52 doubles. Ample car parking. Most major credit/debit cards welcome. Open all year. Brochure on request. Non-smoking establishment. **ETC/AA ◆◆◆**
website: www.dykelands.com

CAMBRIDGE

Victoria Guest House, 57 Arbury Road, Cambridge CB4 2JB (01223 350086). Victoria Guest House is an extremely comfortable Victorian house situated off Milton Road, within walking distance of the City Centre, River Cam and Colleges, with easy access to the M14, M11 and the Cambridge Science Park. Most rooms are en suite or have private facilities. Colour TV, iron, ironing board, hair dryer, tea and coffee making facilities; good parking to the front available. Our guests can enjoy a lovely breakfast served in the dining room, overlooking picturesque gardens to the rear; there we can cater for all your needs. Emma and Duncan strive very hard to offer all their guests a very warm welcome and comfortable stay, which is why guests return to us over and over again. **ETC ◆◆◆◆**

e-mail: victoriahouse@ntlworld.com
website: www.SmoothHound.co.uk/hotels/victori3.html

CAMBRIDGE

Mrs Jean Wright, White Horse Cottage, 28 West Street, Comberton, Cambridge CB3 7DS (01223 262914). A 17th century cottage with all modern conveniences situated in a charming village four miles south-west of Cambridge. Junction 12 off M11 - A603 from Cambridge, or A428 turn off at Hardwick turning. Accommodation includes one double room, twin and family rooms. Own sittingroom with colour TV; tea/coffee making facilities. Full central heating; parking. Golfing facilities nearby. Excellent touring centre for many interesting places including Cambridge colleges, Wimpole Hall, Anglesey Abbey, Ely Cathedral, Imperial War Museum at Duxford, and many more. Bed and Breakfast from £22.50 per person. Children welcome.

CAMBRIDGE

Mrs Dowling, Hamilton Hotel, 156 Chesterton Road, Cambridge CB4 1DA (01223 365664). The Hamilton Hotel is an independent hotel situated approximately one mile from the historic city centre with its famous colleges and close to the River Cam and surrounding parks. Conveniently placed for the guest with time to enjoy the famous colleges, museums, art galleries, theatres and punting on the River Cam. Further a field visit Anglesey Abbey, The American Military Cemetry, Ely Cathedral, Imperial War Museum at Duxford or the National Stud and Racecourse at Newmarket. The hotel has twenty comfortable bedrooms, all with colour television, a hospitality tray, hairdryer and telephone – most rooms have en suite facilities. Ground floor rooms are available but must be requested at time of booking. ETC ◆◆◆
website: www.hamiltonhotelcambridge.co.uk

CAMBRIDGE

Mr and Mrs Salt, Honeysuckle Cottage, 38 High Street, Grantchester, Cambridge CB3 9NF (01223 845977; Mobile: 0797 4767807). Grantchester, the home of Jeffrey Archer, is a beautiful village one-and-a-half miles by car from Cambridge centre, or you can walk for about 30 minutes along the side of the River Cam, through the meadows whilst watching the punts. The house is recently renovated and is a mixture of Gothic and modern. Terms from £38 per person, all rooms en suite.

CAMBRIDGE (near)

Vicki Hatley, Manor Farm, Landbeach, Cambridge CB4 4ED (01223 860165). Five miles from Cambridge and 10 miles from Ely. Vicki welcomes you to her carefully modernised Grade II Listed farmhouse, which is located next to the church in this attractive village. All rooms are either en suite or have private bathroom and are individually decorated. TV, clock radios and tea/coffee making facilities are provided in double, twin or family rooms. There is ample parking and guests are welcome to enjoy the walled gardens. Bed and Breakfast from £25 per person double, and £35 single.

ELY

Mrs Linda Peck, Sharps Farm, Twenty Pence Road, Wilburton, Ely CB6 3PX (01353 740360). Between Ely (six miles) and Cambridge (12 miles) our modern farmhouse offers guests a warm welcome and a relaxed atmosphere. All rooms have en suite or private bathrooms, central heating, colour TV, radio alarm, tea/coffee making facilities, hair dryer and views over surrounding countryside. Breakfast is served in the conservatory, with home-made preserves and free-range eggs. Special diets catered for. Disabled facilities. Ample parking. No smoking. Bed and Breakfast from £24 per person. Short Breaks available.

e-mail: sharpsfarm@yahoo.com

ELY

Mrs C. H. Bennett, Stockyard Farm, Wisbech Road, Welney, Wisbech PE14 9RQ (01354 610433). A warm welcome awaits you at this comfortable former farmhouse in the heart of the Fens, equidistant from Ely and Wisbech. The house makes an ideal base from which to explore the numerous historic sites, watch wildlife at the nearby nature reserves or fish the famous fenland waters. Whatever your interests, Cindy and Tim can offer advice and information. One double and one twin bedroom, both with handbasin, radio, hairdryer and hot drink facilities. Breakfast is served in the conservatory adjoining the guests' TV lounge. Vegetarian breakfast a speciality. Free-range produce. Central heating. Private parking. No smoking. Pets welcome. B&B from £18 per person.

ST NEOTS

Mrs Eileen Raggatt, The Ferns, Berkley Street, Eynesbury, St Neots PE19 2NE (01480 213884). An 18th century house (private family home) in large garden situated on Eynesbury Green. Two rooms available with double bed plus single bed, one with private bathroom, the other with washbasin. Central heating. Charges from £23 per person for Bed and Breakfast, reduced rates for children under 10. St Neots is a market town on the River Ouse just off the A1; one and a half hours north of London, 16 miles west of Cambridge.

website: http://web.onetel.net.uk/~raggatt/

WICKEN

Mrs Valerie Fuller, Spinney Abbey, Wicken, Ely CB7 5XQ (01353 720971). Working farm. Spinney Abbey is an attractive Grade II Listed Georgian stone farmhouse with views across pasture fields. It stands in a large garden with tennis court next to our dairy farm which borders the National Trust Nature Reserve Wicken Fen. One double and one family room, both en suite, and twin-bedded room with private bathroom, all with TV, hospitality tray, etc. Full central heating, guests' sittingroom. Regret no pets and no smoking upstairs. Situated just off A1123, half a mile west of Wicken. Open all year. Bed and Breakfast from £25 per person. ETC ◆◆◆◆

e-mail: spinney.abbey@tesco.net
website: www.spinneyabbey.co.uk

WISBECH

Jayne Best, Four Winds, Mill Lane, Newton, Wisbech PE13 5HZ (01945 870479; Fax: 01945 870274). Charming country house situated in the midst of the Fens countryside, although only four miles from Wisbech and close to King's Lynn, Norfolk coast (28 miles). Ideally situated for touring, fishing and cycling. Accommodation comprises one double en suite with shower, one twin en suite with bath, two singles with washbasins and one main bedroom with Airspa. Private parking. Terms from £23.

WOOD WALTON

The Elephant & Castle Motel & Free House, The Green, Wood Walton, Huntingdon, Cambs PE28 5YN (Tel & Fax: 01487 773337). A family-run establishment in tranquil surroundings yet close to all major routes. 13 en suite motel rooms with TV, tea/coffee making, electric heating, radio and showers. Eight electric hook-ups for touring caravans. Ample parking space. Pets welcome. Full English breakfast served. Bar meals available.

WYTON

Robin and Marion Seaman, The Elms, Banks End, Wyton, Huntingdon PE28 2AA (01480 453523). Edwardian house close to picturesque riverside villages of Houghton and Wyton. Two miles between historic market towns of Huntingdon and St Ives; five minutes from A1 and A14-M11 15 minutes, Stansted 45 minutes - ideal for travel. One double en suite, one twin en suite, and two single rooms. Maximum six guests. All bedrooms have tea/coffee making facilities and colour TV. Central heating. Non-smoking. No pets. Friendly personal service and a warm welcome assured. Bed and Breakfast from £25 per person.
e-mail: elms.wyton@btopenworld.com

Fitzwilliam Museum • *Cambridge, Cambridgeshire* • *01223 332904*
website: www.fitzmuseum.cam.ac.uk
One of the UK's finest collections of armour, antiquities, sculpture, furniture, pottery, paintings, prints, coins and much more.

PLEASE NOTE

All the information in this book is given in good faith in the belief that it is correct. However, the publishers cannot guarantee the facts given in these pages, neither are they responsible for changes in policy, ownership or terms that may take place after the date of going to press. Readers should always satisfy themselves that the facilities they require are available and that the terms, if quoted, still apply.

The FHG Directory of Website Addresses
on pages 387-415 is a useful quick reference guide for holiday accommodation with e-mail and/or website details

CHESHIRE

BALTERLEY (near Crewe)

Mrs Joanne Hollins, Balterley Green Farm, Deans Lane, Balterley, Near Crewe CW2 5QJ (01270 820214). Working farm, join in. Jo and Pete Hollins offer guests a friendly welcome to their home on a 145-acre dairy farm in quiet and peaceful surroundings. Green Farm is situated on the Cheshire/Staffordshire border and is within easy reach of Junction 16 on the M6. An excellent stop-over place for travellers journeying between north and south of the country. We also offer a pets' corner for young children. One family room en suite, one single and one twin-bedded room on ground floor suitable for disabled guests. Tea-making facilities and TV in all rooms. Children welcome, cot provided. Pets welcome. This area offers many attractions; we are within easy reach of historic Chester, Alton Towers and the famous Potteries of Staffordshire. Open all year. Caravans and tents welcome. Bed and Breakfast from £20 per person. **ETC** ◆◆◆◆

CHESTER

Laura and Phillip Abbinante, Vicarage Lodge, 11 Vicarage Road, Hoole, Chester CH2 3HZ (Tel & Fax: 01244 319533). A late Victorian family-run guesthouse offering a warm welcome and peaceful stay. Situated in a quiet residential area just off the main Hoole Road, yet only one mile from the city centre. Accommodation comprises double and twin rooms, en suite available. All rooms are decorated to a high standard with washbasins, central heating, hair dryers, shaver points, remote-control colour TV and tea/coffee facilities. Offering a large selection of breakfast choices. Large private car park on premises. Good-sized patio garden where guests can relax. Bed and Breakfast from £17 per person. Weekly and winter terms available. **AA** and **RAC** *MEMBER*.

CHESTER

Brian and Hilary Devenport, White Walls, Village Road, Christleton, Chester CH3 7AS (Tel & Fax: 01244 336033). White Walls, a 100 year old converted stables, in the heart of award-winning village Christleton, two miles Chester, off the A41, close to A55, M53 and North Wales. Walking distance to village pub and two canalside pub/restaurants, church, Post Office, hairdresser and bus stop. Half hourly bus service to Chester. The village pond is home to swans, mallards, Aylesbury ducks and moorhens. En suite double bedroom, twin bedded room with washbasin all including English Breakfast. Minimum rates from £20 single, £40 per room. Colour TV, tea/coffee making facilities, central heating, overlooking garden. Non-smoking. Sorry, no children or pets.
e-mail: hilary-devenport@supanet.com

CHESTER

Mrs Anne Arden, Newton Hall, Tattenhall, Chester CH3 9NE (01829 770153; Fax: 01829 770655). Part 16th century oak-beamed farmhouse set in large well kept grounds, with fine views of historic Beeston and Peckforton Castles and close to the Sandstone Trail. Six miles south of Chester off A41 and ideal for Welsh hills. Rooms are en suite or have adjacent bathroom. Colour TV in all bedrooms. Guests' own lounge. Fully centrally heated. Bed and Breakfast from £25. Children and pets welcome. Open all year. **ETC** ◆◆◆◆
e-mail: newton.hall@farming.co.uk

CHESTER

Mitchell's of Chester Guest House, 28 Hough Green, Chester CH4 8JQ (01244 679004; Fax: 01244 659567). This elegantly restored Victorian family home is set on the south side of Chester, on a bus route to the city centre. Guest bedrooms have been furnished in period style, with fully equipped shower room and toilet, central heating, TV, refreshment tray and other thoughtful extras. An extensive breakfast menu is served in the elegant dining room, and the guest lounge overlooks the well-maintained garden. The historic city of Chester is ideally placed for touring Wales and the many attractions of the North West of England. **ETC/AA** ◆◆◆◆, *SILVER AWARD.*
e-mail: mitoches@dialstart.net
website: www.mitchellsofchester.com

CHESTER CITY

Frank and Maureen Brady, Holly House, 41 Liverpool Road, Chester CH2 1AB (01244 383484). Holly House is a Victorian townhouse on the A5116, offering a friendly welcome in quiet, elegant surroundings. Comfort and high standards are our priority. Only five minutes' walk from the famous Roman walls which encircle this historic city with its 11th century Cathedral, castle, museum of Roman artifacts, buildings of architectural interest, Amphitheatre, walks by the river, shopping in "The Rows". Spacious accommodation comprises two double/family rooms fully en suite and a double with full private facilities. TV, tea/coffee facilities, own keys. Parking. Bed and Breakfast from £44 for two sharing, or as family rooms at £12 per additional person supplement. Vegetarians catered for. Non-smoking. A warm welcome from Frank and Maureen Brady. **ETC** ◆◆◆

CHESTER (near)

Beryl and John Milner, Green Cottage, The Green, Higher Kinnerton, Chester CH4 9BZ (Tel & Fax: 01244 660137). A homely, friendly, peaceful and comfortable country retreat just over the Welsh border, ideally situated for exploring the historic City of Chester under seven miles away. Easy access to all routes (five minutes from the A55) makes this an ideal base for touring North Wales, West Cheshire and North Shropshire. Beryl and John, previous winners of a Prince of Wales' Award, will offer you warm hospitality and invite you into their home, which has recently been renovated and furnished to a high standard. A double room and a twin room are available, overlooking open countryside. Tea/coffee making facilities, TV, shared private bathroom with bath and shower, central heating, off-road parking, pleasant gardens. There are two pubs within the village offering excellent cuisine. Non-smoking. Bed and Full English Breakfast from £20 per person, with reductions for weekly stays. Please send or telephone for our brochure. ★★★ *GUEST HOUSE.*

CHURCH MINSHULL

Brian and Mary Charlesworth, Higher Elms Farm, Minshull Vernon, Crewe CW1 4RG (01270 522252). A 400-year-old farmhouse on working farm. Oak-beamed comfort in dining and sittingrooms, overlooking Shropshire Union Canal. No dinners served but four pubs within two miles. Interesting wildlife around. Convenient for M6 but tucked away in the countryside; from M6 Junction 18, off A530 towards Nantwich. Family room, double, twin and single rooms are all en suite, with colour TV and tea/coffee facilities. Well behaved pets welcome. Within 15 miles of Jodrell Bank, Oulton Park, Bridgemere Garden World, Stapeley Water Gardens, Nantwich and Chester. Bed and Breakfast from £24. Half price for children under 12 years.

HYDE (near Manchester)

Mrs Charlotte R. Walsh, Needhams Farm, Uplands Road, Werneth Low, Gee Cross, Near Hyde SK14 3AQ (0161 368 4610; Fax: 0161-367 9106). Working farm. A cosy 16th century farmhouse set in peaceful, picturesque surroundings by Werneth Low Country Park and the Etherow Valley, which lie between Glossop and Manchester. The farm is ideally situated for holidaymakers and businessmen, especially those who enjoy peace and quiet, walking and rambling, golfing and riding, as these activities are all close by. At Needhams Farm everyone, including children and pets, receives a warm welcome. Good wholesome meals available in the evenings from Monday to Friday, weekends by arrangement. Residential licence and Fire Certificate held. Open all year. Bed and Breakfast from £24 single minimum to £36 double maximum; Evening Meal £7. ETC/AA ◆◆◆

e-mail: charlotte@needhamsfarm.co.uk **website: www.needhamsfarm.co.uk**

MALPAS

Chris and Angela Smith, Mill House, Higher Wych, Malpas SY14 7JR (01948 780362); Fax: 01948 780566). Modernised mill house on the Cheshire/Clwyd border in a quiet valley, convenient for visiting Chester, Shrewsbury and North Wales. The house is centrally heated and has an open log fire in the lounge. Bedrooms have washbasins, TV and radio and tea-making facilities. One bedroom has an en suite shower and WC. Reductions for children and Senior Citizens. Open January to November. Bed and Breakfast from £22. Evening Meal from £8. **WTB ★★★** *GUEST HOUSE.*

STOCKPORT

Mrs Malik, Further Hey Hotel, 41 Werneth Road, Woodley, Romiley, Stockport SK6 1HP (0161 430 2328). Situated just two miles away from the centre of Stockport and seven miles from Manchester Airport. Further Hey provides comfortable accommodation for the visiting holiday maker or businessman in pleasant surroundings. Built at the turn of the last century, this magnificent building has single and twin bedded rooms en suite with tea/coffee making facilities and colour TVs. Facilities are available for the disabled. Safe parking. Vegetarians catered for. Terms: single room from £25 to £35; double/twin room from £35 to £45.

CORNWALL

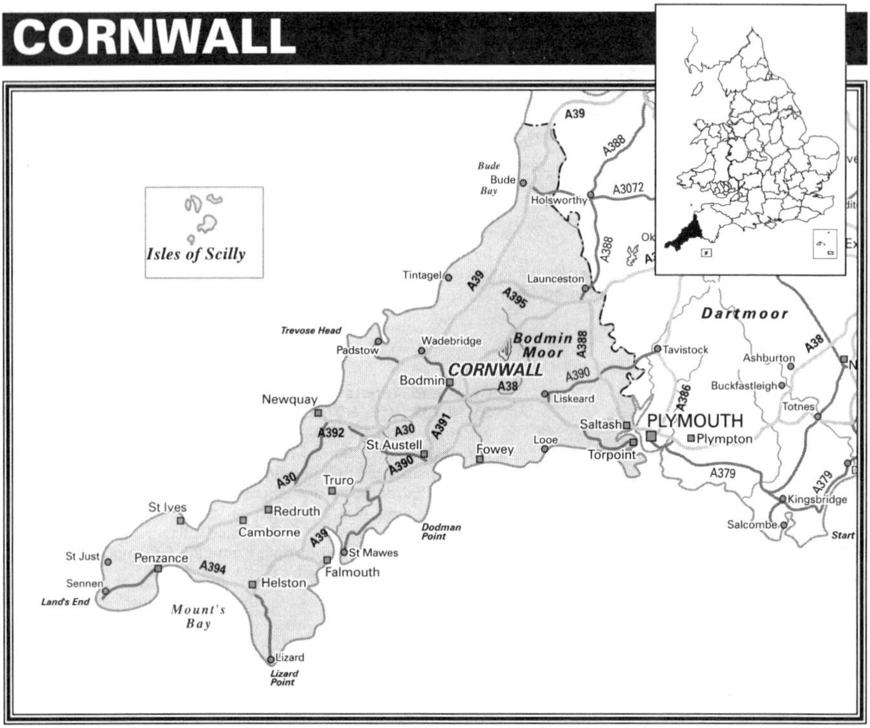

Isles of Scilly

A39
A388
Bude
Bude
Bay
Holsworthy
A3072
Tintagel
A39
Launceston
A395
Trevose Head
Dartmoor
Padstow
Wadebridge
Bodmin Moor
A388
Tavistock
Ashburton
A38
Bodmin
CORNWALL
A390
Buckfastleigh
Newquay
A38
Liskeard
Totnes
A392
A30
A391
Saltash
PLYMOUTH
St Austell
A390
Fowey
Looe
Plympton
A30
Torpoint
Truro
A379
St Ives
Redruth
A379
Camborne
A38
Dodman Point
Kingsbridge
Salcombe
Start
St Just
Penzance
A394
St Mawes
Sennen
Helston
Falmouth
Land's End
Mount's Bay
Lizard
Lizard Point

BODMIN

Mrs Joy Rackham, High Cross Farm, Lanivet, Near Bodmin PL30 5JR (01208 831341). Traditional Victorian granite farmhouse surrounded by fields on this working farm. Lanivet is the geographical centre of Cornwall and thereby central for touring the moor and the north and south coasts. The exciting Eden Project, Lost Gardens at Heligan and Lanhydrock House are close by. Fishing, cycling, golf and horse riding are available within the area. High Cross offers ample off-road parking and modern facilities for guests. Rooms have hot/cold, shaver points and tea and coffee making facilities. One room is en suite. Separate dining room and sitting room for guests. Full English breakfast, optional evening meal. Open all year except Christmas. Bed and Breakfast from £20.

BODMIN

Tremeere Manor

Mrs Margaret Oliver, Tremeere Manor, Lanivet, Near Bodmin PL30 5BG (01208 831513). Tremeere is a 17th Century Manor House set in a 240-acre dairy farm in mid-Cornwall on the halfway mark for the Saints Way, 15 minutes' drive from the Eden Project. There are spacious comfortable rooms comprising two double en suite bedrooms and one twin-bedded room, all with TV, and with lovely views of the surrounding countryside. Central heating, tea/coffee making facilities and a comfortable guests' lounge with TV. Prices are from £22 per person for a double or twin room and £25 per person for a single. No smoking. Nearby is Bodmin town with its ancient Gaol and Steam Railway, Lanhydrock House (NT), The Lost Gardens of Heligan or walking on Bodmin Moor and visiting the famous Jamaica Inn. Coastal walks and beaches are within easy reach as well as walking the Camel Trail. **ETC** ◆◆◆◆

BOSCASTLE

Mrs Jackie Haddy, Home Farm, Minster, Boscastle PL35 0BN (Tel & Fax: 01840 250195). Home Farm is a beautifully situated working farm overlooking picturesque Boscastle and its heritage coastline. The farm is surrounded by National Trust countryside and footpaths through unspoilt wooded valleys to Boscastle village, restaurants and harbour. Traditional farmhouse with beautiful furnishings has three charming en suite rooms with colour TV with satellite link, tea-making facilities; cosy guest lounge with log fire. Good home cooking; walled garden; plenty of friendly farm animals. Beaches, golf courses, riding stables, coastal paths and many other activities for you to enjoy. A warm welcome awaits you. Free golf when booking. **ETC ◆◆◆◆**
e-mail: jackie.haddy@btclick.com
website: www.homefarm-boscastle.co.uk

BOSCASTLE

Mrs P. E. Perfili, Trefoil Farm, Camelford Road, Boscastle PL35 0AD (01840 250606). Set in its own tranquil grounds with ample parking. Trefoil offers non-smoking, centrally heated, en suite accommodation with tea and coffee making facilities and colour TV. Overlooking Boscastle village, with views of the coast and Lundy Island, Trefoil is ideally positioned to explore Cornwall. Two minutes' walk leads you to a local 16th century Inn with real ales and good food. Terms from £22 per person per night. **ETC ◆◆◆**
e-mail: trefoil.farm@tiscali.co.uk
website: myweb.tiscali.co.uk/trefoilfarm

BOSCASTLE

Ruth and Michael Parsons, The Old Coach House, Tintagel Road, Boscastle PL35 0AS (01840 250398; Fax: 01840 250346). Relax in a 300 year old former coach house now tastefully equipped to meet the needs of the new millennium with all rooms en suite, colour TVs, radios, tea/coffee makers and central heating. Accessible for disabled guests. Good cooking. This picturesque village is a haven for walkers with its dramatic coastal scenery, a photographer's dream, and an ideal base to tour both the north and south coasts. The area is famed for its sandy beaches and surfing whilst King Arthur's Tintagel is only three miles away. Come and enjoy a friendly holiday with people who care. Brochure on request. Bed and Breakfast from £20 to £28. **AA ◆◆◆◆**

e-mail: parsons@old-coach.demon.co.uk   **website: www.old-coach.co.uk**

BUDE

Mrs Christine Nancekivell, Dolsdon Farm, Boyton, Launceston PL15 8NT (01288 341264). Dolsdon was once a 17th century coaching inn, now modernised, situated on the Launceston to Bude road within easy reach of sandy beaches, surfing, Tamar Otter Park, leisure centre with heated swimming pool, golf courses, fishing, tennis and horse riding and is ideal for touring Cornwall and Devon. Guests are welcome to wander around the 260 acre working farm. All bedrooms en suite with TV and tea making facilities. Comfortably furnished lounge has colour TV. Plenty of good home cooking assured - full English breakfast. Parking. Bed and Breakfast from £18.50; reductions for children. Brochure available.

BUDE

Mrs Sylvia Lucas, Elm Park, Bridgerule, Holsworthy EX22 7EL (01288 381231). Elm Park is a 205 acre dairy, beef and sheep farm. Six miles from surfing beaches at Bude and ideal for touring Devon/Cornwall. Children are especially welcomed, with pony rides. Games room available with snooker, table skittles, darts, etc, and golf putting. There are spacious family rooms (two en suite) and a twin-bedded room, all with colour TV and tea/coffee making facilities. Ample four-course dinners with freshly produced fare and delicious sweets. Bed, Breakfast and Evening Meal, reasonable terms. Reductions for children and everyone is made welcome and comfortable. Brochure available.

See also Colour Display Advertisement

BUDE

Mrs Cole, Highbre Crest, Whitstone, Holsworthy, Near Bude EX22 6UF (01288 341002). Stunning views to coasts and moors make this very spacious house a special destination for your holiday. With the added bonus of peace, tranquillity and delicious homemade country cooking, how can you resist paying us a visit? We are well situated for the coast and moors in Devon and Cornwall, including The Eden Project. Two double and one twin room - all en suite. Games room with full size snooker table, dining room and comfortable large conservatory with spectacular coastal views. Garden for guests' use. Car parking space. Non-smoking establishment. Children over 12 welcome. Bed and Breakfast from £23, Evening meal from £12 (optional). Open February to November. **ETC** ◆◆◆◆ *SILVER AWARD.*

BUDE

Margaret and Richard Heard, Trencreek Farmhouse, St Gennys, Bude EX23 0AY (01840 230219). Comfortable farmhouse which offers a homely and relaxed family atmosphere. Situated in quiet and peaceful surroundings yet within easy reach of Crackington Haven. Well placed for easy access to coastal and countryside walks. Family, double and twin-bedded rooms, most en suite, all with tea and coffee making facilities. Two comfortable lounges. Games room. Separate diningroom. Generous portions of home-cooked farmhouse food are always freshly prepared. Children welcome, special rates for under twelves. Spring and Autumn breaks available. Non-smoking. Sunday lunches and midday lunches optional.

See also Colour Display Advertisement

BUDE

Mrs E. Turner, Penleaze Farmhouse B&B, Marhamchurch, Bude EX23 0ET (Tel & Fax: 01288 381226). Penleaze is a Victorian farmhouse on a working family farm situated amidst rolling countryside on the North Cornish Coast, renowned for its spectacular views, rugged coastline and sandy beaches to explore, also lovely quaint villages such as Boscastle. One mile to our pretty village and two miles to Bude, also ideally placed for visiting North Devon. We offer three double en suite bedrooms, a twin with private bathroom and a small single; four-poster, roll top bath available. An English breakfast using fresh local produce prepared on the Aga is served in the dining room, separate sitting room for guests to relax. B&B £19.50 to £25pppn. **ETC** ◆◆◆◆ *SILVER AWARD.*

e-mail: liz@penleaze.co.uk   **website: www.penleaze.co.uk**

Terms quoted in this publication may be subject to increase if rises in costs necessitate

BUDE

Mrs Pearl Hopper, West Nethercott Farm, Whitstone, Holsworthy (Devon) EX22 6LD (01288 341394). Working farm, join in. Personal attention and a warm welcome await you on this dairy and sheep farm. Watch the cows being milked, help with the animals. Pony rides, scenic farm walks. Short distance from sandy beaches, surfing and the rugged North Cornwall coast. Ideal base for visiting any part of Devon or Cornwall. We are located in Cornwall though our postal address is Devon. The traditional farmhouse has four bedrooms, two en suite; diningroom and separate lounge with TV. Plenty of excellent home cooking. Access to the house at anytime. Bed and Breakfast from £18, Evening Meal and packed lunches available. Children under 12 years reduced rates. Weekly terms available.
e-mail: pearl@westnethercott.fsnet.co.uk

BUDE (near)

Mr & Mrs R. Holmes, Bears & Boxes Country Guest House, Dizzard, St Gennys, Near Bude EX23 0NX (Tel & Fax: 01840 2303138). Friendly, comfortable accommodation is available in our cottage situated in a peaceful, rural Area of Outstanding Natural Beauty on Cornwall's Heritage Coast, a few minutes' walk from the spectacular Coastal Path. All rooms are equipped with hostess trays, TV and other luxuries; most are en suite. Cot and high chair available. Lounge, reading room and dining room for guests' use. Safe bathing, very good surfing, sea and fly fishing, horse riding, golf and trekking within easy reach; Widemouth Bay, Bude and Bocastle a short drive away. Evening meals by arrangement. No smoking. Pets welcome by arrangement. Open all year. B&B from £25pppn. ETC ◆◆◆◆
website: www.bearsandboxes.com

CALLINGTON

Roger and Geraldine Parkyn, 'Kaedeen', Golberdon, Callington PL17 7LT (01579 384197). A warm welcome awaits you at our home, situated on the outskirts of a quiet village with easy access to Bodmin Moor and Dartmoor. Close to Callington, three miles; Launceston, Tavistock and Liskeard, all nine miles. Convenient for Plymouth or touring the coast. Locally there are opportunities for golfing, swimming, cycling, horse riding or just a stroll in the quiet countryside. En suite room available with TV, teamaking facilities and home-baking. Lounge for relaxation. £19 per person per night. Non-smoking. Ideal for stop-over, mini breaks and holidays. Come and let us spoil you.
e-mail: family@parkyn.charitydays.co.uk

DELABOLE

John and Sue Theobald, Tolcarne, Trebarwith Road, Delabole PL33 9DB. Quiet, comfortable bungalow with private bathroom and shower, TV lounge, double or twin rooms. Pets always welcome in the house. We also have a large kennel and run for dogs left at home during the day. Delabole is situated between Padstow and Bude, with access to many footpaths. Britain's first wind farm and Delabole Slate Quarry have interesting visitor centres. Ample parking. For free brochure please telephone **01840 213558.**

A useful index of towns and counties appears at the back of this book on pages 417-421. Refer also to Contents Pages 2 and 3.

FALMOUTH

Mrs E. Eddy, Trevu House Hotel, 45 Melvill Road, Falmouth TR11 4DG (01326 312852; Fax: 01326 318631). Trevu House is a small family-run hotel with a friendly home-from-home atmosphere, with special emphasis on comfort, cleanliness and personal service. The situation is ideal for a seaside holiday being only about two minutes' walk from Gyllyngvase Beach and within easy reach of the town, harbour and railway station. Spacious accommodation is tastefully furnished with bright modern decor. Large comfortable lounge/reading room. Bedrooms are en suite and have modern divan beds, some 6' wide, colour TV, tea/coffee facilities and central heating. We pride ourselves on our high standard of breakfast cuisine which is well presented and served at separate tables. Trevu House is a non-smoking establishment. Full Fire Certificate held. Small car park. Bed and Breakfast from £17.50. No single room supplement. Brochure available upon request.
e-mail: elaine.eddy@lineone.net   **website: www.trevu-house-hotel.co.uk**

FALMOUTH

Heritage House, 1 Clifton Terrace, Falmouth TR11 3QG (01326 317834). We offer visitors a warm, friendly welcome at our comfortable family-run guesthouse. Centrally located for town and beaches. All bedrooms are tastefully decorated with colour TV, free tea/coffee, vanity basins and central heating, with access available at all times throughout the day. Children are welcome, with cot and highchair available. Bed and full English or vegetarian breakfast from £17 per person nightly. Reduced rates for longer stays. Accommodation includes single, twin, double and family bedrooms. On-street parking available with no restrictions. Open all year (except Christmas). Resident proprietors: **Lynn and Ken Grimes.**
e-mail: heritagehouse@tinyonline.co.uk
website: www.heritagehousefalmouth.co.uk

FALMOUTH

"Wickham", 21 Gyllyngvase Terrace, Falmouth TR11 4DL (01326 311140). A small, friendly, non-smoking guest house situated between the harbour and beach with views over Falmouth Bay. We are close to the railway station and within easy reach of the town. Wickham is the ideal base for exploring Falmouth and South Cornwall's gardens, castles, harbour, coastal footpath and much more. All rooms have television and beverage facilities, some have sea views. Bed and Breakfast from £21 nightly, £140 weekly. Discount for children. Single overnight stays subject to availability.
e-mail: enquiries@wickhamhotel.freeserve.co.uk

FALMOUTH

Mrs D. Nethercot, "Telford", 47 Melvill Road, Falmouth TR11 4DG (01326 314581). Why don't YOU try our guest house this year, where personal service is assured, for your annual holiday or short break? We offer double and twin rooms, all with colour TV and beverage making facilities. En suite rooms with shower and WC. Central heating is available for those early and late season breaks. Private off-road parking. Open March to November. Convenient for town, beaches and station. Tariff: Bed and Breakfast from £126 weekly rate.
website: www.SmoothHound.co.uk/hotels/telfordg.html

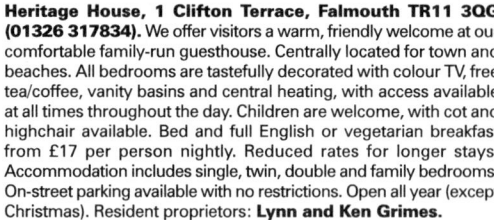

Please mention this guide when making enquiries or bookings

FALMOUTH

Celia and Ian Carruthers, The Clearwater, 59 Melvill Road, Falmouth TR11 4DF (01326 311344). Enjoy quality bed and breakfast accommodation, in a perfect location. Clean, comfortable, tastefully decorated bedrooms with TVs and hot drink making facilities. Internet access for guests. Ten rooms, some en suite. Delicious home cooking. Drinks licence. Close to excellent restaurants, idyllic walks, secluded coves, creekside pubs, watersports, ancient castles and country houses. Two minutes' walk to Falmouth's main beach. Drying and storage facilities for sailing, diving, walking gear, etc. Large car park and near railway station. We welcome guests for short or long stays almost all year, from a very reasonable £20 to £27 per person per night. Please call for a brochure, directions or to check availability. **AA ◆◆◆**

e-mail: clearwater@lineone.net   **website: www.theclearwater.co.uk**

FALMOUTH

See also Colour Display Advertisement

Rosemullion Hotel, Gyllyngvase Hill, Falmouth TR11 4DF (01326 314690; Fax: 01326 210098). Built as a gentleman's residence in the latter part of the 19th century, Rosemullion Hotel offers you a holiday that is every bit as distinctive as its Tudor appearance. Rosemullion is a house of great character and charm, appealing strongly to the discerning guest. The emphasis is very much on that rarest of commodities in today's world – peace. That is why we do not cater for children and do not have a bar of our own. A family-owned hotel continually being refurbished and updated to first class accommodation. Fully centrally heated with 13 bedrooms, some with glorious views over the bay. Large parking area. Non-smoking. B&B £23.50 to £27.50pppn.
e-mail: gail@rosemullionhotel.demon.co.uk
website: www.SmoothHound.co.uk/hotels/rosemullion.html

HAYLE

Mrs Anne Cooper, 54 Penpol Terrace, Hayle TR27 4BQ (01736 752855). Close to lovely beaches and Land's End Peninsula. All rooms with colour TV, beverage making facilities, handbasins and shaver points. Non-smoking establishment. Private parking.
e-mail: annejohn@cooper827.fsnet.co.uk

HELSTON

Mrs Bradley, Myrtle Cottage, Carleen, Breage, Near Helston TR13 9NG (01736 763620). A warm welcome awaits you in this peaceful, relaxing location, situated on the outskirts of the village. The area is steeped in history, with beaches, walks and gardens, something to interest everyone. All rooms are en suite, with tea/coffee making facilities, remote-control colour TV, central heating and a radio alarm. There is ample off-road private parking and the garden is also available to the guests. Non-smoking rooms only. Bed and Breakfast from £20 per person per night. Weekly rates available on request.
e-mail: suzan@pyrope.force9.co.uk

HELSTON

Mrs White, Little Pengwedna Farm, Helston TR13 0AY (01736 850649; Fax: 01736 850489). A friendly Cornish welcome and hearty home cooked breakfast make a stay at this charming farmhouse a real treat. Ideally positioned for touring either coast, you'll find this 19th century granite house prettily and comfortably decorated with original paintings and fresh flowers. All rooms en suite. It is easily reached, on the B3302 between Helston and Hayle. Pets welcome. Terms from £25 to £30. Open from Easter to October. **ETC ◆◆◆◆**
e-mail: ray@good-holidays.demon.co.uk
website: www.good-holidays.demon.co.uk

HELSTON

Mrs P. Roberts, Hendra Farm, Wendron, Helston TR13 0NR (01326 340470). Hendra Farm, just off the main Helston/Falmouth road, is an ideal centre for touring Cornwall; three miles to Helston, eight to both Redruth and Falmouth. Safe sandy beaches within easy reach – five miles to the sea. Two double, one single, and one family bedrooms with washbasins and tea-making facilities; bathroom and toilets; sittingroom and two diningrooms. Cot, babysitting and reduced rates offered for children. No objection to pets. Car necessary, parking space. Enjoy good cooking with roast beef, pork, lamb, chicken, genuine Cornish pasties, fish and delicious sweets and cream. Open all year except Christmas. Evening Dinner, Bed and Breakfast from £150 per week which includes cooked breakfast, three course evening dinner, tea and homemade cake before bed. Bed and Breakfast only from £15 per night also available.

See also Colour Display Advertisement

HELSTON (near)

Mrs D. J. Hill, Rocklands, Pentreath Road, The Lizard, Near Helston TR12 7NX (01326 290339). "Rocklands" is situated overlooking part of Cornwall's superb coastline and enjoys uninterrupted sea views. The Lizard is well known for its lovely picturesque scenery, coastal walks and enchanting coves and beaches, as well as the famous Serpentine Stone which is quarried and sold locally. Open Easter to October. Generations of the Hill family have been catering for visitors on the Lizard since the 1850s. Three bedrooms with sea views, two en suite, tea/coffee making facilities and electric heaters; sittingroom with TV and video; sun lounge; diningroom with separate tables.Children and well trained pets welcome. Bed and Breakfast £23pppn, en suite £25pppn; reductions for children under 10 years.

LAUNCESTON

Mary Rich, "Nathania", Altarnun, Launceston PL15 7SL (01566 86426). A warm welcome awaits you, for accommodation on a small farm on Bodmin Moor within easy reach of coast, moors, towns, lakes and fishing. Visit King Arthur country – Tintagel, Dozmary Pool, the famous Jamaica Inn, Wesley Cottage and cathedral of the moors. One mile from A30, very quiet, ideal for the Eden Project and as an overnight stop for West Cornwall. Double room en suite, twin rooms with bathroom adjoining. Tea making facilities and TV. Payphone. Conservatory and lounge for quiet relaxation. We look forward to meeting you for one night, or why not book your holiday with us and tour Cornwall. You will enjoy the quiet, happy, relaxing atmosphere. Prices from £12.50 per person per night. Please telephone, or write, for details – SAE, thank you. Camping and caravan site also available.

LISKEARD

Mrs Stephanie Rowe, Tregondale Farm, Menheniot, Liskeard PL14 3RG (Tel & Fax: 01579 342407). Working farm, join in. Feeling like a break near the coast? Come and relax, join our family with the peace of the countryside — breathtaking in Spring — on a 200 acre mixed farm, situated near Looe between A38 and A390. See pedigree South Devon cattle and sheep naturally reared, explore the woodland farm trail amidst wildlife and flowers. This stylish, characteristic farmhouse, which dates back to the Domesday Book, has featured in the Daily Telegraph, and is a Cream of Cornwall member, provides exceptional comfort with en suite bedrooms all with colour TV, tea/coffee making facilities, lounge/dining room with log fires. A conservatory to enjoy each day's warmth capturing a beautiful view over the farm, set in an original walled garden including picnic table, tennis court and play area. Special activities can be arranged — fishing, cycling and walking. Home grown and local produce a speciality, full English Breakfast, enjoy a delicious optional evening meal from £15. Bed and Breakfast from £25.00. Open all year. A warm welcome awaits you to discover the beauty of Cornwall. Please phone for a brochure and discuss your requirements. **ETC/AA** ◆◆◆◆ *SILVER AWARD*. Self-catering character cottage also available (**ETC** ★★★★)
e-mail: tregondale@connectfree.co.uk   website: www.tregondalefarm.co.uk

LOOE

Mrs D. Eastley, Bake Farm, Pelynt, Looe PL13 2QQ (Tel & Fax: 01503 220244). Working farm. This is an old farmhouse, bearing the Trelawney Coat of Arms (1610), situated midway between Looe and Fowey. The two double en suite bedrooms and the family room with private bathroom are all decorated to a high standard and have tea/coffee making facilities and TV. Sorry, no pets. No smoking. Open from March to October. A car is essential for touring the area, ample parking. There is much to see and do here – horse riding, coastal walks, golf, National Trust properties, the Eden Project and Heligan Gardens within easy reach. The sea is only five miles away and there is shark fishing at Looe. Bed and Breakfast from £21 to £25. Brochure available on request. **ETC ◆◆◆◆**

MEVAGISSEY

Mrs Dawn Rundle, Lancallan Farm, Mevagissey, St Austell PL26 6EW (Tel & Fax: 01726 842284). Lancallan is a large 17th century farmhouse on a working 700 acre dairy and beef farm in a beautiful rural setting, one mile from Mevagissey. We are close to Heligan Gardens, lovely coastal walks and sandy beaches, and are well situated for day trips throughout Cornwall. Also six to eight miles from the Eden Project (20 minutes' drive). Enjoy a traditional farmhouse breakfast in a warm and friendly atmosphere. Accommodation comprises one twin room and two double en suite rooms (all with colour TV and tea/coffee facilities); bathroom, lounge and diningroom. Terms and brochure available on request. SAE please.
e-mail: dawn@lancallan.fsnet.co.uk

MEVAGISSEY

Helen Blamey, Tregorran, Cliff Street, Mevagissey PL26 6QW (01726 842319). Bed and Breakfast accommodation with magnificent views over the village and harbour. Just a short two minute walk the the harbour itself. All rooms are en suite or have private facilities with colour TV/tea and coffee making facilities. All centrally heated and double glazed. There is also a sauna and a south facing sun deck. Private off-road parking. An ideal touring base. Special promotion for Heligan Gardens or Eden Project tickets (ring for details). For further information telephone Helen Blamey.
website: www.tregorran.homestead.com/home.html

NEWQUAY

Mike and Alison Limer, Alicia, 136 Henver Road, Newquay TR7 3EQ (Tel & Fax: 01637 874328). A warm welcome from your hosts Mike and Alison, who offer you a relaxed and friendly atmosphere in the comfort of their home. Traditional full English breakfast. Four en suite bedrooms, all tastefully furnished, with TV, clock/radio, hairdryer and refreshment tray; one standard with private facilities; iron provided. Relax in the conservatory or spacious lounge. Choose between the golden beaches along Newquay's coastline or a breathtaking coastal walk to Watergate Bay. The Eden Project, quaint fishing villages and the spectacular Cornish coastline, are all within 30 minutes' car ride. Open all year and fully centrally heated. Bed and Breakfast from £20 per person daily. Please telephone or write for brochure. **ETC ◆◆◆◆**

e-mail: aliciaguesthouse@mlimer.fsnet.co.uk   **website: www.cornishlight.freeserve.co.uk/alicia.htm**

NEWQUAY

Meryl and Mark DeWolfreys, Dewolf Guest House, 100 Henver Road, Newquay TR7 3BL (01637 874746). Dewolf Guest House is situated on the A3058 into Newquay Town Centre. All the amenities of Newquay are close at hand with Porth Beach only a short walk from the guest house. We have double or family rooms including two chalets situated in the rear garden. All rooms are non-smoking and offer en suite facilities, colour TV and tea/coffee making facilities. Prices are from £20 per person based on two sharing or from £126 weekly per person. Special Christmas/ New Year Breaks. Off road car parking available, some pets welcome by arrangement. Open all year. *N.A.T.C. APPROVED.*
e-mail: holidays@dewolfguesthouse.com
website: www.dewolfguesthouse.com

NEWQUAY

Terri and Dave Clark, Trewerry Mill, Trerice, St Newlyn East TR8 5GS (Tel & Fax: 01872 510345). A 17th Century watermill which ground corn for the nearby Trerice Manor, now National Trust. Four miles from the north coast in the peaceful Gannel valley; very central for exploring Cornwall, convenient for Eden Project. In seven acres of beautiful grounds with river and wildlife pond. Enjoy Cornish cream teas in the tranquil gardens. The large, beamed mill-room is now the residents' lounge, with TV and bar. Non-smoking throughout. Comfortable bedrooms: two double, one triple, one twin and two single. Some are en suite and all have washbasin and tea making facilities. Large car park. Bed and full Breakfast from £22. Self-catering cottage also available. Please phone for colour brochure or view our website.

e-mail: trewerry.mill@which.net
website: www.trewerrymill.co.uk

NEWQUAY

Mr and Mrs A Slater, St George's Hotel, 71 Mount Wise, Newquay TR7 2BP (01637 873010). The small hotel with a lot to offer. Fabulous sea views. Quality food and service. Clean comfortable accommodation - some en suite with TV. Licensed bar and pool table. Two minutes from town centre and beaches. Large car park. Personal attention. Warm welcome awaits friends old and new. B&B from £140 per week.
e-mail: enquiries@stgeorgeshotel.free-online.co.uk
website: www.st-georges-newquay.co.uk

See also Colour Display Advertisement

NEWQUAY

Margaret and Alan Bird, The Philadelphia, 19 Eliot Gardens, Newquay TR7 2QE (01637 877747; Fax: 01637 876860). Newquay's premier smoke-free guest house, recommended by "Which?" and now twice featured on TV. Quiet tree-lined avenue, award-winning gardens, car park, private patio and hot tub. Bright and spacious quality accommodation, in tastefully themed rooms, all with superb en suite facilities, colour TV and complimentary beverages. Extensive choice for breakfast, short walk to beaches, town and Trenance Gardens. Short drive to the famous Eden Project and Heligan Gardens. Special breaks in quality surroundings, relaxed and friendly atmosphere, comfort, good food and great hospitality, you'll be made very welcome at The Philadelphia. Bed and Breakfast from £25 per person per night. Four-night Eden Break from £99.

e-mail: stay@thephiladelphia.co.uk
website: www.thephiladelphia.co.uk or **www.thephiladelphia.org.uk**

ENGLAND

NEWQUAY

Mrs Carol Lavery, Pensalda, 98 Henver Road, Newquay TR7 3BL (01637 874601). Take a break in the 'heart of Cornwall'. A warm and friendly welcome awaits you at Pensalda. Situated on the main A3058 road, an ideal location from which to explore the finest coastline in Europe. Close to airport and the Eden Project. Single, double and family rooms available, most en suite, all with TV, tea making facilities, etc., including two chalets set in lovely garden. Licensed bar, car park, fire certificate, central heating. Pets welcome. Bed and Breakfast from £18. Four night breaks 1st November to 31st March on special offer (excludes Christmas and New Year).
e-mail: carol@pensalda.fsnet.co.uk
website: www.pensalda-guesthouse.co.uk

NEWQUAY

Mrs B. L. Harvey, Shepherds Farm, Fiddlers Green, St Newlyn East, Newquay TR8 5NW (01872 540502). Working farm. A warm welcome awaits you on our family-run 600 acre mixed working farm. Come and share our warm and friendly atmosphere with first class service in affordable quality accommodation. Cleanliness guaranteed. All rooms en suite and have colour TV and tea making facilities. Large garden. Central location, ideal for touring. The farm is set in rural, small hamlet of Fiddlers Green three miles from beautiful Cornish coastline, five miles from Newquay; 20 minutes from south coast. Glorious sandy beaches, ideal for surfing, little rivers for the very young. Beautiful breathtaking views and walks along scenic clifftops. One-and-a-half miles from National Trust property of Trerice. Good pub food close by. Come and join us! Discounted golf. Bed and Breakfast from £20 to £22. **ETC ◆◆◆◆**

NEWQUAY

Jean & Rob Boston, Highfield Lodge Hotel, Halwyn Road, Crantock, Newquay TR8 5TR (01637 830744). Detached 9 bedroomed licensed hotel situated in one of Cornwall's most beautiful villages. Rooms have panoramic views of sea or countryside and most are en suite. Four-poster bedroom available. Colour TV and tea/coffee facilities in all rooms. Licensed bar. Short walk to one of Cornwall's finest beaches. Highfield Lodge is a no smoking Hotel. Private car park. Open all year. Midweek bookings and short breaks early and late season. Bed and Breakfast from £20 to £30 per night. Special rates for children. Bar meals available. Ring for free brochure. Self-catering flat also available. **ETC ◆◆◆◆**

PADSTOW

Mrs Sandra May, Trewithen Farm, St Merryn, Near Padstow PL28 8JZ (01841 520420). Trewithen farmhouse is a newly renovated Cornish Roundhouse, set in a large garden and situated on a working farm enjoying country and coastal views. The picturesque town of Padstow with its pretty harbour and narrow streets with famous fish restaurants is only three miles away. St Merryn Parish boasts seven beautiful sandy beaches and bays. Also coastal walks, golf, fishing and horse riding on neighbouring farm. Hire a bike or walk along the Camel Trail cycle and footpath - winding for 18 miles along the River Camel. The accommodation has been tastefully decorated to complement the exposed beams and original features. All bedrooms are en suite or have private bathrooms with TVs and hot drink facilities. Parking. Full English breakfast. TV lounge. Bed and Breakfast from £25 to £30 per person per night. Weekly rates and Winter weekend breaks available. **ETC ◆◆◆◆**

A useful index of towns and counties appears at the back of this book on pages 417-421. Refer also to Contents Pages 2 and 3.

PENRYN

Brian and Penny Ward, 62 St Thomas Street, Penryn TR10 8JP (01326 374473). Bed and Breakfast run by husband and wife Brian and Penny, Number 62 is a Grade II Listed house, reputed to be over 250 years old, which offers a friendly welcome. Full English breakfast that can be served early if required. Free tea and coffee and your flasks filled free of charge. Accommodation comprises family, double, twin and single rooms. Situated three minutes' walk from the bus route and a 10 minute walk from the train station, and within easy reach of some of the finest beaches in Cornwall. Open March - October. Bed and Breakfast £12 - £14, children half price.

PENZANCE

"Tradewinds", 21 Regent Terrace, Penzance TR18 4DW (01736 330990). Family-run guest house (non-smoking). Seafront location, convenient for Isle of Scilly boat and parking. TV, tea/coffee making facilities. All rooms en suite. Family room for five. Full English breakfast, vegetarians welcome. Terms from £22 per person. Open all year. Proprietor: **Mrs L. Matthews.**

PENZANCE

Glencree House, 2 Mennaye Road, Penzance TR18 4NG (Tel & Fax: 01736 362026). Large, friendly Victorian guest house echoing the romance of yesteryear, with the comfort and style of today. Peaceful location close to seafront, town centre and sub-tropical gardens. Spacious en suite rooms, some with sea views. All with colour TV and tea/coffee making facilities. Open fires for those cold winter months. Unrestricted parking. Excellent choice of breakfasts. Ideal location for sandy beaches, walking the rugged South West Coastal Path, Scilly Isles. Open all year. Well behaved pets welcome! Bed and Breakfast from £19 per person per night. Please contact **Helen Cahalane** for a brochure/ booking. **website: www.glencreehouse.co.uk**

PENZANCE

Mrs G. Owen, Penalva Private Hotel, Alexandra Road, Penzance TR18 4LZ (01736 369060). The hotel is TOTALLY NON-SMOKING, offering full central heating, fresh immaculate interior, en suite facilities, excellent food and a real welcome with courteous service. Penalva is a well positioned, imposing, late Victorian hotel set in a wide tree-lined boulevard with ample parking, close to promenade and shops. Perfect centre for enjoying the wealth of beautiful sandy coves, historical remains and magnificent walks. Colour TV and tea/coffee making facilities in bedrooms. Open all year. Special diets by prior arrangement. Sorry, no pets. Bed and Breakfast from £18 to £30. Weekly reductions. Children 6 to 12 half-price if sharing family rooms. Highly recommended. SAE, please, for brochure. AA ◆◆◆

PENZANCE

Mr R. Button, Carnson House, East Terrace, Penzance TR18 2TD (01736 365589). A friendly welcome awaits you in our centrally situated, Private Hotel. We specially cater for rail and coach travellers being only yards from the station. A high standard of comfort is maintained together with a reputation for excellent food. We have a comfortable lounge, attractive dining room with separate dining tables, and eight bedrooms, all with heating, tea-makers and colour TV and some with en suite facilities. Penzance is a lively and interesting town with plenty of shops, gardens and promenade, and is the natural centre for exploring the Land's End Peninsula with its beaches, cliffs, coves and villages. We arrange many local excursions, including some to the Isles of Scilly as well as coach tours and car hire. Bed and Breakfast from £21.50 to £26 daily.

AA
◆◆◆◆

Camilla House Hotel
12 Regent Terrace, Penzance TR18 4DW
Tel & Fax: 01736 363771

Susan and Simon would like to welcome you to this lovely Listed building (with own car park) in a quiet terrace close to the harbour and town centre and within easy reach of bus and coach stations. Awarded AA 4 Red Diamonds 2003-2004. Penzance is an ideal base from which you can explore West Cornwall at any time of year. En suite single, double and twin rooms available, many with sea views. We hope that the warm welcome and excellent breakfast plus central heating for your out-of-season visit will make this one of your favourite places. For the safety and comfort of all our guests, smoking is not allowed in the hotel. Bed and Breakfast from £26 to £35 per person per night. Open all year – see web for special offers..

e-mail: enquiries@camillahouse-hotel.co.uk ❖ *website: www.camillahouse-hotel.co.uk*

Boscean Country Hotel
St Just, Penzance, Cornwall TR19 7QP

The Boscean Country Hotel, located amidst some of the most dramatic scenery in West Cornwall, is somewhere very special just waiting to be discovered. This country house offers a wonderful combination of oak panelled walls, a magnificent oak staircase and open log fires. The natural gardens, extending to nearly three acres, are a haven for wildlife including foxes and badgers.

Situated on the Heritage Coast in an Area of Outstanding Natural Beauty close to Cape Cornwall and the Coastal Footpath, this is an ideal base from which to explore the Land's End Peninsula. The moors of Penwith are rich in Iron and Bronze Age relics dating back to 4000BC. Penzance, St Michael's Mount, St Ives, Land's End and the Minack Theatre are all a short distance away.

12 en suite rooms, centrally heated throughout, licensed bar. Excellent home cooking using fresh local produce. *Unlimited Desserts!!*

Open all year.

English Tourism Council ◆◆◆◆
Bed & Breakfast £23.00 Dinner, Bed & Breakfast £36.00

Tel/Fax 01736 788748 E-mail: Boscean@aol.com
Website: www.bosceancountryhotel.co.uk

PENZANCE (near)
Mrs M. D. Olds, Mulfra Farm, Newmill, Penzance TR20 8XP (01736 363940). Near Mulfra Quiot, this hill farm, with cows and calves, high on the edge of the Penwith moors, offers superb accommodation which attracts many of our guests to return year after year. The 17th century, stone built, beamed farmhouse, with far-reaching views, offers two double en suite bedrooms with tea and coffee facilities, TV; comfortable guests' lounge with inglenook fireplace and Cornish stone oven, dining room and sun lounge. Car essential, ample parking, friendly atmosphere, good food, beautiful walking country. Ideal centre for exploring West Cornwall. St Ives eight miles. Eden Project one hour. Bed and Breakfast from £22 - £25. *CORNWALL TOURIST BOARD HIGHLY COMMENDED.*

PENZANCE (near Porthcurno)

Mrs P. M. Hall, Treen Farmhouse, Treen, St Levan, Penzance TR19 6LF (01736 810253). Just off the South West Coastal Footpath, Treen Farm is a family-run, organic dairy farm set in 80 acres of pasture land on the cliffs beside the famous Minack Theatre and the historic Logan Rock. Land's End four miles. Visitors are welcome to use the gardens, walk around the farm and watch milking (children supervised please). Pub, shop, cafe, bus stop and beaches nearby. Ideal for walking, relaxing and sightseeing. Comfortable farmhouse Bed and Breakfast accommodation - twin and double (en suite) rooms with tea/coffee making facilities, garden/sea views; some with TV. Traditional English Breakfast. Guests' lounge with open fire and television. Private parking. Pets welcome. Child reductions. Sorry, no smoking. Bed and Breakfast from £15. Self-catering for two from £120 to £350 per week.
e-mail: paulachrishall@treenfarm.fsnet.co.uk

PERRANPORTH

Chy an Kerensa, Cliff Road, Perranporth TR6 0DR (01872 572470). Licensed Guest House situated by Coastal Path, directly overlooking miles of rolling surf, golden sands, rocks and heathland. Only 200 metres from beach and village centre, which has various restaurants, shops and pubs to suit all tastes and ages. Also tennis, bowls, wetsuit and surfboard hire, with golf and horse riding nearby. Our comfortable bedrooms, most en suite, have colour TV, central heating and tea/coffee making facilities. Many have panoramic sea views, as do our lounge/bar and dining room. Bed and Breakfast from £20 to £28 per person per night. Weekly rates and other reductions. A warm welcome from Wendy Woodcock all year. Please write or telephone for further details. **ETC ♦♦♦**

POLZEATH

Mrs P. White, Seaways, Polzeath PL27 6SU (01208 862382). Seaways is a small family guest house, 250 yards from safe, sandy beach. Surfing, riding, sailing, tennis, squash, golf all nearby. All bedrooms with en suite or private bathrooms, comprising one family, two double, two twin and a single room. Sittingroom; dining room. Children welcome (reduced price for under 10s). Cot, high chair available. Comfortable family holiday assured with plenty of good home cooking. Lovely cliff walks nearby. Padstow a short distance by ferry. Other places of interest include Tintagel, Boscastle and Port Isaac. Non-smoking establishment. Open all year round. Bed and Breakfast from £25; Evening Meal £10.
e-mail: pauline@seaways99.freeserve.co.uk
website: www.seawaysguesthouse.com

PORT ISAAC

Long Cross Hotel & Victorian Gardens, Trelights, Port Isaac PL29 3TF (01208 880243). Stay in one of Cornwall's most unusual hotels set in our own magnificent gardens, visited by thousands of garden lovers annually. We also have our own Free House Tavern for your enjoyment. Area of Outstanding Natural Beauty. Spacious en suite rooms. Pets' corner with animals to feed. Children's adventure play area. Only £60 for three nights September to June.

The Eden Project • *Near St Austell, Cornwall* • *01726 811911*
website: www.edenproject.com
A gateway into the fascinating interaction of plants and people. Two gigantic geodesic conservatories - the Humid Tropics Biome and the Warm Temperate Biome - set amidst landscaped outdoor terraces.

National Maritime Museum • *Falmouth, Cornwall* • *01326 313388*
website: www.nmmc.co.uk
A gateway to the maritime world with interactive displays of boats and their place in the nation's life.

RILLA MILL (near Liskeard)

Woodpeckers, Rilla Mill, Callington PL17 7NT (01579 363717). Woodpeckers is set in a beautiful conservation village, local for hikers to Bodmin Moor (which is only five minutes away), Sterts Theatre and famous Cornish Yarg cheese farm. Central for Eden Project, Looe and Trago Mills. Come and try our candlelit three-course evening meals (£15) with complimentary bottle of wine, served in the conservatory overlooking the countryside and babbling brook. All rooms are fully en suite; the Lilac Haven room also contains a four-poster antique pine bed. Our prices are £23pppn. Woodpeckers' high standards, reflected in the RAC Four Diamond rating, coupled with Sparkling Diamond award and Highly Commended Cornwall Tourism awards, will ensure an enjoyable stay. **RAC ◆◆◆◆,** *SPARKLING DIAMOND AWARD.*
e-mail: alison.merchant@virgin.net

ROSELAND PENINSULA

Mrs Shirley E. Pascoe, Court Farm, Philleigh, Truro TR2 5NB (01872 580313). Working farm, join in. Court Farm is situated in the heart of the Roseland Peninsula, which is undoubtedly one of the loveliest parts of Cornwall with safe, unspoilt beaches on the seaward side, and the beautiful River Fal on the other. The traditionally run farm extends to about 250 acres, 50 of which border the upper reaches of the estuary providing superb walking and bird watching while down river is excellent for sailing, fishing, water skiing etc. The spacious old farmhouse which has over an acre of garden and plenty of parking space, lies in the quiet little village of Philleigh with its lovely old Norman church and 17th century 'Roseland Inn'. There are plenty of good pubs and restaurants within a few miles. For the horse owners who fancy a riding holiday we specialise in providing first class facilities for you and your horse(s). There is also a six-bed cottage available for holiday letting. Please write or telephone for brochure and terms.
e-mail: courtfarm@philleigh.freeserve.co.uk

ST AGNES

Ted and Jeanie Ellis, Cleaderscroft Hotel, 16 British Road, St Agnes TR5 0TZ (01872 552349). This small, detached, family-run Victorian hotel stands in the heart of the picturesque village of St Agnes, convenient for many outstanding country and coastal walks. Set in mature gardens and having a separate children's play area we can offer peace and relaxation after the beach, which is approximately half-a-mile away. Accommodation is provided in generous sized rooms, mostly en suite and all with colour TV. Public rooms comprise lounge, bar, dining rooms and small games room. Private parking. Non-smoking. Regret no pets. Bed and Breakfast from £26 per person per night (sharing). Evening set menu. Self-catering annexe available.
e-mail: tedellis@btinternet.com

ST AGNES

The Sunholme Hotel, Goonvrea Road, St Agnes TR5 0NW (01872 552318). Wonderful countryside and coastal views and a warm welcome await visitors to this country house hotel, standing in its own extensive grounds with ample parking on the southern slope of St Agnes Beacon. Excellent home-cooked meals complement the luxurious en suite accommodation. Children and pets welcome. Open all year. Non-smoking. Please write or phone for brochure. **ETC/AA ★★**
e-mail: info@sunholme.co.uk
website: www.sunholme.co.uk

ST AGNES

PENKERRIS

Dorothy Gill-Carey, Penkerris, Penwinnick Road, St Agnes TR5 0PA (Tel & Fax: 01872 552262). A creeper-clad Edwardian residence with lawned garden in unspoilt Cornish village. A home from home offering real food, comfortable bedrooms with facilities (TV, radio, kettle, H&C). Dining room serving breakfast, with dinner available by arrangement. Bright cosy lounge with a log fire in winter - colour TV, video and piano. Licensed. Ample parking. Dramatic cliff walks and beaches with good surfing available nearby. Easy to find on the B3277 road from big roundabout on the A30 and just by the village sign. Bed and Breakfast from £17.50 to £25.00 per night; Dinner available from £12.50. Open all year. **ETC/AA/RAC** ◆◆
e-mail: info@penkerris.co.uk
website: www.penkerris.co.uk

ST AUSTELL

Mrs Liz Berryman, Polgreen Farm, London Apprentice, St Austell PL26 7AP (01726 75151). Polgreen is a family-run dairy farm nestling in the Pentewan Valley in an Area of Outstanding Natural Beauty. One mile from the coast and four miles from the picturesque fishing village of Mevagissey. A perfect location for a relaxing holiday in the glorious Cornish countryside. Centrally situated, Polgreen is ideally placed for touring all of Cornwall's many attractions. Cornish Way Leisure Trail adjoining farm. Within a few minutes' drive of the spectacular Eden Project and Heligan Gardens. All rooms with private facilities, colour TV, tea/coffee making facilities. Guest lounge. Children welcome. Terms from £23 per person per night. **ETC** ◆◆◆◆
e-mail: polgreen.farm@btclick.com
website: www.polgreenfarm.co.uk

ST CLEER

Trecarne House, Penhale Grange, St Cleer, Liskeard PL14 5EB (Tel & Fax: 01579 343543). At the end of a country lane in a wonderful, tranquil setting on the edge of Bodmin Moor, Trecarne House offers spacious and well decorated bedrooms, with coffee and tea making facilities, hairdryers, colour TV and video. All have uninterrupted views across beautiful open countryside. In the evenings guests are welcome to use the lounge/TV room, and there is a garden with play equipment for young children. The atmosphere is very informal and relaxed, with breakfast served at whatever time you would like. Double rooms start at £30pppn, single from £40; reductions for children sharing. **AA** ◆◆◆◆
e-mail: trish@trecarnehouse.co.uk
website: www.trecarnehouse.co.uk

ST IVES

Mrs N.I. Mann, Trewey Farm, Zennor, St Ives TR26 3DA (01736 796936). Working farm. On the main St Ives to Land's End road, this attractive granite-built farmhouse stands among gorse and heather-clad hills, half-a-mile from the sea and five miles from St Ives. The mixed farm covers 300 acres, with Guernsey cattle and fine views of the sea; lovely cliff and hill walks. Guests will be warmly welcomed and find a friendly atmosphere. Five double, one single and three family bedrooms (all with washbasin); bathroom, toilets; sittingroom, dining room. Cot, high chair and babysitting available. Pets allowed. Car essential, parking. Open all year. Electric heating. Bed and Breakfast only. SAE for terms, please.

ST IVES

Julie Fitzgerald, Horizon Guest House, 5 Carthew Terrace, St Ives TR26 1EB (01736 798069). Do you want a holiday with first-class accommodation and to feel at home instantly? With beautiful sea view rooms overlooking Porthmeor Surf beach. We are close to the coastal footpath to Zennor yet only five minutes from the Tate Gallery, Town Centre and beaches and have some private parking. There is access to your rooms at any time, guests' lounge with colour TV, separate tables for dining and option of home-cooked dinner. Three-night breaks, early and late season £90. All rooms en suite. Private parking. Brochure and colour postcard available.

ST IVES

Angela Walker, Rivendell, 7 Porthminster Terrace, St Ives TR26 2DQ (Tel & Fax: 01736 794923). Our family-run, non-smoking guest house is in a superb location, with a reputation for excellent meals prepared by resident chef. Homely atmosphere. Close to town, beaches and all amenities. Full central heating, en suite rooms available. Colour TV and beverage facilities in all rooms. Television and video in lounge. Fire certificate. Parking available. Open all year (including Christmas and New Year). Phone or send SAE to Angela Walker for brochure. Reduced rates for children and off-peak discounts for over 60s and Countdown cardholders. **RAC ◆◆◆**, *SPARKLING DIAMOND AWARD, DINING AWARD.*
e-mail: rivendellstives@aol.com
website: www.rivendell-stives.co.uk

ST IVES

See also Colour Display Advertisement

Dean Court Hotel, Trelyon Avenue, St Ives TR26 2AD (01736 796023; Fax: 01736 796233). Dean Court overlooks the beach and the beautiful harbour town of St Ives. There is a private terraced garden for the exclusive use of guests, two spacious and comfortable lounges with fine views, and a restaurant with picture windows and comfortable seating. Special attention has been given to making all twelve bedrooms attractive, and they are all en suite, with colour television, radio, hairdryer and hot drinks facilities. Seven rooms have extensive sea views. Full central heating. Level car park in hotel grounds. We regret we cannot allow pets, and do not cater for children. Please write or phone for colour brochure. **RAC ◆◆◆◆.**
e-mail: deancourt@amserve.net
website: www.deancourthotel.com

ST IVES

Roslyn and Keith Pester, Coombe Farmhouse B&B, Lelant Downs TR27 6NW (01736 740843). Off the beaten track and in the heart of the beautiful Cornish countryside, our 150 year old farmhouse lies at the foot of the National Trust's Trencom Hill, yet only three miles from St Ives. We offer a warm welcome, good home cooking and comfortable en suite rooms with lovely views. Our bedrooms are tastefully furnished and decorated. Enjoy a good breakfast in the old dairy, with free-range eggs from our own hens. An excellent location for walking, we are on the St Michael's Way and near the South West Coastal Path. Touring Cornwall or just lazing on the beach, this is the ideal base. The heliport service to the Isles of Scilly is five miles away. Coombe Farmhouse offers away-from-it-all seclusion and an immediate feeling of relaxation and informality. Bed and Breakfast £25 to £35. Cornwall Tourist Board Approved Accommodation.
e-mail: coombefarmhouse@aol.com   **website: www.coombefarmhouse.com**

ST IVES

Linda & Bob Gale, Fairfield House, Porthrepta Road, Carbis Bay, St Ives TR26 2NZ (01736 793771). Linda and Bob welcome you to their homely Edwardian Guest House with fabulous sea views. Ideally situated close to Carbis Bay beach in St Ives Bay, voted one of the most beautiful bays in the world. Two minutes' walk to the Coastal Path, beach and rail line (branch line to St Ives takes three minutes) or walk the beautiful Coastal Path to St Ives. Visit the galleries including the famous Tate, the cobbled streets and harbour, with its many restaurants/pubs. Fairfield House has been recently refurbished with new en suite rooms added in 2003. Lovely rooms, most with sea views across the bay to St Ives. Non-smoking guest house with emphasis on comfort, cleanliness and personal service. Cream teas served in our lovely garden. Bed and Breakfast with varied menus from £22.00 per person per night.

e-mail: info@fairfieldhouse.net **website: www.fairfieldhouse.net**

SENNEN

Mr and Mrs R.A. Comber, Sunny Bank Hotel, Sea View Hill, Sennen TR19 7AR (01736 871278). Sunny Bank is a Highly Recommended hotel standing in large gardens overlooking Sennen Cove. There are 11 bedrooms, all centrally heated with tea and coffee making facilities, some rooms have showers, all have sea or country views. There is a large TV lounge and separate reading room. The grounds provide ample parking. The food is home prepared and cooked using local produce whenever possible. The breakfasts, evening meals and 'Minack Theatre' picnics are delicious. Lands End, the Minack Theatre, sandy beaches and cliff or countryside walks are all within easy reach. Open January – November. Bed and Breakfast from £18.

TINTAGEL

Cate West, Chilcotts, Bossiney, Tintagel PL34 0AY (Tel & Fax: 01840 770324). Without stepping onto a road, slip through the side gate of this 16th Century listed cottage into a landscape owned by the National Trust and designated as an Area of Outstanding Natural Beauty. Closest cottage to nearby Bossiney beach for rock pools, surfing, safe swimming and caves to explore. Walk the airy cliff path north to nearby Rocky Valley or on to picturesque Boscastle Harbour. Southwards takes you to the ruins of King Arthur's Castle and onwards to busy Trebarwith Strand. Notice you have not stepped onto a road yet? Detached traditional country cottage ideal for a small number of guests. Home cooking, warm informal atmosphere, large bright double/family bedrooms with beamed ceilings and olde worlde feel. All rooms have TV, tea/coffee makers. Self-catering annexe available. May I send you a brochure? Bed and Breakfast from £20. Directions: Bossiney adjoins Tintagel on the B3263 (coast road), Chilcotts adjoins large lay-by with telephone box.

TINTAGEL

Bosayne Guest House, Atlantic Road, Tintagel PL34 0DE (01840 770514). Bosayne is situated in an area of natural beauty overlooking the Atlantic Ocean. Close to many amenities, coastal path and King Arthur's Castle, and an excellent touring base. There are two splendid beaches nearby, Bossiney and Trebarwith Strand, ideal for surfing, bathing and beach sports. All the rooms are tastefully decorated,with colour TV, tea-making facilities, clock radio and hairdryer. Many are en suite with fantastic sea views. Our delicious home- cooked breakfast will set you up for the day ahead. We pride ourselves on offering a top class level of service to our customers. A genuine family-run home offering year-round accommodation. **ETC ◆◆◆**
e-mail: clark@clarky100.freeserve.co.uk
website: www.bosayne.co.uk

WADEBRIDGE

Mrs E. Hodge, Pengelly Farm, Burlawn, Wadebridge PL27 7LA (01208 814217). A Listed Georgian farmhouse on a working dairy farm, in a quiet location overlooking wooded valleys. Tastefully decorated and centrally heated throughout, offering one double and one twin room, both en suite with TV, radio, hairdryer and beverage trays. Full English breakfast, using mainly local produce, is served in the traditional style diningroom. Special diets by prior arrangement. Comfortable lounge with TV/video. Large garden with outstanding views for relaxing. An ideal walking, touring and cycling base, only six miles from the coast, with sailing, surfing, golf, riding and coastal walks; Camel Trail, the Saints' Way and Pencarrow House nearby. The Eden Project 35 minutes' drive, Padstow 20 minutes, Wadebridge one and a half miles, with shopping, pubs, restaurants, leisure facilities and The Camel Trail. Static caravan (new 2004) also available. **ETC ◆◆◆◆**
e-mail: hodgepete@hotmail.com   **website: www.pengellyfarm.co.uk**

See also Colour Display Advertisement

WHITSAND BAY (near Downderry)

Mrs S.M. Hoskin, The Copse, St Winnolls, Polbathic, Torpoint PL11 3DX (01503 230205). The Copse is situated in peaceful, unspoilt countryside midway between Plymouth and Looe. The beaches and the golf course at Whitsand Bay are two miles away. We offer en suite rooms with colour television and drinks-making facilities. The Copse is an ideal base for touring Cornwall and South Devon, and visiting the Eden Project. Non-smoking. Regret, no pets. Tariff: £18 to £22 per person per night.

CUMBRIA

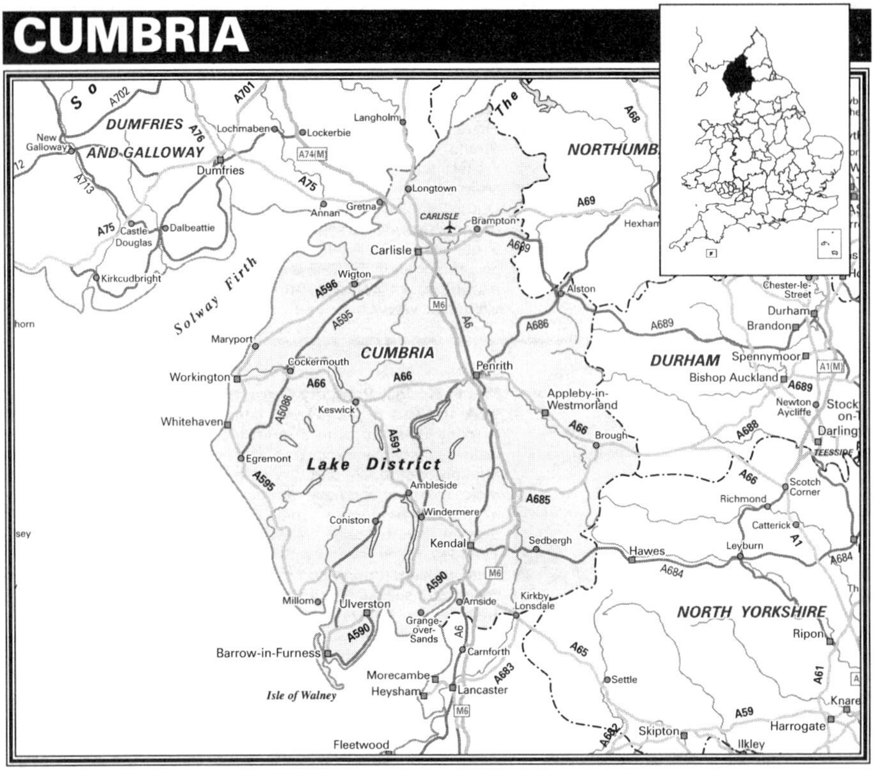

©MAPS IN MINUTES™ 2003 ©Crown Copyright. Ordnance Survey 2003

AMBLESIDE

Mrs Maureen Rushby, Fern Cottage, 6 Waterhead Terrace, Ambleside LA22 0HA (015394 33007). Homely Lakeland stone terraced house situated on the edge of Ambleside only two minutes' walk from the head of Lake Windermere and the Steamer Piers and one mile from the village. Ideal base for touring the Lakes. Kendal approximately 12 miles, Bowness-on-Windermere five miles, Hawkshead and Grasmere about 20 minutes' drive away. The accommodation comprises two double rooms and one twin room, all with tea/coffee making facilities and vanity unit; shared bathroom, lounge/diner with TV. Brochure available. Bed and Breakfast £17 – £19 per person.

AMBLESIDE

Helen and Chris Green, Lyndhurst Hotel, Wansfell Road, Ambleside LA22 0EG (015394 32421). Attractive small Victorian hotel quietly situated in its own garden with private car park. Only two minutes from Ambleside centre. Lovely bedrooms, all en suite. Four poster bedroom or luxury bedroom for that special occasion. Scrumptious food, friendly service. Full central heating for all-year comfort. Cosy bar. Winter and Summer Breaks. A delightful base from which to explore the Lakes either by car or as a walker. Bed and Breakfast from £25. Phone or write for colour brochure, please. **ETC ◆◆◆.**
e-mail: lyndhurst@amblesidehotels.co.uk
website: www.amblesidehotels.co.uk

The Dower House

**Wray Castle, Ambleside
Cumbria LA22 0JA
Tel: 015394 33211**

Lovely old house, quiet and peaceful, stands on an elevation overlooking Lake Windermere, with one of the most beautiful views in all Lakeland. Its setting within the 100-acre Wray Castle estate (National Trust), with direct access to the Lake, makes it an ideal base for walking and touring. Hawkshead and Ambleside are about ten minutes' drive and have numerous old inns and restaurants. Ample car parking; prefer dogs to sleep in the car. Children over five years welcome.

Bed and Breakfast from £28.00
Optional Evening Meal from £14.50
Open all year round

See also Colour Advertisement

See also Colour Advertisement

Ambleside Lodge

Elegant Lakeland home built circa 1875, offering a high standard of accommodation to suit both the discerning traveller or to provide an anchor location while you discover the Lake District.
All bedrooms are en suite and our premier suites and king-size four-poster rooms offer total relaxation and indulgence and have jacuzzi spa baths. Leisure facilities at a private club just five minutes' drive away include swimming pool, sauna, steam room, squash, gymnasium and beauty salon.

Rothay Road, Ambleside LA22 0EJ
Tel: 015394 31681 • Fax: 015394 34547
e-mail: enquiries@ambleside-lodge.com • website: www.ambleside-lodge.com

---

Rothay House is an attractive modern detached guest house set in pleasant gardens with views of the surrounding fells. All bedrooms are comfortable and well furnished with en suite facilities, colour TV, tea and coffee trays. Robin and Margaret combine 20 years quality hotel experience with a friendly atmosphere in clean attractive surroundings. The house is within easy walking distance of the village centre. Ambleside has a variety of interesting shops and restaurants and makes an ideal base for walking, touring or enjoying sailing, watersports and angling on Lake Windermere. Car not essential, but ample parking. Open all year. Children welcome; sorry, no pets. Strictly non-smoking. *Bed and Breakfast from £25 to £30; Winter Weekend Breaks available.*

See also Colour Advertisement

ROTHAY HOUSE

**Rothay Road, Ambleside,
Cumbria LA22 0EE
Tel/Fax: 015394 32434
e-mail: email@rothay-house.com
website: www.rothay-house.com**

Readers are requested to mention this guidebook when seeking accommodation (and please enclose a stamped addressed envelope).

AMBLESIDE

Jack & Barbara Halliday, The Anchorage, Rydal Road, Ambleside LA22 9AY (015394 32046). Situated two minutes' walk from the centre of Ambleside, with its many shops, restaurants and inns, this modern guest house has a private car park, comfortable lounge, tastefully furnished bedrooms with colour TV, tea/coffee making facilities and central heating. Each bedroom has pleasant views over parkland or surrounding fells. En suite rooms available. Choice of English, vegetarian or Continental breakfast. Ideal base for walkers or those wishing to tour the Lake District. Non-smoking. Sorry, no pets. Open all year. Weekly rates/mid-week breaks available at various times. Bed and Breakfast from £18 to £27. **ETC** ◆◆◆
e-mail: info@anchorageonline.force9.co.uk
website: www.anchorageonline.force9.co.uk

AMBLESIDE

Mr D. Sowerbutts, 2 Swiss Villas, Vicarage Road, Ambleside LA22 9AE (015394 32691). A small Victorian terrace house set just off the main road in the centre of Ambleside, near the church, in a slightly elevated position overlooking Wansfell. There is immediate access to the cinema and shops and the wide variety of restaurants and cafes in the town. There are three double bedrooms (one with twin beds) recently refurbished in the traditional style. Each room has central heating, tea-making facilities and colour TV. A full English Breakfast or vegetarian meal available. We are open all year round and you are sure of a friendly welcome and good home cooking. Bed and Breakfast from £24.50 to £26.50 per person. Self-catering accommodation is also available in house next door. See website for details.

e-mail: sowerbutts@tinyworld.co.uk   **website: www.amblesideonline.co.uk**

See also Colour Display Advertisement

AMBLESIDE

Ferndale Hotel, Lake Road, Ambleside LA22 0DB (015394 32207). The Ferndale Hotel is a small, family-run Hotel where you will find a warm, friendly welcome and personal attention at all times. Offering excellent accommodation with good home cooked English or Vegetarian breakfast. Our ten attractive bedrooms have all been individually decorated and furnished, each with full en suite facilities, colour TV and tea/coffee making tray. Full central heating throughout; several rooms have views of the fells, including ground floor bedrooms. Open all year round with car park, licensed, offering packed lunches, hair dryer, clothes/boot drying and ironing facilities. A wide choice of places to dine within minutes' walking distance, ranging from excellent pub food to superb restaurants of many varied cuisines will complete your day. Bed and Breakfast £24 to £26 per person per night. Weekly £155 to £165. Please phone for brochure. **ETC** ◆◆◆
e-mail: info@ferndalehotel.com   **website: www.ferndalehotel.com**

AMBLESIDE

Ian and Helen Burt, The Old Vicarage, Vicarage Road, Ambleside LA22 9DH (015394 33364; Fax: 015394 34734). "Rest awhile in style". Quality Bed and Breakfast accommodation set in tranquil wooded grounds in the heart of the village. All rooms are en suite with kettle, clock/radio, TV, fridge, CD and video player. Washing and drying facilities are also available. Superb English breakfasts are served. Heated indoor swimming pool, sauna, hot tub, sun lounge and roof top terrace. Fishing, riding, climbing, golf, sailing and water sports available nearby. Special breaks available. Friendly service where your pets are welcome. No smoking in bedrooms. Ample free parking.
e-mail: the.old.vicarage@kencomp.net
website: www.oldvicarageambleside.co.uk

ENGLAND

APPLEBY

Mrs Diana Dakin, Morningside, Morland, Penrith CA10 3AZ (01931 714393) Morningside is idyllically situated in the pretty village of Morland, midway between Appleby and Penrith, in the beautiful Eden Valley. Convenient for touring all of Cumbria and only 10 miles from Ullswater, it is perfect for a relaxing break. Friendly, personal service is assured in the beautifully appointed, ground floor twin-bedded room with en suite shower room, colour TV, hot drinks facilities plus the advantage of own entrance from private patio. A delicious breakfast is served in the bedroom overlooking the garden and village views. Central heating. Parking. Bed and Breakfast £25 per person. No smoking please.

APPLEBY

Mrs K.M. Coward, Limnerslease, Bongate, Appleby CA16 6UE (Tel & Fax: 017683 51578). Limnerslease is a family-run guest house five minutes' walk from the town centre. A good half-way stopping place on the way to Scotland. There is a good golf course and an indoor heated swimming pool. Many lovely walks are all part of the charm of Appleby. Two double and one twin bedrooms, all with washbasin, colour TV, tea/coffee making facilities at no extra charge; bathroom, toilet; dining room. Open January to November with gas heating. Ample parking. Bed and Breakfast from £19.50.
e-mail: limnerslease@fsmail.net

APPLEBY

Barbara and Derick Cotton, Glebe House, Bolton, Appleby-in-Westmorland CA16 6AW (017683 61125). Our 17th century former farmhouse is ideally located for exploring the Eden Valley, an area waiting to be discovered by those who seek tranquillity in an Area of Outstanding Natural Beauty. Very quiet location with outstanding views of the Pennines. Approximately one mile from the A66 and four miles west of Appleby, and very convenient for visits to the Lake District, Yorkshire Dales and Scottish Borders. Centrally heated accommodation includes two double (one en suite) and one twin room all with tea-making facilities. Hearty breakfasts are served, with special diets catered for. Children welcome. Non-smoking. Bed and Breakfast from £20 to £25; Evening Meal from £10 to £15. Please send SAE for

brochure. **ETC** ◆◆◆
e-mail: derick.cotton@btinternet.com   **website: www.glebeholidays.co.uk**

BOWNESS-ON-WINDERMERE

Holly Cottages Guest House, 2 Holly Cottages, Rayrigg Road, Bowness-on-Windermere LA23 3BZ (015394 44250). Guest House in the centre of Bowness-on-Windermere, offering four double en suite rooms with colour TV and tea making facilities. Centrally situated to all shops and restaurants. Lake Windermere and boat trips five minutes away. Excellent position for exploring the Lake District. If you enjoy walking, cycling, shopping, steam power, visiting houses and gardens, viewing wonderful scenery or simply pottering about, there is something here for any age or ability. We look forward to welcoming you soon. Sorry, no smoking in house. Private parking and access at all times. Dogs by arrangement. Contact: **Jan or Jim Bebbington (015394 44250).**
website: www.hollycottageguesthouse.co.uk

The *Fish Hotel*

Buttermere, Cockermouth, Cumbria CA13 9XA

Tel: 017687 70253 • Fax: 017687 70287
website: www.fish-hotel.co.uk

Situated in one of Lakeland's most beautiful valleys just five minutes' walk from Buttermere Lake and Crummock Water and at the foot of Honister Pass, this is ideal walking and climbing country with fishing readily available. The needs of climbers are fully understood and catered for. The hotel is full of charm, although modernised for guests' comfort. There is ample parking for all guests' cars. Children are welcome at the Fish Hotel.

The *Richardson* family looks forward to the pleasure of your company and assures you of a warm welcome.

BRAMPTON

Mrs Annabel Forster, High Nook Farm, Low Row, Brampton CA8 2LU (016977 46273). Friendly farmhouse with relaxing atmosphere and good home cooking. Situated one mile from Low Row village and four miles from Brampton in peaceful Irthing Valley. Beef cattle, sheep, goats and poultry are kept and visitors are allowed to wander around the farm. Conveniently situated for touring Northumberland, Lake District and Scottish Borders and only a few miles from Roman Wall, Lanercost Priory and Talkin Tarn. Accommodation comprises one double and one family room, lounge, TV, diningroom. Bed and Breakfast from £14; reductions for children under 12 years. Light snacks and packed lunches available. Well-controlled dogs accepted.

BRAYTON

The Retreat, Brayton, Near Aspatria CA7 3PT (016973 21900). This family-run guest house enjoys superb views of Skiddaw and the Fells from the patio area of the large garden. An en suite room is available, and amenities include tea/coffee facilities, TV and a guest lounge; log fire in winter. Golf and fishing within three-minute walk; bike hire and bike shop on site. Situated off the B5299 which is off the A595 at Mealsgate or the A596 at Aspatria. Open all year. *BRONZE OYSTERCATCHER WINNER IN THE SOLWAY GREENS AWARDS FOR COMMITMENT TO THE ENVIRONMENT.*
website: www.theretreat.lnw.co.uk

Readers are requested to mention this guidebook when seeking accommodation (and please enclose a stamped addressed envelope).

ENGLAND

BUTTERMERE

Dalegarth Guest House, Hassness Estate, Buttermere CA13 9XA (017687 70233). Close to the Lake shore, one-and-a-quarter miles south of village. Bed and Breakfast from £20 including VAT.
website: www.dalegarthguesthouse.co.uk

CALDBECK

Mr and Mrs A. Savage, Swaledale Watch, Whelpo, Caldbeck CA7 8HQ (Tel & Fax: 016974 78409). Ours is a mixed farm of 300 acres situated in beautiful countryside within the Lake District National Park. Easy reach of Scottish Borders, Roman Wall, Eden Valley. Primarily a sheep farm (everyone loves lambing time). Visitors are welcome to see farm animals and activities. Many interesting walks nearby or roam the peaceful Northern fells. Enjoyed by many Cumbrian Way walkers. Very comfortable accommodation with excellent home cooking. All rooms have private facilities. Central heating. Tea making facilities. Bed and Breakfast from £19 to £25; Evening Meal from £12 to £15, Tuesday, Wednesday, Thursday and Saturday only. **AA/ETC** ◆◆◆◆
e-mail: nan.savage@talk21.com
website: www.swaledale-watch.co.uk

CARLISLE

Ronnie and Jackie Fisher, Cornerways Guest House, 107 Warwick Road, Carlisle CA1 1EA (01228 521733). Ronnie and Jackie welcome you to their family-run Guest House. A Grade II Listed building situated in the heart of historic Carlisle just two minutes' walk from city centre with castle, cathedral, bus and railway stations. An ideal base for visiting the Lake District, Hadrian's Wall and Gretna Green. Colour TV, welcome tray, shaver points and central heating in all rooms; en suite rooms available. Payphone and off-street parking. Reasonable rates from £15 per person with reductions for children. To reach us by car turn off M6 at Junction 43. **ETC** ◆◆◆◆

See also Colour Display Advertisement

CARLISLE

Mrs L. Lawson, Craigburn Farm, Catlowdy, Longtown, Carlisle CA6 5QP (01228 577214; Fax: 01228 577014). A warm welcome awaits you at our family-run guest house. Delicious homemade meals, sweets our speciality. Residential licence. Stopover to and from Scotland or ideal for a quiet weekend away exploring Hadrian's Wall, Scottish Borders or shopping in Carlisle. Stay in one of our six cosy en suite rooms furnished with the guests' comfort in mind. A7 to Longtown then follow signs for Catlowdy. **ETC** ◆◆◆◆
e-mail: louiselawson@hotmail.com
website: www.craigburnfarmhouse.co.uk

CARLISLE

Mrs Dorothy Nicholson, Gill Farm, Blackford, Carlisle CA6 4EL (01228 675326; mobile: 07808 571586). In a delightful setting on a beef and sheep farm, this Georgian style farmhouse dated 1740 offers a friendly welcome to all guests breaking journeys to or from Scotland or having a holiday in our beautiful countryside. Near Hadrian's Wall, Gretna Green and Lake District. Golf, fishing, swimming and large agricultural auction markets all nearby; also cycle path passes our entrance. Accommodation is in one double room en suite, one family and one twin/single bedrooms. All rooms have washbasins, shaver points and tea/coffee making facilities. Two bathrooms, shower; lounge with colour TV; separate diningroom. Open all year. Reductions for children; cot provided. Central heating. Car essential, good parking. Pets permitted. Bed and Breakfast from £19 to £24. Telephone for further details or directions.

CARLISLE

Mrs Georgina Elwen, New Pallyards, Hethersgill, Carlisle CA6 6HZ (01228 577308). Ideal location for either North/South stop over or for a longer visit to explore our wonderful countryside. All Bed and Breakfast rooms are en suite with tea/coffee making facilities. Menu choice for dinner. There are also four self catering cottages available, sleeping two to eight. Family-run working farm. Bed and Breakfast from £25; reductions for longer stay). Room Only and Self Catering also available. **ETC** ◆◆◆◆ *GOLD AWARD WINNER.*
e-mail: info@newpallyards.freeserve.co.uk
website: www.newpallyards.freeserve.co.uk

See also Colour Display Advertisement

CARLISLE

Mr G. Shipp, Abberley House, 33 Victoria Place, Carlisle CA1 1HP (01228 521645). An imposing town house offering informal, comfortable high standard en suite rooms with TV, tea and coffee facilities and private parking. We are only a short walk from the excellent town centre with its fine variety of shops, restaurants, pubs and of course the cathedral, castle and award-winning Tullie House museum. Also close by are Stoney Holme and Swift golf courses, the Sands sports and leisure centre and the splendid River Eden. A short drive takes you to historic Hadrian's Wall, the magnificent Lake District and romantic Gretna Green. Our rates start from only £19 per person which includes English breakfast and taxes. **ETC** ◆◆◆◆
e-mail: bbs@abberleyhouse.co.uk
website: www.abberleyhouse.co.uk

COCKERMOUTH

The Allerdale Court Hotel, Market Place, Cockermouth CA13 9NQ (01900 823 645; Fax: 01900 823 033). Situated in the old Market Place of Cockermouth, this Listed building dates back to the 17th century. Original oak beams and open fire help to retain the warm relaxing atmosphere found here. Family-owned and run, we pride ourselves on warm hospitality, good food in our restaurants, and constant attention to detail. The hotel has 24 en suite bedrooms, individually furnished and tastefully equipped to complement the character of the building, all with hospitality trays, TV, radio and phone. Family rooms are available, dogs are welcome. Our concern is your comfort and relaxation throughout your stay.
e-mail: John-H-Carlin@tinyonline.co.uk

COCKERMOUTH

Mr & Mrs R. Mortimer, The Manor House, Oughterside, Aspatria CA7 2PT (Tel & Fax: 016973 22420). Our lovely manor farmhouse dates from the 18th century and retains many original features as well as several acres of land. Rooms are spacious with large en suite bathrooms, tea and coffee making facilities, full size TVs, views and lots of little extras. Our double rooms have kingsize beds and our twin room has double beds. The grounds are home to many species of birds, including barn owls. Set in peaceful surroundings we enjoy easy access to the magnificent scenery of the Western Lakes and Solway Coast. Pets and children welcome. Bed & Breakfast from £21. Evening meals by arrangement.
e-mail: richardandjudy@themanorhouse.net
website: www.themanorhouse.net

COCKERMOUTH

Mrs V. A. Waters, The Rook Guesthouse, 9 Castlegate, Cockermouth CA13 9EU (01900 828496). Interesting 17th century town house, adjacent to historic castle, we offer comfortable accommodation with full English, vegetarian or Continental breakfast. Rooms are equipped with washbasin, colour TV, tea/coffee facilities and central heating. En suite and standard rooms available. Cockermouth is an unspoilt market town located at the North Western edge of the Lake District within easy reach of the Lakes, Cumbrian Coast and Border country. We are ideally situated as a base for walkers, cyclists and holidaymakers. Bed and Breakfast from £17 - £19 per person sharing room, single occupancy £20 - £22. Open all year, except Christmas.
website: www.therookguesthouse.gbr.cc/

COCKERMOUTH (near)

Mrs Bridget Woodward, Whitekeld Farm, Ullock, Near Cockermouth CA14 4RJ (01946 861171). Beautiful double room with large en suite wet room/bathroom in converted sandstone farm outbuildings. Complete privacy and self-contained with magnificent views. Open May 2004, along with converted barn for four, with en suite and top facilities. Terms from £30 to £40 per person per night. Please telephone or e-mail for more details.
e-mail: LBWoodward@aol.com

COCKERMOUTH (near)

Mrs Nicholson, Swinside End Farm, Scales, High Lorton, Near Cockermouth CA13 9VA (01900 85134). Working farm situated in a peaceful part of Lorton Valley, the perfect base for your Lakeland holiday. Ideal for hill walking and touring around the Lake District. All rooms are en suite with central heating, tea/coffee making facilities and hairdryer. TV lounge with open fire. Magnificent views. Packed lunches available. A warm welcome awaits you. Open all year. Pets by arrangement. Bed and Breakfast from £20 to £22 per person per night. **ETC ◆◆◆◆**

GILSLAND

Mrs Packer, The Hill, Gilsland CA8 7DA (016977 47214). In an outstanding hill top location overlooking the Irthing Valley and Hadrian's Wall at Birdoswald, this 16th century fortified farmhouse or "bastle" has three bedrooms. One double en suite, one twin en suite (ground floor) and one twin with private bathroom. A lounge is also provided for guests. One acre of garden and private parking. We provide the greatest of comfort, delicious food and a warm welcome to all who visit this historic and beautiful area. With the introduction of the Hadrian's National Trail in May 2003, The Hill is ideally situated for walkers, being about half a mile from the Wall. **ETC ◆◆◆◆**

HAWKSHEAD (near)

Paul and Fran Townsend, Pepper House, Satterthwaite LA12 8LS (01229 860206, Fax: 01229 860306). A warm welcome awaits in 16th century former farmhouse with elevated position in tranquil valley on edge of Grizedale Forest, four miles from Hawkshead. Red and roe deer and other wildlife abound. Trout fishing nearby. Excellent, peaceful base for exploring the Lakes, close to Beatrix Potter's farm and Ruskin's Brantwood. Miles of forest trails for walking and cycling. Sympathetically updated, all bedrooms have en suite facilities. Two comfortable lounges, one with TV. Central heating, log fires; dining room and terraces with wonderful views. Licensed bar, generous home cooking. Non-smoking. Bed and Breakfast from £24; with Dinner from £36. Weekly rates and special winter rates available.
website: www.pepper-house.co.uk

HESKET NEWMARKET

Howbeck Farmhouse, Hesket Newmarket CA7 8JN (01697 478306). Treat yourself to a great B&B experience in our lovely 17th century home. Howbeck Farmhouse is in a wonderful quiet position a short walk from the village and pub. Cycle rides and fell walks abound, as do drives to local attractions and Lake District beauty spots. Pets welcome.
e-mail: info@howbeckfarmhouse.co.uk
website: www.howbeckfarmhouse.com

IREBY

Woodlands Country House & Cottage, Ireby CA7 1EX (016973 71791; Fax: 016973 71482). A delightful Victorian former vicarage, now a most comfortable hotel with eight en suite bedrooms offering delicious food and affordable wines. We have a fast growing reputation for providing a wonderfully relaxing atmosphere. Ideally situated, in a beautiful rural setting, to explore all of Lakeland, the Solway and the Scottish Border regions. Well behaved pets welcome. Suitable for wheelchair users. Ample parking, Non-smoking. Bed and Breakfast from £35 per person per night. Charming two bedroom self-catering stable conversion also available. **ETC ◆◆◆◆**
e-mail: stay@woodlandsatireby.co.uk
website: www.woodlandsatireby.co.uk

KENDAL

Hollin Root Farm, Garth Row, Skelsmergh, Kendal LA8 9AW (01539 823638). Dating from 1844 Hollin Root Farm is a typical Lakeland farmhouse set in beautiful open countryside with land down to the river. Tranquil settings and large gardens make this an ideal place for longer stays and a good base from which to explore the Lake District. There are many footpaths near the farm including the 84 mile Dales Way. Accommodation consists of three en suite rooms all with colour TV and tea/coffee making facilities. Excellent breakfasts. Packed lunches available. Private car park, safe cycle storage. Children and vegetarians welcome. Open all year. Non-smoking establishment. B&B from £22 to £28 pppn. **ETC ◆◆◆◆**
e-mail: b-and-b@hollin-root-farm.freeserve.co.uk
website: www.hollinrootfarm.co.uk

KENDAL

See also Colour Display Advertisement

Mrs D. M. Swindlehurst, Tranthwaite Hall, Underbarrow, Near Kendal LA8 8HG (015395 68285). Working farm. Highly Commended with the English Tourism Council for excellent standards of comfort and quality. Recommended by Which? Good Bed & Breakfast Guide. Tranthwaite Hall is said to date back to 1186. A charming olde world farmhouse with beautiful oak beams, doors and rare black iron fire range. This working dairy/sheep farm has an idyllic setting half-a-mile up an unspoilt country lane where deer can be seen, herons fishing in the stream and lots of wild flowers. This is a very peaceful and quiet retreat yet only minutes from all Lakes and local attractions. Attractive bedrooms, all are en suite and have TV, tea/coffee making facilities, hair dryer, radio and full central heating. Guest lounge. Full English breakfast is served with eggs from our farm and home-made jam and marmalade. We like guests to enjoy our home and garden as much as we do. Walking, pony trekking, golf and many good country pubs and inns nearby. Bed and Breakfast £23 to £26. **ETC ◆◆◆◆**
e-mail: tranthwaitehall@aol.com   **website: www.tranthwaitehall.co.uk**

KENDAL

Mrs S. Beaty, Garnett House Farm, Burneside, Kendal LA9 5SF (01539 724542). A 15th century farmhouse on a dairy/sheep farm, all bedrooms en suite. Situated half-a-mile from A591 and ten minutes from Windermere. Accommodation comprises double, twin and family bedrooms all with colour TV, clock/radio, tea/coffee making facilities amd hairdryer. Lovely oak panelled lounge with four feet thick walls and a real fire on chilly evenings. Dining room with separate tables - help yourself to starters followed by a choice of cooked breakfast. Good private parking. Short walk to village shops, inn and public transport. Golf and fishing one mile. Winter three-night breaks from £57. No smoking. RAC◆◆◆◆

e-mail: info@garnetthousefarm.co.uk
website: www.garnetthousefarm.co.uk

KENDAL

Mrs A. Taylor, Russell Farm, Burton-in-Kendal, Carnforth, Lancs. LA6 1NN (01524 781334; Fax: 01524 782511). Why not spend a few days at Russell Farm? The proprietors pride themselves on trying to give guests an enjoyable holiday with good food, friendly atmosphere, relaxing surroundings away from the hustle and bustle. The 150-acre dairy farm is set in a quiet hamlet one mile from the village of Burton-in-Kendal, and five miles from the old market town of Kirkby Lonsdale. An ideal centre for touring Lakes and Yorkshire Dales, or going to the coast. Ideal stopover for people travelling south or to Scotland, only five minutes from M6 Motorway. One double, one single and one family bedrooms; bathroom, toilet; sittingroom and diningroom. Children welcome; cot, high chair and babysitting offered. Pets accepted, if well-behaved. Evening Dinner, Bed and Breakfast or Bed and Breakfast. Reductions for children. Car essential, parking. Send large SAE, please, for terms and brochure.

KENDAL (near)

Mrs Pat Metcalfe, Crook Hall, Crook, Near Kendal LA8 8LF (Tel & Fax: 01539 821352). Beautiful, spacious farmhouse dating from the 15th century, with oak beams and beautiful old panelling in guest lounge. The poet, William Wordsworth, used to visit here. Working farm. Magnificent scenery abounds; good walking areas. Conveniently situated between Kendal and Lake Windermere, half-a-mile up our pretty country lane. A warm welcome awaits you. Bed and Breakfast from £25.00 to £27.00 per person. One double and one family en suite room (four-poster bed available). No smoking. No pets. Open April to December. 'Bed & Breakfast Nationwide' Inspected & Approved.

website: www.crookhallfarm.co.uk

KESWICK

Mrs M.A. Illman, Beckstones Farm, Thornthwaite, Keswick CA12 5SQ (017687 78510). Beneath the forest and looking over fields to the magnificent mountain scenery of Skiddaw and the Helvellyn Ranges, Beckstones is peacefully situated off the beaten track and within a short stroll of the southern shores of Bassenthwaite Lake. The Georgian Farmhouse has been extended into the barn, providing quality, centrally heated en suite bedrooms with hospitality trays. Beamed diningroom, TV lounge, ample parking, a large garden and a cycle store. Dogs by arrangement. Bar meals locally, Keswick 10 minutes' drive. Excellent touring and walking base. B&B from £23. Brochure available. ETC ◆◆◆
website: http://website/lineone.net/~beckstones

KESWICK

Anworth House Vegetarian Bed and Breakfast, 27 Eskin Street, Keswick CA12 4DQ (017687 72923). Victorian house with relaxed atmosphere ideally situated for the town centre, theatre, lakes and fells. Two double, one family (double), one four-poster and one twin en suite bedrooms, all individually co-ordinated and tastefully furnished to the highest standards with central heating, hairdryer and tea/coffee making facilities. For the comfort of guests, Anworth House is a non-smoking establishment. Terms from £28 single and from £46 to £52 double. Open all year except Christmas. Special winter breaks available from November to March (excluding Christmas and New Year). ETC ◆◆◆

KESWICK

Cottage in the Wood Country House Hotel & Licensed Restaurant, Whinlatter Pass, Braithwaite, Keswick CA12 5TW (017687 78409). 17th century former Coaching Inn atop Whinlatter Pass has superb views of the Skiddaw range. All seven en suite bedrooms are well appointed, two having four-poster beds. Personally run by Liam and Kath Berney this NON-SMOKING hotel has a wide reputation for its excellent cuisine and fine wines. The convivial atmosphere assures guests of a memorable stay. Pets welcome by arrangement. Ideal base for walking and touring. **ETC/RAC ★★**
e-mail: info@thecottageinthewood.co.uk
website: www.thecottageinthewood.co.uk

KESWICK

Bassenthwaite Hall Farm B&B, Bassenthwaite Village, Near Keswick CA12 4QP (Tel & Fax: 017687 76393). Ideally situated by a stream with ducks, just two miles from Skiddaw and Bassenthwaite Lake and six miles from Keswick and Cockermouth lies Bassenthwaite Hall Farm. A friendly welcome awaits you at this lovely 17th century farmhouse, which is fully modernised whilst retaining its olde worlde character. A charming lounge/diningroom furnished with antiques is available for guests' use any time. Delightful bedrooms with individual period furnishings. Hand basin in rooms. Two bathrooms close by. Tea and coffee making facilities. Good local inn for food nearby.
website: www.bedandbreakfast-lakedistrict.co.uk

KESWICK

Cherry Trees Guest House, 16 Eskin Street, Keswick CA12 4DQ (017687 71048). Comfortable, warm and spacious Victorian guesthouse. Situated within easy access of town centre, lake and fells. Tastefully furnished with king-sized beds!! All double and twin rooms en suite, single room has private facilities. All have colour TV, clock/radio, hairdryer, tea/coffee making facilities and direct dial telephones. Excellent freshly prepared food and home made jams and marmalades. Packed lunches. Secure cycle store. Non-smoking. B&B from £23 - £28.
e-mail: cherry.trees@virgin.net
website: www.cherrytrees-keswick.co.uk

KESWICK

Glencoe Guest House, 21 Helvellyn Street, Keswick CA12 4EN (017687 71016). Cycling, walking or touring, a warm, friendly welcome is guaranteed at our Victorian guest house, situated in a quiet area of town and yet only five minutes' stroll from the centre of Keswick and all its amenities. Glencoe offers spacious en suite and standard rooms, all decorated and furnished to a high standard. Each provides colour TV, hospitality tray and radio alarm; double, twin and single rooms available. Local knowledge and maps are at hand. Here at Glencoe we also provide a drying room, cycle storage and free flask filling. Non-smoking. B&B from £20pp. An enjoyable and comfortable stay awaits.
e-mail: enquiries@glencoeguesthouse.co.uk
website: www.glencoeguesthouse.co.uk

KESWICK

Mrs S. Park, Langdale, 14 Leonard Street, Keswick CA12 4EL (017687 73977). Victorian town house, quietly situated, yet close to town, park, lake and fells. All rooms furnished to a very high standard, having quality en suite facilities, central heating, colour TV, tea/coffee making facilities throughout. Family, double or twin available. Enjoy a good home cooked English or vegetarian breakfast or our popular Continental breakfast. We have a non-smoking policy throughout the house. We will ensure your stay is a pleasant one. Bed and Breakfast from £21; Theatre Breaks. Special three nights midweek/weekend breaks November to March.
website: www.langdaleguesthouse.co.uk

KESWICK

Ian and Janice Picken, Lynwood House Licensed Guest House, 35 Helvellyn Street, Keswick CA12 4EP (017687 72398). Fantastic scenery, fabulous fell-walking; five minutes from town centre, 10 minutes to Lake Derwentwater. Free from smoke. Full Fire Certificate held. Finest cuisine: full breakfast menu including homemade, organic and vegetarian alternatives. Facilities include tea/coffee making facilities and TV. One room en suite, one with private bathroom. Furnished distinctively. Friendly welcome. In short, absolutely fabulous! Bed and Breakfast from £21 per person per night. ETC ◆◆◆◆ *SILVER AWARD*.
e-mail: info@lynwoodhouse.net
website: www.lynwoodhouse.net

KESWICK

Colin and Lesley Smith, Mosedale House, Mosedale, Mungrisdale CA11 0XQ (017687 79371). Traditional 1862 built, lakeland farmhouse. A smallholding with donkeys, hens and ducks. It enjoys a magnificent position, nestling at the foot of Carrock Fell, overlooking the River Caldew, three-and-a-half miles from the A66 Keswick to Penrith road. Four-course dinners, licensed, vegetarians welcome. Home-baked bread, our own free-range eggs. Packed Lunches. No smoking. En suite rooms. Attractive lounge. Bed and Breakfast from £25. Dinner £14.50. Delightful two bedroomed self-catering cottage. Peaceful location, fell-walking from the door. Abundant wildlife. Visit us on our website below. Grade One facilities for disabled guests. ETC ◆◆◆◆
e-mail: mosedale@northlakes.co.uk   **website: www.mosedalehouse.co.uk**

KESWICK

Linda and Ronnie Walker, Watendlath Guest House, 15 Acorn Street, Keswick CA12 4EA (017687 74165). Just a few minutes' walk from Keswick town centre, parks and lake, Watendlath has a quiet and relaxed atmosphere. The attractive rooms are all equipped with en suite shower and toilet, beverage making facilities, radio alarm clock, hairdryer and complimentary toiletries. We have a large family room sleeping four/five with a cot and high chair available if required. Both walkers and cyclists are welcome as we will dry wet clothes, fill flasks, have secure storage for cycles and repairs, and undercover off-road parking for motorbikes - in fact everything to make your holiday a home from home experience. For everyone's comfort we are a non-smoking guest house. Bed and Breakfast from £20 per person per night, weekly from £140. ETC ◆◆◆◆

KESWICK

Ann & Norman Pretswell, Woodside, Penrith Road, Keswick CA12 4LJ (017687 73522). Late 19th century property set in almost an acre of mature grounds with views of Grizedale Pike and surrounding hills. Ideally situated away from the busy town centre yet only a short walk down the C2C bridle path to the town. The property has been extensively refurbished and has larger than average rooms with good-sized en suites. We have a large private car park, and for those using cycles, secure storage, hosepipe, repair stand and associated tools for your use. Being a family-run establishment you are guaranteed a friendly reception and sound advice on anything, from where to go to do extreme rock climbs, to gentle strolls and ferry cruises. After a good night's sleep you will be ready for a hearty English breakfast together with cereal, fruit and yoghurt. We will cater for special needs on request. Credit cards accepted. Dogs welcome by arrangement. Bed and Breakfast from £23.
e-mail: ann@pretswell.freeserve.co.uk   website: www.woodside.uk.net

KESWICK

Annie Scally and Ian Townsend, Latrigg House, St Herbert Street, Keswick CA12 4DF (017687 73068). An attractive Victorian house in a quiet area, only a few minutes' walk from the town centre and Lake, providing an excellent base for visiting the Lake District. We promise a very warm welcome, good food, comfort and hospitality (vegetarian and vegan meals provided if required). We offer a no-smoking environment for the well being and comfort of guests, comfortable rooms, (all with en suite facilities), colour TVs, tea/coffee facilities and central heating. Comfortable residents' lounge with TV. Bed and Breakfast £25 to £28 per person per night. Sorry no pets. ETC ◆◆◆◆
e-mail: info@latrigghouse.com
website: www.latrigghouse.com

KESWICK

Mrs Deborah Mawson, Highside Farm, Bassenthwaite, Keswick CA12 4QG (017687 76952/76328). Fantastic 17th century period working farmhouse, tastefully renovated to the highest standards, featuring oak beams and Inglenook fireplace. Ideally situated for walking, sightseeing, cycling, touring, etc. The farm nestles at the foot of Skiddaw and Ullock Pike, and has tremendous views towards Bassenthwaite Lake. Highside offers a family room sleeping up to four, a double bedroom and a ground-floor bedroom. All rooms are en suite. Highside is the ideal base for your holiday in the Lake District – a hidden jewel waiting to be discovered. Strictly non-smoking. Terms from £27 per person per night. Three night specials £78.
e-mail: deborah@highside.co.uk
website: www.highside.co.uk

KESWICK/BORROWDALE

Mrs S. Bland, Thorneythwaite Farm, Borrowdale, Keswick CA12 5XQ (017687 77237). Thorneythwaite Farm has a beautiful, peaceful position in the Borrowdale Valley standing half- a-mile off the road. The 220 acre sheep farm is seven miles from Keswick and half-a-mile from Seatoller. The 18th century farmhouse has great character inside and out, several rooms having oak beams and panelling and being furnished to suit. Two double and one family bedrooms, all with tea/coffee making facilities; sittingroom with open or electric fire; diningroom; bathroom and toilet. Cot, high chair and reduced rates for children. Sorry no pets. Open from April to November, mid-week bookings accepted. A perfect base for fell walking; Scafell, Great Gable, Glaramara are all within walking distance from the farm. Bed and Breakfast from £19.

KIRKBY STEPHEN

Mrs Sylvia Capstick, Duckintree House, Kaber, Kirkby Stephen CA17 4ER (017683 71073). Duckintree is a working family farm set in the quiet Eden Valley countryside just off the A685 Kirkby Stephen to Brough road. Easy access to the Lakes and Yorkshire Dales or ideal for breaking your journey from the south of England/Midlands to Scotland. Car essential, ample parking. The rooms comprise family, double and twin (cot available) with tea/coffee making facilities. Lounge/dining room with colour TV. All rooms overlook a large garden and countryside. Bed and Breakfast from £17. Reductions for children under 12 years. Pets welcome by arrangement. Evening Meal can be provided. Open from March to October. Campsite available for tourers and tents. Write or phone for details.

KIRKBY STEPHEN

Cocklake House, Mallerstang CA17 4JT (017683 72080). Charming, High Pennine country house Bed and Breakfast in unique position above Pendragon Castle in Upper Mallerstang Dale offering good food and exceptional comfort to a small number of guests. Two double rooms with large private bathrooms. Three acres riverside grounds. Dogs welcome.

LOWESWATER

Mrs Vickers, Askhill Farm, Loweswater, Cockermouth CA13 0SU (01946 861640). Askhill is a family-run farm which has beef and sheep. Situated on the hillside overlooking Loweswater Lake. The area is ideal for fell-walkers; there are plenty of walks (high fells or low walks) to suit everyone's level of ability; we are handy for all the western lakes, Crummock Water, Buttermere, Ennerdale (with lots of woodland walks), Wast Water (the deepest lake). Loweswater is handy for Keswick (10 miles approximately), Cockermouth (eight miles), the city of Carlisle with Roman connections (30 miles approximately), Maryport, steeped in Roman history (12 miles), and we are roughly 12 miles from the Solway coast. B & B from £22 per person; Dinner, B & B from £34 per person. Also 6 berth, self-catering caravan to let from £220 per week. Telephone for a brochure. **ETC ◆◆◆**

e-mail: askhillfarm@aol.com

website: www.countrycaravans.co.uk/askhillfarm

Holker Hall & Gardens • *Near Newby Bridge, Cumbria* • *015395 58328*
website: www.holker-hall.com
A historic hall set in 25 acres of beautiful gardens, plus the Lakeland Motor Museum
featuring the Campbell Bluebird Exhibition.

NEAR SAWREY

Mrs Elizabeth Mallett, Esthwaite How Farmhouse, Near Sawrey, Ambleside LA22 0LB (015394 36450). A warm and friendly welcome awaits you at Esthwaite How Farmhouse, situated in this lovely village where Beatrix Potter wrote her books. Beautiful views of the countryside and the lake (where part of the television film about her life was made) can be seen from bedrooms and the diningroom. Ideal for walking, fishing and touring. Accommodation comprises two double rooms, one en suite, and one twin bedded room. Dining/sitting room with open log fire, central heating. Children welcome; babysitting can be arranged. Open all year. Car essential, parking for three cars. Bed and Breakfast from £17; Bed, Breakfast and Evening Meal from £25. Half rates for children sharing room.

NEWBIGGIN ON LUNE

Mrs Brenda Boustead, Tranna Hill, Newbiggin on Lune, Kirkby Stephen CA17 4NY (015396 23227 or 07989 892368). Tranna Hill offers a relaxing and friendly atmosphere in a non-smoking environment. Five miles from M6 Junction 38, ideal base for all activities with Howgill Fells, nature reserve, fish farm and golf course only minutes away. Well placed for breaking your journey or touring the Lakes and Dales. En suite rooms furnished to a high standard with TV, refreshment trays, central heating and beautiful views. Private parking and large gardens. Delicious breakfasts. All for £20 per person per night. **ETC ◆◆◆◆**
e-mail: trannahill@hotmail.com
website: www.trannahill.co.uk

PENRITH

Elle Jackson, Albany House, 5 Portland Place, Penrith CA11 7QN (01768 863072; Fax: 01768 895527). Close to the town centre, Albany House is a lovely mid-Victorian terraced property. Fine, spacious rooms (two double, two multi, one family), en suite facilities, central heating, colour satellite TV, tea/coffee. Situated close to M6, A6 and A66, an ideal base for touring the Lake District, Eden Valley, Hadrian's Wall and Scottish Borders. An excellent stopover, with the warmest welcome and hearty breakfasts. B&B from £18pp. **ETC ◆◆◆, RAC ◆◆◆,** *SPARKLING DIAMOND AND WARM WELCOME AWARDS.*
e-mail: info@albany-house.org.uk
website: www.albany-house.org.uk

PENRITH

Norcroft Guest House, Graham Street, Penrith CA11 9LQ (Tel & Fax: 01768 862365). Conveniently situated for M6 and just five minutes' walk from town centre, our delightful Victorian house boasts an ideal location. All en suite with a variety of rooms ranging from single, twin, double, triple to family suites with separate connecting children's accommodation. Awarded the RAC Warm Welcome Award and renowned for our delicious Cumbrian breakfast – why not treat yourself to a stay? Non-smoking. Private parking. Credit cards accepted. Rates from £27.50 per person single, £23.50 per person double. Bed and Breakfast. Children welcome. Regret, no pets. For brochure and details please contact **Mr Blagbrough. ETC/RAC ◆◆◆◆,** *WARM WELCOME AWARD.*

PENRITH

Mrs Brenda Preston, Pallet Hill Farm, Penrith CA11 0BY (017684 83247). Pallet Hill Farm is pleasantly situated two miles from Penrith on the Penrith-Greystoke-Keswick road (B5288). It is four miles from Ullswater and has easy access to the Lake District, Scottish Borders and Yorkshire Dales. There are several sports facilities in the area - golf club, swimming pool, pony trekking. Good farmhouse food and hospitality with personal attention. An ideal place to spend a relaxing break. Double, single and family rooms; TV lounge and dining room. Children welcome, cot, high chair. Sorry no pets. Car essential, parking. Open Easter to November. Bed and Breakfast £14 (reduced weekly rates). Reduced rates for children.

PENRITH

Beckfoot Country House, Helton, Penrith CA10 2QB. (01931 713241; Fax: 01931 713391). A beautiful Victorian country house set in three acres of gardens, with wonderful views of the Lowther valley, a tranquil and unspoilt corner of the Lake District National Park. All rooms are en suite, spacious and well appointed with TV, hospitality tray and complimentary toiletries; luxurious executive suite with four-poster. Ironing facilities available. Cumbrian breakfast and home-cooked evening meals served in the oak-panelled diningroom. Activities nearby include walking, cycling, horse riding, fishing, golf, swimming and paragliding, or visit Hadrian's Wall and the Scottish Borders, Eden Valley, historic Carlisle city, historic castles and gardens. Special three night breaks available. AA ◆◆◆◆
e-mail: info@beckfoot.co.uk
website: http//www.beckfoot.co.uk

PENRITH

Mrs Mary Teasdale, Lisco Farm, Troutbeck, Penrith CA11 0SY (017687 79645). Lisco has beautiful views of Saddleback and the Fells. Three miles from Keswick Golf Club, six miles from Derwentwater and five from Ullswater. A good base for touring lovely Lakeland. Comfortable accommodation offered in one double and two en suite family rooms, all with tea/coffee making facilities and washbasins. Bathroom with shower. Lounge and separate diningroom. Bed and Breakfast, optional Evening Meal. Good home cooking. Colour TV. Children welcome. Outside accommodation available for dogs if required. Large dogs also welcome. SAE or phone for further information.

PENRITH

Mrs Ann Toppin, Gale Hall, Melmerby, Penrith CA10 1HN (01768 881254). Working farm. Mrs Ann Toppin welcomes guests to her home on a working beef/sheep farm 10 miles east of Penrith and the M6, a mile-and-a-half from the peaceful village of Melmerby. Beautiful setting at the foot of the Pennines and with extensive views of the Lakeland Fells. Ideal for walking, convenient for the Lake District. Single, double, twin or family rooms available; cot and babysitting. Residents' lounge. Pets welcome by arrangement. Bed and Breakfast from £16; reduction for children under 12 years. Special diets catered for. Full English or Vegetarian Breakfast served. Excellent bar meals available locally.

PENRITH

Mrs Marjorie Whittam, Netherdene Guest House, Troutbeck, Near Penrith CA11 0SJ (01768 483475). Take a break in the Lake District where a warm, friendly welcome awaits you in our non-smoking guest house. Situated in a large pleasant garden amidst lovely countryside with open views in all directions, with the distinctive outline of Blencathra dominating the skyline. Within easy reach of Ullswater and the arboretum at Aira Force with its outstanding waterfall which is a delight to walk in all seasons. All bedrooms are en suite, tastefully furnished to a high standard, with central heating, colour TV and hospitality tray. Enjoy a hearty Aga-cooked English breakfast; take time to relax in the cosy lounge with log fire. Private parking. Bar and restaurant meals available nearby. B&B £21 to £27. ETC ◆◆◆
e-mail: netherdene@aol.com
website: www.netherdene.co.uk

PENRITH

Mrs Jean Ashburner, Lattendales Farm, Berrier Road, Greystoke, Penrith CA11 0UE (017684 83474). Comfortable 17th century farmhouse in quiet attractive village five miles from Penrith. Ideal for touring the Northern Lakes. Accommodation comprises one twin room and two double rooms; lounge with colour TV. Children and pets welcome; reductions for children. Non-smoking. Bed and Breakfast from £17.50 to £18.50 per person. Directions, follow B5288 from Penrith, in Greystoke take Berrier Road and Lattendales Farm is first B&B on left.

PENRITH

Mrs C Bousfield, Trainlands, Maulds Meaburn, Penrith CA10 3HX (017683 51249). David and Carol Bousfield welcome you to this 17th century farmhouse and working farm located away from busy roads and nestling between the Eden and Lyvennet Valleys above the village of Maulds Meaburn. We are five miles west of Appleby and 13 miles south of Penrith. Tea/coffee facilities in the two bedrooms, together with radios. There is a bathroom for the sole use of guests. Lounge with real fire, soft seats and television. A tour of the buildings may be possible. Please remember to bring suitable footwear. Tariff from £18 to £25 per person per night. Evening meal by arrangement, £12 per person. Payment - cheque or cash. A deposit of £20 is required.
e-mail: bousfield@trainlands.u-net.com
website: www.trainlands.co.uk

RAVENGLASS

George and Cath Jones, Holly House Hotel, Main Street, Ravenglass CA18 1SQ. (01229 717230). A small privately-run hotel in a quiet village overlooking the broad estuary on the Irish Sea coast, where visitors will receive a warm welcome and excellent service. Accommodation comprises seven comfortable bedrooms, four en suite, the other three have wash basins. All have colour TV and tea/coffee making facilities. Family rooms available. Ideally situated for walking, fishing and boating activities as well as many places of interest to visit. The cosy public bar offers a wide selection of wines, spirits, beers and real ale. Wholesome home-made food available throughout the day catering for all tastes including a special children's menu. B&B from £21 pppn.
website: www.thehollyhousehotel.com

SHAP

Mr and Mrs D. L. and M. Brunskill, Brookfield, Shap, Penrith CA10 3PZ (01931 716397). Situated one mile from M6 motorway (turn off at Shap interchange No. 39), first accommodation off motorway. Excellent position for touring Lakeland, or overnight accommodation for travelling north or south. Central heating throughout, renowned for good food, comfort and personal attention. All bedrooms are well-appointed and have en suite facilities, remote-control colour TV, hospitality tray and hairdryer. Diningroom where delicious home cooking is a speciality. Well-stocked bar. Residents' lounge. Sorry, no pets. Open from January to December. Terms sent on request, ample parking. Full Fire Certificate. **AA ◆◆◆◆**

ENGLAND

TROUTBECK

Hill Crest, Troutbeck, Penrith CA11 0SH (017684 83935). Stephanie and Andy assure you of a warm and friendly welcome at Hill Crest, their unique Lakeland home which offers two en suite double/family rooms, one twin room. Home cooking, tea/coffee facilities and TV in rooms. Panoramic mountain views. Aira Force waterfalls, Ullswater 10 minutes, Keswick 15 minutes, a good base for walking, boating, touring, Lakes, Hadrian's Wall and the Borders. Books, maps and hints from Stephanie on what to see. Walkers, children and dogs welcome. Bed and Breakfast £20 per person twin or en suite room. Children half-price sharing. 10 minutes Junction 40 M6. At Hill Crest we aim to create a relaxed and informal atmosphere where guests are treated as part of the family. Highly recommended by previous guests. Come as a stranger, leave as a friend. Open all year.

ULLSWATER

Knotts Mill Country Lodge, Watermillock, Penrith CA11 0JN (017684 86699). Spacious guesthouse close to magical Ullswater, in peaceful, scenic surroundings. Ideal for walking, boating or touring the Lake District. Nine en suite bedrooms with stunning views, including family rooms and facilities for the disabled. Our large dining room and lounge have picture windows that overlook the fells. Delicious Evening Meals with generous servings and quality home cooked food and choice of wines. Only 10 minutes from Junction 40 M6 with private grounds and parking. Low season discounts when the Lake District is at its most beautiful with snow on the peaks and you can relax by our log fire. **ETC ◆◆◆**
website: www.knottsmill.com

WINDERMERE

Mrs Dorothy Heighton, Beckmead House, 5 Park Avenue, Windermere LA23 2AR (Tel & Fax: 015394 42757). A small family-run guest house with quality accommodation, delicious breakfasts and a relaxed friendly atmosphere. Single, double or family rooms, with en suite or private showers, all decorated to a high standard with central heating, electric blankets, tea/coffee making facilities, colour TV, hairdryers and clean towels daily. Comfortable residents' lounge. Walking, climbing, sailing, water skiing, pony trekking, golf nearby, or visit historic houses, gardens and museums. **ETC ◆◆◆◆**
e-mail: beckmead_house@yahoo.com
website: www.beckmead.co.uk

WINDERMERE

Mrs J. Seal, Brook House, 30 Ellerthwaite Road, Windermere LA23 2AH (015394 44932). A friendly welcome awaits you at Brook House which is convenient for village and lake. Ideal touring centre. We offer personal service, together with excellent English cooking, under the personal supervision of the proprietors. All rooms are decorated to a high standard; residents' lounge with colour TV; full central heating. All bedrooms have private showers/baths, colour TV, tea/coffee making facilities, and most have private toilets. Access to rooms at all times. Guests' parking. Full Fire Certificate. Open all year. Bed and Breakfast from £18.50 to £27. **ETC ◆◆◆**

WINDERMERE

Mr and Mrs Harvey, College House, College Road, Windermere LA23 1BU (015394 45767). A non-smoking, spacious Victorian family home offering a warm and friendly welcome, in a quiet area close to village centre and railway station. Some rooms have superb mountain views, all are either en suite or have private bathroom, colour TV, tea/coffee making facilities and full central heating. We have plenty of interesting local guides, maps, books, pictures and fresh flowers plus a small private garden with furniture for guests' use. We can pre-arrange local minibus tours, hire of mountain bikes or horse riding facilities. Bed and Breakfast from £18 to £27. Vegetarians welcome. Private car spaces and garage for bikes. **ETC** ◆◆◆

WINDERMERE

Mr and Mrs D. Lennon, Meadow Cottage, Ratherheath Lane, Crook LA8 8JX (015398 21269). Sandra and David Lennon extend a warm welcome to guests who stay at Meadow Cottage. Set in one and a half acres, this old Lakeland cottage has spectacular views and is the ideal location when visiting this beautiful region. All bedrooms are en suite, have tea and coffee facilities and colour TV. We provide Aga-cooked vegetarian or English breakfasts. Some five miles from Lake Windermere, the popular heart of the Lake District, we are conveniently placed for touring, walking or cycling exploration. A flexible service is provided in this non-smoking guesthouse. Please enquire for brochure. Prices from £25 per person.

WINDERMERE

Mylne Bridge House, Brookside, Lake Road, Windermere LA23 2BX (015394 43314; Fax: 015394 48052). Mylne Bridge House is the ideal location for your Lakeland break, situated off the main road between Windermere village and the Lake. There is a large private car park with easy access from Lake Road. There are eight bedrooms, seven of which offer en suite facilities – Room eight has its own private facilities. There is a good mix of single, double, twin and family rooms; all have colour television and tea/coffee making facilities. Most rooms have south-facing windows to capture the sunshine and all are centrally heated for winter comfort. Special diets can be catered for. Non-smoking. No pets. Children welcome. Free fishing permits. Bed and Breakfast from £23 to £30 per person per night.

e-mail: mylnebridgehouse@talk21.com **website: www.s-h-systems.co.uk/hotels/mylne.html**

WINDERMERE

Fir Trees Guest House, Lake Road, Windermere LA23 2EQ (015394 42272; Fax: 015394 42512). Situated mid-way between Windermere village and the lake, built in the traditional Lakeland style, Fir Trees offers delightful accommodation of exceptional quality and charm. Our bedrooms are lovely, all furnished and decorated to a very high standard and all have private en suite facilities, tea/coffee making and television. Breakfasts are traditionally English in style and cooked to perfection.
e-mail: enquiries@fir-trees.com
website: www.fir-trees.com

SANDOWN

Lake Road, Windermere, Cumbria LA23 2JF Tel & Fax: 015394 45275

Superb Bed and Breakfast accommodation. All rooms en suite with colour TV and tea/coffee making facilities. Situated two minutes from Lake Windermere, shops and cafes. Many lovely walks. Open all year. Special out of season rates, also two-day Saturday/Sunday breaks. From £22 to £32 per person, excluding Bank Holidays. Well-behaved dogs welcome. Each room has own safe private car parking. SAE or telephone for further details.

Proprietors: Irene and George Eastwood

See also Colour Advertisement

The Firgarth Hotel

Ambleside Road, Windermere LA23 1EU

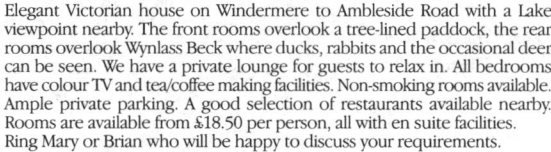

Elegant Victorian house on Windermere to Ambleside Road with a Lake viewpoint nearby. The front rooms overlook a tree-lined paddock, the rear rooms overlook Wynlass Beck where ducks, rabbits and the occasional deer can be seen. We have a private lounge for guests to relax in. All bedrooms have colour TV and tea/coffee making facilities. Non-smoking rooms available. Ample private parking. A good selection of restaurants available nearby. Rooms are available from £18.50 per person, all with en suite facilities. Ring Mary or Brian who will be happy to discuss your requirements.

Tel: 015394 46974 • Fax: 015394 42384
e-mail: thefirgarth@ktdinternet.com
website: www.firgarth.com

See also Colour Display Advertisement

WINDERMERE

St John's Lodge, Lake Road, Windermere LA23 2EQ (015394 43078). This pretty 14 bedroom guest house offers spotlessly clean rooms, a relaxed atmosphere, good service and an excellent choice of breakfasts to suit all tastes. It is ideally situated within ten minutes' leisurely walk of Windermere village and the lake at Bowness Bay and is close to all amenities. The FREE internet access and FREE temporary membership of a nearby luxury leisure club are excellent extras. Personally run by resident chef/proprietors, St John's Lodge offers an ideal location and great value for money.
e-mail: mail@st-johns-lodge.co.uk
website: www.st-johns-lodge.co.uk

See also Colour Display Advertisement

WINDERMERE

Mr and Mrs Tyson, Holly-Wood Guest House, Holly Road, Windermere LA23 2AF (015394 42219). Holly-Wood is a beautiful Victorian house offering clean comfortable accommodation in a quiet position, three minutes' walk from the village centre. A perfect location for your visit to the Lake District and within reach of the Dales and Morecambe Bay. Central heating, tea/coffee makers, television and hair dryer. Traditional or vegetarian breakfasts. Cosy residents' lounge. Bus/station transfer. En suite and budget rooms available. Low season and short break reductions. Bed and Breakfast from £17.50 to £29 per person. Non-smoking. No pets. ETC ◆◆◆◆
website: www.hollywoodaccommodation.co.uk

DERBYSHIRE

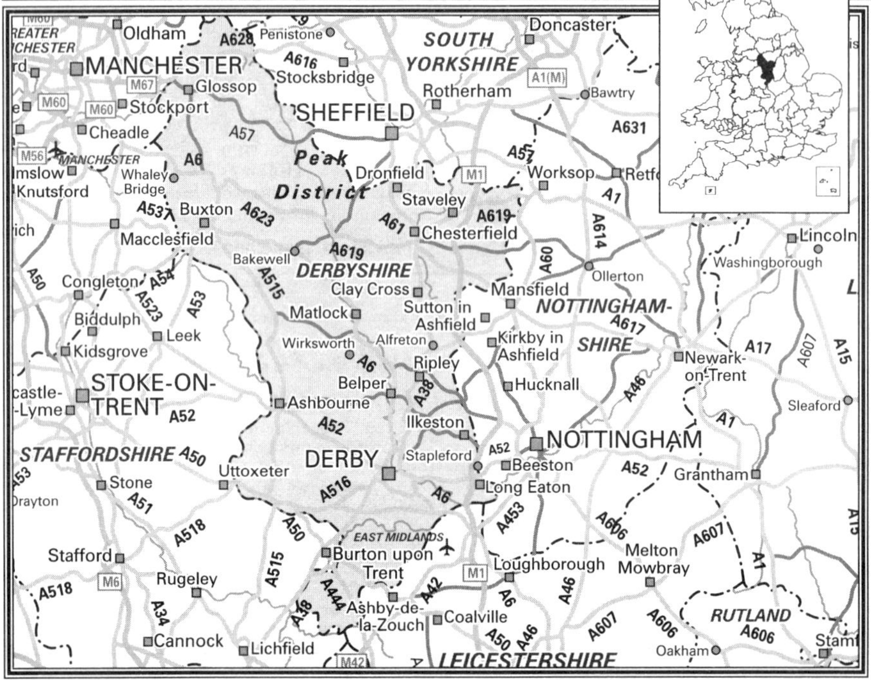

©MAPS IN MINUTES™ 2003 ©Crown Copyright, Ordnance Survey 2003

ASHBOURNE

Mrs A.M. Whittle, Stone Cottage, Green Lane, Clifton, Ashbourne DE6 2BL (01335 343377; Fax: 01335 347117). A charming cottage in the quiet village of Clifton, one mile from Georgian market town of Ashbourne. Ideal for visiting Chatsworth House, Haddon Hall, Dovedale, Carsington Waters and the theme park of Alton Towers. Each bedroom is furnished to a high standard; all rooms en suite with four-poster beds, TV and coffee making facilities. Large garden to relax in. A warm welcome is assured and a hearty breakfast in our delightful cottage. Nearby good country pubs serving evening meals. Bed and Breakfast from £21 per person. Please write or telephone for further details. **ETC/AA ◆◆◆**

e-mail: info@stone-cottage.fsnet.co.uk

ASHBOURNE

Compton House, 27-31 Compton, Ashbourne DE6 1BX (01335 3431000). Situated in the charming market town of Ashbourne, we are a small family-run guest house with accent on good food and quality accommodation in a warm and friendly atmosphere. Originally three terraced cottages, now converted into one rather individual house which has been our home since 1986. As well as a comfortable sitting room, we have five en suite bedrooms, all with colour TV and well-stocked tea tray. Dinner is available if pre-booked. We have safe parking in our delightful garden at the rear of the house. Bed and Breakfast from £22.50 per person. **AA ◆◆◆◆**

e-mail: jane@comptonhouse.co.uk
website: www.comptonhouse.co.uk

ASHBOURNE

Mrs M. Richardson, Throwley Hall Farm, Ilam, Ashbourne DE6 2BB (01538 308202 or 308243). Our Bed and Breakfast accommodation is set in the heart of rural England in the Peak District National Park. Situated on our family farm where the sheep and cattle are nurtured in easy harmony with abundant wildlife and wild flowers. Within a few miles of the nationally renowned beauty of the Manifold Valley and Dovedale. In the spring and summer months you can enjoy watching the new lambs and calves. The bedrooms are comfortable, well-equipped, spacious. All have wash basins, tea and coffee facilities, and are en suite or have private bathrooms. Despite their peaceful rural location we're within easy reach of Alton Towers theme park as well as Chatsworth and the historic pottery works of Stoke-on-Trent. Nearby the charming local market towns of Ashbourne, Leek and Buxton move at a gentler pace. Tariffs from £27 pppn with reduced rates for children.
e-mail: throwleyhall@talk21.com or throwley@btinternet.com
website: www.throwleyhallfarm.co.uk

ASHBOURNE (near)

Mrs Dot Barker, Waterkeepers Cottage, Mappleton, Near Ashbourne DE6 2AB (01335 350444). Set in the Dove Valley on the edge of the Peak District, this 19th century cottage consists of two double rooms with washbasin and two single rooms; sitting room/dining room. Tea making facilities, central heating and open fires on cooler days. The large attractive garden, edged by fields and hills, is a paradise for pets who are welcome in this family atmosphere. The Dove meanders by, forming the boundary between Staffordshire and Derbyshire; approximately 20 miles from Buxton, Bakewell and Matlock while just eight miles away is the popular Alton Towers. Bed and Breakfast £19.50. Reductions for children.

ASHBOURNE (near)

Mr J. Parker, Mona Villas, Church Lane, Middle Mayfield, Mayfield, Near Ashbourne DE6 2JS (01335 343773). A warm, friendly welcome to our home with purpose built en suite accommodation. Beautiful views over open countryside. A local pub serves excellent food within a five minute walk. Situated near Alton Towers, Dove Dale, etc. Bed and Breakfast from £22.50 to £25.00 per night. Three en suite rooms available, single supplement applies. Family rooms available. Parking. **ETC/AA**
◆◆◆
e-mail: info@mona-villas.fsnet.co.uk
website: www.mona-villas.fsnet.co.uk

BAKEWELL

Jenny Bates, Chapel View Farm, Chapel Street, Monyash Near Bakewell DE45 1JJ (01629 814317). Situated in the heart of the Peak District with stunning White Peak scenery and glorious walks. Go sightseeing to places such as Chatsworth House, Haddon Hall and the market town of Bakewell. Sited just off the village green, the accommodation provides a spacious and independent converted 18th century farmhouse. Private parking and own entrance offering one double and one twin room both en suite and separate downstairs WC, lounge with tea and coffee making facilities. Bed and Breakfast from £22 to £25 per person per night, £30 single occupancy. **ETC** ◆◆◆◆

Readers are requested to mention this guidebook when seeking accommodation (and please enclose a stamped addressed envelope).

BAKEWELL

Mrs Julia Finney, Mandale House, Haddon Grove, Bakewell DE45 1JF (01629 812416). Relax in the warm and friendly atmosphere of our peaceful farmhouse situated on the edge of Lathkill Dale. Conveniently located for visiting the many attractions of the area. All rooms are en suite, colour TV and tea making facilities. Ground floor rooms available. A varied breakfast menu is offered, and packed lunches by arrangement. Excellent local inns and restaurants a short drive away. Bed and Breakfast £22 - £25 per person sharing double/twin room. Single occupancy £30 per night. Discount for 3 night stays. No smoking in house. **ETC** ◆◆◆◆

e-mail: julia.finney@virgin.net   website: www.mandalehouse.co.uk

BAKEWELL

Mrs Jenny Spafford, Barleycorn Croft, Sheldon, Near Bakewell DE45 1QS (01629 813636). A well converted small attached barn with private bathroom and TV lounge. Accommodates two, three or four people in a twin and/or double room with washbasin, shaver point, thermostatically controlled heater and tea/coffee making facilities, creating a pleasant private apartment. Also provided: full English or vegetarian breakfast, ironing facilities, hairdryer; independent access with own key and private parking. Sheldon is a unique, unspoilt farming village with no through traffic or public transport, only three miles from Bakewell and ideal for visiting Chatsworth House, Haddon Hall, Matlock, Buxton and all parts of the Peak District. Open all year. Non-smokers only please. Unsuitable for pets or children under 13 years. Bed and Breakfast from £21. **AA** ◆◆◆

BAMFORD

Mr and Mrs D. Treacher, Pioneer House, Station Road, Bamford S30 2BN (01433 650638). Pioneer House is situated in the heart of the Peak District and is the ideal base for a relaxing break in the countryside. Our comfortable home is delightfully furnished in turn of the century style and our well appointed bedrooms are en suite with colour TV and well stocked beverage tray. We have an extensive range of local maps, books and brochures to help you plan your days, whether walking through the breathtaking scenery, sightseeing in the local villages such as Castleton, Hathersage and Hope or visiting the stately homes and heritage sites of Chatsworth House and Haddon Hall. Exclusively for non-smokers. **ETC** ◆◆◆◆
e-mail: pioneerhouse@yahoo.co.uk
website: www.pioneerhouse.co.uk

BUXTON

Roger and Maria Hyde, Braemar, 10 Compton Road, Buxton SK17 9DN (01298 78050). Guests are warmly welcomed into the friendly atmosphere of Braemar, situated in a quiet residential part of this spa town. Within five minutes' walk of all the town's many and varied attractions i.e., Pavilion Gardens, Opera House, swimming pool; golf courses, horse riding, walking, fishing, etc are all within easy reach in this area renowned for its scenic beauty. Many of the Peak District's famous beauty spots including Chatsworth, Haddon Hall, Bakewell, Matlock, Dovedale and Castleton are nearby. Accommodation comprises comfortable double and twin bedded rooms fully en suite with colour TV and hospitality trays, etc. Full English Breakfast served and diets catered for. Non-smokers preferred. Terms from £23.50 inclusive for Bed and Breakfast. Weekly terms available. **ETC** ◆◆◆◆
e-mail: buxtonbraemar@supanet.com   website: www.cressbrook.co.uk/buxton/braemar

BUXTON

Mr Andrew McKerrow, Cotesfield Farm, Parsley Hay, Buxton SK17 0BD (01298 83256). A quiet, easily accessible, Listed farmhouse on a working farm overlooking the High Peak Trail and Upper Long Dale and less than one mile to the cycle hire centre. Guests have the benefit of accommodation separate from the farmhouse, allowing them to go "free range" yet still have the use of TV lounge, bathroom with shower and tea making facilities. En suite rooms available. The farm is central to some of the main natural attractions of the Peak District - Hartington Dale two miles, Bakewell eight miles, Lathkill six miles, Dovedale four miles, the Roaches eight miles, Monsal Dale 11 miles, Buxton eight miles; the High Peak Trail is 100 yards and accessible from the farm.

See also Colour Display Advertisement

CASTLETON

Ye Olde Cheshire Cheese Inn, How Lane, Castleton, Hope Valley S33 8WJ (01433 620330; Fax: 01433 621847). This delightful 17th century free house is situated in the heart of the Peak District and is an ideal base for walkers and climbers; other local attractions include cycling, swimming, gliding, horse riding and fishing. All bedrooms are en suite with colour TV and tea/coffee making facilities. A "Village Fayre" menu is available all day, all dishes home cooked in the traditional manner; there is also a selection of daily specials. Large car park. Full Fire Certificate. B&B from £25.00. All credit cards accepted. Special golf packages arranged. **ETC ◆◆◆**
e-mail: kslack@btconnect.com
website: www.peakland.com/cheshirecheese

CHESTERFIELD

Mrs J. E. Payne, The Clarendon Guest House, 32 Clarence Road, Chesterfield S40 1LN (01246 235004). Located near the town centre and within easy reach of the Peak District, this Victorian town house offers a warm and cheerful welcome, whether on business or pleasure. Comfortable, cosy rooms, each with a TV with satellite channels, and tea/coffee facilities. The rear walled garden offers a peaceful summer retreat. Full English breakfast; home cooked evening meals and special diets by prior arrangement. Bed and Breakfast from £18 single, from £38 double/twin room en suite. **ETC ◆◆◆**

DERBY

Mrs Catherine Dicken, Bonehill Farm, Etwall Road, Mickleover DE3 5DN (01332 513553). This 120 acre mixed farm with Georgian farmhouse is set in peaceful rural surroundings, yet offers all the convenience of being only three miles west of Derby, on the A516 between Mickleover and Etwall. Within 10 miles there is a choice of historic houses to visit; Calke Abbey, Kedleston Hall, Sudbury Hall. Peak District 20 miles, Alton Towers 20 miles. Accommodation in three bedrooms (one twin, one double en suite, one family room with en suite facilities), all with tea/coffee making facilities. Cot and high chair provided. Open all year. Bed and Breakfast from £20. Tennis, croquet available. A warm and friendly welcome awaits you.

HARTINGTON (near Buxton)

The Manifold Inn, Hulme End SK17 0EX (01298 84537). The Manifold Inn is a 200-year-old coaching inn offering warm hospitality and good "pub food" at sensible prices. This lovely mellow stone inn nestles on the banks of the River Manifold opposite the old toll house that once served the turnpike and river ford. All of the guests' accommodation is in the converted old stone blacksmith's shop in the secluded rear courtyard of the inn. The bedrooms have en suite shower, colour TV, tea/coffee making facilities and telephones. Bed and Breakfast £20 to £35. Brochure available. **ETC ◆◆◆**

HOPE VALLEY

Sandra and Mike Oates, Cannon Croft, Cannonfields, Hathersage, Hope Valley S32 1AG (Tel & Fax: 01433 650005). Enjoy panoramic views from the conservatory of our Gold Award-winning B&B. Famous for our breakfasts – try the Sundancer eggs and whisky porridge for example. Flower arranger's garden with sun terrace. Recently refurbished en suite rooms have TV, hospitality tray, hairdryer and many extras. Non-smoking establishment. Private off-road parking and bike storage. Regretfully we cannot take small children or pets. "There are no strangers here, just friends who have not yet met." Double/twin en suite from £25pppn (based on two sharing). Sandra & Mike Oates look forward to meeting you. **ETC** ◆◆◆ *GOLD AWARD.* **website: www.cannoncroft.fsbusiness.co.uk**

MATLOCK

Ruth Lewis, Ellen House, 37 Snitterton Road, Matlock DE4 3LZ (01629 55584; mobile: 07752 598637). Friendly hosts Ruth and Bob welcome you to their extended Edwardian home on the outskirts of Matlock. Conveniently situated in a quiet location close to town centre, station and all amenities. Three double/twin en suite rooms, each centrally heated, double glazed, furnished and equipped to a high standard. Attractive terraced garden with fine town views. Secure parking for bikers. Maps, guide books etc available to borrow. An ideal base for exploring and discovering Derbyshire's heritage and scenery. Whatever your interests a wealth of cultural, outdoor and leisure opportunities await within the beautiful Peak District and beyond. Please note Ellen House is a non-smoking establishment. Bed and Breakfast £23 to £27.50 per person per night - based on a double occupancy, £30 to £40 per night single occupancy of a double room. **ETC** ◆◆◆◆

MATLOCK

Mrs S. Elliott, "Glendon", Knowleston Place, Matlock DE4 3BU (01629 584732). Warm hospitality and comfortable accommodation in this Grade II Listed building. Conveniently situated by the Hall Leys Park and River Derwent, it is only a short level walk to Matlock town centre. Large private car park. Rooms are centrally heated and have washbasin, colour TV and tea/coffee making facilities. En suite available. No smoking. An ideal base for exploring the beautiful Peak District of Derbyshire, with easy access to many places of interest including Chatsworth House, Haddon Hall, National Tramway Museum and Heights of Abraham cable car. Bed and Breakfast from £22 per person. **AA** ◆◆◆◆

TIDESWELL

Mr D.C. Pinnegar, "Poppies", Bank Square, Tideswell, Buxton SK17 8LA (01298 871083). "Poppies" is situated in the centre of an attractive Derbyshire village in the Peak District. Ideal walking country and within easy reach of Castleton, Bakewell, Matlock and Buxton. Accommodation comprises one family room and twin room with washbasins, one double room en suite, all with TV and tea/coffee making facilities. Bathroom and two toilets. Evening meals available by arrangement. Children welcome. Non smoking establishment. Bed and Breakfast from £19.50; Evening Meal from £12.50. **AA** ◆◆◆ **e-mail: poptidza@dialstart.net**

WINSTER

Mrs Jane Ball, Brae Cottage, East Bank, Winster DE4 2DT (01629 650375). In one of the most picturesque villages in the Peak District National Park this 300-year-old cottage offers independent accommodation across the paved courtyard. Breakfast is served in the cottage. Rooms are furnished and equipped to a high standard; both having en suite shower rooms, tea/coffee making facilities, TV and heating. The village has two traditional pubs which provide food. Local attractions include village (National Trust) Market House, Chatsworth, Haddon Hall and many walks from the village in the hills and dales. Ample private parking. Non-smoking throughout. Bed and Breakfast from £22 per person (reduced rates for children). **ETC** ◆◆◆◆ *SILVER AWARD, 'WHICH?' GOOD BED & BREAKFAST GUIDE.*

DEVON

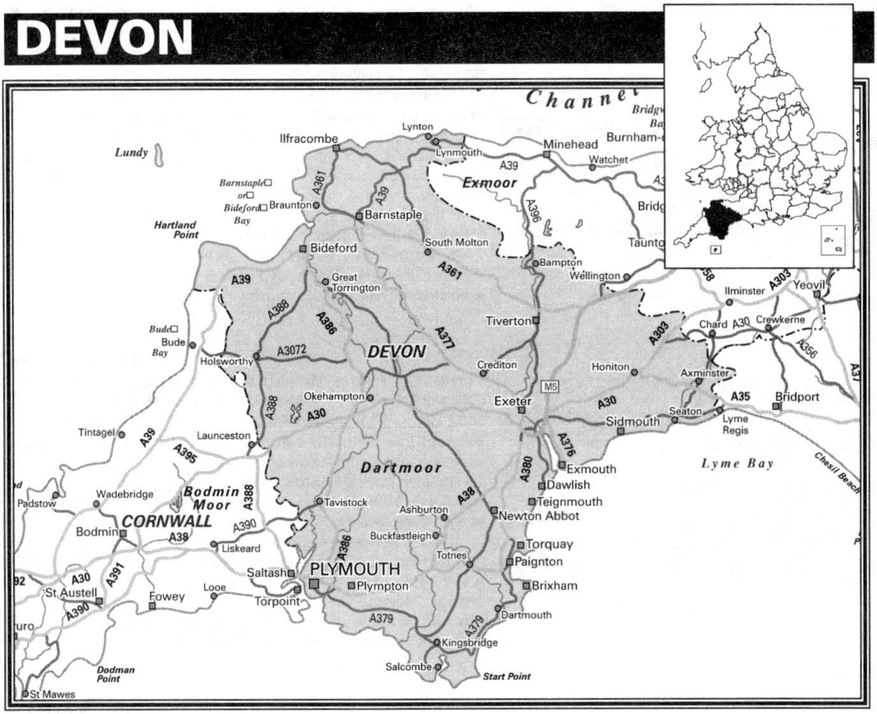

©MAPS IN MINUTES™ 2003. ©Crown Copyright. Ordnance Survey 2003.

[Map of Devon and surrounding region showing Channel, Lundy, Ilfracombe, Lynton, Lynmouth, Minehead, Burnham, Exmoor, Barnstaple, Braunton, Hartland Point, Bideford Bay, Bideford, South Molton, Watchet, Bridg, Taunto, Great Torrington, Bampton, Wellington, Ilminster, Yeovil, Bude Bay, Bude, Holsworthy, A3072, DEVON, Tiverton, Crediton, Honiton, Axminster, Chard, Crewkerne, Bridport, Tintagel, Okehampton, Exeter, Sidmouth, Seaton, Lyme Regis, Launceston, Dartmoor, Exmouth, Lyme Bay, Dawlish, Chesil Beach, Wadebridge, Bodmin Moor, Tavistock, Ashburton, Teignmouth, Newton Abbot, Padstow, CORNWALL, Bodmin, Liskeard, Buckfastleigh, Torquay, Paignton, Totnes, Saltash, PLYMOUTH, Plympton, Brixham, St. Austell, Looe, Fowey, Torpoint, Dartmouth, Kingsbridge, Dodman Point, Salcombe, Start Point, St Mawes, with roads A39, A361, A377, A386, A388, A396, A30, A303, A35, A356, A376, A380, A38, A390, A391, A395, A379 etc.]

ASHBURTON

Lynda Richards, Gages Mill, Buckfastleigh Road, Ashburton TQ13 7JW (Tel & Fax: 01364 652391). Relax in the warm and friendly atmosphere of our lovely 14th century former wool mill, set in over an acre of gardens on the edge of the Dartmoor National Park. Eight delightful en suite rooms, one on the ground floor; all with tea and coffee making facilities, central heating, hairdryers, radio and alarm clocks. We have a large comfortable lounge with corner bar and granite archways leading to the dining room and a cosy sittingroom with colour TV. Licensed. Ample car parking. Being one mile from the centre of Ashburton, this is an ideal base for touring South Devon or visiting Exeter, Plymouth, Dartmouth, the many National Trust properties and other places of interest. Children over 12 years welcome. Sorry no pets. Bed and Breakfast only. **ETC/AA** ◆◆◆, **ETC** *SILVER AWARD FOR EXCELLENCE.*
e-mail: gagesmill@aol.com

ASHBURTON (Dartmoor)

Mrs Joy Hasler, Riversmead, Newbridge, Near Ashburton TQ13 7NT (01364 631224). Riversmead, a detached country house, is situated in the picturesque River Dart valley in the Dartmoor National Park, yet is only three miles from Ashburton and the A38. Set in a one acre garden with stream and spinney, we offer quality en suite accommodation, two double and one twin room, with stunning views from all aspects. Ideally located for river walks only two minutes from the house. There is a guests' sittingroom with TV, full central heating, tea/coffee making facilities, comfortable dining room and ample parking. A drying room is available if required. Bed and Breakfast from £24 per person per night. Restricted smoking. Children over 12. Dogs by arrangement. Open all year.

AXMINSTER

Mrs S.J. Avis, Lea Hill Bed and Breakfast, Membury, Near Axminster EX13 7AQ (01404 881881; Fax: 01404 881890). Lea Hill provides a warm welcome to the pretty village of Membury, a tranquil East Devon parish where the three counties of Devon, Dorset and Somerset meet. Close at hand is the World Heritage Coast at Lyme Regis. Our own "Pitch and Putt" six hole golf course is set against a backdrop of wonderful scenery. Lovely views may be enjoyed from the terrace of Lea Hill's 14th century farmhouse where delicious Devonshire cream teas are served. Four luxuriously appointed B&B rooms and four delightful self-catering cottages available. Evening meals by arrangement. Dogs welcome free of charge. Eight acres of grounds and gardens. Wonderful local walks. **AA/ETC ★★★★★**

e-mail: reception@leahill.co.uk
website: www.leahill.co.uk

BARNSTAPLE

Peter Day, Lower Yelland Farm, Fremington, Barnstaple EX31 3EN (01271 860101/07803 933642). Winner of the 2002 Golden Achievement Award of Excellence for Quality and Service, this tastefully refurbished 16th century farmhouse is situated close to the road between Barnstaple and Bideford on the lovely Taw/Torridge estuary, immediately adjacent to the Tarka Trail. Open all year, the rooms are fully modernised, with colour TV and en suite facilities. With courtyard parking, this is an ideal base for touring Devon and Cornwall. It is within a mile of the sandy beach at Instow, and excellent pubs and restaurants. **ETC ◆◆◆◆**
A self-catering cottage (**ETC ★★★**) is also available, and there are many leisure activities close at hand.
e-mail: peterday@loweryellandfarm.co.uk
website: www.loweryellandfarm.co.uk

BARNSTAPLE

Mrs V.M. Chugg, "Valley View", Guineaford, Marwood, Barnstaple EX31 4EA (01271 343458). Working farm. "Valley View" is a bungalow set in 320 acres of farmland which visitors are free to enjoy. It is near Marwood Hill Gardens and Arlington Court, properties renowned for their beauty, and which are open from March to December. Situated three-and-a-half miles from Barnstaple, the market town. Accommodation comprises two bedrooms each containing a double and single bed. Dining/sittingroom with colour TV and video. Bathroom/toilet. Good English Breakfast. Bed and Breakfast from £16. Evening Meal supplied if required from £6. Children are welcomed, half-price for those under 12 years. Babysitting free of charge. Pets by arrangement. Car essential – parking. Open all year.

BARNSTAPLE

C & M. Hartnoll, Little Bray House, Brayford, Near Barnstaple EX32 7QG (Tel & Fax: 01598 710295). Situated nine miles east of Barnstaple, Little Bray House is ideally placed for day trips to East Devon, Somerset and Cornwall, the lovely sandy surfing beaches at Saunton Sands and Woolacombe, and many places of interest both coastal and inland. Exmoor also has great charm out of season! Come and share the pace of life and fresh air straight from the open Atlantic, and be sustained by a good healthy breakfast. Able to cater for two to ten people staying in a cottage and/or pretty twin-bedded rooms with bathroom. Lovely gardens, walks. Prices from £20 to £25 per person per night.

A useful index of towns and counties appears at the back of this book on pages 417-421. Refer also to Contents Pages 2 and 3.

BARNSTAPLE (near)

Mrs J. Ley, West Barton, Alverdiscott, Near Barnstaple EX31 3PT (Tel & Fax: 01271 858230). Our family-run working farm of 240 acres, with a pedigree herd of suckler cows and sheep, is situated in a small rural village between Barnstaple and Torrington on the B3232. It is an ideal base for your holiday, within easy reach of Exmoor and many sandy beaches on our rugged coastline; also near RHS Rosemoor Gardens, Dartington Glass, the Tarka Trail, golf courses and many beauty spots. Comfortable accommodation with family room, twin beds, single and double rooms available. Guest lounge with TV and tea/coffee making facilities. Good farmhouse cooking including a variety of our own produce when available. Ample parking. Sorry, no pets. No smoking. B&B from £18, Evening Meal optional. Reduced rates for children under 12; weekly terms on request.

BIDEFORD

Mrs S. Wade, Collaberie Farm, Welcombe, Bideford EX39 6HF (01288 331391). Situated on Devon/Cornwall border. Modern farmhouse on 90 acre beef farm overlooking wooded valley to Atlantic Ocean. Just one-and-a-half miles from Welcombe Mouth, voted cleanest beach in Britain in 1993. Clovelly, Hartland Quay, Bideford, Westward Ho! and Bude all within easy reach. Two bedrooms (one family, one double) both with washbasin and tea/coffee making facilities; bathroom, toilet; lounge with colour TV, video; diningroom. Children welcome - high chair, cot; babysitting usually available. Open all year except Christmas. Fire Certificate held. Bed and Breakfast from £18. Evening meal optional. Reductions for children.

BIDEFORD

Hartland Quay Hotel, Hartland Quay, Hartland, Bideford EX39 6DU (01237 441218). Situated at the edge of the Atlantic, you will receive a warm family welcome at any time from resident managers, Chris and Jill Johns. Steeped in history, the main building of this fantastic place has been a hotel since 1886. There is a large dining room offering table d'hôte evening meals and a hearty English breakfast, a peaceful residents' lounge and a public bar. Families are very welcome and we will do our very best to help you with anything you require to make your stay more comfortable. Meals and snacks are available in the bar and packed lunches can be supplied. Free parking for residents' cars. Dogs permitted. Open all year except Christmas.
website: www.hartlandquayhotel.com

Terms quoted in this publication may be subject to increase if rises in costs necessitate

BIDEFORD

Mrs E.M. Curtis, Bracken Haven, Weare Giffard, Bideford EX39 4QR (01237 472918). Welcome to 'Bracken Haven' - a spacious detached bungalow overlooking the scenic river valley where many scenes of "Tarka the Otter" were shot. The picturesque village of Weare Giffard lies off the A386 twixt Bideford and Torrington. A superb walking area and the Tarka Trail for cycling nearby. Village inn 400 yards, golf course one mile, Rosemoor RHS Gardens three and a half miles, and not far distant from the coast and other attractions. Accommodation comprises double en suite with shower and double standard room with basin and shaver points; family bathroom. Guests' lounge with colour TV and video, dining room with separate tables. Full central heating. Regret no pets. Free parking. Terms from £20 en suite, £15 standard room. Some reductions for weekly bookings. Excellent full English breakfasts. Open March till October.

BIDEFORD

Sunset Hotel, Landcross, Bideford EX39 5JA (01237 472962). SOMEWHERE SPECIAL in North Devon. Small country hotel in quiet, peaceful location, overlooking spectacular scenery in an Area of Outstanding Natural Beauty, one and a half miles from Bideford town. Beautifully decorated and spotlessly clean. Highly recommended quality accommodation. All en suite with colour TV, tea/coffee facilities. Excellent reputation. Book with confidence in a NON-SMOKING ESTABLISHMENT. Licensed. Private parking. Visa/Mastercard accepted. Bed and Breakfast from £31. **Mr and Mrs C.M. Lamb,** resident proprietors since 1971. ETC ◆◆◆
e-mail: HazelLamb@hotmail.com

BIDEFORD

The Mount, Northdown Road, Bideford EX39 3LP (01237 473748). A warm welcome awaits you at The Mount in the historic riverside town of Bideford. This small, interesting Georgian building is full of character and charm and is set in its own semi-walled garden, with a beautiful Copper Beech, making it a peaceful haven so close to the town. Within five minutes easy walking, you can be in the centre of the Old Town, with its narrow streets, quay, medieval bridge and park. The Mount is also an ideal centre for exploring the coast, countryside, towns and villages of North Devon. The quiet, restful bedrooms, (single, double, twin and family) are all en suite. Tea and coffee making facilities are available. All rooms have TV. Non-smoking. Bed and Breakfast £30 single, £60 double/twin. Golfing breaks – discounted green fees.
ETC/AA ◆◆◆◆

BIDEFORD (near)

Graham and Liz White, Bulworthy Cottage, Stoney Cross, Alverdiscott, Near Bideford EX39 4PY (01271 858441). Once three 17th century miner's cottages, Bulworthy has been sympathetically renovated to modern standards whilst retaining many original features. Our twin and double guest rooms both offer en suite accommodation, with central heating, colour TV, and many other extras. Standing in quiet countryside, Bulworthy is within easy reach of the moors, Tarka Trail, South West Coastal Path, Rosemoor and numerous National Trust properties. Golf may be prebooked at local courses. We offer a choice of breakfasts and evening meals, using home grown and local produce whenever possible, with a wine list chosen to complement your meal.

BIDEFORD (near)

Mrs Yvonne Heard, West Titchberry Farm, Hartland Point, Near Bideford EX39 6AU (Tel & Fax: 01237 441 287).

Situated on the rugged North Devon coast, West Titchberry is a traditionally run stock farm, half a mile from Hartland Point. The South West Coast Path skirts around the farm, making it an ideal base for walkers. The three guest rooms comprise an en suite family room; one double and one twin room both having wash basins. All rooms have colour TV, radio, hairdryer, tea/coffee making facilities; bathroom/toilet and separate shower room on the same floor. Outside, guests may take advantage of a sheltered walled garden and a games room for the children. Hartland village is three miles away, Clovelly six miles, Bideford and Westward Ho! 16 miles and Bude 18 miles. Bed and Breakfast from £18 per person per night. Evening meal £9. Children welcome at reduced rates for under 12s. Open all year except Christmas. Sorry, no pets.

BISHOPSTEIGNTON

Mrs Nicky Dykes, Whidborne Manor, Ashill, Bishopsteignton, Teignmouth TQ14 9PY (01626 870177). Dating back to 1450, Whidborne Manor retains an abundance of 'olde worlde' charm, yet offers attractive and spacious accommodation with modern day comforts. Situated three miles from the popular seaside town of Teignmouth, this is an ideal place from which to explore the South Devon coast and Dartmoor National Park, along with many other places of beauty and interest. Exeter and Plymouth are easily accessible via main road links/train. Accommodation consists of a twin room and two double rooms, all with tea/coffee facilities and colour TV. Children welcome. Sorry, no pets or smoking. Prices from £20 per person per night Bed and Breakfast. ETC ◆◆◆◆

e-mail: nicky.dykes@btinternet.com

BRAUNTON

Mrs Roselyn Bradford, St Merryn, Higher Park Road, Braunton EX33 2LG (01271 813805). Set in beautiful, sheltered garden of approximately one acre, with many peaceful sun traps to sit and relax. Open all year. Ros extends a warm welcome to all her guests. Rooms (£20 - £25 per person) include single, double and family rooms, all en suite or with private bathroom. Dinner by arrangement. All rooms non-smoking, centrally heated with colour TV and tea/coffee facilities. Guest lounge with books, games, colour TV/video/DVD. Swimming pool, fish ponds, hens, thatched summerhouse, barbecue facilities, excellent parking.

e-mail: Ros@st-merryn.co.uk
website: www.st-merryn.co.uk

See also Colour Display Advertisement

BRIXHAM

Brookside Guest House, 160 New Road, Brixgham TQ5 8DA (01803 858858). Joy and Tony Thompson, the resident proprietors, will be pleased to welcome you to Brookside, a small, friendly guest house situated on a level position on the main approach road into Brixham. All accommodation offers the best in comfort, with tea and coffee making facilities, remote-control colour TV and refrigerators in all rooms. There is ample off-road parking, both at the front and rear of the property. To add further to your comfort, Brookside is a No Smoking, No Children, No Pets establishment. Evening Meals by arrangement. B&B (standard) from £20pppn; B&B (en suite) from £23pppn; B&B (de luxe) from £25pppn.

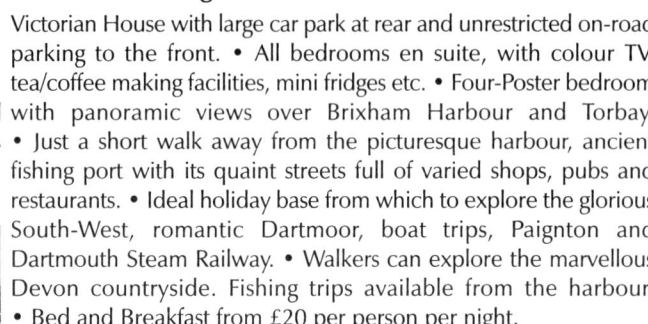

CHUDLEIGH
Jill Shears, Glen Cottage, Rock Road, Chudleigh TQ13 0JJ (01626 852209). 17th century thatched cottage idyllically set in secluded garden, with stream surrounded by woods. Adjoining a beauty spot with rocks, caves and waterfall. A haven for wildlife and birds; kingfishers and buzzards are a common sight. Outdoor swimming pool. Central for touring the moors or sea. Bed and Breakfast from £20. Tea/coffee all rooms.

CLOVELLY
R.C. and C.M. Beck, Stroxworthy Farm, Woolfardisworthy (Woolsery), Near Clovelly EX39 5QB (01237 431333). Stroxworthy Farm is family-run. The picturesque village of Clovelly with its cobbled street leading down to its small harbour and the sea is four-and-a-half miles distant. The area is well known for its scenic beauty and unspoilt coastline, where there are several quiet little beaches between the resorts of Westward Ho! and Bude. Exmoor and Dartmoor are within easy reach. Horse riding, fishing and golf locally. All bedrooms including family suite (two rooms), have duvet, en suite bathrooms, colour TV and tea/coffee making facilities. Large comfortable lounge. Ample parking. Terms: £20.00 Bed and Breakfast. SAE for colour brochure.

COLEBROOKE

Pearl Hockridge, The Oyster, Colebrooke, Crediton EX17 5JQ (01363 84576). The Oyster is a modern bungalow in the pretty, peaceful village of Colebrooke in the heart of Mid Devon. There is a spacious garden for children to play around or sit on the patio. Comfortable accommodation with tea/coffee making facilities, with TV in bedroom and lounge. Bedrooms en suite or with private bathroom - two double and one twin. Walking distance to the New Inn, Coleford, a lovely 13th century free house. Dartmoor and Exmoor are only a short drive away. Central heating. Open all year. Ample parking. Terms from £18 per person for Bed and Breakfast. Children and pets welcome. Smoking accepted. To find us take the Barnstaple road (A377)out of Crediton, turn left after one-and-a-half miles at sign for Colebrooke and Coleford. In Coleford village turn left at the crossroads, then take the left hand turning before the church, the Oyster is the second on the right.

COLYTON

Mrs Norma Rich, Sunnyacre, Northleigh, Colyton EX24 6DA (01404 871422). Working farm, join in. A warm and friendly welcome awaits you. Come and enjoy a relaxing holiday on our working farm, which is set in an Area of Outstanding Natural Beauty amongst the rolling hills of East Devon. Local villages include the fishing village of Beer and picturesque Branscombe. If you enjoy walking, there are plenty of country walks and we are close to the Coastal Footpath. There is a Full English Breakfast. Fresh and mainly homegrown produce is used to make excellent and varied Evening Meals. Sweets are all home-made. Early morning tea. Evening drinks. Three bedrooms with washbasin, separate w.c. TV in lounge, games room, sun room, Wendy house, sandpit. Cot and high chair available. Please enquire for reasonable rates.

COMBE MARTIN

Channel Vista Guest House, Woodlands, Combe Martin EX34 0AT (01271 883514; Fax: 01271 883963). At the sea side in Combe Martin, and just 300 metres from the sea, this elegant and pretty guest house has six guest rooms. All rooms are fully en suite with TV, radio, tea/coffee making facilities, hairdryer and ceiling fan (for the hot weather!). Downstairs there is a relaxing guest lounge with attached licensed Conservatory Bar. Our food is cooked from fresh local produce. Attached private car park. Channel Vista is a non-smoking establishment. Relax with us in lovely Devon. Please contact **Jim and Jen Homer** for a colour brochure and tariff form. ETC ◆◆◆
e-mail: channelvista@freeuk.com
website: www.channelvista.AOneSites.co.uk

CREDITON

Mrs Janet Bradford, Oaklands, Black Dog, Crediton EX17 4QJ (01884 860645). Janet and Ivor warmly welcome you to enjoy a relaxing stay, long or short, in peaceful surroundings with lovely views and countryside walks. Large comfortable bedrooms with en suite, tea/coffee facilities, colour TV and central heating. Large guest lounge with Sky TV and open fire in winter. Large garden with surrounding 20 acres of farmland where guests are free to wander. Walking distance of the 17th century Black Dog Inn pub/restaurant. Oaklands is situated between Dartmoor and Exmoor, ideal for touring all parts of Devon. Bed and Breakfast from £20. Reductions for children. Open all year.

CREDITON

Mrs M Reed, Hayne Farm, Cheriton Fitzpaine, Crediton EX17 4HR (01363 866392). Guests are welcome to our 17th century working beef and sheep farm, situated between Cadeleigh and Cheriton Fitzpaine. Exeter nine miles, Tiverton eight miles. South and North coast, Exmoor and Dartmoor within easy reach. Three local pubs nearby. Good farm fayre. Fishing lake; summer house overlooking duck pond. Bed and Breakfast from £20, reduction for children.

CROYDE

Crowborough B&B, Georgeham, Braunton EX33 1JZ (01271 891005). OPEN ALL YEAR. Peaceful Georgian farmhouse only two miles from Croyde. Ideal location for easy access to the sandy beaches of Croyde (two miles); Putsborough (one mile); Woolacombe (four miles); Saunton (four miles) and Saunton Championship golf course. Five minutes' walk to the village and friendly local Inn. Exmoor National Park is only 45 minutes' drive away and there are many places of interest to visit eg Lundy Island; Arlington Court (National Trust); Clovelly; many gardens (including RHS Rosemoor) etc. Accommodation consists of two double and one twin rooms; breakfast/sitting room with TV, tea/coffee facilities, and wood burner in winter. Ideal for a family or group. Bed and Breakfast from £20 pppn. Details from **Audrey Isaac.**
website: www.crowboroughfarm.co.uk

CULLOMPTON

Mr & Mrs T. Coleman, Town Tenement Farm, Clyst Hydon, Cullompton EX15 2NB (01884 277230). A recommended Bed and Breakfast stop in 16th century farmhouse in quiet village, four miles from M5 Junction 28. Guests are accommodated in one double and one family room with bathroom and one double en suite with kitchen (ground floor). All rooms have tea making facilities. The guests' lounge has inglenook fireplace, exposed beams and panelled screen and is comfortably furnished. A farmhouse breakfast is served and guests may visit the award-winning "Five Bells" in the village for their evening meal. Bed and Breakfast from £18. Reduced rates for children, cots available. Open all year.

DARTMOUTH

Mrs Stella Buckpitt, Middle Wadstray, Blackawton, Totnes TQ9 7DD (01803 712346). Cosy Devon Longhouse on working farm. About one mile from Woodlands Leisure Park and Dartmouth Golf Club, four miles from Dartmouth or beaches, and easy reach of Torbay, Salcombe and Dartmoor. Farm walks and large garden with stream and lake with small boat for guests' use. Children spend hours paddling and fishing in the stream for tadpoles, pond skaters etc. Bring your wellies and have fun anytime of the year Enjoy some evenings playing Scrabble, puzzles or board games. Regret no pets or smoking indoors. Three en suite family/double/ twin rooms. Bed and full English Breakfast daily from £25. Reductions for children and longer stays.

DAWLISH

Mrs Henley, Ocean's Guest House, 9 Marine Parade, Dawlish EX7 9DJ (01626 888139). Sea front location, enjoy the sea views from our balcony. All rooms en suite with tea/coffee facilities and colour TV. Ground floor rooms available with wheelchair access for people with walking disabilities. Partially non-smoking. Bed and Breakfast from £20 per person per night. Children under 14 years old sharing, £14 per night (minimum cost of £40 per room with one parent and one child). Single rooms from £35 per night. 10% discount for Senior Citizens in March, and October.

EXETER

Janet Bragg, Marianne Pool Farm, Clyst St George, Exeter EX3 0NZ (01392 874939). Situated in peaceful rural location two miles from M5 Junction 30, and midway between the seaside town of Exmouth and the historic city of Exeter. This thatched Devon Longhouse offers an en suite family/double room, a twin-bedded room with shared bathroom, all rooms have tea/coffee making facilities. There is a comfortable lounge with colour TV and a dining room in which a full English Breakfast is served. Large lawned garden, ideal for children. Car essential. Open March to November. Bed and Breakfast from £19 to £25 per person.

EXETER

Mrs Gillian Howard, Ebford Court, Ebford, Exeter EX3 0RA (01392 875353; Fax: 01392 876776). 15th century thatched farmhouse set in quiet surroundings yet only five minutes from Junction 30, M5. The house stands in pleasant gardens and is one mile from the attractive Exe Estuary. The coast and moors are a short drive away and it is an ideal centre for touring and birdwatching. The two double bedrooms have washbasins and tea/coffee facilities; sitting/diningroom with colour TV. Non-smoking accommodation. Open all year. Ample parking. Bed and Breakfast from £19 per night; £120 weekly.

EXETER

Mrs Dudley, Culm Vale Guest House, Stoke Canon, Exeter EX5 4EG (Tel & Fax: 01392 841615; mobile: 07855 481765). A fine old country house of great charm and character, giving the best of both worlds as we are only three miles to the north of the Cathedral city of Exeter, with its antique shops, yet situated in the heart of Devon's beautiful countryside on the edge of the pretty village of Stoke Canon. An ideal touring centre. Our spacious comfortable Bed and Breakfast accommodation includes full English breakfast, colour TV, tea/coffee facilities, washbasin and razor point in all rooms, some with bathrooms en suite. Full central heating. Ample free parking. Bed and Breakfast £19 to £27.50 pppn according to room and season. Credit cards accepted. **ETC ◆◆◆, AA** *THREE RED DIAMONDS.*

EXETER

Mrs Sally Glanvill, Rydon Farm, Woodbury, Exeter EX5 1LB (Tel & Fax: 01395 232341). Guests return time and time again to our delightful 16th century Devon Longhouse. We offer a warm and friendly family welcome at this peaceful dairy farm. Ideally situated for exploring the coast, moors and the historic city of Exeter. Only 10 minutes' drive from the coast. Inglenook fireplace and oak beams. All bedrooms have private or en suite bathrooms, central heating, hairdryers and tea/coffee making facilities; one room with romantic four-poster. A traditional farmhouse breakfast is served with free-range eggs and there are several excellent pubs and restaurants close by. Pets by arrangement. Open all year. Highly recommended Bed and Breakfast from £26 to £35. **ETC/AA ◆◆◆◆,** *FARM STAY UK MEMBER.*

EXETER

Karen Williams, Stile Farm, Starcross, Exeter EX6 8PD (Tel & Fax: 01626 890268). Enjoy a peaceful break in beautiful countryside. Close to the Exe Estuary and only two miles to the nearest sandy beach. Take a stroll to the village (only half-a-mile) to discover many eating places, or a little further to some specially recommended ones. Birdwatching, golf, fishing, racing, etc. all nearby, and centrally situated for exploring all the lovely countryside and coastline in the area. Good shopping in Exeter. Comfortable rooms, guests' lounge, English breakfast. Nice garden. Plenty of parking. NON-SMOKING. Personal service and a 'home from home' atmosphere. Bed and Breakfast from £20 per person per night.
website: www.stile-farm.co.uk

See also Colour Display Advertisement

EXETER (near)

The Lord Haldon Country House Hotel, Dunchideock, Near Exeter EX6 7YF (01392 832483; Fax: 01392 833765). The Lord Haldon Country House Hotel is the perfect venue for a quiet get-away break with your beloved pet. Acres of private grounds, mile of driveway for exercise and animals are welcome in guests' bedrooms by arrangement. The hotel stands in its own grounds, four miles south west of Exeter, set 400 feet above sea level above the Haldon Hills. It is family-run by the Preece family, owners for over 20 years. The hotel restaurant is open seven days a week, lunch times and evenings. There is also an intimate Lounge Bar which serves bar food. The Lord Haldon is the only hotel in Devon that is a member of the Relais du Silence, an independent hotel consortium dedicated to fine food, service, peace and quiet. For further information about how you can enjoy the finest part of Devon, please telephone for a free hotel brochure. **ETC ★★★**, **AA ★★★** *TWO ROSETTES*.
e-mail: enquiries@lordhaldonhotel.co.uk　　　　**website: www.lordhaldonhotel.co.uk**

EXMOOR

Mr and Mrs P. Carr, Greenhills Farm, Yeo Mill, West Anstey, South Molton EX36 3NU (01398 341300; mobile: 07974 806099). A warm friendly atmosphere awaits you at Greenhills. Our charming farmhouse on a working farm, situated in the southern foothills of Exmoor, offers an exceptionally high standard of accommodation. Delicious food using home-grown and local produce. Warm, comfortable private suite of rooms, one twin and one double en suite. Separate dining room and lounge, both with beams, inglenooks and log fires. On the Two Moors Way, it's a country-lovers' paradise. Bed and Breakfast from £18 to £22. Evening Meal £10. **ETC ◆◆◆◆** *SILVER AWARD*.

EXMOUTH

Pound House, Pound Lane, Exmouth EX8 4NP (01395 222684). Large Georgian house. All rooms are tastefully furnished and decorated, with private bathroom, colour TV, tea/coffee making facilities. Beautiful sandy beaches and natural beauty of Woodbury Common five minutes by car. Attractions in area include golf, riding, hiking, swimming, National Trust and Heritage properties, Dartmoor and Exmoor National Parks and coastal walks, etc. Large traditional English breakfast. Visitors welcome to use garden. Children and pets welcome. Ample private parking. Terms from £20pppn. Details on request.

EXMOUTH

Devoncourt Hotel, Douglas Avenue, Exmouth EX8 2EX (01395 272277; Fax: 01395 269315). Standing in four acres of mature subtropical gardens, overlooking two miles of sandy beach, yet within easy reach of Dartmoor and Exeter, Devoncourt provides an ideal base for a family holiday. Single, double and family suites, all en suite, well furnished and well equipped; attractive lounge bar and restaurant. Recreational facilities include indoor and outdoor heated pools, sauna, steam room, spa and solarium; snooker room; putting, tennis and croquet; golf, sea fishing and horse riding nearby. Bed and Breakfast from £70 single, £105 double; Self-catering /room only from £55 single, £80 double. Weekly rates available.

GREAT TORRINGTON

Mrs Beryl Heard, Furze Farm Bed and Breakfast, Great Torrington EX38 7HA (01805 623360). A warm welcome is assured at this homely, long established B&B situated one and a half miles from the historic town of Great Torrington. Lovely old character farmhouse with spacious en suite rooms in the heart of Tarka country. Accommodation consists of two double, one family room all with private facilities, TV and tea tray. A hearty breakfast with home-baked bread is provided. Ideal location for RHS Rosemoor Gardens and the Tarka Trail, popular with cyclists and walkers. Cycle hire nearby. Clovelly, Atlantic Village Designer Outlet, Westward Ho!, Instow and Appledore are a short drive away. Bideford, Barnstaple and Holsworthy are within thirty minutes' drive. Dartmoor and Exmoor within easy reach. Non-

smoking establishment. B&B £44 double, £25 single.
e-mail: beryl@furze-farm.co.uk

HONITON

Pamela Boyland, Barn Park Farm, Stockland Hill, Near Stockland, Honiton EX14 9JA (Tel & Fax: 01404 861297; Freephone 0800 328 2605). Working farm. Working dairy farm situated one-and-a-half miles off the A30/A303 Junction, road sign marked Axminster/Stockland. Within reach of many beauty spots. Coast nine miles. Traditional farmhouse breakfast using eggs from our free-range hens. Barn Park Farm has en suite/private bathrooms. All bedrooms have beverage trays (TV on request). A homely atmosphere in a character farmhouse awaits you here. Open all year except Christmas Day. TV lounge, quiet sittingroom. Ground floor bedroom by arrangement. Bed and Breakfast from £18; Evening Meal from £10. No smoking in the house please. **ETC ◆◆◆**
e-mail: Pab@barnparkfarm.fsnet.co.uk
website: www.stockland.cx

See also Colour Display Advertisement

HONITON

Mrs June Tucker, Yard Farm, Upottery, Honiton EX14 9QP (01404 861680). A most attractively situated working farm. The house is a very old traditional Devon farmhouse located just three miles east of Honiton and enjoying a superb outlook across the Otter Valley. Enjoy a stroll down by the River Otter which runs through the farmland. Try a spot of trout fishing. Children will love to make friends with our two horses. Lovely seaside resorts 12 miles, swimming pool, adventure park and garden near by. Traditional English breakfast, colour TV, washbasin, heating, tea/coffee facilities in all rooms. Bed and Breakfast £17.50 to £20. Reductions for children.

Terms quoted in this publication may be subject to increase if rises in costs necessitate

ENGLAND

Varley House, Chambercombe Park, Ilfracombe EX34 9QW
Tel: 01271 863927 • Fax: 01271 879299 • e-mail: info@varleyhouse.co.uk • website: www.varleyhouse.co.uk

Built at the turn of the 20th century for returning officers from the Boer War, Varley generates a feeling of warmth and relaxation, combined with an enviable position overlooking Hillsborough Nature Reserve. Winding paths lead to the Harbour and several secluded coves. Our attractive, spacious, fully en suite, non-smoking bedrooms all have colour TV, central heating, generous beverage tray, hairdryer and clock radio alarm. Superb food, beautiful surroundings and that special friendly atmosphere so essential to a relaxing holiday. Cosy separate bar. Car Park. Children over 5 years of age. Dogs by arrangement. Bed and Breakfast from £26 per person. Weekly from £170 per person. Dinner available £15.

ETC/AA
◆◆◆◆

ILFRACOMBE

Alison and Adrian Homa, Mullacott Farm, Mullacott Cross, Ilfracombe EX34 8NA (01271 866877). Stay on a family-run working farm in the recently converted barn adjacent to the farmhouse. We have many friendly animals to see. It is an ideal base for the beach, walking and riding. All the tastefully decorated rooms have beamed ceilings, with en suite facilities, colour TV and hospitality tray. Ground floor rooms are available. Guests are given their own key. A scrumptious home-produced breakfast, including home-made bread and preserves, our own sausages, bacon and free-range eggs, complements the very high standards of cleanliness and comfort to be found at Mullacott Farm. Children are welcome. Non-smoking. Bed and Breakfast from £25 per person. Special offers available.

See also Colour Display Advertisement

ILFRACOMBE

Geoff and Sharon Burkinshaw, Wentworth House, 2 Belmont Road, Ilfracombe EX34 8DR (Tel & Fax: 01271 863048). Wentworth House, a friendly family-run private hotel built as a gentleman's residence in 1857, standing in lovely gardens only a stone's throw from the town and minutes from the sea, harbour and Torrs Walks. En suite rooms with colour TV and tea/coffee making facilities. Family rooms sleeping up to four persons. Home-cooked food with packed lunches on request. Spacious bar/lounge. Secure storage for bicycles etc. Private parking in grounds. Open all year. Bed & Breakfast from £18.50. Bed, Breakfast and Evening Meal from £25. Discounted rates for weekly bookings. Stay a few days or a week, we will make your visit a pleasant one.

KINGSBRIDGE

Mrs Angela Foale, Higher Kellaton Farm, Kellaton, Kingsbridge TQ7 2ES (Tel & Fax: 01548 511514). Working farm. Smell the fresh sea air and enjoy the delicious Aga-cooked breakfast in the comfort of this lovely old farmhouse. Nestled in a valley, our farm with friendly animals welcomes you. Spacious, well-furnished rooms, en suite, colour TVs, tea/coffee making facilities, own lounge, central heating and log fires. Flexible meal times. Attractive walled garden. Safe car parking. Situated between Kingsbridge and Dartmouth. Visit Salcombe by ferry. One-and-a-half miles to the lost village of Hallsands and Lannacombe Beach. Beautiful, unspoilt coastline with many sandy beaches, paths, wild flowers and wildlife. Ramblers' haven. Good pubs and wet-weather family attractions. Open Easter to October. Non-smoking. Bed and Breakfast from £20. **ETC** ◆◆◆
e-mail: higherkellatonfarm@agriplus.net   website: www.welcome.to/higherkellaton

LYNMOUTH

Tricia and Alan Francis, Glenville House, 2 Tors Road, Lynmouth EX35 6ET (01598 752202). Idyllic riverside setting for our delightful Victorian house built in local stone, full of character and lovingly refurbished, at the entrance to Watersmeet Valley. Award winning garden. Picturesque village, enchanting harbour and unique water-powered cliff railway nestled amidst wooded valleys. Beautiful area where Exmoor meets the sea. Breathtaking scenery, riverside, woodland and magnificent coastal walks with spectacular views to the heather-clad moorland. Peaceful, tranquil, romantic - a very special place. Tastefully decorated bedrooms, most with pretty en suites. Elegant lounge overlooking river. Enjoy a four-course breakfast in our attractive dining room. Non-smoking. Licensed. Bed and Breakfast from £25 per person per night. AA ◆◆◆◆

e-mail: tricia@glenvillelynmouth.co.uk   **website: www.glenvillelynmouth.co.uk**

LYNMOUTH

Rock House, Lynmouth EX35 6EN (01598 753508; Fax: 01598 753472). Share the magic of living at the water's edge in a Grade II Listed building which stands alone at the harbour entrance. Offering peace and tranquillity, it is the perfect place to relax. All rooms have sea views, are centrally heated, en suite, with TV, hairdryer, alarm clock and tea/coffee making facilities. Fresh ingredients used in all meals; vegetarian and special diets catered for. Superb wine list. Fully licensed bar. Putting, tennis and numerous woodland, coastal and riverside walks nearby. Explore the Heritage Coast by boat;i deal for birdwatching. Visit the Valley of Rocks and Doone Valley; the heart of Exmoor is only a short journey away by car or bus.

e-mail: enquiries@rock-house.co.uk
website: www.rock-house.co.uk

LYNMOUTH

Mrs J. Parker, Tregonwell, The Olde Sea Captain's House, 1 Tors Road, Lynmouth, Exmoor National Park EX35 6ET (01598 753369). Truly paradise? Award-winning outstandingly elegant Victorian (former Sea Captain's) riverside home is snuggled into the sunny side of tranquil Lynmouth's deep wooded valleys, alongside beaches, waterfalls, cascades, England's highest cliff tops, enchanting harbour, all steeped in history! A wonderful walking area, where Exmoor meets the sea. Exceptionally dramatic scenery around our Olde Worlde smugglers' village. Wordsworth, Shelley and Coleridge all kept returning here. An all year resort, each season unveiling its own spectacle. Pretty bedrooms, luxury en suites with breathtaking views. Guests' drawing room with open log fires in cooler seasons. Garage, parking. Bed and Breakfast from £22. Come as a resident then return again as a friend!

LYNTON

Mark and Christine Channing, Alford House Hotel, Alford Terrace, Lynton EX35 6AT (Tel & Fax: 01598 752359). Mark and Christine extend a warm welcome to you at Alford House, a beautiful Georgian-style Grade II Listed private hotel, nestling on the slopes of Lynton, with stunning views of the sea and coastline. We have individually decorated and furnished en suite rooms, elegant four-posters, all with colour TV and beverage making facilities. We serve candlelight dinners cooked from freshly prepared produce, with menu choice. Relax in our licensed bar, or quiet TV lounge with beautiful coastal views. Five minutes' walk to Lynton and the cliff railway to Lynmouth. You will enjoy a peaceful and relaxed holiday at Alford House, good food on the table and a genuine warm welcome, whatever the weather!! B&B from £25 to £28 per person. **AA ◆◆◆◆**

e-mail: **enquiries@alfordhouse.co.uk**   website: **www.alfordhouse.co.uk**

LYNTON

Longmead House, Longmead, Lynton EX35 6DQ (01598 752523) One of Lynton's best kept secrets, with a Silver Award for standards of comfort, hospitality and food. Longmead is a small, friendly, family-run hotel providing old-fashioned hospitality and attention to detail in a relaxed and informal atmosphere, with well equipped, en suite rooms. This delightful house is quietly situated in beautiful surroundings towards the Valley of Rocks, yet close to the village centre, with ample car parking. Imaginative evening menu. Licensed. Bed and Breakfast from £23 to £25 pppn. Special short break terms. Details from **Jacqueline and Nigel Poole.** No smoking or pets. **ETC ◆◆◆◆** *SILVER AWARD,* **AA ◆◆◆◆**
e-mail: **info@longmeadhouse.co.uk**
website: **www.longmeadhouse.co.uk**

LYNTON

Pine Lodge, Lynway, Lynton EX35 6AX (01598 753230). A sunny, sheltered, traffic-free location set in landscaped gardens with uninterrupted views of the Watersmeet Estate. A short stroll along the Lynway takes you to Lynton village where you can ride the famous Cliff Railway to Lynmouth. We have spacious en suite rooms and comfortable lounge. All rooms with TV, hairdryer, hospitality tray and central heating. Ground floor bedrooms, level private car park. Children over 12 welcome. Non-smoking. Licensed. Bed and Breakfast from £20 to £25, optional evening meal. **ETC ◆◆◆◆** *SILVER AWARD*, **AA** *FOUR RED DIAMOND AWARD 2003-2004.*
e-mail: **info@pinelodgehotel.com**
website: **www.pinelodgehotel.com**

LYNTON

South View Guest House, 23 Lee Road, Lynton EX35 6BP (01598 752289). South View is a small friendly guest house in the heart of the picturesque Exmoor village of Lynton. Open all year, our aim is to provide a comfortable base from which to explore this beautiful coastal region. We have five rooms, all fully en suite with colour TV, tea/coffee making facilities, hair dryer, alarm clock and individually controlled heating. We serve a full breakfast with a choice of menu. Our comfortable guests' lounge is always open. Private parking is available at the rear. Overnight guests welcome. Bed and Breakfast from £20 to £23 per person per night. **ETC** ◆◆◆

LYNTON

Cliff Bench, Valley House, Lynbridge Road, Lynton EX35 6BD (01598 752285). A secluded Victorian country house, five minutes' walk from Lynton. Set into the rock face high above the West Lyn River, with magnificent views of the National Trust Woodland and sea. All rooms are stylishly decorated, en suite with tea/coffee making facilities, hairdryer, colour TV and beautiful views. Interesting breakfast menu; scrumptious evening meals most days; packed lunches available. Relax in the bar/lounge, the new conservatory room or the front terrace. A walkers' paradise, with some of the best horse riding in the country; also golf and surfing. Rates from £20 pppn. **RAC** ◆◆◆◆
e-mail: info@valley-house.co.uk
website: www.valley-house.co.uk

MORETONHAMPSTEAD

Mrs T. M. Merchant, Great Sloncombe Farm, Moretonhampstead TQ13 8QF (01647 440595). Working farm. Share the magic of Dartmoor all year round while staying in our lovely 13th century farmhouse full of interesting historical features. A working mixed farm set amongst peaceful meadows and woodland abundant in wild flowers and animals, including badgers, foxes, deer and buzzards. A welcoming and informal place to relax and explore the moors and Devon countryside. Comfortable double and twin rooms with en suite facilities, TV, central heating and coffee/tea making facilities. Delicious Devonshire suppers and breakfasts with new baked bread. Open all year. No smoking. **ETC** ◆◆◆
SILVER AWARD, **AA** ◆◆◆◆, *FARM STAY UK MEMBER.*
e-mail: hmerchant@sloncombe.freeserve.co.uk
website: www.greatsloncombefarm.co.uk

MORTEHOE

Lundy House Hotel, Mortehoe EX34 7DZ (01271 870372).
Quality en suite accommodation in small, friendly hotel magnificently situated on cliff-side above secluded cove with spectacular sea views. Superb food, well-stocked licensed bar lounge. TV and tea-making facilities in all rooms. Please write or telephone for full details. Dogs welcome free. **AA ★★**
e-mail: info@lundyhousehotel.co.uk
website: www.lundyhousehotel.co.uk

NORTH TAWTON

Stephen and Elizabeth Parker, Kayden House Hotel, High Street, North Tawton EX20 2HF (01837 82242). A character building in the heart of an historic market town. Located in the centre of Devon, we are ideally situated for exploring the real Devon. Easy reach of South Devon or North Cornwall coasts. We offer a comfortable, relaxing lounge and a bar for residents and diners only. Bar meals or à la carte menu available to suit all palates. Bedrooms are en suite and offer tea/coffee making facilities and colour TV. Family-run, Stephen and Elizabeth look forward to welcoming you and hope your stay with us will be a memorable one.

OKEHAMPTON

Mrs Rosemary Ward, Parsonage Farm, Iddesleigh, Winkleigh EX19 8SN (01837 810318). A warm welcome awaits you at our family-run dairy farm, situated approximately one mile from the picturesque village of Iddesleigh, with an excellent 15th century Inn called The Duke Of York, and three miles from the market town of Hatherleigh. The Tarka Trail passes through our farmyard and 400m salmon/trout fishing is available on the farm boundary. An ideal peaceful haven for touring Devon and Cornwall. Accommodation consists of a two-bedroom family suite and a double room, both en suite, with tea/coffee making facilities, central heating and colour TV. Guests are able to relax in the lounge or in our large walled garden. There is a games room for guests to use with snooker and table tennis. Bed and Breakfast from £25 per person per night. Open Easter to October. Non-smoking and no pets. Reductions for children and weekly bookings. **ETC ◆◆◆◆** *SILVER AWARD.*
website: www.devon-holiday.com/parsonage

OKEHAMPTON

Higher Cadham Farm, Jacobstowe, Okehampton EX20 3RB (01837 851647). Just off the A3072, five miles from Dartmoor, this 16th century farmhouse with barn conversions offers a total of eight rooms, all en suite. There are two non-smoking lounges with TV, games and books, to meet friends or to relax in, as well as a separate bar with a residential licence. You are assured of plenty of hearty Devonshire food and a warm welcome. Babies and well-behaved dogs are welcome by arrangement. We have farm walks, ponies, goats, rabbits, plus a working sheep flock and suckler cow herd. Walkers and cyclists on the Tarka Trail are catered for, with cycle sheds and packed lunches etc. B&B from £25, Dinner £12.50. **AA ◆◆◆◆**
website: www.highercadham.co.uk

OTTERTON

Mrs E.J. Earl, Ropers Cottage, Ropers Lane, Otterton, Budleigh Salterton EX9 7JF (01395 568826; Fax: 01395 568206). In the centre of Otterton, a picturesque village close to the coast, Ropers Cottage waits to welcome you. A quiet retreat to explore East Devon's gentle pleasures, riverside walks, the coastal path, beaches, heathland and never far away, Exeter, the county town, and the seaside resorts of Sidmouth, Exmouth and Budleigh Salterton. Guests have a separate entrance. The dining room has separate tables. There is one double and one single en suite room, both with TV, tea/coffee making facilities and shaver point. Secure off-road parking. Full English Breakfast is served. Snacks and evening meals are available at the King's Arms in the village.

OTTERY ST MARY

Mrs Forth, Fluxton Farm, Ottery St Mary EX11 1RJ (01404 812818) Cat lovers' paradise in charming 16th century farmhouse set in beautiful Otter Valley with two acre gardens including stream and pond. Only four miles from beach at Sidmouth. Central heating. All rooms en suite. Dogs welcome free of charge. Lovely touring and walking country. Terms: Bed and Breakfast £25 per person per day. **AA ◆◆**

PAIGNTON

The Roscrea Hotel, 2 Alta Vista Road, Paignton TQ4 6BZ (01803 558706). Beautifully situated with impressive views over Torbay, close to all beaches and a short stroll to the town centre. Spacious en suite bedrooms, colour TV and tea/coffee making facilities, all with full central heating. Ground floor bedrooms are available, some rooms with sea views and balconies. Honeymoon suite. Cosy bar lounge, beautiful garden. Seasonal entertainment and special Christmas programme. Generous reductions for off-season breaks. Reductions for children. We are well renowned for our excellent food. Kindly write or telephone for our brochure.
website: www.roscreahotel.co.uk

PAIGNTON

Freda Dwane and Steve Bamford, Clifton Hotel, 9-10 Kernou Road TQ4 6BA (Tel & Fax: 01803 556545). In the heart of the English Riviera. A friendly, licensed, no-smoking hotel in an ideal level location just off the sea front and close to shops, rail and coach stations. All rooms en suite with TV and beverages. Superb evening meals available. A perfect spot to leave the car and explore on foot or by public transport South Devon, Dartmoor etc. Open Easter to October. Bed and Breakfast from £23 per person. Spring Breaks available. *WELCOME HOST, COMMITMENT TO QUALITY AWARD HOLDERS*.
e-mail: b&b@cliftonhotelpaignton.co.uk
website: www.cliftonhotelpaignton.co.uk

PAIGNTON

Craigmore Guesthouse, 54 Dartmouth Road, Paignton TQ4 5AN (01803 557373; Fax: 01803 665801). A quality guest house, ideally situated within easy, level walking distance of the seafront, town, coach and railway stations, and leisure centre. This is a non-smoking establishment, with en suite rooms available. All rooms have TV, tea/coffee making facilities, central heating; one ground floor room. Access at all times. Own private car park. Most credit/debit cards accepted. Prices from £18pppn. Brochure available. **ETC ◆◆◆**
e-mail: bookings@craigmore-guesthouse.fsnet.co.uk
website: www.craigmore-guesthouse.fsnet.co.uk

PLYMOUTH

Cranbourne Hotel, 278/282 Citadel Road, The Hoe, Plymouth PL1 2PZ (01752 263858/661400/224646 Fax: 01752 263858). The Cranbourne Hotel is situated just 200 yards from the Hoe Promenade, and a few minutes' walk from train, ferry and bus links. All bedrooms are beautifully decorated, heated, with colour TV and tea/coffee facilities. Keys for access at all times. Licensed Bar. Pets by prior arrangement (no charge). Large secure car park. Under the personal supervision of The Williams Family. **ETC ◆◆◆◆**
e-mail: cran.hotel@virgin.net
website: www.cranbournehotel.co.uk

SALCOMBE

Steve and Laura Girling, Meadow View, 11 Longfield Drive, Salcombe TQ8 8NT (01548 844102). Luxury accommodation with a warm and friendly welcome. Enjoy a leisurely full English or vegetarian breakfast in the comfort of the conservatory overlooking the garden, with far reaching views over North Sands Valley. Ideally situated for the town and beaches at North and South Sands. Salcombe has a range of shops, inns and restaurants. Local activities include boat hire, diving, golf, riding and many superb coastal walks over National Trust land. All rooms have colour television, hairdryer and beverage tray. Double en suite, double/private bathroom and double/shower bathroom. Ample off-road car parking. Regret no smoking inside the house and the accommodation is unsuitable for children or pets. Open all year. Brochure available. Bed and Breakfast from £25 to £30 per person per night.
website: www.meadow-view.com

SHALDON

Glenside House, Ringmore Road, Shaldon TQ14 0EP (01626 872448). Built originally as a private residence in 1820 and in use more recently as a private school, Glenside now offers seven charming en suite rooms, two with their own lounges, and all with armchairs, TV and beverage trays. Being situated on the southern bank of the Teign estuary, it is an easy level riverside walk into the heart of the village with its numerous pubs, restaurants and tearooms, some by the beach. We have a sunny garden; car park. Dogs welcome; children over six years. No smoking. B&B from £23. Proprietors Keith and Tricia Underwood. **ETC ◆◆◆**
e-mail: glensidehouse@amserve.com
website:
www.SmoothHound.co.uk/hotels/glensideho.html

When making enquiries or bookings,
a stamped addressed envelope is always appreciated

Higher Coombe Farm
Tipton St John, Sidmouth EX10 0AX
Tel/Fax: 01404 813385

Farmhouse Bed & Breakfast on working sheep and beef farm. Situated just outside the village of Tipton St John, 4 miles from Sidmouth seafront. Single, double and family rooms.
Open March to December. B&B from £20 to £25. Reductions for children.

e-mail: KerstinFarmer@farming.co.uk   website: www.SmoothHound.co.uk/hotels/higherco

---

SIDMOUTH

Mrs Betty S. Sage, Pinn Barton, Peak Hill, Sidmouth EX10 0NN (Tel & Fax: 01395 514004). A 330-acre farm set peacefully just off the coastal road, two miles from Sidmouth and close to the village of Otterton. Safe beaches and lovely cliff walks. Pinn Barton has been highly recommended, and offers a warm welcome in comfortable surroundings with good farmhouse breakfast. All bedrooms have bathrooms en suite; fridge, colour TV; central heating; free hot drinks facilities; electric blankets. Children very welcome. Reductions for children sharing parents' room. Open all year. Bed and Breakfast including bedtime drink from £22 to £24. Own keys provided for access at all times. **ETC ◆◆◆◆** *SILVER AWARD*
website: www.pinnbartonfarm.co.uk

SIDMOUTH

Mrs Betty Everson, Ambleside, 82 Winslade Road, Sidmouth EX10 9EZ (01395 514423). Ambleside is set in one-third of an acre of ground, approximately 12 minutes from the sea-front. All rooms have TV, tea/coffee making facilities and private bathroom, en suite available. Personal attention guaranteed. Freedom to come and go as you please. Parking available at rear of property. Vegetarians catered for. Pets considered. Please phone or write for further information.

SIDMOUTH

Mrs Elizabeth Tancock, Lower Pinn Farm, Peak Hill, Sidmouth EX10 0NN (01395 513733). Working farm. Lower Pinn is in an Area of Outstanding Natural Beauty, two miles west of the unspoilt coastal resort of Sidmouth and one mile to the east of the pretty village of Otterton. Comfortable, spacious en suite rooms with colour TV, hot drink facilities, electric blankets and central heating. Guests have their own keys and may return at all times throughout the day. Ample parking. Substantial breakfast served in dining room. Local inns and restaurants nearby provide excellent evening meals. Children and pets welcome. Open all year. Bed and Breakfast from £23 to £26. Full details on request. **ETC ◆◆◆◆**
e-mail: liz@lowerpinnfarm.co.uk
website: www.lowerpinnfarm.co.uk

**FREE or REDUCED RATE entry to Holiday Visits and Attractions –
see our READERS' OFFER VOUCHERS on pages 63-90**

SOUTH MOLTON

Mrs J.M. Bray, West Bowden Farm, Knowstone, Near South Molton EX36 4RP (01398 341224). West Bowden is a working farm, mainly beef and sheep. It is situated just north of the A361 about a mile from Knowstone village which has a thatched pub. The house, which is thatched and has inglenook fireplaces, is thought to date from the 17th century. It is spacious and comfortable and has a lounge with colour TV and a separate dining room. Accommodation comprises five en suite bedrooms and others with washbasins; all have tea-making facilities. Guests receive hospitality in the real Devon tradition, plus good home cooking, fresh vegetables and clotted cream. Pets welcome. B & B from £20, evening meal extra. **ETC ◆◆◆**

SOUTH MOLTON (near)

Hazel Milton, Partridge Arms Farm, Yeo Mill, West Anstey, Near South Molton EX36 3NU (01398 341217; Fax: 01398 341569). Now a working farm of over 200 acres, four miles west of Dulverton, "Partridge Arms Farm" was once a coaching inn and has been in the same family since 1906. Genuine hospitality and traditional farmhouse fare await you. Comfortable accommodation in double, twin and single rooms, some of which have en suite facilities. There is also an original four-poster bedroom. Children welcome. Animals by arrangement. Residential licence. Open all year. Fishing and riding available nearby. Bed and Breakfast from £22 to £27; Evening Meal from £10.50. *FARM HOLIDAY GUIDE DIPLOMA WINNER.*
e-mail: bangermilton@yahoo.co.uk

TEIGN VALLEY

S. and G. Harrison-Crawford, Silver Birches, Teign Valley, Trusham, Newton Abbot TQ13 0NJ (01626 852172). A warm welcome awaits you at Silver Birches, a comfortable bungalow at the edge of Dartmoor. A secluded, relaxing spot with two acre garden running down to the river. Only two miles from A38 on B3193. Exeter 14 miles, sea 12 miles. Car advisable. Ample parking. Excellent pubs and restaurants nearby. Good centre for fishing, bird-watching, forest walks, golf, riding; 70 yards salmon/trout fishing free to residents. Centrally heated guest accommodation with separate entrance. Two double-bedded rooms, one twin-bedded room, all with own bath/shower, toilet. Guest lounge with colour TV. Diningroom, sun lounge overlooking river. Sorry, no children under eight. Terms include tea on arrival. Bed and full English Breakfast from £25 per person nightly, £168 per person weekly. Evening Meal optional. Open all year. Self-catering caravans also available from £135.

Glenorleigh HOTEL

26 Cleveland Road
Torquay
Devon TQ2 5BE
Tel: 01803 292135
Fax: 01803 213717

As featured on BBC
Holiday programme

David & Pam Skelly

AA ◆◆◆◆

See also Colour Advertisement

Situated in a quiet residential area, Glenorleigh is 10 minutes' walk from both the sea front and the town centre. •Delightful en suite rooms, with your comfort in mind. •Good home cooking, both English and Continental, plenty of choice, with vegetarian options available daily. •Bar leading onto terrace overlooking Mediterranean-style garden with feature palms and heated swimming pool. •Discounts for children and Senior Citizens. •Brochures and menus available on request. • B&B £26–£36; Dinner £12.
e-mail: glenorleighhotel@btinternet.com • website: www.glenorleigh.co.uk

---

TIVERTON

Mrs L. Arnold, The Mill, Lower Washfield, Tiverton EX16 9PD (01884 255297). A warm welcome awaits you at our newly converted mill, beautifully situated on the banks of the picturesque River Exe. Wonderful views to the National Trust's Knightshayes Court and on the route of the Exe Valley Way. Easy access to both the north and south coasts, Exmoor and Dartmoor. Only two-and-a-half miles from the market town of Tiverton. Relaxing and friendly atmosphere with delicious farmhouse fare. En suite bedrooms with TV and tea/coffee making facilities. Bed and Breakfast from £24.

TORQUAY

Aveland Hotel, Aveland Road, Babbacombe, Torquay TQ1 3PT (Tel/minicom: 01803 326622; Fax: 01803 328940). A warm and friendly welcome awaits you in this family-run licensed hotel. Set in a quiet, level location close to Cary Park, tennis courts and bowling green. Within easy walking distance of Babbacombe Downs with panoramic views across Lyme Bay, with "Blue Flag Beaches" ideal for swimming, watersport or just relaxing in the sun. All rooms are en suite with shower and tea/coffee making facilities. There are two comfortable TV lounges as well as a cosy bar to relax in. Full central heating, car park and gardens. Family rooms available. Well-behaved children welcome. Ideal location to explore the many local attractions, the South West Coastal Walks and Dartmoor National Park. Rates from £18 to £25 B&B pppn. All major credit/debit cards accepted. TCHA recommended. Sign Language OCSL stage one. **AA ◆◆◆◆, WELCOME HOST AND COMMITMENT TO QUALITY AWARDS.**
e-mail: avelandhotel@aol.com   website: www.avelandhotel.co.uk

---

TORQUAY

West Winds, Teignmouth Road, Maidencombe, Torquay TQ1 4TH (01803 314386). Relaxed atmosphere in an attractive family home, centrally heated, all rooms en suite with colour TV, hairdryers and tea/coffee making facilities. Pleasant diningroom with separate tables, overlooking the garden. Large car park. Safe local beach and a Thatched Tavern for a variety of meals is within walking distance. Bed and Breakfast from £18.50pppn, reductions for weekly bookings.

ENGLAND

TORQUAY

Mr & Mrs R.B. Ward, Green Park Licensed Hotel, 25 Morgan Avenue, Torquay TQ2 5RR (01803 293618). GREEN PARK is a small independent licensed hotel situated in a quiet road just 300 yards from the town centre and shops, leading onto Fleet Walk, Torquay's new shopping centre, and then down to the harbour and sea front. Green Park offers our guests en suite rooms, colour TV, tea/coffee facilities, off-road car parking, large TV lounge, comfortable diningroom and bar. Full central heating. Open all year including Christmas and New Year. Bed and Breakfast from £19. Telephone Carole or Rowan for brochure. **AA ◆◆◆**
e-mail: stay@greenparktorquay.co.uk
website: www.greenparktorquay.co.uk

TORQUAY

Dave & Kim Heaslewood, Sea Point Hotel, Old Torwood Road, Torquay, TQ1 1PR (Tel & Fax: 01803 211808). The Seapoint Hotel is a lovely Grade II Listed building ideally situated in a quiet location just 10 minutes' walk to the harbour and the town's many other attractions. Our family-run hotel is open all year and benefits from having en suite rooms equipped with colour TVs, beverage making facilities and central heating. Comfortable TV lounge, cosy residents' bar, off-road parking and evening meals available. Children and pets welcome. Terms £15 to £23pppn. Children under 13 half price, under 2s free. 10% discount on weekly bookings. Please ring Dave or Kim for a brochure. **ETC ◆◆◆**
e-mail: seapointhotel@hotmail.com
website: www.seapointhotel.co.uk

TORQUAY

The Brantwood Hotel, Rowdens Road, Torquay TQ2 5AZ (01803 297241). A warm, friendly welcome, good food and cleanliness are assured at this small family-run hotel located at the end of a tree-lined road, close to Torre Abbey Gardens and the seafront. All rooms are en suite with colour TV, radio, tea/coffee making facilities and hair dryers. Ground floor rooms available. No facilities for children under two. Our large car park guarantees parking for every room. B&B rate per person per night – £20 to £24 pppn. Open all year. Phone **Mr & Mrs Beresford** for a brochure. **ETC ◆◆◆◆**
e-mail: thebrantwood@hotmail.com

TORQUAY

Fairmount House Hotel, Herbert Road, Chelston, Torquay TQ2 6RW (01803 6054460). Enjoy a taste of somewhere special in the tranquillity, warmth and informal atmosphere of our small hotel of character. Set above the picturesque Cockington Valley, Fairmount House, with its mature gardens and sun-filled terraces, is a haven for the discerning visitor seeking a peaceful setting for their holiday or short break. All our bedrooms are tastefully furnished, clean and comfortable, with en suite bathroom or shower, remote-control TV, tea and coffee making facilities. Relax with a drink in our conservatory bar, or choose from an extensive menu in our fully licensed restaurant. Bed and Breakfast from £24. **ETC ◆◆◆◆**, *SILVER AWARD*.
e-mail: stay@fairmounthousehotel.co.uk
website: www.fairmounthousehotel.co.uk

TORRINGTON

Huntshaw Barton, Huntshaw, Torrington EX38 7HH. (01805 625736; mobile: 07855 788512). Grade II Listed family-run farmhouse set in stunning and tranquil North Devon countryside. Bed and Breakfast or self-catering. Evening meals and breakfast in our beautiful dining room with inglenook fireplace. Pets welcome. Four miles from RHS Rosemoor, coast and Tarka Trail.
website: www.huntshawbarton.com

UMBERLEIGH

John & Eileen Chapple, Bouchland Farm, Burrington, Umberleigh EX37 9NF (01769 560394). John and Eileen Chapple welcome you to spend a holiday on their family-run working farm, one mile off the A377 overlooking the lovely Taw Valley. Delicious home-cooking using fresh farm produce - full English breakfasts and varied four-course evening meal (optional). Family, double and twin rooms with washbasins, tea-making facilities and colour TV. En suite available. Lounge with TV, separate dining room, games room with snooker, darts and table tennis. Ideal for exploring North Devon's sandy beaches, moors and many local places of interest. Bed and Breakfast from £22 per person per night, reductions for children.

See also Colour Display Advertisement

WEST DOWN

Robin and Jeannie Hotchkiss, The Long House, The Square, West Down, Near Ilfracombe EX34 8NF (01271 863242). The Long House is a picturesque 18th century guest house situated in a quiet hamlet, yet within 10 minutes' drive of North Devon's famous Blue Flag sandy beaches, the Tarka Trail, and coastal walks in and around Woolacombe and Mortehoe. Exmoor National Park is also nearby, and Lynton, Lynmouth, Rosemoor and Clovelly are all within easy driving distance. The non-smoking Long House has just four enchanting, individually furnished bedrooms, all en suite, with colour TV, beverage facilities, hairdryer and central heating. Breakfast, using local produce whenever possible, is served in what was originally the village smithy. The warmest welcome assured.

e-mail: info@long-house.com   **website: www.long-house.com**

The FHG Directory of Website Addresses

on pages 387-415 is a useful quick reference guide for holiday accommodation with e-mail and/or website details

WOODBURY

David and Belinda Price, Greenacre, Couches Lane, Woodbury, Near Budleigh Salterton EX5 1HL (01395 233574). Secluded guest house surrounded by countryside and stream, only four miles from the sea and five miles from the cathedral city of Exeter. The village centre is only a few minutes' walk away, boasting a Bistro (specialising in fish dishes), two pubs, a Post Office and two antique shops. An old fashioned welcome awaits you in this friendly family home. The comfortable bedrooms - two on the ground floor - all have either en suite or private facilities, colour TV and beverage tray. Well behaved pets and children are welcome. Plenty of car parking. Bed and Breakfast from £20 per person. Brochure available.
e-mail: woodburystone@fsnet.co.uk

YELVERTON

Mrs E. Wills, Callisham Farm, Meavy, Yelverton PL20 6PS (Tel & Fax: 01822 853901). A warm Devonshire welcome and a homely atmosphere awaits you in our traditional Dartmoor Farmhouse. Nestling in the wooded and very pretty valley of Meavy, Callisham is easily accessible from the A386. A perfect centre for walking, cycling and lake or river fishing. Golf, riding and shopping nearby. Guests can enjoy charming en suite bedrooms offering comfortable beds, colour TV and tea making facilities. After a good night's rest you can savour a huge breakfast of your choice with special diets and requests catered for. Cosy in winter with log fires and full central heating. Terms from £20 to £25. **ETC** ♦♦♦, *FARM STAY UK MEMBER.*
e-mail: wills@callishamfarm.fsnet.co.uk
website: www.callishamfarm.fsnet.co.uk

YELVERTON

Mrs Seabrook, Torrfields, Sheepstor, Yelverton PL20 6PF (01822 852161). Torrfields is located on the slopes of Sheepstor within the Dartmoor National Park. The house has direct access to the Moor, in a quiet picturesque location. Ideal for Moorland walking, within easy access to all local amenities, including golf courses, horse riding and game fishing. We are central to all South West attractions. Two double bedrooms en suite. Ground floor bedroom available. Rooms have radio/alarm clock, colour TV, tea and coffee making facilities, hairdryer and central heating. Children welcome. Packed lunch provided on request. Special diets provided by arrangement. Non-smoking. Garden / patio. Ample parking. Bed & Breakfast per night single £18.50 per person per night, £37 per double room. Half board daily £27 to £30. **ETC** ♦♦♦♦
e-mail: lbsrseabrook@aol.com website: http://users.eggconnect.net./seabrook/torrfields.htm

DORSET

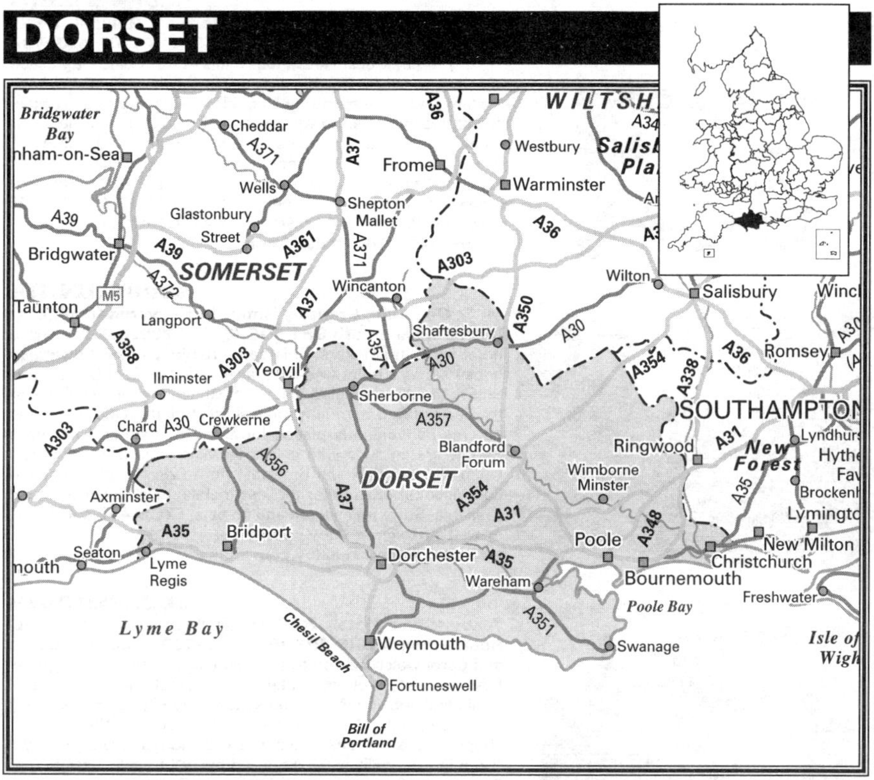

[Map of Dorset and surrounding areas including Somerset, Wiltshire, showing towns such as Bridgwater, Taunton, Yeovil, Sherborne, Shaftesbury, Dorchester, Weymouth, Poole, Bournemouth, Salisbury, Southampton, New Forest, Lyme Bay, Chesil Beach, Bill of Portland, and various A-roads. Inset map of England with region highlighted.]

©MAPS IN MINUTES™ 2003 ©Crown Copyright, Ordnance Survey 2003

BEAMINSTER

Caroline and Vincent Pielesz, The Walnuts, 2 Prout Bridge, Beaminster DT8 3AY (01308 862211). The property is very well situated in this medieval town in the heart of the beautiful Hardy countryside. Just off the main square with private parking and short walk to local inns, restaurants and tasteful little shops. Ideal for the person who enjoys coastal walks, exploring the countryside and visiting large country houses and gardens. The house has been very tastefully refurbished with en suite rooms, tea and coffee making facilities, all the comforts of home. Bed and full English breakfast from £26 per person. Totally non-smoking. **ETC ◆◆◆◆** *SILVER AWARD.*
e-mail: caroline@thewalnuts.co.uk

BOURNEMOUTH

Alan Sibthorpe, Denewood Hotel, 40 Sea Road, Bournemouth BH5 1BQ (01202 309913; Fax: 01202 391155). Warm, friendly hotel in excellent central location, just 500 yards from the beach and close to the shops. Good parking. Single, twin, double and family rooms available, all en suite. Residential and Restaurant licence. TV, tea/coffee and biscuits in rooms. Health salon and spa on site. Open all year. Children and pets welcome. Bed and Breakfast from £22.50 to £25. Special weekly rates available and short break discounts. Please check out our website. **ETC ◆◆◆**
website: www.denewood.co.uk

BOURNEMOUTH

Kath and Dennis Mackie, St Antoine, 2 Guildhill Road, Southbourne, Bournemouth BH6 3EY (01202 433043). Friendly family Guest House four minutes from Blue Flag beach and close to river walks, boating, tennis, bowls and golf. We have two family en suite rooms, two doubles, two twin and one single, all with washbasins, power points and tea/coffee facilities. Off-street parking for five cars. We are on the bus route for Christchurch and Bournemouth centres. Vegetarians, vegans welcome, with option of evening meal on request. Bed and Breakfast from £20-£22 per person. NO SMOKING. *MEMBER OF BOURNEMOUTH AREA HOSPITALITY ASSOCIATION.*.
e-mail: Kath5560@talk21.com

BOURNEMOUTH

Mr S. Goodwin, Cransley Hotel, 11 Knyveton Road, East Cliff, Bournemouth BH1 3QG (01202 290067). A licensed hotel for non-smokers. This comfortable, elegant Edwardian house set in a quiet tree-lined avenue in the East Cliff area of Bournemouth is situated in its own attractive grounds. Close to the heart of Bournemouth and a short stroll from the beach, the hotel is conveniently placed for all major road and rail links. Rooms are en suite with colour television and hospitality tray. Open all year. Bed and Breakfast from £28. Car park. Ground floor accommodation for the less mobile guest. Evening Meals available. Sorry no children and no pets. **ETC/AA ◆◆◆◆**
e-mail: info@cransley.com
website: www.cransley.com

BOURNEMOUTH

Tenby House Hotel, 23 Pinecliff Avenue, Southbourne, Bournemouth BH6 3PY (01202 423696). Melanie, Simon and Carol welcome you to the Tenby House Hotel, a delightful Edwardian-style private hotel with a homely atmosphere and traditional cooking. Mostly en suite and family rooms tastefully decorated, with TV and tea/coffee making facilities. Southbourne shopping area with its variety of cafes and restaurants is only a few minutes' walk away. A short drive or bus ride takes you to Bournemouth centre or Christchurch. Superb beach walk to Hengistbury Head and Boscombe Pier. Bed and Breakfast from £18 to £25 per night, £119 to £168 weekly. Strictly non-smoking.

BOURNEMOUTH

Steve Pini, The Golden Sovereign Hotel, 97 Alumhurst Road, Alum Chine, Bournemouth BH4 8HR (Tel & Fax: 01202 762088). Charming Victorian hotel close to award-winning beaches and wooded Chine walks. Experience our unique atmosphere. Cosy bar, freshly cooked optional evening meals. En suite rooms all with tea/coffee making facilities, television, clock/radio alarm and direct-dial telephone with extra point for internet access. Our priority? – Your comfort and happiness. Prices from £25 per person per night. Brochure on request. **ETC ◆◆◆◆**
e-mail: scott.p@talk21.com
website: www.goldensovereignhotel.com

BOURNEMOUTH

Gervis Court Hotel, 38 Gervis Road, Bournemouth BH1 3DH (01202 556871; Fax: 01202 467066). Gervis Court is a detached Victorian villa set in its own grounds, yet it is only a few minutes' walk to the town centre. The clean sandy beach, B.I.C., shops, attractions and clubs being so close allows you to leave your car in our car park. All rooms are en suite with TV and kettles. Prices start from £23-£30 per person depending on availability and season. For more information please look us up on our website.
e-mail: enquiries@gerviscourthotel.co.uk
website: www.gerviscourthotel.co.uk

Sweet Briar

12 Gardens View, Bournemouth BH1 3QA

Tel: 01202 553028
Fax: 01202 780238

A traditional B&B Guest House for non-smokers. Open all year.
Opposite Knyveton Gardens with bowling greens and tennis courts.
Full central heating. Ideal for shops. Sea and travel
interchange. B&B from £22 pppn. Discounts available.

website: www.sweetbriarbournemouth.co.uk

SOUTHERNHAY HOTEL
42 Alum Chine Rd, Westbourne, Bournemouth BH4 8DX
Tel & Fax: 01202 761251
enquiries@southernhayhotel.co.uk
www.southernhayhotel.co.uk

ETC ◆◆◆

The Southernhay Hotel provides warm, friendly, high standard accommodation with a large car park. All rooms have colour TV, tea/coffee making facilities, hairdryer and radio alarm clock. The hotel is ideally situated at the head of Alum Chine (a wooded ravine) leading down to the sea and miles of safe sandy beaches.

The Bournemouth International Centre, cinemas, theatres, restaurants, clubs and pubs are all within easy reach; minutes by car or the frequent bus service. Seven bedrooms, five en suite. Open all year. Details from Tom and Lynn Derby.

Bed and Breakfast from £20 to £30 per adult per night.

See also Colour Advertisement

BOURNEMOUTH

Mrs S. Barling, Mayfield, 46 Frances Road, Knyveton Gardens, Bournemouth BH1 3SA (Tel & Fax: 01202 551839). Sandra and Mike Barling make your comfort, food and relaxation their concern, offering a high standard of catering and comfort. Ideally situated overlooking Knyveton Gardens with bowls, petanque, tennis and sensory garden. Handy for sea, shops, shows, rail and coach stations. Residential licence. All rooms are en suite, with colour TV, teamaking, central heating, hairdryer, trouser press and radio alarm. Own keys. Parking, evening refreshments. Bed and Breakfast from £24 to £26 daily. Bed, Breakfast and Evening Dinner from £146 to £163 weekly per person. Bargain Breaks October/April.
ETC ◆◆◆ SILVER AWARD.
website: www.mayfieldguesthouse.com

BOURNEMOUTH

The Haven, 16 St Swithun's Road South, East Cliff, Bournemouth BH1 3RQ (01202 556071). Quiet, friendly, family-run hotel. Near beach, shops, rail/coach stations, tennis, bowling and town centre. Colour television, tea/coffee facilities in all bedrooms; most en suite. Car park. Children over 12 years welcome. Bed and Breakfast from £22.50 per person per night. Weekly from £139 to £190. A hotel for NON-SMOKERS.
website: www.thehavenbournemouth.co.uk

ENGLAND

BOURNEMOUTH

Tony and Veronica Bulpitt, Sun Haven Guest House, 39 Southern Road, Southbourne, Bournemouth BH6 3SS (01202 427560). The Sun Haven is in a superb position being only 150 yards from the cliff top, near the cliff lift and zigzag path to a beautiful sandy beach which is regularly awarded the European Blue Flag for superior water quality. Southbourne shopping area with its variety of cafes and restaurants is only a few minutes' walk away. A short drive or bus ride takes you to Bournemouth centre or Christchurch. All day access to rooms. All bedrooms have colour TV, shaver point, washbasin, tea/coffee making facilities and central heating. En suite available. Bed and Breakfast from £19 per person per night. A friendly welcome awaits you. No smoking. **ETC** ◆◆◆

BOURNEMOUTH

Freshfields Hotel, 55 Christchurch Road, Bournemouth BH1 3PA (01202 394023). Small licensed hotel, just a short walk to sandy beach through Boscombe Chine. Close to town and all Bournemouth's attractions, shops and theatres. Golf, tennis, putting and bowling are all nearby. All rooms have colour TV and tea/coffee, most are en suite. Access at all times with own keys. Front car park. BARGAIN BREAKS OCTOBER TO APRIL. Bed and Breakfast from £22. Reductions for Senior Citizens.

BOURNEMOUTH

Lynne and John Scott, Balmer Lodge, 23 Irving Road, Southbourne BH6 5BQ (01202 428545). Lynne and John welcome you to their family-run guest house. Comfortable lounge with colour television. Good home cooking. Tea and coffee making facilities in all rooms. En suite rooms available, full English Breakfast. Children welcome. Senior Citizens' reductions. Access 24 hours. Close to beach, shops and bus routes. Strictly no smoking. No stag or hen parties. All major credit cards accepted. Terms £16 to £30.
e-mail: Balmer@cwcom.net

BOURNEMOUTH

Westcotes House Hotel, 9 Southbourne Overcliff Drive, Bournemouth BH6 3TE (01202 428512). Comfortable private Edwardian house with stylish accommodation for the non-smoker. Situated on the cliff top with panoramic views of the bay, miles of sandy beach lie below with access by a zigzag path or cliff lift. Local shops, cafes and pubs are a short level walk away. All rooms en suite, with shower, toiletries, bathrobes; remote-control TV, clock radio, tea/coffee/chocolate facilities. Pleasant dining room with home cooking a speciality. Private car park for peace of mind. Access at all times with own key. Whatever time of year, whether a few days or a longer stay, a warm welcome awaits you at Westcotes. Bed and Breakfast from £28pp.

BRIDPORT

Mrs K.E. Parsons, 179 St Andrews Road, Bridport (01308 422038). Situated two miles from coast, 10 miles from Lyme Regis and 20 miles from Weymouth. Bedrooms with TV, tea making facilities and washbasins. Parking space available.

BRIDPORT

Britmead House Hotel, West Bay Road, Bridport DT6 4EG (01308 422941; Fax: 01308 422516). An elegant Edwardian house, family-run and ideally situated between Bridport and West Bay Harbour, with its beaches, golf course, Chesil Beach and Dorset Coastal Path. We offer full en suite rooms (two ground floor), all with TV, tea/coffee making facilities, and hairdryer. South facing lounge and dining room overlooking the garden. Licensed, private parking, restricted smoking.
e-mail: britmead@talk21.com
website: www.britmeadhouse.co.uk

BRIDPORT

Mrs Sally Long, Old Dairy House, Walditch, Bridport DT6 4LB (01308 458021). Relax in an Area of Outstanding Natural Beauty, one mile from Bridport town centre. One twin, one double (non smoking) bedrooms. Tea/coffee facilities. Guests' shared bathroom, also downstairs shower/cloakroom. Central heating throughout. Guests' TV lounge with open log fire. Hearty full English breakfast with home-made preserves. Gardens abundant with birds and wildlife. Off-road parking. Rural and coastal walks. Real tennis within short walk; 18 hole golf course two miles. Good selection of restaurants and pubs nearby. Open all year for adults only. You will find an informal, friendly atmosphere and warm welcome.

BRIDPORT (near)

Mrs Sue Norman, Frogmore Farm, Chideock, Bridport DT6 6HT (01308 456159). Working farm. Set in the rolling hills of West Dorset, enjoying splendid sea views, our delightful 17th century farmhouse offers comfortable, friendly and relaxing accommodation. An ideal base from which to ramble the many coastal and country footpaths of the area (nearest beach Seatown one-and-a-half miles) or tour by car the interesting places of Dorset and Devon. Bedrooms with en suite shower rooms, TV and tea making facilities. Guests' dining room and cosy lounge with woodburner. Well behaved dogs welcome. Open all year; car essential. Bed and Breakfast from £20. Brochure and terms free on request.

CERNE ABBAS

Mrs V.I. Willis, "Lampert's Cottage", Sydling St Nicholas, Cerne Abbas DT2 9NU (01300 341659; Fax: 01300 341699). Bed and Breakfast in unique 16th century thatched cottage in unspoilt village. The cottage has fields around and is bounded, front and back, by chalk streams. Accommodation consists of three prettily furnished double bedrooms with dormer windows, set under the eaves, and breakfast is served in the diningroom which has an enormous inglenook fireplace and original beams. The village, situated in countryside made famous by Thomas Hardy in his novels, is an excellent touring centre and beaches are 30 minutes' drive away. West Dorset is ideal walking country with footpaths over chalk hills and through hidden valleys, perfect for those wishing peace and quiet. Open all year. Terms on request.
e-mail: nickywillis@tesco.net

Sherborne Castle • *Sherborne, Dorset* • *01935 813182*
website: www.sherbornecastle.com
Built by Sir Walter Raleigh in 1594 and home to the Digby family since the early 17th century. Splendid collection of art, furniture and porcelain.

ENGLAND

CHARMOUTH

Ann and Andy Gorfin, Kingfishers, Newlands Bridge, Charmouth DT6 6QZ (01297 560232). Come to Kingfishers and relax on your large sunny balcony overlooking the river and garden. Set in beautiful surroundings on the banks of the River Char, Kingfishers offers a secluded setting yet it is only a short stroll to the beach and village amenities. Ann and Andy can assure you of a warm welcome, great food and a friendly atmosphere. From £23 per night we offer a full selection of breakfasts including vegetarian. All rooms are en suite or with private bathroom, balcony, drink making facilities, colour TV and central heating. Home-baked food and clotted cream teas available throughout the day in our lovely Garden Room or outside in the garden. Free access and ample parking. Children and pets welcome.
e-mail: anniegorfin@msn.com

COMPTON ABBAS

Tim and Lucy Kerridge, The Old Forge, Compton Abbas, Shaftesbury SP7 0NQ (Tel & Fax: 01747 811881). Charming 18th century converted wheelwright's with magnificent views to National Trust downland. Ideal for relaxing, walking, wildlife, etc. Choose either Bed and Breakfast in pretty en suite bedrooms (one family, one double and one single), Victorian iron beds and antique furniture, all with colour TV and tea/coffee trays or self-catering (sleeping two) in fully restored smithy (**ETC ★★★★**). A traditional farmhouse breakfast is served using local organic produce. Guests have their own private sitting/dining room, garden and a two acre smallholding to explore. Traditional log burning stove during colder months, we offer a warm welcome all year round. Bed and Breakfast from £25. **ETC ◆◆◆◆**
e-mail: theoldforge@hotmail.com   **website: www.SmoothHound.co.uk/hotels/oldforge.html**

DORCHESTER

Mrs V.A. Bradbeer, Nethercroft, Winterbourne Abbas, Dorchester DT2 9LU (01305 889337). This country house with its friendly and homely atmosphere welcomes you to the heart of Hardy's Wessex. Central for touring the many places of interest that Dorset has to offer, including Corfe Castle, Lyme Regis, Dorchester, Weymouth, Lulworth Cove, etc. Lovely country walks and many local attractions. Two double rooms, one single, en suite or separate bathroom. TV lounge, dining room. Large garden. Open all year. Central heating. Car essential, ample parking. Bed and Breakfast from £18. Take A35 from Dorchester, we are the last house at the western edge of the village.
e-mail: v.bradbeer@ukonline.co.uk

DORCHESTER

Mrs Martine Tree, The Old Rectory, Winterbourne Steepleton, Dorchester DT2 9LG (01305 889468; Fax: 01305 889737). Built in 1850 on one acre of land situated in a quiet hamlet. The grounds have croquet lawns, putting green, children's swing. The outstanding natural surroundings offer country walks giving superb views of the valley. The four guest rooms are all individually furnished to a high standard, each with en suite facilities and containing a welcome basket filled with toiletry items you may have forgotten. No smoking. Breakfast is a delight, enjoyed in The Garden Room with views of the beautiful little courtyard. Special diets. Local pubs and a large selection of restaurants both in Dorchester (six miles) and Weymouth (eight miles) are available. Many activities for all can be enjoyed in Thomas Hardy country. French spoken. Open all year except Christmas. Bed and Breakfast from £28 per person. Brochure available. **ETC ◆◆◆** *SILVER AWARD.*
e-mail: trees@eurobell.co.uk   **website: www.trees.eurobell.co.uk**

DORCHESTER

Mrs Marian Tomblin, Lower Lewell Farmhouse, West Stafford, Dorchester DT2 8AP (01305 267169). This old, historic house, originally a farmhouse, is situated in the Frome Valley, four miles east of Dorchester in the heart of Hardy country. It is two miles from his birthplace and is reputed to be the Talbothays Dairy in his famous novel "Tess of the d'Urbervilles". Situated as it is in quiet countryside yet so near the county town, it makes an ideal base from which to explore Dorset. There are two double bedrooms and one family bedroom, all with washbasin and tea/coffee making facilities. Visitors' lounge with colour TV. Car essential, ample parking. Terms from £20 to £25. Open January to December.

DORCHESTER

Mrs Jacobina Langley, The Stables, Hyde Crook, Frampton DT2 9NW (01300 320075). The Stables is a comfortable country house developed around a 1935 cottage overlooking the valley of Frampton. Set in a small area of woodland off the A37, in the heart of Thomas Hardy country, we enjoy uninterrupted views of open countryside. There is unrestricted off-road parking and 20 acres of ground with wild life, ducks, sheep and horses. All guest accommodation is contained in a separate wing of the house and comprises a comfortable sitting room/TV lounge on the ground floor, with private staircase to a twin en suite bedroom, double bedroom, single bedroom and bathroom on the first floor. The twin beds can be converted to a king-size bed for stays of two nights or more. All rooms are double glazed with central heating and a log fire is lit in the sitting room in the cooler seasons. From £21 per person per night. The Stables specialises in pet friendly facilities for dogs and horses.
e-mail: cobalangley@aol.com   **website: www.framptondorset.com**

See also Colour Display Advertisement

DORCHESTER

Mrs Anita Millorit, Brambles, Woolcombe, Melbury Bubb, Dorchester DT2 0NJ (01935 83672). Set in beautiful, tranquil countryside, Brambles is a pretty, thatched cottage offering every comfort, superb views and a friendly welcome. There is a choice of en suite twin, double or single rooms, all very comfortable and with colour TV and tea/coffee making facilities. Pretty garden available for relaxing in. Full English or Continental breakfast served. Evening meals available by prior arrangement. There are many interesting places to visit and wonderful walks for enthusiasts. B&B from £20 to £28 per person.

DORCHESTER (near)

Michael and Jane Deller, Churchview Guest House, Winterbourne Abbas, Near Dorchester DT2 9LS (Tel & Fax: 01305 889296). Our 17th century Guest House, noted for warm hospitality and delicious breakfasts and evening meals, makes an ideal base for touring beautiful West Dorset. Our character bedrooms are all comfortable and well appointed. Meals, served in our beautiful diningroom, feature local produce, with relaxation provided by two attractive lounges and licensed bar. Your hosts Jane and Michael Deller are pleased to give every assistance with local information to ensure a memorable stay. NON SMOKING. Terms: Dinner, Bed and Breakfast £41 to £52; Bed and Breakfast £27 to £37. Short Breaks available, please call for further details. ETC/AA ◆◆◆◆
e-mail: stay@churchview.co.uk   **website: www.churchview.co.uk**

FURZEHILL

Mrs King, Stocks Farm, Furzehill, Wimborne BH21 4HT (Tel & Fax: 01202 888697). Stocks Farm is a family-run farm and nursery situated in peaceful countryside just one-and-half miles from the lovely country town of Wimborne Minster, off the B3078. Surrounded by lovely Dorset countryside and pretty villages; coastline, beaches and New Forest within easy reach. Bed and Breakfast accommodation consists of one double en suite bedroom and one twin bedroom with private bathroom, both on ground level. Disabled guests are very welcome. Tea and coffee making facilities in both rooms. All accommodation is non-smoking. Situated in secluded garden with patio for guests to enjoy breakfast outside. Local pubs and restaurants offer varied menus. Bed and Breakfast from £20 per person per night.

KIMMERIDGE

Mrs Annette Hole, Kimmeridge Farmhouse, Kimmeridge, Wareham BH20 5PE (01929 480990; Fax: 01929 481503). Relax and take a well earned break in our period 14th Century farmhouse with views of Kimmeridge Bay across 700 acres of farmland. There are many spectacular walks either along the coastal paths or inland over the Purbeck Hills surrounding the ruins of Corfe Castle. Spacious and attractively furnished en suite rooms with colour television, beverage tray and full central heating for those off-season breaks. A delicious home-cooked breakfast of your choice and a warm welcome assured. Bed and Breakfast from £24 to £28 per person. Children over ten years welcome. Open all year except Christmas and Boxing Day. Packed Lunches, Cream Teas and Light Meals available. Non-smoking. Further details on request. **ETC ◆◆◆** *GOLD AWARD.*
e-mail: kimmeridgefarmhouse@hotmail.com

LILLINGTON

Mrs M. E. G. Messenger, Ash House, Lillington, Sherborne DT9 6QX (01935 812490). Ash House is spacious, surrounded by farmland, with delightful views all round. Although so rural and peaceful it is only three miles south of the picturesque town of Sherborne, with its Abbey and other historic buildings. Easy access to Dorchester in one direction and Yeovil in the other. One double or family room (extra bed available) with washbasin, and one twin room with washbasin. Two toilets, bathroom, shower room. Ample parking. Lounge, conservatory, TV, garden. Full English Breakfast and a friendly welcome. Bed and Breakfast £18. Rates reduced for children. South from Sherborne – A352 Dorchester Road.

LULWORTH COVE

John and Jenny Aldridge, Applegrove, West Road, West Lulworth, Wareham BH20 5RY (01929 400592). Comfortable home offering accommodation in central yet quiet off-main road position in old vicarage orchard. Two double rooms and one twin/super king (with balcony). All have en suite shower rooms, beverage trays and colour TVs. Parking in spacious walled garden with mature fruit trees, lawns and garden furniture for guests' use. Generous traditional English, Vegetarian or Vegan breakfast using home grown produce and eggs. 10 minute stroll from Lulworth Cove. Coast path for other beaches, Durdle Door and Fossil Forest nearby. Central for South Dorset Coast. Bed and Breakfast from £22 per person per night. Open from mid March to mid December.
ETC ◆◆◆
e-mail: theorchard@ic24.net

LULWORTH COVE

Mrs Jan Ravensdale, Elads-Nevar, West Road, West Lulworth, Near Wareham BH20 5RZ (01929 400467). The house is set in the beautiful village of West Lulworth, half-a-mile from Lulworth Cove. The rooms are very spacious and all have tea/coffee making facilities and colour TV. West Lulworth is central for many towns and beaches; Weymouth 14, Swanage 18, Poole 23 miles, and there are many places of interest to visit. Reduced rates for Senior Citizens out of season; also weekly bookings. Open all year. Central heating. Bed and Breakfast from £16 per person per night. Vegetarians and vegans catered for. Non-smoking.

Fyrnhams - *Sheila and David Taylor*

A spacious and non-smoking guesthouse, in quiet and unspoilt surroundings with gardens and grounds of about seven acres, with lovely views. Situated about three miles from Lyme Regis and Charmouth, ideal for touring, beaches, fishing, golf course and fossil hunting. Private parking. Access to house all day. A warm and friendly welcome awaits in a real home from home. Excellent accommodation in a comfortable, and well furnished bungalow with one double room with en suite bathroom, one double room with king size and single bed with private facilities, bathroom including a shower. All rooms have CTV, tea/coffee making facilities, clock/radio, hairdryer, towels, heating. Lounge with widescreen TV/video, overlooks rear patio and gardens. Dining area – we serve a good English farmhouse breakfast. Nearby pub for evening meals. *B&B from £20.*

Raymonds Hill, Near Axminster EX13 5SZ
Tel/Fax: 01297 33222 or e-mail: sheilataylor@bucklandfarm.fsnet.co.uk

LYME REGIS
Coverdale Guesthouse, Woodmead Road, Lyme Regis DT7 3AB (01297 442882). Spacious non-smoking guesthouse situated in a residential area of Lyme Regis a short walk from the sea, town, pubs and restaurants. Fine views over Woodland Trust's land to rear and sea to front. Comfortable well furnished bedrooms (double, twin, triple and single) with colour TV, tea making and excellent en suite facilities. Attractive diningroom overlooking patio and cottage garden. Access to house all day. Private parking. Ideal base for exploring countryside and unspoilt scenic coastline on foot or by car. Walkers welcome. South Coast Path/Wessex Ridgeway nearby. Fossil hunting and boat trips available. Bed and Breakfast £25 to £35. Children aged 6 years and above welcome. Brochure available. **AA ◆◆◆◆**

LYME REGIS
Mrs L. Brown, Providence House, Lyme Road, Uplyme DT7 3TH (01297 445704). Comfortable accommodation on the edge of historic Lyme Regis in 200 year old character house with open beamed fireplace, raised gallery area and roof garden. 25 minutes' walk from the sea. Ideal for artists, fossil hunting, walking etc. Easy access by road. Axminster five miles with main line connection to Waterloo. Accommodation comprises one single, one double, one double en suite; all with TV and tea/coffee making facilities. Full English Breakfast and vegetarian option. Rooms available from £18 to £21 per person per night. Secure courtyard area available for bikes/motor bikes, etc.

PORTLAND
Alessandria Hotel, 71 Wakeham, Easton, Portland DT5 1HW (01305 822270/820108; Fax: 01305 820561). This former 18th century inn is situated in a quiet location. Comfortable accommodation; most rooms en suite; colour TV; tea/coffee; free parking. Ground floor rooms. Children welcome. Bed and Breakfast at reasonable prices. Warm and friendly hospitality. **ETC/AA/RAC ◆◆◆**

website: www.s-h-systems.co.uk/hotels/alessand.html

THE THREE HORSESHOES
Powerstock, Dorset DT6 3TF
Tel: 01308 485328

Nestled in the pretty village of Powerstock beneath Edgerton Hill, The Three Horseshoes is reached along winding country lanes – ideal walking country. This family-run inn is featured in many good food guides.

Lunchtime and evening menus offer a wide selection of dishes featuring the finest local produce with an excellent choice of real ales, and interesting wines. Three bedrooms. Children and well-behaved dogs are welcome.

SHERBORNE

Mrs E. Kingman, Stowell Farm, Stowell, Near Sherborne DT9 4PE (01963 370200). A 15th century former Manor House that has retained some lovely historical features. Now a farmhouse on a family-run dairy and beef farm. It is in a beautiful rural location yet only five miles from the A303, two miles from A30 and two hours by train from London. An ideal place to relax and unwind, enjoy traditional home baking and a warm friendly atmosphere. Close to the abbey town of Sherborne, National Trust Properties and many other places of interest to suit all people. Accommodation – one twin room en suite, one double room with a private bathroom, guest bathroom, and lounge with colour TV and log fires. Bed and Breakfast from £22 to £25 per person per night, reductions for children under 10 years and weekly stays. **AA ◆◆◆◆**
e-mail: kingman@stowell-farm.freeserve.co.uk

SHERBORNE

David, Hazel, Mary and Gerry Wilding, White Horse Farm, Middlemarsh, Sherborne DT9 5QN (01963 210222). Set in beautiful Hardy countryside, we offer a warm welcome in comfortable surroundings, with a hearty farmhouse breakfast. The property is surrounded by two acres of paddock and garden with a duck pond. We lie between the historic towns of Sherborne, Dorchester and Cerne Abbas and are situated next door to an inn serving good food and local ales. Within easy reach of many tourist attractions. All rooms have en suite showers, colour TV, central heating and tea/coffee making facilities. There is also a private conservatory/ lounge. Ample parking. Bed and Breakfast from £29. Self-catering cottages also available. **ETC ◆◆◆◆**
e-mail: enquiries@whitehorsefarm.co.uk
website: www.whitehorsefarm.co.uk

Abbotsbury Swannery
Near Bridport, Dorset • 01305 871858
Up to 600 free-flying swans – help feed them twice daily. Baby swans hatch May/June.
AV show, coffee shop and gift shop.

Visit the FHG website
www.holidayguides.com
for details of the wide choice of accommodation
featured in the full range of FHG titles

SHERBORNE

Mrs Helen Knight, Longbar Farm, Level Lane, Charlton Horethorne, Sherborne DT9 4NN (01963 220266). Found up a small lane opposite the village church of this quaint place that appeared in the Doomsday Book. Two miles from the A303 and A30. There are three guest rooms in this charming, spacious, stonebuilt house with open beams, and along with having all the comforts of home, guests are treated to some excellent cooking. Close to the abbey town of Sherborne and the Somerset/Dorset countryside with its 1000 miles of footpaths and tracks (we have secure bicycle storage), Haynes Motor Museum, Longleat, Stourhead, Dorchester and the coast. Centrally heated, hospitality trays, TV and radio/alarm, hairdryer, residents' lounge with TV, stereo and log fires. Village pub five minutes' walk. B&B from £22 per person, reductions for children. **ETC** ◆◆◆

e-mail: longbar@tinyworld.co.uk

website: www.longbarfarm.co.uk

SHILLINGSTONE

Mrs Rosie Watts, Pennhills Farm, Sandy Lane, off Lanchards Lane, Shillingstone, Blandford DT11 0TF (01258 860491). Pennhills Farmhouse, set in 100 acres of unspoiled countryside, is situated one mile from the village of Shillingstone in the heart of Blackmore Vale, ideal for a peaceful retreat, short break or holiday. It offers spacious comfortable accommodation for all ages. Children welcome, pets by arrangement. One downstairs bedroom. All rooms en suite, with TV and tea/coffee making facilities, complemented by traditional English breakfast with home produced bacon and sausages. Bed and breakfast from £22 per person. Good meals available locally. Vegetarians catered for. Brochure sent on request. A warm and friendly welcome is assured by your host, Rosie Watts.

STURMINSTER NEWTON

Mrs J. Miller, Lower Fifehead Farm, Fifehead, St Quinton, Sturminster Newton DT10 2AP (01258 817335). Come and stay with us on our 400 acre dairy farm. Our lovely Listed 17th century farmhouse with interesting mullion windows is pictured and mentioned in Dorset Books. We have three bedrooms - one double en suite, one double and one twin, each with private bathroom, own sitting room, TV and large garden. Tea and coffee making. No evening meals but we can recommend the local places. Bed and Breakfast from £20 per person. Three-day breaks from £60 per person. Right in the heart of the Blackmore Vale and "Hardy" country; lovely walks, fishing and riding can be arranged. **ETC** ◆◆◆◆

SWANAGE

Mrs Rosemary Dean, Quarr Farm, Valley Road, Swanage BH19 3DY (01929 480865). Quarr is a working family farm steeped in history dating back to the Domesday Book. Animals kept naturally – cows, calves, horses, poultry. Bring your children to feed ducks, chickens, peacocks and watch steam trains passing through our meadows. Accommodation in family room with en suite bathroom, own sitting room with colour TV, real log fire, tea making facilities. Two rooms with shared bathroom. Ideal for families, or friends wishing to holiday together. Cot available. Easy reach high class restaurants, pubs; sea three miles. Studland, sandy beach just five miles away. Ideal for walking, cycling, coastal path, RSPB Reserves, golf courses, riding. Bed and Breakfast. Please telephone for further details and terms.

TOLPUDDLE

Paul Wright, Tolpuddle Hall, Tolpuddle, Near Dorchester DT2 7EW (01305 848986). An historic house in village centre in an area of outstanding natural beauty, not far from the coast. Convenient for Bournemouth, Poole, Dorchester, Weymouth, Isle of Purbeck and many small market towns and villages. Centre for local interests e.g., bird-watching, walking, local history, Thomas Hardy, the Tolpuddle Martyrs, etc. Two double, one twin, one family and two single bedrooms. Full English breakfast. Tea/coffee making, TV sitting room. Pets welcome except high season. From £17.50 per person. Weekly rate available. Open all year.

WAREHAM

Mrs Axford, Sunnyleigh, Hyde, Wareham BH20 7NT (01929 471822). Mary offers her guests a friendly welcome to her bungalow with a cup of tea. Situated in the quiet hamlet of Hyde, five miles west of Wareham, adjacent to East Dorset Golf Club; follow the sign from Wareham and we are the first bungalow past the golf club on the right. It is an ideal base for visiting Swanage, Poole and Bovington Tank Museum, with many interesting coastal walks, including Lulworth Cove. Accommodation consists of three double bedrooms (one double, two twin beds), all with tea/coffee facilities, TV, central heating. Bathroom and separate shower room; two toilets. Visitors' lounge with colour TV and log fires in winter. Open all the year except Christmas. Car essential, ample parking. Bed and Breakfast from £20. No smoking.

See also Colour Display Advertisement

WEYMOUTH

Mark and Jean Mitchell, Ferndown Guest House, 47 Walpole Street, Weymouth DT4 7HQ (01305 775228). A friendly welcome awaits you at Ferndown Guest House. A welcoming place to stay, it is family-run by Mark and Jean. Situated just two minutes' walk to the seafront and five minutes into town, it is the ideal place to stay in Weymouth. All rooms have washbasins, colour TV and tea and coffee making facilities; some en suite available. Visitors are welcome to use the lounge with colour TV. Open from April to October. Bed and Breakfast from £18-00. **AA ◆◆**
e-mail: jeanmitchel@amserve.com

WEYMOUTH

Mr S. Green, Florian, 59 Abbotsbury Road, Weymouth DT4 0AQ (01305 773836). The Florian Guest House offers a relaxed, friendly atmosphere, great food and high standards. Breakfast can include prize-winning sausages, smoked fish and fresh fruit. All of our seven tastefully decorated bedrooms are en suite or have private facilities, with colour TVs and hospitality trays. We have a car park, and are only a ten minute walk to the town, beach and harbour, even closer to Radipole Nature Reserve. We are non-smoking, except in the large gardens with seating and water features. Bed and Breakfast from £18 to £26, credit cards accepted. Brochure available. **ETC ◆◆◆**
e-mail: clare@florian-guesthouse.co.uk
website: www.florian-guesthouse.co.uk

See also Colour Display Advertisement

WIMBORNE

Mrs A. C. Tory, Hemsworth Manor Farm, Witchampton, Wimborne BH21 5BN (01258 840216; Fax: 01258 841278). Our lovely old Manor Farmhouse which is mentioned in the Domesday Book, is situated in an exceptionally peaceful location, yet is only half-an-hour's drive from Salisbury, Dorchester, Poole, Bournemouth and the New Forest. Hemsworth is a working family farm of nearly 800 acres, providing some lovely walks. The farm is mainly arable, but is also home to sheep, horses, ponies and various domestic pets. We have three fully equipped en suite bedrooms, all with colour TV. Separate lounge for guests' use. There are excellent pubs locally. Brochure available. **ETC ◆◆◆◆**

DURHAM

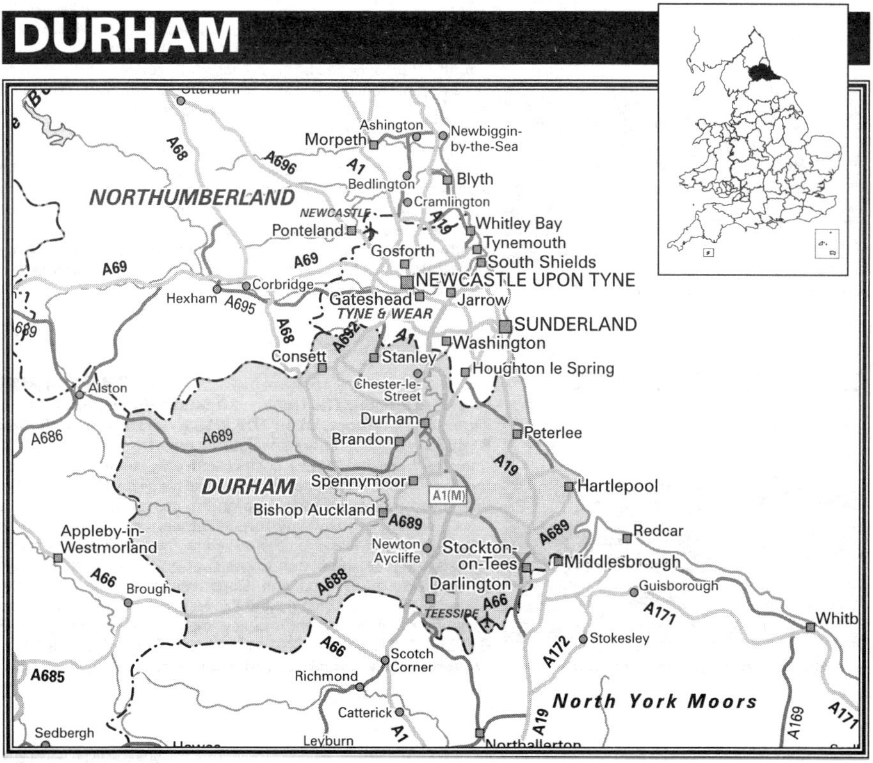

Map showing Durham and surrounding areas including Northumberland, Newcastle Upon Tyne, Tyne & Wear, Sunderland, Durham, and North York Moors.

NORTHUMBERLAND

Otterburn
Ashington
Morpeth
Newbiggin-by-the-Sea
Bedlington
Blyth
Cramlington
NEWCASTLE
Ponteland
Whitley Bay
Gosforth
Tynemouth
South Shields
NEWCASTLE UPON TYNE
Corbridge
Hexham
Gateshead
Jarrow
TYNE & WEAR
SUNDERLAND
Consett
Washington
Stanley
Houghton le Spring
Alston
Chester-le-Street
Durham
Peterlee
Brandon
DURHAM
Spennymoor
A1(M)
Hartlepool
Bishop Auckland
Appleby-in-Westmorland
Newton Aycliffe
Stockton-on-Tees
Redcar
Middlesbrough
Brough
Darlington
Guisborough
TEESSIDE
Whitb
Scotch Corner
Richmond
Stokesley
Catterick
North York Moors
Sedbergh
Leyburn
Northallerton

©MAPS IN MINUTES™ 2003 ©Crown Copyright. Ordnance Survey 2003

BISHOP AUCKLAND

Newlands Hall, Frosterley in Weardale, Bishop Auckland DL13 2SH (01388 529233). Working farm. A warm welcome awaits you on our beef and sheep farm surrounded by beautiful open countryside with its magnificent views of Weardale - an area of outstanding natural beauty. Rich in wildlife, the farm is at the centre of a network of local footpaths. The area has much to offer visitors, ranging from the high wild fells of Weardale and Teesdale, to pretty villages, market towns, and the University City of Durham, with its cathedral, castle and medieval streets. Accommodation comprises a family-size room with stunning views, private bathroom adjacent, tea/coffee making facilities, hairdryer, radio alarm and central heating. Sorry, no pets and no smoking indoors. Full English breakfast is served with home-made bread, own own free-range eggs and other local produce. B&B from £22.50. Open Easter to October.
e-mail: carol.oulton@ukonline.co.uk

CORNFORTH/DURHAM

Mrs D. Slack, Ash House, 24 The Green, Cornforth DL17 9JH (01740 654654; mobile: 07711 133547). Built in the mid-19th Century, Ash House is a beautifully appointed period home combining a delicate mixture of homeliness and Victorian flair. Elegant rooms, individually and tastefully decorated, combining antique furnishings, beautiful fabrics, carved four-posters and modern fittings. Spacious and graceful, filled with character, Ash House offers a warm welcome to both the road-weary traveller and those wishing merely to unwind in the quiet elegance of this charming home on a quiet village green. Private parking. 10 minutes from historic Durham city, and adjacent A1(M) motorway. Well-placed between York and Edinburgh. Excellent value. Terms from £22.50 per person per night.
e-mail: delden@btopenworld.com

e-mail: june@hamsteelshall.co.uk

DURHAM

Hamsteels Hall, Hamsteels Lane, Quebec, Durham DH7 9RS (01207 520388). Hamsteels Hall is an 18th century Country House, Grade II* Listed, tastefully restored but retaining all its original features – inglenook fireplaces, shuttered windows, panelled rooms etc. It is in an elevated position, with fantastic views. The rooms are very spacious and comfortable, and are all en suite with TV/video, hospitality tray etc; all double rooms have four-poster beds. Relax in the gardens, by the pond with its water features, or walk to the nearby garden centre, or the Browney River with its rustic picnic area. Only 10 minutes' drive to Durham City and Beamish Open Air Museum. Ideal for touring Northumbria. Walkers and cyclists welcome. Contact **June Whitfield** for details or check out our website. **ETC** ◆◆◆◆
website: www.hamsteelshall.co.uk

See also Colour Display Advertisement

e-mail: thegablesghouse@aol.com

SPENNYMOOR

Mrs V. Atkinson, The Gables, 10 South View, Middlestone Moor, Spennymoor, DL16 7DF (01388 817544; Fax: 01388 812533). The Gables is a spacious Victorian detached house, 10 minutes from the A1(M) access and only seven miles from medieval Durham city. Ideal touring base for all the North East. We offer five en suite rooms, three on the ground floor. All rooms have colour TV, hospitality tray, toiletries, hairdryer and radio alarm. Breakfast is a choice of seasonal fresh fruit and yoghurt, cereals and toast, traditional English or Continental breakfast. We have private off-road parking. Dogs welcome by arrangement. Room rates from £32 single and £26pppn double/twin. For travel directions and cancellation policy, please see web page. THE GABLES IS STRICTLY NON-SMOKING. **ETC/AA** ◆◆◆◆
website: www.guesthousedurham.co.uk

SPENNYMOOR

John and Jean Thompson, Highview Country House, Kirk Merrington, Near Spennymoor DL16 7JT (01388 811006). Standing in one acre of gardens, in open and rolling countryside, peace and tranquillity awaits. Private and safe parking, situated on the edge of a delightful village with all amenities. Good access from A1(M) and a springboard for the North of England with Durham City only 12 minutes away. Our spacious ground floor rooms are all en suite and furnished to a high standard with colour TV and hospitality tray. Residents' lounge with open balcony and views for miles. Open log fires are a feature of the dining room, with fresh fruit and a full English breakfast (grilled). Bed and Breakfast rates from £25 per person per night (reduced rates for children). Please ring for brochure. **ETC** ◆◆◆◆
e-mail: highviewhouse@genie.co.uk
website: www.highviewcountryhouse.co.uk

STANLEY

Mrs P. Gibson, Bushblades Farm, Harperley, Stanley DH9 9UA (01207 232722). Ideal stop-over when travelling north or south. Only 10 minutes from A1(M), Chester-le-Street. Durham City 20 minutes, Beamish Museum two miles, Metro Centre 15 minutes, Hadrian's Wall and Northumberland coast under an hour. Comfortable Georgian farmhouse set in large garden. Twin ground-floor en suite room plus two double first floor bedrooms. All rooms have tea/coffee making facilities, colour TV and easy chairs. Ample parking. Children over 12 years welcome. Sorry, no pets. Bed and Breakfast from £25 to £30 single, £37 to £42 double. Self catering accommodation also available. Leave A1(M) at Chester-le-Street for Stanley on the A693, then follow sign for Consett. Half-a-mile after Stanley follow signs for Harperley. Farm on right, half-a-mile up from crossroads. **ETC** ◆◆◆

ESSEX

COLCHESTER

Peveril Hotel, 51 North Hill, Colchester CO1 1PY (Tel & Fax: 01206 574001). Town centre hotel with unrestricted parking all weekend and evenings (6pm to 8.30am). Comfortable lounge bar and excellent restaurant providing a comprehensive range of English, Continental and Asian foods, all home cooking. Our hotel is within easy reach of all amenities and only seven miles from Constable Country and six miles from the North Sea. **ETC ◆◆**

COLCHESTER

Mrs Wendy Anderson, The Old Manse, 15 Roman Road, Colchester CO1 1UR (01206 545154). This spacious Victorian family home is situated in a quiet square beside the Castle Park. Only three minutes' walk from bus/coach station or through the Park to town centre. We promise a warm welcome and a friendly, informal atmosphere. All rooms have central heating, TV and tea/coffee making facilities. Ground floor double room has private facilities; two twin-bedded rooms on first floor, one en suite. Full, varied English Breakfast. Bed and Breakfast from £35 single, £50 double. Only 30 minutes' drive from Harwich and Felixstowe. Within easy reach of Constable country and one hour's train journey from London. Sorry, no smoking.
e-mail: wendyanderson15@hotmail.com
website: www.doveuk.com/oldmanse

KELVEDON

Mr and Mrs R. Bunting, Highfields Farm, Highfields Lane, Kelvedon CO5 9BJ (Tel & Fax: 01376 570334). Highfields Farm is set in a quiet area on a 700 acre working farm. This makes a peaceful overnight stop on the way to Harwich or a base to visit historic Colchester and Constable country. Convenient for Harwich, Felixstowe and Stansted Airport. Easy access to A12 and main line trains to London. The accommodation comprises one twin room with private bathroom, one twin room en suite and one double en suite, all with TV and tea/coffee making facilities. Residents' lounge. Good English breakfast is served in the oak beamed dining room. Ample parking. Bed and Breakfast from £28-£30 single and £48 twin or double. **ETC ◆◆◆◆**
e-mail: HighfieldsFarm@farmersweekly.net   **website: www.highfieldsfarm.co.uk**

WESTCLIFF-ON-SEA

The Balmoral Hotel, 32-36 Valkyrie Road, Westcliff-on-Sea SS0 8BU (01702 342947; Fax: 01702 337828). The warmest welcome awaits you at the most luxuriously appointed hotel in Southend. Situated just a short walk from Westcliff's main shopping centre and within easy reach of all major attractions in the area. The hotel offers a range of bedrooms from singles to executive suites, all with full en suite facilities, colour TV with cable channels, tea/coffee tray, direct dial telephone, radio, hairdryer and writing desk. The Sovereigns Restaurant offers a variety of superb cuisine complemented by a selection of fine wines from around the world. The hotel bar offers a choice of wines, beers and spirits as well as tempting bar snacks. Weddings and conferences are catered for. On-site car park.

B&B from £48 single, £73 double. **AA/RAC ★★**
e-mail: enquiries@balmoralsouthend.com   **website: www.balmoralsouthend.com**

GLOUCESTERSHIRE

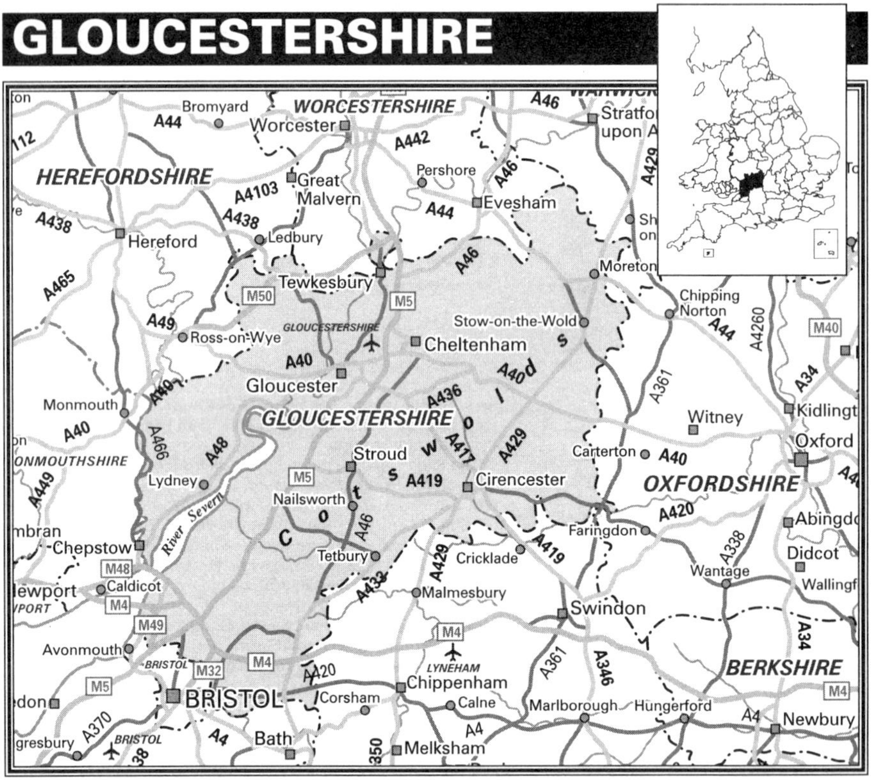

See also Colour Display Advertisement

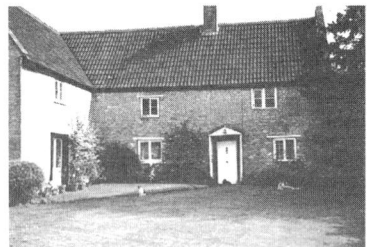

BATH (near)

Mrs Pam Wilmott, Pool Farm, Bath Road, Wick, Bristol BS30 5RL (0117 937 2284). Welcome to our 350 year old Grade II Listed farmhouse on a working farm. On A420 between Bath and Bristol and a few miles from Exit 18 of M4, we are on the edge of the village, overlooking fields, but within easy reach of pub, shops and golf club. We offer traditional Bed and Breakast in one family and one twin room with tea/coffee facilities and TV. Guest lounge. Central heating. Ample parking. Open all year except Christmas. Terms from £20.

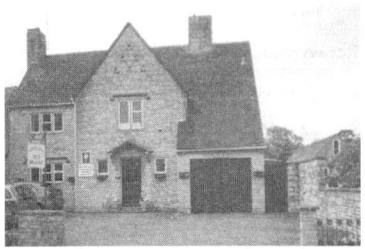

BOURTON-ON-THE-WATER

John and Jean Meadows, Cotswold House, Lansdowne, Bourton-on-the-Water GL54 2AR (01451 822373). Situated close to the centre of this delightful village stands the lovely Cotwold House. It has an elegant hall leading to curved stairs and galleried landing. The spacious and smartly decorated en suite rooms that overlook the beautiful garden are well equipped with colour TV and tea/coffee making facilities. We also have a family bungalow in the garden which can sleep up to six persons. Bed and Breakfast from £22.50 per person. Open all year. Ample parking. We are very central for the beautiful Cotwold walks and tours. **ETC/AA ◆◆◆**

ENGLAND

BRISTOL

Marilyn and Bob Downes, Box Hedge Farm, Coalpit Heath, Bristol BS36 2UW (01454 250786). Box Hedge Farm is set in 200 acres of beautiful rural countryside on the edge of the Cotswolds. Local to M4/M5, central for Bristol and Bath and the many tourist attractions in this area. An ideal stopping point for the South West and Wales. We offer a warm, friendly atmosphere with traditional farmhouse cooking. All bedrooms have colour TV and tea/coffee making facilities. Bed and Breakfast from £25 single standard, £30 single en suite, £40 double standard, £46 double en suite. Family rooms - prices on application. All prices include VAT. Self-catering accommodation also available. Full details on our website.
website: www.bed-breakfast-bristol.com

BRISTOL

e-mail: avril@akitching.fsnet.co.uk

Mayfair Lodge, 5 Henleaze Road, Westbury on Trym, Bristol BS9 4EX (Tel & Fax: 0117 962 2008). A charming Victorian house located in a smart residential area between Westbury on Trym and Clifton. Family-run with a friendly and relaxed atmosphere. Built in 1886 Mayfair Lodge is tastefully furnished retaining much of the character of the period. All rooms have comfortable beds, remote-control TV, hairdryer and hospitality tray. Some are en suite. Telephone facilities readily available to guests. Antiques are themed throughout the house. Conveniently situated for the city, university, theatres and Bristol Zoo and easily reached from the M4 and M5. Terms from £29 single, twin or double £55. Car parking available at rear of property. AA ◆◆◆
website: www.s-h-systems.co.uk/hotels/mayfairlodge.html

CHELTENHAM

Dove House, 128 Cheltenham Road, Bishops Cleeve, Cheltenham GL52 4LZ (01242 679452/679600; Fax: 01242 679600; Mobile: 07973 424358). Dove House is situated on the outskirts of Cheltenham, close to the Racecourse and is ideal as a base for touring/walking the Cotswolds, Forest of Dean, Tewkesbury, Evesham. Golf courses and private fishing lakes close by. All rooms are furnished to a high standard and have central heating, colour TV and tea/coffee making facilities. Ample parking and garden for guests' use. Bed and Breakfast from £20 per person per night; en suite available. Open all year.
e-mail: eric.jenny@lineone.net

COTSWOLD COUNTRY
BED AND BREAKFAST

CHIPPING CAMPDEN

Mrs Gené Jeffrey, Brymbo, Honeybourne Lane, Mickleton, Chipping Campden GL55 6PU (01386 438890; Fax: 01386 438113). A warm and welcoming farm building conversion with large garden in beautiful Cotswold countryside, ideal for walking and touring. Close to Stratford-upon-Avon, Broadway, Chipping Campden and with easy access to Oxford and Cheltenham. All rooms are on the ground floor, with full central heating. The comfortable bedrooms all have colour television and tea/coffee making facilities. Sitting room with open log fire. Breakfast room. Children and dogs welcome. Parking. Maps and guides to borrow. Sample menus from local hostelries for your information. Home-made preserves a speciality. FREE countryside tour of area offered to three-night guests. Rooms: two double, two twin, one family. Bathrooms: three en suite, two shared. Bed and Breakfast: single £24 to £38; double £38 to £50. Brochure available. Credit Cards accepted. **ETC** ◆◆◆◆

e-mail: enquiries@brymbo.com **website: www.brymbo.com**

CHIPPING CAMPDEN

Mrs C. Hutsby, Holly House, Ebrington, Chipping Campden GL55 6NL (01386 593213; Fax: 01386 593181). Holly House is set in the centre of the picturesque thatched Cotswold village of Ebrington. Ideally situated for touring the Cotswolds and Shakespeare's country. Two miles Chipping Campden and Hidcote Gardens, five miles Broadway, 11 miles Stratford-upon-Avon, 19 miles Warwick. Double, twin and family rooms available, all beautifully appointed with en suite facilities, TV and tea and coffee. Laundry facility available. Private parking. Lovely garden room at guests' disposal. Village pub serves meals. Bike hire available locally. Directions: from Chipping Campden take B4035 towards Shipston on Stour, after half-a-mile turn left to Ebrington, we are in the centre of the village. Prices from £25 per person. Child reductions. Non- smoking. **AA** ◆◆◆◆

e-mail: hutsby@talk21.com **website: www.hollyhousebandb.co.uk**

DIDMARTON

Mrs M.T. Sayers, The Old Rectory, Didmarton GL9 1DS (01454 238233; Fax: 01454 238909). This is a charming home, where a happy and relaxed atmosphere prevails. Very comfortable accommodation is offered in three attractively furnished bedrooms, each with an en suite/private bathroom and TV. All bedrooms are non-smoking. There is a cosy sittingroom and pretty garden in which guests may choose to relax. Halfway between Bath and Cirencester, close to Westonbirt Arboretum, Tetbury and M4/5. Pub food a few minutes' walk. Terms: double/twin room £56. Single occupancy £38. **ETC** ◆◆◆◆ *GOLD AWARD.*

e-mail: mt@febCentral.com

See also Colour Display Advertisement

GLOUCESTER (near)

S.J. Barnfield, "Kilmorie Smallholding", Gloucester Road, Corse, Staunton, Gloucester GL19 3RQ (Tel & Fax: 01452 840224). Quality all ground floor accommodation. "Kilmorie" is Grade II Listed (c1848) within conservation area in a lovely part of Gloucestershire, deceptively spacious yet cosy, and tastefully furnished. Double, twin, family or single bedrooms, all having tea tray, colour TV, radio, mostly en suite. Very comfortable guests' lounge, traditional home cooking is served in the separate diningroom overlooking large garden where there are seats to relax, watch our free range hens (who provide excellent eggs for breakfast!) or the wild birds and butterflies we encourage to visit. Perhaps walk waymarked farmland footpaths which start here. Children may "help" with our child's pony, and hens. Rural yet perfectly situated to visit Cotswolds, Royal Forest of Dean, Wye Valley and Malvern Hills. Children over five years. No smoking, please. Bed, full English Breakfast and Evening Dinner from £29; Bed and Breakfast from £20. Ample parking. **ETC** ◆◆◆◆

e-mail: sheila-barnfield@supanet.com

LECHLADE ON THAMES

Mr and Mrs J. Titchener, Cambrai Lodge, Oak Street, Lechlade on Thames GL7 3AY (01367 253173; Mobile: 07860 150467). Situated in an attractive village on the River Thames this family-run guest house is only eight miles from Burford and 12 miles from Swindon. Ideal base for touring the Cotswolds with Kemscott Manor and Buscot House and Gardens nearby. We are close to the river and guests can make use of our lovely garden. One family, two double (en suite), one twin (en suite) and two single rooms available. One room has a Victorian four-poster bed and one room is on the ground floor. Breakfast is served in our airy conservatory overlooking the garden. Non-smoking. Pets by arrangement. Open all year. Bed and Breakfast from £29 to £39 single; £47 to £59 double. A warm and friendly

welcome is assured at Cambrai Lodge. **ETC** ◆◆◆◆ *SILVER AWARD*.

See also Colour Display Advertisement

MINCHINHAMPTON (near Stroud)

Mrs Margaret Helm, Hunters Lodge, Dr Brown's Road, Minchinhampton Common, Near Stroud GL6 9BT (01453 883588; Fax: 01453 731449). Hunters Lodge is a beautiful stone-built Cotswold country house set in a large secluded garden adjoining 600 acres of National Trust common land at Minchinhampton. Accommodation available - one double room en suite; two twin/double-bedded rooms both with private bathrooms. All have tea/coffee making facilities, dressing gowns, central heating and colour TV and are furnished and decorated to a high standard. Private lounge with TV and a delightful new conservatory. Car essential, ample parking space. Ideal centre for touring the Cotswolds, Bath, Cheltenham, Cirencester, with many delightful pubs and hotels in the area for meals. You are

sure of a warm welcome, comfort, and help in planning excursions to local places of interest. Bed and Breakfast from £25 to £27pp; single £35. Non-smoking. Children over 10. No dogs. SAE please, or telephone. **AA** ◆◆◆◆◆
e-mail: hunterslodge@hotmail.com

NAILSWORTH

Mrs Lesley Williams-Allen, The Laurels at Inchbrook, Nailsworth GL5 5HA (Tel & Fax: 01453 834021). A lovely rambling house, part cottage-style and part Georgian. The emphasis is on relaxation and friendly hospitality. All six rooms are en suite and include family, twin and double rooms, each with colour TV and tea making facilities. There is a ground floor room suitable for disabled guests. We have a panelled study/reading room with piano, and a beamed lounge with snooker table and board games. In our licensed dining room we serve excellent breakfasts and home cooked dinners. The secluded streamside garden backs onto fields and offers a swimming pool and the opportunity to observe wildlife. We are ideally situated for touring all parts of the Cotswolds and West

Country, surrounded by a wealth of beautiful countryside and all kinds of activities. Children and pets welcome. Non-smoking. Bed and Breakfast from £21 per person; Dinner by arrangement. Brochure on request. Self-catering cottage also available. **RAC** ◆◆◆
e-mail: laurels@inchbrook.fsnet.co.uk

See also Colour Display Advertisement

NEWNHAM-ON-SEVERN

Philip and Elaine Sheldrake, Swan House Country Guest House, High Street, Newnham-on-Severn GL14 1BY (01594 516504; Fax: 01594 516177). Philip and Elaine extend a warm welcome to our family guesthouse in the picturesque village of Newnham near the beautiful Forest of Dean. Our 17th century house is tastefully furnished with all six bedrooms individually decorated and en suite. The rooms have many comforts including electric blankets for the winter. Elaine cooks a choice of evening meals and can cater for most dietary needs. We have a carefully tended garden which we are happy to share with you. Pets are welcome. Please contact Philip and Elaine Sheldrake for details. Pets and children welcome. **AA** ◆◆◆◆
e-mail: enquiries@swanhousenewnham.co.uk
website: www.swanhousenewnham.co.uk

STONEHOUSE

Mrs D.A. Hodge, Merton Lodge, 8 Ebley Road, Stonehouse GL10 2LQ (01453 822018). A former gentleman's residence situated about three miles from Stroudwater interchange on the M5 (Junction 13), on B4008 (keep going on old road) just outside Stonehouse towards Stroud. Opposite side to Wyevale Garden Centre, 300 yards from the Cotswold Way. Full central heating and washbasins in all bedrooms; one en suite. Only cotton or linen sheets used. Two bathrooms with showers. Large sittingroom with panoramic views of Selsey Common. Well placed for Cotswold villages, Wildfowl Trust, Berkeley Castle, Westonbirt Arboretum, Bath/Bristol, Cheltenham and Gloucester ski slope and Forest of Dean. Satisfaction guaranteed. Excellent cuisine. Carvery/pub 200 yards away. Bed and Breakfast from £20 per person, en suite from £22 per person. Children half price. Friendly welcome. Sorry, no smoking or dogs. ETC ◆◆

See also Colour Display Advertisement

STOW-ON-THE-WOLD

South Hill Farmhouse, Fosseway, Stow-on-the-Wold, GL54 1JU (01451 831888; Fax: 01451 832255). Siân and Mark Cassie welcome you to South Hill Farmhouse. The house is a Listed Cotswold stone farmhouse (no longer a working farm) situated on the ancient Roman Fosse Way on the outskirts of Stow-on-the-Wold. There is ample parking for guests, and it is only 10 minutes' walk to the pubs, restaurants and shops of Stow-on-the-Wold. 2004 prices: single £38, double/twin £52, family (three) £66 per room per night, including generous breakfast. Non-smoking house. ETC ◆◆◆◆
e-mail: info@southhill.co.uk
website: www.southhill.co.uk

STOW-ON-THE-WOLD

Robert Smith & Julie-Anne, Corsham Field Farmhouse, Bledington Road, Stow-on-the-Wold GL54 1JH (01451 831750; Fax: 01451 832247). A traditional farmhouse with spectacular views of Cotswold countryside. Quiet location one mile from Stow, ideally situated for exploring all Cotswold villages including Bourton-on-the-Water, Broadway, Burford and Chipping Campden. Within easy reach of Cheltenham, Oxford and Stratford-upon-Avon; also places of interest such as Blenheim Palace, Warwick Castle and many National Trust houses and gardens. Family, twin and double bedrooms, mostly en suite. TV, tea tray and hairdryer in all rooms. Relaxing guest lounge/dining room. Pets and children welcome. Open all year for Bed and Breakfast from £22.00 (reductions for children). Excellent pub food five minutes' walk away. **ETC/AA ◆◆◆**
e-mail: farmhouse@corshamfield.co.uk   **website: www.corshamfield.co.uk**

See also Colour Display Advertisement

STOW-ON-THE-WOLD

Mrs F.J. Adams, Aston House, Broadwell, Moreton-In-Marsh GL56 0TJ (01451 830475). Aston House is in the peaceful village of Broadwell, one-and-a-half miles from Stow-on-the-Wold, four miles from Moreton-in-Marsh. It is centrally situated for all the Cotswold villages, while Blenheim Palace, Warwick Castle, Oxford, Stratford-upon-Avon, Cheltenham and Gloucester are within easy reach. Accommodation comprises a twin-bedded and a double room, both en suite (first floor), and a double room with private bathroom (ground floor). All rooms have tea/coffee making facilities, radio, colour TV, hairdryer, electric blankets for the colder nights and fans for hot weather. Bedtime drinks and biscuits are provided. Open March to October. No smoking. Car essential, parking. Pub within walking distance. PC and internet access available. Bed and good English breakfast from £25 to £27 per person daily; weekly from £175 per person.
ETC ◆◆◆◆ *SILVER AWARD*, **RAC ◆◆◆◆** *WARM WELCOME AWARD AND SPARKLING DIAMOND AWARD.*
e-mail: fja@netcomuk.co.uk   **website: www.netcomuk.co.uk/~nmfa/aston_house.html**

STOW-ON-THE-WOLD

Graham and Helen Keyte, The Limes, Evesham Road, Stow-on-the-Wold GL54 1EN (01451 830034/831056). The centre of the Cotswolds. Large attractive garden with ornamental pond and waterfall overlooking fields. Only four minutes' walking distance to town centre. Central for places to visit like Stratford-upon-Avon, Burford, Cheltenham, Oxford, Broadway, Evesham, Chipping Campden, etc, all within 20 miles radius. Good sized bedrooms; one four-poster, four rooms en-suite, all with colour TV, hair dryer and tea/coffee making facilities; TV lounge; dining room. Cot, high chair. Established for over 30 years, we have many guests returning each year, even from abroad, and are well recommended. Many guests book for one or two nights then stay for a week. Bed and Breakfast from £20 to £25 per person per night. Central heating. Car park. Open all year except Christmas. Children and pets welcome. **AA** ◆◆◆, **RAC** *LISTED*.
e-mail: theLimes@zoom.co.uk

See also Colour Display Advertisement

STOW-ON-THE-WOLD

The Golden Ball Inn, Lower Swell, Near Stow-on-the-Wold, Cheltenham GL54 1LF (01451 830247). Traditional Cotswold country inn offering Donningtons ales and home-cooked food. Children welcome and small parties catered for. Situated on the beautiful Donnington Way, the inn has parking and a beer garden. En suite B&B from £30pppn. **Steve and Maureen Heath** offer you a warm welcome.
e-mail: maureen@goldenball.fsnet.co.uk

STROUD

Tom and Lesley Williams, Orchardene, Castle Street, Kings Stanley, Stonehouse GL10 3JA (01453 822684; Fax: 01453 821554). Warm welcome at Cotswold Stone cottage. Seven minutes J13 M5. Ideal location to explore undiscovered Cotswolds and Severn Vale. Glorious walks. B&B from £20. Evening Meal optional. Local and organic food. Pets welcome.
e-mail: toranda@btopenworld.com

See also Colour Display Advertisement

TEWKESBURY

Mrs Bernadette Williams, Abbots Court, Church End, Twyning, Tewkesbury GL20 6DA (Tel & Fax: 01684 292515). Working farm. A large, quiet farmhouse set in 350 acres, built on the site of monastery between the Malverns and Cotswolds, half a mile M5-M50 junction. Six en suite bedrooms with colour TV and tea making facilities. Centrally heated. Open all year except Christmas. Large lounge with open fire and colour TV. Spacious diningroom. Licensed bar. Good home cooked food in large quantities, home produced where possible. Children's own TV room, games room and playroom. Tennis lawn. Play area and lawn. Cot and high chair available. Laundry facilities. Ideally situated for touring with numerous places to visit. Swimming, tennis, sauna, golf within three miles. Coarse fishing available on the farm. Bed and Breakfast from £19 to £21. Reduced rates for children and Senior Citizens. **ETC** ◆◆◆
e-mail: bernie@abbotscourt.fsbusiness.co.uk

WINCHCOMBE

Mrs Margaret Warmington, Ireley Farm, Broadway Road, Winchcombe GL54 5PA (01242 602445). Ireley is an 18th century farmhouse located in the heart of gentle countryside, one-and-a-half miles from Winchcombe and within easy reach of Cheltenham, Gloucester, Stratford-upon-Avon and Worcester. The cosy yet spacious guest rooms (one double and two twin) offer either en suite or private bathroom. Relax in the evening beside a traditional open fire and in the morning enjoy a delicious English breakfast. Families are welcomed to enjoy the unique atmosphere of this working farm. B&B from £25 per person.
e-mail: warmingtonmaggot@aol.com

WINCHCOMBE/CHELTENHAM

Bob and Ann, Moors Farm House, 32 Beckford Road, Alderton, Near Tewkesbury GL20 8NL (01242 620523; Freephone: 0800 2989287). Bob and Ann would like to welcome you to their 18th century family farmhouse in a quiet village setting, backing onto fields and woods. The farm house is conveniently located for the motorway, Broadway, Stratford-upon-Avon and many other places of interest. It is also close to local inns and the Cotswolds. All forms of accommodation are available, single, double, twin – some en suite. Prices start from £35 single, £60 double. **ETC ◆◆◆◆** *GOLD AWARD*.

WOODCHESTER

Mrs Wendy Swait, Inschdene, Atcombe Road, South Woodchester, Stroud GL5 5EW (01453 873254). Inschdene is a comfortable family house with magnificent views across the valley, set in an acre of garden near the centre of a quiet village. A double room with private bathroom and a twin-bedded room are available, both being spacious with washbasin and tea/coffee making facilities. Colour TV available in the rooms. Woodchester is an attractive village with excellent local pubs renowned for their food, and all within easy walking distance. An ideal centre for the Cotswolds and close to Slimbridge, Berkeley Castle and Westonbirt Arboretum and more, including Badminton and Gatcombe Horse Trials. Guests are requested not to smoke in the house. Bed and Breakfast from £20 per person.

FHG PUBLICATIONS

publish a large range of well-known accommodation guides. We will be happy to send you details or you can use the order form at the back of this book.

The **FHG** **Directory of Website Addresses**
on pages 387-415 is a useful quick reference guide for holiday accommodation with e-mail and/or website details

HAMPSHIRE

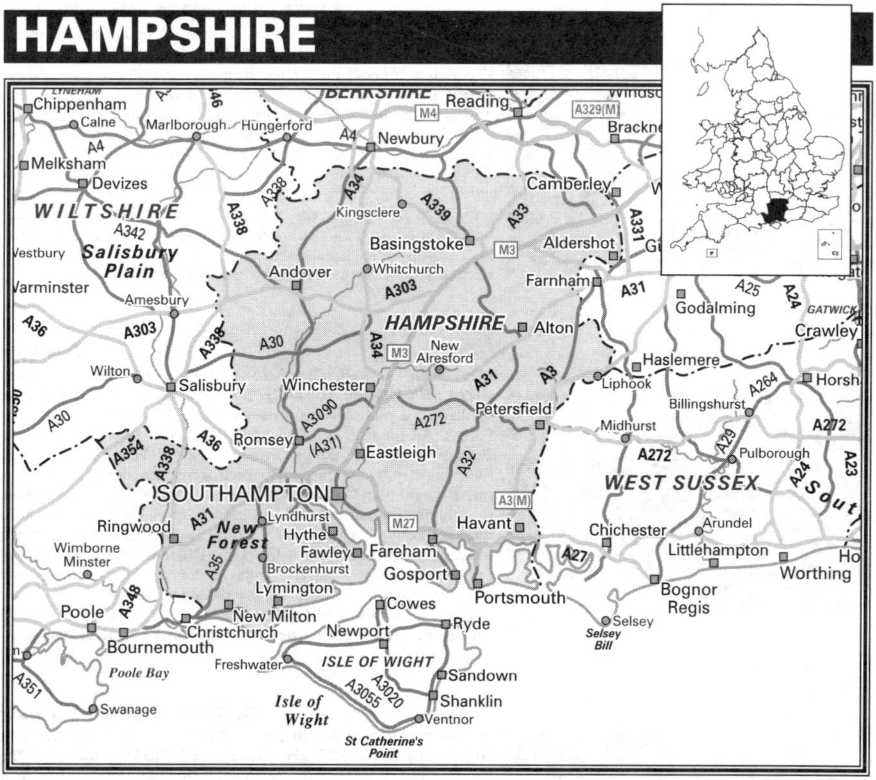

©MAPS IN MINUTES™ 2003 ©Crown Copyright, Ordnance Survey 2003

BARTON-ON-SEA

Lee & Melanie Snook, Laurel Lodge, 48 Western Avenue, Barton-on-Sea, New Milton BH25 7PZ (01425 618309). Ideally situated for the delights of the New Forest, scenic cliff top walks, local beaches, pleasure cruises to the Isle of Wight, the Needles and historic Hurst Castle, horse riding, cycling, golf and a whole host of indoor and outdoor pursuits. Laurel Lodge is a comfortable, centrally heated, converted bungalow, offering twin, double & family rooms. All rooms are fully en suite with tea and coffee making facilities, comfortable chairs, colour TV and alarm clock radio. Ground floor rooms available. Breakfast is served in our conservatory / diningroom with views over the garden. Bed and Breakfast from £25 per person. Special deals for longer breaks. Children welcome, cot and high chair supplied by prior arrangement. Off road parking for all rooms. Strictly no smoking. Open all year. Please phone for further details.

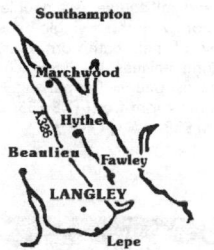

BEAULIEU (near)

Langley Village Restaurant, Lepe Road, Langley, Near Beaulieu, Southampton SO45 1XR (Tel & Fax: 023 8089 1667; Mobile: 07989 781616). A friendly family atmosphere will greet you in this large detached property on the edge of the beautiful New Forest. Ample off-road parking. Each day begins with a hearty full English breakfast. Accommodation comprises one twin, one double and two single rooms, all tastefully decorated and having washbasins, central heating, colour TV and tea-making facilities. A restaurant is attached offering meals all day. Conveniently situated for golf, fishing, horse riding and walking. Close to Exbury Gardens, Lepe Country Park and Beaulieu Motor Museum. Open all year. Bed and Breakfast from £23.50. Special diets catered for by arrangement.
website: www.langley-hampshire.co.uk

BROCKENHURST (New Forest)

Hilden, Southampton Road, Boldre, Brockenhurst (New Forest) SO41 8PT (01590 623682; Fax: 01590 624444). Hilden is a friendly Edwardian home in two-and-a-half acres of gardens and paddock, 50 yards from the open New Forest, offering wonderful cycling, riding and walking. Both the pretty Georgian sailing town of Lymington and the New Forest village of Brockenhurst (80 minutes to Waterloo by train) are about two miles away. There are numerous very good pubs and restaurants nearby, including The Hobler Inn, which serves excellent food, under 200 yards away. Children and dogs welcome, stabling can be arranged, as can cycle hire, and riding from various local stables within five minutes' drive.

website: www.newforestbandb-hilden.co.uk

BURLEY

Mrs Gina Russell, Charlwood, Longmead Road, Burley BH24 4BY (01425 403242). Charlwood is situated on the edge of Burley, a picturesque little village in the midst of the New Forest. An ideal walking and touring base, Bournemouth and Southampton only 16 miles away and Isle of Wight ferry 12 miles. Riding and golf are nearby. The bedrooms, one double, one twin, have washbasin, colour TV and tea/coffee making facilities. Central heating throughout. The friendly family home stands in its own attractive grounds on a no-through forest road offering visitors a peaceful "away from it all" break. A full traditional English Breakfast is served. Pets welcome. No smoking. Open March to November. Bed and Breakfast from £25.

e-mail: charlwoodbnb@aol.com
website: www.newforest.demon.co.uk/charlwood.htm

CADNAM (New Forest)

Simon and Elaine Wright, Bushfriers, Winsor Road, Winsor, Southampton SO40 2HF (02380 812552). Situated in the rural village of Winsor on the quieter northern side of the New Forest. This charming forest cottage offers delightful accommodation with countryside views, comfy beds, TV, spacious en suite bathroom and hospitality tray. Relax in the TV/sitting room with log fire and a delightful secluded garden. Your excellent breakfast is freshly prepared from local farm fresh produce, homemade organic bread along with homemade preserves from our own organically grown fruit. Play golf on a local course or fish in the Hampshire Avon, ride a horse or just relax and enjoy the wonderful flora and fauna of this unique New Forest. 17th century village inn only four minutes' stroll. B&B from £25 per person. Discount three nights. Non-smokers please.

e-mail: bushfriers@waitrose.com   website: www.newforest.demon.co.uk/bushfriers.htm

HAYLING ISLAND

Jane & Phil Taylor, Ravensdale, 19 St Catherines Road, Hayling Island PO11 0HF (Tel & Fax: 023 9246 3203; Mobile: 07802 188259). Jane and Phil welcome you to their home, which is comfortably fitted and in a quiet location within a short walk of the beach and golf course. Two double rooms with en suite facilities, triple room with three single beds, one small double bedroom with use of main bathroom. Central heating, television, tea/coffee making facilities. A full English Breakfast is included and Evening Meal is optional. Car parking. No smoking, and no pets please. Double room from £48-£56, single room from £36, triple room from £58. **AA ◆◆◆◆**

GORSE MEADOW GUEST HOUSE

"The home of Mrs Tee's Wild Mushrooms"

On the first floor there are three double/twin family rooms all en suite with shower and toilet, one of which also has a full bath. The ground floor has easy assisted wheelchair access, a double with en suite bath with shower and toilet. Also a suite consisting of a double with a sitting room and a settee/bed (could sleep four), en suite shower and toilet. All rooms include: shaver plug, TV, tea and coffee making facilities. The restored Edwardian Family Residence stands on an elevated site off a country road a mile-and-a-half from Lymington and a mile from the New Forest. Furnished in its period but with modern conveniences, there is a splendid entrance hall, a galleried staircase, licensed and impressive main dining room. There are paddocks (facilities for guests' horses), gardens, ponds, a bridge, lawn and barbecue area. Beaches are four miles away. Riding a mile away (bookings made from "Gorse Meadow"). Golf courses, tennis courts and boat charter/hire also nearby. We hold Mushroom Seminars for both chefs and amateurs of wild Mushrooms. Fluent in French and German.

For details of residential seminars, please call, write or e-mail:

Sway Road, Lymington, Hampshire SO41 8LR

Tel: (01590) 673354 Fax: (01590) 673336 Mobile: 07774 139731   ETC ◆◆◆

e-mail: gorse.meadow.guesthouse@wildmushrooms.co.uk   website: www.wildmushrooms.co.uk

Terms pppn include full English Breakfast, from £35.
Evening Meals from £25 including ½ bottle of wine per person.

HYTHE

Four Seasons Hotel, Hamilton Road, Hythe, Southampton SO45 3PD (023 8084 5151 or 023 8084 6285). Friendly family-run hotel on the edge of the New Forest. Close to Beaulieu and Exbury, an ideal base for touring. Close to the picturesque market town of Hythe with its marina and a regular ferry service to Southampton and Isle of Wight. Golf, horseriding, windsurfing and other sports within five miles. En suite available, attractive garden. Ample car park. Bed and Breakfast from £24.50.

LYMINGTON

Jane & Mike Finch, "Dolphins", 6 Emsworth Road, Lymington SO41 9BL (Tel & Fax: 01590 676108; Mobile: 07958 727536) "Dolphins" is a very comfortable and homely Victorian cottage in a quiet location, offering warm hospitality and the highest standard of accommodation. Single, twin, double and family rooms all with colour TV and tea/coffee making facilities; ground floor twin or king-size en suite available with patio garden and private entrance. Spacious and very comfortable dining room with open log fire (in winter) and colour satellite TV. Choice of breakfast. Excellent position, just a few minutes' walk from railway/bus/coach stations, ferry and sea, restaurants and town centre. Beautiful Forest walks and excellent cycle rides. Beach chalet, leisure club facilities, and mountain bikes available. Also walking distance of Marinas and beautiful Nature Reserve. Bed and Breakfast from £27 per person per night; children half price. ETC/AA ◆◆◆◆, *WELCOME HOST.*

e-mail: dolphins@easynet.co.uk   mike and janefinch@hotmail.com
website: www.dolphinsnewforestbandb.co.uk

LYMINGTON

Mrs Patricia Ellis, Efford Cottage, Everton, Lymington SO41 0JD (01590 642315; Fax: 01590 641030/642315). Guests receive a warm and friendly welcome to our home, which is a spacious Georgian cottage. All rooms are en suite with many extra luxury facilities. We offer a four-course, multi-choice breakfast, with homemade bread and preserves. Patricia is a qualified chef and uses our homegrown produce. An excellent centre for exploring both the New Forest and the South Coast with sports facilities, fishing, bird watching and horse riding in the near vicinity. Private parking. Dogs welcome. Sorry, no children. Bed and Breakfast from £25 to £35 per person. **ETC ◆◆◆◆◆** *GOLD AWARD, RAC SPARKLING DIAMOND AND WARM WELCOME ACCOLADES, WELCOME HOST, ENGLAND FOR EXCELLENCE AWARD, FHG DIPLOMA WINNER 1997, 1999 AND 2000.*
e-mail: effordcottage@aol.com   **website: www.effordcottage.co.uk**

See also Colour Display Advertisement

LYMINGTON

Mrs R. Sque, Harts Lodge, 242 Everton Road, Lymington SO41 0HE (01590 645902). Bungalow (non-smoking) set in three acres. Large garden with small lake and an abundance of bird life. Quiet location. Three miles west of Lymington. Friendly welcome and high standard. Accommodation comprises double, twin and family en suite rooms, each with tea/coffee making facilities and colour TV. Delicious four-course English breakfast. The sea and forest are five minutes away by car. Horse riding, golf and fishing are nearby. The village pub, serving excellent home-made meals, is half a mile away. Children and pets welcome. Bed and Breakfast from £25pp. **AA ◆◆◆◆**

LYMINGTON (near)

Mrs Deborah Fairhurst, The Firs, 25A Everton Road, Hordle, Near Lymington SO41 0FF (01425 618857; mobile: 0772 9127157). Situated in the village of Hordle, between Lymington and New Milton, within easy reach of the New Forest and the coast, where a warm welcome awaits you from your hosts Debbie and Phil Fairhurst. Accommodation consists of one double room on the ground floor, beautifully furnished with ceiling fan, TV, trouser press, hairdryer and tea/coffee making facilities. Adjacent to your bedroom is a wc. Private bathroom with bath and shower over is on the first floor. Dressing gowns supplied. Non-smoking home. Private parking. Bed & Breakfast from £48 per room per night.
e-mail: p.fairhurst@tiscali.co.uk
website: www.newforest.demon.co.uk/thefirs.htm

See also Colour Display Advertisement

LYNDHURST

Whitemoor House Hotel, Southampton Road, Lyndhurst SO43 7BU (023 8028 2186). Situated just a few minutes' walk away from the centre of Lyndhurst and opposite open forest, this hotel is, in the words of the Visitors' Book, 'friendly, welcoming, comfortable and quiet'. All bedrooms have en suite bath or shower and toilet, colour TV, tea/coffee making facilities and a view of either the forest or the garden. Families with children are welcome and there is a no-smoking policy in operation. The hotel is licensed and dinner is available on request. Bed and Breakfast from £28 per person per night for double or twin room, single from £35 per person per night. **AA ◆◆◆**
e-mail: whitemoor@aol.com
website: www.whitemoorhotel.co.uk

Terms quoted in this publication may be subject to increase if rises in costs necessitate

COTTAGE BED & BREAKFAST AT APPLEDORE

Holmsley Road, Wootton, New Milton, Hants, BH25 5TR
Tel: 01425 629506 • Mobile: 07773 527626

This graciously decorated New Forest Cottage is presented by myself, Mariette, whose home-cooked breakfasts are a veritable joy, served in the conservatory overlooking the garden. The Cottage is located in the heart of the New Forest where you can enjoy all the verdant tranquil beauty and step back in time as you traverse the leafy glades. Take care to observe the spectacular wildlife in their natural environment. There are many local pubs and restaurants which will happily welcome your pet. For pets and families alike there is a warm and friendly welcome. All en suite rooms, Tea/Coffee making facilities, TV, Towels and Toiletries.

website: www.appledorecottage.co.uk

LYNDHURST

Penny Farthing Hotel, Romsey Road, Lyndhurst SO43 7AA (023 802 84422; Fax: 023 802 84488). The Penny Farthing is a cheerful small Hotel ideally situated in Lyndhurst village centre, the capital of "The New Forest". The Hotel offers en suite single, twin, double and family rooms with direct-dial telephone, tea/coffee tray, colour TV and clock radio. We also have some neighbouring cottages available as Hotel annexe rooms or on a self-catering basis. These have been totally refitted, much with "Laura Ashley" decor, and offer quieter, more exclusive accommodation. The hotel has a licensed bar, private car park and bicycle store. Lyndhurst has a charming variety of shops resturants, pubs and bistros and "The New Forest Information Centre and Museum". All major credit cards accepted. **AA/RAC/ETC ◆◆◆◆**
website: www.pennyfarthinghotel.co.uk

MILFORD-ON-SEA (New Forest)

Carolyn and Roy Plummer, Ha' Penny House, 16 Whitby Road, Milford-on-Sea, Lymington SO41 0ND (01590 641210). Ha' Penny House is a delightful character house with a warm, friendly atmosphere. Set in a quiet area of the unspoilt village of Milford-on-Sea and just a few minutes' walk to both sea and village, it is ideally situated for visiting the New Forest, Bournemouth, Salisbury and the Isle of Wight. The comfortable bedrooms are all en suite and beautifully decorated, with TV, hospitality tray and many extra touches. Four course, multi-choice breakfast. Large sunny diningroom and cosy guest lounge. Attractive gardens and summer house. Ample private parking. Three double, one twin. Non-smoking. Bed and Breakfast from £25 to £29 per person per night for double or twin room. Three-night short breaks for two people sharing, including breakfast from £156. Self-catering apartment also available. Open all year. **ETC ◆◆◆◆◆** SILVER AWARD, **AA ◆◆◆◆◆** BREAKFAST AWARD,.
e-mail: info@hapennyhouse.co.uk   **website: www.hapennyhouse.co.uk**

See also Colour Display Advertisement

NEW MILTON

Toad Hall, New Lane, Bashley Cross Road, Bashley, New Milton BH25 5SZ (01425 611951). Welcome to Toad Hall, a period cottage once used as a Mission Hall. Dating back to the 17th century, it is tastefully furnished, with a relaxed, friendly atmosphere. Bashley is situated on the southern fringe of the New Forest, and is home to the 'Sammy Miller Motorcycle Museum'. Forest and links golf courses, superb riding stables, and just the best walking and cycling country, plus the sea – all available within a few minutes. Charming double bedroom offering colour TV/video, tea/coffee making facilities and en suite bathroom. Full English breakfast using local farm produce. Regret, non-smoking. Bed and Breakfast from £25pppn.
e-mail: info@toadhallnewforest.co.uk
website: www.toadhallnewforest.co.uk

PETERSFIELD

Mrs Mary Bray, Nursted Farm, Buriton, Petersfield GU31 5RW (01730 264278). Working farm. This late 17th century farmhouse, with its large garden, is open to guests throughout most of the year. Located quarter-of-a-mile west of the B2146 Petersfield to Chichester road, one-and-a-half-miles south of Petersfield, the house makes an ideal base for touring the scenic Hampshire and West Sussex countryside. Queen Elizabeth Country Park two miles adjoining picturesque village of Buriton at the western end of South Downs Way. Accommodation consists of three twin-bedded rooms (two with washbasin), two bathrooms/toilets; sittingroom/breakfast room. Full central heating. Children welcome, cot provided. Sorry, no pets. Car essential, ample parking adjoining the house. Non- smoking. Bed and Breakfast only from £21 per adult, reductions for children under 12 years. Open all year except Christmas, March and April.

PORTSMOUTH

Graham and Sandra Tubb, "Hamilton House", 95 Victoria Road North, Southsea, Portsmouth PO5 1PS (Tel & Fax: 023 928 23502). Delightful Victorian townhouse B&B, centrally located five minutes by car from Continental and Isle of Wight Ferry Terminals, M27/A27, Stations, City Centres, University, Sea-front, Historic Ships/Museums and all the tourist attractions that Portsmouth, and its resort of Southsea, has to offer. Bright, modern, centrally heated rooms with remote-control colour TV, hairdryer, clock, cooler fan and generous tea/coffee making facilities. Some rooms have en suite facilities. Ideal touring base for southern England. Full English, vegetarian and Continental breakfasts are served in lovely Spanish style dining room. Also Continental breakfasts served from 6am (for early morning travellers). Nightly/weekly stays welcome all year. Bed and Breakfast £23 to £24 per person nightly in standard rooms and £26 to £27 per person in en suite rooms. **ETC/AA** ◆◆◆◆
e-mail: sandra@hamiltonhouse.co.uk   website: www.hamiltonhouse.co.uk

RINGWOOD (New Forest)

Joan and Brian Peck, Old Stacks, 154 Hightown Road, Ringwood BH24 1NP (Tel & Fax: 01425 473840). Joan and Brian warmly welcome you to Old Stacks, their delightful spacious bungalow where home from home hospitality awaits. The twin en suite room with its own garden entrance and patio and the double room with its large private bathroom adjoining have colour TV and tea and coffee facilities and are both attractively decorated and comfortable. Relaxation awaits in their lovely garden and cosy log fires warm the lounge in winter. A country inn is conveniently close by and Ringwood with its weekly Wednesday market and many excellent restaurants and pubs is a mile away. Explore the beautiful New Forest and walk along Bournemouth's sandy beaches, 15 minutes' drive by car. An ideal centre for your holiday. For non-smokers only. Bed and Breakfast from £22 per person. **ETC/AA** ◆◆◆◆
e-mail: oldstacksbandb@aol.com   website: www.SmoothHound.co.uk/hotels/oldstacks.html

ROPLEY

David and Sue Lloyd-Evans, Thickets, Swelling Hill, Ropley, Alresford SO24 0DA (01962 772467). This spacious country house, surrounded by a two acre garden, has fine views across the Hampshire countryside. There are two comfortable twin-bedded rooms with private bath or shower room. Tea/coffee making facilities available. Guests' sitting room with TV. Full English Breakfast. Local attractions include Jane Austen's House, ten minutes by car; Winchester, with its fine cathedral, is 20 minutes away and Salisbury, Chichester and the New Forest are all within easy reach. Heathrow Airport is one hour away. Several good pubs in the area. Restricted smoking. Children welcome from the age of 10 years. Regret, no pets. Open all year, except Christmas and New Year. Bed and Breakfast from £23.

SOUTHAMPTON

Dormy House Hotel, 21 Barnes Lane, Sarisbury/Warsash, Southampton SO31 7DA (01489 572626; Fax: 01489 573370). The Dormy House Hotel is a tranquil Victorian House, set in a quiet residential area, fully modernised and located within half a mile of the River Hamble and Warsash, perfect for all activities on the river. Accommodation consists of a charming dining room, comfortable lounge, twelve tastefully decorated, en suite bedrooms, each with tea/coffee making facilities, direct-dial telephones and remote-control TV. Ground floor bedrooms have access to the attractive and peaceful garden. Fully licensed. Local restaurants offer a broad range of traditional, light or ethnic menus. Easy access to the many attractions along the South Coast, Isle of Wight and the New Forest and within easy reach of Business Parks at Whitely, Segensworth and Hedge End. **AA** ◆◆◆◆

e-mail: dormyhousehotel@warsash.globalnet.co.uk   website: www.dormyhousehotel.net

SOUTHAMPTON

Mrs Rose Pell, Verulam House, 181 Wilton Road, Shirley, Southampton SO15 5HY (023 8077 3293 or 07790 537729). Guests are warmly welcomed to this comfortable, warm, roomy Edwardian establishment, in a nice residential area. Good cuisine. Two twin and one double room (used as singles when necessary) all with TV and tea/coffee making facilities; two bathrooms - plenty of hot water. Car parking space. Five minutes by car to historic Southampton city noted for its parks; railway station 10 minutes. Airport, Cross Channel ferries and Isle of Wight within easy reach and not far from M27, M3, Portsmouth, Winchester, Bournemouth, New Forest and coast. Bed and Breakfast from £24 per person per night. Non-smokers only.

STOCKBRIDGE

Mr and Mrs A.P. Hooper, Carbery Guest House, Stockbridge SO20 6EZ (01264 810771). Ann and Philip Hooper welcome you to Carbery Guest House situated on the A30, just outside the village of Stockbridge, overlooking the famous trout fishing River Test. This fine old Georgian House has one acre of landscaped gardens, with swimming pool. Stonehenge and numerous places of interest nearby; sporting and recreational facilities close at hand. Accommodation includes double, twin, family and single rooms, available with private facilities. Centrally heated with colour TV, tea and coffee making equipment, hair dryers, radio alarms. Cots, high chairs. Car essential, parking. Open January to December for Evening Dinner, Bed and Breakfast or Bed and Breakfast only. Terms on application. **ETC/AA/RAC** ◆◆◆

WICKHAM

Mrs Patricia Toogood, 23 School Road, Wickham, Fareham PO17 5AA (01329 832457). Comfortable and friendly B&B close to picturesque 13th century village with shops, pubs and restaurants. We are four miles from Fareham, 20 minutes from Portsmouth Ferry Port and historic ships. Ideal overnight stop. Accommodation comprises family, double, twin and single rooms; guests' TV lounge. Excellent breakfast which can be served early if required. Free tea and coffee, flasks filled free of charge. No smoking anywhere in the house. Cooling fans in all rooms. Parking available. Deposit required for all bookings. Bed and Breakfast £20 per person per night.

**FREE or REDUCED RATE entry to Holiday Visits and Attractions —
see our READERS' OFFER VOUCHERS on pages 63-90**

WINCHESTER

Mrs S. Buchanan, "Acacia", 44 Kilham Lane, Winchester SO22 5PT (01962 852259; Mobile: 07801 537703). First class Tourist Board inspected accommodation in a peaceful location on the edge of the countryside, yet only a five minute drive from Winchester city centre. Excellent and easy access to road and rail communications to many tourist areas, all within one hour including London (by rail), Portsmouth, the New Forest, Salisbury, Stonehenge, etc. The accommodation consists of two doubles and one twin bedroom, all of which have en suite or private bathroom and tea/coffee making facilities. Charming sitting room with satellite TV. Excellent choice of breakfast. Non-smokers only. Off-street parking. Leave Winchester by the Romsey road, Kilham Lane is right at the second set of traffic lights. "Acacia" is 200 metres on the right. Bed and Breakfast from £54 to £56; single £45. **ETC/AA ◆◆◆◆** *SILVER AWARD*
e-mail: ericbuchanan@btinternet.com   **website: www.btinternet.com/~eric.buchanan**

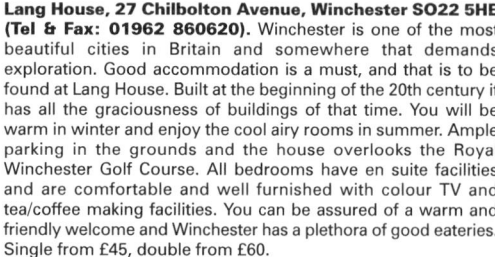

WINCHESTER

Lang House, 27 Chilbolton Avenue, Winchester SO22 5HE (Tel & Fax: 01962 860620). Winchester is one of the most beautiful cities in Britain and somewhere that demands exploration. Good accommodation is a must, and that is to be found at Lang House. Built at the beginning of the 20th century it has all the graciousness of buildings of that time. You will be warm in winter and enjoy the cool airy rooms in summer. Ample parking in the grounds and the house overlooks the Royal Winchester Golf Course. All bedrooms have en suite facilities and are comfortable and well furnished with colour TV and tea/coffee making facilities. You can be assured of a warm and friendly welcome and Winchester has a plethora of good eateries. Single from £45, double from £60.
website: www.langhouse.co.uk

WINCHESTER (near)

Mays Farm, Longwood Dean, Near Winchester SO21 1JS (01962 777486; Fax 01962 777747). Twelve minutes' drive from Winchester, (the eleventh century capital city of England), Mays Farm is set in rolling countryside on a lane which leads from nowhere to nowhere. The house is timber framed, originally built in the sixteenth century and has been thoroughly renovated and extended by its present owners, James and Rosalie Ashby. There are three guest bedrooms, (one double, one twin and one either), each with a private bathroom or shower room. A sitting room with log fire is usually available for guests' use. Ducks, geese, chickens and goats make up the two acre "farm". Prices from £23 per person per night for Bed and Breakfast. Booking is essential. Please telephone or fax for details.

Marwell • *Near Winchester, Hants* • *07626 943163*
website: www.marwell.org.uk
World famous for its dedication to the conservation of endangered species.
Nearly 1000 animals in acres of beautiful parkland.

FHG PUBLICATIONS publish a large range of well-known accommodation guides. We will be happy to send you details or you can use the order form at the back of this book.

HEREFORDSHIRE

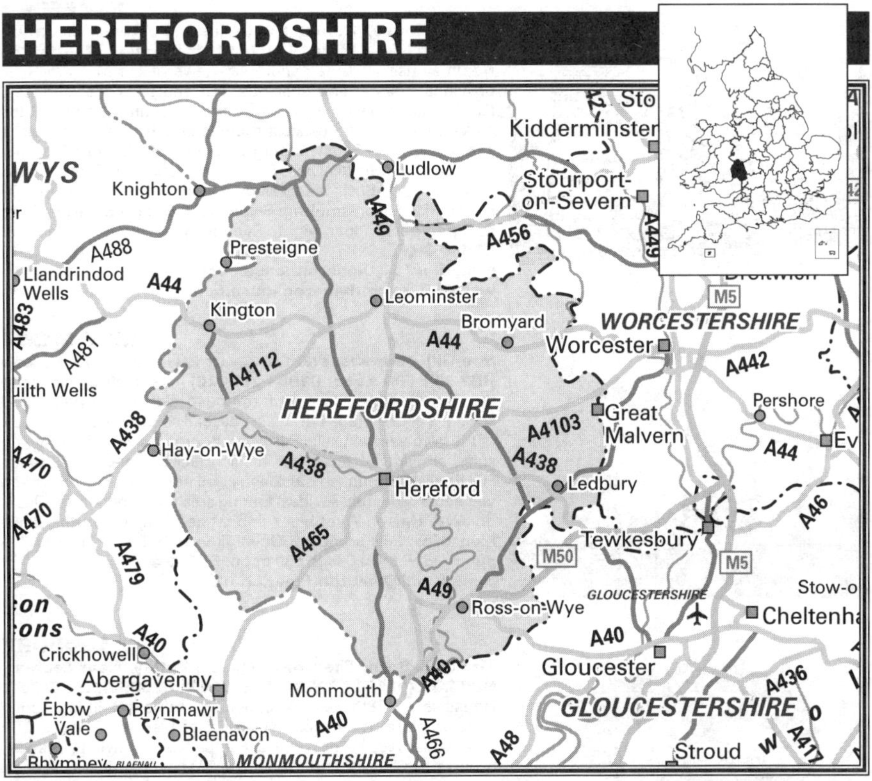

Map showing Herefordshire and surrounding areas including Knighton, Ludlow, Presteigne, Llandrindod Wells, Kington, Leominster, Bromyard, Worcester, Great Malvern, Pershore, Hay-on-Wye, Hereford, Ledbury, Tewkesbury, Ross-on-Wye, Cheltenham, Gloucester, Monmouth, Abergavenny, Stroud, with roads A488, A49, A456, A44, A4112, A438, A4103, A442, A46, A465, A49, A40, A466, A48, A436 and county labels WORCESTERSHIRE, GLOUCESTERSHIRE, MONMOUTHSHIRE.

© MAPS IN MINUTES™ 2003 ©Crown Copyright. Ordnance Survey 2003

GOLDEN VALLEY

Melvin and Joyce Powell, The Old Vicarage, Vowchurch, Hereford HR2 0QD (Tel & Fax: 01981 550357). Described as 'an oasis of care and attention'. A wonderful escape in the Heart of the Golden Valley, where comfort and warm hospitality are guaranteed. Interesting family treasures abound in this one-time home of Lewis Carroll's brother. Attractive rooms to suit everyone's requirements, whether single, twin, double or family (en suite and private bathrooms). We are proud to offer you the finest of local produce - home made bread and preserves too. Why not arrange a small celebratory/surprise party break. Come and Taste the Difference by Experiencing the Special. Go on – be pampered! Bed and Breakfast from £24; Dinners from £16. A non-smoking establishment. Award-winners for creative cooking with local foods. **ETC ◆◆◆◆** *SILVER AWARD.*
website: www.golden-valley.co.uk/vicarage

See also Colour Display Advertisement

HEREFORD

David Jones, Sink Green Farm, Rotherwas, Hereford HR2 6LE (01432 870223). Working farm. A friendly welcome awaits you at our 16th century farmhouse overlooking the picturesque Wye Valley, yet only three miles from Hereford. Our individually decorated en suite rooms, one four-poster, all have tea/coffee facilities, colour TV and central heating. Relax in our extensive garden, complete with summer house and hot tub, or enjoy a stroll by the river. Pets by arrangement; children welcome. Terms from £23 per person. **AA ◆◆◆◆**
e-mail: SinkGreenFarm@msn.com
website: www.sinkgreenfarm.co.uk

HEREFORD

Heron House, Canon Pyon Road, Portway, Burghill, Hereford HR4 8NG (01432 761111; Fax: 01432 760603). Heron House, with its panoramic views of the Malvern Hills, provides friendly and spacious Bed and Breakfast services. Facilities include en suite, family room, vanity units, colour TV, tea making equipment, breakfast room/lounge with stone fireplace and real log fire. Situated four miles north of Hereford in a rural location, this is an ideal base for walking, fishing, golf, cycling and bird-watching. Business facilities available on site. Secure off-road parking. Non-smoking. Bed and full English Breakfast from £20 per person per night. Evening meal by arrangement. **ETC ◆◆◆**
e-mail: info@theheronhouse.com
website: www.theheronhouse.com

KINGSTONE

Mrs Gill Andrews, Webton Court Farmhouse, Kingstone HR2 9NF (Tel & Fax: 01981 250220) An attractive, family-run black and white Georgian farmhouse with comfortable and spacious accommodation, set in peaceful countryside in the heart of the Wye Valley. A selection of bedrooms is available, some en suite, all with TV, tea/coffee making facilities and washbasins. Full English farmhouse breakfast, good home cooking with fresh vegetables and fruit. An ideal touring area for Symonds Yat, Ross-on-Wye, Hay-on-Wye, black and white villages and the Black Mountains. Pets accepted. Open all year. B&B from £18 to £20 pppn. DB&B from £28 to £30 pppn. **ETC ◆◆**
e-mail: gill@webton.fsnet.co.uk

LEDBURY

Mrs S.W. Born, The Coach House, Putley, Near Ledbury HR8 2QP (01531 670684; Fax: 01531 670992). The Coachh House is an 18th century coaching stable set in gorgeous Herefordshire. It lies six miles west of historic Ledbury. The spectacular Wye Valley National Footpath is only five miles away, browse the "Black and White Trail", Malvern Hills or Brecon Beacons. The accommodation comprises double, twin and single rooms all en suite. Guests have their own private lounge with TV, radio and woodburning stove, also the use of an adjacent kitchen. A hearty, full English breakfast is served in the stable dining room. Tariffs are £22pppn double and twin, £27 per night single, reduced by £1.50 pppn for three nights and more.
e-mail: wendyborn@putley-coachhouse.co.uk   **website: www.putley-coachhouse.co.uk**

LEOMINSTER

Rossendale House, 46 Broad Street, Leominster HR6 8BS (01568 612464). This 17th century Listed townhouse in the heart of the charming and historic centre for the Marches is perfectly located amid the famous black and white villages in the foothills of the Welsh mountains. Ideally situated for leisure pursuits in the beautiful surrounding countryside of Herefordshire, Shropshire and Worcestershire and convenient to main travel networks. You will enjoy the friendly hospitality and comforts of home in this curious, ancient house. You will long remember the delicious food prepared from local produce and want to return again and again. Bed and Breakfast from £20. Private parking.
e-mail: enquiries@rossendalehouse.co.uk

LEOMINSTER

Catherine and Marguerite Fothergill, Highfield, Newtown, Ivington Road, Leominster HR6 8QD (01568 613216). Highfield stands in a large garden with unspoilt views of open farmland and distant hills, just one and a half miles from the old market town of Leominster. Accommodation comprises one twin en suite, and one twin and one double room with private facilities, all with radio alarm and tea/coffee making facilities. Guests are requested not to smoke in bedrooms. There are two sitting rooms, one with TV and French windows opening onto the patio, and both with open fires for chillier seasons. Full central heating. Meals are prepared from fresh ingredients, using local produce where possible. Ample parking. Regret no children and no dogs. Prior booking essential. **ETC ◆◆◆◆**

e-mail: info@stay-at-highfield.co.uk   **website: www.stay-at-highfield.co.uk**

The Coach House

ROSS-ON-WYE

Mrs Maggie Adams, Brookfield House, Over Ross Street, Ross-on-Wye HR9 7AT (01989 562188). A Grade II Listed building, part Georgian, part Queen Ann house, which has been recently refurbished to a high standard by the new owners. Accommodation comprises large, tastefully decorated en suite rooms with king-size beds, colour TV and hospitality trays. All rooms are non-smoking. Within an easy stroll of the centre of Ross-on-Wye but with the advantage of a large private car park. Price includes Full English Breakfast with a Vegetarian option. Bed and Breakfast £24.50 pppn (double or twin).

ROSS-ON-WYE

Mrs H. Smith, Old Kilns, Howle Hill, Ross-on-Wye HR9 5SP (Tel & Fax 01989 562051). A high quality bed and breakfast establishment in picturesque, quiet village location. Centrally heated, private parking. Some rooms with super king-size bed plus en suite shower, toilet; also brass king-size four-poster bed with private bathroom and jacuzzi. Colour TV and tea/coffee making facilities in bedrooms. Lounge with log fire. Full English breakfast. Central for touring Cotswolds, Malvern, Stratford-upon-Avon, Wye Valley and Royal Forest of Dean. Open all year. Bed and Breakfast from £20 per person. Children and pets welcome (high chair, cots and babysitting service provided). Please telephone for free brochure. Self-catering cottages also available sleeping 2–14 with four-poster beds and jacuzzi. **AA/RAC** ◆◆◆, *SPARKLING DIAMOND AWARD.*

HERTFORDSHIRE

RICKMANSWORTH

Mrs Elizabeth Childerhouse, Tall Trees, 6 Swallow Close, Nightingale Road, Rickmansworth WD3 7DZ (01923 720069). Large detached house situated in a quiet cul-de-sac with the centre of Rickmansworth only a short walk away. It is a small picturesque old town where there are many places to eat. We are five minutes' walk from the Underground station, half-an-hour to central London. Full breakfast served with homemade bread and preserves. Vegetarians and coeliacs catered for. Tea and coffee making facilities in rooms. Off-street parking. Convenient for M25 and Watford. No pets. This is a non-smoking household. Bed and Breakfast from £28.

WATFORD

Grove End Hotel, 73 Bushey Hall Road, Bushey, Watford WD23 2EN (01923 226798; Fax: 01923 210877). Situated in an acre of lovely gardens, this small, welcoming, family-run establishment has been in business for the past 35 years. It has 29 rooms to suit most people's pockets and taste, from basic single rooms to family rooms through to en suite. All rooms have satellite TV, washhand basin, and tea making facilities. En suite rooms also have shower, toilet, hairdryer, direct-dial phone and radio alarm. All rooms include a full English cooked buffet breakfast. There is a small bar, open from Monday to Thursday, which serves bar food from a varied menu. Weekend stays on a Bed and Breakfast basis only.
e-mail: grove.end@ntlworld.com
website: www.groveendhotel.co.uk

ISLE OF WIGHT

CARISBROOKE

Mrs V.A. Skeats, The Mount, 1 Calbourne Road, Carisbrooke, Near Newport PO30 5AP (01983 522173/524359). "The Mount" is superbly situated in the charming village of Carisbrooke, overlooking Carisbrooke Castle. Ideally located for all amenities. Delightful lanes and downs for walking. Information/requirements of maps and details on local activities can be provided. Rooms are comfortably furnished with washbasins/razor points. Own keys. Private car park. Lock-up cycle shelter. Children welcome. We offer homely accommodation in a Victorian house with personal service. Bed and Breakfast from £16. Reductions for children. Any day bookings accepted. For further details, please write or telephone.

CHALE

Mrs Whittington, Cortina, Gotten Lane, Chale PO38 2HQ (01983 551292). Cortina is ideally situated in country surroundings on the south side of the island with lovely views, one mile from the coast road. We offer home cooking and all rooms have hot and cold water and colour TV. There is a large garden and space for car parking. Mid-week bookings are acceptable and we can assure you of a warm welcome.

TOTLAND BAY

Sandy Lane Guest House, Colwell Common Road, Totland Bay PO39 0DD (Tel & Fax: 01983 752240). Enjoy the comfort and friendly atmosphere of our family-run Bed and Breakfast. All the bedrooms are comfortably furnished and offer colour TV and tea and coffee making facilities. All rooms are en suite. We offer a varied breakfast menu using local produce. Sandy Lane has a large garden with a pleasant aspect. There is ample parking on the quiet road outside the house. Four minutes walk from safe sandy beach; selection of pubs and restaurants within walking distance.
ETC ◆◆◆◆
e-mail: jane@sandylaneguesthouse.fsnet.co.uk

KENT

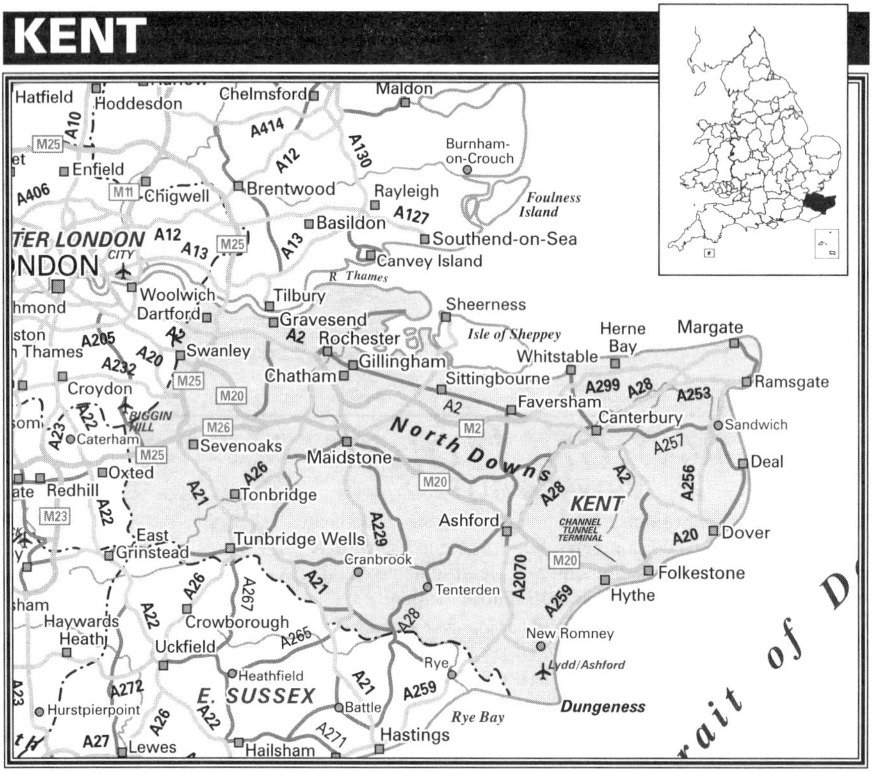

(Map of Kent showing towns including Chelmsford, Maldon, Brentwood, Basildon, Southend-on-Sea, Tilbury, Gravesend, Rochester, Gillingham, Chatham, Sittingbourne, Faversham, Canterbury, Margate, Ramsgate, Sandwich, Deal, Dover, Folkestone, Hythe, New Romney, Ashford, Maidstone, Tonbridge, Tunbridge Wells, Cranbrook, Tenterden, and bordering areas of E. Sussex and Greater London.)

ASHFORD

Mrs Janet Feakins, Old Farm House, Soakham Farm, Whitehill, Bilting, Ashford TN25 4HB (01233 813509). Soakham is a working farm situated on the North Downs Way between Boughton Aluph and Chilham and adjoining Challock Forest. It is ideally located both for walking and visiting many places in the South East area. Canterbury and Ashford are ten miles and five miles respectively. The farmhouse was originally a Hall House and Grade II Listed with much exposed woodwork. It offers the following accommodation; two double rooms including one with a four-poster bed and a twin-bedded room. Prices are from £20 per person for Bed and Breakfast. Ample parking is available and we are open all year round.

ASHFORD

Mrs Veronica Johnson, Yew Tree Cottage, Pluckley, Ashford TN27 0QS (01233 840547). Fifteenth century Kentish Hall House hiding within a Georgian exterior in attractive village location overlooking the Weald of Kent. Excellent for exploring the varied scenery and many places of interest in the 'Garden of England'. Within easy reach of Channel Tunnel, Port of Dover and coast. Many footpaths, including Greensand Way. Several good pubs locally serving a range of excellent food. Two spacious double rooms one with private bathroom and one with en suite shower room. Tea and coffee making facilities. Off-road parking. Sorry, no smoking or pets. Bed and Breakfast from £21. Open April to September inclusive.

ENGLAND

BROADSTAIRS
Hanson Hotel (Lic.), 41 Belvedere Road, Broadstairs CT10 1PF (01843 868936). A small friendly Georgian hotel with relaxed atmosphere, centrally situated for beach, shops and transport. Most rooms are en suite. Renowned for excellent food, we offer Bed and Breakfast only or, a five course Evening Dinner with a choice of menu. Children and pets welcome. Open all year. Spring and winter breaks available. Telephone for brochure to **Trevor and Jean Webb.**

BROADSTAIRS
Keston Court Hotel, 14 Ramsgate Road, Broadstairs CT10 1PS (01843 862401). The Keston Court is a small hotel of charm and character, with friendly service and a homely atmosphere. It is only five minutes' walk to the shops and beach. Parking is free, and our licensed bar will cater for all your needs. All rooms have tea/coffee making appliances, also colour TV. The hotel holds a full fire certificate. Central heating in all rooms. Adults only. Closed during winter months. Room tariff (per night): single £19, standard double or twin £38, twin with shower £42, en suite double £44.
e-mail: kestoncourt@tinyonline.co.uk
website: www.SmoothHound.co.uk/hotels.html

CANTERBURY
Mrs Prudence Latham, Tenterden House, The Street, Boughton, Faversham ME13 9BL (01227 751593). Stay in one of the en suite bedrooms (one double, one twin) in this delightful gardener's cottage and stroll through the shrubbery to the 16th century diningroom, in the main house, for a traditional English breakfast, beneath the Dragon Beam. Close to Canterbury, Whitstable and the Channel Ports. It makes an ideal base for exploring Kent, then walk to one of the historic inns in the village for your evening meal. Tea/coffee making facilities. Off-road parking. Open all year. Bed and Breakfast from £23 per person.

CANTERBURY
Mrs Lewana Castle, Great Field Farm, Misling Lane, Stelling Minnis, Canterbury CT4 6DE (01227 709223). Situated in beautiful countryside, our spacious farmhouse is about eight miles from Canterbury and Folkestone, 12 miles from Dover and Ashford. We are a working farm with some livestock, including friendly ponies and chickens. We provide a friendly and high standard of accommodation with full central heating and double glazing, traditional breakfasts cooked on the Aga, courtesy tray and colour TV in each of our suites/bedrooms. Our annexe suite has private staircase, lounge, kitchen, double bedroom and bathroom, also available for self-catering holidays. Our cottage suite has its own entrance stairs, lounge, bathroom and twin-bedded room. Our large double/family bedroom has en suite bathroom with airbath. There is ample off road parking and good pub food nearby. Bed and Breakfast from £25 per person, reductions for children. Non-smoking establishment. **ETC** ♦♦♦ *SILVER AWARD.*

CANTERBURY
Frances Mount, South Wootton House, Capel Road, Petham, Canterbury CT4 5RG (01227 700643; Fax: 01227 700613). A beautiful farmhouse with conservatory set in extensive garden, surrounded by fields and woodland. Fully co-ordinated bedroom with private bathroom. Tea/coffee facilities, colour TV. Children welcome. Canterbury four miles. Non-smoking. Bed and Breakfast from £25. Open all year. **ETC** ♦♦♦

CANTERBURY

Mr and Mrs R. Linch, Upper Ansdore, Duckpit Lane, Petham, Canterbury CT4 5QB (01227 700672; Fax: 01227 700840). Beautiful secluded Listed Tudor farmhouse with various livestock, situated in an elevated position with far-reaching views of the wooded countryside of the North Downs. The property overlooks a Kent Trust Nature Reserve, is five miles south of the cathedral city of Canterbury and only 30 minutes' drive to the ports of Dover and Folkestone. The accommodation comprises one family, three double and one twin-bedded rooms. All have shower and WC en suite and tea making facilities. Dining/sitting room, heavily beamed with large inglenook. Pets welcome. Car essential. Bed and Breakfast from £22.50 per person. Credit cards accepted. **ETC** ◆◆◆

e-mail: roger@ansdore.fsnet.co.uk   website: www.SmoothHound.co.uk/hotels/upperans.html

CANTERBURY

Maria and Alistair Wilson, Chaucer Lodge Guest House, 62 New Dover Road, Canterbury CT1 3DT (01227 459141). A highly recommended friendly guest house which is elegantly decorated and immaculately clean. Fully double glazed and centrally heated. Secure parking. Seven bedrooms en suite, including family rooms, with colour TV, tea/coffee making facilities, radio/alarm and hairdryer. Open all year round. 10 minutes' walk to city centre, cathedral, bus and rail stations. Hospital and cricket ground only five minutes' walk. Ideal base for touring Kent and for trips to the Continent. Bed and Breakfast from £19 per person.

DEAL

Sutherland House Hotel, 186 London Road, Deal CT14 9PT (01304 362853; Fax: 01304 381146). Situated on the A258 Deal to Sandwich Road, 200 yards from the Deal Hospital. This stylish hotel offers charming bedrooms which are decorated and furnished with great style and taste. The yellow and blue dining room provides a charming venue for home cooked dinners and breakfasts and guests have the use of a comfortable lounge well stocked with books and magazines. Four en suite non-smoking bedrooms. No smoking area in diningroom. TV, tea/coffee facilities and direct dial telephone in bedrooms. Licensed. Central heating. Sorry, no children under five years. Parking. Bed and Breakfast from £45 to £47 per night single occupancy of a double room, £57 to £60 per night double. Major Credit Cards accepted. **AA** ◆◆◆◆◆

e-mail: info@sutherlandhouse.fsnet.co.uk   website: www.sutherlandhousehotel.co.uk

See also Colour Display Advertisement

DOVER

Penny Farthing Guest House, 109 Maison Dieu Road, Dover CT16 1RT (01304 205563; Fax: 01304 204439). Close to docks and town centre, the A2, the A20 and only ten minutes from the Channel Tunnel. Impressive Victorian house with spacious en suite accommodation offering extra facilities. Choice of breakfast, early starters catered for. Penny Farthing is an excellent base for touring Kent and ideal for the one night ferry client or the cruise passenger. Our house is non-smoking.

e-mail: pennyfarthingdover@btinternet.com
website: www.pennyfarthingdover.com

BLERIOT'S - DOVER

A Victorian residence set in a tree-lined avenue, in the lee of Dover Castle. Within easy reach of trains, bus station, town centre, hoverport and docks. Channel Tunnel approximately 10 minutes' drive. Off-road parking. We specialise in one night 'stop-overs' and mini-breaks. Single, double, twin and family rooms with full en suite. All rooms have colour TV, tea and coffee making facilities, and are fully centrally heated. Full English breakfast served from 7am. Reduced rates for room only. Open all year. *MasterCard & Visa Accepted* ETC ◆◆◆

Rates: Bed and Breakfast: £23.00 to £26.00 per person per night.
Mini-Breaks January to April and October to December £20.00 per person per night.

47 Park Avenue, Dover, Kent CT16 1HE Tel: (01304) 211394

DOVER

St Mark's Guest House, 23 Castle Street, Dover CT16 1PT (01304 201894). St Mark's Guest House in White Cliffs country is within sight of the famous Dover Castle and in walking distance of the ferry port and town centre with all its shops and cosmopolitan restaurants. Fifteen minutes' drive from the Channel Tunnel. We offer a comprehensive range of facilities. Most rooms are en suite and all have showers and washbasins. All rooms have tea/coffee making facilities, TV and are clean, comfortable and centrally heated. We offer an excellent English breakfast and cater for vegetarians. Bed and Breakfast from £18 to £27 pppn. Family rooms available.

DOVER

Alkham Court, Meggett Lane, South Alkham, Near Dover CT15 7DG (01303 892056). Peaceful location in an Area of Outstanding Natural Beauty overlooking the Alkham Valley, with ponies and sheep on our farm, and a homely atmosphere. Hearty English breakfasts with local produce served in our conservatory dining room which enjoys spectacular views. Excellent accommodation comprising double/family room with en suite facilities, and double room with private bathroom. Ground floor rooms with antique furniture and private entrance. Ideal touring base; Dover Castle and White Cliffs nearby; 10 minutes from Eurotunnel and ferries, 20 minutes Canterbury. ETC ◆◆◆◆
e-mail: wendy.burrows@alkhamcourt.co.uk
website: www.alkhamcourt.co.uk

See also Colour Display Advertisement

FOLKESTONE

Duncan and Alison Taylor, Bolden's Wood, Fiddling Lane, Stowting, Near Ashford TN25 6AP (Tel & Fax: 01303 812011). Between Ashford/Folkestone. Friendly atmosphere, modern accommodation (one double/twin, two singles) on our smallholding, set in unspoilt countryside. Non-smoking throughout. Log-burning stove in TV lounge. Full English breakfast. Country pubs (meals) nearby. Children love the old-fashioned farmyard, free range chickens, friendly sheep and...Llamas, Alpacas and Rheas! Treat yourself to a Llama-led picnic trek to our private secluded woodland and downland, and enjoy watching the bird life, rabbits, foxes, badgers and occasionally deer. You could round off your trip booking a short sightseeing or fishing trip on our Folkestone fishing boat! Easy access to Channel Tunnel and Ferry Ports. Bed and Breakfast £23 per person.
e-mail: StayoverNight@aol.com
website: www.countrypicnics.com

FOLKESTONE

Mr and Mrs M. Sapsford, Wycliffe Hotel, 63 Bouverie Road West, Folkestone CT20 2RN (Tel & Fax: 01303 252186). However long, or short, your stay, a warm welcome is guaranteed at our friendly, family hotel offering clean, comfortable and affordable accommodation. We are based centrally and are close to all amenities. Our menu is interesting and varied, and guests have their own keys for freedom of access at all times. If you are travelling to or from the Continent we can offer an ideal stopover as we are conveniently situated just a short distance from the Channel Tunnel and Folkestone is an easy drive from the port of Dover. Off-street parking. Pets and children welcome - family rooms available. All major credit cards accepted. Bed and Breakfast from £22.50, Evening Meal £14. Discount for four or more nights. Please write or call for our brochure.

e-mail: sapsford@wycliffhotel.freeserve.co.uk   website: www.wycliffehotel.com

HEADCORN

Mrs Dorothy Burbridge, Waterkant Guest House, Moat Road, Headcorn, Ashford TN27 9NT (01622 890154). Waterkant is a small guest house situated in tranquil Wealdon Village of olde worlde charm. A warm and friendly welcome is assured and the relaxed and informal atmosphere is complemented by fine cuisine, excellent service and comfortable surroundings. Bedrooms have private or en suite bathrooms, four-poster beds, tea/coffee making facilities, colour TV and are centrally heated and double glazed. Lounge with colour TV. The beautifully landscaped secluded garden bounded by a stream provides a large pond, summerhouse for visitors' use and ample parking. Fast trains to London and a wealth of historic places to visit nearby. Open all year. Visitors return year after year. Bed and Breakfast from £20, with reduced rates for children, Senior Citizens, mid-week and winter season bookings, and referrals from FHG. Participants in ETC's Quality Assurance schemes.

MAIDSTONE

Mrs Clifford, Langley Oast, Langley Park, Langley, Maidstone ME17 3NQ (01622 863523). Langley Oast was built in 1873 as part of Langley Park Farm, which was owned at that time by "Fremlins", the local brewery. The farm was a working farm until 1985 when the farm buildings were sold for conversion to homes. Langley Park, as it is now known, forms a secluded hamlet of about twelve homes, a quarter of a mile from the main road, the A274, about two miles from the centre of Maidstone and two miles from Leeds Castle. The Oast is set in the heart of Kentish countryside with fields as far as the eye can see, with a lake at the bottom of the nearest field. Maidstone is the county town of Kent and an ideal touring base for London or to visit the many tourist attractions in Kent. Or as a 'Stop Over' to or from the Continent, we are only 35 minutes from Folkestone and Dover. The Oast has been luxuriously converted by its present owners, Peter and Margaret Clifford. Bedrooms are either in the large Roundel rooms (24 ft across), one with jacuzzi en suite, or in twin rooms with Half Tester Canopies. Peter and Margaret look forward to welcoming you and will do everything in their power to ensure that your stay will be a happy and enjoyable one. Single room from £30, twin room from £45, Double round room from £65 to £75. **AA** ◆◆◆◆, *MEMBER SOUTH EAST ENGLAND TOURIST BOARD.*

See also Colour Display Advertisement

MARGATE

Malvern Hotel, Eastern Esplanade, Cliftonville, Margate CT9 2HL (Tel & Fax: 01843 290192). Small seafront private hotel, ideally situated within easy reach of Dover, Folkestone, Channel Tunnel and Canterbury. En suite facilities and TV in all rooms. TV lounge, tea/coffee making facilities, telephone, ironing facilities & hairdryer. Licensed bar and themed restaurant; special diets catered for. Non-smoking facilities. Conference facilities. Parking. Credit cards accepted. Children welcome.

e-mail: themalvern@aol.com
website: www.malvern-hotel.co.uk

TENTERDEN/BIDDENDEN

Mrs Susan Twort, Heron Cottage, Biddenden, Ashford TN27 8HH (01580 291358). Peacefully situated in own grounds of six acres amidst acres of arable farmland, boasting many wild animals and birds, a stream and pond for coarse fishing. Within easy reach of Leeds Castle and many National Trust Properties including Sissinghurst Castle. You can choose between five tastefully furnished rooms with en suite and TV, or two rooms with separate bathroom. All rooms are centrally heated and have tea/coffee making facilities. There is a residents' lounge with log fire. Evening meals by arrangement. Bed and Breakfast from £20 to £25 per person per night.

TUNBRIDGE WELLS

Number Ten, 10 Modest Corner, Southborough, Tunbridge Wells TN4 0LS (Tel & Fax: 01892 522450). Traditional Bed and Breakfast accommodation in a lovely, tranquil hamlet, yet within easy reach of the M25, and one hour from Dover. Tastefully decorated, with comfortable beds, friendly hospitality and a homely atmosphere. One double room en suite and two twin rooms (two bedrooms and bathroom on ground floor), all well equipped, with colour TV, tea/coffee making facilities and individually controlled central heating; bathrooms with power showers. Excellent full English or Continental breakfast. Evening Meals by prior arrangement; excellent restaurants and pubs nearby. Well situated for walking and visiting National Trust and English Heritage properties. Children and dogs welcome. Restricted smoking policy. **ETC ◆◆◆**

e-mail: modestanneke@lineone.net

website: www.s-h-systems.co.uk/hotels/numberten.html

• • *Some Useful Guidance for Guests and Hosts* • •

Every year literally thousands of holidays, short breaks and overnight stops are arranged through our guides, the vast majority without any problems at all. In a handful of cases, however, difficulties do arise about bookings, which often could have been prevented from the outset.

It is important to remember that when accommodation has been booked, both parties – guests and hosts – have entered into a form of contract. We hope that the following points will provide helpful guidance.

GUESTS:

- When enquiring about accommodation, be as precise as possible. Give exact dates, numbers in your party and the ages of any children.
- State the number and type of rooms wanted and also what catering you require – bed and breakfast, full board etc. Make sure that the position about evening meals is clear – and about pets, reductions for children or any other special points.
- Read our reviews carefully to ensure that the proprietors you are going to contact can supply what you want. Ask for a letter confirming all arrangements, if possible.
- If you have to cancel, do so as soon as possible. Proprietors do have the right to retain deposits and under certain circumstances to charge for cancelled holidays if adequate notice is not given and they cannot re-let the accommodation.

HOSTS:

- Give details about your facilities and about any special conditions. Explain your deposit system clearly and arrangements for cancellations, charges etc. and whether or not your terms include VAT.
- If for any reason you are unable to fulfil an agreed booking without adequate notice, you may be under an obligation to arrange suitable alternative accommodation or to make some form of compensation.

While every effort is made to ensure accuracy, we regret that FHG Publications cannot accept responsibility for errors, omissions or misrepresentations in our entries or any consequences thereof. Prices in particular should be checked because we go to press early. We will follow up complaints but cannot act as arbiters or agents for either party.

LANCASHIRE

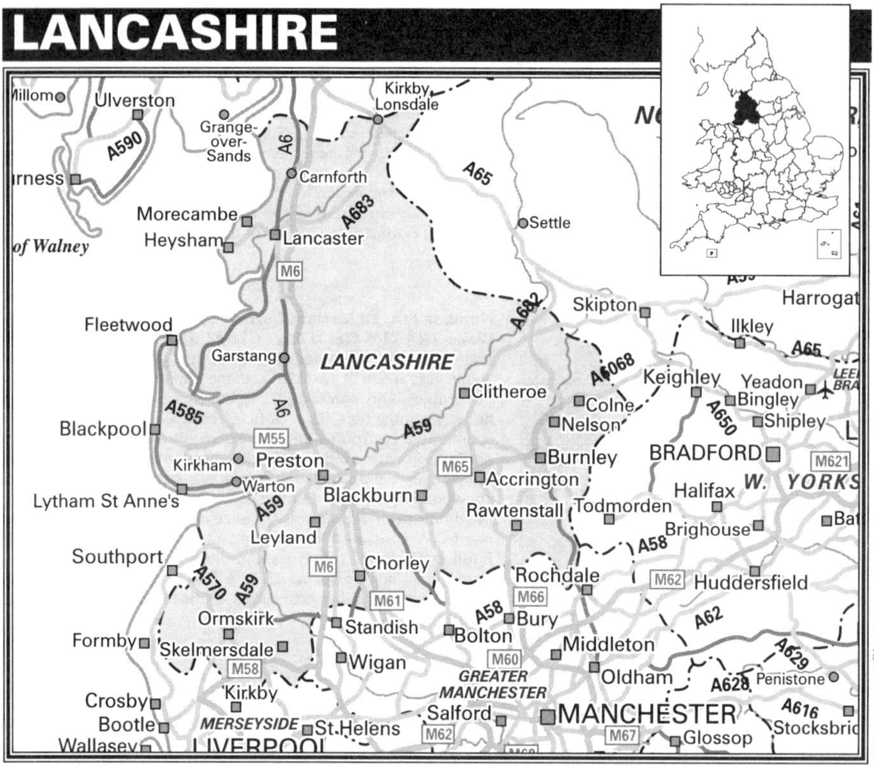

Millom ○ Ulverston
Grange-over-Sands
A590
A6
ness
of Walney
Morecambe
Heysham
Lancaster
M6
Carnforth
A683
Kirkby Lonsdale
A65
Settle
Skipton
Ilkley
A65
Harrogat

Fleetwood
Garstang ○
LANCASHIRE
Clitheroe
Colne
Nelson
Keighley
Yeadon
Bingley
Shipley
A6068
A650

Blackpool
A585
A6
M55
Kirkham ○
Warton
Preston
A59
M65
Burnley
Accrington
BRADFORD
M621
W. YORKS
Halifax
Lytham St Anne's
Blackburn
A59
Rawtenstall
Todmorden
Brighouse
Bat
A58

Southport
A570
A59
M6
Chorley
Leyland
Rochdale
M62 Huddersfield
M66
A58
Bury
A62
Ormskirk
Standish
Bolton
Middleton
Oldham
A629
Penistone ○
Formby
Skelmersdale
M58
Wigan
M60
GREATER MANCHESTER
A628
A616
Crosby
Kirkby
MERSEYSIDE St.Helens
Salford
MANCHESTER
Stocksbrid
Bootle
M62
M67
Glossop
Wallasey
LIVERPOOL

BLACKBURN (near)

The Brown Leaves Country Hotel, Longsight Road, Copster Green, Near Blackburn BB1 9EU (01254 249523; Fax: 01254 245240). Family-run hotel conveniently situated on the A59 about halfway between Preston and Clitheroe, five miles from Junction 31 on the M6 in the beautiful Ribble Valley. Twelve well-furnished, individually designed en suite bedrooms, all on the ground floor, with TV, tea/coffee making facilities, hairdryer and trouser press. Guests' lounge and bar lounge. Full English breakfast is served in the spacious dining room using only the finest local produce, Evening Meals optional. Car parking facilities. Pets by arrangement. Winner of 1998 Casserole Award and 1998 House-keeping Award. All credit cards welcome.
website: www.brownleavescountryhotel.co.uk

See also Colour Display Advertisement

BLACKPOOL

Elsie and Ron Platt, Sunnyside and Holmsdale Hotel, 25-27 High Street, North Shore, Blackpool FY1 2BN (01253 623781). Two minutes from North Station, five minutes from Promenade, all shows and amenities. Colour TV lounge. Full central heating. No smoking. Children welcome; cots available. Reductions for children sharing. Senior Citizens' reductions May and June, always welcome. Special diets catered for, good food and warm friendly atmosphere awaits you. Bed and Breakfast from £18. Morning tea available. Overnight guests welcome when available. Small parties catered for.
e-mail: elsieandron@amserve.net

The Birchley Hotel

64 HOLMFIELD ROAD, NORTH SHORE, BLACKPOOL FY2 9RT
YVONNE AND ALAN JONES ~ TEL: 01253 354174

The Birchley is situated in a pleasant, select North Shore area adjacent to Queens Promenade. Open most of the year and totally non-smoking. Seven bedrooms, all en suite, tea and coffee tray, colour TV and central heating, lounge area, separate dining tables and a small licensed bar for residents' use. Stair lift. Full English or light breakfast, optional 3 course evening dinner with choice of menu, excellent food and generous portions. Bed and Breakfast from £18 per person per night.
H.O.A.S.T. Silver Award. Blackpool Private Hotels Association. Visit our website for full details.

e-mail: alan123@lineone.net   **website: www.birchley.com**

BLACKPOOL

Brabyns Hotel, Shaftesbury Avenue, Blackpool FY2 9QQ (01253 354263). The Brabyns Hotel, is a well maintained private hotel. Situated just off Queens Promenade, close to the cliffs in the quiet North Shore area of Blackpool, but still conveniently placed for visiting the famous Blackpool attractions i.e. Tower, Pleasure Beach, live shows, night clubs and the famous Blackpool Illuminations. Within a 10 mile radius of the hotel is a choice of nine golf courses, including the renowned Royal Lytham St Annes. An ideal base for touring the rural Fylde coast, English Lakes and Yorkshire Dales. Comfortable, friendly hotel with 22 tastefully decorated bedrooms all with en suite facilities, direct-dial telephones, hairdryers, tea/coffee making facilities, colour TV. Licensed. Free car parking and open all year. Bed and Breakfast from £25. **ETC/AA/RAC ★★**

BLACKPOOL

Castlemere Hotel, 13 Shaftesbury Avenue, North Shore, Blackpool FY2 9QQ (Tel & Fax: 01253 352430). Licensed, family-run hotel run for the past twelve years by resident proprietors Dave and Sue Hayward, who have established an excellent clientele. Situated in the very pleasant North Shore area of Blackpool, adjacent to the delightful Queen's Promenade with lovely views across the Irish Sea. The busy town centre, bus and train stations are convenient and a range of entertainment opportunities including a Casino and Golf Course, are within an easy walk or a short tram ride. Ideally situated for visiting the Dales, Lake District, "Bronte" Country and the Fylde Coast. Easy access to M55. All rooms en suite with central heating, colour TV, alarm clock radios, tea-making facilities and hairdryers. Ironing facilities are also available. Cosy bar, where evening snacks are available. Evening Dinner is optional. Open all year. Car Park. All major credit cards accepted. Terms from £25 per day per person, Bed & Breakfast. **AA ◆◆◆**, *FHG DIPLOMA WINNER, WELCOME HOST, WELCOME TO EXCELLENCE.*
e-mail: bookings@hotelcastlemere.co.uk   or   sue@hotelcastlemere.co.uk
website: www.hotelcastlemere.co.uk

National Football Museum • *Preston, Lancashire•* 01772 908442
www.nationalfootballmuseum.com
The story of the world's greatest game. In two distinctive halves, it can be enjoyed by supprters of all ages. Shop and restaurant.

CARNFORTH

Mrs Melanie Smith, Capernwray House, Capernwray, Carnforth LA6 1AE (01524 732363). Situated in the Lower Lunesdale Valley on the North Lancashire and Cumbria borders (M6 Junction 35, off B6254) where the peace and solitude of the countryside are yours to enjoy. The house is beautifully furnished to ensure a delightful and comfortable stay for the non-smoking guest. Centrally heated en suite bedrooms with tea/coffee facilities, TV, shoe cleaning, clock radio and hair dryer. Panoramic views can be enjoyed over the Cumbrian or Pennine Hills. Superb location in eighteen acres of rolling countryside, ideal for the coast, Lakes, Dales, Lancaster bird reserves, historic houses, steam railways or a break en route London-Scotland. Spacious lounge. Ample parking. Sorry, no pets. Bed and Breakfast from £25 single, £48 double en suite and £50 twin en suite; Dinner £12.50. Open all year. Brochure available. Also small select touring caravan park. All major credit cards accepted. **ETC ◆◆◆◆** *SILVER AWARD, FHG DIPLOMA WINNER.*
e-mail: thesmiths@capernwrayhouse.com   **website: www.capernwrayhouse.com**

CHORLEY

Mrs Val Hilton, Jepsons Farm, Moor Road, Anglezarke, Chorley PR6 9DQ (01257 481691). Jepsons Farm, formerly a 17th century inn, is a stone built farmhouse with oak beams and wood burning stoves and is situated in Anglezarke, next to Rivington in the West Pennine Moors. Non-working farm apart from horses. It boasts excellent views and is surrounded by beautiful countryside for all outdoor activities including riding, walking, climbing, abseiling, cycling and fishing or simply relaxing. Good food assured and bedrooms have colour TV and tea/coffee trays; en suite facilities. Accommodation for horses in spacious looseboxes; bridleways in abundance for all riding requirements. Places of interest include Wigan Pier, Martin Mere, Astley Hall, Camelot and coastal resorts of Blackpool and Southport. Bed and Breakfast from £25; Evening Meal from £7.50. Reductions for children. Special rates for longer stays.

CLITHEROE

Mrs Margaret A. Berry, Lower Standen Farm, Whalley Road, Clitheroe BB7 1PP (01200 424176; mobile: 07905 458138). This farmhouse is situated 20 minutes' walk from town centre, one mile from A59 road. Convenient for M6, 20 minutes' drive from Junction 31. There are two double rooms en suite, one twin-bedded room with washbasin only and an additional single room if required. TV and tea/coffee making facilities; cot also available. Own lounge with electric fire and TV; dining room. Full central heating. Pets and children are welcome, reduced rates for children under 12 years. Open all year except Christmas and New Year. Golf club nearby. Bed and Breakfast from £18.50 per person, £22 in en suite room.

CLITHEROE (near)

Mrs Marje Adderley, Rose Cottage, Longsight Road (A59), Clayton-le-Dale, Ribble Valley BB1 9EX (01254 813223; Fax: 01254 813831). A warm welcome awaits at our picturesque cottage situated at the gateway to the Ribble Valley, five miles from M6 and M65 on A59. Excellent night-stop travelling to and from Scotland, easy access to Yorkshire Dales, Lake District and Blackpool. Full English breakfast included in price; single occupancy from £28 to £32, double £23pp. Weekend breaks, shared occupancy: two nights £42pp; three nights £64pp. Stay seven nights, pay only for six nights. Comfortable well equipped rooms offering tea/coffee, TV, radio alarm, heated towel rail, hair dryer, shoe cleaning, smoke detectors; all have private facilities. Phone for our brochure. Nearby Ribbleway, cycling, walking, fishing. Trace your family at Records Office, Preston. Major credit cards accepted.
e-mail: bbrose.cott@talk21.co.uk   **website: www.SmoothHound.co.uk/hotels/rosecott.html**

Bell Farm Bradshaw Lane, Scronkey, Pilling, Preston PR3 6SN. Tel: 01253 790324

Beryl and Peter welcome you to their 18th century farmhouse situated in the quiet village of Pilling, which lies between the Ribble and Lune Estuaries. The area has many public footpaths and is ideal for cycling. From the farm there is easy access to Blackpool, Lancaster, the Forest of Bowland and the Lake District. Accommodation consists of one family room, one double and one twin; all rooms en suite. Tea and coffee making facilities. Lounge and dining room. All centrally heated. Children and pets welcome. Full English Breakfast is served. Open all year, except Christmas and New Year. Bed and Breakfast from £22.50.

LANCASTER

Roy and Helen Domville, Three Gables, Chapel Lane, Galgate, Lancaster LA2 0PN (01524 752222). A large detached bungalow, three miles south of Lancaster and 400 yards from Lancaster University. Access from M6 Junction 33 and A6 in Galgate village. Two double bedrooms each with shower, toilet, colour TV and tea/coffee making facilities. One bedroom also has a private TV lounge. Open all year with full central heating. Spacious parking. A good location for visiting Blackpool, Morecambe, the Lake District and Yorkshire Dales. You will be sure of a friendly welcome and a homely atmosphere. Sorry, no pets. Non-smokers only please. Bed and Breakfast £20 per person.

LANCASTER/KENDAL

Mrs Jean Scrase, The Old Police Station, 6 Dykes Lane, Yealand Conyers, Carnforth LA5 9SP (01524 735142). Bed and Breakfast in a genuine Victorian Police Station in a small village on the North Lancashire/Cumbria borders. The house has magnificent views onto the Lakeland Fells and Pennine Hills. It is ideally situated for the RSPB at Leighton Moss and Silverdale. The Lake District and Yorkshire Dales are a short drive away. The village has ancient woods, hills and the Lancaster Canal on its doorstep. Two miles from Junction 35 on M6, off A6. En suite twin room, central heating, tea/coffee facilities and parking. English breakfast with home made bread and preserves. Vegetarian food, packed lunches available on request. Why not stop over en route to or from Scotland! From £20 per person. Regret no pets.

See also Colour Display Advertisement

MORECAMBE

Mrs R. Holdsworth, Broadwater Hotel, 356 Marine Road, East Promenade, Morecambe LA4 5AQ (01524 411333). The Broadwater is a small friendly hotel, situated on the select East Promenade with glorious views of Morecambe Bay and Lakeland Mountains. Only five minutes' walk from the town centre, shops and amusements. We offer every comfort and the very best of foods, varied and plentiful with choice of menu. All rooms en suite with heating, colour TV and tea making facilities. A perfect base for touring, the Broadwater is only 45 minutes' drive away from Blackpool, Yorkshire Dales and the Lake District, and 10 minutes from the historic city of Lancaster. Open all year. Dinner available. Bed and Breakfast from £18.

SOUTHPORT

Rosedale Hotel, 11 Talbot Street, Southport PR8 1HP (Tel & Fax: 01704 530604). One of Southport's most centrally situated hotels, ideally placed for the beach, parks, entertainment, golf courses and the famous Lord Street. The perfect location whether you are on holiday or on business. Resident proprietors, Joan and Alan Beer, make every effort to ensure that all their guests have a happy and comfortable stay. Full central heating and private parking. All rooms have tea/coffee making facilities and colour TV. Residents' bar and separate TV lounge. A lovely secluded rear garden is available for guests' enjoyment. Children welcome. Sorry, no pets. Bed and Breakfast from £26. ETC/AA/RAC ◆◆◆◆
e-mail: info@rosedalehotelsouthport.co.uk   website: www.rosedalehotelsouthport.co.uk

LEICESTERSHIRE

BELTON-IN-RUTLAND (near Uppingham)

The Old Rectory, Belton-in-Rutland, Oakham LE15 9LE (01572 717279; Fax: 01572 717343). Guest Accommodation. Victorian country house and guest annexe in charming village overlooking Eyebrook valley and rolling Rutland countryside. Comfortable and varied selection of rooms, mostly en suite, with direct outside access. Prices from £20 per person per night including breakfast. Small farm environment (horses and sheep) with excellent farmhouse breakfast. Public house 100 yards. Lots to see and do: Rutland Water, castles, stately homes, country parks, forestry and Barnsdale Gardens. Non-smoking. Self-catering also available. **RAC** ◆◆◆

e-mail: bb@iepuk.com

LOUGHBOROUGH

L. & K. Charwat, Charnwood Lodge, 136 Leicester Road, Loughborough LE11 2AQ (01509 211120; Fax 01509 211121). Charnwood Lodge is a quality Bed and Breakfast which is tastefully decorated throughout. It has superior en suite rooms, colour TV/satellite, tea/coffee facilities, its own car park, quiet surroundings and private gardens with conservatory. We have single, twin/double, family and four-poster bedrooms. Available on request (free of charge) cot, high chair, ironing board and hair dryer. We are close to all local amenities within the Charnwood area. East Midlands airport is eight miles, Derby 18 miles, Donington Park nine miles, Nottingham 15 miles, Leicester 12 miles. We hope you enjoy your stay with us, and will recommend us to your friends. Rates from £30 to £57 per night. Guests can enjoy a drink in the bar or lounge. We accept Visa, Mastercard and Eurocard. **ETC** ◆◆◆◆

website: www.charnwoodlodge.com

MEDBOURNE

Mrs J.A. Wainwright, Homestead House, 5 Ashley Road, Medbourne, Market Harborough LE16 8DL (01858 565724; Fax: 01858 565324). Situated in an elevated position overlooking the Welland Valley on the outskirts of picturesque Medbourne with a meandering brook running through the centre. Surrounded by open countryside, the village has two public houses, post office/shop, etc. Local places of interest include Foxton Locks on Grand Union Canal, Rockingham Castle, Rutland Water (sailing, fishing, windsurfing), Eyebrook Reservoir (fishing, bird watching), Naseby Battlefield, various houses and halls, gliding, riding, nature trails and many delightful picnic spots. Accommodation comprises three twin/double rooms, all en suite and having TV, telephone and hospitality tray; sittingroom, dining room. Children welcome. Central heating. Illuminated car parking. Bed and Breakfast £45 for double/twin room, £27 single occupancy. Evening meals available at local pub. Reductions for children. Sorry, no pets. Open all year. **ETC** ◆◆◆◆ *SILVER AWARD.*

e-mail: june@homesteadhouse.co.uk   **website: www.homesteadhouse.co.uk**

MELTON MOWBRAY

Hillside House, 27 Melton Road, Burton Lazars, Melton Mowbray LE14 2UR (01664 566312; Fax: 01664 501819). Situated on the edge of the village with views over rolling countryside, Hillside House is a comfortable, converted old farm building, offering one double and one twin room both en suite, and one twin with private bathroom. All have colour TV and tea/coffee making facilities. There is a guests' lounge; Rutland Water, Geoff Hamilton's Garden and Belvoir Castle are close by. Melton Mowbray with its bustling market is one and a half miles away. Bed and Breakfast from £21 to £24pp. Children over ten only. Closed Christmas and New Year. **ETC** ◆◆◆◆

e-mail: hillhs@aol.com

website: www.hillside-house.co.uk

OAKHAM

The Exeter Guest House, Wakerley, Oakham, Rutland LE15 8PA (01572 747817; Fax: 01572 747339). Welcome to this homely, family-run Bed & Breakfast. Set in the picturesque Welland Valley with a host of interesting walks for ramblers. Burghley House, Rockingham Castle and Kirby Hall are nearby, as is Rutland Water, Europe's largest man-made lake which offers excellent fishing, sailing and bird watching. A newly-renovated and extended annexe provides attractive accommodation. All seven bedrooms have en suite facilities, colour television, tea/coffee-makers and underfloor heating. Children welcome. Cots available. Parking. Garden area. A wholesome, wide ranging, Continental breakfast is included. This is a quiet and well-run hostelry ideal for a break that is just that little bit different.
website: www.ExeterGuestHouse.co.uk

LINCOLNSHIRE

ALFORD

Westbrook House, Gayton Le Marsh, Alford LN13 0NW (01507 450624). At Westbrook House we offer carefully designed, thoughtfully equipped, quality en suite accommodation in a tranquil village location, between superb beaches and the Lincolnshire Wolds. Breakfasts and optional evening meals are served in the conservatory overlooking the patio garden and feature "Tastes of Lincolnshire". There is a galleried TV/sitting area with tourist information. Ideal base for local market towns, countryside, walking, cycling etc. (bikes available). Discover the "Real Lincolnshire". Open all year. Central heating. On-site parking. Bed & Breakfast from £20. **ETC** ◆◆◆◆
e-mail: westbrook_house@hotmail.com
website: www.bestbookwestbrook.co.uk

CLEETHORPES

The Anchorage, 16 The Kingsway, Cleethorpes DN35 8QU (Tel & Fax: 01472 696757). A small, friendly, sympathetically restored hotel in a Victorian house, overlooking the Humber and the sea. Furnished and decorated to a very high standard, giving an old-fashioned and welcoming ambience. All bedrooms are centrally heated and have en suite facilities. On the ground floor is the breakfast room and also the guests' lounge where you can look out on the ever-changing scenery. Two single and two family/double/twin rooms available, some with sea views. Buses and trains are within easy reach and we are conveniently situated for the local attractions and amenities. Unrestricted street parking available; some private parking planned for 2004. B&B from £22.50 per person per night. **ETC** ◆◆◆◆ For further details please contact: **Meg and Pete Hayselden**.
e-mail: hotel@anchorage.f9.co.uk

GAINSBOROUGH

The Black Swan Guest House, 21 High Street, Marton, Gainsborough DN21 5AH (Tel and Fax: 01427 718878). We offer a warm and friendly stay at our delightfully converted 18th century coaching inn, so get away from the 'hurly burly' of modern life, and escape to the peace and quiet, although Lincoln is only 12 miles away and many other attractions are nearby. All our rooms are en suite, with full facilities; we also have a comfortable guest lounge with ample reading matter. Our breakfasts are made with the best quality local produce and should set you up for the day. We are a non-smoking establishment. Single from £30, double from £55. **AA** ◆◆◆◆
e-mail: info@blackswan-marton.co.uk

HORNCASTLE

Mrs C.E. Harrison, Baumber Park, Baumber, Near Horncastle LN9 5NE (01507 578235; Fax: 01507 578417; mobile: 07977 722776). Spacious elegant farmhouse of character in quiet parkland setting on a mixed farm. Large gardens, wildlife pond and grass tennis court. Fine bedrooms with lovely views, period furniture and log fires. Central in the county and close to the Lincolnshire Wolds, this rolling countryside is little known and quite unspoilt. Bridleways and lanes ideal for walking, cycling or riding: stabling for horses available. Two championship golf courses at nearby Woodhall Spa. Well located for historic Lincoln, interesting market towns and many antique shops. Single, double and twin en suite with private bathroom. Bed and Breakfast from £22.50. A warm welcome awaits. **ETC** ◆◆◆◆
website: http://uk.geocities.com/baumberpark/thehouse

LANGTON-BY-WRAGBY

Miss Jessie Skellern, Lea Holme, Langton-by-Wragby, Market Rasen LN3 5PZ (01673 858339). Ground floor accommodation in comfortable, chalet-type house set in own half-acre peaceful garden. All amenities. Central for touring Wolds, coast, fens, historic Lincoln etc. So much to discover in this county with wonderful skies and room to breathe. Attractive market towns, Louth, Horncastle (famed for antiques), Boston, Spilsby, Alford, Woodhall Spa (noted for golf). Accommodation offered in two double bedrooms (can be let as single at no extra charge), with washbasins and TV; bathroom, toilet adjoining; lounge with colour TV always available to guests, separate diningroom. Drinks provided. Children welcome at reduced rates. Pets welcome (no charge). Car almost essential, parking. Numerous eating places nearby. Bed and Breakfast from £20 per person. Open all year.

LINCOLN

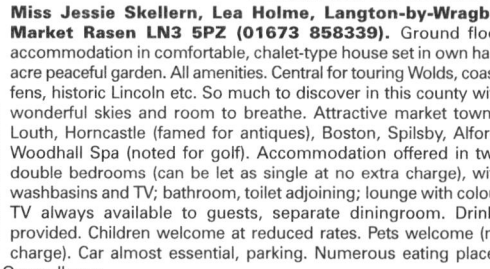

EDWARD KING HOUSE

Edward King House, The Old Palace, Lincoln LN2 1PU (01522 528778; Fax: 01522 527308). A former palace of the Bishops of Lincoln, Edward King House offers Bed and Breakfast accommodation in a friendly and informal atmosphere. It is in a wonderful setting at the heart of historic uphill Lincoln, next to the Cathedral and Medieval Bishops' Palace overlooking the modern city with views over many miles to the west and south. Single and twin-bedded rooms (non-smoking) are all centrally heated and have washbasins and tea/coffee making facilities. Prices from £20 single, £39 twin with Continental breakfast (full breakfast £2 extra per person). **AA** ◆◆
e-mail: enjoy@ekhs.org.uk
website: www.ekhs.org.uk

LOUTH

Tony and Beverly Moss, Keddington House Host Home, 5 Keddington Road, Louth LN11 0AA (01507 603973/ 604248; Fax: 01507 600691). Tony and Beverly offer personal accommodation in our beautiful Victorian house, set back 100 yards from the road, in our quiet grounds with ample parking. Just 10 minutes from the 'capital of the wolds', Louth town centre and Cadwell Park; and half-an-hour from Humberside airport. Also convenient for Lincoln, Skegness, Cleethorpes, etc. Tea/coffee served in lounge. Excellent food. TV in all rooms, en suite available. Games room. Heated outdoor swimming pool in summer months. 'A Hidden Oasis'.
e-mail: beverly@keddingtonhouse.co.uk
website: www.keddingtonhouse.co.uk

LOUTH

The Priory Hotel, Eastgate, Louth LN11 9AJ (01507 602930; Fax: 01507 609767). The Priory is a Grade II Listed building dating from 1818. With its stunning Victorian-Gothic style architecture, set in beautiful tranquil surroundings, it is the ideal location for those seeking a relaxing break – business or social. The hotel is set in three acres with mature trees, a lake with a fountain, old folly and a ruined mausoleum. 12 en suite bedrooms, recently refurbished. Restaurant, Cafe Bar, conference room, marquee facilities, wedding receptions, private parties, weekend breaks, French, Anglo cuisine, car parking. Our friendly and caring staff are just as impressive as the setting. Please telephone for further information.
website: www.theprioryhotel.com

MARKET RASEN

Mrs Vivienne Klockner, Redhurst, Holton-cum-Beckering, Market Rasen LN8 5NG (Tel & Fax: 01673 857927). A warm welcome awaits guests at Redhurst B&B, set in gardens, orchard and copse in a small village nestling on the edge of the Lincolnshire Wolds. Enjoy swimming in the heated outdoor pool in summer and warmth from a crackling log fire in winter. An ideal centre from which to explore the many and varied attractions of Lincolnshire. Two twin rooms en suite (one ground floor); one single room with private facilities. English or Continental breakfast. From £22 per person per night. Self-catering also available. Non-smoking; sorry, no pets. Open all year. Brochure on request. ETC grading awaited.

NORTH HYKEHAM

See also Colour Display Advertisement

The Gables Guesthouse, 546 Newark Road, North Hykeham, Lincoln LN6 9NG (01522 829102; Fax: 01522 850497). This smart guesthouse enjoys a convenient location just off the A46 Lincoln bypass, ten minutes south of the city centre. We have two en suite double and two twin bedrooms, all are brightly decorated and thoughtfully equipped, with cable TV and tea/coffee making facilities. There is also a pool table and sauna available for guests' use. Breakfast is served at individual tables in the attractive lounge/dining room. Vegetarians welcome. Full central heating. Ample parking. Terms from £25 to £35 single, from £45 to £50 double. Credit cards welcome. **RAC ◆◆◆**
e-mail: thegables@ntlworld.com
website: www.gablesguesthouse.com

PETERBOROUGH

See also Colour Display Advertisement

Jenny Dixon, Bed & Breakfast at No.19 West Street, Kings Cliffe, Near Stamford, Peterborough PE8 6XB (01780 470365; Fax 01780 470623). A beautifully restored 500-year-old Listed stone house, reputedly one of King John's Hunting Lodges, situated in the heart of the stone village of Kings Cliffe on the edge of Rockingham Forest. Both the double and twin rooms have their own private bathrooms, and there is colour TV and a welcome tray in each. In the summer breakfast can be served on the terrace overlooking a beautiful walled garden. Off street parking is behind secure gates. Within 10 miles there are seven stately homes including Burghley House famous for the Horse Trials, Rutland Water, and the beautiful old towns of Stamford and Oundle. Imaginative evening meals are available on request and prices range from £12 to £18. Open all year. A non-smoking house. Bed and Breakfast from £20pp.
e-mail: kjhl_dixon@hotmail.com   **website: www.kingjohnhuntinglodge.com**

SCUNTHORPE

The Beverley Hotel, 55 Old Brumby Street, Scunthorpe DN16 2AJ (01724 282212; Fax: 01724 270422). Situated between Scunthorpe and Ashby in a quiet residential area in one of the oldest parts of town, with easy access to all main routes; nine miles from Humberside airport and within easy reach of five golf courses, the Humber Bridge, Beverley, Hull, York and Doncaster. Comfortable residents' lounge with colour TV, where you can sit and relax; charmingly decorated dining room for both evening meals and breakfasts; well-stocked bar. Double rooms are tastefully decorated with all modern fittings, colour TV, tea/coffee making facilities and all are en suite with shower; some also with bath. Executive rooms are available for that extra comfort with luxury fittings and bedding. Please contact us for more information. **website: www.beverleyhotelscunthorpe.co.uk**

See also Colour Display Advertisement

THORPE FENDYKES

Mrs S. Evans, Willow Farm, Thorpe Fendykes, Wainfleet, Skegness PE24 4QH (01754 830316). In the heart of the Lincolnshire Fens, Willow Farm is a working smallholding with free range hens, goats, horses and ponies. Situated in a peaceful hamlet with abundant wildlife, ideal for a quiet retreat – yet only 15 minutes from the Skegness coast, shops, amusements and beaches. Bed and Breakfast is provided in comfortable en suite rooms from £17 per person per night, reductions for children (suppers and sandwiches can be provided in the evening on request). Rooms have tea and coffee making facilities and a colour TV and are accessible to disabled guests. Horse riding available. Friendly hosts! Ring for brochure.
e-mail: willowfarmhols@aol.com
website: www.willowfarmholidays.co.uk

WOODHALL SPA

Barbara and Tony Hodgkinson, Kirkstead Old Mill Cottage, Tattershall Road, Woodhall Spa LN10 6UQ (01526 353637; mobile: 07970 040401). A warm welcome awaits you at this peaceful, sunny, detached non-smoking house, which is set beside the River Witham on the outskirts of Woodhall Spa, a village which is noted for its 'old world' charm, park with open-air heated swimming pool, Kinema in the woods and championship golf course. A new garden, three-acre woodland garden, rowing boat, riverbank walks and membership of a local leisure club are also yours to enjoy, plus seasonal coarse fishing. There are numerous pubs and restaurants locally, or you are welcome to bring back a takeaway. We have a telephone, e-mail, fridge, iron and hairdryer for guests to use, and our three guest bedrooms (two en suite) each has a TV, clock radio and hot drinks tray. A video, piano and open fire help to make the lounge a relaxing area. From £21 per person, a cooked, typical English breakfast is served or you can choose a lighter, healthy option.
website: www.woodhallspa.com

National Fishing Heritage Centre • *Grimsby, N.E. Lincs* • *01472 323345*
Tells the story of fishermen, their boats, and the waters they fished in. The dangers and hardships of life at sea are vividly re-created.

ENGLAND

NORFOLK

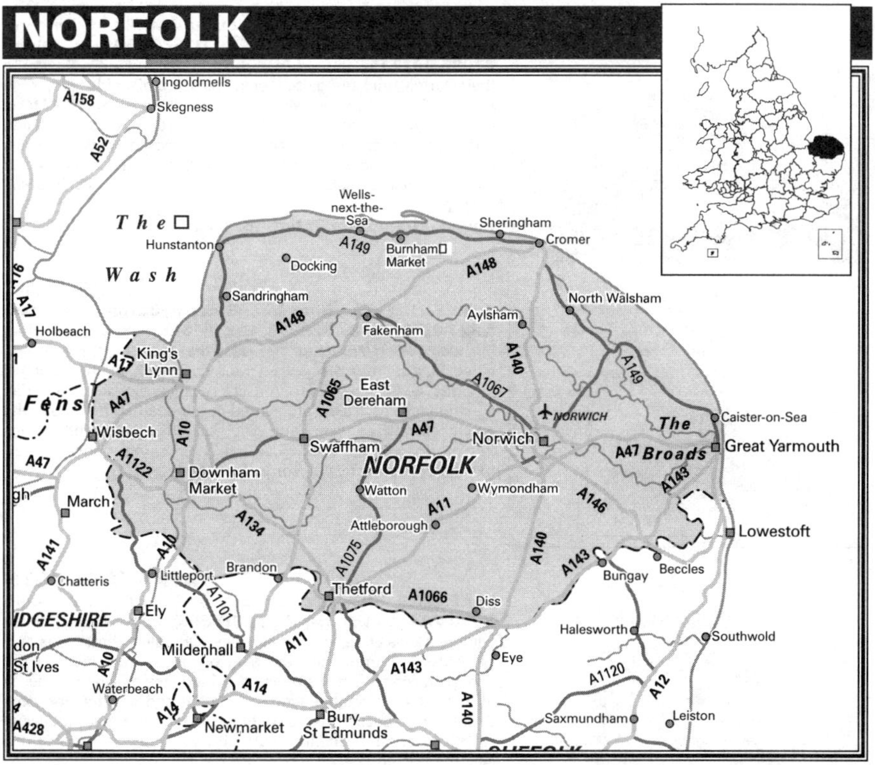

Map of Norfolk showing towns including Ingoldmells, Skegness, Hunstanton, Wells-next-the-Sea, Sheringham, Cromer, Burnham Market, Docking, Sandringham, North Walsham, Holbeach, King's Lynn, Fakenham, Aylsham, Wisbech, East Dereham, Norwich, Caister-on-Sea, Swaffham, Great Yarmouth, Downham Market, Watton, Wymondham, Lowestoft, March, Attleborough, Chatteris, Littleport, Brandon, Thetford, Diss, Bungay, Beccles, Ely, Halesworth, Southwold, Mildenhall, Eye, Waterbeach, Newmarket, Bury St Edmunds, Saxmundham, Leiston. The Wash, The Fens, The Broads, NORFOLK, CAMBRIDGESHIRE, SUFFOLK.

AYLSHAM

The Old Pump House, Holman Road, Aylsham, Norwich NR11 6BY (01263 733789). This comfortable 1750's house, facing the thatched pump a minute from Aylsham's church and historic marketplace, has six bedrooms, four en suite, with colour TV and tea/coffee facilities. English Breakfast with free-range eggs and local produce (or vegetarian breakfast) is served in the pine-shuttered sitting room overlooking the peaceful garden. Aylsham is central for Norwich, the coast, the Broads, National Trust houses, steam railways and unspoilt countryside. Well-behaved children are very welcome. Bed and Breakfast from £22 to £30. Dinner by prior arrangement from October to May. Non-smoking. Off-road parking for six cars. **ETC ◆◆◆◆**

See also Colour Display Advertisement

DISS

4B&B Strenneth Country Bed & Breakfast, Airfield Road, Fersfield, Diss IP22 2BP (01379 688182; Fax: 01379 688260). Well-established, family-run businesss, situated in unspoiled countryside, a short drive from Bressingham Gardens, Snetterton Motor Racing Circuit and the picturesque market town of Diss. Offering first-class accommodation, the original 17th century building has been renovated to a high standard with exposed oak beams and a newer single storey courtyard wing. There is ample off-road parking and plenty of nice walks nearby. All seven bedrooms, including a four-poster and an executive, are tastefully furnished, each having colour TV, hospitality tray, central heating and full en suite facilities. The establishment is smoke-free and the guest lounge has a log fire on cold winter evenings. Extensive breakfast menu using local produce. Ideal touring base. Pets most welcome at no extra charge. Outside kennels with runs if required. Bed and Breakfast from £25. **ETC ◆◆◆◆**
e-mail: pdavey@strenneth.co.uk   website: www.strenneth.co.uk

FAKENHAM

Mrs Brown, Abbot Farm, Walsingham Road, Binham, Fakenham NR21 0AW (Tel & Fax: 01328 830519; Mobile: 07986 041715). Liz and Alan Brown offer a warm welcome to their Norfolk brick bungalow set in 150 acres of arable land, close to Little Walsingham and the north Norfolk coastline. Breakfasts are taken in the sunny conservatory, comfortable accommodation is found in the attractive loft conversion. Accommodation consists of one double and two twin bedrooms, all en suite; colour TV and tea/coffee making facilities. No smoking. Terms from £20. **ETC/AA** ◆◆◆

e-mail: abbot.farm@btinternet.com

FAKENHAM

Julie Sadler, The Boar Inn, Great Ryburgh, Fakenham NR21 0DX (01328 829212; Fax: 01328 829421). The Boar Inn, with its Listed Frontage nestles in the verdant Wensum Valley, close by the round towered Saxon Church in the heart of Norfolk. The five en suite rooms all have television and tea/coffee making facilities. Meals are served in the beamed bar and in the newly refurbished restaurant. Well situated for tourist attractions in Norfolk; wild life park close by. The resident ghost is more mischievous than troublesome. **ETC** ◆◆◆

GREAT YARMOUTH

Mrs E. Dack, `Dacona', 120 Wellesley Road, Great Yarmouth NR30 2AP (01493 856863 or 855305). Homely guest house with own keys and access at all times. Centrally situated, it is only two/three minutes from the seafront and five minutes from shopping centre. Every amenity provided - tea making facilities in all rooms, comfortable accommodation and an ideal location. Bed and Breakfast terms from £14 to £16 nightly. Small parties (up to 24) welcomed. Children catered for (half-price rates). Dogs accepted on enquiry.

See also Colour Display Advertisement

GREAT YARMOUTH

Swiss Cottage Hotel, 31 North Drive, Great Yarmouth NR30 4EW (01493 855742; mobile: 07734 980289). Located on the seafront with superb views across the Venetian Waterways to the sandy beach and sea. Close to all amenities and and a good base for Norfolk Broad attractions. Single, twin and double rooms, most en suite, all with colour TV, radio/alarm, tea/coffee making; sea view rooms available. Full English breakfast with fresh local produce. Spacious residents' lounge with colour TV. Private car park. B&B: single room from £20, double room from £30. Open all year.

KING'S LYNN (near)

Amanda Case, Lower Farm, Harpley, King's Lynn PE31 6TU (01485 520240). Lower Farm is a lovely old farmhouse with large, comfortable rooms. Two double rooms en suite, and one double room with private bathroom. It is close to Sandringham and Houghton Hall; the Peddars Way is nearby for walkers, and there is good golfing, sailing and shooting in the area. It is 20 minutes from the coast, where there are good pubs, also Burnham Market with good shopping. Stabling available; dogs must be kept outside. Terms from £25 to £28 per person, single £30 to £35.

LONG STRATTON (near Norwich)

Mrs Joanna Douglas, Greenacres Farmhouse, Woodgreen, Long Stratton, Norwich NR15 2RR (01508 530261). Period 17th century farmhouse on 30 acre common with ponds and natural wildlife, 10 miles south of Norwich (A140). The beamed sittingroom with inglenook fireplace invites you to relax. A large sunny dining room encourages you to enjoy a leisurely traditional breakfast. All en suite bedrooms (two double/twin) are tastefully furnished to complement the oak beams and period furniture, with tea/coffee facilities and TV. Full size snooker table and all-weather tennis court for guests' use. Jo is trained in therapeutic massage, aromatherapy and reflexology and is able to offer this to guests who feel it would be of benefit. Come and enjoy the peace and tranquillity of our home.Bed and Breakfast from £25. Reductions for two nights or more. Non-smoking. **ETC** ◆◆◆

See also Colour Display Advertisement

LUDHAM

Malthouse Farmhouse, Malthouse Lane, Ludham NR29 5QL (01692 678747). The farmhouse dates back to 1700 and has retained lots of its period features. It is situated in quiet countryside on the edge of Ludham village in the heart of the Norfolk Broads, where country walks and cycle rides start at the gate. We are five minutes' walk from Womack Water and boat hire; within easy reach of the coast; 15 minutes' drive to Yarmouth races. B&B accommodation comprises one double bedroom (making yours a completely exclusive stay) with private bathroom/shower; use of the barn room for TV viewing, use of garden, tea-making facilities. Full farmhouse or vegetarian breakfast; evening meals available from village pub five minutes' walk. B&B £30.00 to £35.00pppn. Brochure on request.

NORTH WALSHAM

Mrs G. Faulkner, Dolphin Lodge, 3 Knapton Road, Trunch, North Walsham NR28 0QE (01263 720961). Friendly welcome from the proprietors of this bungalow accommodation. Bed and Breakfast in a village setting just two-and-a-half miles from beaches. Many rural walks locally; within easy reach of all Norfolk's attractions including the Norfolk Broads. All rooms en suite, with tea/coffee making facilities, TV, hairdryer. **ETC** ◆◆◆

NORWICH

Foxwood Guest House, Fakenham Road, Taverham, Norwich NR8 6HR (01603 868474). For those preferring the country rather than the city, why not try Foxwood Guest House. We are set in the middle of twenty acres of woodland, on the outskirts of the village of Taverham, approximately six miles from Norwich. All rooms have comfortable beds and tea/coffee making facilities; en suite available. There are many rivers and lakes nearby for the fishermen as well as many golfing areas and a new Sportspark. In Norwich there are lots of restaurants, café/bars, shops, art galleries and the Maddermarket Theatre, Castle Museum and cathedrals; National Trust properties miles of coastline, bird reserves and many other places of interest in the area. Bed & Breakfast from £25 single, £50 double. **e-mail: yvonne@foxwoodguesthouse.fsnet.co.uk**

A useful index of towns and counties appears at the back of this book on pages 417-421. Refer also to Contents Pages 2 and 3.

NORWICH

Mr Brian and Mrs Diane Curtis, Rosedale Guest House, 145 Earlham Road, Norwich NR2 3RG (01603 453743; Fax: 01603 259887). Friendly, family-run Victorian Guest House pleasantly situated within short walking distance of city centre and University, on the B1108. All rooms have colour TV, tea/coffee making facilities and own keys for your convenience. A full English breakfast is served in the diningroom and vegetarians are made very welcome. There are several good eating places nearby and once you have parked your car you can relax and enjoy Norwich. The Norfolk Broads are just seven miles away and the coast 20 miles. Full central heating. Bed and Breakfast from £20 per person. Completely no smoking. All major credit cards accepted. **ETC ◆◆**
e-mail: drcbac@aol.com

RACKHEATH

Judy Bell, Barn Court, Back Lane, Rackheath, Norwich NR13 6NN (Tel & Fax: 01603 782536). Friendly and spacious accommodation in a traditional Norfolk Barn conversion built around a courtyard. Situated five miles from the historic city of Norwich and two miles from the heart of the Norfolk Broads at Wroxham. Our accommodation consists of one double en suite room with a four-poster and two double/twin rooms. All rooms have colour TV and facilities for making tea/coffee. We are within walking distance of a very good Norfolk pub which serves reasonably priced meals. Packed lunches and dinners are available on request. Children are very welcome. Bed and Breakfast from £20 to £25. **ETC ◆◆◆**
e-mail: barncourtbb@hotmail.com

RACKHEATH

Mr & Mrs R. Lebbell, Manor Barn House, Back Lane, Rackheath, Norwich NR13 6NN (01603 783543). 17th century converted barn with a wealth of exposed beams. A family home with lovely gardens in quiet surroundings, situated just off A1151. Very convenient for Norwich (five miles), and two miles from Wroxham, heart of Broadland. Accommodation includes twin/double rooms with central heating, tea/coffee facilities, TV and own bathroom. Separate lounge area with colour TV. We are 100 yards from traditional old Norfolk pub, "The Green Man", where it is possible to eat very well and inexpensively. Open all year for Bed and Breakfast from £25 to £32 single, £44 to £50 double. **ETC ◆◆◆◆**
website: www.manorbarnhouse.co.uk

See also Colour Display Advertisement

SHERINGHAM

Beeston Hills Lodge, 64 Cliff Road, Sheringham NR26 8BJ. Bed and Breakfast seaside holiday accommodation. Our Edwardian lodge which is marvellously located next to the Norfolk Coastal Path, cliffs and ocean, obtains good views of the sea and green. Beeston Hills Lodge is one of the highest dwellings here, located opposite the putting green and the sea and set back from the road so there is no passing traffic. The house is equipped with a four-poster, king-size bed, an old piano, satellite system, home cinema with giant screen TV in lounge, video player and several colour TVs with boosted feeds to the bedrooms, and DVD. One shower and separate bathroom with shower. Garden with garden furniture. Car parking for two cars. Ten to twenty minutes' drive from the golf course and cinema. The Lodge can accommodate up to eight people in four bedrooms (cot available if required), with sea views. Children, Senior Citizens and well behaved pets welcome. Terms from £20 pppn. Non-smoking. Creative writing courses available, as the owner, a writer and poet, has recently reached the finals of an International Writing competition. Please contact for further details. **(01263 825333; Mobile: 0788 7751760 ; Fax: 001 775 542 2519).**
e-mail: enquiries@bhlodge.co.uk   **website: www.bhlodge.co.uk/lodge.htm**

SWAFFHAM

Mrs Green, "Paget", Lynn Road, Narborough, King's Lynn PE32 1TE (01760 337734). Private house offering Bed and Breakfast. Lounge available, log fire. Tea/coffee making facilities, TV in bedrooms. Ample parking. Pleasant local river, lakes and rural walks. Various water sports and horse riding nearby. Situated between the old market town of Swaffham and King's Lynn. Trout and coarse fishing lakes nearby. Pets welcome. Bed and Breakfast £17.50 per person. SAE please.

WELLS-NEXT-THE-SEA

Mrs Dorothy MacCallum, Machrimore, Burnt Street, Wells-next-the-Sea NR23 1HS (01328 711653). A warm welcome awaits you at this attractive barn conversion. Set in quarter-of-an-acre in quiet location close to the shops and picturesque harbour of Wells. Three en suite guest bedrooms (two twin and one double) at ground floor level overlook their own patio and garden area. Ample car parking. Sorry no smoking in the bedrooms. Ideal for the bird watching sanctuaries at Cley, Salthouse and Titchwell. Close to Sandringham, Holkham and the Shrines at Walsingham. Prices from £26 to £30 daily; £165 to £185 weekly. 10% reduction three nights or more. **ETC** ◆◆◆
e-mail: dottiemac39@hotmail.com
website: www.machrimore.co.uk

WEST RUNTON

Pauline and Tony White, "Timney's" 126 Cromer Road, West Runton, Cromer NR27 9QA (01263 837456). Single storey Bed and Breakfast accommodation. Easy off-road parking facilities. Sea view to front elevation, golf course and National Trust land to rear. Pleasant garden available to guests. All rooms are en suite, with tea and coffee making facilities and TV. Extensive walking, horse riding, golfing and beach within ten minutes' walking distance. In season rates: double room £24 per person per night. Sorry no children under 12 or pets.

PLEASE NOTE

All the information in this book is given in good faith in the belief that it is correct. However, the publishers cannot guarantee the facts given in these pages, neither are they responsible for changes in policy, ownership or terms that may take place after the date of going to press. Readers should always satisfy themselves that the facilities they require are available and that the terms, if quoted, still apply.

Holkham Hall & Bygones Museum • *Wells-next-the-Sea, Norfolk* • *01328 710227*
website: www.holkham.co.uk
One of Britain's most majestic stately homes. It has splendid state rooms with wonderful paintings, fine furniture and ancient statues.

Pettitts Animal Adventure Park • *Near Great Yarmouth, Norfolk* • *01493 701403*
Three parks in one - fun for all the family. Rides, play area, adventure golf course, animals galore. Children's entertainment daily.

WOODTON

Mrs J. Read, George's House, The Nurseries, Woodton, Near Bungay NR35 2LZ (01508 482214). A charming 17th century cottage with a six acre free-range egg unit and working forge/ blacksmith's showroom, situated in the centre of the village, just off the main Norwich to Bungay road. Wonderful holiday area, ideal for touring Norfolk and Suffolk. Within 10 miles is historic Norwich, with its castle, cathedral, theatre and excellent shops. Coast 18 miles. Guest accommodation comprises three double bedrooms with washbasins. Bathroom, shower, toilet, dining room, lounge/TV, sun room. Ample parking. Bed and Breakfast £23 per person per night. Excellent pub meals available 100 yards.
e-mail: georgeshouse@bushinternet.com
website: www.rossmag.com/georges/

WROXHAM

Wroxham Park Lodge, 142 Norwich Road, Wroxham NR12 8SA (01603 782991). Friendly Bed and Breakfast in an elegant Victorian house, situated in Wroxham 'Capital of Norfolk Broads'. Ideal for touring, day boats and boat trips on the beautiful Broads, fishing, steam railways, National Trust Houses, Wroxham Barns. Near north Norfolk coast, Great Yarmouth and Norwich. Good local restaurants and pubs. Guests arriving by train will be met. Open all year. All rooms en suite, tea/coffee making facilities, colour TV. Conservatory, garden, car park, ground floor room, central heating and public telephone. Pets by arrangement. Bed and Breakfast from £22 per person. Ring for brochure.
ETC ◆◆◆◆

NORTHAMPTONSHIRE

See also Colour Display Advertisement

KETTERING

Mrs A. Clarke, Dairy Farm, Cranford St Andrew, Kettering NN14 4AQ (01536 330273). Enjoy a holiday in our comfortable 17th century farmhouse with oak beams and inglenook fireplaces. Four-poster bed now available. Peaceful surroundings, large garden containing ancient circular dovecote. Dairy Farm is a working farm situated in a beautiful Northamptonshire village just off the A14, within easy reach of many places of interest or ideal for a restful holiday. Good farmhouse food and friendly atmosphere. Open all year, except Christmas. Bed and Breakfast from £25 to £35 (children under 10 half price); Evening Meal £16. **ETC ◆◆◆◆** *SILVER AWARD.*

LONG BUCKBY

Carrie Hart, Murcott Mill, Long Buckby NN6 7QR (01327 842236; Fax: 01327 844524). Murcott Mill is an imposing Georgian mill house set within a working farm. It has a large garden and lovely outlook over open countryside. All rooms are en suite with colour TV. Central heating throughout and visitors have their own lounge and dining room with open log fires. An ideal stopover, close to M1 and good location for touring the area. Children and pets welcome. Bed and Breakfast from £28 single; double £50. Open all year.
e-mail: carrie.murcottmill@virgin.net

NORTHUMBERLAND

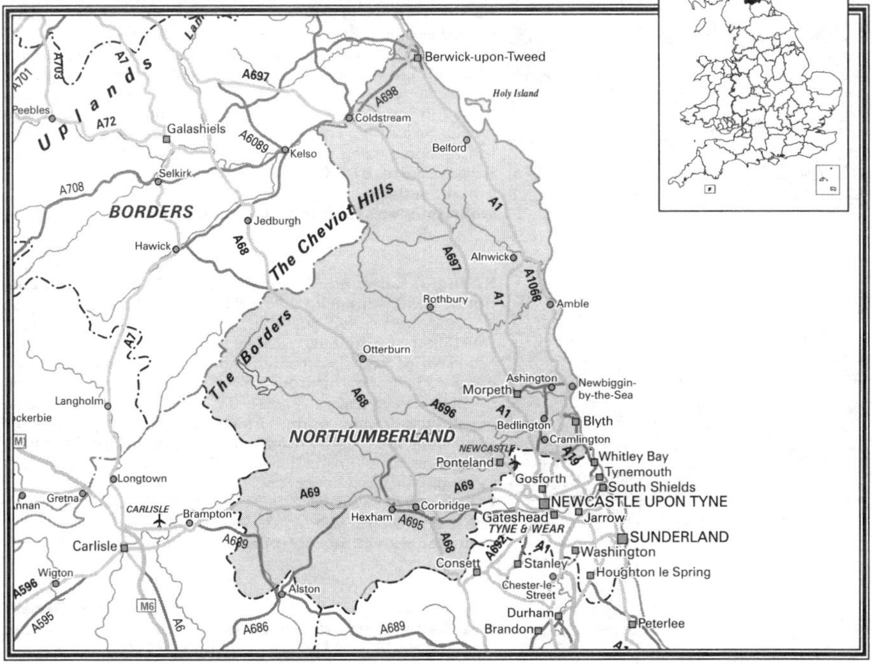

© MAPS IN MINUTES™ 2003 ©Crown Copyright. Ordnance Survey 2003

ALLENDALE

Mrs Eileen Ross Finn, Thornley House, Allendale NE47 9NH (01434 683255). Beautiful country house in spacious grounds surrounded by field and woodland, one mile out of Allendale, 10 miles south of Hexham, near Hadrian's Wall. Two large beautifully furnished lounges, one with TV, one with Steinway Grand Piano; three bedrooms all with private facilities, tea maker and radio. Marvellous walking country where you don't see anybody. Golf course nearby. Home baking. Bring your own wine. Packed lunches, vegetarians catered for. Ample parking. Bed and Breakfast from £22. Dinner £15. Bed and Breakfast weekly from £130. Cat lovers' delight – resident Manx and Maine Coon; wonderful feline art collection. A no smoking house. **ETC ◆◆◆◆**
e-mail: e.finn@ukonline.co.uk
website: web.ukonline.co.uk/e.finn

THORNLEY HOUSE

See also Colour Display Advertisement

ALNMOUTH

Janice Edwards, Westlea, 29 Riverside Road, Alnmouth NE66 2SD (01665 830730) We invite you to relax in the warm, friendly atmosphere of "Westlea" situated at the side of the Aln Estuary. We have an established reputation for providing a high standard of care and hospitality. Guests start the day with a hearty breakfast of numerous choices and in the evening a varied and appetising four-course traditional meal is prepared using local produce. All bedrooms are bright, comfortable and en suite with colour TVs, hot drinks facilities, central heating and electric blankets. Two bedrooms on the ground floor. Large visitors' lounge and diningroom overlooking the estuary. Ideal for exploring castles, Farne Islands, Holy Island, Hadrian's Wall. Fishing, golf, pony trekking, etc within easy reach. Private parking. Bed and Breakfast from £22; Bed, Breakfast and Evening Meal from £34. Numerous Hospitality awards. **ETC ◆◆◆**

ALNWICK

Sheila Dodds, South Hazelrigg, Chatton, Alnwick NE66 5RZ (01668 215216; Mobile: 07710 346076). South Hazelrigg is situated between the market town of Wooler and the coastal village of Belford, approximately ten minutes off the A1 road, ideally placed for trips to the beach, Farne Islands, Holy Island, the Cheviot Hills and the many castles. Rooms are spacious and comfortable with hospitality trays and colour TV. Breakfast is served in the elegant dining room and the local village inns provide an extensive menu. Local activities include birdwatching, fishing, horse riding and golf, Bamburgh being the most scenic English course. **ETC** ◆◆◆ *SILVER AWARD*
e-mail: sed@hazelrigg.fsnet.co.uk
website: www.farmhousebandb.co.uk

ALNWICK

K. and J. Bateman, Charlton House, 2 Aydon Gardens, South Road, Alnwick NE66 2NT (01665 605185). Charlton House is a very special guest house, where our guests are always welcomed in a friendly, relaxed atmosphere. All rooms are beautifully decorated, some with original fireplaces and patchwork quilts. All bedrooms have private facilities, alarm clock radio, hair dryer, hospitality trays and colour TV. There is also a comfortable guest lounge. Choose from Traditional English, vegetarian or Continental breakfasts. Private and off-street parking. Tariff from £24 per person per night. (includes Breakfast). We think you will remember Charlton House fondly, long after your stay has ended. **ETC** ◆◆◆. *WHICH?' 'GOOD BED AND BREAKFAST' GUIDE, PRIDE OF NORTHUMBRIA FOOD HYGIENE AWARD.*
website: www.SmoothHound.co.uk/hotels/charlt2.html

ALNWICK (near)

Mrs Celia Curry, Howick Scar Farm House, Craster, Alnwick NE66 3SU (Tel & Fax: 01665 576665). Comfortable farmhouse accommodation on working mixed farm situated on the Heritage Coast between the villages of Craster and Howick. Ideal base for walking, golfing, bird-watching or exploring the coast, moors and historic castles. The Farne Islands, famous for their colonies of seals and seabirds, and Lindisfarne (Holy Island) are within easy driving distance. Accommodation is in two double rooms with washbasins. Guests have their own TV lounge/dining room with full central heating. Non-smoking. Bed and Breakfast from £20. Open Easter to November. **ETC** ◆◆◆, *FARM STAY UK.*
e-mail: stay@howickscar.co.uk
website: www.howickscar.co.uk

BERWICK-UPON-TWEED

Mrs Margo Newington-Bridges, High Steads, Lowick TD15 2QE (Tel & Fax: 01289 388689). High Steads is a Georgian farmhouse some four miles from the A1, close to Holy Island and Berwick-upon-Tweed. We are an ideal base from which to explore the many castles, coastline and Cheviot Hills. Close by there is fishing, horse riding, shooting, golf and beautiful walking country. We have two en suite rooms, one double, one twin and guests' sittingroom. Our house is non-smoking except in the summer house. Ample courtyard parking. Extensive grounds with magnificent views and croquet on the lawn. Varied and interesting breakfasts including Eggs Benedict and Gentleman's Victorian Omelette. Bed and Breakfast from £25.00 per person per night. **AA** *FOUR RED DIAMONDS AND EGGCUP AWARD FOR THE VERY BEST BREAKFAST, NORTH NORTHUMBRIA LOCAL FOOD AWARD (BRONZE).*
e-mail: highstead@aol.com

Readers are requested to mention this guidebook when seeking accommodation (and please enclose a stamped addressed envelope).

BERWICK-UPON-TWEED

Mrs Chater, West Mains House, Beale, Berwick-upon-Tweed TD15 2PD (01289 381227). West Mains House sits in the beautiful county of Northumberland, overlooking the Holy Island of Lindisfarne. It has unrestricted views on all sides and is ideal for walkers, cyclists and of course, birdwatchers. The county is very diverse, holding appeal for history buffs and country lovers. It is noted for its castles, peel towers and stately homes; many of which are just a short distance from the West Mains House. We are a family-run B&B, very child and dog friendly. We cater for a variety of diets where possible, our hope being to make your stay as enjoyable as possible.

BERWICK-UPON-TWEED

Fred and Lynda Miller, The Cobbled Yard Hotel, 40 Walkergate, Berwick-upon-Tweed TD15 1DJ (01289 308407, Fax: 01289 330623). Situated one minute from Berwick-upon-Tweed's main thoroughfare this hotel is surrounded by walls and ramparts built by Queen Elizabeth I to protect Berwick. Accommodation consists of three family rooms, one double and one twin room (can sleep up to 15). All are en suite with colour TV, tea/coffee, central heating, hairdryer, trouser press and ironing facilities. A wide range of attractions and activities are on offer with lots of beaches and picnic areas within easy walking distance. Ideal centre point for visits to Edinburgh and Newcastle. Private parking. Restaurant and bar lounge. Vegetarians also catered for.

e-mail: cobbledyardhotel@berwick35.fsnet.co.uk   website: www.cobbledyardhotel.com

CORBRIDGE

Mrs L. Adamson, Low Fotherley Farm, Riding Mill, Corbridge NE44 6BB (Tel & Fax: 01434 682277). Low Fotherley is an impressive Victorian farmhouse built around 1895 situated on the A68 south of Riding Mill in the beautiful Northumbrian countryside with outstanding views. The market towns of Hexham and Corbridge are nearby. Explore Hadrian's Wall, Durham, Beamish, Kielder, the Scottish Borders, Northumberland's coastline, Bamburgh and the Farne Islands. The farmhouse has lots of character, with open fireplaces and beams. The house is spacious and comfortable. Both rooms are of a high standard with full central heating, TV, tea/coffee making facilities, hairdryer and radio. Farmhouse breakfast is cooked on the Aga with toast, home-made jams and marmalade. Families welcome. No smoking. £22.50 per person, discounts for children. ETC ◆◆◆◆, *FARM STAY UK MEMBER*.
e-mail: hugh@lowfotherley.fsnet.co.uk   website: www.westfarm.freeserve.co.uk

HEXHAM

Mrs Ruby Keenleyside, Struthers Farm, Catton, Allendale, Hexham NE47 9LP (01434 683580). Struthers Farm offers a warm welcome in the heart of England, with many splendid local walks from the farm itself. Panoramic views. Situated in an area of outstanding beauty. Double/twin rooms, en suite, central heating. Good farmhouse cooking. Ample safe parking. Come and share our home and enjoy beautiful countryside. Children welcome, pets by prior arrangement. Open all year. Near Hadrian's Wall (half an hour's drive). Bed and Breakfast from £22; Optional Evening Meal from £12.

HEXHAM

Mr and Mrs D. Maughan, Greencarts Farm, Humshaugh, Hexham NE46 4BW (01434 681320; mobile: 07752 697355). Greencarts is a working farm situated in Roman Wall country, ideally placed for exploring by car, bike or walking. It has magnificent views of the Tyne Valley. It is warm and homely, with central heating and log fires. Home-cooked food is provided. En suite accommodation with safe car/bike parking. Convenient for Hexham Racecourse; fishing available locally. All welcome. Bed and Breakfast from £22 to £25. Open all year.
e-mail: Sandra.Maughan2@200m.co.uk

STAMFORDHAM

Mrs Crowe, Stamfordham Bay Horse Inn, South Side, Stamfordham NE18 0PB (01661 886244). Family-run 16th century village inn serving lunches and evening meals; real ales, pool and darts. Four double, one twin/family and one single en suite rooms with TV and hot drinks facilities; central heating. Newcastle Airport six miles. Children and pets welcome. Parking available. Open January to December. B&B from £33 single, £58 double and £68 to £78 (for four) family room.
e-mail: stay@stamfordham-bay.co.uk
website: www.stamfordham-bay.co.uk

WARKWORTH

Sue and Geoff Lillico, Aulden, 9 Watershaugh Road, Warkworth NE65 0TT (01665 711583; Fax: 01665 711652). Enjoy a high standard of care and hospitality, as you relax in an Area of Outstanding Natural Beauty. With Warkworth as a base, you can explore the coastline, hills and castles from Berwick in the north to Hadrian's Wall in the west. Situated in a quiet part of the village, off the main road, we provide one double en suite and one twin-bedded room with private facilities. Each room has TV, hospitality tray and hairdryer. Extensive breakfast menu. Bed and Breakfast from £20. Weekly rates available. Light supper available on request. Non-smoking.
e-mail: auldenbandb@hotmail.com

WARKWORTH

John and Edith Howliston, 7 Woodlands, Warkworth NE65 0SY (01665 711263). John and Edith, previously of North Cottage, welcome you to No.7 Woodlands, situated at the south end of the village and offering comfortable and homely bed and breakfast accommodation throughout the year. One double/twin en suite bedroom and one twin with own toilet; both rooms with TV, electric blanket, hospitality tray and clock radio. Delicious breakfasts served in the dining room; sitting room. Warkworth, just a few miles south of Alnwick, is an ideal base from which to explore the area and has a wide sandy beach, several excellent restaurants and a lovely river. All Northumberland's many attractions are within easy reach, including seaside villages, Farne Islands and Holy Island. B&B from £24pppn, weekly from £160.
e-mail: edithandjohn@another.com
website: www.accta.co.uk/north

NOTTINGHAMSHIRE

BURTON JOYCE

Mrs V. Baker, Willow House, 12 Willow Wong, Burton Joyce, Nottingham NG14 5FD (0115 931 2070). A large period house (1857) in quiet village location yet only four miles from city. Attractive, interesting accommodation with authentic Victorian ambience. Bright, clean rooms with tea/coffee facilities, TVs. Walking distance of beautiful stretch of River Trent (fishing). Ideally situated for Holme Pierrepont International Watersports Centre; golf course; National Ice Centre; Trent Bridge (cricket); Sherwood Forest (Robin Hood Centre) and the unspoiled historic town of Southwell with its Minster and Racecourse. Good local eating. Evening Meal by arrangement. Private parking. From £19 per person per night. Reduced rates for children. Dogs welcome. Please phone first for directions.

EDWINSTOWE (near Mansfield)

Robin Hood Farmhouse B&B, Rufford Road, Edwinstowe NG21 9JA (Tel & Fax: 01623 824367). Traditional Olde English farmhouse in Robin Hood's village in the middle of Sherwood Forest. We are in close proximity of Clumber and Rufford Country Parks and adjacent to Center Parcs and South Forest Leisure Complex. Easy access to Nottingham and Lincoln. The farmhouse, which is set in extensive gardens, is open and centrally heated all year round. Accommodation comprises double/family and twin room, colour TV, tea/coffee making facilities in all rooms. Tariff from £17.50 per person per night. Reductions for children and extra nights. Pets and special requirements available on request. Ample secure parking.
e-mail: robinhoodfarm@aol.com

FARNSFIELD

Ken and Margaret Berry, Lockwell House, Lockwell Hill, Old Rufford Road, Farnsfield, Newark NG22 8JG (01623 883067). Set in 25 acres with 10 acres of woodland and situated on the edge of Sherwood Forest near Rufford Park on the A614, we are within easy reach of Nottingham, Newark, Mansfield, Worksop and all local country parks and tourist attractions. Small family-run Bed and Breakfast offering friendly service and comfort. All bedrooms are en suite and have tea/coffee making facilities, TV. Full English Breakfast. Ample car parking. Good pubs and restaurants nearby. Brochure available. Rates from £22.

ENGLAND

MANSFIELD

Mrs L. Palmer, Boon Hills Farm, Nether Langwith, Mansfield NG20 9JQ (01623 743862). This is a stone-built farmhouse, standing 300 yards back from A632 on edge of village. It is on a 155-acre mixed farm with dogs, cats, goats, chicks, calves. Situated on the edge of Sherwood Forest, six miles from Visitors' Centre, eight miles from M1, 10 miles from A1. Chatsworth House, Newstead Abbey, Hardwick Hall and Creswell Crags all within easy reach. One double en suite, one double and one twin shared bathroom; toilet; fitted carpets throughout. Open fires. Background central heating for comfort all year round. Large sittingroom/diningroom with colour TV. Children welcome; babysitting. No pets. Car essential – parking. Bed and Breakfast from £18 per night, which includes bedtime drink. Evening Meal available nearby. Non-smokers only. Rates reduced for children. Open March to October inclusive.

SUTTON-IN-ASHFIELD

Mr P. Jordan, Dalestorth Guest House, Skegby Lane, Skegby, Sutton-in-Ashfield NG17 3DH (01623 551110). Dalestorth Guest House is an 18th century Georgian family home converted in the 19th century to become a school for young ladies of the local gentry and a boarding school until the 1930s. In 1976 it was bought by the present owners and has been modernised and converted into a comfortable, clean and pleasant guest house serving the areas of Mansfield and Sutton-in-Ashfield, offering overnight accommodation of Bed and Breakfast or longer stays to businessmen, holidaymakers or friends and relations visiting the area. Please send for further information.

OXFORDSHIRE

[Map of Oxfordshire and surrounding counties showing towns including Stratford upon Avon, Pershore, Evesham, Banbury, Shipston-on-Stour, Moreton-in-Marsh, Chipping Norton, Stow-on-the-Wold, Cheltenham, Witney, Oxford, Carterton, Cirencester, Faringdon, Cricklade, Malmesbury, Swindon, Chippenham, Calne, Marlborough, Hungerford, Newbury, Reading, Wantage, Didcot, Wallingford, Abingdon, Thame, Bicester, Kidlington, Aylesbury, Wendover, Henley-on-Thames, Maidenhead, Marlow, High Wycombe, Beaconsfield, Amersham, Berkhamsted, Tring, Hemel Hempstead, Windsor, Slough, Bracknell, Towcester, Brackley, Buckingham, Milton Keynes, Leighton Buzzard, Dunstable, and major roads. Inset map of England. ©MAPS IN MINUTES™ 2003 ©Crown Copyright, Ordnance Survey 2003]

BANBURY

Mrs Rosemary Cannon, High Acres Farm, Great Bourton, Banbury OX17 1RL (Tel & Fax: 01295 750217). New Farmhouse situated on edge of village off A423 Southam Road, three miles north of Banbury overlooking the beautiful Cherwell Valley. Ideally situated for touring Cotswolds, Stratford, Warwick, Oxford, Blenheim Palace. Local pubs serving evening meals Tuesdays to Saturdays. Very comfortable accommodation comprising one twin room, one family room (one double and one single bed). Tea/coffee making facilities, hair dryers; central heating; shower room with electric shower; guests' sittingroom with colour TV. All rooms fully carpeted. Non-smoking. Parking. Bed and Breakfast from £20. Child under 10 sharing family room £10. Sorry, no pets. A warm welcome awaits you.

BANBURY (near)

Mrs E. J. Lee, The Mill Barn, Lower Tadmarton, Near Banbury OX15 5SU (01295 780349). Tadmarton is a small village, three miles south-west of Banbury. The Mill, no longer working, was originally water powered and the stream lies adjacent to the house. The Mill Barn has been tastefully converted, retaining many traditional features such as beams and exposed stone walls, yet it still has all the amenities a modern house offers. Two spacious en suite bedrooms, one downstairs, are available to guests in this comfortable family home. Base yourself here and visit Stratford, historic Oxford, Woodstock and the beautiful Cotswolds, knowing you are never farther than an hour's drive away. Open all year for Bed and Breakfast from £25, reductions for children. Weekly terms available.

BLADON (near)

Tom and Carol Ellis, Wynford House, 79 Main Road, Long Hanborough OX29 8JX (01993 881402). Wynford House is situated in the village of Long Hanborough a mile from the Bladon burial place of Sir Winston Churchill, three miles from Woodstock and Blenheim Palace. Oxford is twelve miles away and the Cotswolds are close by. Comfortable non-smoking accommodation. Family or double en suite, double and twin rooms with colour TV, tea/coffee making facilities. Pubs serving good food within walking distance. Bed and Breakfast from £24.

HENLEY-ON-THAMES

The Old Bakery, Skirmett, Near Henley-on-Thames RG9 6TD (01491 638309; Fax: 01491 638086). This welcoming family house is situated on the site of an old bakery, seven miles from Henley-on-Thames and Marlow; half-an-hour from Heathrow and Oxford; one hour from London. It is in the Hambleden Valley in the beautiful Chilterns, with many excellent pubs selling good food. Excellent village pub in Skirmett within easy walking distance. One double en suite, one twin-bedded room and one double with use of own bathroom. All with TV and tea making facilities. Open all year. Parking for five cars (car essential). Children and pets welcome. Bed and Breakfast from £30 single; £60 double, £75 en suite. **ETC ◆◆◆◆**
e-mail: liz.roach@euphony.net

MINSTER LOVELL

Mrs Katharine Brown, Hill Grove Farm, Crawley Road, Minster Lovell OX29 0NA (01993 703120). Hill Grove is a mixed, family-run, 300 acre working farm situated in an attractive rural setting overlooking the Windrush Valley. Ideally positioned for driving to Oxford, Blenheim Palace, Witney (Farm Museum) and Burford (renowned as the Gateway to the Cotswolds and for its splendid Wildlife Park). New golf course one mile. Hearty breakfasts. One double/private shower, one twin/double en suite. Children welcome. Open all year except Christmas. Bed and Breakfast from £26pppn for double/private shower; £27pppn for double or twin en suite. Non- smoking. **ETC ◆◆◆◆**
e-mail: kbrown@eggconnect.net
website: www.country-accom.co.uk/hill-grove-farm

OXFORD

Mr and Mrs L. Price, Arden Lodge, 34 Sunderland Avenue (off Banbury Road), Oxford OX2 8DX (01865 552076; 07702 068697). Modern detached house in select part of Oxford, within easy reach of Oxford Centre. Excellent position for Blenheim Palace and for touring Cotswolds, Stratford, Warwick etc. Close to river, parks, country inns and golf course. Easy access to London. All rooms have tea/coffee making and private facilities. Parking. Bed and Breakfast from £24 per person per night.

OXFORD

D. J. Underwood, Conifer Lodge, 159 Eynsham Road, Botley OX2 9NE (01865 862280; Fax: 01865 865135). Luxury stone house on the outskirts of Oxford city, only two and a half miles bus route to the city centre, yet in the peace and quiet of the countryside. Very accessible to all tourist areas. Central heating in all rooms, double glazed throughout, colour television, large garden and patio, plenty of parking space. Bed and breakfast, business persons welcome, reasonable rates. **ETC ◆◆◆**
website: www.smoothhound.co.uk/oxford

OXFORD

Tilbury Lodge, 5 Tilbury Lane, Botley, Oxford OX2 9NB (01865 862138; Fax: 01865 863700). Tilbury Lodge is a modern guest house situated in a quiet country lane within a short distance of Oxford city centre. Nine immaculately presented rooms, all en suite; our four-poster has added luxuries including a foot spa, use of the jacuzzi and a complimentary bottle of wine. Ample off-street parking. Guests can relax in the guest lounge with internet facilities; dinner available on request. Stefan and Melanie are passionate about hospitality and look forward to welcoming you to Tilbury Lodge and providing a service never to be forgotten! One room suitable for pets. Some ground floor rooms suitable for disabled visitors. Vegetarian/ vegan and alternative diets available. Non-smoking. **ETC/RAC** ◆◆◆, *SPARKLING DIAMOND AWARD.*
website: www.oxfordcity.co.uk/hotels/tilbury

OXFORD

Mr Stratford, The Bungalow, Cherwell Farm, Mill Lane, Old Marston, Oxford OX3 0QF (01865 557171). Modern bungalow on five acres set in countryside but only three miles from the city centre. Offering comfortable accommodation and serving traditional breakfast. Colour TV, tea/coffee facilities in all rooms. Private parking. Non-smoking. Not on bus route. Bed and Breakfast from £23 to £27 per person. **ETC** ◆◆◆

OXFORD

Artemis House, 240 Abingdon Road, Oxford OX1 4SP (01865 244357). Artemis is an Edwardian house, recently restored, ideally located three-quarters of a mile from the city centre. Proprietor, Diane Jelfs, has used her many years of experience in welcoming visitors to Oxford to create a guest house that combines originality with respect for the house's period features. There is a variety of accommodation, from budget to en suite. All bathrooms have showers and toiletries; some also have baths. English, Continental or vegetarian breakfasts; special diets by arrangement. Parking available. Regular bus service to city centre from outside house.
e-mail: Artemis.house@btopenworld.com

SOULDERN

Toddy and Clive Hamilton-Gould, Tower Fields, Tusmore Road, Near Souldern, Bicester OX27 7HY (01869 346554; Fax: 01869 345157). Tower Fields is in an unspoilt elevated position with outstanding views, situated half-a-mile from the village of Souldern. A recently renovated farmhouse and barn provide comfortable en suite bedrooms on the ground floor, all with colour TV and tea/coffee making facilities. This is a working smallholding where you will see rare breeds of cattle, sheep, poultry and pigs. Full English breakfast using home produce is available. Stabling and garaging available on request. Non-smoking. Disabled guests accommodated. Three miles Junction 10 M40. Ideally situated Cotswolds, Silverstone, Birmingham, Oxford. Bed and Breakfast single from £35, double from £55. Full details on request. **ETC** ◆◆◆
e-mail: hgould@strayduck.com

TETSWORTH (near Thame)

Mrs Julia Tanner, Little Acre, Tetsworth, Thame, Oxford OX9 7AT (01844 281423; mobile: 07798 625252). Charming country retreat with pretty landscaped gardens and paddocks to walk the dog. Quiet location but only two miles from J6 M40. Near Chilterns, Oxford, Cotswolds, Heathrow Airport. Comfy beds, hearty breakfasts, 'olde worlde' style dining room. Open all year with friendly, relaxed atmosphere. En suite rooms; ground floor bedrooms. Tea/coffee making facilities and TV in rooms. Pets welcome. Highly recommended by previous guests. Bed and Breakfast from £22.50. **ETC/AA** ◆◆◆◆

Little Acre B & B, Tetsworth, Oxon

WITNEY

Mrs Elizabeth Simpson, Field View, Wood Green, Witney OX28 1DE (01993 705485; Mobile: 07768 614347). Witney is famous for blankets, made here for over 300 years. Our house was built in 1959, of Cotswold stone. Set in two acres and situated on picturesque Wood Green, with football and cricket pitches to the rear, yet only 10 minutes' walk from the centre of this lively, bustling market town. An ideal touring centre for Oxford University (12 miles), Blenheim Palace (eight miles), Cotswold Wildlife Park (eight miles) and country walks. Ample parking. Three delightful en suite bedrooms with central heating, tea/coffee making facilities and colour TV. Non- smoking. A peaceful setting and a warm, friendly atmosphere await you. Bed and full English Breakfast from £25.50. **ETC ◆◆◆** *SILVER AWARD*.

e-mail: bandb@fieldview-witney.co.uk   **website: www.fieldview-witney.co.uk**

WOODSTOCK

The Leather Bottel, East End, North Leigh, Near Witney OX8 6PY (01993 882174). Joe and Nena Purcell invite you to The Leather Bottel guest house situated in the quiet hamlet of East End near North Leigh, convenient for Blenheim Palace, Woodstock, Roman Villa, Oxford and the Cotswolds. Breathtaking countryside walks. Two double en suite bedrooms, one family room with own bathroom, one single bedroom, all with colour TV and tea/coffee making facilities. Bed and Breakfast £30 per night for single room, from £45 for double. Children welcome. Open all year. Directions: follow signs to Roman Villa off A4095. **ETC ◆◆◆**

WOODSTOCK

Mrs Kay Bradford, Hamilton House, 43 Hill Rise, Old Woodstock OX20 1AB (Tel & Fax: 01993 812206; Mobile: 07778 705568). Highly recommended Bed and Breakfast establishment with parking, overlooking Blenheim Park, Blenheim Palace and the town centre with good selection of restaurants, pubs and shops within walking distance. Accommodation offered - one twin-bedded room and two double rooms, all en suite with colour TV and tea making facilities. Excellent selection of Continental and full English breakfast. Comfortable and relaxed atmosphere with informative and very hospitable hostess. Ideal base for Blenheim Palace, Bladon, the Cotswolds, Stratford-upon-Avon, Oxford and major airports. Access off A44 northern end of Woodstock, one-third-of-a-mile up the hill from the Black Prince Pub. Children and pets welcome. Bed and Breakfast from £23 per person, based on two people sharing.

e-mail: kay@hamiltonhousewoodstock.co.uk   **website: www.hamiltonhousewoodstock.co.uk**

SHROPSHIRE

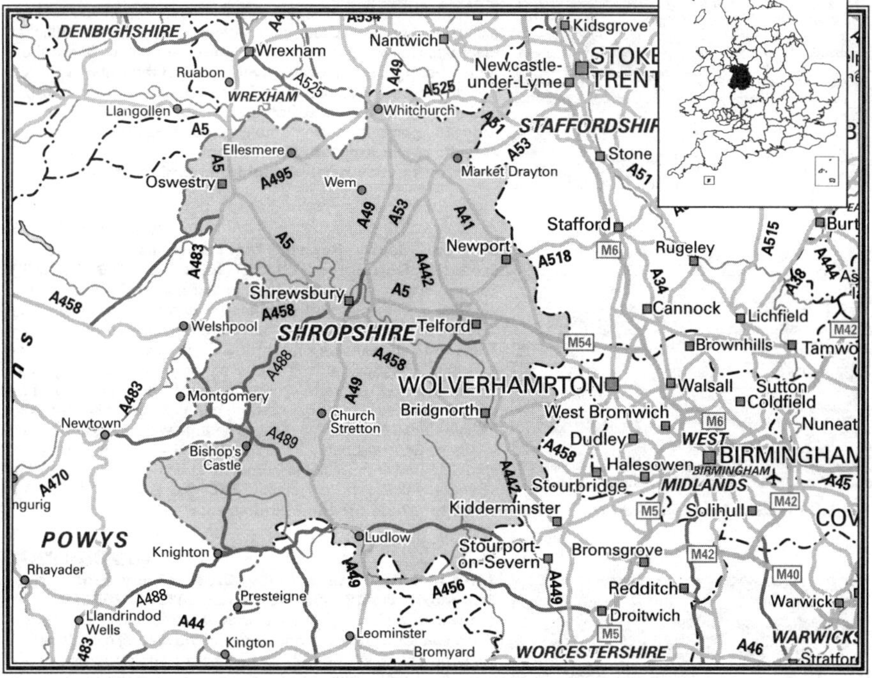

©MAPS IN MINUTES™ 2003 ©Crown Copyright, Ordnance Survey 2003

[Map of Shropshire and surrounding areas showing towns including Shrewsbury, Telford, Oswestry, Ludlow, Church Stretton, Bishop's Castle, Wolverhampton, Birmingham, and neighbouring counties Denbighshire, Wrexham, Staffordshire, West Midlands, Worcestershire, Powys]

BISHOP'S CASTLE

Mrs Ann Williams, Shuttocks Wood, Norbury, Bishop's Castle SY9 5EA (01588 650433; Fax: 01588 650492). Shuttocks Wood is a Scandinavian house in woodland setting situated within easy travelling distance of the Long Mynd and Stiperstone Hills. Accommodation consists of one double and two twin-bedded rooms, all en suite and with tea/coffee facilities and colour TV. Good walks and horse riding nearby and a badger set just 20 yards from the door! Ample parking. Non-smoking establishment. Children over 12 years welcome. Sorry, no pets. Open all year. Bed and Breakfast from £25 per person per night. Credit cards accepted.

CHURCH STRETTON

See also Colour Display Advertisement

Mrs Mary Jones, Acton Scott Farm, Acton Scott, Church Stretton SY6 6QN (01694 781260; Fax: 0870-129 4591). Lovely 17th century farmhouse in peaceful village amidst the beautiful hills of South Shropshire, an area of outstanding natural beauty. The house is full of character and the rooms, which are all heated, are comfortable and spacious with en suite or private bathroom and beverage making facilities. Colour TV lounge. We are a working farm, centrally situated for visiting Ironbridge, Shrewsbury and Ludlow, each being easily reached within half-an-hour. Visitors' touring and walking information available. No smoking. Bed and full English Breakfast from £20 per person. Weekly rate £135 per person. ETC ◆◆◆, *FARM STAY UK*.
e-mail: bandb@actonscottfarm.co.uk
website: www.actonscottfarm.co.uk

CHURCH STRETTON

Mrs Chris Brandon-Lodge, North Hill Farm, Cardington, Church Stretton SY6 7LL (01694 771532; mobile: 07929 278764). Farmhouse Bed and Breakfast accommodation in the beautiful Shropshire hills, one mile from Cardington village, itself a conservation gem. Quiet, rural setting with plenty of wildlife, an ideal base for walking and riding. Central for Ludlow, Shrewsbury and Ironbridge. Rooms have lovely views of the valley with TV & hot drinks tray. Well-behaved dogs and horses welcome. Bed and full English breakfast from £22 per person. Luxury en suite room £30 per person. Non-smoking. **AA** ◆◆◆◆
e-mail: cbrandon@btinternet.com
website: www.virtual-shropshire.co.uk/northhill

DORRINGTON

Ron and Jenny Repath, Meadowlands, Lodge Lane, Frodesley, Dorrington SY5 7HD (Tel & Fax: 01694 731350). Former farmhouse, set in eight acres of gardens, paddocks and woodland, with pleasant woodland trail for guests' use. Quiet location in a delightful hamlet seven miles south of Shrewsbury. The guest house lies on a no-through road to a forested hill rising to 1000ft. Meadowlands features panoramic views over open countryside to the Stretton Hills. Guest accommodation includes en suite facilities and every bedroom has a colour TV, drink-making facilities and a silent fridge. Guests' lounge with maps and guides for loan. Central heating. Plenty of parking space. Strictly no smoking. Bed and Breakfast from £20; Evening Meal from £12 by arrangement. Brochure available. **ETC** ◆◆◆

e-mail: meadowlands@talk21.com
website: www.meadowlands.co.uk

IRONBRIDGE

Jutta and Alan Ward, Linley Crest, Linley Brook, Near Bridgnorth WV16 4SZ (Tel & Fax: 01746 765527). Very convenient for the medieval towns of Shrewsbury, Bridgnorth, Much Wenlock, Ludlow, Ironbridge and the dramatic landscape of the Long Mynd. We offer three generous double rooms with TV, beverage tray, hairdryer – two of which have a shower en suite, guest-controlled heating and EASY ACCESS; additionally, one has a private conservatory. The third bedroom has a private bathroom. Delicious English breakfast provided and special diets catered for. Winners of the Bridgnorth District Council Healthy Eating Gold Award since 1999. Pub serving food within staggering distance. Open all year; off-road parking; drying facilities. No smoking, no pets, no cards. Children very welcome. From £22.50 per person per night. Weekly rate available. Euro payment accepted. Wir sprechen Deutsch – Herzlich willkommen! Warm welcome assured. **ETC** ◆◆◆◆ *SILVER AWARD.*

e-mail: linleycrest@easicom.com
website: www.linleycrest.co.uk

LUDLOW

M.A. and E. Purnell, Ravenscourt Manor, Woofferton, Ludlow SY8 4AL (01584 711905). Ravenscourt is a superb, newly renovated Tudor Manor set in two acres of lovely gardens. Beautifully furnished and equipped bedrooms. Wonderful area for walking or touring. Two miles from Ludlow, famous for its restaurants and architecture, eight miles from Leominster, famous for antiques, and 15 miles from Hereford and Worcester with their historic cathedrals. Close to National Trust properties and only 40 minutes from Ironbridge and Stratford. Excellent home cooked food. All rooms are en suite with remote-control colour TV, tea/coffee facilities and central heating. Bed and Breakfast from £30 per person; £5 discount for three nights or more. Warm welcome assured. Also self-catering cottages available, £120 to £330 per week, 10% discount for two weeks. **ETC** ◆◆◆◆ *GOLD AWARD.*

e-mail: ravenscourtmanor@amserve.com
website: www.SmoothHound.co.uk

NEWPORT

Sambrook Manor, Sambrook, Newport TF10 8AL (01952 550256; mobile: 07811 915535). Sambrook is centrally situated in the heart of Shropshire,15 minutes from Telford and Market Drayton, 30 minutes from Shrewsbury, Potteries, Stafford, and 40 minutes from Birmingham, Alton Towers and the Welsh Borders. The Manor House, which is a Listed building, is the focal point of the farm which has beef and dairy cattle, sheep, horses and of course the farm dogs. On the ground floor is a large sitting room and conservatory for guests' use, while upstairs are three guest bedrooms, all en suite. Full English Breakfast cooked to your individual taste. Visitors' room with colour TV. Tea and coffee facility in bedrooms. Private parking. Stabling available for horses – many accessible bridle paths. Bed and Breakfast £25, reduction for children. **ETC** ◆◆◆
website: www.go2.co.uk/sambrookmanor

OSWESTRY

Mrs Margaret Jones, Ashfield Farm House, Maesbury, Near Oswestry SY10 8JH (Tel & Fax: 01691 653589; mobile 07989 477414). Scented roses and scarlet creepers ramble over this delightful 16th century coaching house and farmhouse, nestling in the English/Welsh borderland, one mile from Oswestry and A5. Lovely mountain views. Exceptionally pretty, cosy and spacious rooms, en suite or private luxury bath/ shower room, with TV, hostess tray. Many original features and period decor. Complimentary tea/coffee on arrival. Five minute walk to canalside inn, excellent Warehouse restaurant and boat hire. Visit this beautiful area overflowing with castles, lakes, mountains and woodlands. Chester, Llangollen and Shrewsbury within 30 minutes' drive. Bed and Breakfast from £23 per person per night. Also Garden Coach House self-catering available. Short Breaks .Brochure available. **ETC** ◆◆◆◆ *SILVER AWARD.*
e-mail: marg@ashfieldfarmhouse.co.uk   website: www.ashfieldfarmhouse.co.uk

OSWESTRY (near)

Pam Morrissey, Top Farm House, Knockin, Near Oswestry SY10 8HN (01691 682582). Full of charm and character, this beautiful 16th century Grade I Listed black and white house is set in the delightful village of Knockin. Enjoy the relaxed atmosphere and elegant surroundings of this special house with its abundance of beams, open fires in winter, and fresh flowers all year round. Sit in the comfortable drawing room where you can read, play the piano, listen to music, or just sit and relax. Hearty breakfasts from our extensive menu are served in the lovely diningroom which looks out over the flower-filled garden. The large bedrooms are all en suite, attractively decorated and furnished. All have tea/coffee making facilities, colour TV, etc. The main bathroom has a sauna cabinet and spa bath for guests' use. Convenient for the Welsh Border, Shrewsbury, Chester and Oswestry. Bed and Breakfast from £24 per person. **ETC** ◆◆◆◆ *SILVER AWARD*, **AA** ◆◆◆◆
e-mail: p.a.m@knockin.freeserve.co.uk   website: www.topfarmknockin.co.uk

LYTHWOOD HALL
**BAYSTON HILL
SHREWSBURY SY3 0AD**

Quality Bed and Breakfast accommodation in a comfortable, spacious Georgian house. Enjoy the peaceful rural surroundings, our beautiful gardens or the log fire in winter. Relax in the guests' lounge, visit our spotted horses or walk on the Shropshire Way.

We are centrally placed for guests to tour Shropshire and the Welsh Borders. The medieval town of Shrewsbury is just three miles away and we are within easy reach of several excellent golf courses. Shropshire also has a great range of garden centres and specialist nurseries for keen gardeners to visit. There is easy access to all main routes, e.g. A5, A49, M54, M6. We are open all year. Kennel and run available for dogs. Bed and Breakfast £25, double room £45. Evening meal £14. Home-grown produce, vegetarians welcome.

Tel: 01743/07074 874747 • Fax: 01743 874747 • e-mail: lythwoodhall@amserve.net

SHREWSBURY
Mrs Sheila Griffiths, Sowbath Farm, Shawbury, Shrewsbury SY4 4ES (Tel & Fax: 01939 250064). Set in 120 acres of farmland, centrally located in the heart of the beautiful county of Shropshire, in a peaceful location with easy access to the local towns and attractions. Accommodation consists of one single room, one double room, two twin rooms, one on the ground floor with an en suite bathroom and Mobility 1 Access. Lounge and dining area. Attractions in the area include Hodnet Hall Gardens, Hawkstone Park Follies, Ironbridge Gorge museums, Secret Hills – the Shropshire Hills Discovery Centre, and Shrewsbury town centre shopping. ETC ◆◆◆
**e-mail: info@sowbathfarm.co.uk
website: www.sowbathfarm.co.uk**

See also Colour Display Advertisement

SHREWSBURY (near)
Mrs Gwen Frost, Oakfields, Baschurch Road, Myddle, Shrewsbury SY4 3RX (01939 290823). Visiting Shropshire? Why not enjoy the warm welcome and home-from-home atmosphere at Oakfields, which is in a quiet, idyllic setting located in the picturesque village of Myddle made famous by Gough's "History of Myddle" written in 1700. All ground floor bedrooms, each tastefully decorated and equipped with colour TV, tea-making facilities, washbasin, hairdryer and shaver point; cot and high chair also available; guests' TV lounge. Central heating throughout. Large and pleasant garden for guests to enjoy. 15 minutes from Shrewsbury and Hawkstone Park and convenient for Ironbridge, Wales, Chester, etc. Golf and riding nearby. Extensive car park. Non-smoking. Bed and Breakfast from £20 pppn. Nearest main road A528, also straight road from A5. ETC ◆◆◆

TELFORD
Mrs Mary Jones, Red House Farm, Longdon-on-Tern, Wellington, Telford TF6 6LE (01952 770245). Red House Farm is a late Victorian farmhouse in the small village of Longdon-on-Tern, noted for its aqueduct, built by Thomas Telford in 1796. Two double bedrooms have private facilities, one family room has its own separate bathroom. All rooms are large and comfortable. Excellent breakfast. Farm easily located, leave M54 Junction 6, follow A442, take B5063. Central for historic Shrewsbury, Ironbridge Gorge museums or modern Telford. Several local eating places. Open all year. Families most welcome, reductions for children. Pets also welcome. Bed and Breakfast from £20.
**e-mail: rhf@virtual-shropshire.co.uk
website: www.virtualshropshire.co.uk/red-house-farm**

SOMERSET

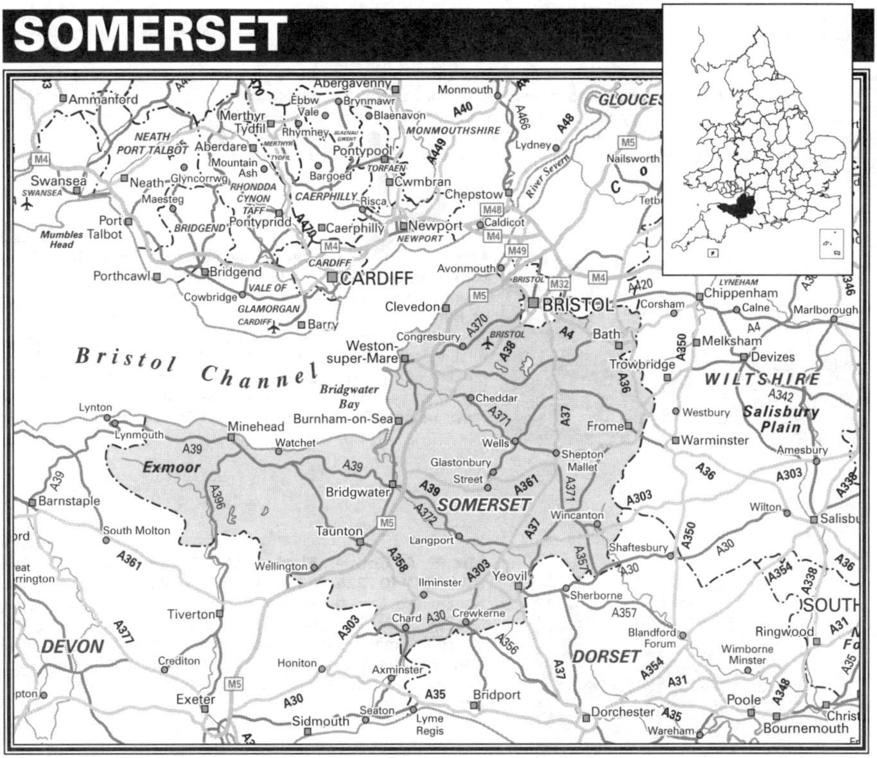

©MAPS IN MINUTES™ 2003. ©Crown Copyright, Ordnance Survey 2003.

BARTON ST DAVID

Mr & Mrs T. Norton, Watercress Cottage, Jarmany Hill, Barton St David, Somerton TA11 6DA (01458 850905). Deep in the heart of Somerset this comfortable Bed and Breakfast awaits you. We guarantee you a peaceful stay with excellent rural views and good food. The accommodation available is a double room with a single bed and a twin room. There is a comfortable lounge which has a TV and tea and coffee making facilities. Ample parking. Sorry no pets. Bed and Breakfast from £20. Children half price. We look forward to hearing from you.

BATH

Mrs Judith Goddard, Cherry Tree Villa, 7 Newbridge Hill, Bath BA1 3PW (01225 331671). Friendly Victorian home approximately one mile from centre of Bath, at the start of the A431. Very frequent bus service, or for those who enjoy walking, a stroll through Victoria Park will take you comfortably into the city. Bright comfortable bedrooms, all with washbasin, colour TV and tea/coffee making facilities. Full central heating and off-street parking. Bed and full English Breakfast from £18 per person per night. Children welcome. From city centre take main A4 Upper Bristol road, at Weston Pub take A431 and Cherry Tree Villa lies on the left hand side. Winner of an FHG Diploma awarded by readers. **ETC ◆◆◆**

BATH

Michael and Carole Bryson, Walton Villa, 3 Newbridge Hill, Bath BA1 3PW (01225 482792; Fax: 01225 313093). Our immaculate Victorian family-run B&B offers non-smoking accommodation in a relaxed and friendly atmosphere. Just a short bus journey or 25 minute stroll to town centre, via the beautiful gardens of the Royal Victoria Park. Our three en suite bedrooms are delightfully decorated and furnished for your comfort, with colour TV, hairdryer and hospitality tray. Enjoy a delicious Full English or Continental breakfast served in our gracious dining room. Sorry, no pets. Off street parking. Bed and Breakfast from £25. **ETC** ◆◆◆

e-mail: walton.villa@virgin.net   website: www.walton.izest.com

BATH

Mrs June E. A. Coward, Box Road Gardens, Box Road, Bathford, Bath BA1 7LR (01225 852071). Homely, comfortable country house in two acres, situated on A4 road three miles east of Bath City Centre. Easy access to M4, local beauty spots. Accommodation in twin, double and family rooms with central heating, tea/coffee making facilities; TV. Shower en suite. Ample parking and good local "pub food". Open all year for Bed and Breakfast from £19 per person. This is a non-smoking house. Sorry, no pets. Phone June on **01225 852071** for further details.

BATH

Mrs M. A. Cooper, Flaxley Villa, 9 New Bridge Hill, Bath BA1 3PW (01225 313237). Follow A4 through Bath to Queen Square, take top left-hand exit and follow one mile to Weston Pub, take right hand lights A431. Flaxley Villa is a comfortable Victorian house five minutes from town centre. All rooms with colour TV, also showers and tea/coffee making facilities. En suite room available. Parking. Full English Breakfast. Terms from £25 per person per night.

BRISTOL

Downs View Guest House, 38 Upper Belgrave Road, Clifton, Bristol BS8 2XN (0117 9737046; Fax: 0117 9738169). A well established, family-run Victorian guest house situated on the edge of Durdham Downs. All rooms have panoramic views over the city or the Downs. We are one-and-a-half miles north of the city centre, just off Whiteladies Road where there are plenty of restaurants, shops and buses. We are within walking distance of Bristol Zoo and Clifton Suspension Bridge. All rooms have tea/coffee making facilities, washbasin, colour TV and central heating. There are seven en suite rooms. We offer a varied menu including traditional English breakfast. Bed and Breakfast from £35 single, £45 double. **ETC/RAC** ◆◆◆

BRISTOL

Mrs M. Hasell, The Model Farm, Norton Hawkfield, Pensford, Bristol BS39 4HA (01275 832144). Working farm. Model Farm is situated two miles off the A37 in a peaceful hamlet, nestling under the Dundry Hills. A working arable and beef farm in easy reach of Bristol, Bath, Cheddar and many other interesting places. The spacious accommodation is in two en suite rooms, one family and one double, with tea/coffee facilities. Separate dining room and lounge with colour TV for visitors. Private parking. Open all year (except Christmas and New Year). Bed and Breakfast from £20. **ETC** ◆◆◆

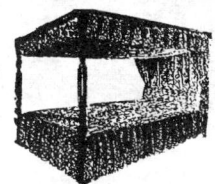

BURNHAM-ON-SEA

Mrs F. Alexander, Priors Mead, 23 Rectory Road TA8 2BZ (Tel & Fax: 01278 782116; Mobile: 07990 595585). Peter and Fizz welcome guests to enjoy their enchanting Edwardian home set in half-an-acre of beautiful gardens with weeping willows, croquet and swimming pool. All three rooms have either twin or king-size beds, en suite/private facilities, washbasins, hospitality trays, colour TVs, etc. Peaceful location, walk to the sea, town, golf and tennis clubs. Ideal touring base for Bristol, Bath, Wells, Glastonbury, Wookey Hole, Cheddar and Dunster. A no-smoking home. Parking. Easy access to Junction 22 M5 for Wales, Devon and Cornwall. Bed and Breakfast from £22.50. Reductions for three nights. *"WHICH?" RECOMMENDED.*
e-mail: priorsmead@aol.com
website: www.priorsmead.co.uk

CHARD

Mrs Jean Watkis, Keymer Cottage, Buckland St Mary, Chard TA20 3JF (01460 234226 or 07940 051439). Keymer Cottage is a stone-built Victorian farmhouse, with inglenook, attractively furnished, offering friendly and comfortable hospitality. Good local eating venues and many places of interest in the area, including National Trust properties, cider mills, museums, gardens etc. It is one mile from the A303, five miles from Chard and Ilminster, and nine miles from Taunton, the county town. Exmoor, Dartmoor and the North Somerset coast are within easy reach and Lyme Regis is only 19 miles away. There is a guest sittingroom with colour TV and three bedrooms, either en suite or with private bathroom and tea making facilities. Non-smoking. Sorry, no children. Bed and full English Breakfast from £22.50 per person per night.

CHURCHILL

Winston Manor Hotel, Bristol Road, Churchill, Winscombe BS25 5NL (01934 852348). Nestling at the foot of the Mendip Hills, the Winston Manor Hotel is set in its own grounds of one and a half acres. The hotel is within easy motorway access and is perfectly located for visiting either the historic sites of Bath, Bristol, Wells, Cheddar and Glastonbury, or the coastal towns of Weston-Super-Mare or Clevedon. Outdoor pursuits nearby include golf, rambling, cycling, potholing, angling and sailing. Newly renovated and personally managed by the owners, the hotel comprises fourteen en suite rooms. At the end of the day the lounge bar enables you to relax with a pre-dinner drink before dining in our excellent "Clementine's" restaurant. Rates from £27.50 per person inclusive of VAT. Non-smoking. **AA ★★**
e-mail: info@winstonmanorhotel.co.uk   website: www.winstonmanorhotel.co.uk

CREWKERNE

Mrs Catherine Bacon, Honeydown Farm, Seaborough Hill, Crewkerne TA18 8PL (Tel & Fax: 01460 72665). We are a working dairy farm on the Somerset/Dorset border, one and a half miles from Crewkerne, in peaceful countryside with panoramic views. National Trust properties, private gardens and numerous other places of interest are within easy reach, and the coast is only 14 miles away. Centrally heated accommodation comprises one double room en suite, and one double and one twin with washbasins. All rooms have television, clock/radio and hospitality tray. Enjoy the patio or garden or relax in the guest lounge. Evening meals by arrangement. Non-smoking. Single room from £28, double/twin room from £48.
e-mail: cb@honeydown.freeserve.co.uk
website: www.honeydown.freeserve.co.uk

A useful index of towns and counties appears at the back of this book on pages 417-421. Refer also to Contents Pages 2 and 3.

DULVERTON

e-mail: info@winsbere.co.uk

Mrs M. Rawle, Winsbere House, Dulverton TA22 9HU (01398 323278). Attractive private house set in pretty gardens on the edge of Dulverton, 10 minute walk from the centre and a short drive to Tarr Steps and the moors. Comfortable, tastefully decorated rooms with lovely country views and a friendly informal atmosphere. One double, one twin both with luxury en suite plus one double/single with private bathroom. Superb full English breakfast. Cyclists welcome. Route Three West Country Way on doorstep. Ample private parking and lockup cycle shed. No dogs. Non-smoking. Children welcome aged 8 or over. Excellent location for touring Exmoor, West Somerset and North Devon. Open all year (except Christmas and New Year). Terms: £20 to £22.50 per person per night (single from £20). **ETC ◆◆◆**
website: www.winsbere.co.uk

DULVERTON

Mrs Gill Summers, Higher Langridge Farm, Exbridge, Dulverton TA22 9RR (01398 323999). Find our 17th century farmhouse hidden amid picturesque countryside two miles south-west of Dulverton - off the beaten track. Guests' accommodation is a private wing of the farmhouse; relax in our cosy guests' lounge with TV and inglenook fireplace with woodburner for winter months. Guests' bedrooms are furnished with country pine furniture, decorated in pastel colours and pretty linen; one double with shower en suite, one family room to sleep two to four with private bathroom. Full English breakfast cooked on the Aga is served with farm eggs and local sausages. Wonderful views over fields and woodland with resident wildlife. Prices from £22 to £28 based on two sharing.
e-mail: info@langridgefarm.co.uk
website: www.langridgefarm.co.uk

See also Colour Display Advertisement

ENMORE (near Bridgwater)

Mrs Doreen Cole, Little Paddock, Stone Hall Lane, Enmore, Bridgwater TA5 2AL (01278 671188). At Little Paddock we will provide you with a high standard of accommodation. Our double room has an en suite shower, tea/coffee facilities, colour TV, radio, hairdryer plus other little extras to make your stay special. The Quantock Hills are nearby for those who enjoy walking. Enmore Park Golf Course with its 71 Par 18-hole course is half a mile away. The towns and cities of Taunton, Bath, Wells and Glastonbury, to name a few, are within easy reach, as is the M5. Car essential. No smoking. Bed and Breakfast from £20 per person per night.

EXFORD

Edgcott House, Exford, Near Minehead TA24 7QG (Tel & Fax: 01643 831495). Edgecott is a 17th century country house of great charm and character set in the village of Exford, right in the heart of the magnificent Exmoor National Park, amidst mature, secluded gardens in beautiful lush countryside. Experience the sound of birdsong and bubbling brook, the comfort of open log fires, newly refurbished bedrooms - all with en suite, and delicious full English breakfast. The location may be new, but Marc's warm hospitality is unchanging.

FREE or REDUCED RATE entry to Holiday Visits and Attractions – see our READERS' OFFER VOUCHERS on pages 63-90

GLASTONBURY

Mrs J.M. Gillam, Wood Lane House, Butleigh, Glastonbury BA6 8TG (01458 850354). Charming old AA Listed house with lovely views over open countryside and woods. Quiet yet not isolated and only 200 yards from excellent village "local". Ideal touring centre for Cheddar, Wells, Bath and many beauty spots and only 20 miles from coast. Attractions include Butterfly Farm, Fleet Air Arm Museum, Rural Life Museum, cheese making, steam engines and many places of historic interest. Accommodation comprises three double rooms with well equipped en suite facilities, tea/coffee and TV. Comfortable and warm sitting/dining room. Open all year round except Christmas and New Year. Car essential. Parking. Bed and Breakfast from £22.50; single £30. Half price for children.

GLASTONBURY

Mrs D. P. Atkinson, Court Lodge, Butleigh, Glastonbury BA6 8SA (01458 850575). A warm welcome awaits at attractive, modernised 1850 Lodge with homely atmosphere. Set in picturesque garden on the edge of Butleigh, three miles from historic Glastonbury. Only a five minute walk to pub in village which serves lovely meals. Accommodation in one double and two single bedrooms; constant hot water, central heating. Bathroom adjacent to bedrooms. TV lounge. Tea/coffee served. Bed and Breakfast from £18.50; Evening Meal by arrangement. Children welcome at reduced rates.

GLASTONBURY (near)

Sue Chapman, Meare Manor, 60 St Mary's Road, Meare, Glastonbury BA6 9SR (Tel & Fax: 01458 860449). 200 year old Manor House set in own grounds with beautiful gardens and views over Mendip Hills. Peaceful setting in the heart of King Arthur country. Ideal base for tourist attractions including Glastonbury Abbey, Chalice Well, Wells Cathedral, Cheddar Gorge and Clarks Shopping Village. Warm welcome assured with friendly help and advice. Family rooms and suite available. Hospitality trays, colour TV. Some rooms suitable for disabled guests. Ample car parking. Open all year. From M5, Junction 23 follow A39 Glastonbury - Street, take B3151 Glastonbury to Wedmore, approximately three miles from Glastonbury. Bed and Breakfast from £35 per person per night.
e-mail: info@mearemanor.com

See also Colour Display Advertisement

GLASTONBURY (near)

Mrs M. White, Barrow Farm, North Wootton, Near Glastonbury BA4 4HL (Tel & Fax: 01749 890245). Working farm. Barrow is a dairy farm of 146 acres. The house is 15th century and of much character, situated between Wells, Glastonbury and Shepton Mallet. It makes an excellent touring centre for visiting Somerset's beauty spots and historic places, for example, Cheddar, Bath, Wookey Hole and Longleat. Guest accommodation consists of two double rooms, one family room, one single room and one twin-bedded room, each with washbasin, TV and tea/coffee making facilities. Bathroom, two toilets; two lounges, one with colour TV; dining room with separate tables. Guests can enjoy farmhouse fare in generous variety, home baking a speciality. Bed and Breakfast, with optional four-course Dinner available. Car essential; ample parking. Children welcome; cot and babysitting available. Open all year except Christmas. Sorry, no pets. Bed and Breakfast from £16; Dinner £12.

ILMINSTER

Mrs G. Phillips, `Hermitage', 29 Station Road, Ilminster TA19 9BE (01460 53028). Enjoy the friendly atmosphere of a lovely Listed 17th century house with beams and inglenook. Four-poster beds. Acres of delightful gardens, woods and hills beyond. Twin or double rooms with washbasin; en suite available. Lounge with log fire and colour TV. Tea or coffee with homemade biscuits on arrival. Full English breakfast. Traditional inns nearby for evening meals. Ideal touring centre for Quantock Hills, Wells, Glastonbury, Lyme Regis and many picturesque villages. Several National Trust properties, gardens and historic houses within a few miles. Ten miles from M5, one mile from A303. Bed and Breakfast from £40 for two people, double/twin. £47 en suite, double/twin. Non-smoking. **ETC** ◆◆◆
website: //home.freeuk.net/hermitage/

See also Colour Display Advertisement

ILMINSTER

Mrs Grace Bond, Graden, Peasmarsh, near Donyatt, Ilminster TA19 0SG (01460 52371). Comfortable home with pretty garden in peaceful location within easy reach of M5 and A303. Situated on the A358 Ilminster to Chard road. Close to Devon and Dorset borders, the nearest beach being at Lyme Regis. Multi-screen cinema, ten pin bowling and popular eating place at nearby Taunton. Many local rural attractions and pubs serving good food. One family and two double rooms with hot drink facilities, washbasin and central heating. Bathroom with bath, shower and toilet upstairs, separate shower and toilet downstairs. Commode, cot and high chair available. Good home cooking assured. We would be happy to provide further details. Bed and Breakfast from £18, reductions for children.

MARK VILLAGE (near Highbridge)

Mrs B. M. Puddy, Laurel Farm, Mark Causeway, Near Highbridge TA9 4PZ (01278 641216; Fax: 01278 641447). Laurel Farm is on the Wells to Burnham-on-Sea B3139 road; M5 Junction 22 two miles; 12 miles from the cathedral city of Wells, five miles from Burnham-on-Sea; Highbridge two miles. Ideal for overnight or short breaks to tour our lovely area. Nicely furnished and decorated, with a large well kept lawn and flower garden at the back. Doubles, singles and family rooms available. All en suite with tea/coffee facilities. Large sitting room, colour TV. Central heating, electric blanket and log fires for cooler evenings. Bed and Breakfast from £20. **ETC** ◆◆◆

See also Colour Display Advertisement

MELLS

Claveys Farm, Mells, Near Frome BA11 3QP (01373 814651). This tranquil and welcoming haven offers you exactly what you expect of a farmhouse bed and breakfast. Warm and friendly atmosphere with log fires. Double, single and twin bedrooms. Large and peaceful sitting room. Home-made bread and free range eggs. Good wholesome home-grown and home-cooked fare. Three-course evening meals by arrangement (BYOB). Mells is a picturesque village in the Mendips, 17 miles from Bath and close to Frome.
e-mail: bandb@fleurkelly.com
website: www.fleurkelly.com/bandb

Readers are requested to mention this guidebook when seeking accommodation (and please enclose a stamped addressed envelope).

MINEHEAD

Glendower House, 30-32 Tregonwell Road, Minehead TA24 5DU (01643 707144; Fax 01643 708719). A family-run hotel offering quality accommodation with a personal welcome. Glendower House is situated in an attractive Edwardian residential terrace in the popular seaside resort of Minehead, the Gateway to Exmoor, and is only a few minutes' level walk from both the town centre and seafront. All rooms are centrally heated and have modern en suite shower rooms, colour TV, tea and coffee making facilities, radio/clock alarms and hairdryers. Non-smoking. Licensed bar. Large private car park. Ground floor rooms. Freshly prepared evening meals. Bed & Breakfast from £25 per person. **AA** *FOUR RED DIAMONDS*.
e-mail: info@glendower-house.co.uk
website: www.glendower-house.co.uk

MONTACUTE

Paterson and Sue Weir, Slipper Cottage, 41 Bishopston, Montacute TA15 6UX (01935 823073; mobile: 07812 145402; Fax: 01935 826868). A friendly welcome awaits you at this charming 17th century cottage, in one of Somerset's prettiest villages. Montacute House, excellent pubs and restaurants just around the corner. Tintinhull House Gardens, Barrington Court, Stourhead, Lytes Cary, Wells Cathedral, Sherborne Abbey, Glastonbury Abbey and Lyme Regis not far away. Four golf courses within ten miles. Accommodation consists of two double rooms, both with vanity basin, shaver point, colour TV, central heating and tea/coffee making facilities. Terms from £40 to £44 per room, per night including breakfast. Single occupancy £26 to £40. Sorry, no pets, no smoking. Open all year except Christmas and New Year. *FHG DIPLOMA WINNER 2001, 2002.* **ETC** ◆◆◆

e-mail: pat.weir@ntlworld.co.uk

website: www.slippercottage.co.uk

PORLOCK

Margery and Henry Dyer, West Porlock House, West Porlock, Near Minehead TA24 8NX (01643 862880). Imposing country house in Exmoor National Park on the wooded slopes of West Porlock commanding exceptional sea views of Porlock Bay and countryside. Set in five acres of beautiful woodland gardens unique for its variety and size of unusual trees and shrubs and offering a haven of rural tranquillity. The house has large spacious rooms with fine and beautiful furnishings throughout. Two double, two twin and one family bedrooms, all with en suite or private bathrooms, TV, tea/coffee making facilities, radio-alarm clock and shaver point. Licensed. Non-smoking. Private car park. Bed and Breakfast from £27.50 to £30.00 per person. Credit Cards accepted. Sorry, no pets. **ETC** ◆◆◆◆

PORLOCK

Mr & Mrs Cotterell, The Ship Inn, High Street, Porlock TA24 8QD (01643 862507; Fax: 01643 863224). The thatched 13th century Ship Inn is within walking distance of sea and moor. There is a genuine old bar with stone floors and roaring log fires in winter. There are 10 bedrooms, mainly en suite. Local produce used. Traditional English cooking with a modern twist, real ales. Gardens to enjoy. Ship's log details special events. **RAC** ◆◆◆
e-mail: mail@shipinnporlock.co.uk
website: www.shipinnporlock.co.uk

Ralegh's Cross Inn

Brendon Hill, Exmoor, Somerset TA23 0LN
Tel: 01984 640343 • Fax: 01984 641111

High in the beautiful Brendon Hills, Exmoor National Park, Ralegh's Cross Inn offers the warmest of welcomes, a million miles from the stresses of modern life. All rooms en suite, with colour TV and hospitality tray. An extensive menu, with freshly prepared starters, home-cooked main courses and home-made desserts, is available daily. We're also famous locally for our tasty Farmer's Carvery. A walker's, rider's and fisherman's paradise with many nearby places of interest for the tourist too. Open all year. Seasonal leisure breaks. Colour brochure available.

e-mail: enquiry@raleghscross.co.uk • website: www.raleghscross.co.uk

See also Colour Advertisement

SHEPTON MALLET

Mr and Mrs J. Grattan, Park Farm House, Forum Lane, Bowlish, Shepton Mallet BA4 5JL (01749 343673; Fax: 01749 345279). A 17th century house, formerly a working farm, situated in a conservation area. The accommodation comprises one twin-bedded room (bathroom en suite) and a suite of a double bedroom and a twin bedroom with private facilities. There is ample car parking. Conveniently situated close to the ancient Cathedral City of Wells (four miles), Cheddar Gorge and caves, Clarks village at Street and Longleat within 12 miles. The Georgian city of Bath, and Bristol, are only 18 miles away. Shepton Mallet has good restaurants, many local pubs and easy access to the scenic Mendip Hills. Bed and Breakfast from £18.50 per person per night: no single person supplement.
e-mail: john.marjorie@ukonline.co.uk

TAUNTON

Anne and Bill Slipper, The Old Mill, Bishop's Hull, Taunton TA1 5AB (Tel & Fax: 01823 289732). Relax and enjoy the hospitality in this Grade II Listed former Corn Mill, situated on the edge of a conservation village just two miles from Taunton. We have two lovely double bedrooms, The Mill Room with en suite facilities overlooking the weir pool, and The Cottage Suite with its own private bathroom, again with views over the river. Both rooms are centrally heated, with TV, generous beverage tray and thoughtful extras. Guests have their own lounge and dining area overlooking the river, where breakfast may be taken from our extensive breakfast menu amidst machinery of a bygone era. We are a non-smoking establishment. Double en suite £27 pppn, double with private bathroom £24 pppn. **ETC** ◆◆◆◆◆ *SILVER AWARD*.

TAUNTON

The Falcon Hotel, Henlade, Taunton TA3 5DH (01823 442502; Fax: 01823 442670). You can always expect a warm welcome at this historic villa, with just the right blend of comfortable, spacious accommodation, friendly efficient staff and the personal attention of its family owners. Located one mile from the M5 motorway, it makes an ideal base for business stays, or as a touring centre for this attractive corner of the West Country. Facilities include ten en suite bedrooms with colour TV, tea/coffee making facilities, direct dial telephone, etc. Honeymoon suite, conference facilities, restaurant and ample parking. Superbly accessible to Quantock, Blackdown Hills, Exmoor, North and South Devon coasts. Our tariff is inclusive of a Full English Breakfast. **ETC** ★★★, **AA** ★★

TAUNTON

Mr and Mrs P.J. Painter, Blorenge House, 57 Staplegrove Road, Taunton TA1 1DG (Tel & Fax: 01823 283005). Spacious Victorian residence set in large gardens with a swimming pool and large car park. Situated just five minutes' walking distance from Taunton town centre, railway, bus station and Records Office. 24 comfortable bedrooms with washbasin, central heating, colour TV and tea making facilities. Five of the bedrooms have traditional four-poster beds, ideal for weekends away and honeymoon couples. Family and twin rooms are available. The majority of rooms have en suite facilities. Large dining room traditionally furnished; full English breakfast/ Continental breakfast included in the price. Please send for our colour brochure. **ETC/AA** ◆◆◆◆
website: www.blorengehouse.co.uk

TAUNTON

John and Ann Bartlett, The Spinney, Curland, Taunton TA3 5SE (Tel & Fax: 01460 234362). Six miles from Taunton, convenient for A303 and M5. Ann and John welcome you to their home on the slopes of the Blackdown Hills. Nestling in a designated Area of Outstanding Natural Beauty, The Spinney is an ideal base for holidays, day excursions, walking or visiting places of interest. The double, twin or family bedrooms all have colour TV, beverage tray and central heating with quality en suite facilities. Ground floor rooms available. Evening meals are recommended. Non-smokers only please. Open all year. Bed and Breakfast: double/twin £25 per person per night, single £40 per person per night. **ETC** ◆◆◆◆, **AA** *FOUR RED DIAMONDS*
e-mail: bartlett.spinney@zetnet.co.uk
website: www.somerweb.co.uk/spinney-bb

TAUNTON (near)

Peter McGuire, Rydon Farm, West Newton TA7 0BZ (01278 663472). Rydon Farm is a large rural farmhouse set in beautiful landscaped gardens. It dates from 1540 with many period features including beams and inglenooks. We have two large double bedrooms and a twin, en suite facilities and a guests' lounge with woodburner. Bedrooms are tastefully furnished with courtesy tray, hairdryer, selection of books and TV. Midway between Taunton and Bridgwater, within two miles of the M5, we are ideally located for walkers, cyclists or holidaymakers, with the Quantock Hills and Somerset Levels nearby. Ample parking. Bed and Breakfast from £25. Non-smoking. Open all year. **ETC** ◆◆◆◆
e-mail: info@rydonfarm.com
website: www.rydonfarm.com

See also Colour Display Advertisement

TAUNTON (near)

Mrs Pam Parry, Pear Tree Cottage Thatched Country Cottage & Garden B&B, Stapley, Churchstanton, Taunton TA3 7QA (Tel & Fax: 01823 601224). An old thatched country cottage halfway between Taunton and Honiton, set in the idyllic Blackdown Hills, designated an Area of Outstanding Natural Beauty. Picturesque countryside laced with winding lanes full of natural flora and fauna. Wildlife abounds. Three-quarters of an acre traditional cottage garden leading off to two-and-a-half acres of meadow garden planted with specimen trees. Central for north/south coasts of Somerset, Dorset and Devon. Exmoor, Dartmoor, Bristol, Bath, etc within little more than an hour's drive. Many gardens and National Trust properties encompassed in a day's outing. Double/single and family suite with own facilities, TV, tea/coffee. Conservatory/ Garden Room. Evening Meals available. Open all year. **ETC** ◆◆◆
e-mail: colvin.parry@virgin.net
www.SmoothHound.co.uk/hotels/thatch.html or www.best-hotel.com/peartreecottage

THEALE

Gilly & Vern Clark, Yew Tree Farm, Theale, Near Wedmore BS28 4SN (01934 712475). This 17th century farmhouse is equidistant between Wells and Cheddar both approximately ten minutes away by car. The seaside towns of Weston, Burnham and Brean are close by and the cities of Bath and Bristol, both served with park and ride facilities, are approx. 40 minutes' drive. There is a very warm welcome awaiting you at this farm, which has been in the Clark family for over 120 years. Lovely accommodation with en suite facilities, colour TV (one room with video) and full coffee and tea making facilities. Two and three-course meals available. Children welcome; occasional pets at discretion of the owners. From £21 per person per night. Please telephone for brochure.
e-mail: enquiries@yewtreefarmbandb.co.uk

See also Colour Display Advertisement

WASHFORD

Mrs Sarah Richmond, Hungerford Farm, Washford, Watchet TA23 0JZ (01984 640285). Hungerford Farm is a comfortable 13th century farmhouse on a 350 acre mixed farm, three-quarters of a mile from the West Somerset Steam Railway; quarter-of-a-mile from Cleeve Abbey and Washford Mill offering local arts and crafts. Situated in beautiful countryside on the edge of the Brendon Hills and Exmoor National Park. Within easy reach of the North Devon coast, two-and-a-half miles from the Bristol Channel and Quantock Hills. Marvellous country for walking, riding, and fishing on the reservoirs. Family room and twin-bedded room, both with colour TV; own bathroom, shower. Breakfast room with TV and open fire on colder days. Children welcome at reduced rates, cot and high chair. Pets by arrangement. Bed and Breakfast from £20, reduced rates for longer stays. Evening drink included. Open February to November.
e-mail: sarah.richmond@virgin.net

See also Colour Display Advertisement

WELLS

Mrs Sheila Stott, Lana, Hollow Farm, The Hollow, Westbury-sub-Mendip, Near Wells BA5 1HH (Tel & Fax: 01749 870635). Modern farmhouse on working farm. Comfortable family home in beautiful gardens with views of Somerset Levels and the Mendip Hills. Quiet location. Breakfast room for sole use of guests. Full English breakfast (meals available at local pub five minutes' walk away). En suite rooms including fridge, hairdryer, tea/coffee facilities, shaver point, colour TV and central heating. Non-smoking. Terms from £23 per person per night. Reduced rates for three nights or more.
e-mail: sheila@stott.2366

WESTON-SUPER-MARE

Mr and Mrs H. Wallington, Braeside Hotel, 2 Victoria Park, Weston-super-Mare BS23 2HZ (Tel & Fax: 01934 626642). Delightful family-run hotel, ideally situated near sandy beach; shops and park are close by. All our nine bedrooms have bath/shower and toilet en suite, colour TV and coffee/tea making facilities and are tastefully decorated, creating just the right atmosphere in which to relax after a busy day. Some rooms with sea views. Unrestricted on-street parking. Good base for exploring Mendip and Quantock Hills, Exmoor, etc. Directions: with sea on left, take first right after Winter Gardens, then first left into Lower Church Road, Victoria Park is the cul-de-sac on the right after the left hand bend. Special Bed and Breakfast offer: Nov - April inclusive (excluding Easter weekend) - THIRD NIGHT FREE. ETC/AA ◆◆◆
e-mail: braeside@tesco.net
website: www.braesidehotel.co.uk

ENGLAND

WESTON-SUPER-MARE

John and Katie Nelson, The Owl's Crest, 39 Kewstoke Road, Kewstoke, Weston-super-Mare BS22 9YE (01934 417672). Situated within the small country village of Kewstoke, just one and three quarters of a mile from Weston and just minutes from the M5. Ideally placed for walks through National Trust countryside or relaxing strolls along the unspoilt beach at Sand Bay. A friendly, personal service is offered with the flexibility to make your stay as enjoyable as possible. Relax in our comfortable guest lounge or in fine weather enjoy the sheltered sunny garden terrace. All our individually decorated rooms are en suite with TV, radio alarm clock, hairdryer and tea/coffee tray. Recommended restaurant/carvery within village. Bed and Breakfast from £23.50 per person per night. Non-smoking throughout. *WELCOME HOST AWARD. GOLD COMMENDED AWARD WINNERS – WESTON HOTELS ASSOCIATION.* e-mail: **theowlscrest@talk21.com**

WESTON-SUPER-MARE

Mrs Margaret Holt, Moorlands, Hutton, Weston-super-Mare BS24 9QH (Tel & Fax: 01934 812283). Enjoy fine food and warm hospitality at this impressive late Georgian house set in landscaped gardens below the slopes of the Western Mendips. A wonderful touring centre, perfectly placed for visits to beaches, sites of special interest and historic buildings. Families with children particularly welcome; reduced terms and pony rides. Full central heating, open fire in comfortable lounge. Licensed. Open all year. Bed and Breakfast from £21 per person. **ETC ◆◆◆**

WESTON-SUPER-MARE

Sunset Bay Hotel, 53 Beach Road, Weston-Super-Mare BS23 1BH (01934 623519). Sunset Bay Hotel is a non-smoking, small, family-run hotel enjoying an unrivalled position on the seafront, with superb views to Weston Bay and the Welsh coastline. A guest lounge on the first floor overlooks the bay, with games and books for the enjoyment of our guests. Breakfast is served in the dining room/bar overlooking the beach and lawns, and though we do not provide evening meals, there is a menu of hot and cold snacks. Packed lunches can be supplied on request. All rooms are en suite, or with a private bathroom, and TV, tea/coffee making facilities, hairdryers and towels are supplied in all rooms. On arrival we would like to welcome you with a complimentary tray of tea and cakes. Sunset Bay is ideal for family holidays, weekend breaks, short breaks and holidays at any time of year. e-mail: **relax@sunsetbayhotel.co.uk**

WIVELISCOMBE

Jenny Cope, North Down Farm, Pyncombe Lane, Wiveliscombe, Taunton TA4 2BL (Tel & Fax: 01984 623730). In tranquil, secluded surroundings on the Somerset/ Devon Border. Traditional working farm set in 100 acres of natural beauty with panoramic views of over 40 miles. M5 motorway seven miles and Taunton ten miles. All rooms tastefully furnished to high standard include en suite, TV, and tea/coffee facilities. Double, twin or single rooms available. Dining room and lounge with log fires for our guests' comfort; centrally heated and double glazed. Drying facilities. Delicious home produced food a speciality. Fishing, golf, horse riding and country sports nearby. Dogs welcome. Bed and Breakfast from £25 pppn, £195 weekly. North Down Break: three nights Bed and Breakfast and Evening Meal £95 per person. **ETC ◆◆◆◆** *SILVER AWARD.* e-mail: **jennycope@tiscali.co.uk**

STAFFORDSHIRE

ALTON

Church Grange Guest House, Bradley in the Moors, Alton ST10 4DF (01889 507525). A licensed country guest house in a spectacular location just a five-minute drive from world-famous Alton Towers; also convenient for Uttoxeter Racecourse. Church Grange is a wonderful base for families visiting the Peak District - after one of our hearty breakfasts you'll be ready to enjoy the UK's favourite place all the more! We offer our guests a warm welcome and spacious, beautifully furnished bedrooms, all with TV and tea/coffee making facilities. Three rooms en suite; one with private shower and WC. Central heating. Ample parking. Please contact Maureen Salt for details. ETC ◆◆◆◆
e-mail: enquiries@chgrange.co.uk
website: www.chgrange.plus.com

See also Colour Display Advertisement

ECCLESHALL

M. Hiscoe-James, Offley Grove Farm, Adbaston, Eccleshall ST20 0QB (01785 280205). You'll consider this a good find! Quality accommodation and excellent breakfasts. Small traditional mixed farm surrounded by beautiful countryside. The house is tastefully furnished and provides all home comforts. Whether you are planning to book here for a break in your journey, stay for a weekend or take your holidays here, you will find something to suit all tastes among the many local attractions. Situated on the Staffordshire/Shropshire borders we are convenient for Alton Towers, Stoke-on-Trent, Ironbridge, etc. Just 15 minutes from M6 and M54; midway between Eccleshall and Newport, four miles from the A519. Reductions for children. Play area for children. Open all year. Bed and Breakfast all en suite from £24. Many guests return. Self-catering cottages available. Brochure on request.
RAC ◆◆◆ *WARM WELCOME AWARD AND SPARKLING DIAMOND AWARD.*
e-mail: accomm@offleygrovefarm.freeserve.co.uk   website: www.offleygrovefarm.co.uk

HARLASTON/TAMWORTH

Mrs Joyce Rowe, Harlaston Post Office, Main Road, Harlaston, Tamworth B79 9JU (01827 383324; Fax: 01827 383746). Situated within the Mease Valley, the Post Office is in the centre of the attractive village of Harlaston, opposite the church. Lichfield and Tamworth and their many attractions are within easy reach. Accommodation features a conservatory overlooking the garden, five en suite rooms in the main building and three annexe rooms, all with tea/coffee making facilities and TV. Family room available on request. No smoking. Secure parking available. Excellent pub in village for evening meals. Single from £25, double or twin from £45, excluding VAT. AA ◆◆◆◆

OAKAMOOR

Mr and Mrs C. Franks, The Beehive, Churnet View Road, Oakamoor ST10 3AE (01538 702420). The Beehive is a family-run, non-smoking guest house overlooking the River Churnet, offering Bed and Breakfast accommodation in the peaceful village of Oakamoor. All rooms en suite with central heating, colour TV and tea/coffee making facilities. Private parking. Ideally situated for visiting the Peak District National Park and the Staffordshire Moorlands. The world famous Potteries are only 12 miles away. Enjoy the antique shops of Ashbourne and Leek. The thrill of Alton Towers is only one mile away. Enjoy a romantic break in one of our four-poster beds. Open from January to December. Prices from £23 per person per night. ETC/AA ◆◆◆◆
e-mail: thebeehiveoakamoor@btinternet.com   website: www.thebeehiveguesthouse.co.uk

TAMWORTH

Mrs Jane Davies, Middleton House Farm, Middleton, Near Tamworth B78 2BD (01827 873474; Fax: 01827 872246). Middleton House Farm is a family-run dairy and arable farm of 400 acres. The farmhouse dates back to the 18th century and, after extensive refurbishment, consists of five bedrooms, all individually and tastefully furnished to a very high standard with locally crafted old pine furniture. Situated just two miles from J9 of M42 opposite the Belfry Golf Course, 15 minutes from Birmingham and NEC, 10 minutes from Tamworth (Castle, Snowdome and Drayton Manor). Guests' own lounge and diningroom with individual tables. Bedrooms all with colour TV, hospitality tray, hairdryer and extras; full central heating. Bed and Breakfast from £27.50 per person. Non-smoking. Ample car parking. **ETC** ◆◆◆ *SILVER AWARD.*

e-mail: rob.jane@tinyonline.co.uk   **website: www.middletonhousefarm.co.uk**

UTTOXETER

Glenda Lovatt, Bowmore House, Stone Road, Bramshall, Uttoxeter ST14 8SH (Tel & Fax: 01889 564452). Bowmore House is a 200-year-old former farmhouse which has been extensively renovated and modernised. It is set in the middle of beautiful countryside, two miles from Uttoxeter and six miles from Alton Towers. One double and one single room on the ground floor share a bathroom, and upstairs there is a double room with private bathroom. Rooms have courtesy tray, kettle, colour TV and radio. Bed and full farmhouse Breakfast with eggs from our own hens from £25pppn; special rates for children and short breaks. There is a small paddock suitable for anyone wishing to take a horse riding holiday. **ETC** ◆◆◆◆
e-mail: glovatt@furoris.com

• • *Some Useful Guidance for Guests and Hosts* • •

Every year literally thousands of holidays, short breaks and overnight stops are arranged through our guides, the vast majority without any problems at all. In a handful of cases, however, difficulties do arise about bookings, which often could have been prevented from the outset.

It is important to remember that when accommodation has been booked, both parties – guests and hosts – have entered into a form of contract. We hope that the following points will provide helpful guidance.

GUESTS:

• When enquiring about accommodation, be as precise as possible. Give exact dates, numbers in your party and the ages of any children.

• State the number and type of rooms wanted and also what catering you require – bed and breakfast, full board etc. Make sure that the position about evening meals is clear – and about pets, reductions for children or any other special points.

• Read our reviews carefully to ensure that the proprietors you are going to contact can supply what you want. Ask for a letter confirming all arrangements, if possible.

• If you have to cancel, do so as soon as possible. Proprietors do have the right to retain deposits and under certain circumstances to charge for cancelled holidays if adequate notice is not given and they cannot re-let the accommodation.

HOSTS:

• Give details about your facilities and about any special conditions. Explain your deposit system clearly and arrangements for cancellations, charges etc. and whether or not your terms include VAT.

• If for any reason you are unable to fulfil an agreed booking without adequate notice, you may be under an obligation to arrange suitable alternative accommodation or to make some form of compensation.

While every effort is made to ensure accuracy, we regret that FHG Publications cannot accept responsibility for errors, omissions or misrepresentations in our entries or any consequences thereof. Prices in particular should be checked because we go to press early. We will follow up complaints but cannot act as arbiters or agents for either party.

SUFFOLK

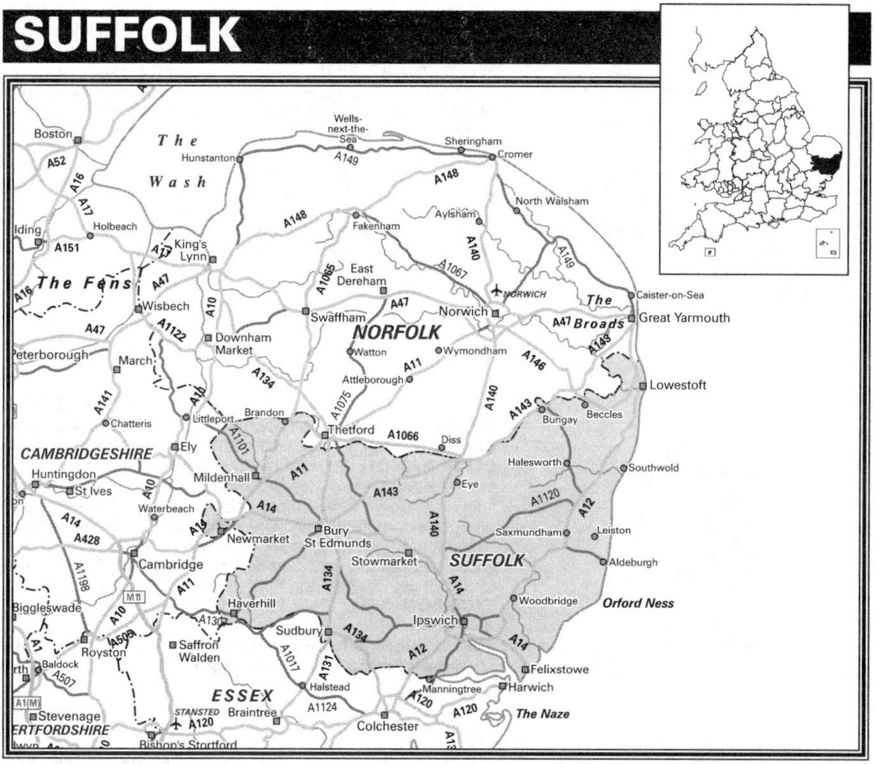

ENGLAND

[Map of Suffolk and surrounding counties showing Norfolk, Cambridgeshire, Essex, Hertfordshire, with towns, A-roads including Bury St Edmunds, Ipswich, Norwich, Cambridge, Colchester, Great Yarmouth, Lowestoft, Orford Ness, The Naze, and inset map of England.]

BURY ST EDMUNDS

John Kemp, Gifford's Hall, Hartest, Near Bury St Edmunds IP29 4EX (01284 830464; Fax: 01284 830964). Gifford's Hall is a vineyard and small country living set in some of Suffolk's most beautiful and tranquil surroundings, midway between Bury, Lavenham and Sudbury. It is a Listed Georgian farmhouse with large comfortable rooms including one twin and one double with en suite bathrooms. Guests have the use of the large drawing/TV/games room and breakfast is usually taken in the conservatory. You will be welcome to explore our 33 acres which includes 12 acres of vines and a winery, wild flower meadows grazed by rare breed sheep, pigs, goats and pure breed free range hens, an acre rose garden, sweet peas and chrysanthemums, an organic vegetable garden and even a shop and tea room where you can enjoy a cream tea or taste the wines. Bed and Breakfast £50 double, £55 twin. Brochures on request.

e-mail: john@giffordshall.co.uk

BURY ST EDMUNDS

Kay Dewsbury, Manorhouse, The Green, Beyton, Near Bury St Edmunds IP30 9AF (01359 270960). You will find a welcoming and relaxed atmosphere at this lovely timbered 15th century farmhouse, set in large gardens overlooking village green. Pretty, spacious, en suite bedrooms – two twin and two double, king-size, with sofas; all with colour TV, tea-making, radio and hairdryer. Choice of breakfasts at individual tables. A non-smoking house. Parking. Good local inns. Terms from £27 per person per night. Beyton signposted off A14. **ETC** ◆◆◆◆◆ *GOLD AWARD, WHICH? GUIDE RECOMMENDED.*
e-mail: manorhouse@beyton.com
website: www.beyton.com

CLARE

Alastair and Woolfy Tuffill, "Cobbles", 26 Nethergate Street, Clare, Near Sudbury CO10 8NP (01787 277539; Fax: 01787 278252). Situated in one of the loveliest parts of East Anglia, a friendly welcome awaits you at Cobbles - this Grade II Listed beamed house dates back to the 14th century. Clare is an historic market town and the area abounds in history and ancient buildings, with many antique shops and places of interest to visit. The house is within easy walking distance of the ancient castle and country park, and the town centre with pubs and restaurants which provide excellent food. Accommodation is provided in one twin and one single bedroom in the house with bathroom. Within the pretty walled garden is the charming beamed twin-bedded en suite cottage with private access. All rooms have central heating, colour TV, handbasins and tea/coffee making facilities. Bed and Breakfast from £26 per person per night. Easy parking. We are strictly non-smoking.

FELIXSTOWE

Geoffrey & Elizabeth Harvey, The Grafton Guest House, 13 Sea Road, Felixstowe IP11 2BB (01394 284881; Fax: 01394 279101). Situated by the sea front, the Grafton offers quality Bed and Breakfast accommodation. All en suite and standard rooms have colour TV, clock radio, hairdryer and tea/coffee making facilities. Owners Geoffrey and Elizabeth are committed to providing a first class service and extend a warm welcome to all guests. Non-smoking throughout. Single rooms from £23.50, double from £40, per night, including breakfast. ETC/RAC ◆◆◆◆ *SPARKLING DIAMOND, WARM WELCOME AWARD.*
e-mail: info@grafton-house.com
website: www.grafton-house.com

FRAMLINGHAM

Mr & Mrs Jones, Bantry, Chapel Road, Saxtead, Woodbridge IP13 9RB (01728 685578). Bantry is situated in the picturesque village of Saxtead close to the historic castle town of Framlingham. Saxtead is best known for its working windmill beside the village green. Bantry is set in half an acre of gardens overlooking open countryside and three-quarters-of-a-mile along Tannington Road on right-hand side from Saxtead Windmill. We offer you accommodation in one of three purpose-built self-contained en suite apartments (one ground floor), separate from the house. For secluded comfort each comprises an en suite bedroom leading through to its own private lounge/diningroom with TV and drink-making facilities. Bed and Breakfast from £20 per person per night. Non-smoking.

e-mail: cheryl.jones@sleepysuffolk.co.uk   **website: www.sleepysuffolk.co.uk**

FRAMLINGHAM

Brian and Phyllis Collett, Shimmens Pightle, Dennington Road, Framlingham, Woodbridge IP13 9JT (01728 724036). Shimmens Pightle is situated in an acre of landscaped garden, surrounded by farmland, within a mile of the centre of Framlingham, with its famous castle and church. Ideally situated for the Heritage Coast, Snape Maltings, local vineyards, riding, etc. Cycles can be hired locally. Many good local eating places. Double and twin bedded rooms, with washbasins, on ground floor. Comfortable lounge with TV overlooking garden. Morning tea and evening drinks offered. Sorry, no pets or smoking indoors. Bed and traditional English Breakfast using local cured bacon and home made marmalade, from £23.50 per person, reduced weekly rates. Vegetarians also happily catered for. SAE please. Open Mid-April to October. ETC ◆◆◆

IPSWICH

Mrs Rosanna Steward, High View, Back Lane, Washbrook, Ipswich IP8 3JA (01473 730494). A comfortable modernised Edwardian house set in a large secluded garden located four miles south of Ipswich, the county town of Suffolk. Ideally situated to explore the Suffolk heritage coast and countryside, we are within easy reach of "Constable Country", Lavenham, Kersey, the historic market town of Bury St Edmunds plus many other picturesque locations. There is a maze of public footpaths in and around the village providing a good variety of walks through woodland and open countryside. Twin, double and single bedrooms; guests' bathroom with shower and toilet, lounge with TV. Good pub meals available in the village. Double and Twin from £22 and Single £22 per person per night. No smoking. **ETC ◆◆◆◆**
e-mail: rosanna.steward@virgin.net

PEASENHALL

Mrs Fiona Burley, Bay House, Rendham Road, Peasenhall IP17 2NQ (01728 660221). A comfortable Country House in peaceful surroundings on the outskirts of a pleasant unspoilt Suffolk village. Eight miles from the sea and close to Aldeburgh, Snape Maltings and the bird reserve at Minsmere. Numerous places of historic interest close by. Private sitting room. En suite facilities with tea/coffee in the bedroom which looks out on to open countryside and woodland. Regret, no pets. Evening meals not provided, but there are several good pubs and restaurants close by. Bed and Breakfast £25.

WOODBRIDGE

Sue Bagnall, Abbey House, Monk Soham, Woodbridge IP13 7EN (01728 685225). Abbey House is a Victorian rectory set in ten acres of quiet Suffolk countryside in the village of Monk Soham, between Debenham and Framlingham, and within easy reach of Southwold, Lavenham and Aldeburgh. The house is surrounded by secluded gardens with ponds and woodland. The remainder of the grounds are occupied by some Jersey cows, sheep, chickens and waterfowl. Guest accommodation comprises double bedrooms, with either en suite or private bathroom and tea making facilities; exclusive use of dining room and drawing room, with log fire. Bed and Breakfast en suite £27.50 pppn (double); £30 pppn (twin); £25 pppn with private facilities. Please write or phone for further information.

WOODBRIDGE

Grange Farm, Dennington, Woodbridge IP13 8BT (01986 798388; mobile: 07774 182835). A warm welcome awaits you at our exceptional moated farmhouse dating from the 13th Century, and set in extensive grounds including ace all weather tennis court, in a superb spot two and a half miles north of Dennington. A comfortable base with log fires in winter and plenty of beams. Close to Snape Maltings, the coast, Minsmere and many places of interest. Accommodation comprises one single, one double, two twin bedrooms, guests' own bathroom and sitting room. Good pubs nearby. Bread and marmalade home made. Parking available. Children welcome. Non-smoking. B&B from £22 single, £44 double/twin. **ETC ◆◆◆**
website: www.framlingham.com/grangefarm

FREE or REDUCED RATE entry to Holiday Visits and Attractions —
see our **READERS' OFFER VOUCHERS** on pages 63-90

SURREY

FARNHAM

Mariners Hotel, Millbridge, Frensham, Farnham GU10 3DJ (01252 792050; Fax: 01252 792649). Within easy reach of Gatwick and Heathrow Airports and ideally placed for visits to London, this country-style hotel has a tranquil situation by the River Wey. Guests of all ages are warmly welcomed and for parents there are baby sitting and listening arrangements and a useful laundry and ironing service. Bedrooms are spacious and provided with a private bathroom, colour television, direct-dial telephone and tea and coffee-making facilities. For disabled guests, there is easy access to ground-floor rooms which overlook well-kept gardens. Dining here presents an interesting choice in a bistro-style restaurant with a range of Italian dishes as well as an extensive buffet and à la carte menu. Food is also served in the cosy lounge bar. **ETC ◆◆◆**
e-mail: info@themarinershotel.co.uk   **website: www.themarinershotel.co.uk**

GATWICK

Carole and Adrian Grinsted, The Lawn Guest House, 30 Massetts Road, Horley RH6 7DE (01293 775751; Fax: 01293 821803). The Lawn, a totally non-smoking establishment, is a lovely Victorian house in a pleasant garden, two minutes from the centre of Horley and one-and-a-half miles from Gatwick. All rooms are en suite with colour TV, hairdryers, tea/coffee/chocolate trays and direct dial telephones. Horley, with its restaurants, shops and pubs is 150 yards away. The mainline railway station (300 yards) has services to London (Victoria 40 minutes) and Brighton (45 minutes). The Lawn is ideal for those 'overnighting' before or after a flight from Gatwick Airport. On site holiday parking by arrangement. Bed and Breakfast from £55 per en suite double/twin room. **ETC/AA/RAC ◆◆◆◆**, *ETC SILVER AWARD, RAC SPARKLING DIAMOND*

e-mail: info@lawnguesthouse.co.uk   **website: www.lawnguesthouse.co.uk**

HORLEY (near Gatwick)

Mrs G. McLean, Gorse Cottage, 66 Balcombe Road, Horley RH6 9AY (01293 784402). Friendly, welcoming accommodation, two miles from Gatwick Airport in residential area with pubs and restaurants within walking distance. Five minutes from railway station serving London (45 minutes) and the South East. Early breakfast catered for, light breakfast served after 7.30am - cereal, scrambled eggs (free-range), toast, coffee, tea and juice. Centrally heated, pleasant room with tea and coffee making facilities. Terms £38 double/twin, £26 single.

Brooklands Museum • *Weybridge, Surrey* • *01932 857381*
website: www.motor-software.co.uk
Set on 30 acres of the original motor racing circuit. Racing cars, motorcycles and bikes, and the new 'Fastest on Earth' exhibition.

FHG PUBLICATIONS publish a large range of well-known accommodation guides. We will be happy to send you details or you can use the order form at the back of this book.

KINGSTON-UPON-THAMES

Chase Lodge Hotel, 10 Park Road, Hampton Wick, Kingston-upon-Thames KT1 4AS (020 8943 1862; Fax: 020 8943 9363). An award-winning hotel with style and elegance, set in tranquil surroundings at affordable prices. Quality en suite bedrooms. Full English breakfast. À la carte menu. Licensed bar. Wedding receptions catered for. Honeymoon suite available with jacuzzi and steam area. Only 20 minutes from Heathrow Airport. Close to Kingston town centre and all major transport links. All Major credit cards accepted. **AA/RAC ★★★,** *LES ROUTIERS.*
e-mail: info@chaselodgehotel.com
website: www.chaselodgehotel.com

LEATHERHEAD

Mrs Robin Reilly, Chalklands, Beech Avenue, Effingham, Leatherhead KT24 5PJ (01372 454936; Fax: 01372 459569). Bed and Breakfast available within easy reach of central London. Facilities include en suite rooms, TV lounge with satellite TV and tea/coffee making. Parking. Children welcome, dogs by arrangement. Single from £30 to £35, double from £50 to £55, triple/family from £60 to £65. **ETC ◆◆◆**
e-mail: rreilly@onetel.net.uk
web: www.SmoothHound.co.uk/hotels/chalklands.html

LINGFIELD

Mrs Vivienne Bundy, Oaklands, Felcourt Road, Lingfield RH7 6NF (01342 834705). Oaklands is a spacious country house of considerable charm dating from the 17th century. It is set in its own grounds of one acre and is about one mile from the small town of Lingfield and three miles from East Grinstead, both with rail connections to London. It is convenient to Gatwick Airport and is ideal as a "stop-over" or as a base to visit many places of interest in south-east England. Dover and the Channel Ports are two hours' drive away whilst the major towns of London and Brighton are about one hour distant. One family room en suite, one double and one single bedrooms with washbasins; three bathrooms, two toilets; sittingroom; diningroom. Cot, high chair, babysitting and reduced rates for children. Gas central heating. Open all year. Parking. Bed and Breakfast from £23; Evening Meal by arrangement.
e-mail: oaklands@ukonline.co.uk

LINGFIELD

Mrs V. Manwill, Stantons Hall Farm, Eastbourne Road, Blindley Heath, Lingfield RH7 6LG (01342 832401). Stantons Hall Farm is an 18th century farmhouse, set in 18 acres of farmland and adjacent to Blindley Heath Common. Family, double and single rooms, most with WC, shower and wash-hand basins en suite. Separate bathroom. All rooms have colour TV, tea/coffee facilities and are centrally heated. There are plenty of parking spaces. We are conveniently situated within easy reach of M25 (London Orbital), Gatwick Airport (car parking for travellers) and Lingfield Park racecourse. Enjoy a traditional English breakfast in our large farmhouse kitchen. Bed and Breakfast from £23.50 per person, reductions for children sharing. Cot and high chair available. Well behaved dogs welcome by prior arrangement.

OXTED

Pinehurst Grange Guest House, East Hill (A25), Oxted RH8 9AE (01883 716413). Victorian ex-farmhouse offers one double, one twin and one single bedroom. All with washbasin, tea/coffee making facilities, colour TV; residents' dining room. Private parking. Close to all local amenities. Only 20 minutes' drive from Gatwick Airport and seven minutes' walk to the station with good trains to London/Croydon. Also close to local bus and taxi service. There are many famous historic houses nearby including "Chartwell", "Knole", "Hever Castle", and "Penshurst Place". Very handy for Lingfield Park racecourse. WALKERS NOTE: only one mile from North Downs Way. No smoking.

REDHILL

Mrs Trozado, Lynwood Guest House, 50 London Road, Redhill RH1 1LN (01737 766894). Gatwick Airport 12 minutes by train or car; London 35 minutes by train. Six minutes' walk to Redhill Station and town centre. Comfortable rooms with en suite facilities, colour TV and tea/coffee facilities. Car park. English Breakfast.

SURBITON

Mrs Menzies, Villiers Lodge, 1 Cranes Park, Surbiton KT5 8AB (020 8399 6000). Excellent accommodation in small Guest House. Every comfort, tea/coffee making facilities in all rooms. Close to trains and buses for London, Hampton Court, Kew, Windsor and coast. Reasonable terms.

SUSSEX

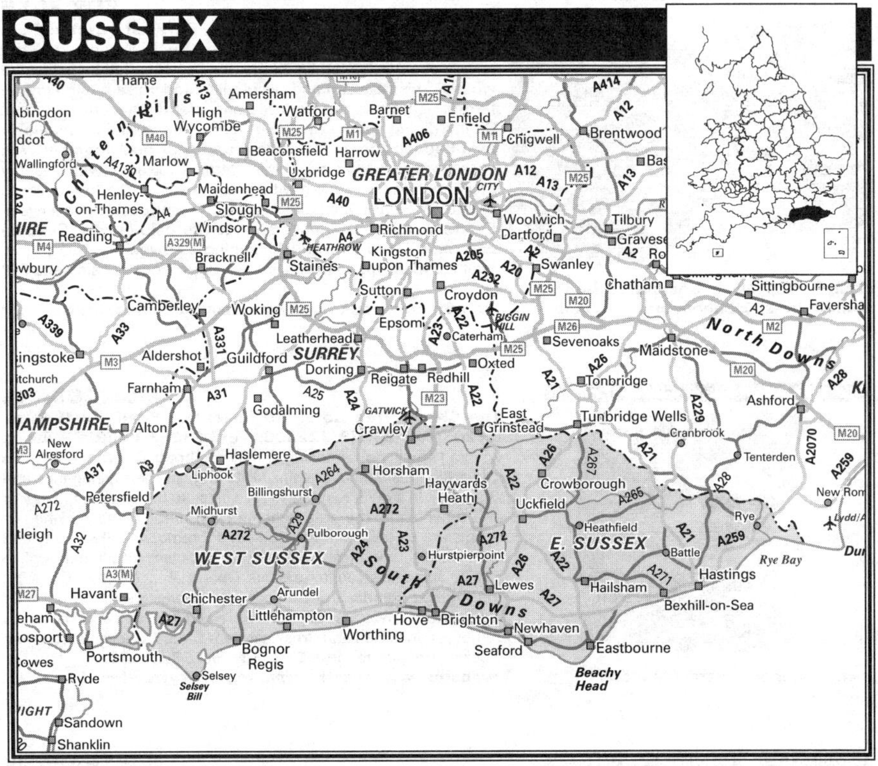

ENGLAND

[Map of Sussex and surrounding areas showing towns and roads including: Thame, Amersham, Watford, Barnet, Enfield, Brentwood, Abingdon, High Wycombe, Beaconsfield, Harrow, Chigwell, Didcot, Marlow, Uxbridge, GREATER LONDON, Wallingford, Maidenhead, LONDON CITY, Henley-on-Thames, Slough, Woolwich, Tilbury, Basildon, SHIRE, Reading, Windsor, Richmond, Dartford, Gravesend, Bracknell, HEATHROW, Kingston upon Thames, Swanley, Rochester, Newbury, Staines, Sutton, Croydon, Chatham, Sittingbourne, Faversham, Camberley, Woking, Epsom, Caterham, Sevenoaks, Maidstone, North Downs, Basingstoke, Aldershot, Guildford, SURREY, Leatherhead, Oxted, Tonbridge, Ashford, Farnham, Dorking, Reigate, Redhill, East Grinstead, Tunbridge Wells, HAMPSHIRE, Alton, Godalming, GATWICK, Crawley, Cranbrook, Tenterden, New Alresford, Haslemere, Horsham, Crowborough, New Romney, Liphook, Billingshurst, Haywards Heath, Uckfield, Petersfield, Midhurst, WEST SUSSEX, Pulborough, Hurstpierpoint, Heathfield, E. SUSSEX, Battle, Rye, Lydd, Leigh, South Downs, Lewes, Hailsham, Hastings, Rye Bay, Havant, Chichester, Arundel, Newhaven, Bexhill-on-Sea, Portsmouth, Littlehampton, Hove, Brighton, Seaford, Eastbourne, Cowes, Ryde, Bognor Regis, Worthing, Beachy Head, Selsey, Selsey Bill, IGHT, Sandown, Shanklin]

EAST SUSSEX

BURWASH

Mrs E. Sirrell, Woodlands Farm, Burwash, Etchingham TN19 7LA (Tel & Fax: 01435 882794). Woodlands Farm stands one third of a mile off the road, surrounded by fields and woods. This peaceful and beautifully modernised 16th century farmhouse offers comfortable and friendly accommodation. Sitting/dining room; two bathrooms, one en suite, double or twin-bedded rooms (one has four-poster bed) together with excellent farm fresh food. This is a farm of 108 acres with a variety of animals and is situated within easy reach of 20 or more places of interest to visit and half an hour from the coast. Open all year. Central heating. Literature provided to help guests. Children welcome. Dogs allowed if sleeping in owner's car. Parking. Evening Meal optional. Bed and Breakfast from £22 single to £48 double. Telephone or SAE, please. Non-smoking.
e-mail: liz_sir@lineone.net   website: www.SmoothHound.co.uk/hotels/woodlands.html

See also Colour Display Advertisement

EASTBOURNE

The Cherry Tree Hotel, 15 Silverdale Road, Eastbourne BN20 7AJ (01323 722406; Fax: 01323 648838). Award winning small, non-smoking, family-run hotel. Converted from an Edwardian residence it retains all its original charm, elegance and character. In a quiet residential area close to the sea front, theatres and downlands, the area benefits from unrestricted parking. All rooms are en suite and have colour TV, radio, hospitality tray and direct dial telephones. Noted for its excellent traditional English cuisine and is licensed to residents. Open March to October, offering the highest standard of facilities and service which you would expect from a Two Star Silver Award Hotel. Bed and Breakfast from £31.50, Dinner, Bed and Breakfast from £44.50. Special Breaks and weekly terms on request. **ETC ★★** *SILVER AWARD.*
e-mail: anncherrytree@aol.com   website: www.eastbourne.org/cherrytree-hotel

See also Colour Display Advertisement

EASTBOURNE

Tony and Trish Callaghan, Far End Private Hotel, 139 Royal Parade, Eastbourne BN22 7LH (01323 725666). From the moment you arrive you are assured of a warm welcome and real "home from home" atmosphere. Our centrally heated bedrooms with colour TV and tea/coffee making facilities are tastefully decorated, most have en suite facilities and sea views. Residents have their own lounge and private car park. Enjoy freshly prepared traditional home cooking. Special diets can be catered for. We are adjacent to the popular Princes Park with boating lake, lawns, bowling greens and pitch'n'putt, close by you can enjoy sailing, fishing, bowling, tennis and swimming. We are in easy reach of Beachy Head, the South Downs and Newhaven. We will be delighted to provide information on the many local attractions and services, and shall do our best to make your stay as memorable and pleasant as possible. Bed and Breakfast from £22; Evening Meal available. Low season short breaks. Please call or write for our colour brochure. **AA ◆◆◆**

EASTBOURNE

Pamela & Lyall Davidson, The Alfriston Hotel, 16 Lushington Road, Eastbourne BN21 4LL (Tel & Fax: 01323 725640). Elegant Victorian townhouse hotel in town centre conservation area. Nearest hotel to railway/bus station and shopping and business centre. Near sea, theatres, conference centre and South Downs. 10 bedrooms (all non-smoking), eight en suite and one ground floor two-bedroom suite sharing shower room. All with colour television and tea/coffee making facilities. Full English breakfast in spacious dining room. Licensed. Numerous restaurants nearby. Golf '2 for 1' green fees packages for six local 18-hole courses. Small functions/workshops/seminars catered for. No pets or children under 12. Open all year. **ETC ◆◆◆**
e-mail: alfristonhotel@fsbdial.co.uk

EASTBOURNE

Hotel Iverna, 32 Marine Parade, Eastbourne BN22 7AY (01323 730768). Close to pier, shops and theatres. Magnificent sea views. All rooms with private facilities, colour TV, fridge and tea making facilities. Probably the best breakfast in Eastbourne. Bed and Breakfast from £25 per night. Open all year. Please visit our website for more information. Contact **Dave and Sandra Elkin**. **website: www.hoteliverna.fsnet.co.uk**

See also Colour Display Advertisement

EASTBOURNE

St Omer Hotel, 13 Royal Parade, Eastbourne BN22 7AR (01323 722152; Fax: 01323 723400). A family-run, non-smoking hotel in a prominent seafront position, with panoramic views of the sea, beach and promenade. The comfortable bedrooms are all en suite, with colour TV, clock radio and tea/coffee making facilities. There is an elegant dining room serving fine English cuisine, and a comfortable guest lounge and sun lounge. **ETC/AA ◆◆◆** **e-mail: stomerhotel@hotmail.com** **website: www.st-omer.co.uk**

HAILSHAM (near)

David and Jill Hook, Longleys Farm Cottage, Harebeating Lane, Hailsham BN27 1ER (Tel & Fax: 01323 841227). Situated in quiet private country lane one mile north of the market town of Hailsham with its excellent amenities including modern sports centre and leisure pool, surrounded by footpaths across open farmland. Ideal for country lovers. Dogs and children welcome. The coast at Eastbourne, South Downs, Ashdown Forest and 1066 country are all within easy access. The non-smoking accommodation comprises one twin room, double room en suite; family room en suite and tea/coffee making facilities. Bed and Breakfast from £20 Reductions for children. **ETC ◆◆◆**

HALLAND

Ms Rosi Baynham, Tamberry Hall, Eastbourne Road, Halland, Lewes BN8 6PS (Tel & Fax: 01825 880090). Enjoy the warm and friendly surroundings of this delightful country house with exposed beams. Surrounded by woodland and fields. Centrally situated for touring this Area of Outstanding Natural Beauty. Famous gardens, National Trust, Brighton, Eastbourne and Tunbridge Wells. National golf course three minutes, Glyndebourne 10 minutes. Relax in the comfort of your beautiful room, with tea/coffee, TV, hairdryer and trouser press. Savour our extensive breakfast menu, English, vegetarian or continental. Village pub and restaurant 200 yards. Doubles, family, twin, all en suite. Private parking, non-smoking. B&B from £25 to £45pp. **ETC ◆◆◆◆** *SILVER AWARD.* Self-catering (**ETC ★★★★**) in private wing also available. **e-mail: bedandbreakfast@tamberryhall.fsbusiness.co.uk**

HARTFIELD

Bolebroke Castle, Hartfield TN7 4JJ (01892 770061; Fax: 01892 771041). Henry VIII's hunting lodge is set in a stunningly beautiful location on a 30 acre estate away from main roads and noise. There are two lakes, woodlands and views to the Ashdown Forest where you will find Pooh Bridge. The castle has antique furniture, original beamed ceilings and the second largest fireplace in England. Four-poster suite. Colour TV. Tea/coffee facilities. Bed and Breakfast and self-catering available. Tunbridge Wells five miles. Eastbourne and Brighton 30 miles. Telephone for brochure. **ETC** ◆◆◆◆
website: www.bolebrokecastle.co.uk

HASTINGS

Peter Mann, Grand Hotel, Grand Parade, St Leonards, Hastings TN38 0DD (Tel & Fax: 01424 428510 or 0870 2257025). Seafront family-run hotel, half-a-mile west of Hastings Pier. Spacious lounge, licensed bar, central heating. Some rooms have colour TV, radio/room-call/baby-listening and some have en suite facilities. Free access at all times. Unrestricted/disabled parking. Non-smoking throughout hotel. In the heart of 1066 country close to Battle Abbey, Bodiam and Hever Castles, Kipling's Bateman and historic Cinque Ports plus Hastings Castle, Caves, Sealife Aquarium, local golf courses and leisure centres. Open all year. Bed and Breakfast from £15; Evening Meal from £15. Children welcome, half price when sharing room. SAE for further information. **ETC** ◆◆◆

RYE

Pat and Jeff Sullivan, Cliff Farm, Iden Lock, Rye TN31 7QE (Tel & Fax: 01797 280331 – long ring please). Our farmhouse is peacefully set in a quiet elevated position with extensive views over Romney Marsh. The ancient seaport town of Rye with its narrow cobbled streets is two miles away. We are an ideal touring base although the town and immediate district have much to offer - golden beaches, quaint villages, castles, gardens etc. Comfortable guest bedrooms with washbasins and tea/coffee making facilities; two toilets; own shower; diningroom and sittingroom. Home produce. Open March to October for Bed and Breakfast from £20 per person. Reduced weekly rates. **AA** ◆◆◆
e-mail: pat@cliff-farm.co.uk
website: www.cliff-farm.co.uk

RYE

Mr & Mrs Cogan, Aviemore Guest House, 28/30 Fishmarket Road, Rye TN31 7LP (Tel & Fax: 01797 223052). Guests are assured of a genuinely warm welcome and clean, comfortable accommodation at Aviemore, which overlooks the park and the River Rother, just two minutes' walk from the town centre. Four double rooms (two en suite) and four twin rooms (two en suite); all with remote-control colour TV and complimentary tea, coffee, hot chocolate and biscuit tray. Central heating throughout. 24-hour access. Bathroom/toilet, separate shower/toilet. Guest lounge, separate breakfast room with Bar. Credit cards accepted. Car park nearby. Excellent full English breakfast with choices. Bed and Breakfast (based on two sharing) £50 per room per night en suite, £42 per room per night standard double or twin. **ETC** ◆◆◆
e-mail: aviemore@lineone.net

RYE

Barbara and Denys Martin, Little Saltcote, 22 Military Road, Rye TN31 7NY (01797 223210; Fax: 01797 224474). Situated in a quiet road, just ten minutes' walk from the centre of medieval Rye, Little Saltcote is an Edwardian family home which offers off-road parking and five comfortable rooms (one at ground floor), all with TV, radio and beverage tray. With a 'nothing is too much trouble' philosophy we aim to ensure our guests leave relaxed and refreshed. We welcome families and are pleased to offer tourist advice or arrange bike hire. Ideally located for touring Sussex and Kent's varied attractions, including everything from sandy beaches to castles, historic houses and gardens. Rates, including acclaimed full English or vegetarian breakfast, start from £20 per person. Special offer available from November to February. Pets welcome by arrangement. **AA** ◆◆◆
e-mail: littlesaltcote.rye@virgin.net

RYE

Geoff and Gillian Woods, The Strand House, Winchelsea, Near Rye TN36 4JT (01797 226276; Fax 01797 224806). Nestling beneath the cliff of the ancient medieval town of Winchelsea lies the 15th century Strand House, previously the town workhouse. Full of atmosphere with oak beams and inglenook fireplaces, but with the comfort of en suite facilities, central heating, colour TV and beverage tray. Romantic four-poster bedroom available. A lounge with log fires in winter leads onto a pretty garden for your enjoyment in summer. A residents' bar, payphone, and ample parking in the grounds make your visit relaxed and enjoyable. An ideal place to stay while you explore the many places of interest within easy reach. Tariff from £28 to £42 per person. Visa/Mastercard/Eurocard accepted. Non-smoking. *ETC* ◆◆◆ *SILVER AWARD*, **AA** *FOUR RED DIAMONDS.*
e-mail: strandhouse@winchelsea98.fsnet.co.uk

RYE

Mrs Wanda Bosher, The Old Vicarage at Rye Harbour, Rye TN31 7TT (01797 222088). Enjoy quality bed and breakfast of the highest standard in our former Victorian vicarage. Very quietly situated, with original features, open fires, linen and lace, antique furniture and oil paintings – be transported back to the genteel pace and ambience of times past. Breakfasts are taken in the elegant diningroom and with fresh local produce, it is certainly a meal to remember. During the winter a crackling log fire adds to the pleasure. Monica Edwards, the well-known children's author, lived here once – one can imagine her planning her tales of intrigue and adventure in Westling Harbour (Rye Harbour). Excellent walking, bird-watching and private parking. Less than an hour from Channel ports and Tunnel, and offering a perfect base for exploring many local towns, historic houses and gardens. Bed and Breakfast from £19.50 to £29.50. **AA ★★★**

Battle Abbey & Battlefield • *Battle, East Sussex* • *01424 773792*
website: english-heritage.org.uk
Discover what really happened in 1066 with an interactive tour of the atmospheric abbey ruins and battlefield. Museum and shop.

The FHG Directory of Website Addresses

on pages 387-415 is a useful quick reference guide for holiday accommodation with e-mail and/or website details

ENGLAND

ST LEONARDS-ON-SEA

Mrs J. Turner, Seaspray Guest House, 54 Eversfield Place, St Leonards-on-Sea, Hastings TN37 6DB (01424 436583). Recently refurbished family-run B&B, ideally situated on Hastings seafront. Near pier and White Rock Theatre; five minutes' level walk to the town centre, station and tourist attractions. Family, double and twin rooms are all en suite; single rooms with shared bathrooms. All rooms have tea/coffee making, colour TV, radio alarm, double glazing and central heating; access at all times. Extensive breakfast menu. Children welcome. No smoking. Short breaks available October to April (excluding Christmas and New Year) – details on request. **ETC ◆◆◆◆**
e-mail: jo@seaspray.freeserve.co.uk
website: www.seaspraybb.co.uk

WINCHELSEA

Mrs Wendy Hysted, Orchard Spot, Broad Street, Icklesham, Winchelsea TN36 4AS (01424 814681). A very private detached room in a garden setting with own patio and ample parking. Freedom to come and go as you please. Picturesque area, near to the historic towns of Winchelsea, Rye and Battle. Good walking and cycling and within close proximity of many seaside resorts. Many good local pubs serving a vast variety of excellent food. Twin bedded non-smoking room, with colour TV, tea/coffee making facilities and private en suite. Friendly atmosphere and a good English breakfast is served. Bed and Breakfast from £23. Open April to October. Home-made cakes available.

WEST SUSSEX

ARUNDEL

Mrs Vicki Richards, Woodacre, Arundel Road, Fontwell, Arundel BN18 0QP (01243 814301). Woodacre offers Bed and Breakfast in a traditional family home with accommodation for up to 10-12 guests. The house is set in a beautiful garden surrounded by woodland. We are well positioned for Chichester, Arundel, Goodwood and the seaside and easily accessible from the A27. Our rooms are clean and spacious and two are on the ground floor. We serve a full English breakfast in our conservatory or diningroom overlooking the garden. Plenty of parking space. Everyone is very welcome. Bed and Breakfast from £24 per person. Credit cards accepted. Pets welcome. **ETC ◆◆◆◆**
e-mail: wacrebb@aol.com
website: www.woodacre.co.uk

BOGNOR REGIS

Deborah S. Collinson, The Old Priory, 80 North Bersted Street, Bognor Regis PO22 9AQ (01243 863580; Fax: 01243 826597). A charming 17th century Priory restored to its former glory with a blend of historic charm. Situated in a picturesque rural village close to Bognor Regis, Chichester, Arundel, Goodwood, Fontwell and within easy access of Portsmouth, Brighton, Continental ferry port and all major commuting routes. Facilities include superb en suite rooms equipped to 4 star standard, four-poster water bed with jacuzzi bath, secluded outdoor swimming pool, Cordon Bleu cuisine, homemade bread and jams, residential licence, open all year. Tariff: single £35, doubles from £27.50 to £35 per person per room inclusive of full English Breakfast. **AA ◆◆◆◆**

e-mail: old.priory@btconnect.com
website: www.old-priory.com

THE Aldwick Hotel

Aldwick Road,
Aldwick, Bognor Regis,
West Sussex PO21 2QU
www.aldwickhotel.co.uk

Bognor Regis, sunniest town in mainland Britain, provides a splendid point from which to explore the coast and countryside of West Sussex and Hampshire. The Aldwick Hotel has been caring for the needs of holidaymakers since 1947, and is well practised in providing home-from-home comforts, quality food and service. So whether visiting the seaside for sunshine; Chichester for its history, Cathedral and Festival Theatre; or Goodwood for historic car racing on circuit and hill climb, and horse racing over arguably Britain's most scenic racecourse, choosing the Aldwick Hotel will ensure your comfort for short breaks and holidays.

Tel: 01243 821945
Fax: 01243 821316
e-mail: info@aldwickhotel.co.uk

HENFIELD

Mrs J. Forbes, Little Oreham Farm, off Horne Lane, Near Woodsmill, Henfield BN5 9SB (01273 492931). Delightful old Sussex farmhouse situated in rural position down lane, adjacent to footpaths and nature reserve. One mile from Henfield village, eight miles from Brighton, convenient for Gatwick and Hickstead. Excellent base for visiting many gardens and places of interest in the area. The farmhouse is a Listed building of great character; oak-beamed sittingroom with inglenook fireplace (log fires), and a pretty diningroom. Three comfortable attractive bedrooms with en suite shower/ bath; WC; colour TV; tea making facilities. Central heating throughout. Lovely garden with views of the Downs. Situated off Horne Lane, one minute from Woodsmill Countryside Centre. Winner of Kellogg's award: "Best Bed and Breakfast" in the South East. You will enjoy a friendly welcome and pleasant holiday. Sorry, no children under 10. Bed and Breakfast from £23 per person. Evening Meals by arrangement. Non-smoking. Open all year.

See also Colour Display Advertisement

HENFIELD

Mrs J.A. Pound, The Squirrels, Albourne Road, Woodmancote, Henfield BN5 9BH (01273 492761). The Squirrels is a country house with lovely large garden set in a secluded area convenient for south coast and downland touring. Brighton and Gatwick 20 minutes. Good food at pub five minutes' walk. One family, one double, one twin and one single rooms, all with colour TV, washbasin, central heating and tea/coffee making facilities. Ample parking space. A warm welcome awaits you. Open all year. Directions: from London take M25, M23, A23 towards Brighton, then B2118 to Albourne. Turn right onto B2116 Albourne/Henfield Road – Squirrels is approximately one-and-a-half miles on left. Bed and Breakfast £20.

ENGLAND

HORLEY

Collendean Farm, Collendean Lane, Norwood Hill, Near Horley RH6 0HP (01293 862433; Fax: 01293 863102). Collendean Farm is a 16th Century farmhouse. Bed and Breakfast is available in our converted barn in our farmyard set in the green belt countryside with stunning views and scenery. Three family rooms, one double and two singles. All rooms have en suite facilities with TV and tea/coffee tray; hairdryer, fridge, microwave and hob. Full Continental breakfast available. Non-smoking throughout. Excellent local pubs for evening meals and snacks. Horley, with restaurants for eating out, ten minutes away. Gatwick ten minutes by car, Brighton 30 minutes by train. Courtesy transport by arrangement.
e-mail: collendean.barn@amserve.net

LITTLEHAMPTON

Carol and Roger Roberts, Arun Sands, 84 South Terrace, Littlehampton BN17 5LJ (Tel & Fax: 01903 732489). Arun Sands is situated on Littlehampton seafront overlooking the green and Oyster Pond, just a short walk to the town centre. All our rooms are en suite, independently heated, and have colour television, tea/coffee making facilities, radio alarm clock, hairdryer, electric shaver point, a bedtime story book and a teddy bear. Cooked breakfast is served at your own table in our comfortable dining room. Bed and Breakfast from £25 per person per night.
ETC ◆◆◆
website: www.arun-sands.co.uk

See also Colour Display Advertisement

MIDHURST

Mrs R.M. Reeves-Fisher, Meadowhills, Stedham, Midhurst GU29 0PT (01730 812609; mobile: 07776 262147). This small, comfortable, homely country estate, dating from 1908, is set in grounds of 25 acres with magnificent views over the South Downs. Amenities include fishing rights, and the area is a walker's paradise; riding stables nearby. Local attractions include leisure centres at Midhurst and Petersfield, Cowdray Park with golf and polo, horse racing at Fontwell and Goodwood; the South Coast is 20 miles away. Places of interest include Uppark, the Weald and Downland Museum, National Trust properties and Chichester Festival Theatre.
website: www.meadowhills.co.uk

SELSEY

Mrs Margaret Pizzey, Windfall Cottage, 29 Woodland Road, Selsey PO20 0AL (01243 602205) Guests are assured of a relaxed and friendly welcome at Windfall Cottage, which is situated just five minutes from the sea. Accommodation is available in two double and one twin bedroom, all with TV and tea/coffee making facilities. Just nine miles from historic Chichester, this is an ideal base for exploring the attractions of the South Coast, as well as for shopping and golf. Pets welcome. Open all year. Bed and breakfast from £18.50 pppn in winter, to £22.00 pppn in summer. Short break details on request.
ETC ◆◆

WORTHING

Mrs Jill Colbourn, Tudor Lodge, 25 Oxford Road, Worthing BN11 1XQ (01903 234401). Large Victorian house in central position near all amenities offering spacious accommodation. All rooms with washbasins, colour TV, tea/coffee facilities, central heating. Access at all times. Some off-street parking. No smoking. Bed and Breakfast from £20 per person per night.

TYNE & WEAR

NEWCASTLE-UPON-TYNE

New Kent Hotel, 127 Osborne Road, Jesmond, Newcastle-upon-Tyne NE2 2TB (0191-281 7711; Fax: 0191-281 3369). This privately owned hotel is situated in a quiet location, but only minutes from the city centre. It has built up a reputation for good food and friendly, efficient service in a warm and congenial atmosphere. All bedrooms are en suite, with hospitality tray, direct-dial telephone, colour TV with satellite, and radio. There is a spacious cocktail lounge and a restaurant serving the best of modern and classic cuisine. Local attractions include the Metro Centre, Northumbria National Park, Holy Island and Bamburgh Castle. Single from £47.50, double from £69.50. **AA ★★★**

NEWCASTLE-UPON-TYNE

Imperial Guest House, 194 Station Road, Wallsend, Newcastle-upon-Tyne NE28 8RD (Tel & Fax: 0191 236 9808). Behind the plain and unassuming terraced frontage lies a guest house with a difference. At the Imperial we are committed to giving you the highest standards of service and comfort. This Victorian house has been superbly restored to create an elegant and supremely stylish interior. There are two guest lounges: the Drawing Room which is non-smoking, and the Empire Lounge in which smoking is permitted. The bedrooms are beautifully decorated, with attention to detail being our watchword, and as they are located on the ground floor, are ideal for the elderly. The Lord Armstrong Room has a shower, whilst the Lord Collingwood is our stunning en suite room. The guest house is ideally situated for exploring the city centre, the coast, Hadrian's Wall and the beauty of Northumbria and County Durham. With direct Metro links from the airport, coach and rail stations, it is only 10 minutes from the city centre and only a few minutes from the International Ferry Terminal. B&B from £24. **ETC/AA ◆◆◆◆**
e-mail: enquiries@imperialguesthouse.co.uk   website: www.imperialguesthouse.co.uk

WARWICKSHIRE

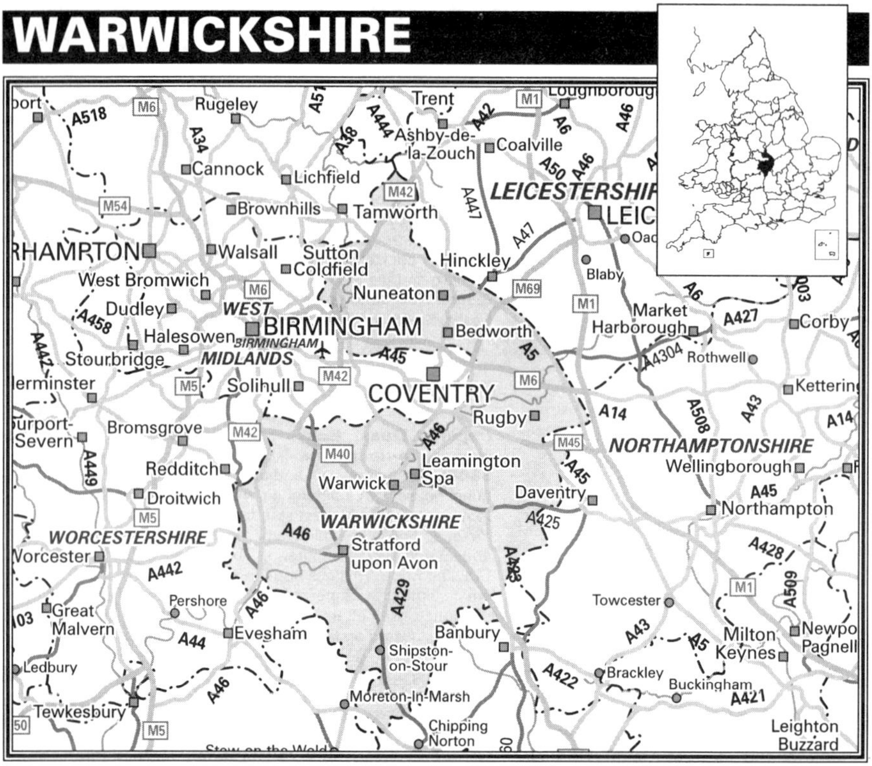

See also Colour Display Advertisement

ALCESTER

The Globe Hotel, 54 Birmingham Road, Alcester B49 5EG (Tel & Fax: 01789 763287). A warm and friendly hotel in the historic market town of Alcester (seven miles from Stratford-upon-Avon). Stylish and spacious en suite bedrooms with remote-control TV, radio alarm clock, direct dial telephones, modem connection and hospitality trays. Ideally placed for Stratford-upon-Avon, motorways M40/42 and M5, Airport/NEC (30 minutes) and touring the Cotswolds. Rooms from £35 to £65. Totally refurbished in 2000. **ETC/AA** ◆◆◆◆

ALCESTER

Mrs Hammersley, Sambourne Hall Farm, Sambourne, Alcester B96 6NZ (01527 852151). Beautiful 16th Century Farmhouse set in 500 acres of farmland in picturesque village. Large comfortable bedrooms, own sitting room. Walled garden. Excellent local pubs nearby. Coughton Court one mile. Ragley Hall five miles and Stratford-upon-Avon 10 miles. Ideal for business or vacation. National Exhibition Centre and Cotswolds easy access.

COVENTRY (near)

Conrad and Barbara Chamberlain, Bourne Brook Lodge, Mill Lane, Fillongley, Near Coventry CV7 8EE (Tel & Fax: 01676 541898). Experience the peace and tranquillity of our Country House offering high standards of comfort and cleanliness in picturesque surroundings. Modern luxury en suite chalet rooms with colour TV and hostess tray. Full English breakfast. Terms per person: double/twin £50; single £25 to £35; family room £75. Private car park and gardens. No smoking. **ETC ◆◆◆◆**
e-mail: bournebrooklodge@care4free.net

KENILWORTH

Trudi and Ken Wheat, The Hollyhurst Guest House, 47 Priory Road, Kenilworth CV8 1LL (01926 853882; Fax: 01926 855211). A comfortable Victorian guest house close to the town centre and a pleasant stroll from Kenilworth Castle. A bustling town with excellent restaurants, located in the heart of the Warwickshire countryside, Kenilworth is well connected by road and convenient for the NEC, NAC and the University of Warwick. You'll find the Hollyhurst perfect as a business base or holiday stopover. In either case we offer real hospitality and home comforts in our seven bedroomed, fully licensed guest house. Three rooms are en suite and we have private parking for up to seven vehicles. Non-smoking. No pets. Bed and Breakfast from £22 per person. **AA ◆◆◆**
e-mail: admin@hollyhurstguesthouse.co.uk

LIGHTHORNE (near Warwick)

Mrs J. Stanton, Redlands Farm, Banbury Road, Lighthorne, Near Warwick CV35 0AH (01926 651241). A beautifully restored 15th century farmhouse built of local stone, the "Old Farm House" is set in two acres of garden with its own swimming pool, well away from the main road yet within easy travelling distance of Stratford and Warwick, and handy for the Cotswolds. Guest accommodation is one double (with bathroom), one single and one family bedrooms, all with tea making facilities; bathroom; beamed lounge with TV; diningroom. Rooms are centrally heated and the farmhouse also has open fires. Children welcome – reduced rates and facilities available. No pets. A car is recommended to make the most of your stay. B&B from £20.

See also Colour Display Advertisement

STRATFORD-UPON-AVON

Mrs Julia Downie, Holly Tree Cottage, Birmingham Road, Pathlow, Stratford-upon-Avon CV37 0ES (Tel & Fax: 01789 204461). Period cottage dating from 17th Century, with antiques, paintings, collection of porcelain, fresh flowers, tasteful furnishings and friendly atmosphere. Picturesque gardens, orchard, paddock and pasture with wildlife and extensive views over open countryside. Situated 3 miles north of Stratford-upon-Avon towards Henley-in-Arden on A3400. Rooms have television, radio/alarm, hospitality trays and hairdryers. Breakfasts are a speciality. Pubs and restaurants nearby. Ideally located for Theatre, Shakespeare Country, Heart of England, Cotswolds, Warwick Castle, Blenheim Palace and National Trust Properties. Well situated for National Exhibition Centre, Birmingham and National Agricultural Centre, Stoneleigh. Children welcome, pets by arrangement. Non-smoking. Bed & Breakfast from £27.
e-mail: john@hollytree-cottage.co.uk   website: www.hollytree-cottage.co.uk

e-mail: linhill@bigwig.net

STRATFORD-UPON-AVON

Ms Diana Tallis, Linhill, 35 Evesham Place, Stratford-upon-Avon CV37 6HT (01789 292879; Fax: 01789 299691). Linhill is a comfortable Victorian Guest House run by a friendly young family. It is situated only five minutes' walk from Stratford's town centre with its wide choice of fine restaurants and world famous Royal Shakespeare Theatre. Every bedroom at Linhill has central heating, colour TV, tea/coffee making facilities and washbasin. En suite facilities are also available, as are packed lunches and evening meals. Bicycle hire and babysitting facilities if desired. Leave the children with us and re-discover the delight of a candlelit dinner in one of Stratford's inviting restaurants. Bed and Breakfast from £20 to £35; Evening Meal from £7 to £10. PRIVATE HOUSE SLEEPS 5 AVAILABLE. **ETC ◆◆◆**
website: www.linhillguesthouse.co.uk

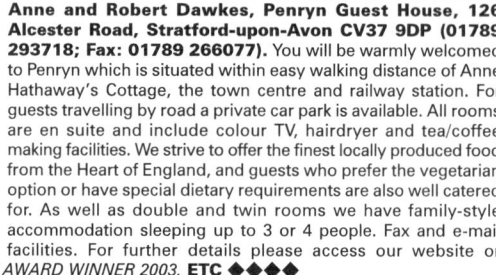

telephone for brochure. *INSPIRED BREAKFAST AWARD WINNER 2003.* **ETC ◆◆◆◆**
e-mail: penrynhouse@btinternet.com

STRATFORD-UPON-AVON

Anne and Robert Dawkes, Penryn Guest House, 126 Alcester Road, Stratford-upon-Avon CV37 9DP (01789 293718; Fax: 01789 266077). You will be warmly welcomed to Penryn which is situated within easy walking distance of Anne Hathaway's Cottage, the town centre and railway station. For guests travelling by road a private car park is available. All rooms are en suite and include colour TV, hairdryer and tea/coffee making facilities. We strive to offer the finest locally produced food from the Heart of England, and guests who prefer the vegetarian option or have special dietary requirements are also well catered for. As well as double and twin rooms we have family-style accommodation sleeping up to 3 or 4 people. Fax and e-mail facilities. For further details please access our website or
website: www.penrynguesthouse.co.uk

e-mail: thehuntersmoon@ntlworld.com

STRATFORD-UPON-AVON

Mrs Austin, Hunter's Moon Guest House, 150 Alcester Road, Stratford-upon-Avon CV37 9DR (01789 292888; Fax: 01789 204101). Stratfordians Rosemary and David Austin, welcome you to Shakespeare's town to enjoy your visit at our family-run guest house, which is situated on the A422, five miles from the M40 motorway link, half-a-mile from the town centre and close to Anne Hathaway's Cottage and other Shakespearean properties. All bedrooms have en suite facilities, colour TV, hairdryer, tea/coffee making facilities; singles, doubles, twin and family rooms. An excellent English or vegetarian breakfast is served. Private car parking. Please ring for reservations. **AA/RAC ◆◆◆**, *ARTHUR FROMMER RECOMMENDED 2001, WELCOME HOST AWARD.*
website: www.huntersmoonguesthouse.com

STRATFORD-UPON-AVON

Mrs M. Turney, Cadle Pool Farm, The Ridgeway, Stratford-upon-Avon CV37 9RE (01789 292494; mobile: 07973 722217). Working farm. Situated in picturesque grounds, this charming oak-panelled and beamed family home is part of a 450-acre farm. It is two miles from Stratford-upon-Avon, between Anne Hathaway's Cottage and Mary Arden's House. Only eight minutes by car from the Royal Shakespeare Theatre and the race course. Ideal touring centre for Warwick and the Cotswolds. Accommodation comprises one family and one double room en suite, with TV and one double room with private bathroom. All have central heating, tea/coffee facilities, hairdryers. There is an antique oak dining room and guest sitting room. The gardens and ornamental pool are particularly attractive with peacocks and ducks roaming freely. Children over ten welcome at reduced rates. Sorry, no pets. Non-smoking accommodation available. Bed and Breakfast from £26 per person per night. **AA ◆◆◆◆**

STRATFORD-UPON-AVON

Susan and Derek Learmount, Green Haven Guest House, 217 Evesham Road, Stratford-upon-Avon CV37 9AS (01789 297874). A cosy and prettily refurbished Guest House, centrally heated with colour TV, courtesy trays and many thoughtful extras. Within easy walking distance of the Town Centre, and easily accessible to historic Warwick and the beautiful Cotswolds. Our bedrooms are all en suite and comprise two family rooms, doubles and twins, with extra large showers and plenty of hot water. Our competitive rates include a delicious English, vegetarian/vegan or Continental breakfast. Private parking and payphone for guests. ETC ◆◆◆◆
e-mail: susanlearmount@green-haven.co.uk
website: www.green-haven.co.uk

ENGLAND

WARWICK

Mrs Elizabeth Draisey, Forth House, 44 High Street, Warwick CV34 4AX (01926 401512; Fax: 01926 490809). Our rambling Georgian family home within the old town walls of Warwick provides two luxurious, peaceful guest suites hidden away at the back of the house. One family-sized ground floor suite opens onto the garden, while the other overlooks it. Both are en suite with private sitting and dining rooms. TV, fridge, telephone, hot and cold drink facilities. Ideally situated for holidays or business. Stratford, Oxford, Birmingham and Cotswold villages within easy reach. Breakfasts, full English or Continental, at times agreed with our guests. Private parking. Junction 15 of M40 only two miles away. Terms from £34 to £37 per person in double or twin room.

e-mail: info@forthhouseuk.co.uk   website: www.forthhouseuk.co.uk

Heritage Motor Centre • Gaydon, Warwickshire • 01926 641188
website: www.heritage.org.uk
The largest collection of British cars in the world. 4-wheel drive demonstration circuit, children's roadway, cafe and gift shop.

Hatton Country World • Hatton, Warwickshire • 01926 843411
website: www.hattonworld.com
Rural crafts, farm park and shopping village. Craft gifts and antiques, plus factory outlets and speciality foods. Children can enjoy the soft play centre; displays of traditional farming methods and lots of animals.

FHG PUBLICATIONS publish a large range of well-known accommodation guides. We will be happy to send you details or you can use the order form at the back of this book.

WEST MIDLANDS

Boxtrees Farm

Stratford Road, Hockley Heath, Solihull B94 6EA

Telephone: 01564 782039 • Fax: 01564 784661

Boxtrees Farm is on the A3400, just one mile from Junction 4 of the M42 and is within easy reach of Birmingham International Airport/NEC/Rail link (10 minutes) and Stratford-upon-Avon (20 minutes). The 18th century farmhouse has all the comforts of modern living whilst retaining its traditional features. The delightful farm courtyard has a 12 unit craft centre and coffee shop-bistro. Tastefully converted large twin bedded, family and double rooms available. All rooms are en suite with TV and tea/coffee making facilities. Bed and Breakfast from £45 per room per night.

E-mail: bandb@boxtrees.co.uk Website: www.boxtrees.co.uk

BIRMINGHAM

Ian and Angela Kerr, Awentsbury Hotel, 21 Serpentine Road, Selly Park, Birmingham B29 7HU (0121-472 1258). A Victorian country house set in its own large garden. Close to Birmingham University, buses, trains, BBC Pebble Mill, Queen Elizabeth and Selly Oak Hospitals, and only two miles from the city centre. All rooms have colour TV, telephone, tea/coffee making facilities, washbasin and central heating. Some rooms en suite, some with showers. TV lounge. Ample car parking. Open all year. Pets and children welcome. Reductions for children. Terms from £40 single room, from £54 twin room, inclusive of breakfast and VAT; Evening Meals if required. Light supper or bedtime drink at small charge. **AA** and **RAC** *LISTED.*

BIRMINGHAM

Woodville House Bed and Breakfast, 39 Portland Road, Edgbaston, Birmingham B16 9HN (0121 454 0274; Fax: 0121 454 5965). First class accommodation one mile from the city centre. All rooms with colour TV, tea/coffee making facilities. En suite available. Car parking. Bed and Breakfast from £20 single, £30 double and £35 double en suite. **ETC** ◆

WOLVERHAMPTON

Featherstone Farm Hotel, New Road, Featherstone, Wolverhampton WV10 7NW (01902 725371; Fax: 01902 731741; mobile: 07836 315258). This is a small, high-class country house hotel set in five acres of unspoiled countryside, only one mile from Junction 11 on the M6 or Junction 1 on the M54. The main house has eight en suite bedrooms with all the facilities one would expect in a hotel of distinction. Self-contained fully furnished cottages with maid service are also available. Kings Repose Indian Restaurant, serving freshly prepared dishes, and licensed bar. Secure car park. Children and pets welcome. **ETC** ★★★
e-mail: lewisprice@featherstonefarm.co.uk
website: www.featherstonefarm.co.uk

WILTSHIRE

CHIPPENHAM

Jeffrey and Victoria Lippiatt, Manor Farm, Alderton, Chippenham SN14 6NL (Tel & Fax: 01666 840271). Working farm. Manor Farm is a beautiful 17th century farmhouse which may be found nestling near the church in picturesque Alderton. Home to the Lippiatt family, the house offers warmth and comfort coupled with high standards. The lovely bedrooms are spacious and well equipped, with delightful views. The farm is only four miles from Junctions 17 and 18 of the M4. Bath, Malmesbury, Badminton and Castle Combe are all a short drive away. We have a selection of super English country pubs and excellent golf courses nearby. Bed and Breakfast from £30 per person. One twin, two double rooms, all en suite. Non-smoking household. Children from 12. Pets by arrangement. Open all year except Christmas and New Year.
e-mail: jlippiatt@farmline.com
website: www.themanorfarm.co.uk

CHIPPENHAM (near)

Mrs Diana Barker, Manor Farm, Sopworth, Near Chippenham SN14 6PR (01454 238676). Working farm. Manor Farm is a working mixed farm on the Beaufort estate near Badminton. The Jacobean farmhouse was updated in Georgian and Victorian times. It is very quietly situated in lovely countryside yet near many places of interest: Malmesbury, Tetbury and South Cotswolds, Berkeley Castle, Bristol, Bath, Castle Combe, Lacock Abbey, Avebury. Ideal overnight stop for travellers to South West and Wales. Junction 18, M4 six miles and close to Fosse Way and M5. Spacious comfortable rooms with heating, and tea and coffee making facilities. En suite available. Lounge/diningroom with open fires in winter. Personal attention and a warm welcome. Bed and Breakfast from £20 to £35 per person, reductions for children.
e-mail: manor.farm@virgin.net

DEVIZES

Mrs Stratton, The Gate House, Wick Lane, Devizes SN10 5DW (01380 725283; Fax: 01380 722382; mobile: 07889 637047). The Gatehouse is located on a quiet road, just a few minutes from country walks, yet only three quarters of a mile from the lovely old market town of Devizes. It is totally peaceful, either for a journey's break or a weekend in Wiltshire. We have three bedrooms – the double is en suite, the twin and single use the guest bathroom. All rooms have colour TV, tea/coffee making facilities and hairdryer. A full English breakfast is served in the dining room overlooking the large, well-maintained garden. Sorry, no pets and no smoking. Please write, telephone or fax for our brochure.
e-mail: info@visitdevizes.co.uk
website: www.visitdevizes.co.uk

DEVIZES

Littleton Lodge, Littleton Panell (A360), West Lavington, Devizes SN10 4ES (01380 813131; Fax: 01380 816969). Superb Victorian family house set in one acre of private grounds, overlooking vineyard within pretty conservation village. Five minutes' drive from historic Devizes. All rooms en suite with beverage tray, TV and radio/alarms. Choice of scrumptious breakfast. Excellent meals are available at two pubs within five/ten minutes' walk. Stonehenge is only 15 minutes' drive and Littleton Lodge is an ideal base to explore the Wiltshire White Horses, prehistoric Avebury, Georgian Bath (30 mins), Salisbury (30 mins), the National Trust village of Lacock, as well as numerous country houses and gardens. Private parking. Mastercard, Visa and Switch accepted. Single occupancy from £40, Double from £55.
ETC/AAA ◆◆◆◆
e-mail: stay@littletonlodge.co.uk
website: www.littletonlodge.co.uk

MALMESBURY

Mrs Fitzgerald, Manby's Farm, Oaksey, Malmesbury SN16 9SA (01666 577399). Our new farmhouse, situated within stunning countryside on the Wiltshire/Gloucestershire border is close to the Cotswold Water Park. We offer luxury accommodation from where you can enjoy the peace and quiet or plan a visit to one of the many places of interest, such as Malmesbury, Castle Combe, Oxford, Stratford-upon-Avon, Stonehenge, Longleat and many more. Our farmhouse has full central heating and snooker room with indoor swimming pool adjacent. Three double/twin en suite bedrooms with tea/coffee making facilities, radio alarm and colour TV; family room also available. A hearty English breakfast is served. Bed and Breakfast from £25pppn based on two sharing. Visa and Mastercard accepted. **ETC** ◆◆◆◆

e-mail: enquiries@manbysfarm.com

website: www.manbysfarm.com

MALMESBURY

Mrs Susan Barnes, Lovett Farm, Little Somerford, Near Malmesbury SN15 5BP (Tel & Fax: 01666 823268; mobile: 07808 858612). Working farm. Enjoy traditional hospitality at our delightful farmhouse just three miles from the historic town of Malmesbury with its wonderful Norman abbey and gardens and central for Cotswolds, Bath, Stratford, Avebury and Stonehenge. Two attractive en suite bedrooms with delightful views, each with tea/coffee making facilities, colour TV and radio. Delicious full English breakfast served in our cosy dining room/lounge. Central heating throughout. Bed and Breakfast from £25. Credit cards accepted. Non-smoking accommodation. Open all year. **ETC/AA** ◆◆◆◆, *FARM STAY UK MEMBER.*
e-mail: lovettfarm@btinternet.com
website: www.lovettfarm.co.uk

MARLBOROUGH

Mrs Maggie Vigar-Smith, Wernham Farm, Clench Common, Marlborough SN8 4DR (01672 512236). This working farm is set in picturesque countryside on Wansdyke, off the A345. It is close to Marlborough, Avebury, Pewsey and the Kennet & Avon Canal. Accommodation is available in two family bedrooms, one en suite and one with private bathroom. Terms: £35 single, from £50 double. **ETC** ◆◆◆. Five caravan and camping pitches are also available.
e-mail: margglvsf@aol.com

MELKSHAM

Beechfield House Hotel and Restaurant, Beanacre, Melksham SN12 7PU (01225 703700; Fax: 01225 790118). A comfortable Victorian country house set in eight acres of beautiful gardens in a quiet country location near the National Trust village of Lacock, yet only twenty minutes away from Junction 17 of M4 motorway. The hotel has twenty-one en suite bedrooms, including four-poster and half-tester beds. Private rooms are available for conferences and meetings, private lunches and dinner parties. Banqueting for up to sixty persons. Daily lunches and dinners are available in our elegant restaurant.
e-mail: csm@beechfieldhouse.co.uk
website: www.beechfieldhouse.co.uk

MERE

Mrs Jean Smith, The Beeches, Chetcombe Road, Mere BA12 6AU (01747 860687). A comfortable, old Toll House with interesting carved stairway and gallery, standing in beautiful garden at entrance to early English village. Centrally situated for Bath, Wells, Salisbury, Bournemouth, New Forest and Sherborne. In close proximity to the famous Stourhead Gardens and Longleat House and Wildlife Park. We have two double and family rooms. The house is furnished to a very high standard, is centrally heated with TV, tea/coffee making facilities, washbasin and shaver point in all rooms, one room having en suite shower, another room en suite bath and bidet. Large lounge. Large enclosed car park. Open all year. Bed and Breakfast from £19. Reductions for children. **ETC ◆◆◆**

SALISBURY

Audrey Jerram, Chicklade Lodge, Chicklade, Hindon, Salisbury SP3 5SU (01747 820389). Ideally situated for exploring this interesting area - Salisbury, Stonehenge, Shaftesbury, Stourhead, Longleat, Bath, Wells, Glastonbury, etc. This is a 19th century house of character set amidst lovely countryside. Charming twin-bedded rooms with washbasins, shaver points and tea/coffee making facilities. Pets welcome. Open all year. Painting Holidays are also available, full details on request. Ample parking space. Location: A303 nearby, about 28 miles west of Andover. Going through Chicklade turn right at the small crossroads (signposted Hindon on left). Bed and Breakfast from £20. Non-smoking.
e-mail: audreyjerram@aol.com

SALISBURY

Dawn and Alan Curnow, Hayburn Wyke Guest House, 72 Castle Road, Salisbury SP1 3RL (Tel & Fax: 01722 412627). Hayburn Wyke is a Victorian house, situated adjacent to Victoria Park, and a ten minute riverside walk from the city centre. Salisbury and surrounding area have many places of interest to visit, including Salisbury Cathedral, Old Sarum, Wilton House and Stonehenge. Most bedrooms have en suite facilities, all have washbasin, television, and tea/coffee making equipment. Children are welcome at reduced rates. Sorry, no pets (guide dogs an exception). Private car parking for guests. Open all year. Bed and full English Breakfast from £23. Credit cards and Switch accepted. **AA/RAC ◆◆◆**
e-mail: hayburn.wyke@tinyonline.co.uk
website: www.hayburnwykeguesthouse.co.uk

See also Colour Display Advertisement

SALISBURY

Mrs Sue Combes, Manor Farm, Burcombe, Salisbury SP2 0EJ (01722 742177; Fax: 01722 744600). Working farm. An attractive stone-built farmhouse with a lovely walled garden, set in a quiet village amid downland and water meadows, five miles west of Salisbury. The two bedrooms are very comfortable with en suite facilities, TV, tea trays and clock-radios. Large lounge and access to garden. This is an ideal location for Salisbury, Wilton and Stonehenge and easy access to many places of historic interest and gardens. For those seeking peace this is an idyllic place to stay with various walks and the local pub only a five minute stroll. Children welcome. Bed and Breakfast from £23 to £24. **ETC ◆◆◆◆**
e-mail: s.a.combes@talk21.com

SALISBURY

Scotland Lodge, Winterbourne Stoke, Salisbury SP3 4TF (01980 620943; Fax: 01980 621403; mobile: 07957 863183). This 16th century cottage has been transformed into a substantial house with additions in successive centuries. The front garden was turfed from the surrounding downland, which had never been ploughed, providing a profusion of wild Spring flowers including a multitude of cowslips. Within the house there is a feeling of peace and tranquillity. All rooms are en suite with bath and shower, TV and tea/coffee making facilities. Two rooms in the Victorian part are particularly large and airy, with comfortable chairs, a fridge, and one has the added benefit of a small, fully equipped kitchen which may be used for self-catering. Also available is a smaller double with en suite bath and shower. Regret no smoking in the house. Ample car parking. **ETC/AA** ◆◆◆

SWINDON

County View Guest House, 31/33 County Road, Swindon SN1 2EG (01793 610434/618387; Fax: 01189 394100). This Victorian property is situated on the main road and is only five minutes' walk from town centre, coach and rail stations and only five minutes' drive from Junction 15 and 16 M4. It is ideally placed for business and leisure visits to Swindon and Wiltshire area. All rooms have tea/coffee making facilities and TV. En suite and shower rooms. Private parking. Evening meals. It is like home from home. Children and pets accepted by arrangement. Cot and high chair available. Ground floor bedrooms. Bed and Breakfast single room from £18, twin room from £30 per night. *PILGRIMS PROGRESS COMMENDATION*.

SWINDON

Mrs Mary Richards, Little Cotmarsh Farm, Broad Town, Wootton Bassett, Swindon SN4 7RA (01793 731322). Little Cotmarsh Farm is a lovely 17th Century farmhouse nestling quietly in the little hamlet of Cotmarsh. Enjoy the relaxed atmosphere of our home, the attractive bedrooms are spacious and well equipped – two en suite, one with private bathroom. We are just seven miles from Avebury, the largest monument in Britain. Hungerford, Tetbury and Bradford-on-Avon are full of glorious antique shops or visit Swindon's new Great Western Designer Outlet Village. Best of all, borrow "100 Walks in Wiltshire" and explore our wonderful countryside. Good local pub food. M4 Junction 16 approximately four miles. Bed and Breakfast from £22 to £28 per person. No smoking. **AA** ◆◆◆◆
website: www.littlecotmarshfarm.co.uk

STEAM - Museum of GWR • *Swindon, Wiltshire* •*01793 466650*
website: www.steam-museum.org.uk
The story of the people who built the Great Western Railway, using sounds and smells, real objects and world-famous locomotives. Hands-on exhibits and special events.

The FHG Directory of Website Addresses
on pages 387-415 is a useful quick reference guide for holiday accommodation with e-mail and/or website details

WORCESTERSHIRE

e-mail: salli@middletongrange.com

DROITWICH

Mrs Salli Harrison, Middleton Grange, Salwarpe, Droitwich Spa WR9 0AH (01905 451678; Fax: 01905 453978). Enjoy high quality accommodation and hospitality in this traditional 18th century country house surrounded by peaceful and picturesque gardens. All rooms have en suite/private facilities with colour TV, generous beverage tray, hairdryer, radio alarm and more. Excellent breakfast. Wedding nights catered for. Children welcome. Babysitting service. Dogs by arrangement. Superbly situated for exploring the Heart of England. Stratford-upon-Avon, Warwick, Cotswolds, Birmingham and Wales all with one hour. M5 motorway six minutes. Many traditional eating establishments close by. Single from £30, double from £50. **ETC** ◆◆◆ *SILVER AWARD.*

website: www.middletongrange.com

DROITWICH SPA

David and Tricia Havard, Phepson Farm, Himbleton, Droitwich Spa WR9 7JZ (01905 391205). Working farm. In our 17th century oak beamed farmhouse and converted buildings, we offer a warm welcome, good food and a relaxed and informal atmosphere. All rooms en suite with colour TV, hairdryers and tea/coffee facilities. Situated on a small sheep farm with scenic fishing lake; walking on Wychavon Way. Convenient for touring the beautiful Heart of England. Five miles from motorway network. Featured on 'Wish You Were Here'. Self-catering also available. Credit cards accepted. **ETC** ◆◆◆, *WINNER OF BEST WORCESTERSHIRE BREAKFAST AWARD 2003.*

website: www.phepsonfarm.co.uk

See also Colour Display Advertisement

MALVERN

David Watkins, The Red Gate, 32 Avenue Road, Great Malvern WR14 3BJ (Tel & Fax: 01684 565013). Come, relax and be pampered in a centrally heated, beautifully restored Victorian hotel. Situated on a tree-lined road near to Great Malvern railway station, town centre and hills. Parking on the premises. Renowned for friendly informal atmosphere - "It's like coming home". Seven individually decorated bedrooms with en suite facilities, all non-smoking with colour TV and tea/coffee facilities. There is a breakfast menu to suit all tastes. Vegetarians welcome. Residential licence. Enjoy a good book from a wide selection in our attractive lounge. On better days relax on the verandah or sit in the south-walled garden and forget your cares. Bed and Breakfast from £42. **ETC** ◆◆◆ *SILVER AWARD, GUESTACCOMM, WHICH? HOTEL GUIDE.*

e-mail: enquiries@the-red-gate.co.uk   website: www.the-red-gate.co.uk

See also Colour Display Advertisement

MALVERN (near)

Ann and Brian Porter, Croft Guest House, Bransford, Worcester WR6 5JD (01886 832227; Fax: 01886 830037). 16th-18th century part black and white cottage-style country house situated in the River Teme Valley, four miles from Worcester and Malvern. Croft House is central for visiting numerous attractions in Worcester, Hereford, Severn Valley and surrounding countryside. There is fishing close by and an 18-hole golf course opposite. Facilities include three en suite rooms (two double, one family) and two double rooms with washbasins, hospitality trays; TV in all bedrooms. Double glazing, central heating, residential licence and home-cooked dinners. There is a TV lounge for guests' use. A cot and baby listening service are provided. Bed and Breakfast from £23 to £33 single, £41 to £56 double. Festive Christmas and New Year Breaks available. **AA** ◆◆◆

MALVERN WELLS

Dave and Janet Vale, The Old Coach House Bed & Breakfast, Wells Road, Malvern Wells WR14 4HD (01684 564382). Welcome to The Old Coach House, situated on the eastern slopes of the Malvern Hills, with easy access from the A449. Convenient for touring the area by car and only a short walk from The Three Counties Showground. All bedrooms have en suite shower and WC, colour TV, hairdryer, clock radio, and hospitality tray. Hearty English Breakfast is prepared with local produce whenever possible. Dave and Janet Vale look forward to welcoming you to The Old Coach House where you will be made to feel completely at home.
e-mail: info@coachhousemalvern.co.uk
website: www.coachhousemalvern.co.uk

MALVERN WELLS

Mrs J.L. Morris, Brickbarns Farm, Hanley Road, Malvern Wells WR14 4HY (016845 61775). Working farm. Brickbarns, a 200-year-old mixed farm, is situated two miles from Great Malvern at the foot of the Malvern Hills, 300 yards from the bus service and one-and-a-half miles from the train. The house, which is 300 years old, commands excellent views of the Malvern Hills and guests are accommodated in one double, one single and one family bedrooms with washbasins; two bathrooms, shower room, two toilets; sitting room and dining room. Children welcome and cot and babysitting offered. Central heating. Car essential, parking. Open Easter to October for Bed and Breakfast from £16 nightly per person. Reductions for children and Senior Citizens. Birmingham 40 miles, Hereford 20, Gloucester 17, Stratford 35 and the Wye Valley is just 30 miles.

NEWNHAM BRIDGE

Deepcroft Farm House, Newnham Bridge, Tenbury Wells WR15 8JA (01584 781412). Set in the Teme Valley, off the A456, on the borders of Worcestershire, Herefordshire and Shropshire this secluded old farmhouse, with five acres of garden and orchard, offers easy access to the Severn Valley Railway, the historic towns of Ludlow and Worcester as well as to the Welsh Marches and the Shropshire Hills. Ideal for fishermen, cyclists and tourists the accommodation comprises two twin-bedded and one single room, all with hand basins, shaver points, and tea/coffee making facilities. A comfortable sitting room with colour TV is also available for guests. Bed and full English breakfast from £20.

OMBERSLEY

Mrs M. Peters, Tytchney, Boreley, Ombersley WR9 0HZ (01905 620185). 16th Century black-and-white medieval Hall House in peaceful country lane. Views over Severn Valley to Malvern Hills. Quaint olde worlde cottage atmosphere. Inglenook log fires and beams. Within easy reach of Worcester, Malvern, Bewdley. Two-and-a-half miles Ombersley, a picturesque black-and-white village with pubs and restaurants, local shop, bakery and Post Office. Nearby attractions: Worcester Cathedral, Royal Worcester Porcelain, Commandery Civil War Museum, Severn Valley Railway, Witley Court (English Heritage), Hanbury Hall (NT), Bewdley Safari Park, Coughton Court (Guy Fawkes), Elgar's Birthplace, Webb's Garden Centre. Double, family and single rooms; cot available. Bed and Breakfast from £17.

YORKSHIRE

PLEASE NOTE

All the information in this book is given in good faith in the belief that it is correct. However, the publishers cannot guarantee the facts given in these pages, neither are they responsible for changes in policy, ownership or terms that may take place after the date of going to press. Readers should always satisfy themselves that the facilities they require are available and that the terms, if quoted, still apply.

EAST YORKSHIRE

White Lodge Guest House

9 Neptune Street, Bridlington YO15 3DE • 01262 670903

Very relaxing guest house, personally run by Caitlyn and Toni Greene. We have an excellent reputation for food and can cater for all diets, with adequate notice. Situated opposite South Beach and Conference Centre, with the harbour and town only a short walk away. The ground floor room has its own patio area, garden furniture and purpose built store for motorised wheelchair. All seven bedrooms are centrally heated and have colour TV with satellite, tea/coffee facilities and five rooms en suite. Guests' lounge; diningroom and toilet on ground floor. Own keys. Special reductions for children and Senior Citizens. Special offers on Christmas breaks. Ideal base for conference delegates, golfers, fishing trips, bird watchers, walkers and in fact everyone! Open all year.

e-mail: Caitlyn@whitelodgeguesthouse.fsnet.co.uk
website: www.whitelodgeguesthouse.co.uk

BEVERLEY

Rudstone Walk Country Accommodation, South Cave, Near Beverley HU15 2AH (01430 422230; Fax: 01430 424552). A RELAXING RETREAT FOR LEISURE AND BUSINESS GUESTS. Nestled in its own secluded corner of the Yorkshire Wolds with fine views, Rudstone Walk provides superb breakfasts and highly commended en suite bedrooms and suites, surrounding the farmhouse and its walled garden courtyard. Self-catering Short Breaks, B&B weekend rates and special three nights Bed & Breakfast for the price of two. Ring or e-mail for brochure.
e-mail: office@rudstone-walk.co.uk
website: www.rudstone-walk.co.uk

BRIDLINGTON

John and Helen Gallagher, Rosebery House, 1 Belle Vue, Tennyson Avenue, Bridlington YO15 2ET (01262 670336; Fax: 01262 608381). Grade II Listed Georgian house with character. It has a long sunny garden and superb views of the gardens and sea. Amenities are close by making it an ideal centre for walking, bird-watching, golfing, wind and sailboarding or touring the historic, rolling Wolds. A high standard of comfort, friendliness and satisfaction guaranteed. All rooms are en suite, centrally heated, have colour TV and tea/coffee facilities. Vegetarians are most welcome. Some car parking available. Open all year except Christmas and New Year. Bed and Breakfast from £19.50 per person. **ETC ◆◆◆◆**
e-mail: roseberyhouse@zexus.co.uk
website: www.roseberyhouse.biz

BRIDLINGTON

See also Colour Display Advertisement

The Seacourt Hotel and Annabel's Restaurant, 76 South Marine Drive, Bridlington YO15 3NS (01262 400872). This large Edwardian house standing quietly in a prime position overlooking the beautiful South Bay, with panoramic views of the Old Harbour, town and Flamborough Head, has been refurbished and transformed into a delightful, small hotel of distinction. Luxuriously appointed. 12 standard and de luxe bedrooms, some with stunning sea views, all en suite with colour TV, direct-dial telephones, hospitality trays, toiletries and central heating. Annabel's Restaurant situated within the hotel; bar meals are also available. Miles of safe sandy beaches, 18 hole golf course, bowling green all within walking distance.
e-mail: seacourt.hotel@tiscali.co.uk

See also Colour Display Advertisement

BRIDLINGTON

South Dene Hotel, 94 Horsforth Avenue, Bridlington YO15 3DF. (01262 674436). A warm and friendly family-run hotel situated on Bridlington's South Side, just 150 yards from The Royal Spa and approximately five minutes' walk to the central shops. Our B&B at £20 is excellent value with a quality breakfast provided. Short breaks/weekend stays are most welcome. Major credit cards accepted. Colour brochure available on request. **ETC ◆◆.**

BRIDLINGTON

Christine and Peter Young, The White Rose, 123 Cardigan Road, Bridlington YO15 3LP (01262 673245). We are a small hotel situated in a quiet residential area close to the South Beach and within walking distance of the Spa and Harbour. We offer comfortable accommodation with most bedrooms en suite with colour TV, hospitality tray and gas heating. We have a non-smoking bedroom and dining room. We offer choice of menus at all meals; choice of early or late evening dinner. Open all year including Christmas. Bed and Breakfast from £20 per person. Weekend winter breaks with two nights bed and breakfast and candle-lit meal on Saturday £82 per couple; mid-week winter breaks of four nights Monday to Friday bed and breakfast, one adult pays full price £80, second adult pays £48 when sharing double/twin room. Available October to February inclusive, except during Christmas and New Year. **ETC ◆◆◆**

DRIFFIELD

Mrs Katrina Gray, The Wold Cottage, Wold Newton, Driffield YO25 3HL (Tel & Fax: 01262 470696). The Wold Cottage is a spacious Georgian farmhouse, set in its own grounds. We can offer you peace and tranquillity with views of new and mature woodlands and continuous Wold Land. So come and relax and forget the pressures of everyday life, stroll around and observe the wildlife and history, or explore the wonders of the East Coast, York and Moors. We have a twin, double, and four-poster room with air spa bath, all en suite and tastefully furnished and decorated. There are beverage making facilities in each room. We pride ourselves on our cleanliness and do not allow any smoking or pets in the house. A warm friendly, family atmosphere awaits you. Bed and Breakfast £28 to £35 per person per night. Evening Meal £16. **ETC/AA ◆◆◆◆◆** *SILVER AWARD.*
website: www.woldcottage.com

NORTH YORKSHIRE

BEDALE

Mrs M. Keighley, Southfield, 96 South End, Bedale DL8 2DS (01677 423510). This is a quiet country town only five minutes from A1, so is ideal for breaking journey from South to Scotland. With the Dales immediate and the Lakes only one hour away, it is a good base for touring. Area attractions include Fountains Abbey, Ripon Cathedral, Harewood House, Bolton Castle, Lightwater Valley (as on TV) and many more. Four 18-hole golf courses and swimming, to keep husband and children happy. Free off-road parking for four/five cars. Two double en suite bedrooms, one twin and one single both with washbasins and tea/coffee making facilities and sittingroom. SAE please. Now open all year. Established 1977. **AA/RAC** ◆◆◆, *"WHICH?" RECOMMENDED.*

BEDALE

The White Rose Hotel, Bedale Road, Leeming Bar, Northallerton DL7 9AY (01677 422707/424941; Fax: 01677 425123). Family-run, 18 bedroom private hotel situated in village on A684, half a mile from A1 motorway. Warm, friendly atmosphere. Ideal base for touring North York Moors, Dales and coastal resorts. All bedrooms have en suite bathrooms, colour TV, radio, telephone, trouser press and tea/coffee making facilities. Fully licensed; restaurant. Bed and Breakfast from £42 single, £56 double/twin, £62 family room, some budget rooms available. Pets welcome. Please write or telephone for further details. **AA/RAC ★★**
e-mail: John@whiterosehotel.co.uk
website: www.whiterosehotel.co.uk

See also Colour Display Advertisement

BEDALE

Mrs D. Layfield, Little Holtby, Leeming Bar, Northallerton DL7 9LH (01609 748762). A period farmhouse with beautiful views at the gateway to the Yorkshire Dales, within easy distance of many places of great interest, just 100 yards off the A1 between Bedale and Richmond. Little Holtby has been restored and furnished to a high standard whilst still retaining its original character; polished wood floors, open fires and original beams in many of the rooms. All bedrooms have colour TV, tea/coffee making facilities and are centrally heated. One double bedroom (en suite), one four-poster room, one twin-bedded room with washbasin. Bed and Breakfast from £25 to £30pppn; Evening Meal available. **ETC** ◆◆◆ *SILVER AWARD.*
e-mail: littleholtby@yahoo.co.uk

Eden Camp Modern History Museum • *Malton, North Yorkshire* • *01653 697777*
website: www.edencamp.co.uk
This award-winning museum will take you back to wartime Britain where you can experience the sights, sounds and smells of World War II.

Blacksheep Brewery Visitor Centre • *Masham, North Yorkshire* • *01765 689227*
website: www.blacksheepbrewery.com
Traditional working brewery with excellent visitor facilities including guided tours, bistro and gift shop.

COVERDALE

Mrs Julie A. Clarke, Middle Farm, Woodale, Leyburn DL8 4TY (01969 640271). Middle Farm is a peacefully situated traditional Dales farmhouse, with adjoining stable block for guests' accommodation. Situated on the unclassified road linking Wensleydale and Wharfedale. Ideal place to escape the 'madding crowd'. Good base for walking and touring any of the Dales' many beauty spots. Noted for excellent home cooking, offering Bed and Breakfast with optional Dinner. Two double and one twin-bedded rooms all en suite. Separate lounge, diningroom. Guests' privacy assured. Pets and children welcome. Ample private off-road parking. Open all year round. Brochure available on request. Directions – 5 miles Kettlewell, 10 miles Leyburn, unclassified road.
e-mail: julie-clarke@amserve.com

FILEY

Leonard & Diane Hunter, "Sea Cabin" 16 Gap Road, Hunmanby Gap, Near Filey YO14 9QP (01723 891368). Unique Bed & Breakfast accommodation. En suite for two people only. Own private lounge. Located on the clifftop with access to the golden sands of Filey Bay. Quiet location. Good Yorkshire food, 3-course English breakfast. Bookings for evening meals as required. The perfect venue for a relaxing break. Private parking. Pets welcome. By car: five minutes Filey, 10 minutes Flamborough, 15 minutes Bridlington, 20 minutes Scarborough. Please contact for brochure and terms.

GRASSINGTON

Grassington House Hotel and Restaurant, The Square, Grassington, Skipton BD23 5AQ (01756 752406; Fax: 01756 752135). The hotel is situated in the quaint cobbled square and is renowned for its atmosphere of warmth and friendliness. Our restaurant, serving à la carte, is very popular for its good food where we use produce from local suppliers. We also serve a large selection of meals and snacks in the bar and conservatory. The hotel is well situated for walking in the beautiful dales or touring. Large private car park. **ETC/AA ★★**

HARROGATE

Mrs E. Gourlay, Glenayr, 19 Franklin Mount, Harrogate HG1 5EJ (01423 504259). Whether you visit Harrogate for business or pleasure you won't find a warmer welcome or enjoy genuine hospitality anywhere to match the comfortable Victorian home of Elizabeth Gourlay who treats her guests as invited friends. Harrogate's elegant town centre is a leisurely five minute walk and the International Conference and Exhibition Centre a mere 200 yards from the hotel. Six light and pleasantly furnished bedrooms with en suite bathroom offer home from home comfort. You can savour a traditional and substantial English breakfast. Brochure available.

See also Colour Display Advertisement

HARROGATE

Mrs Judy Barker, Brimham Guest House, Silverdale Close, Darley, Harrogate HG3 2PQ (01423 780948). The family-run guest house is situated in the centre of Darley, a quiet village in unspoilt Nidderdale. All rooms en suite and centrally heated with tea/coffee making facilities and views across the Dales. Full English breakfast served between 7am and 9am in the dining room; a TV lounge/conservatory is available for your relaxation. Off street parking. Central for visits to Harrogate, York, Skipton and Ripon, or just enjoying drives through the Dales and Moors where you will take in dramatic hillsides, green hills, picturesque villages, castles and abbeys. Children welcome. Bed and Breakfast from £20 per person per night double, £22 per person twin room and £30 single room, reductions for three nights or more. Yorkshire in Bloom Winner. **ETC** ◆◆◆◆

HARROGATE

Chris and Cliff Naylor, Parnas Hotel, 98 Franklin Road, Harrogate HG1 5EN (01423 564493; Fax: 01423 563554). A family-run licensed, spacious 10 bedroomed Hotel where a friendly atmosphere is our priority plus comfort and a hearty breakfast. An easy walk to town and conference centre. Single, double, twin or family rooms, all en suite. All have TV and tea/coffee facilities. Harrogate is a sophisticated Spa Town with beautiful buildings and exclusive shops. Take an evening stroll to beautiful Valley Gardens and then enjoy a drink in the hotel. Ideal base for touring – York 19 miles, Leeds Royal Armoury 17 miles, and near Dales. Ample parking. Prices from £25 per person. Children's rates available. Brochure on request.
e-mail: info@parnashotel.co.uk
website: www.parnashotel.co.uk

HARROGATE

Mr Derek and Mrs Carol Vinter, Spring Lodge, 22 Spring Mount, Harrogate HG1 2HX (01423 506036). Attractive Edwardian guest house situated in a quiet cul-de-sac, yet close to all the amenities of Harrogate, Britain's floral spa town, with its elegant and outstanding architecture and gardens, antique shops and restaurants. Ideal tourist base for visiting the Dales and North York Moors, historic York and bustling Leeds. Children welcome, cot and high chair provided. All year round a warm welcome awaits you from the resident proprietors. Short breaks available. Accommodation comprises three double rooms, one triple/family and one single. En suite rooms available. Coffee and tea making facilities in all rooms. Residential licence. We are a non-smoking guesthouse. Bed and Breakfast from £20 pppn. **ETC** ◆◆◆

e-mail: dv22harrogate@aol.com
website: www.spring-lodge.co.uk

A high standard of comfortable accommodation awaits you at The Coppice, with a reputation for excellent food and a warm friendly welcome. All rooms en suite with telephones. Quietly located off Kings Road, five minutes' walk from the elegant shops and gardens of the town centre. Just three minutes' walk from the Conference Centre. Ideal location to explore the natural beauty of the Yorkshire Dales. Midway stop Edinburgh–London.

Free Yorkshire touring map - ask for details.

Bed and Breakfast £35 single, £55 double, twin from £60, family from £68; Evening Meal £17.

The Coppice

9 Studley Road, Harrogate HG1 5JU
Tel: 01423 569626 • Fax: 01423 569005
e-mail: coppice@harrogate.com • website: www.harrogate.com/coppice

ETC ◆◆◆◆

See also Colour Advertisement

HARROGATE

Mrs C.E. Nelson, Nidderdale Lodge Farm, Fellbeck, Pateley Bridge, Harrogate HG3 5DR (01423 711677). Working farm. Homely, comfortable, Christian accommodation. Spacious stone built bungalow in beautiful Nidderdale which is very central for touring the Yorkshire Dales; Pateley Bridge two miles, Harrogate 14 miles, Ripon nine miles. Museums, rocks, caves, fishing, bird watching, beautiful quiet walks, etc all nearby. En suite rooms (one twin, two double), TV. Private lounge. Tea making facilities available. Choice of breakfast. Evening meals available one mile away. Ample parking space on this working farm. Open Easter to end of October. **ETC ◆◆◆**

HELMSLEY

Mrs J. Milburn, Barn Close Farm, Rievaulx, Helmsley YO6 5HL (01439 798321). Barn Close Farm is nicely situated in the North York Moors National Park. This family offers homely accommodation to holidaymakers all year round. The farmhouse is in beautiful surroundings. Within easy reach of Rievaulx Abbey, and many other places of interest. It is an ideal centre for tourists. Pony trekking nearby. Good walking terrain! Home produced meat, eggs, vegetables served. Highly commended for good food. Sorry, no pets. En suite double and one family bedrooms; bathroom; toilets; sitting room and dining room. Children are welcome. Cot, high chair and babysitting available. Bed and Breakfast from £22 to £25, Evening Meal £12. **ETC ◆◆◆**

HELMSLEY

Virginia Collinson, Hall Farm, Gilling East, York YO62 4JW (01439 788314). Come and stay with us at Hall Farm. A beautifully situated 400 acre working stock farm with extensive views over Ryedale. Completely away from all the traffic, we are half-a-mile away from the road, as you drive up to the farm you may see cows with their calves and in the spring and early summer ewes with their lambs. We offer a friendly, family welcome with home made scones on arrival. A ground floor double en suite room is available and includes hospitality tray with home made biscuits. Sittingroom with TV and open fire on chilly evenings, diningroom with patio doors to conservatory. You will be the only guests so the breakfast time is up to you. Full English Breakfast includes home made bread and preserves with our own free range eggs. There are lots of excellent places to eat in the evenings in the historic market town of Helmsley and nearby villages. York, Castle Howard and the North York Moors within half-an-hour drive. Terms from £22 per person.
e-mail: virginia@collinson2.fsnet.co.uk

HELMSLEY

Mrs C Swift, Stilworth House, 1 Church Street, Helmsley YO62 5AD (01439 771072). Helmsley is beautifully situated for touring the North York Moors National Park, East Coast, York, "Herriot" and "Heartbeat" country. There is a wealth of footpaths and bridleways to explore. Stilworth House overlooks the All Saints Church to the front and Helmsley Castle to the rear. A warm welcome awaits you in the comfortable relaxed atmosphere of this elegant Georgian town house just off the market square. Highly recommended for good food. All rooms are en suite, with tea/coffee making facilities, colour TV, radio alarms, hairdryer, central heating. Private gardens and car park. Bed and Breakfast from £25 per person per night. Please telephone, or write, for colour brochure. As recommended by the "Which?" Good B&B Guide. **ETC** ◆◆◆

KIRKBYMOORSIDE

Janet Trousdale, Brickfields Farm, Kirby Mills, Kirkbymoorside YO62 6NS (01751 433074). Brickfields Farm enjoys a secluded location, at the end of a tree-lined lane, yet only a mile from the amenities of Kirkbymoorside. Ideal base for visiting North York Moors and Steam Railway, also Castle Howard, Rievaulx Abbey, York, Scarborough and Whitby. Golf locally. The newly converted guest rooms are well equipped, with tea/coffee tray, mini-fridge, clock/radio/CD, hairdryer, colour TV/video. All have en suite facilities, with heated towel rails, modern efficient showers and fluffy bathrobes. Quiet, informal atmosphere with a warm, friendly welcome and my personal attention. Ground floor rooms. Ample on-site parking. Open all year. Evening meals by arrangement. No smoking. No pets. B&B from £30. Brochure available. **ETC** ◆◆◆◆ *SILVER AWARD*, **AA** *FOUR RED DIAMONDS.*

KIRKBYMOORSIDE

Mr Chris Tinkler, The Cornmill Luxury Guest House, Kirby Mills, Kirkbymoorside, York YO62 6NP (01751 432000; Fax: 01751 432300). This sympathetically restored 18th century watermill and Victorian farmhouse provide a warm and friendly welcome and tranquil, well-appointed accommodation on the River Dove. The large (no smoking) bedrooms with en suite baths and/or powerful showers, fluffy towels, kingsize or twin beds, themed four-poster rooms, guest lounge with self-service honesty bar and wood-burning stove, plus boot room, are in the farmhouse. Our sumptuous breakfasts and pre-booked dinners are served in the Mill, with glass-floored viewing panel over the millrace. Wheelchair friendly. Golf and horse riding nearby. On site parking. Open all year round. Self-catering accommodation also available.

e-mail: cornmill@kirbymills.demon.co.uk   **website: www.kirbymills.demon.co.uk**

LEYBURN

Mrs H.M. Richardson, Sunnyridge, Argill Farm, Harmby, Leyburn DL8 5HQ (01969 622478). Situated on a small sheep farm in Wensleydale, Sunnyridge is a spacious bungalow in an outstanding position. Magnificent views are enjoyed from every room. In the heart of the Yorkshire Dales and the midst of Herriot country, it is an ideal centre for exploring the wide variety of activities and attractions; or a restful stop-over for travellers. Sample Yorkshire hospitality and relax in comfortable ground floor accommodation comprising one double or twin bedroom and one family/double/twin-bedded room, both en suite, each with colour TV and tea/coffee facilities. Non-smoking. Guest lounge. Children welcome. Pets by arrangement. Bed and Breakfast from £20. **ETC** ◆◆◆
e-mail: richah@freenet.co.uk

BANAVIE

Banavie is a large semi-detached house set in a quiet part of the picturesque village of Thornton-le-Dale, one of the prettiest villages in Yorkshire with its famous thatched cottage and bubbling stream flowing through the centre. We offer our guests a quiet night's sleep and rest away from the main road, yet only four minutes' walk from the village centre. One large double or twin bedroom and two double bedrooms, all tastefully decorated with en suite facilities, colour TV, hairdryer, shaver point etc. and tea/coffee making facilities. There is a large guest lounge, tea tray on arrival. A real Yorkshire breakfast is served in the dining room. Places to visit include Castle Howard, Eden Camp, North Yorkshire Moors Railway, Goathland ("Heartbeat"), York etc. There are three pubs, a bistro and a fish and chip shop for meals. Children and dogs welcome. Own keys.

B&B from £21 to £24 pppn • SAE please for brochure
Welcome Host. Hygiene Certificate held.

Mrs Ella Bowes ~ Tel: 01751 474616
ROXBY ROAD, THORNTON-LE-DALE, PICKERING YO18 7SX
e-mail: ella@banavie.fsbusiness.co.uk • www.banavie.uk.com

ETC ◆◆◆◆

MALTON

Mrs Ann Hopkinson, The Brow, 25 York Road, Malton YO17 0AX (01653 693402). The Brow is a large house with beautiful views. It was the home of the Walker family who owned the oldest of the five breweries for which Malton was famous. Captain Walker of Whitby (to whom Captain Cook was apprenticed) was a member of the same Walker family. A visit to The Brow should not be missed. A warm welcome awaits you here with TV and tea/coffee making facilities in all rooms. Children welcome, reduced rates. Bed and Breakfast from £25 to £30 per person per night.

NORTHALLERTON

Ann Saxby, Hallikeld House, Stokesley Road, Brompton, Northallerton DL6 2UE (01609 773613; Fax: 01609 770262; mobile: 077300 58807). Two miles east of Northallerton in open countryside, ideal for travelling from coast to Dales. Easy access to A19 and A1. Central heating, lounge. Bed and Breakfast from £17 per person per night.

PICKERING

Mrs S. Wardell, Tangalwood, Roxby Road, Thornton-le-Dale, Pickering YO18 7SX (01751 474688). Tangalwood provides a warm welcome. Very clean and comfortable accommodation and good food. Situated in a quiet part of this picturesque village, which is in a good central position for Moors, "Heartbeat" country, coast, North York Moors Railway, Flamingo Park Zoo and forest drives, mountain biking and walking. Good facilities for meals provided in the village. Accommodation in one twin and one double en suite rooms, one single with private bathroom; all with tea/coffee making facilities and TV; alarm clock/radio and hairdryer also provided; diningroom; central heating. Open Easter to October for Bed and Breakfast from £21 each. Private car park. Secure motorbike and cycle storage. ETC ◆◆◆
website: www.accommodation.uk.net/tangalwood

PICKERING

Mrs Sandra M. Pickering, "Nabgate", Wilton Road, Thornton-le-Dale, Pickering YO18 7QP (01751 474279). Situated at the eastern end of this beautiful village "Nabgate" was built at the turn of the century. Accommodation comprises two double and one twin rooms, all en suite, all with TV, tea making facilities, shaver point. Central heating. Diningroom and lounge for guests' use. Keys provided for access at all times. Car park. Children and pets welcome. Thornton Dale has three pubs all providing meals, also cafes, fish and chip shop and bistro. Situated in the North York Moors National Park it is an ideal base for East Coast, Steam Railway, Flamingoland, Castle Howard, York and "Heartbeat" village. Open all year. Bed and Breakfast from £20 to £25. Welcome Host and Hygiene Certificate held. Self-catering cottage also available. ETC ◆◆◆
website: www.nabgateguesthouse.co.uk

RICHMOND

Browson Bank Farmhouse Accommodation, Browson Bank Farmhouse, Browson Bank, Dalton, Richmond DL11 7HE (01325 718504 or 01325 718246). A newly converted granary set in 300 acres of farmland. The accommodation consists of three very tastefully furnished double/twin rooms all en suite, tea and coffee making facilities, colour TV and central heating. A large, comfortable lounge is available to relax in. Full English breakfast served. Situated six miles west of Scotch Corner (A1). Ideal location to explore the scenic countryside of Teesdale and the Yorkshire Dales and close to the scenic towns of Barnard Castle and Richmond. Terms from £20.00 per night.

RICHMOND

Mrs S. Lawson, Stonesthrow, Dalton, Near Richmond DL11 7HS (01833 621493). With a welcoming fire, private garden and conservatory, Stonesthrow offers you a friendly, family atmosphere. Unmistakable Yorkshire hospitality from the moment you arrive – we greet you with a tea or coffee and home made cakes. Situated midway between the towns of Richmond and Barnard Castle, it offers you an ideal base for exploring the Yorkshire Dales, Teesdale, and York. Stonesthrow, a non-smoking Bed and Breakfast, has well appointed bedrooms with TV, tea/coffee facilities and full central heating. Off-road parking. Children eight and over are welcome. Sorry, no pets. B&B £18pppn, £20 single.

ROBIN HOOD'S BAY

Mrs B. Reynolds, 'South View', Sledgates, Fylingthorpe, Whitby YO22 4TZ (01947 880025). Pleasantly situated, comfortable accommodation in own garden with sea and country views. Ideal for walking and touring. Close to the moors, within easy reach of Whitby, Scarborough and many more places of interest. There are two double rooms, lounge and diningroom. Bed and Breakfast from £18, including bedtime drink. Parking spaces. Phone for further details.

ROBIN HOOD'S BAY (near)

David and Angela Pattinson, Hogarth Hall, Boggle Hole Road, Near Robin Hood's Bay, Whitby YO22 4QQ (01947 880547). Hogarth Hall is set in 145 acres of habitat attracting a variety of wildlife. Wonderful views over ancient woodlands, heather-covered moorland and down the valley to the sea. Enjoy wonderful sunsets and sunrises. All rooms are en suite with TV. Tea/coffee making facilities are available. Scarborough 12 miles, Whitby nine miles, York 40 miles, Rievaulx Abbey 30 miles. Walks around the farm and further afield. Robin Hood's Bay is an 80 minute walk along the road, unused railway, cliff path or beach. Use your car to visit points of interest listed on our tour. New fishing lake available shortly. Bed and Breakfast £20 per person per night, reducing nightly to £100 per person for seven nights.

SCARBOROUGH

Mrs V. Henson, Brinka House, 2 Station Square, Ravenscar, Scarborough YO13 0LU (01723 871470). Brinka House Bed & Breakfast is situated in Ravenscar midway between Scarborough and Whitby, with stunning views across to Robin Hood's Bay and is surrounded by the moors. The village boasts a variety of walks, cycle tracks, golf course, pony and llama trekking, and a bus service from the front door to town. A warm welcome and tasty breakfast awaits, vegetarians and special diets catered for. We have a romantic double room with a large corner bath en suite and a twin/family room en suite. All rooms have TV, drinks facilities and sea views. Terms from £19 per person per night, £25 single.

SCARBOROUGH

Sue and Tony Hewitt, Harmony Country Lodge, Limestone Road, Burniston, Scarborough YO13 0DG (0800 2985840; Tel & Fax: 01723 870276). DISTINCTIVELY DIFFERENT. Peaceful and relaxing retreat, octagonal in design and set in two acres of private grounds with 360° panoramic views of the National Park and sea. An ideal centre for walking or touring. Two miles from Scarborough and within easy reach of Whitby, York and the beautiful North Yorkshire countryside. Tastefully decorated en suite centrally heated rooms with colour TV and all with superb views. Attractive dining room, guest lounge and relaxing conservatory. Traditional English breakfast, including vegetarian. Fragrant massage available. Bed and Breakfast from £24 to £34. Non smoking, licensed, private parking facilities. Personal service and warm, friendly Yorkshire hospitality. Spacious five-berth caravan also available for self-catering holidays. Children over seven years welcome. Christmas packages. ETC ◆◆◆◆
e-mail: tony@harmonylodge.net   website: www.harmonylodge.net

SCARBOROUGH

Mrs M.M. Abbott, Howdale Hotel, 121 Queens Parade, Scarborough YO12 7HU (Freephone: 0800 056 6622; Tel & Fax: 01723 372696). Overlooks beautiful North Bay. Close to town. Licensed. Excellent food. Clean, comfortable rooms with colour TV, tea/coffee making facilities and hairdryer. Most en suite. Terms from £20 per person.
e-mail: mail@howdalehotel.co.uk   website: www.howdalehotel.co.uk

SCARBOROUGH

Mrs M. Edmondson, Plane Tree Cottage Farm, Staintondale, Scarborough YO13 0EY (01723 870796). This small mixed farm is situated off the beaten track, with open views of beautiful countryside and the sea. We have sheep, hens, two ginger cats and special sheep dog "Bess". This very old beamed cottage, small but homely, has one twin with bathroom and two double en suite rooms with tea maker. Meals of very high standard served with own fresh eggs and garden produce are available. Staintondale is about half-way between Scarborough and Whitby and near the North York Moors. Pretty woodland walks nearby. Car essential. Bed and Breakfast from £23 per person per night. Also six-berth caravan available. SAE please for details, or telephone. ETC ◆◆◆

ENGLAND

e-mail: gantongreyhound@supanet.com

SCARBOROUGH

The Ganton Greyhound, Ganton, Near Scarborough YO12 4NX (01944 710116; Fax: 01944 712705). Hosts, Terry and Margaret Bennett, are deservedly proud of their excellent reputation for providing good hospitality, good food, and a warm, friendly atmosphere. En suite bedrooms (double, twin, family and disabled) are tastefully furnished, with tea/coffee facilities and colour television, and there is a lounge for the exclusive use of guests. Drinks and meals can be enjoyed in the pleasant bar, where large open fireplaces and oak beams add to the welcoming ambience; meals are also available in the light and airy conservatory restaurant. Its location on the main A64 York to Scarborough road is ideal for exploring this scenic area; the North York moors and several golf courses, including Ganton Championship Course, are within easy reach.
website: www.gantongreyhound.com

SCARBOROUGH

Michael and Angela Saville, The Leeway Hotel, 71 Queen's Parade, Scarborough YO12 7HT (01723 374371). The Leeway is a family-run Guest House which is ideally situated close to the North Bay beach, and yet near to the local amenities. A superb base from which to explore the North York Moors, York, Whitby, etc. All double rooms are en suite and have tea/coffee making facilities, TV and radio. Sea views are available. Car parking for six cars, and free on-street parking is available outside the hotel. For your comfort and safety, bedrooms are non-smoking. Bed and Breakfast from £18 to £22.

e-mail: info@windmill-hotel.co.uk

SCARBOROUGH

Angela and Roland Thompson, The Windmill Hotel, Mill Street, Off Victoria Road, Scarborough YO11 1SZ (01723 372735). 18th century windmill. Built around the windmill is The Old Mill Hotel, comprising 12 attractively decorated en suite rooms surrounding the mill courtyard. All are tastefully furnished with tea/coffee making facilities, colour TV and central heating. Four-poster beds available. Breakfast is served on the ground floor of the Mill itself. There is private parking in the courtyard. Within the Mill is the contemporary Toy Museum, tea rooms and play area for children. The Mill is a few minutes' walk from the town centre, rail and bus stations. Pets welcome by arrangement. Bed and Breakfast from £26. Children aged 2 to 14 years £10; children aged under 2 £5. **ETC** ◆◆◆
website: www.windmill-hotel.co.uk

SCARBOROUGH

Sylvia and Chris Kirk, The Terrace Hotel, 69 Westborough, Scarborough YO11 1TS (01723 374937). A small family-run Hotel situated between North and South Bays, close to all Scarborough's many attractions and only a short walk from the town centre, rail and bus stations. Private car park. Three double bedrooms (one en suite), three family rooms (one en suite) and one single bedroom, all with colour TV and tea making facilities. Full Fire Certificate. Non-smoking accommodation available. Bed and full English Breakfast from £17. En suite facilities £3 extra per person per night. Children (sharing room with adults) under four years FREE, four to 11 years half price.
websites: www.s-h-a.dircon.co.uk
www.s-h-systems.co.uk

FREE or REDUCED RATE entry to Holiday Visits and Attractions — see our READERS' OFFER VOUCHERS on pages 63-90

SKIPTON

Mrs Heather Simpson, Low Skibeden Farmhouse, Harrogate Road, Skipton BD23 6AB (07050 207787/01756 793849). Detached 16th century farmhouse in private grounds one mile east of Skipton (five minutes from town centre) off the A59/A65 gateway to the Dales, eg Bolton Abbey - Malham, Settle. Luxury bed and breakfast with fireside treats in the lounge. All rooms are quiet, spacious, have panoramic views, washbasins, tea facilities and electric overblankets. Central heating October to May. All guests are warmly welcomed and served tea/coffee and cakes on arrival, bedtime beverages are served from 9.30pm. Breakfast is served from 7am to 8.45am in the dining room. No smoking. No pets and no children under 12 years. Safe parking. New arrivals before 10pm. Quality and value guaranteed. Bed and Breakfast from £22.50 per person per night for standard room with washbasin, shared facilities, two-piece en suite from £24.50 per person per night shared; single occupancy from £30-£48. Full en suite from £26.50 per person per night. Farm cottage sometimes available (**ETC ★★★**). A deposit secures a room. Open all year. Credit cards accepted. **AA ◆◆◆◆**, *"WELCOME HOST"*, *"WHICH?"* **website: www.yorkshirenetco.uk/accgde/lowskibeden**

STOKESLEY

Sue & Mike Barnfather, Four Wynds, Whorl Hill, Faceby, Stokesley TS9 7BZ (01642 701315). A warm and friendly welcome awaits you at 'Four Wynds', a smallholding set in beautiful, quiet and tranquil countryside on the edge of the North Yorkshire Moors and within easy commuting distance of Teeside (15 minutes) and only five minutes from the A19. We are the perfect location for visiting York and Whitby, or for touring Herriot, Captain Cook and Heartbeat Country, and an ideal stopover for 'Coast to Coast', 'Cleveland Way' and 'Lykewake' walkers – transport can be arranged from a pick-up point. All bedrooms have tea/coffee making facilities, colour TV and radio alarm, some en suite. Traditional hearty breakfast served at a time to suit and evening meal on request. Ample free and safe parking. Bed & Breakfast from £22 to £25 per person per night. Sorry no dogs. **ETC ◆◆◆**

See also Colour Display Advertisement

THIRSK

Joyce Ashbridge, Mount Grace Farm, Cold Kirby, Thirsk YO7 2HL (01845 597389; Fax: 01845 597872). A warm welcome awaits you on working farm surrounded by beautiful open countryside with magnificent views. Ideal location for touring or exploring the many walks in the area. Luxury en suite bedrooms with tea/coffee facilities. Spacious guests' lounge with colour TV. Garden. Enjoy delicious, generous helpings of farmhouse fayre cooked in our Aga. Children from 12 years plus. No smoking. No pets. Bed and Breakfast from £28. Open all year except Christmas.
e-mail: joyce@mountgracefarm.com
website: www.mountgracefarm.com

THIRSK

Mrs Julie Bailes, Glen Free, Holme-on-Swale, Sinderby, Near Thirsk YO7 4JE (01845 567331). Glen Free is an old Lodge Bungalow set in a very peaceful situation, but still only one mile from the B6267 Masham/Thirsk road). Approximately seven miles from Ripon, Thirsk, Bedale. York and Harrogate 40 minutes approximately. One double room and one double with single bed with washbasin. Central heating, tea making facilities and TV. All rooms ground floor. Golf, fishing, swimming and riding available locally. Ideal for touring the Dales and Herriot country. Bed and Breakfast from £16 per person.

THORNTON-LE-DALE

Bridgefoot Guest House, Chestnut Avenue, Thornton-le-Dale, Pickering Y018 7RR (01751 474749). Bridgefoot Guest House is situated in the village of Thornton-le-Dale, by the trout stream, in a wall-enclosed garden next to the thatched cottage. Ideal touring base for the moors, east coast, countryside, forestry, and York. Centrally heated throughout. Family room; several double and twin-bedded rooms; ground floor double (all rooms en suite), tea and coffee facilities, shaver points. Colour TV. Dining room. B&B from £24.00. Car parking. Non-smoking. Open all year. Contact **Mr and Mrs Evans. ETC ◆◆◆ website: www.bridgefoot-house.co.uk**

WENSLEYDALE

Barbara and Barrie Martin, The Old Star, West Witton, Leyburn DL8 4LU (01969 622949). Formerly a 17th century coaching inn, now a family-run guest house. You are always welcome at the Old Star. The building still retains many original features. Comfortable lounge with oak beams and log fire. Dinner available if ordered in advance. Bedrooms mostly en suite with central heating and tea/coffee making facilities. In the heart of the Yorkshire Dales National Park we are ideally situated for walking and touring the Dales. Large car park. Open all year except Christmas. Bed and Breakfast from £18 to £22 with special breaks available. **ETC ◆◆◆**

WHITBY

Heather and John Hall, Endeavour B&B, 28 Upgang Lane, Whitby Y021 3EA (01947 821110). Situated in the historic town of Whitby, this luxuriously appointed detached residence is on the West Cliff, with sea views yet close to the centre of town. Recently refurbished, this lovely home offers top class accommodation with three en suite bedrooms, two with fabulous sea views and all having hospitality trays, colour TVs and central heating. Full English breakfasts are served in the lovely dining room, which has separate tables. Parking for three cars. Heather and John offer friendly and personal service to ensure guests are comfortable and content during their stay. Bed & Breakfast from £23 pppn; special rate midweek short breaks available. Non-smoking. **e-mail: hhall49@hotmail.com website: www.endeavourbedandbreakfast.co.uk**

WHITBY

John and Jane King, Serendipity, 17 Abbey Terrace, West Cliff, Whitby YO21 3HQ (01947 603868). Serendipity is family-run, close to sea and town. Our comfortable rooms are all en suite or have private bathrooms with colour TV and refreshment tray. You can choose an excellent breakfast from our breakfast bar and hot servery. Easy access to the North York Moors, villages and other major attractions. Our rates are £30 per person per night for Bed and Breakfast, single occupancy from £35. Non-smoking hotel. For further information please visit our website. **e-mail: enquiries@serendipityhotel.co.uk website: www.serendipityhotel.co.uk**

WHITBY

Janice and Donna Hillier, Ashford Non-Smoking Guest House, 8 Royal Crescent, Whitby YO21 3EJ (01947 602138). "Come as a Guest - Leave as a Friend". The Ashford is a family-run guest house providing a relaxed, informal atmosphere and friendly service. Situated on Whitby's West Cliff, the Ashford occupies a superb position in Royal Crescent, overlooking Crescent Gardens and the sea. It is ideally situated for coastal and country walks, and makes an excellent base for exploring the North York Moors. Take a short drive inland and visit "Heartbeat Country", the North York Moors Railway, Rievaulx Abbey, Pickering and a myriad of pretty moorland villages, or take the coast road to discover the attractions of Scarborough, Bridlington and Filey. A little further afield you will find the historic city of York and Harrogate. Full central heating. Comfortable lounge. All bedrooms have en suite facilities, courtesy tray and colour TV. Good home cooking. Access at all times. Bed and Breakfast from £22. **ETC** ◆◆◆
e-mail: info@ashfordguesthouse.co.uk   website: www.ashfordguesthouse.co.uk

WHITBY

Mr and Mrs Richardson, Egton Banks Farm, Glaisdale, Whitby YO21 2QP (01947 897289). Beautiful old farmhouse situated in a lovely valley close to quiet roadside. Set in 120 acres of pastureland and woods. Centre of National Park. Warm and friendly atmosphere. Diningroom/Lounge for guests with TV and books. Close to river, one mile from Glaisdale village and mainline railway, eight miles to Whitby, four miles steam railway and Heartbeat country. Both bedrooms have pretty decor and TV. One double/twin and one family room, both en suite. Full Yorkshire Breakfast. Packed lunches. All diets catered for. **ETC** ◆◆◆◆
e-mail: egtonbanksfarm@agriplus.net
website: www.egtonbanksfarm.agriplus.net

See also Colour Display Advertisement

WHITBY (near)

Mrs Pat Beale, Ryedale House, Coach Road, Sleights, Near Whitby YO22 5EQ (Tel & Fax: 01947 810534). Exclusive to non-smokers, welcoming Yorkshire house of character at the foot of the moors, National Park "Heartbeat" country. Three-and-a-half-miles from Whitby. Magnificent scenery, moors, dales, picturesque harbours, cliffs, beaches, scenic railways, superb walking - it's all here! Highly commended, beautifully appointed rooms with private facilities, many extras. Guest lounge; breakfast room with views over Esk Valley. Enjoy the large south-facing terrace and landscaped gardens. Extensive traditional and vegetarian breakfast choice. Local inns and restaurants - two within a short walk. Parking available, also public transport. Bed and Breakfast double £22 to £24, single £21 to £26, minimum stay two nights. Weekly reductions and Monday-Friday offers available. Regret, no pets or children. **ETC** ◆◆◆◆

PLEASE NOTE

All the information in this book is given in good faith in the belief that it is correct. However, the publishers cannot guarantee the facts given in these pages, neither are they responsible for changes in policy, ownership or terms that may take place after the date of going to press. Readers should always satisfy themselves that the facilities they require are available and that the terms, if quoted, still apply.

ENGLAND

Mr and Mrs G. Steel, Alder Carr House, York Road, Barmby Moor, York YO42 5HT (Tel & Fax: 01759 380566; mobile: 07885 277740). A Georgian-style house in 10 acres with a large garden for guests to relax in. Rooms are spacious with good views over countryside. The nearby market town of Pocklington has a National Water Lily collection and a Gliding Club. A wide range of local restaurants and country pubs offer an excellent choice for evening meals. Within easy reach of the York 'Park and Ride', Yorkshire Coast, Moors and Wolds. Your historian hostess will be happy to share her local knowledge to help you make the most of your visit. Closed Christmas and New Year. Twin, double/family rooms, all en suite or private facilities. Children welcome. Restricted smoking. Prices from £22.50 per person per night.

June, Keith and Rob Wood, Ascot House, 80 East Parade, York YO31 7YH (01904 426826; Fax: 01904 431077). An attractive Victorian villa built in 1869 with easy access to the historic city centre by walking or by public transport. All bedrooms have central heating, colour TV and complimentary tea/coffee making facilities while the family and double rooms are en suite. Most rooms have four-poster or canopy beds. Comfortable residents' lounge with TV; attractive dining room. There is also a sauna which can be hired by the hour. York has much to offer with its ancient narrow streets, medieval churches, Roman, Viking and National Railway museums and the Minster. Private parking. Single from £26 to £56 per room per night, double £56 to £68 per room per night, including Traditional English Breakfast and VAT.

ETC/AA/RAC ◆◆◆◆, ETC *SILVER AWARD*.
e-mail: admin@ascothouseyork.com   website: www.ascothouseyork.com

Briar Lea House, 8 Longfield Terrace, Bootham, York YO30 7DJ (01904 635061; Fax: 01904 330356). This comfortable Victorian terrace house is situated in a quiet leafy suburb, just a seven minute riverside walk into the heart of the city. Bedrooms are comfortable and well-equipped with double, twin and family rooms, which are able to accommodate a mixture of friends and family. All rooms are en suite and have colour TV, tea and coffee making facilities as standard. Both on-street and limited off-street parking is available. Full English breakfast is served together with fresh fruit options and vegetarian diets will be catered for. All major credit/debit cards accepted. No smoking throughout.
ETC/AA ◆◆◆
e-mail: briarleahouse@msn.com
website: www.briarlea.co.uk

Crossways Guest House, 23 Wigginton Road, York YO31 8HJ (01904 637250). Crossways Guest House is a three-storey Victorian Town House, situated ten minutes' walk from the city wall. It is an excellent base for exploring the city's famous attractions as well as touring the North York Moors and Dales. All rooms are en suite with TV and tea/coffee making. Twin room on the ground floor. Patio with a garden available for guests. City bus stop at the end of the garden. Bed and Breakfast £40 per room per night for two nights or more, £50 per room for one night, £20 -£30 per room per night single occupancy of double room. Bargain breaks out of season, prices on request. No smoking.
e-mail: info@crosswaysguesthouse.freeserve.co.uk
website: www.crosswaysguesthouse.freeserve.co.uk

A useful index of towns and counties appears at the back of this book on pages 417-421. Refer also to Contents Pages 2 and 3.

YORK

Cumbria House, 2 Vyner Street, Haxby Road, York YO31 8HS (01904 636817). A warm and friendly welcome awaits you at Cumbria House - an elegant, tastefully decorated Victorian guest house, where comfort and quality are assured. We are convenient for the city, being only 15 minutes' walk from York's historic Minster and yet within minutes of the northern by-pass (A1237). A launderette, post office and children's park are close by. All rooms have colour TV, radio alarms and tea/coffee facilities. Most are en suite and all are non-smoking. Central heating. Fire Certificate. Guests' car park. Full English breakfast or vegetarian alternative. £23 to £28 per person. **AA** ◆◆◆
e-mail: candj@cumbriahouse.freeserve.co.uk
website: www.cumbriahouse.com

YORK

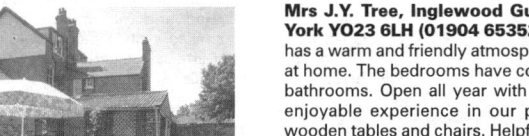

Mrs J.W. Harrison, Fairthorne, 356 Strensall Road, Earswick, York YO32 9SW (Tel & Fax: 01904 768609). John and Joan Harrison invite you for a restful holiday in a peaceful country setting - a dormer bungalow with central heating, TV, shaver points, tea making facilities and en suite in bedrooms; TV lounge and dining room. Pleasant family atmosphere. Situated three miles north of York, within easy reach of East Coast and Yorkshire Moors and near golf course. Bus stop 50 yards if required. Bed and Breakfast from £20 per night. Reductions for children. Private car park and large garden. Open all year. **ETC** ◆◆◆

YORK

Mrs J.Y. Tree, Inglewood Guest House, 7 Clifton Green, York YO23 6LH (01904 653523). The Inglewood Guest House has a warm and friendly atmosphere where guests will really feel at home. The bedrooms have colour TV and some have en suite bathrooms. Open all year with central heating. Breakfast is an enjoyable experience in our pleasant diningroom with dark wooden tables and chairs. Helpful information is given on where to go and what to see. It is an ideal centre for exploring York and making day excursions to many market towns and villages around York. There are many places of historic interest also to visit. Children are welcome. Sorry, no pets. A car is not essential, but there is parking. Bed and Breakfast from £25; reductions for children. Non-smoking.
website: www.SmoothHound.co.uk/hotels/inglewood.html

YORK

Newton House, Neville Street, Haxby Road, York YO31 8NP (01904 635627). Diana and John offer all their guests a friendly and warm welcome to their Victorian end town house a few minutes' walk from the city centre, York's beautiful Minster, medieval walls and museums. We are only a 40 mile drive from coastal resorts, the lovely Yorkshire Moors and Dales. Three double/twin en suite rooms, colour TV, tea/coffee tray, central heating. Breakfast menu. Car park. Non-smoking. Fire Certificate. Terms from £25pp.

YORK

Mav and Maureen Davidson, "Oaklands" Guest House, 351 Strensall Road, Old Earswick, York YO32 9SW (01904 768443). A very warm welcome awaits you at our attractive family house set in open countryside, yet only three miles from York with close access to the York ring road (A1237), A64, A1 and A19. Ideally situated for City, Coast, Dales and Moors. Our comfortable bedrooms are centrally heated with vanity unit, colour TV, razor point, tea and coffee tray, radio alarms and hairdryers. En suite facilities available. A more than ample full breakfast is served in a light airy diningroom. Your hosts, Maureen and Mav, very much look forward to seeing you. Bed and full English Breakfast from £22. Discounts available. Open all year. No pets. Smoking in garden only. **ETC** ◆◆◆◆

YORK

Mrs Helen Butterworth, Wellgarth House, Wetherby Road, Rufforth, York YO23 3QB (01904 738592; mobile: 07711 252577). A warm welcome awaits you at Wellgarth House, ideally situated in Rufforth (B1224) three miles from York, one mile from the Ring Road (A1237) and convenient for "Park and Ride" into York City. This country guest house offers a high standard of accommodation with en suite. Bed and Breakfast from £25pppn. All rooms have complimentary tea/coffee making facilities, colour TV. Excellent local pub just two minutes' walk away which serves lunches and dinners. Large private car park. **ETC** ◆◆◆

YORK

Mrs J. Woodland, Cavalier Hotel, 39 Monkgate, York YO31 7PB (Tel & Fax: 01904 636615). The Cavalier is an early Georgian Listed building, recently refurbished to provide very comfortable accommodation. It is ideally located close to the city centre and yards from the ancient city walls and most of the historic sites. Also convenient for touring North York Moors, Dales and East Coast resorts. Most rooms are en suite, and all have washbasins, colour TV, shaver points, radio alarms, and tea/coffee making facilities. Hairdryer and ironing facilities are available on request. Bed and full English breakfast with vegetarian options. Amenities include pay phone, parking, full central heating. Full Fire Certificate. Open all year. Winter/Spring mini-breaks available, details on request.

YORK

Astley House, 123 Clifton, York YO30 6BL (01904 634745; Fax: 01904 621327; mobile 07830 109215). Elegant Victorian house, family-run, within walking distance of the city centre. Beautiful en suite accommodation, some four-posters; all with colour TV and tea/ coffee facilities. Traditional English or lighter breakfasts are freshly cooked and served in a relaxed atmosphere. Evening meals available. Car parking. Discounted rates available throughout the year.
e-mail: astleyhousehotel@aol.com
website: www.astleyhouseyork.co.uk

YORK

David and Katherine Leedham, York House, 62 Heworth Green, York YO31 7TQ (Tel & Fax: 01904 427070). A short stroll from the heart of one of Europe's most historic cities, York House is the perfect base for a visit to beautiful York or the surrounding areas. Recently refurbished luxury rooms, each individually decorated, are complete with all the conveniences you could need for a relaxing and enjoyable stay. A few of the facilities offered: en suite shower or bath; four-poster, double, twin, family and single rooms; tea/coffee making facilities; off-street parking; full English breakfast; non-smoking establishment. Prices from £25pppn. Children welcome. Discounts available. **ETC** ◆◆◆◆
e-mail: yorkhouse.bandb@tiscali.co.uk
website: www.yorkhouseyork.com

YORK

Mr and Mrs G. Hudson, Orillia House, 89 The Village, Stockton on Forest, York YO3 9UP (01904 400600). A warm welcome awaits you at Orillia House, conveniently situated in the centre of the village, three miles north east of York, one mile from A64. The house dates back to the 17th century and has been restored to offer a high standard of comfort with modern facilities yet retaining its original charm and character. All rooms have private facilities, colour TV and tea/coffee making facilities. Our local pub provides excellent evening meals. We also have our own private car park. Bed and Breakfast from £22. Telephone for our brochure. **ETC** ◆◆◆◆
website: www.orilliahouse.co.uk

YORK

St Paul's Hotel, 120 Holgate Road, York YO2 4BB (01904 611514). St Paul's is situated a short walk from the centre of the historic city of York, which has something to offer everyone, with museums, shopping, tours, restaurants and nightlife ranging from olde worlde pubs to the very latest in bars. Deep in the heart of Yorkshire, it is only a short drive to breathtaking views of the Yorkshire Moors and Dales. Situated in a pleasant residential location, we have six stylish rooms with en suite facilities, colour television and tea/coffee making facilities. We can provide twin, double or family accommodation and even have a four-poster room. Our residents' lounge offers the opportunity to meet other guests, relax and unwind. We pride ourselves on friendly and reliable service to make sure your stay with us is an enjoyable one. Bed and full English Breakfast from £27.50. Reductions for longer stays.

YORK

Simon Usher and Mark Reilly, The Park View, 34 Grosvenor Terrace, Bootham YO30 7AG (Tel & Fax: 01904 620437). A period townhouse with a friendly welcome. We are a short walk from the historic city centre of York. En suite rooms with colour TV, tea/coffee making facilities, central heating, hairdryer and radio alarm. Attractive dining room offering a choice of breakfasts including Full English and Vegetarian option. Bed and Breakfast from £29 per person. Simon and Mark offer a high standard of comfort and hospitality at "The Park View". A totally non-smoking establishment. **ETC** ◆◆◆
e-mail: theparkviewyork@aol.com

YORK (near Castle Howard)

See also Colour Display Advertisement

Sandie and Peter Turner, High Gaterley Farm, Near Welburn, York YO60 7HT (Tel & Fax: 01653 694636). High Gaterley enjoys a unique position, located within the boundaries of Castle Howard's magnificent country estate. It is ideally situated for easy access to the City of York, East Coast and the North Yorkshire Moors renowned for ruined abbeys and castles. The tranquil ambience with panoramic views over the Howardian Hills make it a perfect location for a peaceful and relaxing stay in a comfortable well-appointed farmhouse with the option of fine cuisine. En suite facilities with tea and coffee in all rooms, log fire in the drawing room, TV, non-smoking, dogs by prior arrangement. Open all year. Bed and Breakfast from £20. Optional evening meal and special diets by arrangement. **ETC** ◆◆◆◆
e-mail: admin@highgaterley.com
website: www.highgaterley.com

WEST YORKSHIRE

HAWORTH (near)

Newsholme Manor Hotel & Restaurant, Slaymaker Lane onto Slack Lane, Oakworth, Keighley, Near Haworth BD22 0RQ (01535 642964; Fax: 01535 645629). Pleasant accommodation with beautiful gardens and view over the valley. The en suite bedrooms all have facilities. Open all year round. Bar meals, lunches and evening meals served, fully licensed bar. Golf, horse riding and caravan site close by. For further details please contact **Mr C.T. Sexton.**
website: www.SmoothHound.co.uk

HALIFAX

Mr and Mrs G. Horrocks-Taylor, Fieldhouse, Staups Lane, Stump Cross, Halifax HX3 6XW (01422 355457). Spacious Listed 18th century farmhouse in the picturesque Shibden Valley and Brontë Country. Jacob sheep, horses, home grown produce, log fires, beamed rooms and antiques, walking, dry stonewalling and Brontë Breaks organised. A warm welcome is assured whether you stay for business or pleasure. Terms from £27 to £30, Evening meal from £8 to £12. Children welcome. Open all year.
ETC ◆◆◆◆

e-mail: stayatfieldhouse@yahoo.co.uk
website: www. fieldhouse-bb.co.uk

PONTEFRACT/WENTBRIDGE

Mrs I. Goodworth, The Corner Cafe, Wentbridge, Pontefract WF8 3JJ (01977 620316). A sixteenth century cottage featuring oak beams and a lovely secluded garden with plenty of car parking space, set in a small village but within easy reach of main roads (a quarter-of-a-mile A1). Accommodation includes two single, one double, one twin with private bathroom and two family rooms en suite, all with washbasin, TV, tea and coffee making facilities and full central heating. Non-smoking accommodation available. Two family rooms en suite in annexe. This picturesque village has three very nice old inns and restaurants where evening meals or snacks can be obtained. Children welcome. Terms from £20. Open all year round, except Christmas.

The FHG **Directory of Website Addresses**
on pages 387-415 is a useful quick reference guide for
holiday accommodation with e-mail and/or website details

Scotland

FHG

SCOTLAND

𝔉𝔥𝔊 𝔇iploma 𝔚inners 2003

Each year we award a small number of diplomas to holiday proprietors whose services have been specially commended by our readers. The following were our FHG Diploma Winners for 2003.

England

DERBYSHIRE

Mr Tatlow
Ashfield Farm, Calwich
Near Ashbourne
Derbyshire DE6 2EB

DEVON

Mrs Tucker
Lower Luxton Farm, Upottery
Near Honiton
Devon EX14 9PB

◆

Royal Oak
Dunsford Near Exeter
Devon EX6 7DA

GLOUCESTERSHIRE

Mrs Keyte
The Limes, Evesham Road
Stow-on-the-Wold
Gloucestershire GL54 1EN

HAMPSHIRE

Mrs Ellis, Efford Cottage,
Everton, Lymington,
Hampshire SO41 0JD

◆

R. Law
Whitley Ridge Hotel
Beauly Road, Brockenhurst
Hampshire SO42 7QL

HEREFORDSHIRE

Mrs Brown
Ye Hostelrie, Goodrich
Near Ross on Wye
Herefordshire HR9 6HX

NORTH YORKSHIRE

Charles & Gill Richardson
The Coppice, 9 Studley Road
Harrogate
North Yorkshire HG1 5JU

◆

Mr & Mrs Hewitt
Harmony Country Lodge
Limestone Road, Burniston,
Scarborough
North Yorkshire YO13 0DG

Wales

POWYS

Linda Williams
The Old Vicarage
Erwood, Builth Wells
Powys LD2 3SZ

Scotland

ABERDEEN, BANFF & MORAY

Mr Ian Ednie
Spey Bay Hotel
Spey Bay
Fochabers
Moray IV32 7PJ

PERTH & KINROSS

Dunalastair Hotel
Kinloch Rannoch
By Pitlochry
Perthshire PH16 5PW

**HELP IMPROVE BRITISH
TOURISM STANDARDS**

As recommendations are submitted from readers of the FULL RANGE of FHG titles the winners shown above may not necessarily appear in this guide.

ABERDEEN, BANFF & MORAY

Map showing SCOTLAND region with locations including Dornoch, Tarbat Ness, Lossiemouth, Cullen, Macduff, Fraserburgh, Elgin, Buckie, Banff, Cromarty, Nairn, Forres, MORAY, Keith, Turriff, Peterhead, Aberlour, Dufftown, Huntly, Ellon, Drumnadrochit, Grantown-on-Spey, Rhynie, Oldmeldrum, Inverurie, Monadhliath Mountains, Aviemore, Alford, ABERDEENSHIRE, ABERDEEN CITY, Aberdeen, Cairngorm Mountains, Kingussie, Newtonmore, Laggan, Braemar, Ballater, Banchory, Stonehaven, Dalwhinnie, Grampian Mountain, PERTH AND KINROSS, Pitlochry, ANGUS, Brechin, Montrose, Kirriemuir, Aberfeldy, Blairgowrie, Forfar, Arbroath

ABERDEEN

Aberdeen Springbank Guest House, 6 Springbank Terrace AB11 6LS (Tel & Fax: 01224 592048). A warm welcome awaits you at our comfortable family-run Victorian Guest House, well located five minutes from the city centre, rail, bus and ferry terminals. All rooms are en suite, with TV, tea/coffee making facilities, hairdryer and clock radio. Special diets and vegetarians catered for. Close to pubs, restaurants and nightlife. Other amenities include riding, swimming, and fishing nearby, with easy access to a region of historic interest and scenic beauty. Children welcome. Non-smoking.
e-mail: betty@springbank6.fsnet.co.uk
website: www.aberdeen-guesthouse.co.uk

ABERDEEN

University of Aberdeen, Hospitality Services, King's College, Aberdeen AB24 3FX (01224 273444; Fax: 01224 276246). Situated in the historic Old Aberdeen area, the University of Aberdeen has a wide variety of Bed & Breakfast accommodation available. At King's Hall rooms are available all year round and are fully en suite. Facilities also include TV, trouser press, hairdryer, telephone, tea and coffee. During the Easter and Summer vacations additional B&B accommodation is available in the student residences at very attractive rates. Some rooms are en suite and most offer coffee, tea, telephone and linen. TV lounges are also available to visitors. **STB** ★/★★ *B & B.*
e-mail: accommodation@abdn.ac.uk
website: www.abdn.ac.uk/catering

SCOTLAND

ABERDEEN

Mrs D. Pyper, The Globe Inn, 13–15 North Silver Street, Aberdeen AB10 1RJ (01224 624258; Fax: 01224 622893). Traditional city centre inn, full of character and atmosphere. Seven luxurious en suite bedrooms, all with satellite TV, telephone, tea-making facilities and hairdryer. An extensive, mainly home-cooked menu is available , and a good selection of draught beer including real ales. Live music Thursday to Sunday. Open January to December. B&B from £30 to £34.50 per person single, £17.50 to £19.50 per person double. Short breaks available. **STB** ★★★ *INN.*

ABERDEEN

Balvenie Guest House, 9 St Swithin Street, Aberdeen AB10 6XB (01224 322559). Isobel and Edward welcome you to their comfortable, family-run guest house in a quiet location in Aberdeen's West End. The house is within easy walking distance of the city centre and is also adjacent to major bus routes to the beach, city centre, airport, railway station and universities. All five rooms have central heating and double glazing, beverage facilities, washbasin and colour TV. Prices include full Scottish or Continental breakfast; evening meals are available on request. For further information, please telephone or see our website. Terms from £17 to £22 per night single, double/twin from £32 to £34; four nights or more negotiable.
e-mail: balveniegh@aol.com
website: thebalvenieguesthouse.co.uk

BALLINDALLOCH

Glenavon Hotel, Tomintoul, Ballindalloch AB37 9ET (01807 580218; Fax: 01807 580733). This small, family-run hotel offers a relaxed atmosphere, with home cooking and open fires. Accommodation is available in two single, one twin, two double and two family rooms. Families and pets are always welcome. The hotel is situated close to the Lecht ski slopes and is a popular venue for fishing holidays. Open all year. Bed and Breakfast from £17 to £30pp; Evening Meals available. **STB** ★★ *INN.*

BRODIE

Mrs E. Malim, Invercairn House, Brodie, Forres IV36 2TD (Tel & Fax: 01309 641261). Visit our intriguing home – adjacent to Brodie Castle and previously the Castle's railway station. We are situated between Forres and Nairn and provide an excellent base for exploring historic castles, distilleries and the Moray Firth coast, or drive through the Highlands to the West coast. Golf, fishing, riding and birdwatching all available locally. Four bedrooms available, one double; two twin (one en suite) and one single. Dinners by arrangement. Licensed. Bed and Breakfast from £19.
e-mail: invercairnhouse@supanet.com
website: www.invercairnhouse.co.uk

BUCKIE

Mrs Catherine Crawford, Glenelg, 26 Richmond Terrace, Portgordon, Buckie AB56 2RA (01542 833221). Detached Victorian house in quiet residential area, with fine views, overlooking the Moray Firth. One single, one twin, one double, one family room, all with TV and tea/coffee making facilities. Short walk to beaches. B&B £18 per person. Open all year. **STB** ★★★★ *B&B.*

Built in 1760 as a coaching inn for Invercauld Estate, the Inver Hotel has over the centuries established an enviable reputation for warm Scottish hospitality in what nowadays are distinctly elegant surroundings. All attractively furnished bedrooms are fully equipped with en suite facilities, tea/coffee hospitality tray, colour TV (incl Sky satellite - 8 individual channels) and enjoy outstanding views over the surrounding countryside. Family-owned and run, The Inver Hotel is famed for its outstanding cuisine served in the spacious lounge with its open hearth fire. There is a cosy, warm atmosphere in the public bar where visitors can 'meet the locals'. The beer garden with its picturesque outlook over the surrounding mountains has a wealth of colour during the summer months and here visitors can enjoy a drink or meal 'al fresco'. Activities include golfing, fishing, deer-stalking, pony-trekking, hill-walking, climbing and ski-ing.

Rates from: £25 per person double/twin B&B, £35 per person single B&B.

Inver Hotel
Crathie, By Balmoral,
Aberdeenshire AB35 5UL
Tel: 013397 42345 • Fax: 013397 42009
e-mail: enquiries@theinver.co.uk • website: www.theinverhotel.co.uk

See also Colour Advertisement

SCOTLAND

FORRES

Mrs Hilda Massie, Milton of Grange Farm, By Forres IV36 2TR (01309 676360). A warm welcome to our family farm, situated close to Forres, Findhorn and Kinloss. En suite rooms are tastefully furnished to a high standard, with TV and tea/coffee facilities; delicious Scottish cuisine is offered. The farm adjoins the Findhorn Nature Reserve which is popular with birdwatchers. Findhorn village has watersports and a lovely sandy beach. Nearby Findhorn Foundation, with its Eco Village, is world famous, or spend the day touring the coastline dolphin spotting. To the east is Elgin, with Johnston's cashmere outlet. This is an excellent base for golf; Coastal, Castle and Malt Whisky Trails; places of historic interest including the Pictish Stone (Sueno) at Forres; to the west Culloden Battlefield and Fort George. Inverness, Gateway to the Highlands, is 30 miles (also airport). Rates - double from £22.50 to £25.00 (high season). STB ★★★★ *B&B*.
e-mail: hildamassie@aol.com   **website: www.forres-accommodation.co.uk**

GRANTOWN-ON-SPEY

Mrs Val Dickinson, An Cala Guest House, Woodlands Terrace, Grantown-on-Spey PH26 3JU (01479 873293). An Cala is a lovely Victorian granite house set in half an acre and offers comfort in a friendly and cosy atmosphere, only a ten minute walk from the town centre. Four delightful en suite guest bedrooms with tea/coffee tray and colour TV, hairdryers. Doubles have king-size beds. Ideally situated for Spey walks, Munros, RSPB Reserves at Boat of Garten and Loch Insh, the Whisky Trail and as a base for visiting castles and most places in the Highlands. Excellent local golf and tennis clubs. Non-smoking. On-site parking. Terms from £24 to £26 per person. STB ★★★★ *GUEST HOUSE*.
e-mail: ancala@globalnet.co.uk
website: www.ancalahouse.co.uk

INVERURIE

Mrs P.A. Milne, Earlsmohr Guest House, 85 High Street, Inverurie AB51 3QJ (01467 620606). Situated on the southern side of the town near the River Don, Earlsmohr offers Bed and Breakfast accommodation in three comfortable twin rooms, all en suite. All rooms have tea and coffee making facilities and colour TV, and there is private parking. Bed and Breakfast £20 per person per night.
e-mail: earlsmohr@aol.com

KEITH

Mrs Smart, Errolbank, 134 Fife Street, Dufftown, Keith AB55 4DP (01340 820229). Small friendly guest house on Whisky Trail. Children and pets welcome. Full Scottish breakfast our speciality. From £16 per person. En suite family room from £18 per person (children under twelve half price). Please mention guide when booking.

See also Colour Display Advertisement

MACDUFF

The Knowes Hotel and Restaurant, 78 Market Street, Macduff AB44 1LL (Tel & Fax: 01261 832229). Situated high on a hill, overlooking Macduff Harbour, The Knowes Hotel and Restaurant enjoys magnificent views over Banff Bay and across the Moray Firth to the Caithness coastline. This friendly, family-run hotel provides an ideal base from which to explore a wide variety of features and activities available to visitors to this unique part of North-East Scotland. Renowned for food prepared from fresh local produce, the Knowes Restaurant specialises in seafood, fresh salmon, Aberdeen Angus steak and local game, producing imaginative and traditional dishes. Come along and experience the cuisine, the views, and the ambience. Lorenzo and Kimberly look forward to welcoming you. **STB ★★** *HOTEL.*
e-mail: enquiries@knoweshotel.co.uk
website: www.knoweshotel.co.uk

PORTSOY

Mrs Helen Christie, The Boyne Hotel, 2 North High Street, Portsoy AB45 2PA (01261 842242). This cosy, privately owned, coastal village hotel has recently been refurbished to a high standard. The hotel boasts twelve en suite bedrooms, two dining rooms, a TV and video lounge, public bar and a cocktail lounge bar complete with a small dance floor. Meals are served daily using the finest local produce. Portsoy has lovely sandy beaches and a natural outdoor pool. Situated on the Moray Firth Coast, it is an ideal centre for touring North East Scotland. Activities include golf, pony trekking, bird watching, sea angling, curling and bowls. Follow the Whisky, Castle and Coastal trails. Visit the Agricultural Heritage Centre, Baxters Visitor Centre and Portsoy Boat Festival. **STB ★★** *HOTEL.*
e-mail: enquiries@boynehotel.co.uk
website: www.boynehotel.co.uk

Ballindalloch Castle • *Ballindalloch, Moray* • *01807 500206*
website: www.ballindallochcastle.co.uk
16th century castle, home of the Macpherson-Grant family since 1546 with many interesting artefacts. Famous Aberdeen-Angus herd, gardens, tearoom and shop.

ARGYLL & BUTE

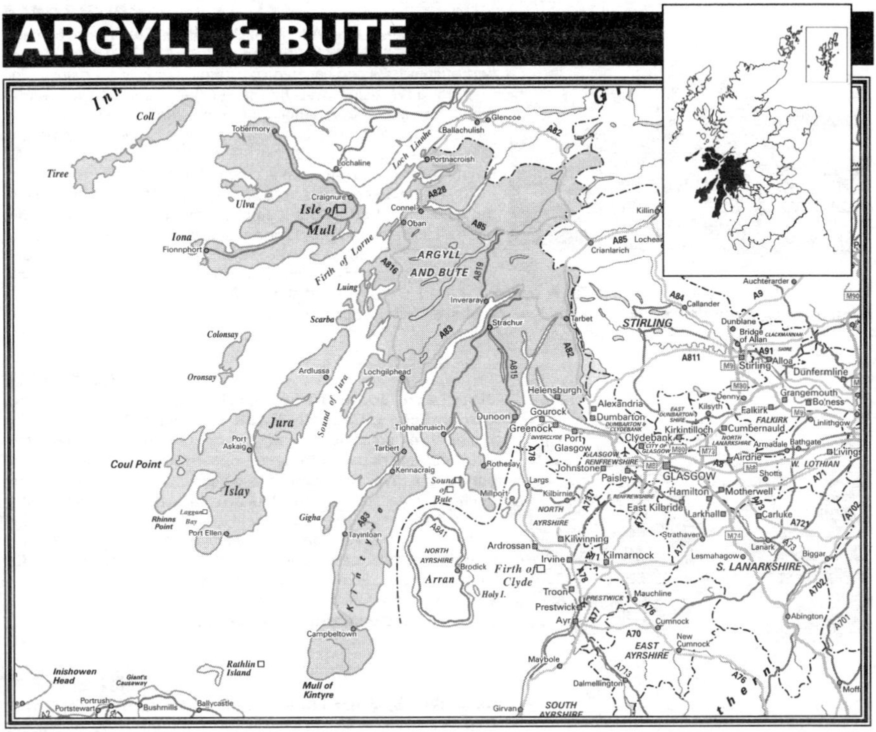

SCOTLAND

ARDMADDY (near Oban)

Mrs D. Gilbert, Ardshellach Farm, Ardmaddy, Near Oban PA34 4QY (01852 300218). Working beef-cattle and sheep farm situated on the Ardmaddy road 12 miles from Oban on the B844 to Easdale and approximately one mile before the Bridge over the Atlantic and Ardmaddy Castle Gardens. This quiet accommodation is 400 yards from the sea overlooking Luing and Scarba and comprises one room sleeping two/four. Bathroom with bath and shower adjacent. TV lounge. Children welcome. Highland Games in August. Bed and Breakfast from £17 includes evening cup of tea. Bar meals available by Atlantic Bridge.

See also Colour Display Advertisement

BALLACHULISH (near Glencoe)

Mr & Mrs J.A. MacLeod, Lyn-Leven Guest House, Ballachulish PA39 4JW (01855 811392; Fax: 01855 811600). Lyn-Leven, a superior award-winning licensed guest house overlooking Loch Leven, with every comfort, in the beautiful Highlands of Scotland, is situated one mile from historic Glencoe village. Four double, two twin and two family bedrooms, all rooms en suite; sittingroom and diningroom. Central heating. Excellent and varied home cooking served daily. Children welcome at reduced rates. An ideal location for touring. Fishing, walking and climbing in the vicinity. The house, open all year, is suitable for disabled guests. Car not essential but private car park provided. Bed and Breakfast from £22. Dinner, Bed and Breakfast from £200 to £220 per person per week. Credit and debit cards accepted. STB ★★★★ GUEST HOUSE, AA/RAC ◆◆◆◆ website: www.LynLeven.co.uk

CARRADALE

Mr A. Milstead, Dunvalanree, Port Righ, Carradale, Kintyre PA28 6SE (01583 431226; Fax: 01583 431339). Dunvalanree was built in 1939 and has been welcoming guests ever since. The owners' advertising grab line is "at the water's edge", and it would be difficult to imagine a place closer to the sea with great views across the golf course and Arran hills across Kilbrannan Sound. Alyson has been awarded both 'Taste of Scotland' and two RAC Dining Awards and has been accredited by the Vegetarian Society. In 2001 Dunvalanree was voted by guests to be the best hotel in the local tourist area. The area abounds with wildlife (there are often seals in the bay), and history (this is where Robert the Bruce landed in 1306), or just come and chill out. From £55 per person for Dinner, Bed and Breakfast. Room for disabled guests. Also self-catering cottage for two available. **STB** ★★★★ *SMALL HOTEL*, **RAC** ◆◆◆◆◆
e-mail: fhg@dunvalanree.com   **website: www.dunvalanree.com**

DALMALLY

Jinty and John Burke, Orchy Bank Guest House, Stronmilchan, Dalmally PA33 1AS (01838 200370). You will be sure to receive a friendly, warm welcome at this 120-year-old Victorian house with seven guest rooms. Situated on the bank of the River Orchy with a 200-year-old bridge at the bottom of the large garden. The area has very good river and loch fishing, a nine hole golf course and is ideal for bird watching, hill walking and deer stalking. All rooms have tea making facilities, heaters and electric blankets. Large guest lounge with log fire. Bed and full Breakfast from £20 per person. **STB** ★★ *GUEST HOUSE*.
e-mail: a.j.burke@talk21.com
website: www.loch-awe.com/orchybank

INVERARAY

Mr R. Gayre, Minard Castle, Minard PA32 8YB (Tel & Fax: 01546 886272). Stay in style in our 19th Century Scottish castle which stands in its own grounds in beautiful countryside beside Loch Fyne, three-quarters-of-a-mile from the A83 Inveraray to Lochgilphead road. A peaceful location for a quiet break, you can stroll in the grounds, walk by the loch, explore the woods, or use Minard Castle as your base for touring this beautiful area with its lochs, hills, gardens, castles and historic sites. Breakfast in the Morning Room and relax in the Drawing Room. The three comfortable bedrooms have colour television, tea/coffee making facilities and en suite bathrooms. No smoking in the house. Evening Meals available within five miles. Bed and Breakfast £45 per person, children half price. Open April to October. We offer a warm welcome in a family home. Self-Catering properties also available, £120 to £370 per week. **STB** ★★★★ *B&B*.
e-mail: reinoldgayre@minardcastle.com   **website: www.minardcastle.com**

INVERARAY

Mrs Semple, Killean Farmhouse, Inveraray PA32 8XT (01499 302474). Killean Farmhouse is located just a few miles outside Inveraray. Ideally situated for walking, climbing, pony trekking or just touring. There is fishing for trout, pike or salmon, and opportunities to enjoy boating, water skiing or windsurfing. The whole area is steeped in history and the town of Inveraray itself is a classic example of 18th century Scottish town planning. With all this in mind, the cottages provide high quality accommodation for family holidays.

A useful index of towns and counties appears at the back of this book on pages 417-421. Refer also to Contents Pages 2 and 3.

OBAN

Mrs Morven Stewart, Glenview, Soroba Road, Oban PA34 4JF (01631 562267). At Glenview we aim to make your stay as comfortable as possible. All rooms have central heating, colour TV and hospitality trays; some also have en suite facilities. A full Scottish breakfast is served, although Continental is available if preferred. We have ample private parking at the rear of the house. Situated ten minutes' walk from the town centre, train, ferry and bus terminals. Oban boasts regular sailings to the Islands, and an excellent golf course, as well as walking, cycling, fishing, or just letting the world go by. Open all year.

OBAN

Ian and Carol Harris, Alltavona Guest House, Corran Esplanade, Oban PA34 5AQ (01631 565067; mobile: 07771 708301). This very attractive Victorian building is situated on the Esplanade, with spectacular views over to the islands of the West Coast. Restaurants and shops are within 10 minutes' walk, and Alltavona is ideally placed for day trips to Mull, Staffa and Iona, as well as activities such as hill walking, bird watching, fishing, canoeing, sailing, and horse-riding. Aonach Mhor and the White Corries are approximately one hour's drive, for some of the best skiing in Scotland. Accommodation is available in two twin rooms and four double rooms, all en suite. Special rates available out of season, and discounts for longer booking. **STB** ★★★★ *GUEST HOUSE.*
e-mail: carol@alltavona.co.uk
website: www.alltavona.co.uk

OBAN

Margaret and Archie MacDonald, Kings Knoll Hotel, Dunollie Road, Oban PA34 5JH (01631 562536; Fax: 01631 566101). The hotel enjoys magnificent views standing in its own grounds overlooking Oban Bay and is the first hotel that visitors meet when entering on the A85. Most bedrooms are en suite with colour TV and hospitality tray. The elegant Kings Rest lounge bar has a Highland theme and is ideal for a cosy dram before dinner in the Knoll restaurant, which specialises in fresh local produce. Oban is ideally located for visiting the Western Isles and exploring the spectacular local scenery. **STB** ★★★ *GUEST HOUSE*, **RAC** ★★
e-mail: kingsknoll@aol.com
website: www.kingsknollhotel.co.uk

OBAN

Mrs C. MacDonald, Bracker, Polvinister Road, Oban PA34 5TN (01631 564302; Fax: 01631 571167). Bracker is a modern bungalow built in 1975 and extended recently to cater for visitors. We have three guest rooms, two double and one twin-bedded, all en suite with TV and tea/coffee making facilities. Small TV lounge and diningroom. Private parking. The house is situated in a beautiful quiet residential area of Oban and is within walking distance of the town (approximately eight to 10 minutes) and the golf course. Friendly hospitality and comfortable accommodation. Bed and Breakfast from £18. Non-smoking. **STB ★★★** *GUEST HOUSE.*
website: www.bracker.co.uk

See also Colour Display Advertisement

OBAN

Mr and Mrs I. Donn, Palace Hotel, Oban PA34 5SB (01631 562294). A small family hotel offering personal supervision situated on Oban's sea front with wonderful views over the Bay, to the Mull Hills beyond. All rooms en suite, with colour TV, tea/coffee making facilities, several non-smoking. The Palace is an ideal base for a real Highland holiday. By boat you can visit the islands of Kerrera, Coll, Tiree, Lismore, Mull and Iona, and by road Glencoe, Ben Nevis and Inveraray. Fishing, golf, horse riding, sailing, tennis and bowls all nearby. Children and pets welcome. Reductions for children. Please write or telephone for brochure. Competitive rates.
website: www.thepalacehotel.activehotels.com

TARBERT

Mrs Linda Whyatt, Rhu House, Tarbert PA29 6YF (Tel & Fax: 01880 820231). Rhu House is found in a quiet rural location, set in mature gardens, on the shore of West Loch Tarbert. Situated four miles south of Tarbert on the Campbeltown Road, close to Kennacraig Ferry Terminal. Ideal base for exploring the Kintyre Peninsula or making day trips to the Southerly Hebrides. This is a non-smoking establishment. En suite facilities available, all rooms have scenic views, tea/coffee making facilities and wash hand basins. There is a spacious residents' lounge with television. Ample parking, but sorry no dogs in the house. Prices from £20 per person. **STB ★★★** *B&B.*
e-mail: rhuhouse@ukonline.co.uk

AYRSHIRE & ARRAN

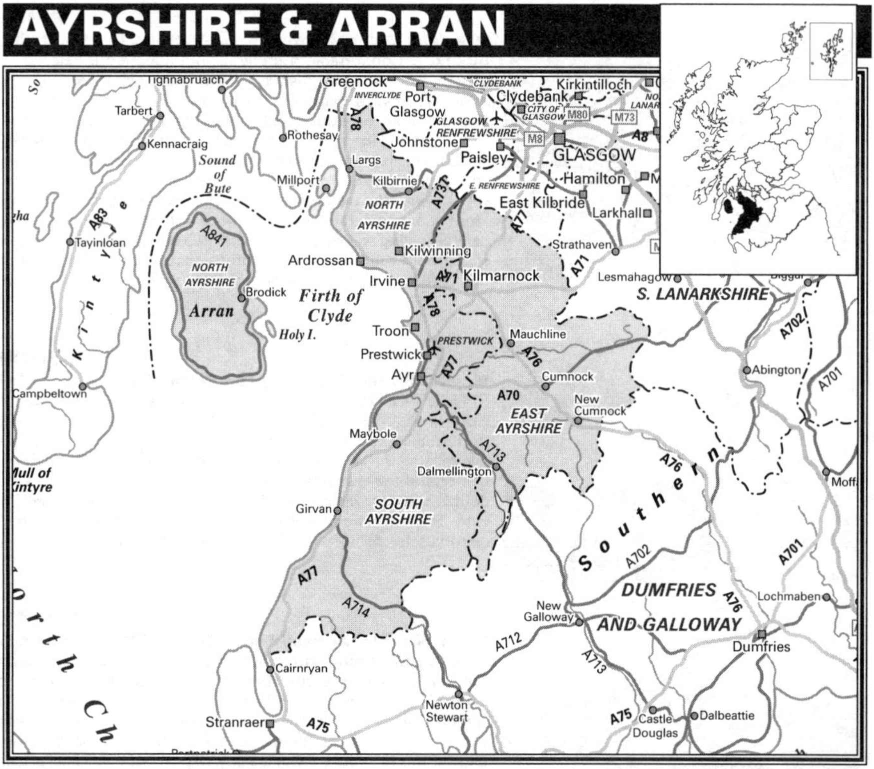

SCOTLAND

AYR

Mrs Wilcox, Fisherton Farm, Dunure, Ayr KA7 4LF (Tel & Fax: 01292 500223). Traditional stone-built farmhouse on working mixed farm with extensive sea views to Arran. Convenient for golf, walking and Burns Country. Also convenient for Culzean Castle and Prestwick Airport. From Ayr take A719 coast road past Haven Craig Tara; farm is five miles south of Ayr. Accommodation comprises one double and one twin en suite, ground floor bedrooms with TV and tea/coffee making facilities; also a family unit. Central heating throughout. Children welcome. Pets by arrangement. Please write, telephone or fax for further information. Prices from £20 to £25. Also self-catering. **STB ★★★ B&B. WELCOME HOST.**
website:

www.fishertonfarm.homestead.com/webpage.html

AYR

See also Colour Display Advertisement

Mrs Agnes Gemmell, Dunduff Farm, Dunure, Ayr KA7 4LH (01292 500225; Fax: 01292 500222). Welcome to Dunduff Farm where a warm, friendly atmosphere awaits you. Situated just south of Ayr at the coastal village of Dunure, this family-run beef and sheep unit of 600 acres is only 15 minutes from the shore providing good walks and sea fishing and enjoying close proximity to Dunure Castle and Park. Accommodation is of a high standard yet homely and comfortable. Bedrooms have washbasins, radio alarm, tea/coffee making facilities, central heating, TV, hair dryer and en suite facilities (the twin room has private bathroom). There is also a small farm cottage available sleeping two/four people. Bed and Breakfast from £25 per person; weekly rate £170. Cottage from £250 per week. Colour brochure

available. **STB ★★★★ B&B, AA/RAC ◆◆◆◆◆**
e-mail: gemmelldunduff@aol.com   website: www.gemmelldunduff.co.uk

BEITH

Mrs Jane Gillan, Shotts Farm, Beith KA15 1LB (01505 502273). Comfortable friendly accommodation is offered on this 160 acre dairy farm situated one-and-a-half miles from the A736 Glasgow to Irvine road; well placed to visit golf courses, country parks, or leisure centre, also ideal for the ferry to Arran or Millport and for many good shopping centres all around. A high standard of cleanliness is assured by Mrs Gillan who is a first class cook holding many awards, food being served in the diningroom with its beautiful picture windows. Three comfortable bedrooms (double en suite, family and twin), all with tea-making facilities, central heating and electric blankets. Two bathrooms with shower; sittingroom with colour TV. Children welcome. Bed and Breakfast from £16. Dinner can be arranged. **STB ★★★** *B&B*, **AA ★★★**

DUNLOP

Mrs W. Burns, East Langton Farm, Dunlop KA3 4DS (01560 482978). A warm welcome in peaceful surroundings, close to all amenities. Twenty minutes to Glasgow or Prestwick Airport, also 20 minutes from the coast with spectacular views overlooking the Isle of Arran, Dalry and the Kilbirnie hills, and Ben Lomond in the distance. Very quiet, peaceful countryside. One double and two twin rooms, all with private bathroom/shower, TV with Teletext, radio alarm, tea/coffee making facilities and hairdryer. Terms from £20.50 to £22.50 per person.

GIRVAN

Mrs I. Melville, Ardwell Farm, Girvan KA26 0HP (01465 713389). Working farm, join in. Our traditional farmhouse is on the A77 Girvan to Stranraer road, three miles south of the town of Girvan itself and within 45 minutes of the ferries at Cairnryan and Stranraer. Accommodation comprises one double and two twin rooms (two with washhand basins), bathroom and separate shower room. TV room with tea tray. Drying facilities. Local places of interest include Culzean Castle, Galloway Forest Park, Burns Cottage and Burns Experience. We are just yards from a sandy beach for shore walks, or take advantage of local golf courses. Children are welcome, pets by arrangement. Bed and Breakfast from £17.50; Evening Meal by arrangement. **STB ★★** *B&B*.

KILMARNOCK

Mrs M. Howie, Hill House Farm, Grassyards Road, Kilmarnock KA3 6HG (Tel & Fax: 01563 523370). Enjoy a peaceful holiday on a working dairy farm two miles east of Kilmarnock. We offer a warm welcome with home baking for supper, choice of farmhouse breakfasts with own preserves. Four large comfortable bedrooms with lovely views over Ayrshire countryside, en suite facilities, tea/coffee, electric blankets, central heating; TV lounge, sun porch, diningroom and garden. Excellent touring base with trips to coast, Arran, Burns Country and Glasgow nearby. Easy access to A77 and numerous golf courses. Children very welcome. Bed and Breakfast from £20 (including supper). Self-catering cottages also available. **STB ★★★★** *B&B*.

KILMARNOCK (near)

Mrs Nancy Cuthbertson, West Tannacrieff, Fenwick, Kilmarnock KA3 6AZ (01560 600258; mobile: 07773 226332; Fax: 01560 600914). A warm welcome awaits all guests to our dairy farm, situated in the peaceful Ayrshire countryside. Relax in spacious well furnished en suite rooms with all modern amenities, colour TV and tea/coffee making facilities. Large parking area and garden. Situated off the A77 on the B751 road to Kilmaurs, so easily accessible from Glasgow, Prestwick Airport, and the south. An ideal base for exploring Ayrshire's many tourist attractions. Enjoy a hearty breakfast with home-made breads and preserves and homebaking for supper. Children welcome. Cost from £20 per person. Brochure available. **STB ★★★★ B&B.**

e-mail: westtannacrieff@btopenworld.com
website: www.SmoothHound.co.uk/hotels/westtannacrieff.html

LARGS

South Whittlieburn Farm, Brisbane Glen, Largs KA30 8SN (01475 675881; Fax: 01475 675080). Warm, friendly hospitality, enormous delicious breakfasts, all rooms en suite, ample parking. Enjoy a great holiday on our peaceful working sheep farm in lovely Brisbane Glen, only five minutes' drive from the popular tourist resort of Largs and near the ferries to the islands of Cumbrae, Bute, Arran and Dunoon. 40 minutes from Glasgow and Prestwick airports and the ferry terminal at Troon to Belfast. Certified caravan and camping site with electric hook-ups, toilet and shower, from £8 per night. Please enquire about holiday caravan to hire. Also self-catering flat available at Dunoon, five minutes from pier, swimming pool, sea and shops. Bed and Breakfast from £23pppn; reduced rates for children under 11. Special diets, packed lunches. A warm welcome from **Mary Watson.** STB ★★★★ B&B, AA ◆◆◆◆, CHOSEN BY "WHICH?" 'BEST BED & BREAKFAST', WELCOME HOST.

e-mail: largsbandb@southwhittlieburnfarm.freeserve.co.uk
website: www.SmoothHound.co.uk/hotels/whittlie.html

MAUCHLINE

Mrs J. Clark, Auchenlongford, Sorn, Mauchline KA5 6JF (01290 550761). The farm is situated in the hills above the picturesque village of Sorn, with its castle set on a promontory above the River Ayr, and its 17th century church nearby. It is only 19 miles east of the A74 and 20 miles inland from the town of Ayr. Accommodation comprises three attractive, furnished bedrooms and a large, well appointed residents' lounge. Full Scottish breakfast is served with home-made jams and marmalade; traditional High Tea and/or Dinners are also available on request. Bed and Breakfast £18; Bed, Breakfast and Evening Meal £28. Brochure available.

Culzean Castle and Country Park • Maybole, Ayrshire • 01655 884400
website: www.nts.org.uk/culzean.html
Robert Adam's masterpiece set in beautifully landscaped gardens. Investigate the Eisenhower connection and visit the Interpretation Centre, swan pond and aviary. Restaurant and tea rooms, picnic areas.

BORDERS

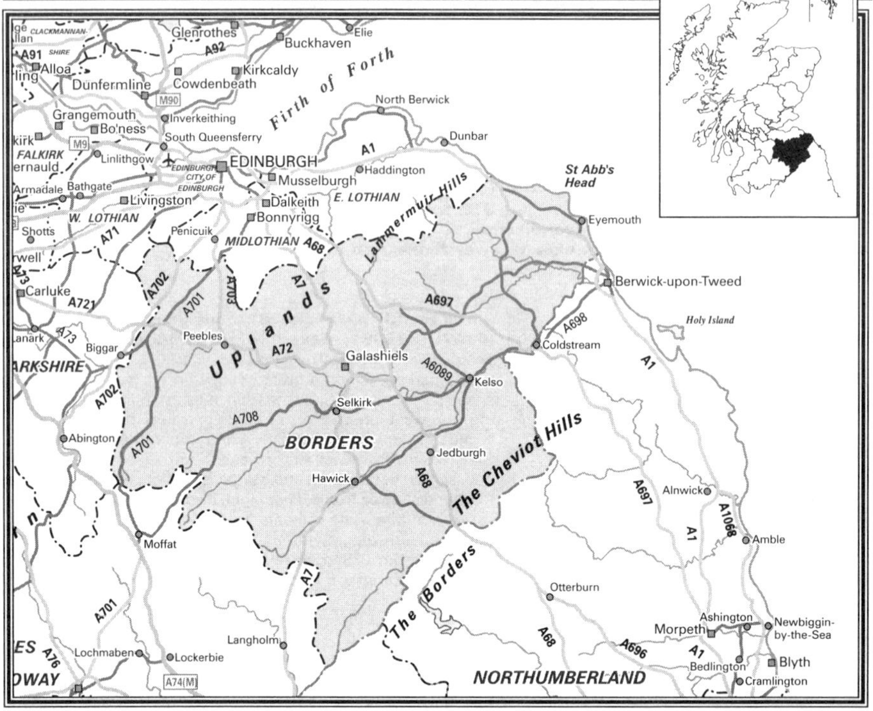

[Map of the Borders region of Scotland showing towns including Edinburgh, Peebles, Galashiels, Selkirk, Hawick, Jedburgh, Kelso, Coldstream, and surrounding areas with roads and the Cheviot Hills. Inset map of Scotland in top right corner.]

©MAPS IN MINUTES™ 2003 ©Crown Copyright. Ordnance Survey 2003

ASHKIRK

Mrs Betty Lamont, Ashkirktown Farm, Ashkirk, Selkirk TD7 4PB (Tel & Fax: 01750 32315). Working farm. Situated off the A7 midway between Hawick and Selkirk. Ashkirktown Farm offers a warm welcome in a peaceful and tranquil setting. Whether en route to Edinburgh or exploring the beautiful Borders area of Scotland a comfortable stay is assured. The old farmhouse has been tastefully furnished. Large private lounge with colour TV, tea/coffee making facilities. Golf, fishing and horse riding available within one mile. Open April to October. Bed and Breakfast from £20. Reduced rates for children. Non-smoking accommodation available.

BIGGAR

Mrs Rosemary Harper, South Mains Farm, Biggar ML12 6HF (01899 860226). Working farm. South Mains Farm is a working family farm, situated in an elevated position with good views, on the B7016 between Biggar and Broughton. An ideal place to take a break on a North/South journey. Edinburgh 29 miles, Peebles 11 miles. Well situated for touring the Border regions in general. A comfortable bed and excellent breakfast provided in this centrally heated and well furnished farmhouse. The lounge has a log fire and the bedrooms, two double and one single, have hand-basins and electric blankets. Open all year. Car essential, parking. Terms £17 per night which includes light supper of home made scones, etc. If you are interested just ring, write or call in. Warm welcome assured.

JEDBURGH

Sheila Whittaker, Hundalee House, Jedburgh TD8 6PA (Tel & Fax: 01835 863011). Large historic Manor House set in 15 acres of secluded gardens and woodland. The house is decorated in a charming Victorian style. All rooms are en suite, two with four-posters, and all with the expected luxuries including TV, tea/coffee making facilities, hairdryer, central heating etc. We would be delighted to welcome you to Hundalee House; we love the place and firmly believe that it should be shared with others. We hope by our efforts we have created a warm and welcoming atmosphere and that you take away with you many happy memories. Bed and Breakfast from £20 to £25 per person per night. Single supplement £10 (single person in a double room). **e-mail: sheila.whittaker@btinternet.com**

JEDBURGH

Mrs Susan Forster, Hoolet's Nest, Mount Hooly, Jedburgh TS8 6TJ (Tel & Fax: 01835 850764). Hoolet's Nest is a modern bungalow with a self-contained flat, set in a large garden. One twin–double room. It is situated half a mile from the A68 north of Jedburgh, on the A698 Kelso road. There is a restaurant next door which has an award for the best food in the Borders. We are 400 yards from St Cuthbert's Walk. The lovely towns of Kelso, Melrose and Jedburgh are within 15 minutes' drive.

MELROSE

Mrs Ann O'Neill, Old Abbey School, Waverley Road, Melrose TD6 9SH (01896 823432). This comfortable family home in a 150-year-old converted school house is situated within easy walking distance of the town centre and River Tweed. Ideal as a centre for visiting the abbeys, castles and museums in the Scottish Borders, and close to Abbotsford House, the home of Sir Walter Scott. Also a good centre for walking holidays. Two double and one twin room with tea-making facilities and TV; one with private facilities. Non-smoking. Private parking. Open from March to November. B&B single £28, double £22 to £25. **STB ★★★** *B&B.* **e-mail: oneill@abbeyschool.fsnet.co.uk**

NEWCASTLETON

See Also Colour Display Advertisement

Pamela Copeland, Bailey Mill Courtyard Apartments and Trekking Centre, Bailey Mill, Newcastleton TD9 0TR (016977 48617; Fax: 016977 48074). A warm welcome awaits you from Pam and Ian on this small farm holiday complex, nestling on the Roxburghshire/Cumbrian border. The rural self-contained apartments create a courtyard setting or enjoy Bed and Breakfast or Full Board riding holidays in the farmhouse. Forest trekking and lessons in outdoor school. Colour TV, heating (oil), electricity and linen included in the rent. On site sauna, jacuzzi, toning table, games room, laundry, babysitting, fully licensed bar and meals. Enjoy walking or trekking through surrounding forests. Central touring area for Lake District, Hadrian's Wall and Scotland. Colour brochure available. Self-catering £88-£498; Bed and Breakfast from £20 per person. **ETC ★★/★★★** *SELF-CATERING.* **e-mail: pam@baileymill.fsnet.co.uk** **website: www.holidaycottagescumbria.co.uk**

Readers are requested to mention this guidebook when seeking accommodation (and please enclose a stamped addressed envelope).

PEEBLES

Sheena Brown, 'Shalem', March Street, Peebles EH45 8EP (Tel & Fax: 01721 721047). 'Shalem' is centrally situated in the beautiful Scottish Borders town of Peebles. Peebles is an ideal location for day trips to historic homes, gardens, abbeys or castles, and boasts lovely forest and hill walks, cycling, fishing in the River Tweed and golf. You are assured of a warm, friendly welcome with excellent accommodation. The family room has en suite shower room and the double room has a private bathroom (not en suite). Both rooms have tea/coffee making facilities and colour TV. Dogs welcome by arrangement; reduced rates for children sharing. Family room £25pppn, double room £22pppn, single in double room £23-£25. **STB ★★★** *B&B.*

PEEBLES

Mrs Mary Sweeney, The Steading, Venlaw Castle Road, Peebles EH45 8QG (01721 720293). Tastefully converted steading with spacious rooms peacefully situated on an elevated position with panoramic views over Peebles. Surrounded by countryside, yet only a short distance from the town centre. Two double and one one twin room, all en suite, with hairdryer, TV and tea/coffee making facilities. Large garden and cobbled courtyard. Ideal base for touring. Ample parking. Pets welcome. Non-smoking. **STB ★★★★** *B&B.*

•• *Some Useful Guidance for Guests and Hosts* ••

Every year literally thousands of holidays, short breaks and overnight stops are arranged through our guides, the vast majority without any problems at all. In a handful of cases, however, difficulties do arise about bookings, which often could have been prevented from the outset.

It is important to remember that when accommodation has been booked, both parties – guests and hosts – have entered into a form of contract. We hope that the following points will provide helpful guidance.

GUESTS:

• When enquiring about accommodation, be as precise as possible. Give exact dates, numbers in your party and the ages of any children.

• State the number and type of rooms wanted and also what catering you require – bed and breakfast, full board etc. Make sure that the position about evening meals is clear – and about pets, reductions for children or any other special points.

• Read our reviews carefully to ensure that the proprietors you are going to contact can supply what you want. Ask for a letter confirming all arrangements, if possible.

• If you have to cancel, do so as soon as possible. Proprietors do have the right to retain deposits and under certain circumstances to charge for cancelled holidays if adequate notice is not given and they cannot re-let the accommodation.

HOSTS:

• Give details about your facilities and about any special conditions. Explain your deposit system clearly and arrangements for cancellations, charges etc. and whether or not your terms include VAT.

• If for any reason you are unable to fulfil an agreed booking without adequate notice, you may be under an obligation to arrange suitable alternative accommodation or to make some form of compensation.

While every effort is made to ensure accuracy, we regret that FHG Publications cannot accept responsibility for errors, omissions or misrepresentations in our entries or any consequences thereof. Prices in particular should be checked because we go to press early. We will follow up complaints but cannot act as arbiters or agents for either party.

DUMFRIES & GALLOWAY

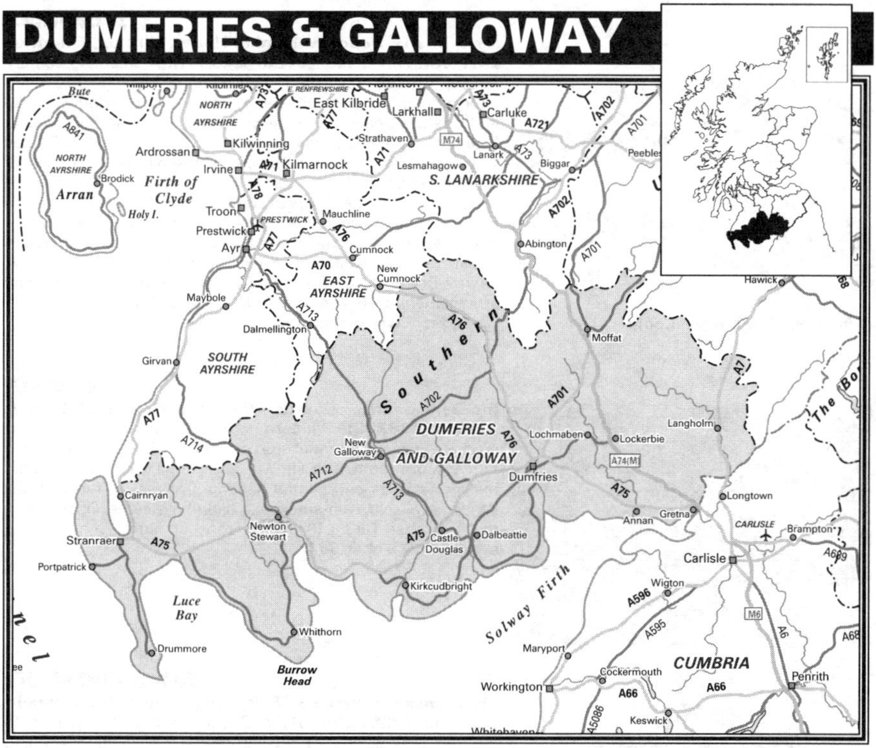

SCOTLAND

CANONBIE

Miss G. Matthews, Four Oaks, Canonbie DG14 0TF (013873 71329). Bed and Breakfast accommodation in comfortable, peaceful family home, with open views of lovely rolling countryside and farmland. Near the village of Canonbie, off the A7 just north of Carlisle, providing an excellent base for touring the Borderlands. Near River Esk. Accommodation provided in one twin room en suite, one double room with en suite bathroom with bath and shower. Cot available. Visitors' lounge with TV, tea/coffee making facilities. Garden and good parking. Terms £20 to £22. **STB ★★★** *B&B*.

See also Colour Display Advertisement

CASTLE DOUGLAS

Mrs P. Kirk, Albion House, 49 Ernespie Road, Castle Douglas DG7 ILD (Tel & Fax 01556 502360). A warm Galloway welcome awaits you at Albion House which was built around 1860. Well positioned on the outskirts of town within an acre of private grounds yet only a few minutes' walk to all amenities. We have a variety of rooms and suites with individual decor providing a high standard of accommodation. Castle Douglas is an ideal location to experience all that Galloway has to offer – stunning scenery, historic buildings, gardens, fishing, golfing and interesting walks. Cycling is now very popular and Castle Douglas has its own cycle hire business. Price £23 to £27 per person sharing twin/double. Dinner by prior arrangement. **STB ★★★★** *B&B*.
e-mail: pikoe007@aol.com

e-mail: wallamhill@aol.com

DUMFRIES

Mr & Mrs G. Hood, Wallamhill House, Kirkton, Dumfries DG1 1SL (Tel & Fax: 01387 248249). A charming country house, tastefully furnished, with a warm, friendly, welcoming atmosphere. The spacious en suite bedrooms - two double/family and one twin, have lovely views over garden and countryside. Beautifully appointed, each room has colour and satellite TV plus video, tea/coffee making facilities, shower and toilet and full central heating. Small health suite, steam room and sauna available for guests' use. Situated in peaceful countryside only three miles from Dumfries town centre with excellent shopping, swimming pool, ice bowl for curling, green bowling, fishing and golf. Hill and forest walks, birdwatching, cycling and mountain bike trails all nearby. Bed and Breakfast from £23 per person. Evening meal by arrangement. **STB ★★★★** *B&B,* **AA ◆◆◆◆◆**
website: www.wallamhill.co.uk

GRETNA

Mr Gary Beattie, Guards Mill Farm, Gretna DG16 5JA (01461 338358). Modern farmhouse accommodation in separate units on this family-run mixed farm. One double and one family room, both with shower en suite, TV, radio, tea/coffee making facilities and central heating. Convenient for M74/M6. Parking available. Non-smoking. Children welcome. Open March to November. B&B £18 per person per night. Short breaks available. **STB ★★** *B&B.*

KIRKCUDBRIGHT

Miriam Baker, Number 3 – B&B, 3 High Street, Kirkcudbright DG6 4JZ (01557 330881). A 'B' Listed Georgian property with a 17th century dining area, situated opposite Broughton House and behind MacLellan's Castle at the end of Kirkcudbright's historic old High Street. This is the oldest part of the "Artists' Town", peaceful, yet only three minutes' walk from shops, restaurants and the harbour. Rich in ambience, this property will charm those seeking comfort in delightful period surroundings. The house has a period drawing room for guests and three bedrooms, two twin en suite and one double with private bathroom. B&B from £27.50pp; reductions for children. Non-smoking. **STB ★★★★** *B&B,* *MEMBER SCOTLAND'S BEST B&BS.*
e-mail: ham_wwk@hotmail.com
website: www.number3-bandb.co.uk

MOFFAT

Morlich House Guest House, Ballplay Road, Moffat DG10 9JU (01683 220589; Fax: 01683 220887). In beautiful 'Burns Country', this superb, award-winning, Victorian country guest house is set in quiet elevated grounds overlooking the town and surrounding hills. Just five minutes' walk from town centre. Rooms are en suite with colour TV, radio alarm, tea/coffee; four-poster available. Private car park. Well behaved dogs welcome. Open all year. B&B from £22 per person. Weekly terms available. *JPC MERIT AWARDS 1998.*
e-mail: info@morlichhouse.co.uk
website: www.morlichhouse.co.uk

Shambellie Museum of Costume • *Dumfries, Dumfriesshire* • *01387 850375*
Step back in time and experience Victorian and Edwardian grace and refinement. Set in wooded grounds, it offers the chance to see period clothes in appropriate settings.

SCOTLAND

MOFFAT

Mrs Deakins, Annandale House, Moffat DG10 9SA (01683 221460). Situated just five minutes' walk from Moffat town centre and one mile off the M74, Annandale House is a haven of peace, surrounded by mature gardens with private parking. The three well-appointed spacious bedrooms all have central heating, tea/coffee making facilities and hairdryers. There is one en suite double with king-size bed, one twin and one family room. Well behaved pets welcome. TV lounge. Open all year. An ideal base for exploring South-West Scotland and the Scottish Borders. Bed and Breakfast from £18 per person per night (reduced rates for children). Non-smokers please.
e-mail: june@annandalehouse.com
website: www.annandalehouse.com

MOFFAT

Mr and Mrs W. Gray, Barnhill Springs Country Guest House, Moffat DG10 9QS (01683 220580). Barnhill Springs is an early Victorian country mansion standing in its own grounds overlooking Upper Annandale. Situated half-a-mile from the A74/M, the house and its surroundings retain an air of remote peacefulness. Internally it has been decorated and furnished to an exceptionally high standard of comfort. Open fire in lounge. Accommodation includes family, double, twin and single rooms, some en suite. Children welcome. Pets welcome free of charge. Open all year. Bed and Breakfast from £22; Evening Meal (optional) from £15. **STB ★★** *GUEST HOUSE*, **AA ◆◆◆**

MOFFAT

Katherine Clemmens, Limetree House, Eastgate, Moffat DG10 9AE (01683 220001; Fax: 01683 221947). Limetree House is an 18th century Grade C Listed building in stunning countryside. Accommodation comprises one family, two double, two twin and one four-poster bedroom, all bedrooms en suite with colour TV, tea/coffee making facilities; one bedroom with VCR. Private and lock-up garage parking is available. Open January to December. No smoking. Pets by arrangement. **STB ★★★** *GUEST HOUSE*. **AA ◆◆◆◆**. *WALKERS AND CYCLISTS WELCOME.*
e-mail: limetree-house@btconnect.com
website: www.limetreehouse.co.uk/

WHITHORN

Mrs M. Forsyth, Old Bishopton, Whithorn, Newton Stewart DG8 8DE (01988 500754). Bed and Breakfast with home cooking is available at farm bungalow with en suite facilities for couples who enjoy a quiet, relaxing holiday, on this working farm with cows and sheep. You can sit out on the sun porch overlooking the walled patio or explore the various places of interest in our area. Wigtown has created much interest in its selection as the Scottish Book Town. Golf is available nearby, or visit the National Forest Park of Glentrool. Self catering also available in our double glazed, self contained bungalow sleeping six. Pets welcome. (**STB ★★** *SELF CATERING).*

The FHG Directory of Website Addresses
on pages 387-415 is a useful quick reference guide for holiday accommodation with e-mail and/or website details

SCOTLAND

DUNBARTONSHIRE

LUSS by

Mrs K. Carruthers, The Corries, Inverbeg, By Luss G83 8PD (Tel & Fax: 01436 860275). In beautiful, easily accessible rural location, with panoramic views of Loch Lomond. Accommodation available in one twin, one double, one family rooms, all en suite. Children welcome. Ideal base for exploring the Trossachs, Rob Roy Country; Glasgow and Stirling within easy reach. Expect a very warm welcome to this family home. Bed and Breakfast from £25 single, from £20 per person in double/twin room.

PLEASE NOTE

All the information in this book is given in good faith in the belief that it is correct. However, the publishers cannot guarantee the facts given in these pages, neither are they responsible for changes in policy, ownership or terms that may take place after the date of going to press.

Readers should always satisfy themselves that the facilities they require are available and that the terms, if quoted, still apply.

DUNDEE & ANGUS

BRECHIN

Rosemary Beatty, Brathinch Farm, By Brechin DD9 7QX (01356 648292; Fax: 01356 648003). Working farm. Brathinch is an 18th century farmhouse on a family-run working arable farm, with a large garden, situated off the B966 between Brechin and Edzell. Rooms have private or en suite bathroom, TV and tea/coffee making facilities. Shooting, fishing, golf, castles, stately homes, wildlife, swimming and other attractions are all located nearby. Easy access to Angus Glens and other country walks. Open all year. Double £20, twin £21, single £22 to £25. We look forward to welcoming you. **STB ★★★** *B&B.*
e-mail: adam.brathinch@btinternet.com

BROUGHTY FERRY

Mrs M. Stafford, Abertay Guest House, 65 Monifieth Road, Broughty Ferry, Dundee DD5 2RW (01382 730381). Abertay Guest House is situated close to Broughty Ferry's town centre with its wealth of shops, restaurants and pubs. Dundee city centre is approximately five miles away, easily reached by bus. There are many golf courses within reasonable driving distance, and the Angus countryside and glens are easily accessible. There are two single rooms, two family, one double and one twin room, all en suite. All rooms are centrally heated, have tea/coffee making facilities and TV. Private parking is available at the rear of the house. Bed and Breakfast from £20 per person per night. **STB ★★★** *GUEST HOUSE.*

EDZELL

Mrs A. McMurray, Inchcape, High Street, Edzell DD9 7TF (01356 647266). Inchcape is situated within the lovely village of Edzell, four miles off the A90 Dundee to Aberdeen road. With the Angus glens and rivers all within easy reach we are the perfect base for walking, cycling, fishing and golfing. Edzell golf course is just across the road and 10% off green fees can be arranged. Three bedrooms all recently refurbished and all en suite. Tea/coffee making facilities, drying room available. TV lounge. Double/twin £18 per person. Single £20. **STB ★★★** *B&B.*
e-mail: alison.mcm@btinternet.com

MURRAY LODGE
h o t e l

MONTROSE

Murray Lodge Hotel, 2-8 Murray Street, Montrose DD10 8LB (01674 678880; Fax: 01674 678877). Ideally located on the main A92 in the north end of the town centre, Murray Lodge Hotel offers the best in comfort and hospitality. Developed from an 18th century linen mill, the hotel offers excellent serviced accommodation at very reasonable prices. All bedrooms are clean and modern, with en suite showers, toilets and washbasins. Each has direct dial telephone, remote control colour TV (satellite channels), study desk, tea/coffee tray and tourist information pack. Non-smoking rooms available. Coffee shop offers a superb daily selection of home baking and light lunches. Specialities include homemade soups, prawn or smoked salmon salads, cheeseboard with bannocks, gateaux or cheesecakes for sweet. **STB ★★★** *SMALL HOTEL..*
e-mail: alison.mcm@btinternet.com

EDINBURGH & LOTHIANS

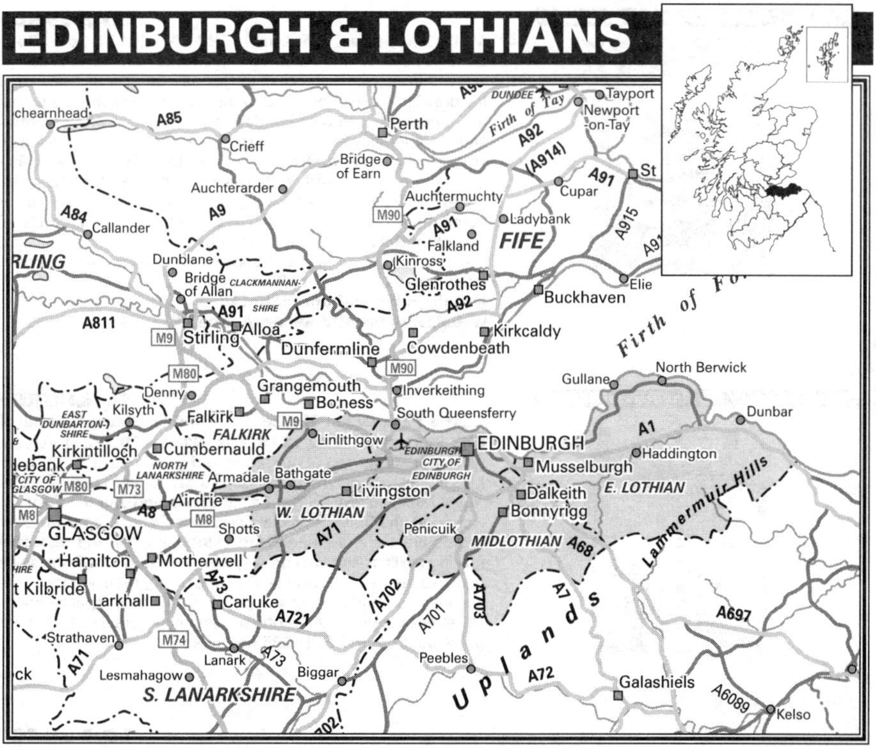

SCOTLAND

BATHGATE (near)

Mrs F. Gibb, Tarrareoch Farm, Station Road, Armadale, Near Bathgate EH48 3BJ (01501 730404). This 17th century farmhouse is situated two miles from M8 Junction 4, which is midway between Glasgow and Edinburgh. This peaceful location overlooks panoramic views of the countryside. All rooms are on the ground flooor, ideal for disabled visitors, and have central heating, colour TV and tea/coffee making facilities. We are within easy reach of golf, fishing, cycling (15 mile cycle track runs along back of property). Ample security parking. Open January to December. Terms from £18 per person per night. **STB ★★★** *B&B*.

BLACKBURN

Cruachan B&B, 78 East Main Street, Blackburn EH47 7QS (01506 655221; Fax: 01506 652395). A relaxed and friendly base is provided at Cruachan from which to explore central Scotland. The centre of Edinburgh can be reached by train in only 30 minutes from nearby Bathgate, and Glasgow is only 35 minutes by car. All rooms en suite/private facilities, full hospitality tray, fresh towels daily, colour TV and central heating. Hosts Kenneth and Jacqueline ensure you receive the utmost in quality of service, meticulously presented accommodation and of course a full Scottish breakfast. They look forward to having the pleasure of your company. Bed and Breakfast from £23 per person per night. **STB ★★★** *B&B*.
e-mail: cruachan.bb@virgin.net
website: www.cruachan.co.uk

EDINBURGH

40 Dublin Street, Edinburgh EH3 6NN (0131-557 1355).
Luxury B&B in Central Edinburgh, 150 yards from Harvey Nichols, and within walking distance of all the main attractions. Located on the drawing room floor of a Georgian townhouse, this is a private residence with one twin-bedded room available with bathroom and electric shower. Double with four-poster bed available on special request and at extra charge. Established since 1991, guests are welcomed with tea or coffee and home-made brownies. Tea and coffee making facilities in room, with fruit and home-made biscuits. Transport to or from station or airport is "all part of the service". Price: £80 double, £55 single High Season; £70 double, £40 single Low Season, with full Breakfast (home-made breads, scones, muffins, preserves).
e-mail: robinws@onetel.net.uk
website: www.40dublinstreet.co.uk

EDINBURGH

Castle Park Guest House, 75 Gilmore Place, Edinburgh EH3 9NU (0131-229 1215; Fax: 0131-229 1223). A warm welcome awaits you at our family-run guest house, close to the King's Theatre, conference centre and city centre. Travel along the Royal Mile with Edinburgh Castle at one end and the Palace of Holyrood, the Queen's official Scottish residence, at the other. All rooms are tastefully decorated with colour TV and tea/coffee making facilities and are centrally heated throughout. Twin, single and en suite rooms available. Pleasant dining room where guests can enjoy a hearty breakfast. Children welcome; special prices. Off-street parking. Full Scottish/Continental breakfast. Bed and Breakfast from £17.50 to £25 per person.

EDINBURGH

Mr Ian McCrae, 44 East Claremont Street, Edinburgh EH7 4JR (Tel & Fax 0131-556 2610). Situated in the Victorian part of Edinburgh's New Town, McCrae's is only 15 minutes' walk from the city centre giving easy access to all attractions. The comfortable accommodation comprises three twin/double rooms, all at ground level. All rooms have en suite facilities, central heating, colour TV, radio/alarm, fridge, hairdryer and tea/coffee trays. Iron available on request. A full traditional breakfast is served using fresh local produce. Unrestricted on-street parking immediately outside. Rates from £24.50 per person per night sharing or from £28.50 for single occupation. Reductions available for long stays. Visa/Mastercard accepted. Open all year. **STB ★★★** *B&B.*
e-mail: mccraes.bandb@lineone.net
website: http://website.lineone.net/~mccraes.bandb

EDINBURGH

Mr T. C. Borthwick, Belford Guest House, 13 Blacket Avenue, Edinburgh EH9 1RR (0131- 667 2422; Fax: 0131-667 7508). Belford House, lying only a short distance from the city centre, is an ideal base from which to explore Edinburgh's historic past, and rests in a quiet tree-lined avenue running between the A7 and the A701. An attractive stone Victorian terrace house, Belford House is one mile from Princes Street and close to Holyrood Park, and the Royal Commonwealth Pool. The house is only four miles from the Straiton Junction on the Edinburgh City By-Pass. An excellent bus service provides easy transport to all the attractions of the capital. Some bedrooms have en suite facilities and all are comfortably furnished with washbasins, tea/coffee hospitality tray and colour TV. An attractive dining room offers wholesome full Scottish breakfasts to prepare guests for a full day's touring in the capital. Bed and Breakfast double/twin en suite from £25, single en suite from £35, double/twin standard £20, single standard £25. **STB ★★** *GUEST HOUSE.*

INTERNATIONAL GUEST HOUSE

AA ◆◆◆◆   37 Mayfield Gardens, Edinburgh EH9 2BX   STB ★★★★
Tel: 0131 667 2511   Fax: 0131 667 1112   Mrs Niven
E-mail: intergh@easynet.co.uk
Internet: www.accommodation-edinburgh.com

The International is an attractive, stone-built Victorian terrace house conveniently situated one-and-a-half-miles south of Princes Street on the main A701 and only four miles from the Straiton junction on the Edinburgh city by-pass. Lying on the main bus route, access to the city centre is easy. **The International** has ample private parking. Visitors who require a touch of luxury a little out of the ordinary can do no better than visit **The International**. All bedrooms have en suite, direct dial telephone, colour television and tea/coffee maker facilities. The decor is outstanding with ornate plasterwork on the ceilings as fine as in 'The New Town.' Some rooms enjoy magnificent views across to the extinct volcano of Arthur's Seat. The full Scottish breakfasts served on the finest bone china are a delight.

B&B from £30 to £60 single; £50 to £120 double
19th century setting with 21st century facilities!
In Britain magazine has rated **The International** as their 'find' in all Edinburgh.

EDINBURGH
Mrs Rhoda Mitchell, Hopetoun, 15 Mayfield Road, Edinburgh EH9 2NG (0131-667 7691; Fax 0131-466 1691). "Which?" Good Bed and Breakfast Guide. COMPLETELY NON-SMOKING. Hopetoun is a small, friendly, family-run B&B situated close to Edinburgh University, one-and-a-half miles south of Princes Street, and with an excellent bus service to the city centre. Very comfortable accommodation is offered in a completely smoke-free environment. Having only three guest bedrooms, and offering private facilities, the owner prides herself in ensuring personal attention to all guests in a friendly, informal atmosphere. All rooms have central heating, washbasin, colour TV and tea/coffee making facilities. Parking is also available. Bed and Breakfast from £20 to £40. Visa/ Mastercard/Delta. **STB ★★★** *B&B*.
website: www.hopetoun.com

e-mail: hopetoun@aol.com

EDINBURGH
A-Haven Townhouse, 180 Ferry Road, Edinburgh EH6 4NS (0131-554 6559, Fax: 0131-554 5252). Victorian town house hotel close to Edinburgh city centre. The 14 well-equipped en suite bedrooms have individually controlled heating, colour TV, hospitality tray, telephone, and hairdryer. There is a charming lounge to relax in after a busy day out, and a well stocked bar. Bed and a hearty breakfast are provided, with evening meal by prior arrangement. Children are most welcome; family bedrooms, cots and a safe play area are available. There is a free secure car park and the hotel is convenient for public transport. Short break details on request. **STB ★★★** *SMALL HOTEL.*
e-mail: reservations@a-haven.co.uk
website: www.a-haven.co.uk

EDINBURGH

Sonas Guest House, 3 East Mayfield, Edinburgh EH9 1SD (0131-667 2781) Sonas Guest House is a lovely stone terraced building, with well proportioned bright rooms all with en suite bathrooms. Friendly, warm and comfortable, Sonas offers a delightful stay for your trip to Edinburgh. Just over one mile from the city centre, leave your car in our free car park and walk into town or take one of several frequent buses. Sonas is an old Gaelic word for bliss!
e-mail: info@sonasguesthouse.com
website: www.sonasguesthouse.com

EDINBURGH

Susie Berkengoff, Barony House, 23 Mayfield Gardens, Newington, Edinburgh EH9 2BX (Freephone: 0800 980 4806; Tel: 0131-667 5806; Fax: 0131 667 6833). One of the most comfortable guest houses in Edinburgh imbued with a personal touch, with tasteful furnishings and traditionally furnished bedrooms, and offering personal, friendly service. Close to Edinburgh Castle, Holyrood Palace, historic New Town, Princes Street and the Royal Mile. Real Scottish breakfast served every morning. Special dietary requirements catered for. **STB** ★★★★ *GUEST HOUSE.*
e-mail: susieb@baronyhouse.co.uk
website: www.baronyhouse.co.uk

EDINBURGH

Janette and Graham Gibson, Cruachan Guest House, 53 Gilmore Place, Edinburgh EH3 9NT (Tel & Fax: 0131-229 6219). Dating from 1890, this Victorian villa has bedrooms on all floors. All rooms have central heating and most are en suite. Single, double and family rooms available. Excellent breakfasts are served in the bright conservatory and there is a residents' lounge with TV. Children welcome. Non-smoking. Private parking by arrangement. Situated close to the heart of the beautiful city of Edinburgh, Cruachan is only minutes' walk from the Castle, Conference Centre, theatres and Princes Street. Terms from £25 to £40 per person. **STB** ★★★ *GUEST HOUSE.*
e-mail: janette@cruachan9.freeserve.co.uk
website: www.cruachan9.freeserve.co.uk

EDINBURGH

Mr and Mrs Derek Mowat, Dunstane House Hotel, 4 West Coates, Haymarket, Edinburgh EH12 5JQ (Tel & Fax: 0131 337 6169). Impressive Victorian mansion, dating back to the 1850s and retaining its spectacular original features. All rooms have been luxuriously refurbished; four-poster bed available. We offer fine dining in our unique 'Skerries' restaurant, and more informal meals in the Stane bar. Only fresh produce from the Orkney Isles is used. City centre location only minutes from Princes Street and the castle. Private parking. Bed and Breakfast from £44 to £65 per person per night. **STB** ★★★★ *HOTEL*, **AA** ◆◆◆◆◆
website: www.dunstane-hotel-edinburgh.co.uk

EDINBURGH

Mr and Mrs Oussellam, Granville Guest House, 13 Granville Terrace, Edinburgh EH10 4PQ (0131-229 1676; Tel & Fax: 0131-229 4633). A warm, family-run guest house in central Edinburgh. We are close to all local amenities, not to mention the city's most prized attraction, Edinburgh Castle. All our rooms have tea/coffee facilities and colour television; six en suite. Limited off-street parking available. A warm welcome on your arrival. B&B from £20 per person per night. **STB** ★★ *GUEST HOUSE.*
e-mail: granvilleguesthouse@tinyworld.co.uk

EDINBURGH

The Inverleith Hotel, 5 Inverleith Terrace, Edinburgh EH3 5NS (0131-556 2745). The Inverleith Hotel is a small private hotel, dating back to 1860, nestling in the quiet area of Inverleith yet only 10 minutes' away from the hub of city life. We have a residents' bar with a selection of fine wines, Scottish malt whiskies, beers and spirits. All rooms are en suite, with direct-dial telephones and tea and coffee making facilities. To start your day, cereals and Full Scottish Breakfast are offered in our Victorian breakfast room, on the ground floor. The hotel has a completely non-smoking policy. Credit cards accepted. Group discounts available. Free on-street parking. STB ★★★ *SMALL HOTEL.*
e-mail: info@inverleithhotel.co.uk
website: www.inverleithhotel.co.uk

EDINBURGH

The Ivy Guest House, 7 Mayfield Gardens, Edinburgh EH9 2AX (0131-667 3411; Fax: 0131-620 1422). Bed and Breakfast in a comfortable Victorian villa. Open all year round. Private car park. Close to city centre and all its cultural attractions with excellent public transport and taxi services available on the door step. Many local sports facilities (booking assistance available). All rooms have central heating, washbasins, colour TV and tea/coffee making facilities. Choice of en suite or standard rooms, all power showers. Public phone. Large selection of eating establishments nearby. A substantial Scottish breakfast and warm welcome is assured, courtesy of Don and Dolly Green. Terms from £18 per person per night. STB ★★★ *GUEST HOUSE.* **AA ◆◆◆, RAC ◆◆◆◆**

e-mail: don@ivyguesthouse.com   **website: www.ivyguesthouse.com**

EDINBURGH

Kenvie Guest House, 16 Kilmaurs Road, Edinburgh EH16 5DA (0131-668 1964; Fax: 0131-668 1926). A charming and comfortable Victorian town house situated in a quiet and pleasant residential part of the city, approximately one mile south of the centre and one small block from Main Road (A7) leading to the City and Bypass to all routes. Excellent bus service. We offer for your comfort, complimentary tea/coffee, central heating, colour TV and No Smoking rooms. En suite rooms available. Lovely breakfasts and lots of additional caring touches. A warm and friendly welcome is guaranteed from Richard and Dorothy.
e-mail: dorothy@kenvie.co.uk

EDINBURGH

Mrs Ritchie, Ingleneuk, 31 Drum Brae North, Edinburgh EH4 8AT (0131-317 1743). Comfortable detached bungalow approximately four miles west of city centre and three miles from airport. Close to Forth Road Bridge and City bypass. Good bus service. Ample car parking. No smoking. Our self-contained family unit comprises a twin-bedded room with seating and breakfasting area, a double bedroom and a shower room. All bedrooms have private entrance and look onto landscaped gardens with birds and squirrels. All rooms are en suite with hospitality trays, colour TV, iron, hairdryer, etc. and the family unit has a fridge. Breakfast is served to your room. Bed and Breakfast from £20 per person. Stuart and Lynda look forward to welcoming you to their home.
e-mail: ingleneukbnb@btinternet.com
website: www.accommodata.co.uk/110999.htm

EDINBURGH

Alan and Angela Vidler, Rowan House, 13 Glenorchy Terrace, Edinburgh EH9 2DQ (Tel & Fax: 0131-667 2463). Elegant Victorian home, quietly located in an attractive area of the city only 10 minutes by bus from the centre. Rooms have colour TV, tea/coffee making facilities and are mostly en suite. Children welcome at reduced rates. Convenient for Castle, Royal Mile, University, theatres and restaurants. Located just off the A701 from the south (turn left at Bright's Crescent, just off Mayfield Gardens) and close to major roads A1, A7 and A702. Unrestricted street parking. Bed and Breakfast from £24 per person. **STB/AA** ★★★ *B&B*.
e-mail: angela@rowan-house.co.uk
website: www.rowan-house.co.uk

EDINBURGH

Heather & James McWilliams, Ben Craig House, 3 Craigmillar Park, Edinburgh EH16 5PG (0131-667 2593; Fax: 0131-667 1109). Ben Craig is an attractive detached Victorian villa lying only one-and-three-quarter miles south of Princes Street, the Royal Mile and Waverley Station, and is situated on a major bus route, allowing guests to travel easily into the city centre. Tastefully restored and decorated to the highest standards, all bedrooms are elegantly furnished and have private bathrooms all of which have shower or shower over bath, colour TV, hospitality tray and hairdryer. Full Scottish breakfasts are served in the delightful conservatory overlooking the landscaped garden. Non-smoking house. Double/twin £29 to £40, single £35 to £60. **STB** ★★★★ *GUEST HOUSE*.
e-mail: bencraighouse@dial.pipex.com
website: www.bencraighouse.co.uk

EDINBURGH

Mrs Kay, Blossom House, 8 Minto Street, Edinburgh EH9 1RG (0131-667 5353; Fax: 0131-667 2813). Blossom House is a traditional stone-built town house attractively situated within the Newington district of Edinburgh, less than one mile from the City Centre and on a main bus route. All bedrooms are tastefully furnished with en suite facilities, colour TV and tea/coffee hospitality tray. Some rooms enjoy attractive views to the extinct volcano of Arthur's Seat. Full Scottish breakfasts are served in the spacious dining room. Many fine restaurants are situated nearby, providing a wide range of cuisine to suit everyone's taste and pocket. Central heating. Private car park. B&B from £19 per person per night. **STB** ★★ *GUEST HOUSE*.
e-mail: blossom_house@hotmail.com
website: www.blossomguesthouse.co.uk

GULLANE

Mrs Mary Chase, Jadini Garden, Goose Green, Gullane, East Lothian EH31 2BA (01620 843343). Comfortable family home in a delightful secluded walled garden, which guests are welcome to use. Private parking for up to eight cars. Gullane is a charming coastal village, well-known for its famous golf courses. Gullane Golf Club is just a few minutes' walk from Jadini Garden, and Muirfield is at the other end of the village. Nearby also are the beautiful sandy beaches bordered by cliffs and dunes, providing spectacular walks and seabird nature trails. Edinburgh is only 30 minutes by car, four miles from North Berwick. French, German and Spanish spoken. Bed and Breakfast from £20 to £30 per person. **STB** ★★★ *B&B*.
e-mail: marychase@jadini.com
website: www.jadini.com

Terms quoted in this publication may be subject to increase if rises in costs necessitate

LINLITHGOW

Mr and Mrs R. Inglis, Thornton, Edinburgh Road, Linlithgow EH49 6AA (01506 844693; Fax: 01506 844876). Comfortable family-run Victorian house with original features retained. Central situation in a peaceful location near the Union Canal in historic Linlithgow - only five minutes' walk from the town centre, Linlithgow Palace and railway station. This is a real home from home offering quality accommodation in a friendly and relaxing atmosphere. Open February to November inclusive. Excellent base for visiting Edinburgh, Stirling, Glasgow and the Falkirk Wheel. Early booking advisable. Credit cards accepted. Terms from £25 per person. **STB ★★★★** *B&B,* **AA ◆◆◆◆,** *WINNER AA 'BEST BREAKFAST' SCOTLAND AWARD, RECOMMENDED BY "WHICH?" B&B GUIDE.*
e-mail: inglisthornton@hotmail.com
website: www.thornton-scotland.co.uk

MUSSELBURGH

Inveresk House, Inveresk Village, Musselburgh EH21 7UA (0131-665 5855; Fax: 0131-665 0578). Historic Mansion house and award- winning Bed & Breakfast. Family-run "home from home". Situated in three acres of garden and woodland. Built on the site of a Roman settlement from 150 AD, the remains of a bathhouse can be found hidden in the garden. Three comfortable en suite rooms. Original art and antiques adorn the house. Edinburgh's Princes Street seven miles from Inveresk House. Good bus routes. Families welcome. Off-street parking. Telephone first. B&B from £40 per person. Family room £100 to £120.
e-mail: chute.inveresk@btinternet.com
website: http://travel.to/edinburgh

See also Colour Display Advertisement

FAIRSHIELS

PATHHEAD

Mrs Anne Gordon, "Fairshiels", Blackshiels, Pathhead EH37 5SX (01875 833665). We are situated on the A68, three miles south of Pathhead at the picturesque village of Fala. The house is an 18th century coaching inn (Listed building). All bedrooms have washbasins and tea/coffee making facilities; one is en suite. All the rooms are comfortably furnished. We are within easy reach of Edinburgh and the Scottish Borders. A warm welcome is extended to all our guests – our aim is to make your stay a pleasant one. Cost is from £18.50 per person; children two years to 12 years £11.50, under two years FREE.

ROSLIN

Mrs Rosemary Noble, Glenlea House, Hawthornden, Lasswade EH18 1EJ (0131-440 2079). Glenlea is one mile from the picturesque village of Roslin. Large 150-year-old family house standing in one acre of garden, overlooking historic Rosslyn Chapel and the Pentland Hills. Plenty of good eating places in the area also walking and riding but within easy reach of Edinburgh which is seven miles away. Accommodation comprises one large family room, two double and one single. One of the double rooms is on the ground floor with bathroom adjacent. Full Scottish breakfast. Fully centrally heated. Ample parking. Bed and Breakfast from £25.

FIFE

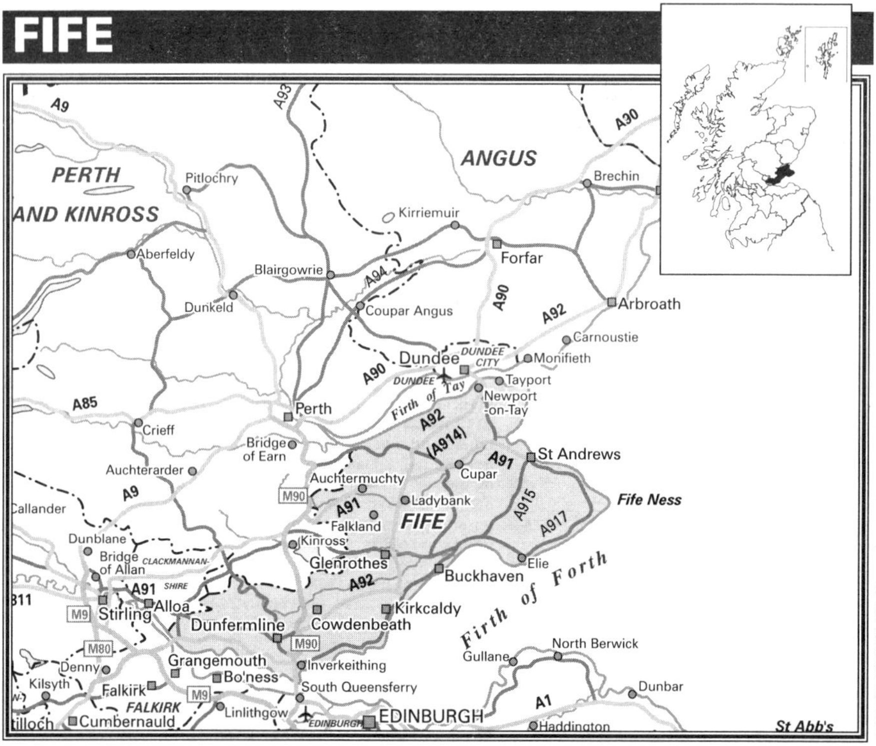

A9 · A93 · A9 · PERTH AND KINROSS · Pitlochry · ANGUS · A30 · Brechin · Aberfeldy · Kirriemuir · Blairgowrie · Forfar · A94 · A90 · A92 · Dunkeld · Coupar Angus · Arbroath · Carnoustie · A90 · DUNDEE CITY · Monifieth · Dundee · DUNDEE · Tayport · Firth of Tay · Newport-on-Tay · A85 · Perth · A92 · Crieff · Bridge of Earn · (A914) · A91 · St Andrews · Auchterarder · Auchtermuchty · Cupar · A915 · Callander · A9 · M90 · A91 · Ladybank · Fife Ness · Dunblane · Kinross · Falkland · FIFE · A917 · Bridge of Allan · CLACKMANNAN-SHIRE · Glenrothes · Buckhaven · Elie · Firth of Forth · 311 · A91 · SHIRE · A92 · Kinross · M9 · Stirling · Alloa · Kirkcaldy · Dunfermline · Cowdenbeath · M90 · North Berwick · M80 · Inverkeithing · Gullane · Denny · Grangemouth · Bo'ness · South Queensferry · Dunbar · Kilsyth · Falkirk · M9 · FALKIRK · Linlithgow · EDINBURGH · A1 · tilloch · Cumbernauld · EDINBURGH · Haddington · St Abb's

©MAPS IN MINUTES™ 2003 ©Crown Copyright. Ordnance Survey 2003.

SCOTLAND

CULROSS

Judith Jackson, St Mungo's B&B, Low Causeway, Culross KY12 8HJ (01383 882102). 17th century Listed building on the outskirts of the best preserved medieval village in Scotland. Culross has a range of National Trust buildings and an historic abbey. This is an ideal location for touring Central Scotland – Edinburgh, Glasgow, Stirling, Perth, St Andrews and the Trossachs are all within easy reach. All rooms have views over the Forth Estuary and TV, hairdryer, tea and coffee etc. One family room en suite (sleeps three), one double and one twin with shared bathroom. Full central heating. Beautiful mature gardens extending to one acre. Off-street parking. Non-smoking. Bed and Breakfast from £18pp.
e-mail: martinpjackson@hotmail.com
website: www.milford.co.uk/scotland/accom/h-a1763.html

KIRKCALDY

Mrs A. Crawford, Crawford Hall, 2 Kinghorn Road, Kirkcaldy KY1 1SU (01592 262658). Crawford Hall is a large rambling old house over 100 years old and was once the local vicarage. Spacious rooms and some sea views. Teasmaid and colour TV in all rooms. Guests have use of hairdryer and iron on request. Pay phone. Ample private parking. Lovely walled gardens. Five minutes' walk to town centre. Handy for golf course, cinema, theatre and ice rinks. Kirkcaldy also boasts two beautiful parks. Evening meal by arrangement. Double and twin rooms £18 per person, single room £20 per person.

See also Colour Display Advertisement

LEVEN

Mrs Pam MacDonald, Dunclutha Guest House, 16 Victoria Road, Leven KY8 4EX (01333 425515; Fax: 01333 422311). This quiet Victorian former rectory provides the ideal location for touring. Ideal base for golf enthusiasts, within easy reach of 46 golf courses and only 14 miles from St Andrews. Forty minutes from Edinburgh Airport, Perth and 30-35 minutes from Dundee. Facilities include three en suite rooms - one double, one twin, one family (sleeps three to four), one family (sleeps three) with private bathroom. Colour TV and tea/coffee facilities in all rooms, cot available. Visitors' lounge with TV. Most credit cards accepted. Open all year. Terms from £25 pppn. Non-smoking. **STB ★★★★** *GUEST HOUSE.*

e-mail: pam.leven@dunclutha-accomm.demon.co.uk
website: www.dunclutha-accomm.demon.co.uk

ST ANDREWS

Mrs Duncan, Spinkstown Farmhouse, St Andrews KY16 8PN (01334 473475). Only two miles from St Andrews on the picturesque A917 coast road to Crail, Spinkstown is a uniquely designed farmhouse with views of the sea and surrounding countryside. Bright and spacious, it is furnished to a high standard. Accommodation consists of double and twin rooms, all are en suite and have tea/coffee making facilities and colour TV; diningroom and lounge. Substantial farmhouse breakfast to set you up for the day. The famous Old Course, historic St Andrews and several National Trust properties are all within easy reach, as well as swimming, tennis, putting, bowls, horse riding, country parks, nature reserves, beaches and coastal walks. Plenty of parking available. Bed and Breakfast from £23. **STB ★★★★** B&B, **AA ◆◆◆◆**

e-mail: anne@spinkstown.com

website: www.spinkstown.com

ST ANDREWS

Mrs Linzi Taylor, The Paddock, Sunnyside, Strathkinness, By St Andrews KY16 9XP (01334 850888; Fax: 01334 850870). A warm welcome awaits you for Bed & Breakfast at this attractive and comfortable modern family home, located in a quiet and peaceful village just two miles from St Andrews, the 'Home of Golf'. The house sits in its own secluded grounds with uninterrupted views over beautiful rolling countryside, and offers the ideal base for golfing, cycling, walking and touring, or simply relaxing with a good book. Ample private parking. Major credit cards accepted. Garage available for bikes. **STB ★★★★** B&B. **AA ◆◆◆◆◆**

e-mail: thepaddock@btinternet.com
website: www.thepadd.co.uk

GLASGOW & DISTRICT

GLASGOW

Mrs P. Wells, "Avenue End" B&B, 21 West Avenue, Stepps, Glasgow G33 6ES (0141-779 1990; Fax: 0141-779 1951). Stepps village is situated north-east of Glasgow just off the A80. This self-built family home nestles down a quiet leafy lane offering the ideal location for an overnight stay or touring base with the main routes to Edinburgh, Stirling and the North on our doorstep. Easy commuting to Loch Lomond, the Trossachs or Clyde Valley. M8 exit 12 from the south, or A80 Cumbernauld Road from the north. Glasgow only ten minutes away, Glasgow Airport 12 miles. Ample parking. All rooms offer colour TV, compliments tray and en suite or private facilities. Home from Home – warm welcome assured! All from £22.50 per person per night. Self-catering also available. **STB ★★★** *B&B*.
e-mail: avenueEnd@aol.com

See also Colour Display Advertisement

GLASGOW

Kirkland House, 42 St Vincent Crescent G3 8NG (0141-248 3458; Fax: 0141-221 5174). City Centre Guest House located in Glasgow's Little Chelsea, a beautiful Victorian Crescent in the area known as Finnieston, offers excellent rooms, most with en suite facilities, full central heating, colour TV, tea/coffee makers. The house is located within walking distance of the Scottish Exhibition Centre, the Museum & Art Gallery, and Kelvingrove Park. We are very convenient for all City Centre and West End facilities and only 10 minutes' drive from Glasgow's International Airport. Short Break details on request. **STB ★★★** *GUEST HOUSE*.
e-mail: info@kirkland.net43.co.uk
website: www.kirkland.net43.co.uk

HIGHLANDS

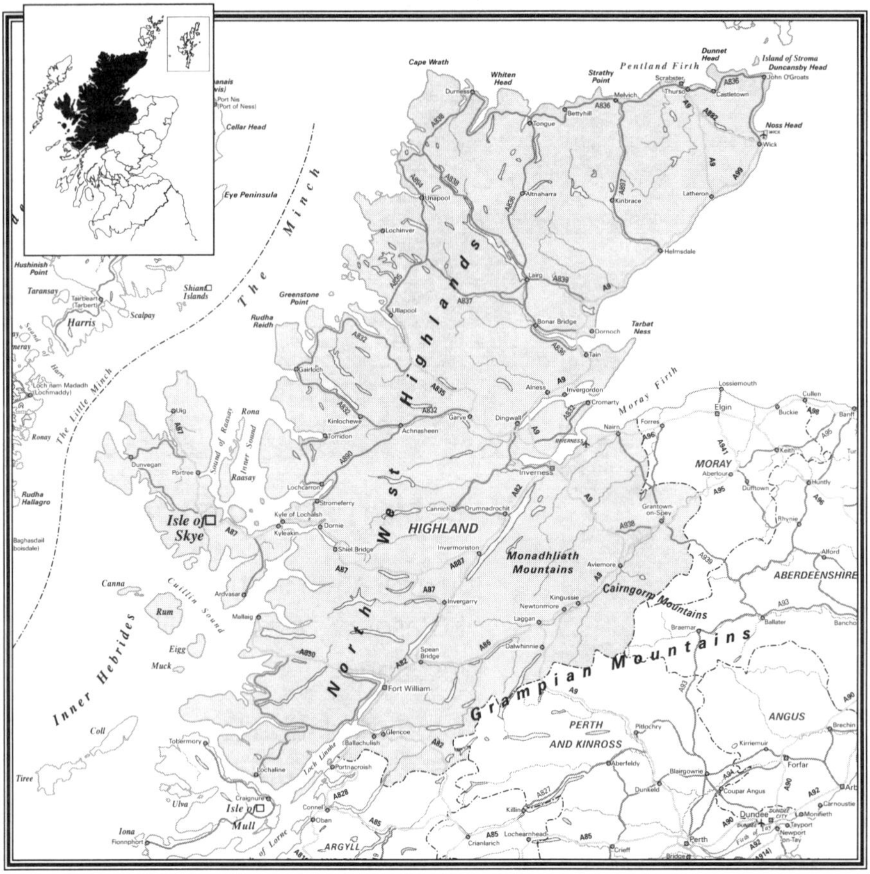

Cape Wrath
Whiten Head
Strathy Point
Pentland Firth
Dunnet Head
Island of Stroma
Duncansby Head
John O'Groats
Noss Head
Wick
Thurso
Castletown
Scrabster
Melvich
Bettyhill
Tongue
Durness
Lochinver
Unapool
Altnaharra
Kinbrace
Latheron
Helmsdale
Lairg
Ullapool
Bonar Bridge
Dornoch
Tarbat Ness
Tain
Alness
Invergordon
Cromarty
Moray Firth
Lossiemouth
Elgin
Cullen
Buckie
Forres
Nairn
MORAY
Keith
Dingwall
Garve
Achnasheen
Kinlochewe
Torridon
Gairloch
Greenstone Point
Rudha Reidh
Inverness
Lochcarron
Stromeferry
Kyle of Lochalsh
Kyleakin
Dornie
Shiel Bridge
Cannich
Drumnadrochit
HIGHLAND
Invermoriston
Monadhliath Mountains
Aviemore
Grantown-on-Spey
Cairngorm Mountains
Kingussie
Newtonmore
Laggan
Dalwhinnie
Invergarry
Spean Bridge
Fort William
Glencoe
Ballachulish
Portnacroish
North West Highlands
Grampian Mountains
ABERDEENSHIRE
Ballater
Braemar
ANGUS
PERTH AND KINROSS
Pitlochry
Kirriemuir
Forfar
Brechin
Aberfeldy
Blairgowrie
Coupar Angus
Dunkeld
Dundee
Killin
Crianlarich
Crieff
Perth
ARGYLL
Oban
Connel
Isle of Mull
Craignure
Tobermory
Lochaline
Iona
Ulva
Tiree
Coll
Muck
Eigg
Rum
Canna
Cuillin Sound
Mallaig
Ardvasar
Inner Hebrides
Isle of Skye
Portree
Uig
Dunvegan
Raasay
Rona
Inner Sound
Sound of Raasay
The Little Minch
The Minch
Harris
Scalpay
Taransay
Hushinish Point
Shiant Islands
Eye Peninsula
Cellar Head
Ronay
Rudha Hallagro
Loch nam Madadh (Lochmaddy)

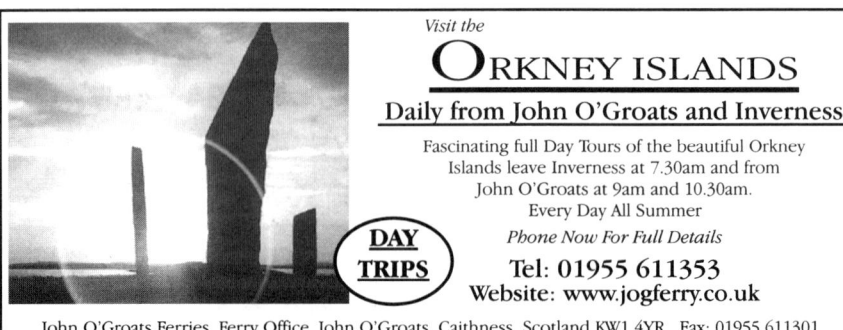

HIGHLANDS (North)

The Kinlochbervie Hotel

Kinlochbervie, By Lairg, Sutherland IV27 4RP
Tel: 01971 521275 • Fax: 01971 521438
e-mail: klbhotel@aol.com
www.kinlochberviehotel.com

In one of the most stunning locations on the North West coast of Scotland. Wide open seas, majestic hills and unforgettable sunsets – these views can be yours when you stay in one of our supremely comfortable guest rooms. Each room has en suite bathroom, colour TV, telephone and tea/coffee making facilities. Standard and Premier rooms available, also one suite. All public rooms are relaxing and comfortable and we take special pride in our cuisine, with fresh fish and seafood, hill lamb and venison. The Garbet Bistro offers a more informal atmosphere for an excellent selection of lunches and snacks.

See also Colour Advertisement

SCOTLAND

ARDGAY

Mrs Moffat, Sgodachail, Braelangwell, Ardgay IV24 3BP (01863 755322). Warm Highland welcome in a peaceful location with views over the river to the beautiful hills. Ideal for nature lovers. The house is situated in a typical Highland glen where the hills and sky dominate the land, scenery unique to this part of Scotland. Accommodation comprises three bedrooms, one with private bathroom, two twin bedrooms share a bathroom. Situated six miles from Ardgay village, two miles from Croick Church, the centre of the Highland clearances. Railway station is six miles away. No bus service. Activities include golf, horse riding and fishing with permits. Bed and Breakfast is £16; £18 including private facilities. No evening meals.

DORNOCH

Amalfi Bed and Breakfast, River Street, Dornoch IV25 3LY (01862 810015). A friendly, family-run B&B located alongside Royal Dornoch's Struie Course, close to the beach and all other attractions. All bedrooms are on the ground floor, are comfortably furnished and have en suite shower rooms with washbasin and wc, colour TV, hairdryer and complimentary hostess tray. One room is twin-bedded and the other has a double and single bed. There is private off-street parking and a garden for your enjoyment. Reductions on Royal Dornoch's green fees for our guests. Rates from £18pppn.
e-mail: EMackayAmalfi@aol.com

LOCHINVER

Arthur and Meryl Quigley, Ardglas Guest House, Inver, Lochinver IV27 4LJ (01571 844257; Fax: 01571 844632). The guest house gives panoramic views of Lochinver village, the loch, the harbour and the mountains around, including Suilven, in an area distinguished for its walking and angling. We can advise on local walks and attractions. For anglers we issue fishing permits, hire fishing gear and boats. We have boats on over twenty lochs and can advise on where fishing is currently best. Accommodation comprises one single, five double/twin rooms and two family rooms, with shared facilities. Guest lounge with TV. Ample parking. Terms from £19 per person, children under four years free. Evening meals by prior arrangement. Open all year.
STB ★★★ *GUEST HOUSE.*

e-mail: ardglas@btinternet.com
website: www.ardglas.co.uk

HIGHLANDS (Mid)

ACHNASHEEN

David and Lilah Ford, Hillhaven, Kinlochewe, Achnasheen IV22 2PA (0845 6448641/01445 760204). A modern bungalow set back from the road situated on the Wester Ross coastal trail amidst spectacular mountain scenery. Ideal base for touring and exploring the West Highlands and Islands, central to the Torridon Mountains and Loch Maree. Ben Eighe National Nature Reserve within walking distance. Accommodation comprises two double rooms and one twin room, all en suite; television lounge. Drying facilities available. Wheelchair access. Special diets catered for. Ample parking. Bed & Breakfast £25 per person per night double, £30 per night single. No smoking. **STB** ★★★ *B&B*.
e-mail: hillhaven@kinlochewe.info

GAIRLOCH

Mrs A. MacIver, Heatherdale, Charleston, Gairloch IV21 2AH (01445 712388). A warm welcome awaits at Heatherdale, situated on the outskirts of Gairloch, overlooking the harbour and bay beyond. Within easy walking distance of the golf course and sandy beaches. Ideal base for hill walking. All rooms have en suite facilities, some with sea view. Excellent eating out facilities nearby. Ample parking. Residents' lounge with open fire. Bed and Breakfast prices from £21 per person per night. **STB** ★★★★ *B&B*.
e-mail: BrochoD1@aol.com

PLOCKTON

Mrs Janet MacKenzie Jones, "Tomacs", Frithard Road, Plockton IV52 8TQ (Tel & Fax: 01599 544321). Fine views overlooking Loch Carron and Applecross Hills. Double and twin bedrooms. One room has en suite facilities and one has private facilities; all have washbasin, central heating, TV and tea/coffee making facilities. Bed and Breakfast from £18. **STB** ★★★ *GUEST HOUSE*.
e-mail: janet@tomacs.freeserve.co.uk

STRATHPEFFER

Dunraven Lodge, Golf Course Road, Strathpeffer IV14 9AS (01997 421210). Beautiful Listed period house with all rooms en suite; recently refurbished to a very high standard of comfort and design. Guest lounge, dining room, full-size snooker room and lovely gardens provide an excellent base for your holiday or business trip. Open all year with many seasonal specials. Golf course, restaurants, bars and shops are just a short distance away, and we are ideally situated for exploring both the East and West coasts of the Highlands, Aviemore, Ullapool, Dornoch, Inverness, the Isle of Skye and Loch Ness. Bed and Breakfast from £25 to £30 pppn. **STB** ★★★★ *B&B*, **AA** ◆◆◆◆◆
e-mail: sandra.iddon@ntlworld.com
website: www.milford.co.uk/scotland/accom/h-a-1865.htm

HIGHLANDS (South)

SCOTLAND

BOAT OF GARTEN

Heathbank House, Drumuillie Road, Boat of Garten PH24 3BD (01479 831234). With a friendly welcome, Heathbank House is the perfect base for your short break or longer stay in an unhurried and relaxed atmosphere. The house, which is non-smoking throughout, has six en suite rooms, two with four-poster beds. Five course dinner menus change daily and are served in a Charles Rennie Mackintosh style dining room. Heathbank House is well situated for traditional and modern outdoor pursuits, cycling, walking, climbing, golf, fishing, bird watching, etc. If you prefer, just take a tour and admire the scenery.
e-mail: enquiries@heathbankhotel.co.uk
website: www.heathbankhotel.co.uk

CULLODEN MOOR

Mrs Margaret Campbell, Bay View, Westhill, By Inverness IV2 5BP (01463 790386). Bay View is set in a rural area on famous Culloden Moor, offering comfortable homely accommodation in one twin-bedded room with en suite shower, one double room with en suite bathroom, and one double room with private bathroom. An excellent touring base for the Highlands of Scotland and many famous historic sites. All home made food, local produce used. Bed and Breakfast from £20. **STB ★★★** *B&B.*
website: www.bayviewguest.com

DRUMNADROCHIT

Carol and Ewan Macleod, Glenurquhart House Hotel, Balnain, Drumnadrochit IV63 6TJ (01456 476234). Escape to the Scottish Highlands for peace and tranquillity and stay in our comfortable, friendly hotel with fantastic views of Loch Meiklie and Glen Urquhart. The hotel nestles in six acres of wooded grounds close to Loch Ness and Glen Affric nature reserve and is ideally suited for touring the Highlands. Most rooms are en suite and all have tea/coffee making facilities, hairdryer, colour TV, plus video in family rooms. There is a residents' lounge warmed by a log fire, restaurant serving freshly cooked meals and a cosy bar with ample supply of malt whiskies. Bikes can be hired and there is fishing available. **STB ★★★** *SMALL HOTEL.*
e-mail: carol@glenurquhartlodges.co.uk

FORT AUGUSTUS

Brenda Graham, Caledonian Cottage, Station Road, Fort Augustus PH32 4AY (Tel & Fax: 01320 366401; Mobile: 07967 740329). Offering a warm Highland welcome, the cottage is set in the quiet picturesque village of Fort Augustus, where the famous locks flow down into Loch Ness. The beautiful landscape is a walker's paradise (Great Glen Way); fishing, boating, canoeing, cycling and golf are all available. Pubs, restaurants and entertainment are just steps away from the cottage. Comfortable modern accommodation with TV, tea/coffee facilities. Non-smoking offering double/twin/family room en suite; double with private facilities. Pleasant garden to relax in and take in the view. Private parking. Children and small pets welcome. Open all year. Single and Short Break supplement. Rates from £15 to £29 per person according to season.
e-mail: brenda@ipw.com   website: www.ipw.com/calcot

FORT WILLIAM

John and Julie Mackin, Braeburn B&B, Badabrie, Fort William PH33 7LX (01397 772047). A warm welcome awaits you at Braeburn, a spacious family-run house with panoramic views of the surrounding area; Ben Nevis four miles. Situated in its own private grounds with ample off-road parking and storage for bikes and skiing equipment. Three miles from the town centre; local hotels and bars serving good food and drink all within walking distance. Ideally situated for touring the West Highlands of Scotland. All rooms are en suite with colour TV, hairdryer and hospitality tray, relax in the residents' lounge or on our sunny patio. Enjoy a hearty breakfast to set you up for the day. Prices range from £22.50 to £25 per person. **STB ★★★** *B&B.*
e-mail: mackinjj@hotmail.com
website: www.accommodation-fort-william.com

FORT WILLIAM

Mr Nielson, Glenshiel, Achintore Road, Fort William PH33 6RW (Tel & Fax: 01397 702271). Modern purpose-built guest house situated near the shore of Loch Linnhe with panoramic views of the surrounding mountains. Accommodation comprises three en suite double bedrooms and one twin-bedded en suite, all with colour TV and tea making facilities. Non-smoking. Large car park. Garden. Directions: on the A82 one-and-a-half-miles south of Fort William. Bed and Breakfast from £18 to £25. **STB ★★** *B&B.*

FORT WILLIAM

Norma and Jim McCallum, "The Neuk", Corpach, Fort William PH33 7LR (01397 772244). The Neuk is fully centrally heated and double glazed throughout to ensure maximum comfort of guests. Two family and two double bedrooms, all en suite, with colour TV and refreshment facilities. Guests' dining room and smoking lounge. Payphone. Situated north-west of Fort William in the village of Corpach offering panoramic views over Mamore Mountains, Ben Nevis and Loch Linnhe. An ideal base for exploring the surrounding area either walking, cycling or motoring. Open all year. Whatever the weather you can always be sure of a warm welcome. Bed and Breakfast from £18 to £40. Evening meal £11. Brochure available.
e-mail: normamccallum@theneuk10.fsbusiness.co.uk
website: www.fortwilliamguesthouse.com

FORT WILLIAM

John and Jeanette Mooney, Ben Nevis View Bed and Breakfast, Station Road, Corpach, Fort William PH33 7JH (01397 772131). Bed and Breakfast establishment located adjacent to the Caledonian Canal basin on the outskirts of Fort William, affording superb views across the water to Ben Nevis. Providing all the modern comforts for today's traveller, Ben Nevis View is open from February to October and caters for two to six people in one double and one family room (one double and two single beds), both en suite with colour TV, hairdryer and tea/coffee making facilities. Enjoy a hearty cooked breakfast in our bright, cheery dining room in true Scottish style. Tariff from £18 to £22 per person per night, subject to season. Family room prices available on request. Non-smoking; sorry, no dogs. **STB ★★★** *B&B.*

e-mail: bennevisview@amserve.net
website: www.bennevisview.co.uk

A useful index of towns and counties appears at the back of this book on pages 417-421. Refer also to Contents Pages 2 and 3.

FORT WILLIAM

Mrs Wallace, Ossian's Hotel, High Street, Fort William PH33 6DH (01397 700857). Ossian's can provide the traveller to the Scottish Highlands a comfortable, friendly and informal hotel, right in the centre of town. Shops, pubs and entertainment are just outside our front door. Relax and enjoy some of our good home cooking. All rooms are en suite. Budget/family rooms available. Some rooms have loch views. Lift access to all floors. Well-behaved pets and children are welcome. We are only a four minute walk from train or bus stations. Fort William makes an excellent base for touring the West Highlands, and with some of the best climbing in Britain, walkers and climbers are very welcome here. Bed and Breakfast from £18 to £32.

e-mail: mburnsmaclean@aol.com

FORT WILLIAM

Mrs Mary MacLean, Innishfree, Lochyside, Fort William PH33 7NX (01397 705471). Set against the background of Ben Nevis, this spacious Bed and Breakfast house offers a high level of service. Just two miles from the town centre and three miles from Glen Nevis. Visitors are guaranteed a warm friendly welcome and excellent accommodation. All rooms have en suite facilities and also offer remote-control colour TV and tea/coffee making facilities. Breakfast is served in the conservatory, which is overlooked by panoramic views. Enthusiastic advice on pursuits and activities are given. Access to private car park is available. This house has a non-smoking policy and pets are not allowed. Open all year. Prices range from £19 to £25 per person per night. **STB ★★★★ B&B.**

website: www.innishfree.co.uk

e-mail: fhg@allt-nan-ros.co.uk

FORT WILLIAM

Allt-nan-Ros Hotel, Onich, By Fort William PH33 6RY (01855 821210; Fax: 01855 821462). Named in Gaelic after the cascading stream that runs through the beautiful and colourful four acres of gardens, this fine hotel will hold special appeal for lovers of wild and romantic mountain and loch scenery. Situated on the A82 in the crofting village of Onich, Allt-nan-Ros is an imposing building of Victorian origin that has been modernised with skill and imagination. Guest rooms have magnificent views, and are appointed with private bath and toilet facilities, radio, central heating, electric blankets and tea and coffee makers. Under the attentive care of an expert chef, the cuisine is superbly prepared and presented, from the full Scottish breakfast to dinner which features many imaginative specialities. **STB ★★★★ HOTEL, AA ★★★ and TWO ROSETTES.**

website: www.allt-nan-ros.co.uk

e-mail: glenmhorhotel@btconnect.com

INVERNESS

Glen Mhor Hotel, 8-13 Ness Bank, Inverness IV2 4SG (01463 234308; Fax: 01463 713170). Established in 1957, the Glen Mhor Hotel is situated in a beautiful, tranquil location on the River Ness in the heart of Inverness. Our business and leisure visitors have enjoyed friendly, attentive service from Management and Staff, many with many years service well into double figures. We are just a few minutes' walk away from the city centre, railway station, Eden Court Theatre and other attractions. The bedrooms are spread over four adjacent properties, all of the same high standard and individually decorated. Our restaurants, Nico's and The Riverview, are by far the longest established Seafood Restaurants in Inverness and are renowned for the excellence of the Made In Scotland cuisine. Innovative, international and traditional themes on poultry, beef, lamb, vegetarian and game in season.

website: www.glen-mhor.com

The Loch Ness Monster Visitor Centre • *Drumnadrochit, Inverness* • 01456 450342
website: www.lochness-centre.com
All you ever wanted to know about the monster! Superb documentary, including
eye-witness accounts. Shop with souvenirs.

SCOTLAND

INVERNESS

The Waterside Hotel, 19 Ness Bank, Inverness IV2 4SF (01463 233065; Fax: 01463 241075). Beautifully located on the river bank and within five minutes' walk of the city centre, The Waterside is a family-owned and professionally run hotel where Management and Staff will ensure all your needs are catered for. The new owners, Mr and Mrs Manson, have recently refurbished the Function Suite as well as refitting the reception and function area and it is intended that by March 2004 all the bedrooms will have undergone significant upgrading to maintain the hotel's position at the upper end of the three star hotel market. The Waterside Brasserie, with its fabulous river views, and the Cocktail Bar offer freshly prepared and imaginatively presented food with an impressive range of wines, beers, malts and spirits. A sound base to tour the Highlands, offering a warm welcome and Highland hospitality.
e-mail: info@thewatersideinverness.com   **website: www.thewatersideinverness.com**

INVERNESS

Mrs E. MacKenzie, The Whins, 114 Kenneth Street, Inverness IV3 5QG (01463 236215). Comfortable, small homely non-smoking accommodation. 10 minutes bus and railway stations, with easy access to many golf courses, walking and cycling areas, and a great base for touring North, East and West by car, rail or bus. Bedrooms have TV, tea making, washbasins and heating off season. Bathroom, shared toilet and shower; £17 per person. Write or phone for full details.

INVERNESS

Mrs A. MacLean, Waternish, 15 Clachnaharry Road, Inverness IV3 8QH (01463 230520). Delightful bungalow in beautiful setting overlooking Moray Firth and Black Isle. On main A862 road to Beauly, and just five minutes to Inverness town centre. Ideal touring centre for North and West. Canal cruises and golf course nearby and lovely walks by banks of Caledonian Canal. Loch Ness is just 15 minutes' drive. Accommodation comprises three double/twin rooms, one en suite, all with tea/coffee making facilities and colour TV. Comfortable lounge. Full Scottish breakfast. Private car park. Open March to October. Bed and Breakfast from £17.

See also Colour Display Advertisement

INVERNESS

Moray Park House, 1 Moray Park, Island Bank Road, Inverness IV2 4SX (01463 233528). Moray Park is a lovely old house overlooking Cavell Gardens and the River Ness, and just a few minutes from the main shopping streets. The Mathieson Family purchased Moray Park House in August 2003 and have carried out refurbishment during the winter. Seven rooms have en suite facilities and one a private bathroom. All are freshly decorated and all but two have river views. One large ground floor room is designed for use by disabled people, with extra space and suitable en suite facilities. There is a car park for residents. Moray Park House is ideally positioned for access to the lovely Island Bank Walk, the Eden Court Theatre, the Castle, city parks and numerous restaurants, all of which are within a few minutes' walk. Bed and Breakfast rates vary from £20 to £50.

e-mail: MorayParkHotel@aol.com   **website: www.MorayParkHotel.co.uk**

KINGUSSIE

Valerie J. Johnston, Ardselma, The Crescent, Kingussie PH21 1JZ (Tel & Fax: 01540 661809; mobile: 07786 696384). An imposing Victorian villa situated in an elevated position within two acres of private grounds, Ardselma commands magnificent views of the Cairngorm Mountains. Accommodation comprises two family and one double en suite rooms, one twin room with private facilities, and one single and one twin room with shared facilities. TV lounge available with tea/coffee making facilities; central heating. A three minute walk to the high street or to the golf course. Evening meals by prior arrangement, fresh local produce and game our speciality. Packed lunches available. Groups catered for, discounts available. Children and pets welcome. Smoking. Safe cycle storage. **e-mail: valeriedunmhor@aol.com**

MORAR (by Mallaig)

Mrs U. Clulow, Sunset Guest House, Morar, by Mallaig PH40 4PA (01687 462259; Fax: 01687 460085). Situated in the peaceful west coast village of Morar, overlooking the renowned silver sands and the beautiful Inner Hebrides. With the island studded Atlantic in front and backdrop of the mountain wilds of Knoydart, Sunset is superbly placed for those wishing to find the tranquillity, scenic beauty and romantic history for which this part of Scotland is famous. AUTHENTIC THAI FOOD is also on the menu to provide some inner warmth after a long and energetic day. Children welcome. Prices from £15.00.
e-mail: sunsetgh@aol.com   website: www.sunsetguesthouse.co.uk

ONICH

Mrs J. MacLean, Forester's Bungalow, Inchree, Onich PH33 6SE (01855 821285). Situated in the hamlet of Inchree in the village of Onich, eight miles south of Fort William (nearest town). This is a Swedish design bungalow with full central heating. Letting two twin-bedded rooms and a family room which sleeps four. Tea making facilities in rooms with TV. Not en suite. One public bathroom plus extra toilet. Bed and breakfast at £17 per person. Children in family rooms half price.

SPEAN BRIDGE

See also Colour Display Advertisement

Mr M. Jenkinson, The Braes Guest House, Tirindrish, Spean Bridge PH34 4EU (01397 712437; Fax: 01397 712108). The Braes Guest House is a family-run guest house set in one and a half acres of secluded grounds with magnificent views of The Grey Corries. This is an ideal base to relax or tour some of the very best scenery in Scotland. We cater for all outdoor activities with purpose-built drying rooms and pick-up and drop-off facilities available by prior arrangement. Early breakfast, packed lunches and dinners can be provided from quality local produce and must be pre-booked. Five double en suite rooms, one twin with private bathroom and one single en suite room. The residents' lounge with TV has superb mountain views from the large picture windows. Ample car parking set back 100 yards from main A86. Pets welcome. A non-smoking establishment. All rooms are centrally heated and have tea making facilities. We hope that you arrive as a guest and leave as a friend. Credit/debit cards accepted.
STB ★★★ *GUEST HOUSE, WALKERS AND CYCLISTS WELCOME.*
e-mail: enquiry@thebraes.co.uk   website: www.thebraes.co.uk

SPEAN BRIDGE (by)

Dreamweavers, Earendil, Mucomir, By Spean Bridge PH34 4EQ (Tel & Fax: 01397 712548). Come to the heart of the Highlands and experience the ultimate in Scottish hospitality. Comfortable spacious accommodation, plentiful home cooking and beautiful surroundings. Artists, birdwatchers, photographers and walkers all welcome, with plenty to do, see and inspire you. We are the ideal centre for all mountain and water sports and golf is available nearby. Special Theme Weekends available. Children welcome. Specially adapted to meet the needs of all disabled with easy access and a range of aids available. Bed & Breakfast £20pp; Dinner, Bed and Breakfast £30pp. Please contact for further details.
e-mail: helen@dreamweavers.co.uk
website: www.dreamweavers.co.uk

TOMATIN

Robert Coupar and Lesley Smithers, Glenan Lodge (Licensed), Tomatin IV13 7YT (01808 511217; Fax: 01808 511356). The Glenan Lodge is a typical Scottish Lodge situated in the midst of the Monadhliath Mountains in the valley of the Findhorn River, yet only one mile from the A9. It offers typical Scottish hospitality, home cooking, warmth and comfort. The seven bedrooms, including two family rooms, are all en suite, with central heating, tea-making facilities and colour TV. There is a large comfortable lounge and a homely diningroom. The licensed bar is well stocked with local malts for the guests. Glenan Lodge caters for the angler, birdwatcher, hillwalker, stalker and tourist alike whether passing through or using as a base. Open all year round. Bed and Breakfast; Dinner optional. Non-smoking. Credit cards accepted. **AA ◆◆◆**

e-mail: enquiries@glenanlodge.co.uk   **website: www.glenanlodge.co.uk**

LANARKSHIRE

CALDERBANK

Mrs Betty Gaines, Calder Guest House, 13 Main Street, Calderbank ML6 9SG (01236 769077; Fax: 01236 750506). Calder Guest House is a spacious Victorian house which is over 100 years old and has recently been tastefully refurbished. With its close proximity to the motorway network, and within two miles of the railway station, it is ideally situated for the holiday or business traveller, as a convenient stopover or as a base to tour or visit the surrounding countryside. The spacious accommodation has a choice of bedrooms to suit the family or the person travelling alone, some are en suite, and all rooms are equipped with colour TV and tea/coffee making facilities. The conservatory to the rear of the house, overlooking the garden and the children's play area, contains the diningroom and lounge, giving a bright and cheerful setting to enjoy a hearty Scottish breakfast, or to relax in the evening after a hard day. There is ample off-road parking. Games room with pool and darts or watch "the big match", golf or cricket on television. Bed and Breakfast from £25 pp. **STB ★★★** *GUEST HOUSE.*

PERTH & KINROSS

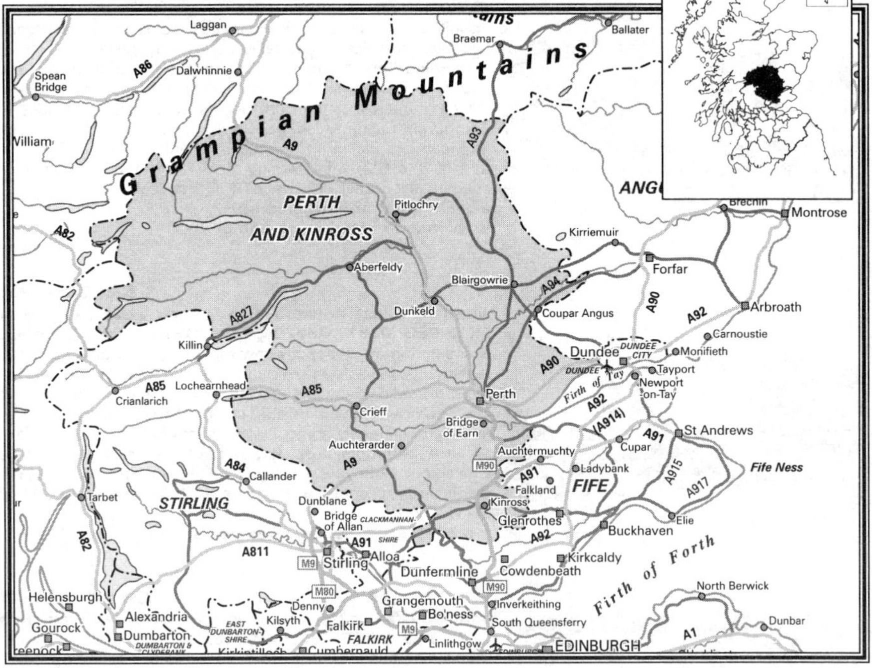

Map of Perth & Kinross region showing towns including Pitlochry, Aberfeldy, Blairgowrie, Dunkeld, Perth, Crieff, Auchterarder, Dundee, Forfar, Arbroath, St Andrews, Stirling, Dunfermline, and Edinburgh, within the Grampian Mountains area of Scotland.

©MAPS IN MINUTES™ 2003 ©Crown Copyright. Ordnance Survey 2003

SCOTLAND

AUCHTERARDER

Mrs Brodie, Allandale House, 17 High Street, Auchterarder PH3 1DB (01764 663329; mobile: 07801 479056; Fax: 01764 664451). Allandale House is a stylish Bed and Breakfast of great comfort and character, which has been refurbished to a very high standard, yet still retains many of its original features. Each spacious bedroom has tea/coffee making facilities, colour TV and central heating. Most rooms have private facilities, one is a family room. Auchterarder is perfectly situated as a base for touring Scotland. Perth, Stirling, Pitlochry, The Trossachs, Loch Lomond and Edinburgh are all less than one hour away and Gleneagles is only two miles away. Highchairs and cots provided. Car parking available. **STB ★★★ B&B, AA ◆◆◆◆**
e-mail: AllandaleHouse@aol.com
website: http://freespace.virgin.net/allandale.house/

BIRNAM

The Waterbury Guest House, Murthly Terrace, Birnam PH8 0BG (01350 727324; Fax: 01350 727023). This lovely Victorian terraced house, situated in the heart of Birnam, is the home of Jane and David, whose warm and friendly welcome awaits you. Our rooms are tastefully decorated, with many period features retained. The bedrooms have en suite or private facilities, colour TV, radio and hospitality tray. Breakfast is generous and our daily specials are always popular. Evening meals (by prior arrangement) are freshly prepared using local and Scottish produce. Non-smoking. Bed and Breakfast from £25 pppn.
e-mail: info@waterbury-guesthouse.co.uk
website: www.waterbury-guesthouse.co.uk

BLAIRGOWRIE

Rosalind Young, Holmrigg, Wester Essendy, Blairgowrie PH10 6RD (Tel & Fax: 01250 884309). One double/family, one double four-poster and one double on ground floor. All rooms are en suite with tea/coffee making facilities, radio and TV; ironing and hair drying facilities. Comfortable lounge with open fire and colour TV; diningroom. Heating throughout. Vegetarian meals and packed lunches; home cooking and baking; full cooked breakfast. Places of interest range from Scott's 'Discovery' in Dundee to Edinburgh Castle. Also golf, fishing and walking. Pets by arrangement. Parking. Non-smoking house. Bed and Breakfast from £20 to £23; with Evening Meal £31 to £34. Discounts for children and Senior Citizens. **STB** ★★★ *B&B*.
e-mail: info@holmrigg.co.uk
website: www.holmrigg-bnb.co.uk

CALLANDER

Annfield Guest House, North Church Street, Callander FK17 8EG (01877 330204; Fax: 01877 330674). Annfield is situated in a quiet spot a few minutes' walk from shops and restaurants. Ideal as an overnight stop or as a centre for visiting the surrounding Scottish Highlands. You will receive the warmest of welcomes from your hosts, Janet and Mike Greenfield, to their fine Victorian family home. All bedrooms have en suite facilities or private bathroom, hospitality tray and hairdryer. Guests' lounge with colour TV. Private parking. Open all year. No smoking. Major credit cards accepted. **STB** ★★★ *B&B*. **AA** ◆◆◆, *WELCOME HOST AWARD*.
e-mail: janet-greenfield@amserve.com

CRIANLARICH

John and Janice Christie, Inverardran House, Crianlarich FK20 8QS (01838 300240). Set just outside the village of Crianlarich, Inverardran House is sited in an elevated position with views across Strathfillan to Ben Challum. This property offers excellent fishing, walking and touring prospects. We can offer you Bed and Breakfast accommodation for up to eight people in three en suite double rooms and one twin room with a private bathroom. Tea/coffee making facilities in the rooms. Open all year. Prices from £16 to £20 per person per night based on two sharing, £5 to £7.50 surcharge for a single person. Discounts for longer stays. Evening meals on request.
e-mail: janice@inverardran.demon.co.uk
website: www.inverardran.demon.co.uk

CRIEFF

Glenearn House, Perth Road, Crieff PH7 3EQ (01764 650000). A warm welcome awaits visitors to this beautifully kept Victorian house situated within half a mile of Crieff town centre, the Hydro Hotel and Crieff Golf Club. The house offers spacious, finely furnished accommodation with TV, video recorder, tea/coffee trays, trouser press and radio alarm in all bedrooms. Video and book libraries are available to guests. For further comfort two guest lounges are provided. Glenearn is set back from the road and provides generous private car parking and well maintained gardens. Terms from £32 Bed and Breakfast single, £27 double/twin. Open all year. **STB** ★★★★ *GUEST HOUSE*.
e-mail: bookings@glenearnhouse.f9.co.uk

CRIEFF

Mr and Mrs Clifford, Merlindale, Perth Road, Crieff PH7 3EQ (Tel & Fax: 01764 655205). Merlindale is a luxurious Georgian house situated close to the town centre. All bedrooms are en suite (two with sunken bathrooms) and have tea/coffee making facilities. We have a jacuzzi available plus garden, ample parking and satellite television. We also have a Scottish library for the use of our guests. Cordon Bleu cooking is our speciality. A warm welcome awaits you in this non-smoking house. Terms from £40 Bed and Breakfast single, £27.50 double/twin. Dinner £20. Open February to December. **STB ★★★★** *B&B*, **AA ◆◆◆◆**

DUNNING

Mrs Elspeth Dunbar, 6 The Glebe, Dunning PH2 0RF (01764 684953). The house is set in its own grounds at the top of a very quiet cul-de-sac with spectacular views to the Grampian mountains, five minutes from the A9 and 15 minutes from the M90. Dunning is convenient for Gleneagles, Stirling, Central Scotland and the way North. The village has a Norman Church, and is the site where in 1656 the last witch was burned at the stake. Also available is a nine-hole golf course, tennis courts and two restaurants. Elspeth is a trained cook and will provide for all tastes. Accommodation, available from £22.50 per person per night, comprises a large double bedroom with en suite shower and a single with private bathroom.
e-mail: cckdunbar@aol.com

KIRKMICHAEL

Log Cabin Hotel, Kirkmichael PH10 7NA (01250 881288; Fax: 01250 881206). Unique, family-run hotel, set in the picturesque hills of Perthshire, less than half-an-hour from Glenshee, Pitlochry and Blairgowrie. The bar is fully licensed, with a good range of malt whiskies; guests can enjoy panoramic views of Strathardle from the dining room. All bedrooms are en suite. A good central base for touring Perthshire and beyond; many golf courses are within easy reach; skiing at Glenshee in the winter; ideal for walking holidays. Please call for brochure or further information. Pets and children welcome. Bed and Breakfast from £25 pppn. **STB ★★** *HOTEL.*
website: www.logcabinhotel.co.uk

PERTH

Stuart and Trisha Honeyman, Auld Manse Guest House, Pitcullen Crescent, Perth PH2 7HT (Tel & Fax: 01738 629187). Victorian semi-villa, former manse just a short walk from city centre, parks and sport amenities. Situated on the A94 Coupar Angus road the Manse offers comfortable rooms all with private facilities, colour TV and hospitality tray. Guest lounge with satellite TV. Payphone and fax for guests' use. Ample car parking. Fire and Food Hygiene Certificates. Perth is an ideal base for touring and is only a short drive from most major cities; or try our many beautiful golf courses with a choice of nine or 18 hole play. Open all year. Bed and Breakfast from £18.50. Reductions for party bookings. **STB ★★★** *GUEST HOUSE.*
e-mail: trishaatauldmanse@hotmail.com
website: www.guesthouseperth.com

The FHG Directory of Website Addresses
on pages 387-415 is a useful quick reference guide for
holiday accommodation with e-mail and/or website details

STANLEY

Mrs Ann Guthrie, Newmill Farm, Stanley PH1 4QD (01738 828281). This 330 acre farm is situated on the A9, six miles north of Perth. Accommodation comprises twin and double en suite rooms and a family room with private bathroom; lounge, sittingroom, diningroom; bathroom, shower room and toilet. Bed and Breakfast from £19; Evening Meal on request. The warm welcome and supper of excellent home baking is inclusive. Reductions and facilities for children. Pets accepted. The numerous castles and historic ruins around Perth are testimony to Scotland's turbulent past. Situated in the area known as "The Gateway to the Highlands" the farm is ideally placed for those seeking some of the best unspoilt scenery in Western Europe. Many famous golf courses and trout rivers in the Perth area. STB ★★★ *B&B*.

e-mail: guthrienewmill@sol.co.uk   website: www.newmillfarm.co.uk

See also Colour Display Advertisement

STRATHYRE

Ben Sheann Hotel, Main Street, Strathyre FK18 8NA (Tel & Fax: 01877 384609). Victorian hotel situated in the friendly village of Strathyre in the Trossachs. Surrounded by the beautiful scenery of Scotland's new National Park with golf, walking, fishing, canoeing and shooting all available nearby and yet only one hour from the cities of Glasgow, Edinburgh and Perth. Ten bedrooms available (including family rooms), all with TV, tea/coffee making facilities and central heating. Public bar and lounge, dining room and residents' lounge. Pool table, Sky TV. Entertainment available at weekends - quiz nights, etc. Bar lunches and evening meals available. Prices from £20 Bed and Breakfast per person. We can also cater for small weddings, functions and meetings.
e-mail: colin@bensheannhotel.co.uk
website: www.bensheannhotel.co.uk

STIRLING & THE TROSSACHS

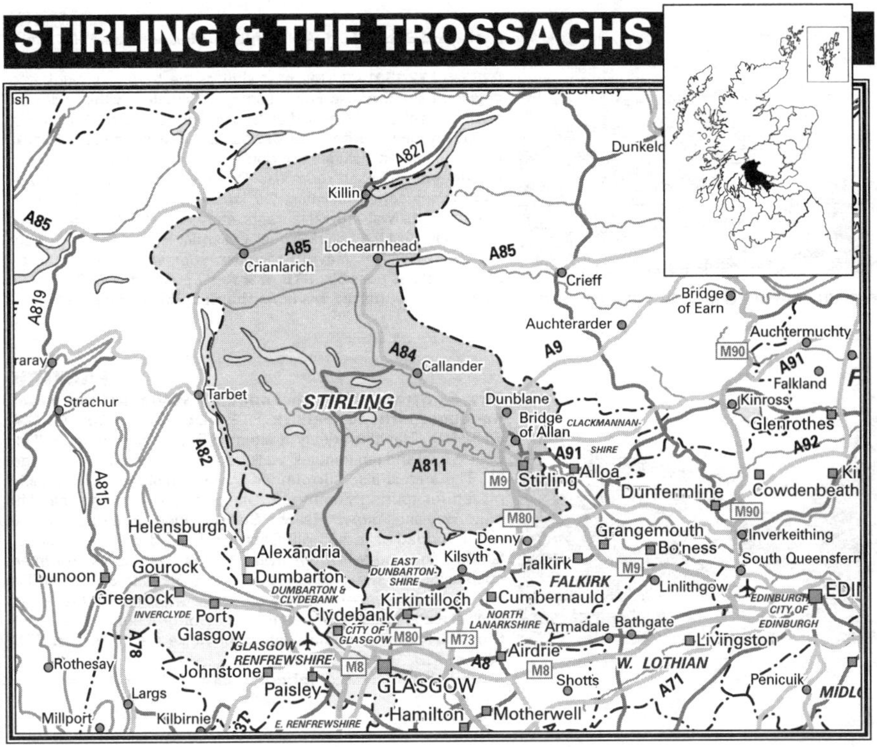

©MAPS IN MINUTES™ 2003 ©Crown Copyright, Ordnance Survey 2003

ABERFOYLE

Forth House, Lochard Road, Aberfoyle, Stirling FK8 3TD (Tel & Fax: 01877 382696). Within Loch Lomond and Trossachs National Park you'll find FORTH HOUSE, an attractive, Victorian home that offers both Bed and Breakfast and The Hayloft, a self-catering flat. The Bed and Breakfast accommodation is stylishly decorated and furnished. The ground floor double room (sleeps two/four) has private shower adjacent and guest TV lounge. The secluded Hayloft (sleeps two/four) has a well appointed kitchen, utility room and is heated throughout. French doors open on to a garden patio. It is an ideal location for summer and winter breaks in a most beautiful part of Scotland.
e-mail: stay@forthhouse.com
website: www.forthhouse.com

See also Colour Display Advertisement

CALLANDER

Riverview Guest House, Leny Road, Callander FK17 8AL (01877 330635; Fax: 01877 339386). Excellent value for money accommodation in the Trossachs area which forms the most beautiful part of Scotland's first National Park. Ideal centre for walking and cycling holidays with cycle storage being available. GUEST HOUSE - all rooms en suite, TV and tea making facilities. Bed and Breakfast from £21. Low season and long stay discounts available. Private parking. SELF CATERING - stone cottages sleep three or four from £225 per week. Call Drew or Kathleen Little for details. Sorry no smoking and no pets.
STB ★★★ *B&B*, STB ★★★★ *SELF-CATERING*.
e-mail: auldtoll@aol.com
website: www.nationalparkscotland.co.uk

FALKIRK

Betty and Bede Ward, Ashbank Bed & Breakfast, 105 Main Street, Redding, Falkirk FK2 9UQ (01324 716649; Fax: 01324 712431). On the east side of the town, Ashbank is a detached stone house (100 years old), situated within pleasant gardens on all sides. Off-road parking and good views to Braveheart Country, together with Scottish hospitality await you at Ashbank. Accommodation includes two double en suite rooms and two twin en suite rooms. Each room has TV with four channels, remote-control; tea/coffee facilities. No smoking or pets. Golf, tennis, swimming, hillwalking, restaurants, etc. all nearby. Near trains and motorway. Visit the Falkirk Wheel, Callendar House and Linlithgow Palace. We will endeavour to make your stay at Ashbank as comfortable as possible. **STB ★★★** *B&B.* **AA ◆◆◆◆**

e-mail: ashbank@guest-house.freeserve.co.uk   website: www.ashbank.falkirkwheel.net

FALKIRK

Mrs E. Strain, "Hawthorndean", Wallacestone Brae, Reddingmuirhead, Falkirk FK2 0DQ (Tel & Fax: 01324 715840). "Hawthorndean" is situated five miles from the Falkirk Boat Wheel and ten minutes' walk from the Union Canal, at Bridge 56. The area is also surrounded by local history and is ideally placed for touring Edinburgh, Glasgow and Stirling; near M9 motorway and Polmont Railway Station. Open all year; traditional accommodation to suit all. Centrally heated double en suite, family, single and twin rooms with TV, radio alarm clock, hairdryer, hospitality tray and ironing facilities. Lounge with 32" digital TV. Interesting garden. Ample parking. Traditional Scottish breakfast, special dietary needs catered for. Send for brochure. Prices from £16 to £25. Ideal accommodation for walkers and cyclists. **STB ★★★** *B&B.*

e-mail: eileenstrain@yahoo.co.uk

•• *Some Useful Guidance for Guests and Hosts* ••

Every year literally thousands of holidays, short breaks and overnight stops are arranged through our guides, the vast majority without any problems at all. In a handful of cases, however, difficulties do arise about bookings, which often could have been prevented from the outset.

It is important to remember that when accommodation has been booked, both parties – guests and hosts – have entered into a form of contract. We hope that the following points will provide helpful guidance.

GUESTS:

• When enquiring about accommodation, be as precise as possible. Give exact dates, numbers in your party and the ages of any children.

• State the number and type of rooms wanted and also what catering you require – bed and breakfast, full board etc. Make sure that the position about evening meals is clear – and about pets, reductions for children or any other special points.

• Read our reviews carefully to ensure that the proprietors you are going to contact can supply what you want. Ask for a letter confirming all arrangements, if possible.

• If you have to cancel, do so as soon as possible. Proprietors do have the right to retain deposits and under certain circumstances to charge for cancelled holidays if adequate notice is not given and they cannot re-let the accommodation.

HOSTS:

• Give details about your facilities and about any special conditions. Explain your deposit system clearly and arrangements for cancellations, charges etc. and whether or not your terms include VAT.

• If for any reason you are unable to fulfil an agreed booking without adequate notice, you may be under an obligation to arrange suitable alternative accommodation or to make some form of compensation.

While every effort is made to ensure accuracy, we regret that FHG Publications cannot accept responsibility for errors, omissions or misrepresentations in our entries or any consequences thereof. Prices in particular should be checked because we go to press early. We will follow up complaints but cannot act as arbiters or agents for either party.

SCOTLAND

SCOTTISH ISLANDS

Isle of Coll

ARINAGOUR

Ruth Sturgeon, Tigh-na-Mara FHG, Arinagour PA78 6SY (01879 230354). This licensed guest house offers spectacular views to Mull and the Treshnish Isles. Explore magnificent sandy beaches, visit the RSPB Reserve - perhaps spot an elusive corncrake? Roam amidst a profusion of wild flowers or relax in the lounge whilst keeping a watchful eye for otters and admire the ever changing moods of the sea. All rooms have washbasin, electric blankets, tea/coffee making facilities and mini bar. Interesting 9 hole golf course and fishing nearby; cycle and boat hire available. Bed and Breakfast from £23, Evening Meal £15. A self-catering cottage is also available.

e-mail: ruth@tighnamara.info

SCOTLAND

Isle of Lewis

STORNOWAY

Mr G. Lowder, Hal 'O' The Wynd Guest House, Newton Street, Stornoway HS1 2RE (01851 706073). Hal 'O' The Wynd is a large three storey building painted white and dates back some 300 years. The property has four large bedrooms, two en suite and two standard. All rooms have a sea view and a panoramic view of Lewis Castle grounds and beyond to Arnish Point. It also has a comfortable guest lounge and a well laid out diningroom. There is also a public payphone in the front hall. All rooms are centrally heated with a thermostatic control, colour teletext TV and tea/coffee making facilities. Fully licensed. A la carte menu. The town centre is a five minute walk where you will find the bus station which has a good service to all major attractions on the island. We can arrange guided tours of the island. We also have an attractive rear garden that you may wish to use for a barbecue to taste our local fresh seafood etc. Whatever you decide to do on your holiday we will try to make it a pleasant and happy one to remember and hope you enjoy your stay with us. **STB ★★★** *GUEST HOUSE.*

website: www.lowders@madasafish.com

FHG PUBLICATIONS publish a large range of well-known accommodation guides. We will be happy to send you details or you can use the order form at the back of this book.

Isle of Skye

PORTREE

The Royal Hotel, Portree IV51 9BU (01478 612525; Fax: 01478 613198). Set overlooking the picturesque harbour of Portree, The Royal Hotel offers you a quiet, relaxing retreat during your stay on Skye. Recently refurbished, offering new standards in comfort and style. Accommodation consists of 21 well appointed rooms, some equipped to accommodate families, most overlooking the harbour and featuring private bathroom facilities and colour TV. Room service is available as well as a fitness centre and sauna for guests to use. The Royal Hotel offers a wide and varied menu serving sea food, lamb, venison and tender Highland beef. Vegetarians are also catered for. There is something for everyone; from walking, climbing and watersports. **STB** ★★★ *HOTEL*. **RAC** ★★

e-mail: info@royal-hotel-skye.com

website: www.royal-hotel-skye.com

Orkney

KIRKWALL

John D. Webster, Lav'rockha Guest House, Inganess Road, Kirkwall KW15 1SP (Tel & Fax: 01856 876103). Situated a short walk from the Highland Park Distillery and Visitor Centre, and within reach of all local amenities. Lav'rockha is the perfect base for exploring and discovering Orkney. We offer high quality accommodation at affordable rates. All our rooms have an en suite WC and power shower, tea/coffee tray, hairdryer, radio alarm clock and remote-control colour TV. Those with young children will appreciate our family room with reduced children's rates, children's meals and child minding service. We also have facilities for the disabled, with full unassisted wheelchair access from our private car park. All our meals are prepared to a high standard using fresh, local produce as much as possible. Bed and Breakfast from £22 per person. Special winter break prices available. **STB** ★★★★ *GUEST HOUSE, WINNER OF BEST B&B ORKNEY; FOOD AWARDS, TASTE OF SCOTLAND ACCREDITED.*

e-mail: lavrockha@orkney.com

website: www.lavrockha.co.uk

Shetlands

BRAE

Mrs E. Wood, Westayre Bed and Breakfast, Muckle Roe, Brae ZE2 9QW (01806 522368). A warm welcome awaits you at our working croft on the picturesque island of Muckle Roe, where we have breeding sheep, pet lambs, ducks and cats. The island is joined to the mainland by a small bridge and is an ideal place for children. The accommodation is of a high standard and has en suite facilities. Guests can enjoy good home cooking and baking. In the evening sit by the open peat fire and enjoy the views looking out over Swarbacks Minn. Spectacular cliff scenery and clean safe sandy beaches, bird watching and hill walking and also central for touring North Mainland and North Isles. Bed and Breakfast from £22 (standard room); from £24 (en suite). **STB** ★★★★ *B&B*.

e-mail: westayre@ukonline.co.uk

website: www.westayre.shetland.co.uk

𝔉𝔥𝔊 Diploma Winners 2003

Each year we award a small number of diplomas to holiday proprietors whose services have been specially commended by our readers. The following were our FHG Diploma Winners for 2003.

England

DERBYSHIRE

Mr Tatlow
Ashfield Farm, Calwich
Near Ashbourne
Derbyshire DE6 2EB

DEVON

Mrs Tucker
Lower Luxton Farm, Upottery
Near Honiton
Devon EX14 9PB

◆

Royal Oak
Dunsford Near Exeter
Devon EX6 7DA

GLOUCESTERSHIRE

Mrs Keyte
The Limes, Evesham Road
Stow-on-the-Wold
Gloucestershire GL54 1EN

HAMPSHIRE

Mrs Ellis, Efford Cottage,
Everton, Lymington,
Hampshire SO41 0JD

◆

R. Law
Whitley Ridge Hotel
Beauly Road, Brockenhurst
Hampshire SO42 7QL

HEREFORDSHIRE

Mrs Brown
Ye Hostelrie, Goodrich
Near Ross on Wye
Herefordshire HR9 6HX

NORTH YORKSHIRE

Charles & Gill Richardson
The Coppice, 9 Studley Road
Harrogate
North Yorkshire HG1 5JU

◆

Mr & Mrs Hewitt
Harmony Country Lodge
Limestone Road, Burniston,
Scarborough
North Yorkshire YO13 0DG

Wales

POWYS

Linda Williams
The Old Vicarage
Erwood, Builth Wells
Powys LD2 3SZ

Scotland

ABERDEEN, BANFF & MORAY

Mr Ian Ednie
Spey Bay Hotel
Spey Bay
Fochabers
Moray IV32 7PJ

PERTH & KINROSS

Dunalastair Hotel
Kinloch Rannoch
By Pitlochry
Perthshire PH16 5PW

HELP IMPROVE BRITISH TOURISM STANDARDS

As recommendations are submitted from readers of the FULL RANGE of FHG titles the winners shown above may not necessarily appear in this guide.

Wales

FHG

Ratings You Can Trust

ENGLAND

The English Tourism Council (formerly the English Tourist Board) has joined with the **AA** and **RAC** to create a new, easily understood quality rating for serviced accommodation, giving a clear guide of what to expect.

HOTELS are given a rating from One to Five **Stars** – the more Stars, the higher the quality and the greater the range of facilities and level of services provided.

GUEST ACCOMMODATION, which includes guest houses, bed and breakfasts, inns and farmhouses, is rated from One to Five **Diamonds**. Progressively higher levels of quality and customer care must be provided for each one of the One to Five Diamond ratings.

HOLIDAY PARKS, TOURING PARKS and CAMPING PARKS are now also assessed using **Stars**. Standards of quality range from a One Star (acceptable) to a Five Star (exceptional) park.

Look out also for the new **SELF-CATERING** Star ratings. The more **Stars** (from One to Five) awarded to an establishment, the higher the levels of quality you can expect. Establishments at higher rating levels also have to meet some additional requirements for facilities.

SCOTLAND

Star Quality Grades will reflect the most important aspects of a visit, such as the warmth of welcome, efficiency and friendliness of service, the quality of the food and the cleanliness and condition of the furnishings, fittings and decor.

THE MORE STARS,
THE HIGHER THE STANDARDS.

The description, such as Hotel, Guest House, Bed and Breakfast, Lodge, Holiday Park, Self-catering etc tells you the type of property and style of operation.

WALES

Places which score highly will have an especially welcoming atmosphere and pleasing ambience, high levels of comfort and guest care, and attractive surroundings enhanced by thoughtful design and attention to detail

STAR QUALITY GUIDE FOR

HOTELS, GUEST HOUSES AND FARMHOUSES

SELF-CATERING ACCOMMODATION
(Cottages, Apartments, Houses)

CARAVAN HOLIDAY HOME PARKS
(Holiday Parks, Touring Parks, Camping Parks)

★★★★★   *Exceptional quality*
★★★★   *Excellent quality*
★★★   *Very good quality*
★★   *Good quality*
★   *Fair to good quality*

In England, Scotland and Wales, all graded properties are inspected annually by Tourist Authority trained Assessors.

ANGLESEY & GWYNEDD

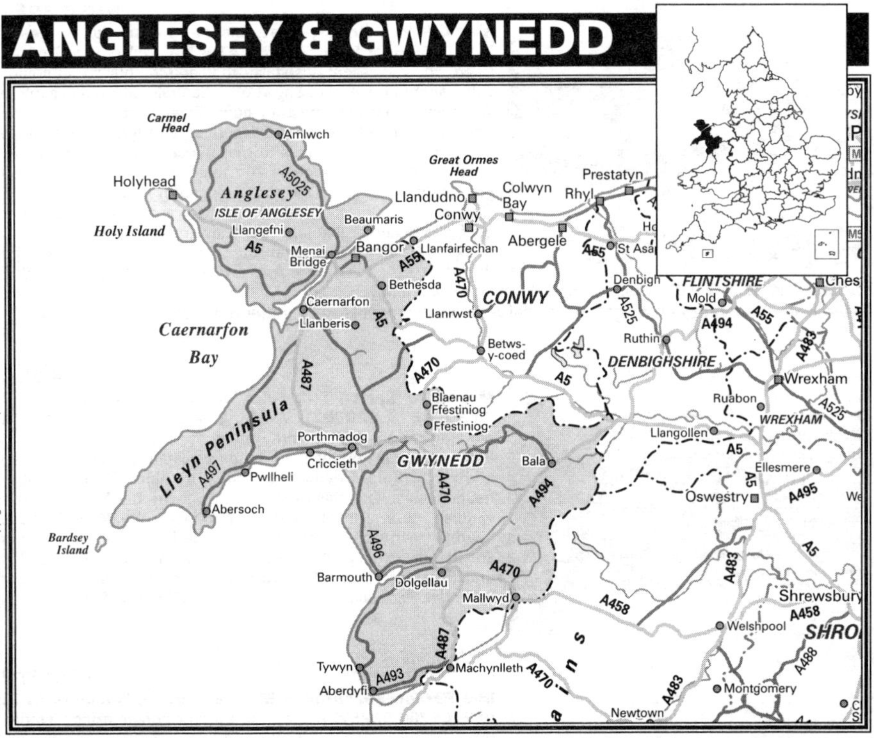

WALES

ABERDOVEY

Jim and Marion Billingham, Preswylfa, Aberdovey LL35 0LE (01654 767239; Fax: 01654 767983). Preswylfa is a non-smoking very attractive Edwardian family home, private and secluded with a lovely mature garden filled with old-fashioned fragrant flowers and safe car parking area. A footpath leads down to the old fishing village of Aberdovey, also famous for its sailing, walking and golf. All three luxury en suite bedrooms, two of which enjoy breathtaking views over Cardigan Bay, have full facilities and kingsize beds. A relaxing guest lounge with period furniture and grand piano awaits you, the dining room beyond leading into the garden. Evening meals are available by arrangement. Excellent cuisine, catering for organic and special diets. A warm welcome guaranteed. Price per room £60 to £70.

WTB ★★★ COUNTRY HOUSE, WHICH? GOOD BED & BREAKFAST GUIDE.
e-mail: info@preswylfa.co.uk   **website: www.preswylfa.co.uk**

ANGLESEY

Richard and Shirley Murphy, Ingledene, Ravenspoint Road, Trearddur Bay LL65 2YU (Tel & Fax: 01407 861026). Ingledene, a large Edwardian seaside home with magnificent views across Trearddur Bay, provides a warm and friendly welcome for your stay. Spacious twin/double rooms (two en suite), most with sea views. Relax and watch the glorious sunsets and wake up to the sound of the waves. All rooms are centrally heated with colour TV and tea/coffee making facilities. Parking is to the rear of the property with ample space for boats, etc. Holyhead ferry terminal is only 10 minutes away, with day trips to Ireland from £12. Bed and Breakfast from £20 per person. Open all year. Self-catering cottage (sleeps 2+2) also available.
e-mail: info@Ingledene.co.uk
website: www.ingledene.co.uk

ANGLESEY

Mrs J. Bown, Drws-y-Coed, Llannerch-y-medd, Anglesey LL71 8AD (Tel & Fax: 01248 470473). Welcome to Drws-y-Coed. Enjoy excellent hospitality, food and tranquil surroundings with panoramic views of Snowdonia. Centrally situated to explore Anglesey's coastline and attractions. Twenty-five minutes to the port of Holyhead. Beautifully decorated and furnished en suite bedrooms with all facilities to make your stay most enjoyable. Inviting spacious lounge with a log fire. The freshly cooked breakfasts are served in the cosy diningroom with separate tables. Games room. Interesting historic farmstead and walks on a 550 acre beef, sheep and arable farm. Attractive garden with a gazebo to relax in. Non-smoking establishment. Open all year. Bed and Breakfast £26. **WTB** ★★★★ *FARM, FARM HOLIDAY GUIDE DIPLOMA,* **WTB** *RURAL TOURISM AWARD, FARMSTAY UK MEMBER.*
e-mail: drws.ycoed@virgin.net   website: www.SmoothHound.co.uk/hotels/drwsycoed.html

BALA

Mrs C. A. Morris, Tai'r Felin Farm, Frongoch, Bala LL23 7NS (01678 520763). Working farm. Tai'r Felin Farm is a working farm, situated three miles north of Bala (A4212 and B4501). Double and twin bedrooms available with beverage tray and clock radio. Beamed lounge with colour TV and central heating. Excellent base for touring Snowdonia National Park, watersports, walking, fishing, etc. National White Water Centre is nearby. Hearty breakfast. Recommended for excellent cooking and friendly atmosphere. Relax and enjoy a homely welcome. Bed and Breakfast from £20. Walkers and cyclists welcome. Car essential. Reductions for longer stays. **WTB** ★★ *FARM.*

CRICCIETH

Mrs Parker, Seaspray, 4 Marine Terrace, Criccieth LL52 0EF (01766 522373). Seaspray is a large non-smoking Victorian terrace house, situated on the sea front, west side of Criccieth Castle on the Lleyn Peninsula. Some rooms are en suite, others have private facilities, affording sea views across Cardigan Bay. Evening meals are available on request at breakfast, vegetarian meals an option. Pets are welcome. Criccieth is only a short distance away from the Snowdonia National Park, which boasts some of the most beautiful and spectacular scenery in the country. Ample facilities are available for golfers, sailors, fishermen and ramblers. **WTB** ★★★ *B&B.*
website: www.seasprayguesthouse.co.uk

DOLGELLAU

Mr and Mrs J. S. Bamford, Ivy House, Finsbury Square, Dolgellau LL40 1RF (01341 422535; Fax: 01341 422689). A country town guesthouse offering a welcoming atmosphere and good homemade food. Guest accommodation consists of six double rooms, four with en suite toilet facilities, all with colour TV, tea/coffee making facilities and hair dryer. The diningroom, which is licensed, has a choice of menu, including vegetarian dishes. The lounge has tourist information literature and there are maps available to borrow. Dolgellau is an ideal touring, walking and mountain biking region in the southern area of the Snowdonia National Park. Bed and Breakfast from £20, en suite from £26. **WTB** ★★ *GUEST HOUSE,* **AA** ◆◆◆
e-mail: marg.bamford@btconnect.com
website: www.ukworld.net/ivyhouse

Terms quoted in this publication may be subject to increase if rises in costs necessitate

MAENTWROG

Belinda Wain, Bryn Maen, Maentwrog LL41 4HN (01766 590417). Upon your arrival, you will be warmly greeted with a cup of tea in the guest lounge which overlooks the Vale of Maentwrog. In an Area of Outstanding Natural Beauty, Maentwrog offers excellent walking, mountain climbing, cycling, beaches, castles, mountain railways and many other tourist attractions. Luxurious rooms with king-size beds, en suite and own bathrooom facilities (with bath), television, hairdryers, tea/coffee making facilities, ironing on request, drying, and secure storage for bikes. Vegetarians welcome. Aromatherapy, Therapeutic Massage, Shiatsu and Reiki treatments available. **website: www.brynmaen.com**

PWLLHELI

Marine View, The Promenade, South Beach, Pwllheli LL53 5AL (01758 612758). Situated in a quiet, sunny position on the sea front commanding an excellent view of Cardigan Bay and the Cambrian mountain range, centrally situated for touring with Snowdonia National Park nearby. Accommodation comprises ground floor double room with shower; two doubles on the first floor; toilet and bathroom. One mile of sandy beach, ideal for bathing and wind surfing. Golf, tennis, fishing and marina for boating not far from house. Ideal for a quiet relaxing holiday. Free parking. Bed and Breakfast £25 per night.

WALES

TALYLLYN

Gwesty Minffordd Hotel, Talyllyn LL36 9AJ (01654 761665; Fax: 01654 761517). Small 17th century Drovers' Inn at the base of Cader Idris (2697ft), ideal as a centre for touring. Enjoy a Minffordd dinner, cooked on an Aga using local Welsh produce, organic vegetables, Welsh flavouring. Residential and restaurant licence. Seven bedrooms all en suite, two on the ground floor; non-smoking. Pets welcome; no children under 12. Dolgellau six miles, Machynlleth eight. **WTB ★★★** *HOTEL*, **AA ★★**, *FOUNDER MEMBER TASTE OF WALES, GOOD FOOD GUIDE 2000.*
e-mail: hotel@minffordd.com
website: www.minffordd.com

A useful index of towns and counties appears at the back of this book on pages 417-421. Refer also to Contents Pages 2 and 3.

NORTH WALES

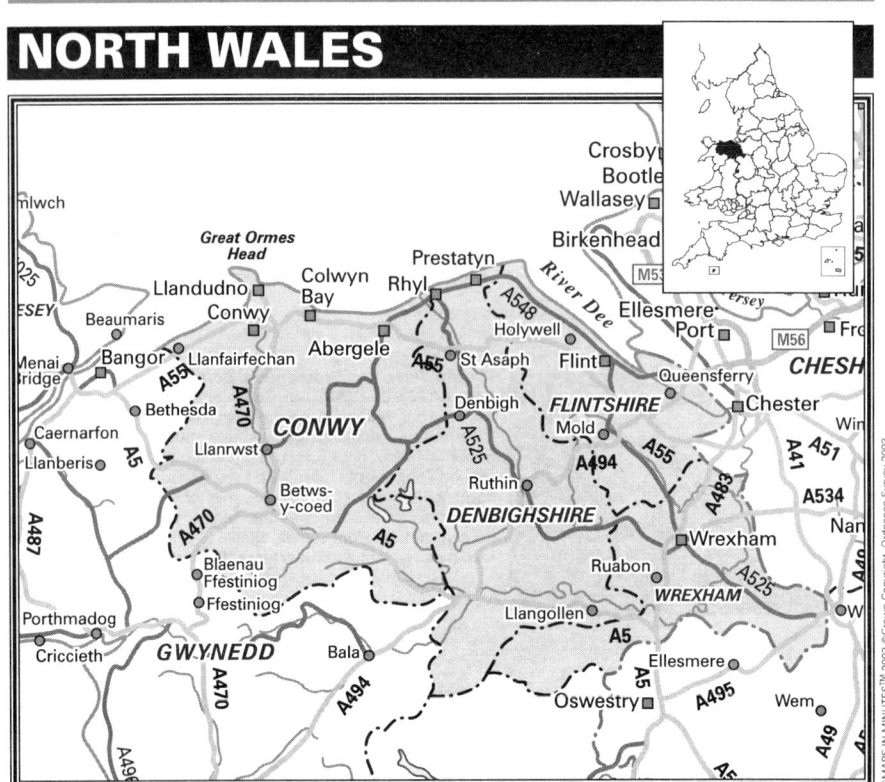

BETWS-Y-COED

Mark and Joan Edwards, Bryn Bella Guest House, Llanrwst Road, Betws-y-Coed LL24 0HD (Tel & Fax: 01690 710627). Bryn Bella is a small but select Victorian guest house enjoying an elevated position overlooking the beautiful village of Betws-y-Coed and the surrounding mountains of the Snowdonia National Park. All rooms are beautifully furnished and have en suite shower rooms. All rooms have colour TV and tea/coffee making facilities. The house enjoys glorious views of the village and surrounding mountains and there is ample private parking. Garaging for motorcycles and mountain bikes is also available. If travelling by train or bus there is a free pick-up service from the local station. Non-smoking throughout. Bed and Breakfast from £22 per person. Open all year. Discount on seven days. On line booking. **WTB ★★★★** *GUEST HOUSE,* **AA ◆◆◆◆**
website: www.bryn-bella.co.uk

e-mail: brynbella@clara.net

BETWS-Y-COED

e-mail: welcome@broncelyn.co.uk

Jim and Lilian Boughton, Bron Celyn Guest House, Lôn Muriau, Llanrwst Road, Betws-y-Coed LL24 0HD (01690 710333; Fax: 01690 710111). A warm welcome awaits you at this delightful guest house overlooking the Gwydyr Forest and Llugwy/Conwy Valleys and village of Betws-y-Coed in Snowdonia National Park. Ideal centre for touring, walking, climbing, fishing and golf. Also excellent overnight stop en route for Holyhead ferries. Easy walk into village and close to Conwy/Swallow Falls and Fairy Glen. Most rooms en suite, all with colour TV and beverage makers. Lounge. Full central heating. Garden. Car park. Open all year. Full hearty breakfast, packed meals, evening meals - special diets catered for. Bed and Breakfast from £22 to £30, reduced rates for children under 12 years. Special out of season breaks. **WTB ★★★** *GUEST HOUSE.*
website: www.broncelyn.co.uk

BETWS-Y-COED

Mrs Florence Jones, Maes Gwyn Farm, Pentrefoelas, Betws-y-Coed LL24 0LR (01690 770668). Maes Gwyn is a mixed farm of 90-97 hectares, situated in lovely quiet countryside, about one mile from the A5, six miles from the famous Betws-y-Coed. The sea and Snowdonia Mountains about 20 miles. Very good centre for touring North Wales, many well-known places of interest. House dates back to 1665. It has one double and one family bedrooms with washbasins and tea/coffee making facilities; bathroom with shower, toilet; lounge with colour TV and diningroom. Children and Senior Citizens are welcome at reduced rates and pets are permitted. Car essential, ample parking provided. Good home cooking. Six miles to bus/railway terminal. Open May/November for Bed and Breakfast from £20. SAE, please, for details.
e-mail: Florence.Jones1@btinternet.com

BETWS-Y-COED

Summer Hill Non-Smokers' Guest House, Coedcynhelier Road, Betws-y-Coed LL24 0BL (01690 710306). Especially for the non-smoker, Summer Hill is delightfully situated in a quiet, sunny location overlooking the River Llugwy and Fir Tree Island; 150 yards from main road, shops and restaurants. Seven comfortable bedrooms (four en suite), tea/coffee making facilities. Residents' lounge with colour TV. Ideal for walkers. Flasks filled. Vegetarians, special diets catered for. Private car parking. Betws-y-Coed is the gateway to Snowdonia, with spectacular mountains, forests and rivers. Golf, fishing, gardens, castles all accessible. Bed and Breakfast from £18. **WTB ★★** *GUEST HOUSE.*

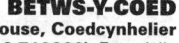

BETWS-Y-COED

Mrs E.A. Jones, Pant Glas, Padoc, Pentrefoelas Road, Betws-y-Coed LL24 0PG (01690 770248). Peaceful and quiet, but with a friendly atmosphere, this beef and sheep farm of 181 acres, with scenic views, is situated five miles from Betws-y-Coed. Ideal for touring, within easy reach of Snowdon, Bodnant Gardens, Caernarvon Castle, Llandudno, Black Rock Sands, Ffestiniog Railway, Llechwedd Slate Mines, Swallow and Conwy Falls and woollen mills. Accommodation comprises two double and one twin bedrooms, all with washbasins and tea/coffee making facilities; bath and shower, two toilets. Use of colour TV lounge. Sorry no pets. Car essential, parking for three/four cars. Bed and Breakfast from £18. Open Easter to November.

See also Colour Display Advertisement

BETWS-Y-COED

Brian and Enid Youe, Fairy Glen Hotel, Beaver Bridge, Betws-y-Coed LL24 0SH (01690 710269). Fairy Glen Hotel offers you a warm and friendly welcome, comfortable accommodation and excellent home-cooked food, in a relaxed and convivial atmosphere. All our rooms are well equipped with central heating, colour TV, alarm clock-radio, hairdryer and tea/ coffee making facilities. We have a TV lounge, and cosy licensed bar for our residents to relax in. Our private car park is for guests only. Evening meals available from £14.50 per person. Bed and Breakfast from £23 per person per night. **WTB ★★** *HOTEL*, **AA ★★**
e-mail: hotelfairyglen@amserve.com
website: www.fairyglenhotel.co.uk

CHESTER (near)

Mrs Christine Whale, Brookside House, Brookside Lane, Northop Hall, Mold CH7 6HN (01244 821146). Relax and enjoy the hospitality of our recently refurbished 18th century Welsh stone cottage. The home-from-home accommodation offers a double, twin or family room, en suite upon request. All rooms have colour TV and tea-making facilities. Within a short walk the village has an excellent restaurant and two pubs (one of which serves bar meals). Suitable for touring North Wales and Chester or just a short break away from it all. Bed and Breakfast from £32 per night single, £47 per night double. **WTB ★★★** *B&B*.
e-mail: christine@brooksidehouse.fsnet.co.uk
website: www.brooksidehouse.fsnet.co.uk/

COLWYN BAY

Lyndale Hotel and Restaurant, Abergele Road, Colwyn Bay LL29 9AB (01492 515429). Centrally situated near Old Colwyn Village, the Lyndale, with sea views, is in an ideal location. All North Wales attractions, including Snowdonia National Park Anglesey, Caernarfon, Conwy, LLandudno and Colwyn Bay, are within easy reach. All bedrooms with full en suite facilities, colour TV, in-house video, radio, telephones, tea/coffee making facilities and central heating, offering a high standard of comfort. The restaurant has an excellent reputation for high quality cuisine. Fully licensed and open all year. Private car park. Bed and Breakfast from £29 per person. **AA ★★, RAC ★★**

WALES

CONWY

Glan Heulog Guest House, Llanrwst Road, Conwy LL32 8LT (01492 593845). Spacious Victorian house, tastefully decorated. With off-road parking. Short walk from historic castle and town walls of Conwy. Ideally situated for touring Snowdonia and North Wales with its many attractions. We have a selection of twin, double and family rooms with en suite facilities, TV and tea/coffee making facilities. There is a large garden with seating to enjoy the far-reaching views. Children welcome. Pets by arrangement. Vegetarians catered for. Bed and Breakfast from £20–£26 per person per night. **WTB ★★★** *GUEST HOUSE*, **AA ◆◆◆**

e-mail: glanheulog@no1guesthouse.freeserve.co.uk
website: www.walesbandb.com

See also Colour Display Advertisement

CONWY

Kate Jones, The Lodge, Tal-y-Bont, Conwy LL32 8YX (01492 660766; Fax: 01492 660534; Freephone: 0800 9176593). Nestling in the lovely rolling hills of the beautiful Conwy Valley, our family-run, 14-bedroomed hotel has all the ingredients for a wonderful holiday. Enjoy peace and quiet, superb food, and attention from our friendly and efficient staff. Our lovely en suite bedrooms have that extra touch to make you feel at home. All major attractions are within easy reach, including Bodnant Gardens. Large private car park; extensive established grounds. Children and pets welcome. Restaurant meals, non-smoking areas. Conwy six miles. **WTB ★★★** *HOTEL*, **AA ★★**
website: www.lodgehotel.co.uk

CONWY

Park Hill Hotel/Gwesty Bryn Parc, Llanrwst Road, Betws-y-Coed, Conwy LL24 0HD (Tel & Fax: 01690 710540). OUR HOTEL IS YOUR CASTLE. Family-run country house hotel. Ideally situated in Snowdonia National Park. Breathtaking views of Conwy/Llugwy Valleys. Renowned for excellent service, cuisine and its teddy bear collection. Indoor heated swimming pool with sauna free and exclusively for our guests. Secluded free car park. Golf course and village within six minutes' walking distance. Walkers welcome; guided walks on request. Free shuttle service to nearest railway stations. All our rooms with en suite bathroom facilities, coffee/tea tray, CTV etc. Full cooked English Breakfast. Multilingual staff. Bed and Breakfast from £27.50 per person per night. **WTB ★★★** *HOTEL*, **AA/RAC ★★**. *SPECIAL HOSPITALITY AWARD. ASHLEY COURTENAY AND WHICH? RECOMMENDED.*
e-mail: welcome@park-hill-hotel.co.uk   website: www.park-hill-hotel.co.uk

CONWY

Mrs Sylvia Baxter, Glyn Uchaf, Conwy Old Road, Dwygyfyichi, Penmaenmawr, Conwy LL34 6YS (Tel & Fax: 01492 623737). Enjoy a quiet, peaceful holiday at this old mill house set in 11 acres of National Parkland in beautiful mountainous countryside. Ideal touring centre for Snowdonia. Accommodation comprises three bedrooms, all en suite and having lovely views. Lounge with colour TV; diningroom. Excellent cuisine with varied menus and home produce. Tea/coffee making facilities, and colour TV in bedrooms. Children welcome. Two-and-a-half miles to Conwy, five to Llandudno and Colwyn Bay; three minutes' walk to village. Pony trekking, golf and fishing locally. Ample parking. Guests have access to house at all times. Bed and Breakfast from £20. Reductions for children under 12. Highly recommended. SAE or phone please. **WTB ★★★** *COUNTRY HOUSE*.

WALES

CORWEN

Bob and Kit Buckland, Corwen Court Private Hotel, London Road, Corwen LL21 0DP (01490 412854). Situated on the main A5, this converted old police station and courthouse has six prisoners' cells turned into single bedrooms. Hot and cold in each, with a bathroom to service three on the first floor and a shower room for three on the ground floor. All double bedrooms have bathrooms en suite. The dining room in the old courthouse is where the local magistrates presided, and the comfortable lounge spreads over the rest of the court. Central heating throughout and colour TV in the lounge. Fire Certificate. Bed and Breakfast from £17; Evening Meal £9. Children and pets welcome. Convenient base for touring North Wales.

LLANDUDNO

Roger and Merril Pitblado, Chilterns, 19 Deganwy Avenue, Llandudno LL30 2YB (01492 875457). Chilterns is a guest house for non-smokers. It has full central heating and is near the Great Orme, promenade, beach and shops. Our forecourt provides invaluable parking in this busy seaside town. This family-run guest house has just five trading bedrooms - double, family and twin rooms with en suite facilities, colour television, beverage tray and some with king-size bed. Our basic tariff is £20 per person per night, with reductions for stays of three or more nights. Children stay at a reduced rate. We look forward to welcoming you to our home. **WTB ★★★** *GUEST HOUSE.*
e-mail: info@chilternsguesthouse.co.uk
website: www.chilternsguesthouse.co.uk

LLANDUDNO

Mrs Ruth Hodkinson, Cranleigh, Great Orme's Road, West Shore, Llandudno LL30 2AR (01492 877688). A comfortable, late Victorian private residence and family home situated on the quieter West Shore of Llandudno. Only yards from beach and magnificent Great Orme Mountain. Parking: no problem. Town centre is a short pleasant walk away. Many places of interest in surrounding area, and opportunities for sports and recreational activities. Excellent home cooked food. Two en suite rooms with bath and wc, both with views of sea and mountains. Conforms to high standards of S.I. 1991/474. Most highly recommended. Bed and Breakfast £20 per person.

LLANGOLLEN

Mrs T. Bryant, Bryant Rose, 31 Regent Street, Llangollen LL20 8HN (01978 860389). Comfortable Bed and Breakfast accommodation in this centrally heated Guest House in the North Wales Borderlands. Two bedrooms, both en suite, with tea/coffee making facilities and TV. Special diets catered for. Non-smoking. Off-street parking. B&B from £19pppn. Short Breaks available. Open March to December.
website: www.borderlands.co.uk/bryant-rose.main.htm

RHOS-ON-SEA

Sunnydowns Hotel, Rhos-on-Sea, Colwyn Bay, Conwy LL28 4NU (01492 544256; Fax: 01492 543223). A three star hotel, situated close to the beach and shops, with car park, bar, games room, sauna, restaurant and TV lounge. All rooms en suite with remote-control TV, video and satellite channels, radio, tea/coffee facilities, hairdryer, mini-bar/refrigerator, safe and telephone. The towns of Llandudno, Colwyn Bay and Conwy are only five minutes' drive away and it is just ten minutes to the mountains and castles of Snowdonia. Dogs welcome. **WTB ★★★** *HOTEL.*
e-mail: sunnydowns-hotel@tinyworld.co.uk
website: www.hotelnorthwales.co.uk

The FHG Directory of Website Addresses on pages 387-415 is a useful quick reference guide for holiday accommodation with e-mail and/or website details

RHOS-ON-SEA
W.D. & M. Pryce, "Sunnyside", 146 Dinerth Road, Rhos-on-Sea LL28 4YF (01492 544048). A warm welcome awaits you in our home, which is situated between Llandudno and Colwyn Bay. Central for the mountains, sea, shops and also golf course, bowling and cricket at Rhos-on-Sea, where tournaments are held. We are a non-smoking establishment with one double and one twin bedroom. A good breakfast starts off your day. Children welcome. Bed and Breakfast from £18 per person, £20 single. **WTB ★★** *B&B.*

RHYL
Barratts Restaurant, Ty'n Rhyl, 167 Vale Road, Rhyl LL18 2PH (Tel & Fax: 01745 344138; Mobile: 07730 954994). This delightful 16th century house lies in a secluded location surrounded by attractive gardens. It is really a restaurant with rooms and the quality of food reflects the skill of the owner/chef. Public areas are smartly furnished and include a panelled lounge and separate bar. The three en suite bedrooms are comfortable and have many extra facilities. No smoking in dining room or in bedrooms. Credit cards accepted. Parking. **AA ◆◆◆◆** **e-mail: ebarratt5@freeuk.com**

TREFRIW
Mrs B. Cole, Glandwr, Trefriw, Near Llanrwst LL27 0JP (01492 640431). Large country house on the outskirts of Trefriw Village overlooking the Conwy River and its Valley, with beautiful views towards the Clwydian Hills. Good touring area; Llanrwst, Betws-y-Coed and Swallow Falls five miles away. Fishing, walking, golfing and pony trekking all close by. Comfortable rooms, lounge with TV, dining room. Good home cooking using local produce whenever possible. Parking. Bed and Breakfast from £22.50.

WALES

CARMARTHENSHIRE

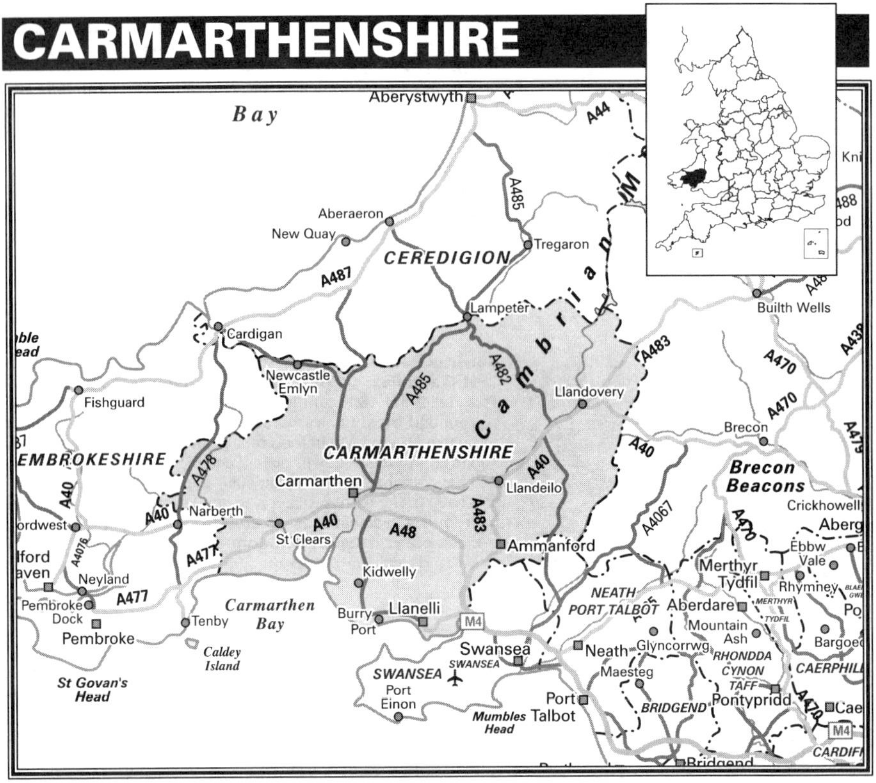

WALES

CARMARTHEN

Mrs Margaret Thomas, Plas Farm, Llangynog, Carmarthen SA33 5DB (Tel & Fax: 01267 211492). Working farm.
"Welcome Host". Situated six miles west of Carmarthen town along the A40 towards St Clears. Quiet location, ideal touring base. Working farm run by the Thomas family for the past 100 years. Very spacious, comfortable farmhouse. All rooms en suite, with tea/coffee making facilities, colour TV and full central heating. TV lounge. Evening meals available at local country inn nearby. Good golf course minutes away. Plas Farm is en route to Fishguard and Pembroke Ferries. Ample safe parking. Bed and Breakfast from £20 per person. Children under 16 years sharing family room half price. A warm welcome awaits. **WTB ★★★** *FARM.*
website: www.ukworld.net/plasfarm

LLANDEILO

Pant Y Bas Bed and Breakfast, Pentrefelin, Llandeilo SA19 6SD (01558 822809). Separate luxury ground floor units set within extensive landscaped grounds situated on the banks of the Mydffi River in beautiful countryside. All rooms en suite, colour television, tea/coffee making facilities, hairdryer. Breakfast served in our delightful 16th century home. All year round warmth and comfort with your own key. Within walking distance of friendly country pub offering bar meals or restaurant cuisine. Hometown to three great gardens – Aberglassny, National Botanical Gardens and Dynevor, and situated amongst the fabulous Brecon Beacons. Ample parking. Reductions for three nights or more. Non-smoking. Bed and Breakfast from £22.50 pppn. **WTB ★★★** *B&B.*
website: www.southwestwalesbandb.co.uk

LLANELLI

Mrs Elizabeth Hedges, Bryngwenyn Farm, Pontyberem, Llanelli SA15 5NG (01269 843990; mobile: 07786 985196; Fax: 01269 843990). Situated in peaceful countryside with panoramic views across the Gwendraeth Valley, Bryngwenyn Farm offers self-catering or B&B accommodation. Just five miles from the motorway and ideally situated for the many local attractions, castles, gardens and the beautiful beaches of Gower. Farmhouse accommodation comprises an en suite double bedroom, fully-equipped with tea/coffee making facilities, hairdryer and colour TV. Meals are taken in the dining room; sitting room for guests' use. Terms from £40 per night double, £25 single occupancy. Evening meals by prior arrangement £12.50. We can also accommodate up to five in each of our cottages with meals taken in the farmhouse.

e-mail: Elizabeth.Hedges@btinternet.com   **website: www.bryngwenynfarm.co.uk**

CEREDIGION

ABERYSTWYTH

Marine Hotel, The Promenade, Marine Terrace, Aberystwyth SY23 2BX (Freephone: 0800 0190020; Tel: 01970 612444; Fax: 01970 617435). Large seafront hotel with a lift to all floors. Bars, restaurant, bistro and lounges all on ground level. This family-run hotel is highly recommended for its warm, friendly atmosphere, good home cooking, and attention to guests' comfort. The 42 en suite refurbished bedrooms have TV and tea/coffee making facilities, and most have magnificent views of Cardigan Bay. Complimentary use of leisure suite with sauna, steam room, jacuzzi and gym. The hotel has facilities for disabled guests. Bargain breaks and mini-holidays offer excellent value. Golf parties welcome. **WTB ★★** *HOTEL.*
e-mail: marinehotel1@btconnect.com
website: www.marinehotelaberystwyth.co.uk

Vale of Rheidol Railway • *Aberystwyth, Cardiganshire* • *01970 625819*
An unforgettable journey by narrow gauge steam train , climbing over 600 feet in 12 miles from Aberystwyth to Devil's Bridge. There are many sharp turns and steep gradients, and the journey affords superb views of the valley.

FHG PUBLICATIONS publish a large range of well-known accommodation guides. We will be happy to send you details or you can use the order form at the back of this book.

PEMBROKESHIRE

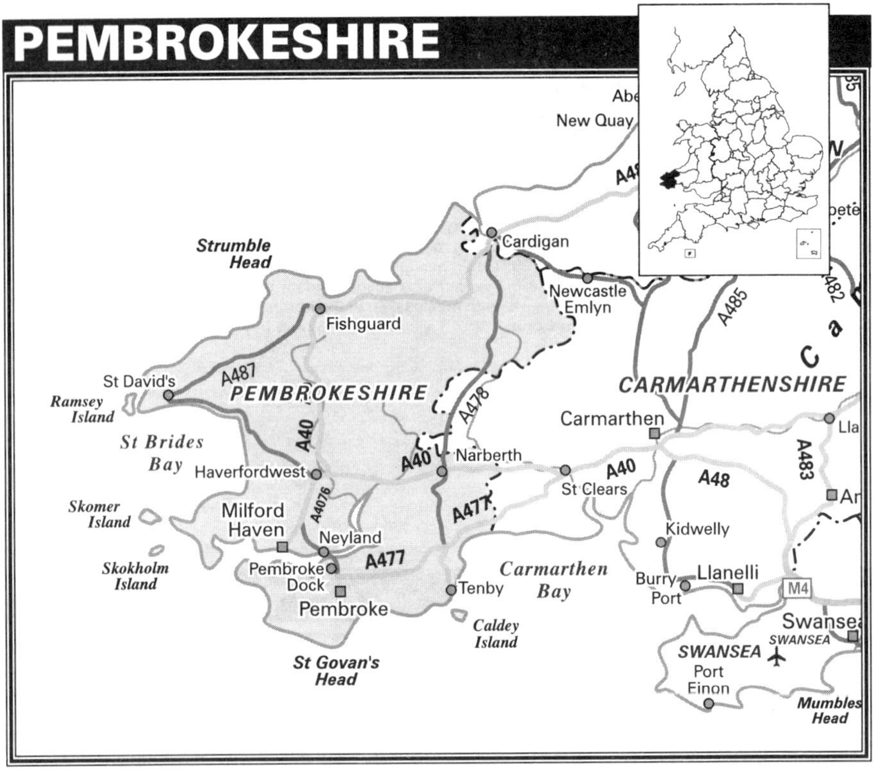

Map of Pembrokeshire showing Strumble Head, Fishguard, St David's, Ramsey Island, St Brides Bay, Skomer Island, Skokholm Island, Milford Haven, Neyland, Pembroke Dock, Pembroke, St Govan's Head, Haverfordwest, Narberth, St Clears, Tenby, Caldey Island, Carmarthen, Kidwelly, Llanelli, Swansea, Mumbles Head, Cardigan, Newcastle Emlyn, New Quay. Roads A487, A40, A4076, A477, A478, A485, A48, A483, M4. CARMARTHENSHIRE, Carmarthen Bay, SWANSEA, Port Einon. WALES.

©MAPS IN M NUTES™ 2003 ©Crown Copyright, Ordnance Survey 2003

See also Colour Display Advertisement

AMROTH

East Llanteg Farmhouse B&B, Near Amroth SA67 8QA (01834 831336). Only two miles from the coast, the comfortable farmhouse is ideally located for exploring Pembrokeshire's renowned beaches and also the "Garden County" of Carmarthenshire. The resorts of Saundersfoot and Tenby are close at hand, and the seaside village of Amroth just minutes away. Irish Ferryport 20 minutes. The bedrooms are roomy and comfortably furnished, with private or en suite bathrooms. Two double, one family and one twin, all with colour TV; there is a comfortable private guests' lounge. Guests are assured of a warm welcome and traditional home cooking. £22-£25pppn; Evening Meals by request. No pets, no smoking. Ample safe parking. **WTB ★★** *B&B.*
e-mail: mail@eastllanteg.freeserve.co.uk
website: www.pembrokeshireholiday.co.uk

**FREE or REDUCED RATE entry to Holiday Visits and Attractions —
see our READERS' OFFER VOUCHERS on pages 63-90**

Twmpath GUEST HOUSE

TWMPATH GUEST HOUSE has a Tourist Board **THREE STAR** rating and a Welcome Host **GOLD** Award. It offers home comforts, with full facilities for families, elderly and disabled guests. Set in the heart of the Pembrokeshire countryside, ideal for cyclists and walkers. Luxury rooms with full en suite facilities and cuisine of a high standard, combined with a warm, friendly, family atmosphere. We will ensure that your visit to Pembrokeshire is a memorable one. Twmpath Guest House overlooks the picturesque Preseli Mountains, just 20 minutes away from Haverfordwest and Fishguard.

Tel: 01437 532990
Twmpath Guest House,
Maenclochog, Pembs SA66 7RL

See also Colour Advertisement

Helen and Chris welcome you to the Gumfreston Hotel, a fine Victorian house in a quiet residential street. There are 9 en suite bedrooms, all non-smoking, with tea/coffee facilities,

colour TV, radio and central heating. A tasty English breakfast will start your day, and an excellent menu of home-cooked dishes is available with varied starters, main courses and desserts. Vegetarian and children's meals also catered for. Smoking is permitted in the bar. Attended parking only 30 yards away.

GUMFRESTON HOTEL,
CULVER PARK, TENBY SA70 7ED
TEL/FAX: 01834 842871
e-mail: gumf@supanet.com

Tenby has four beautiful, safe, sandy beaches; other leisure activities include golf, bowling, tennis, horse riding, sailing, surfing, sea and river fishing, and walking. ★★

AA ♦♦♦ Guest Accommodation

See also Colour Advertisement

BROADHAVEN

Mrs F. Morgan, Albany Guest House, 27 Millmoor Way, Broadhaven, Haverfordwest SA62 3JJ (01437 781051; Fax: 01437 781050. Albany is a friendly, family-run Bed & Breakfast. Three en suite rooms, double, single or twin, all with tea/coffee making facilities, TV, central heating, and access at all times (some rooms have sea views). Parking. Two minutes from sandy beach of Broadhaven and leading to Little Haven. Within walking distance are shop/Post Office, cafe, pub/restaurant and Coastal Path. Windsurfing, swimming, diving and boat trips to Skomer and Grassholm bird islands (puffins, razorbills etc); seal pups in bays September/October. Coastal bus May to September. Nearby are St David's, Tenby, Oakwood etc and sandy beaches. **WTB ★★★** *GUEST HOUSE.*
e-mail: info@albanyguesthouse.fsnet.co.uk
website: www.albanyguesthouse.co.uk

Marine Life Centre • *St David's, Pembrokeshire* •*01437 721665*
All-weather attraction giving a unique insight into the undersea world. Simulation of underwater caves, shipwreck tank and touch tanks; gift shop, refreshments, play areas.

Pembroke Castle • *Pembroke, Pembrokeshire* • *01646 681510*
The birthplace of Henry VII, this is the oldest castle in West Wales, dating back to the 13th century, with a fine five-storey circular keep. Exhibitions, displays, videos and tableaux give a fascinating insight into history and heritage.

BROADHAVEN (near)

Sandra Davies, Barley Villa, Walwyns Castle, Near Broadhaven, Haverfordwest SA62 3EB (01437 781254). Our 20 acre smallholding with friendly horses offers peace, tranquillity and walks and overlooks Rosemoor Nature Reserve in Pembrokeshire's National Park. Our spacious house, furnished for the comfort of our guests, has three bedrooms, two of which are en suite, complete with hospitality trays; lounge/dining room with colour TV, coal fire and board games for restful evenings. We are centrally situated for visiting Pembokeshire's many sandy bays, famous bird islands, coastal paths and historic places. Many sport and leisure activities within easy travelling distance. We offer hearty breakfasts, packed lunches and special diets. Non-smoking establishment catering for adults and young persons over 14. Private car and boat parking. Bed and Breakfast from £23 to £27 en suite. Comfortable two-bedroomed caravan also available for hire. **WTB ★★★** *FARM.*
e-mail: sandra.barleyvilla@btinternet.com   website: **www.barleyvilla.co.uk**

CILGERRAN

Pam and Mike Bousfield, Wyndarra B&B, Cilgerran, Near Cardigan SA43 2RY (01239 621243). We are situated near the market town of Cardigan and close to the Welsh Wild Life Centre and the Pembrokeshire Coastal Path. In the village there are organised canoe trips on the River Tiefi, where one can see the very interesting Cilgerran Castle. There are a great many family attractions nearby. Wyndarra offers a twin room, private bathroom, family room en suite, sleeps four plus cot. Tea and coffee facilities in both rooms. Tariff: low season £18, high season £20. Children half price. **WTB ★★★** *B&B.*
e-mail: elvina.bousfield@tesco.net

VINE COTTAGE

SAUNDERSFOOT

David and Helen Trimmings, Vine Cottage, The Ridgeway, Saundersfoot SA69 9LA (01834 814422). Former farmhouse on outskirts of picturesque harbour village in the heart of Pembrokeshire National Park. Beaches, shops, restaurants within ten minute walk. A non-smoking establishment providing comfortable accommodation and a hearty breakfast in a relaxed and friendly atmosphere. All rooms en suite, centrally heated with alarm clock/radio, colour TV, hairdryer and hospitality tray. Children over six years welcome – half price when sharing with two adults. Pets welcome by arrangement. Private parking.
WTB ★★★ *GUEST HOUSE,* **AA ◆◆◆◆**
e-mail: enquiries@vinecottageguesthouse.co.uk
website: www.vinecottageguesthouse.co.uk

POWYS

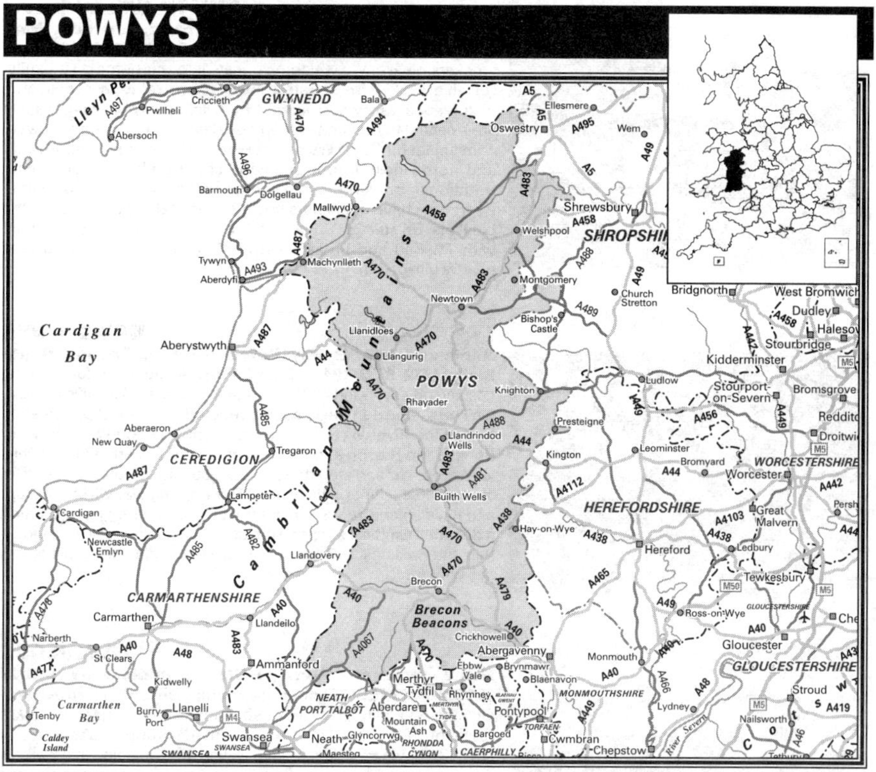

WALES

BRECON

Stephen and Melanie Dale, The Beacons Restaurant & Accommodation, 116 Bridge Street, Brecon LD3 8AH (Tel & Fax: 01874 623339). A recently restored Georgian house situated close to the river in the historic small market town of Brecon. Surrounded by magnificent scenery in the heart of the National Park. This 17th/18th century house is full of warmth and character, and offers a variety of individually styled, well equipped bedrooms including four-poster and king-size luxury period rooms. Elegant lounge, cosy cellar bar and a candlelit restaurant serving fine food and wines (five nights) in a relaxed and informal atmosphere. Private parking and secure bike store. **WTB ★★★** *GUEST HOUSE,* **AA/RAC ◆◆◆**
e-mail: beacons@brecon.co.uk
website: www.beacons.brecon.co.uk

BUILTH WELLS

Mrs N. Jones, Ty-Isaf Farm, Erwood, Builth Wells LD2 3SZ (01982 560607). Ty-Isaf is a mixed working farm in the Wye Valley, with cattle, sheep, ponies and plenty of dogs. All bedrooms have washbasin, tea/coffee making facilities and full central heating. It is situated just off the A470 near Erwood village, and is an ideal spot from which to tour Mid-Wales, being within easy reach of Elan Valley, the Black Mountains and Brecon Beacons, Llangorse Lake and Hay-on-Wye, famous for its bookshops, including what is claimed to be the largest second-hand bookshop in the world. Bed and Breakfast or Bed and Breakfast and Evening Meal with good home cooking. Bed and Breakfast from £18 per person.

BUILTH WELLS (near)

Mrs Margaret Davies, The Court Farm, Aberedw, Near Builth Wells LD2 3UP (Tel & Fax: 01982 560277). Non-smokers please. We welcome guests into our home on a family-run livestock farm situated away from traffic in a peaceful, picturesque valley surrounded by hills. Lovely walking, wildlife area, central to Hay-on-Wye, Brecon Beacons, Elan Valley and very convenient for Royal Welsh Showground. We offer comfort, care and homeliness in our spacious stone-built farmhouse with traditional cooking using home produce where possible. Bedrooms have adjustable heating, hospitality trays and electric blankets. En suite or private bathroom available. Guests' lounge with TV. Bed and Breakfast from £18. Good food available at nearby village inn.

HAY-ON-WYE

Annie and John McKay, Hafod-y-Garreg, Erwood, Builth Wells LD2 3TQ (01982 560400). A medieval farmhouse, nestling on a wooded hillside in a Site of Special Scientific Interest, well off the beaten track, above, reputedly, the most picturesque part of the River Wye. A short drive from Hay-on-Wye 'Town of Books', and Brecon and the Beacons National Park. Alternatively, leave your car and step through our gate into a walkers' paradise, steeped in ancient Celtic history. Drink spring water from the tap, and have an enormous breakfast with our free-range eggs. Enjoy a delicious candlelit supper with log fires in the massive inglenook. Bed and Breakfast £48 per double en suite, dinner available at £15 per person.

LLANIDLOES

Mrs Janet Evans, Dyffryn Glyn, Llanidloes SY18 6NE (01686 412129). Dyffryn is centrally situated in an Area of Outstanding Natural Beauty two miles from the friendly market town of Llanidloes, one mile from Clywedog Lake with its spectacular views where sailing, fishing, birdwatching and walking can be pursued. Ideal area for touring. Accommodation comprises one en suite room and one double and one twin-bedded room with washbasin and use of bathroom; both rooms have towels and tea making facilities. Visitors' own sitting room with TV, separate dining room. Ample parking. Bed and Breakfast from £20. **WTB ★★★** *B&B.*

LLANIDLOES

Jean Bailey, Glangwy, Llangurig, Llanidloes SY18 6RS (01686 440697). Local river stone (Wye) built house offering comfortable Bed and Breakfast accommodation in beautiful countryside. Traditional English breakfast served; all home cooked evening meals; special diets catered for, vegetarians included. Accommodation comprises two doubles (can be used as family rooms as single bed also in each) and one twin bedroom with washbasin, tea/coffee facilities and storage heater (all beds have electric underblanket); bathroom, separate shower room; diningroom (separate tables per party); lounge with colour TV. Pets welcome. Parking. Central for touring and local walks. Bed and Breakfast £14 per person; reductions for children under nine years. Ideal for birdwatching – 'Kite Country'.

Upper Genffordd Farm Guest House
Talgarth, Brecon LD3 0EN • Tel: 01874 711360
website: www.SmoothHound.co.uk/hotels/uppergenffordd.html

Selected 16th century farmhouse, suitable for disabled guests. Set in 200 acres in the Brecon Beacons National Park, Upper Genffordd Farm is an ideal base for exploring the Black Mountains, Wye Valley and the Brecon Beacons, an area of outstanding beauty, rich in historical and archaeological interest, with Roman camps and Norman castles. Picturesque mountain roads will lead you to reservoirs, the Gower coast with its lovely sandy beaches and Llangorse Lake – well known for all kinds of water sports. Livestock markets and open markets, leisure centres, **Please contact Mrs Prosser** pony trekking centres all within a few miles. The charming Guest House accommodation includes one double and one twin-bedded room, both with en suite facilities, tea/coffee making facilities, central heating, colour TV and hairdryer. The cosy lounge has a wealth of personal bric-a-brac, maps and paintings. Guests are made welcome with home-made cakes and tea on arrival. The local pub and restaurant is nearby and Hay-on-Wye, 'The Town of Books', is a short distance away. Bed & Breakfast from £20 to £25pp. AA ◆◆◆◆.

Awarded Plaque of Recommendation from the WTB • Nominated "Landlady of the Year" 1999 • Winner of FHG Diploma.

See also Colour Advertisement

MACHYNLLETH

Gwernstablau, Llanwrin, Machynlleth SY20 8QH (01650 511688). Gwernstablau is a tranquil 17th century farmhouse set in its own five acre grounds. It tastefully combines the old world charm of a wealth of beamed ceilings and open log fires with the convenience of modern central heating and en suite accommodation. Visitors can enjoy a leisurely wander around the gardens, feed the ducks or just sit and relax by the stream. Dinner can be enjoyed in the distinctive dining room with its galleried landing, crystal chandelier and antique furniture.
website: www.gwern-stablau.com

NEWTOWN

e-mail: info@greenfields-bb.co.uk

Mrs Vi Madeley, Greenfields, Kerry, Newtown SY16 4LH (01686 670596; Fax: 01686 670354). A warm welcome awaits you at Greenfields. All rooms are tastefully decorated and are spacious in size, each having panoramic views of the rolling Kerry hills. There is a good choice of breakfast menu and evening meals can be provided by prior arrangement; packed lunches are also available. Licensed for residents. Accommodation available in twin, double, family and single rooms, all en suite (twin rooms let as singles if required). Hostess tray and TV in all rooms. The diningroom has individual tables. A good place for stopping for one night, a short break or longer holiday. Excellent off-road parking. Bed and Breakfast from £20 to £22 per person; Evening Meal £4.50 to £10. Brochure available. **WTB ★★** *GUEST HOUSE.*
website: www.greenfields-bb.co.uk

WELSHPOOL

Mrs Joyce Cornes, Cwmllwynog, Llanfair, Caereinion, Welshpool SY21 0HF (Tel & Fax: 01938 810791). Built in the early 17th century, Cwmllwynog is a traditional long farmhouse of character on a working dairy farm. We have a spacious garden with a stream at the bottom and a lot of unusual plants. All bedrooms have colour TV and drink making facilities. Double room en suite, twin with washbasins and private bathroom. Delicious home-cooked meals cooked. We can help you with routes. Open January to November. Bed and Breakfast from £22, Evening Meal £12. **WTB ★★★★** *FARMHOUSE.*

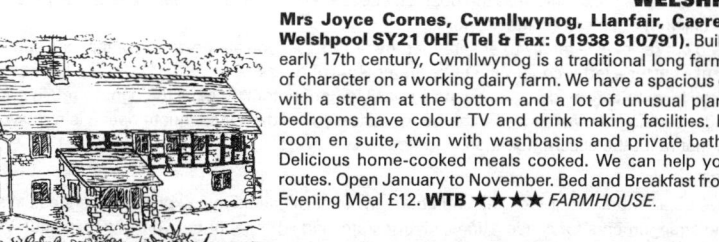

FREE or REDUCED RATE entry to Holiday Visits and Attractions – see our READERS' OFFER VOUCHERS on pages 63-90

WELSHPOOL

Mrs Jane Jones, Trefnant Hall, Berriew, Welshpool SY21 8AS (01686 640262). Trefnant Hall offers a warm welcome in a Grade II Listed farmhouse built in 1742. All rooms are comfortably furnished with tea/coffee making facilities, colour TV and are en suite. This sheep and beef farm is set in beautiful peaceful countryside away from the busy roads with superb views and gardens. Powis Castle and gardens are just two miles away with the market town of Welshpool close by. An ideal centre for exploring mid-Wales with the seaside less than an hour away. Bed and Breakfast from £21 per person. Self-catering property available. **WTB ★★★** *B&B*, **WTB ★★★★★** *SELF-CATERING.*

WELSHPOOL

Mrs Freda Emberton, Tynllwyn Farm, Welshpool SY21 9BW (01938 553175/553054). Working farm. A warm welcome is assured at Tynllwyn Farm, built 1861, which stands on a hillside with breathtaking views of the Long Mountain and Severn Valley. We are a working beef farm. Large comfortable lounge with open fires in winter. Also licensed bar. All bedrooms en suite with colour TV, tea/coffee facilities and central heating. All home cooking. Large parking area. Nearby are the lovely market town of Welshpool, Powis Castle, Welshpool and Llanfair Steam Railway, canal trips, also exciting quad trekking and mountain bike hire. Easy reach of the lakes and mountains of Mid Wales. Children welcome, pets by arrangement. Bed and Breakfast from £23 to £30. Two self-catering cottages available. **WTB ★★★** *FARM.*

WALES

•• *Some Useful Guidance for Guests and Hosts* ••

Every year literally thousands of holidays, short breaks and overnight stops are arranged through our guides, the vast majority without any problems at all. In a handful of cases, however, difficulties do arise about bookings, which often could have been prevented from the outset.

It is important to remember that when accommodation has been booked, both parties – guests and hosts – have entered into a form of contract. We hope that the following points will provide helpful guidance.

GUESTS:

• When enquiring about accommodation, be as precise as possible. Give exact dates, numbers in your party and the ages of any children.

• State the number and type of rooms wanted and also what catering you require – bed and breakfast, full board etc. Make sure that the position about evening meals is clear – and about pets, reductions for children or any other special points.

• Read our reviews carefully to ensure that the proprietors you are going to contact can supply what you want. Ask for a letter confirming all arrangements, if possible.

• If you have to cancel, do so as soon as possible. Proprietors do have the right to retain deposits and under certain circumstances to charge for cancelled holidays if adequate notice is not given and they cannot re-let the accommodation.

HOSTS:

• Give details about your facilities and about any special conditions. Explain your deposit system clearly and arrangements for cancellations, charges etc. and whether or not your terms include VAT.

• If for any reason you are unable to fulfil an agreed booking without adequate notice, you may be under an obligation to arrange suitable alternative accommodation or to make some form of compensation.

While every effort is made to ensure accuracy, we regret that FHG Publications cannot accept responsibility for errors, omissions or misrepresentations in our entries or any consequences thereof. Prices in particular should be checked because we go to press early. We will follow up complaints but cannot act as arbiters or agents for either party.

SOUTH WALES

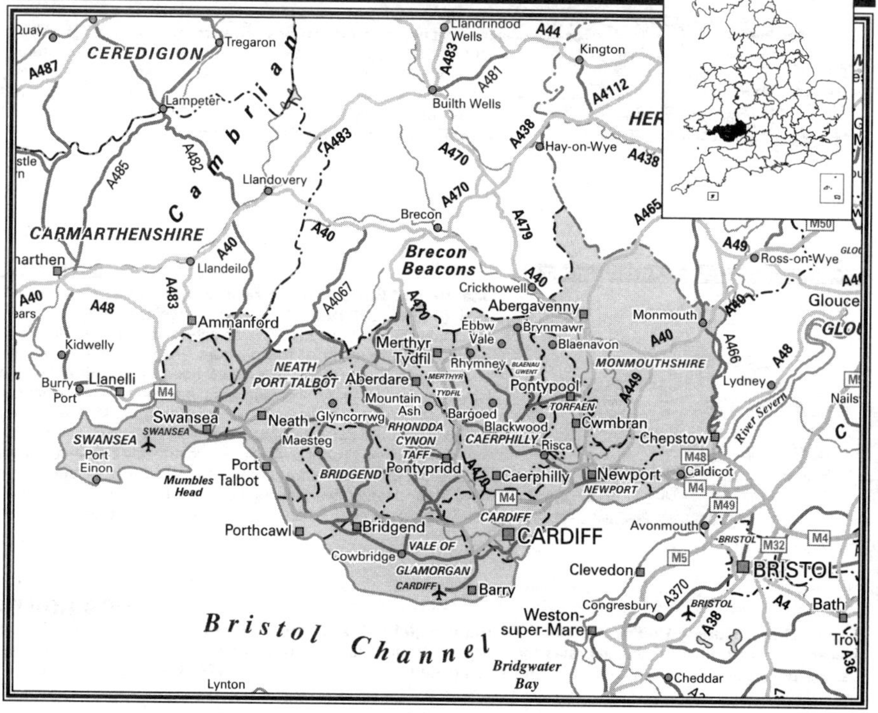

Map showing South Wales including Cardiff, Swansea, Newport, the Brecon Beacons and surrounding areas, with an inset map of England and Wales.

CARDIFF

Mrs Sarah Nicholls, Preste Gaarden Hotel, 181 Cathedral Road, Cardiff CF11 9PN (029 2022 8607; Fax: 029 2037 4805). This spacious Victorian family home offers olde worlde charm with modern amenities, including en suite facilities in most rooms. You will immediately feel relaxed by the warm welcome given by Sarah. Situated in the heart of the City, close to the Castle, museums, shops and an international array of restaurants and only 100 yards from Sophia Gardens offering walking, fishing and horse riding. Bed and Breakfast from £22 to £35 per person includes tea/coffee and biscuits in your room. Well established and independently recommended. **WTB ★★** *HOTEL, WELCOME HOST GOLD.*
e-mail: stay@cosycardiffhotel.co.uk
website: www.cosycardiffhotel.co.uk

COWBRIDGE (near)

Mrs Sue Beer, Plas Llanmihangel, Llanmihangel, Near Cowbridge CF71 7LQ (01446 774610). Plas Llanmihangel is the finest medieval Grade 1 Listed manor house in the beautiful Vale of Glamorgan. We offer a genuine warmth of welcome, delightful accommodation, first class food and service in our wonderful home. The baronial hall, great log fires, the ancient tower and acres of beautiful historic gardens intrigue all who stay in this fascinating house. Its long history and continuous occupation have created a spectacular building in romantic surroundings unchanged since the 16th century. A great opportunity to experience the ambience and charm of a past age. Three double rooms. Bed and Breakfast from £28. High quality home cooked evening meal on request. **WTB ★★★** *GUEST HOUSE, CONSUMER ASSOCIATION'S 'WHICH?' GOOD BED & BREAKFAST GUIDE.*
e-mail: plasllanmihangel@ukonline.co.uk

WALES

GOWER

Mrs Anne Main, Tallizmand, Llanmadoc, Gower SA13 1DE (01792 386373). Located near the splendid Gower coastline and surrounded by beautiful countryside. Miles of unspoilt beaches, pine woods and salt marshes. Ideal for walking, surfing, birdwatching and wild flowers. Tallizmand has tastefully furnished en suite bedrooms with tea/coffee making facilities; TV lounge. Home cooking, packed lunches, vegetarians catered for. Ample parking. Bed and Breakfast from £22.50.
e-mail: davidgeraldmain@aol.com

See also Colour Display Advertisement

GOWER PENINSULA

Joanne and Chris Allder, Heathfield, Llethryd, Gower SA2 7LH (01792 390198). All guests are welcomed by a friendly atmosphere. Our house is set in an acre of mature garden with a heated swimming pool that visitors are welcome to use by arrangement. Llethryd village is a quiet hamlet on the B4271 on the Gower Peninsula, an Area of Outstanding Natural Beauty. From our house there are lovely tranquil woodland walks and sandy beaches. We are close to restaurants serving locally caught fish and home grown produce. We are approximately 20 minutes from Swansea's extensive shopping centre and theatres. All rooms have TV and tea/coffee making facilities. Children welcome. Non-smokers preferred. Bed and Breakfast from £22.50 per person.

MONMOUTH

Tresco Guest House, Redbrook, Near Monmouth (01600 712325). Situated in the Wye Valley. Snacks available. Packed lunches. Special rates for children. Ground floor bedrooms have views of flower gardens. Fishing, pony trekking, walking and canoeing. Parking. Bed and Breakfast £17.50. **WTB ★★★** *GUEST HOUSE.*

MONMOUTH

Rosemary and Derek Ringer, Church Farm Guest House, Mitchel Troy, Monmouth NP25 4HZ (01600 712176) A spacious and homely 16th century, Grade II Listed, former farmhouse with oak beams and inglenook fireplaces, set in large attractive garden with stream. An excellent base for visiting the Wye Valley, Forest of Dean and Black Mountains. All bedrooms have washbasin, tea/coffee making facilities and central heating; most are en suite. Own car park. Terrace, barbecue. Colour TV. Non-smoking. Bed and Breakfast from £22 to £26 per person, Evening Meals by arrangement. **WTB ★★** *GUEST HOUSE,* **AA ◆◆◆**

MONMOUTH

Mrs Rosemary Townsend, Lugano, Llandogo, Monmouth NP25 4TL (01594 530496; Fax: 01594 530956). Lugano is a modern bungalow standing in its own beautiful gardens just off the A466 between Monmouth and Chepstow. Accommodation comprises one family/twin room and two double rooms (one en suite), all the non-smoking bedrooms tastefully furnished and decorated, with washbasins, TV and tea/coffee making facilities. There is a large collection of books and tourist literature which guests are welcome to borrow. The conservation village of Lugano is in the heart of the Wye Valley, an Area of Outstanding Natural Beauty, within easy reach of the Forest of Dean, Tintern Abbey and the Brecon Beacons. B&B from £21 per person per night. Brochure available. **WTB ★★★** *B&B.*
e-mail: TOWNSEND@lugano.freeserve.co.uk

RAGLAN (MONMOUTH)
Mrs J.E. Thom, The Grange, Penrhos, Raglan NP15 2LQ (01600 780202). Organic mixed farm (115 acres) in open peaceful countryside with breathtaking views, but not remote. (Monmouth six miles, Abergavenny nine miles). The Rolls of Monmouth golf course is two miles. Good for touring and walking - Offa's Dyke path runs through. We welcome families, dogs and horses. We have stables and menage. Large en suite rooms and superb home cooked evening meals if required. Bed and Breakfast from £22 per person. Self-catering property also available to suit two/three persons. Please telephone for further details. Come and share this beautiful place. **WTB ★★★** *FARMHOUSE.*

ST BRIDES WENTLOOG (near Newport)
Mrs C.A. Bushell, Chapel Guest House, Church Road, St Brides Wentloog, Near Newport NP10 8SN (01633 681018; Fax: 01633 681431) Comfortable accommodation in a converted chapel situated in a village between Newport/Cardiff, near Tredegar House. Restaurant and inn adjacent, car park available. Guest lounge with TV. Single, double and twin rooms en suite or private bathroom. Beverage trays, TV, shaver points in all rooms. From £25. Children under three years FREE, three to 12 year olds half price sharing parents' room. Pets by arrangement. Leave M4 at Junction 28, take A48 towards Newport, at roundabout take third exit signposted St Brides, B4239. Drive to centre of village, turn right into Church Road and left into Church House Inn car park; the guest house is on the left and a warm welcome awaits. Credit/Debit Cards accepted. **WTB ★★★** *GUEST HOUSE.*
e-mail: chapelguesthouse@hotmail.com   **website: www.SmoothHound.co.uk/**

Carlton Hotel, Mumbles

SWANSEA
Carlton Hotel, 654-656 Mumbles Road, Mumbles, Gower, Swansea SA3 4EA (Tel & Fax: 01792 360450). A warm and friendly welcome awaits you at the Carlton Hotel, in the village of Mumbles on the Gower Peninsula. The hotel is located on the sea front, offering panoramic views across Swansea Bay, and is a short walk from the attractions of Mumbles and the picturesque village of Oystermouth. The Carlton has 20 en suite bedrooms all with TV, tea/coffee making facilities, radio clock alarms and central heating. Ground floor rooms available. Fredrick's Restaurant provides a varied menu, snacks and a comprehensive wine list; well stocked bar. Excellent facilities for water skiing, sailing and power boating opposite the hotel. Swansea's modern city centre, with shops, cinemas, night clubs etc. is a short trip from the hotel. Well behaved pets welcome.
e-mail: mail@carltonmumbles.co.uk   **website: www.carltonmumbles.co.uk**

WALES

IRELAND

Co. Donegal

LETTERKENNY

Nuala and Michael Duddy, Pennsylvania House B&B, Curraghleas, Mountain Top, Letterkenny (00 353 74 9126808; Fax: 00 353 74 9128905). Pennsylvania House is a luxurious smoke-free B&B overlooking the hills, valleys and mountains of Donegal, four minutes away from Letterkenny town. It is tucked away off the main road and provides a secluded retreat for those who desire the very finest in accommodation. Spacious en suite bedrooms, TV, phone, alarm clock radio, luggage racks, arm chairs, etc. Pennsylvania House is unique and truly outstanding and provides everything and more that any visitor could desire. Guests will feel right at home in this picturesque corner of the Emerald Isle, where you arrive a stranger and leave a friend. Rates from 45 euros to 51 euros per person. **AA ◆◆◆◆**

e-mail: info@accommodationdonegal.com or nualasbandb@eircom.net
website: www.accommodationdonegal.com

Co. Kildare

A warm welcome at this period Georgian country house set in attractive gardens and retaining the original style. Offering the highest levels of service, care and hospitality, including generous breakfasts with freshly baked bread in the comfortable dining room. Ideally situated for outdoor activities including golf, fishing and horseriding. Non-smoking. Ample parking. Open all year.

For further information contact Joan and Myles at Tel: 00 353 45 892087
e-mail: ballinagappahouse@eircom.net • website: www.ballinagappa.com

Ballinagappa Country house
clane, county kildare, Republic of Ireland

RaC
◆◆◆◆◆
Sparkling
Diamond &
Warm Welcome
Award

See also Colour Advertisement

SPECIAL WELCOME SUPPLEMENT

Are you looking for a guest house where smoking is banned, a farmhouse that is equipped for the disabled, or a hotel that will cater for your special diet? If so, you should find this supplement useful. Its three sections, NON-SMOKERS, DISABLED, and SPECIAL DIETS, list accommodation where these particular needs are served. Brief details of the accommodation are provided in this section; for a fuller description you should turn to the appropriate place in the main section of the book.

Non-smoking • England

LONDON, HAMMERSMITH. Anne and Sohel Armanios, 67 Rannoch Road, Hammersmith, London W6 9SS (020 7385 4904; Fax: 020 7610 3235). Comfortable, centrally located Edwardian family home. Great base for sightseeing. Excellent transport access. Bed and Continental Breakfast £24 pppn Double; £34 single. Smoking only in garden.

BEDFORDSHIRE, SANDY. Mrs M. Codd, Highfield Farm, Tempsford, Sandy SG19 2AQ (01767 682332; Fax: 01767 692503). Tranquil welcoming atmosphere on attractive arable farm. All rooms have tea/coffee making facilities, most have bathroom en suite and two are on the ground floor. No smoking. **ETC ◆◆◆◆◆** *SILVER AWARD.*

CAMBRIDGESHIRE, ELY. Mrs C. H. Bennett, Stockyard Farm, Wisbech Road, Welney, Wisbech PE14 9RQ (01354 610433). Comfortable former farmhouse. One double and one twin bedroom, both with handbasin, radio, hairdryer and hot drink facilities. Vegetarian breakfast a speciality. Central heating. Private parking. No smoking. Pets welcome. B&B from £18 per person.

CUMBRIA, KESWICK. Anworth House Vegetarian Bed and Breakfast, 27 Eskin Street, Keswick CA12 4DQ (01768 772923). Ideally situated for the town centre, theatre, lakes and fells. Five en suite bedrooms. Non-smoking. Open all year except Christmas. Special winter breaks available. **ETC ◆◆◆**

CUMBRIA, KESWICK. Annie Scally and Ian Townsend, Latrigg House, St Herbert Street, Keswick CA12 4DF (017687 73068). An attractive detached Victorian house situated in a quiet area, only a few minutes' walk from the town centre and Lake, offering a non-smoking environment for the well-being and comfort of guests. **ETC ◆◆◆◆**

CUMBRIA, TROUTBECK. Hill Crest, Troutbeck, Penrith CA11 0SH (017684 83935). A unique warm and friendly Lakeland home. Non-smoking establishment where children and dogs are welcome. En suite rooms available.

DERBYSHIRE, MATLOCK. Ruth Lewis, Ellen House, 37 Snitterton Road, Matlock DE4 3LZ (01629 55584; mobile: 07752 598637). Extended Edwardian home on outskirts of Matlock, ideal base for exploring Derbyshire's heritage and scenery. A non-smoking establishment.

DEVON, SALCOMBE, Steve and Laura Girling, Meadow View, 11 Longfield Drive, Salcombe TQ8 8NT (01548 844102). Luxury accommodation with a warm and friendly welcome. Ideally situated for the town and beaches. No smoking inside the house. Regret no children or pets.

DEVON, WEST DOWN. Robin and Jeannie Hotchkiss, The Long House, The Square, West Down, Near Ilfracombe EX34 8NF (01271 863242). Picturesque 18th century guest house in quiet hamlet, yet within 10 minutes' drive of Blue Flag beaches and Exmoor. Comfortable en suite rooms, delicious breakfast and non-smoking throughout.

DORSET, BEAMINSTER. Caroline and Vincent Pielesz, The Walnuts, 2 Prout Bridge, Beaminster DT8 3AY (01308 862211). Very well situated in this medieval town, the house has been very tastefully refurbished with en suite rooms, tea and coffee making facilities, all the comforts of home. Totally non-smoking. ETC ◆◆◆ *SILVER AWARD*.

DORSET, LULWORTH COVE. Mrs J.S. Ravensdale, Elads-Nevar, West Road, West Lulworth, Wareham BH20 5RZ. Set in the beautiful village of West Lulworth, half-a-mile from Lulworth Cove. Spacious rooms all with tea/coffee making facilities and colour TV. Vegetarians and Vegans catered for. Non-smoking. Open all year.

DORSET, LYME REGIS. Mrs L. Brown, Providence House, Lyme Road, Uplyme DT7 3TH (01297 445704). Character house in village location on edge of historic Lyme Regis. Accommodation comprises one single, one double, one double en suite, all with TV and tea/coffee making facilities.

HEREFORDSHIRE, GOLDEN VALLEY. Melvin and Joyce Powell, The Old Vicarage, Vowchurch, Hereford HR2 0QD (Tel & Fax: 01981 550357). Warm hospitality guaranteed in this Victorian house of character. Individually decorated rooms, refreshment trays, fresh fruit and flowers, home-made bread and preserves. Non-smoking.

HEREFORDSHIRE, HEREFORD. Heron House, Canon Pye Road, Portway, Burghill, Hereford HR4 8NG (01432 761111; Fax: 01432 760603). Friendly welcome at rural location four miles north of Hereford. En suite, vanity units, tea making facilities, colour TV, log fire, parking. Non-smoking. ETC ◆◆◆

ISLE OF WIGHT, TOTLAND BAY. Mrs Westerhoff, Sandy Lane Guest House, Colwell Common Road, Totland Bay PO39 0DD (Tel & Fax: 01983 752240). Family-run B&B ideally situated for west Wight's tourist attractions. Non-smoking establishment. ETC ◆◆◆◆

LANCASHIRE, BLACKPOOL. Yvonne & Alan Jones, The Birchley Hotel, 64 Holmfield Road, North Shore FY2 9RT (01253 354174). Situated in a pleasant, select area adjacent to Queens Promenade. Seven en suite bedrooms. Stair lift. Excellent food. Open most of the year. Totally non-smoking.

NORFOLK, SHERINGHAM. Beeston Hills Lodge, 64 Cliff Road, Sheringham NR26 8BJ (01263 825333; mobile: 0788 7751760; Fax: 001 775 542 2519). Bed and Breakfast seaside holiday accommodation. Edwardian lodge which is marvellously located next to the Norfolk Coastal Path, cliffs and ocean. Children, Senior Citizens and well behaved pets welcome. Non-smoking.

NORTHUMBERLAND, ALNMOUTH. Janice Edwards, Westlea, 29 Riverside Road, Alnmouth NE66 2SD (01665 830730) All bedrooms are bright, comfortable and en suite with colour TVs, hot drinks facilities, central heating and electric blankets. Two bedrooms on the ground floor. Private parking. ETC ◆◆◆

OXFORDSHIRE, OXFORD. Tilbury Lodge, 5 Tilbury Lane, Botley, Oxford OX2 9NB (01865 862138; Fax: 01865 863700). Modern guest house situated in quiet country lane within a short distance of Oxford city centre. All rooms en suite; one four-poster with added luxuries. Non-smoking. ETC/RAC ◆◆◆, *SPARKLING DIAMOND AWARD.*

OXFORDSHIRE, WITNEY. Mrs Elizabeth Simpson, Field View, Wood Green, Witney OX28 1DE (01993 705485; Mobile: 07768 614347). Set in two acres and situated on picturesque Wood Green, yet only ten minutes from the centre of town. Non-smoking. ETC ◆◆◆ *SILVER AWARD*

SHROPSHIRE, IRONBRIDGE. Jutta and Alan Ward, Linley Crest, Linley Brook, Near Bridgnorth WV16 4SZ. (Tel & Fax: 01746 765527). Extremely comfortable accommodation; quiet and pretty location; excellent base for exciting tourist attractions; wholesome breakfasts, almost every wish granted, however, most definitely no smoking in the house. Euro payment accepted. ETC ◆◆◆ *SILVER AWARD*

SOMERSET, BATH. Michael and Carole Bryson, Walton Villa, 3 Newbridge Hill, Bath BA1 3PW (01225 482792; Fax: 01225 313092). All bedrooms tastefully decorated and furnished with en suite facilities, hospitality tray, colour TV, hairdryer and central heating. No smoking policy throughout. ETC ◆◆◆

SOMERSET, BURNHAM-ON-SEA. Mrs F. Alexander, Priors Mead, 23 Rectory Road TA8 2BZ (Tel & Fax: 01278 782116; Mobile: 07990 595585). Enchanting Edwardian home set in half-an-acre of beautiful gardens with weeping willows, croquet and swimming pool. Peaceful location, walk to the sea, town, golf and tennis clubs. Parking. Bed and Breakfast from £22.50. Reductions for three nights. *"WHICH?" RECOMMENDED.*

SOMERSET, CHARD. Mrs Jean Watkis, Keymer Cottage, Buckland St Mary, Chard, Somerset TA20 3JF (01460 234226 or 07940 051439). Stone built Victorian Farmhouse, with inglenook, attractively furnished, offering friendly and comfortable hospitality. Guest sitting room with colour TV.

SOMERSET, WESTON-SUPER-MARE. Mrs Katie Nelson, The Owls Crest, 39 Kewstoke Road, Kewstoke, Weston-Super-Mare BS22 9YE (01934 417672). Situated within the small country village of Kewstoke minutes from the M5. En suite with TV, radio alarm clock, hairdryer and tea/coffee tray. Non-smoking throughout.

SURREY, GATWICK. Carole and Adrian Grinsted, The Lawn Guest House, 30 Massetts Road, Horley RH6 7DE (01293 775751; Fax: 01293 821803). Imposing Victorian house, five minutes from Gatwick Airport. All rooms en suite with TV, hairdryer, tea/coffee/chocolate tray, direct dial phone and computer modem sockets. Central heating. Children welcome. Totally non-smoking.

SUSSEX (EAST), HASTINGS. Peter Mann, Grand Hotel, Grand Parade, St Leonards, Hastings TN38 0DD (Tel & Fax: 01424 428510 or 0870 2257025) Seafront family-run hotel; some rooms with colour TV, radio; some en suite. Unrestricted/disabled parking. Non-smoking restaurant. Licensed bar. **ETC ◆◆◆**

YORKSHIRE (NORTH), SCARBOROUGH. Sue and Tony Hewitt, Harmony Country Lodge, Limestone Road, Burniston, Scarborough YO13 0DG (0800 2985840; Tel & Fax: 01723 870276). Relaxing octagonal retreat, superb 360° views of the National Park and sea. Licensed, private parking, completely non-smoking. Warm and friendly. **ETC ◆◆◆◆**

Non-smoking • Scotland

AYRSHIRE, LARGS. Mrs M. Watson, South Whittlieburn Farm, Brisbane Glen, Largs KA30 8SN (01475 675881; Fax: 01475 675080). Superb farmhouse accommodation, enormous delicious breakfasts, warm, friendly hospitality. Highly recommended. All rooms en suite. Open all year except Christmas. **STB ★★★★ B&B, AA ◆◆◆◆**

PERTH & KINROSS, CALLANDER. Annfield Guest House, North Church Street, Callander FK17 8EG (01877 330204; Fax: 01877 330674). Ideal as an overnight stop or as the centre for visiting the surrounding Scottish Highlands. All bedrooms have en suite facilities or private bathroom, hospitality tray and hairdryer. Private parking. No smoking. **AA ◆◆◆, STB ★★★ B&B.**

Non-smoking • Wales

NORTH WALES, LLANDUDNO. Roger and Merril Pitblado, Chilterns, 19 Deganwy Avenue, Llandudno LL30 2YB (01492 875457). Chilterns is entirely non-smoking with full central heating. Double, family and twin rooms with en suite facilities, colour televisions, beverage trays and some with king-size beds. **WTB ★★★ GUEST HOUSE.**

POWYS, BUILTH WELLS (NEAR). Mrs Margaret Davies,The Court Farm, Aberedw, near Builth Wells LD2 3UP (Tel & Fax: 01982 560277). Guests are welcome into our home on a family-run livestock farm set in a peaceful, picturesque valley surrounded by hills. En suite or private bathroom available. Guests' lounge. Traditional cooking. Non-smokers please.

SOUTH WALES, ST BRIDES WENTLOOG (Near Newport). Mrs C.A. Bushell, Chapel Guest House, Church Road, St Brides Wentloog, Near Newport NP10 8SN (01633 681018; Fax: 01633 681431) Comfortable accommodation in a converted chapel. Guest lounge with TV. Single, double and twin rooms en suite or private bathroom. Beverage trays, TV, shaver points in all rooms. From £25. **WTB ★★★ GUEST HOUSE.**

Special Diets • England

LONDON, HAMMERSMITH. Anne and Sohel Armanios, 67 Rannoch Road, Hammersmith, London W6 9SS (020 7385 4904; Fax: 020 7610 3235). Comfortable, centrally located Edwardian family home. Great base for sightseeing. Excellent transport access. Bed and Continental Breakfast £24 pppn Double; £34 single. Smoking only in garden.

CAMBRIDGESHIRE, ELY. Mrs C. H. Bennett, Stockyard Farm, Wisbech Road, Welney, Wisbech PE14 9RQ (01354 610433). Comfortable former farmhouse. One double and one twin bedroom, both with handbasin, radio, hairdryer and hot drink facilities. Vegetarian breakfast a speciality. Central heating. Private parking. No smoking. Pets welcome. B&B from £18 per person.

CHESHIRE, BALTERLEY. Mrs Joanne Hollins, Balterley Green Farm, Deans Lane, Balterley, Near Crewe CW2 5QJ (01270 820214). One family room en suite, one single and one twin-bedded room on ground floor. Children welcome, cot provided. Pets welcome. Open all year. ETC ◆◆◆◆

CUMBRIA, KESWICK. Anworth House Vegetarian Bed and Breakfast, 27 Eskin Street, Keswick CA12 4DQ (01768 772923). Ideally situated for the town centre, theatre, lakes and fells. Five en suite bedrooms. Non-smoking. Open all year except Christmas. Special winter breaks available. ETC ◆◆◆

CUMBRIA, KESWICK. Annie Scally and Ian Townsend, Latrigg House, St Herbert Street, Keswick CAI2 4DF (017687 73068). We promise a very warm welcome, good food, comfort and hospitality; vegetarian and vegan meals provided if required. ETC ◆◆◆◆

CUMBRIA, TROUTBECK. Hill Crest, Troutbeck, Penrith CA11 0SH (017684 83935). A unique warm and friendly Lakeland home with tea/coffee and twin rooms, where children and dogs are welcome, En suite rooms available. No smoking

DERBYSHIRE, CHESTERFIELD. Mrs J. E. Payne, The Clarendon Guest House, 32 Clarence Road, Chesterfield S40 1LN (01246 235004). Located near the town centre and within easy reach of the Peak District. Full English breakfast; home cooked evening meals and special diets by prior arrangement. ETC ◆◆◆

DEVON, SALCOMBE, Steve and Laura Girling, Meadow View, 11 Longfield Drive, Salcombe TQ8 8NT (01548 844102). Luxury accommodation with a warm and friendly welcome. Ideally situated for the town and beaches. Enjoy a leisurely full English or vegetarian breakfast. Regret no children or pets.

DORSET, LYME REGIS. Mrs L. Brown, Providence House, Lyme Road, Uplyme DT7 3TH (01297 445704). Accommodation comprises one single, one double, one double en suite, all with TV and tea/coffee making facilities. Full English Breakfast and vegetarian option.

HEREFORDSHIRE, GOLDEN VALLEY. Melvin and Joyce Powell, The Old Vicarage, Vowchurch, Hereford HR2 0QD (Tel & Fax: 01981 550357). Warm hospitality guaranteed in this Victorian house of character. Individually decorated rooms, refreshment trays, fresh fruit and flowers, home-made bread and preserves. Non-smoking. Vegetarian and special diets catered for.

SHROPSHIRE, IRONBRIDGE. Jutta and Alan Ward, Linley Crest, Linley Brook, Near Bridgnorth WV16 4SZ (Tel & Fax: 01746 765527). The setting is tranquil and pleasing. The cosy bedrooms have king-sized beds and every home comfort. The breakfasts are generous, wholesome and varied. We happily cater for special dietary requirements. Euro payment accepted. ETC ◆◆◆ *SILVER AWARD.*

SUSSEX (EAST), HASTINGS. Peter Mann, Grand Hotel, Grand Parade, St Leonards, Hastings TN38 0DD (Tel & Fax: 01424 428510 or 0870 2257025) Seafront family-run hotel; some rooms with colour TV, radio; some en suite. Unrestricted/disabled parking. Non-smoking restaurant. Licensed bar. ETC ◆◆◆

PLEASE NOTE

All the information in this book is given in good faith in the belief that it is correct. However, the publishers cannot guarantee the facts given in these pages, neither are they responsible for changes in policy, ownership or terms that may take place after the date of going to press. Readers should always satisfy themselves that the facilities they require are available and that the terms, if quoted, still apply.

Special Diets • Scotland

AYRSHIRE, LARGS. Mrs M. Watson, South Whittlieburn Farm, Brisbane Glen, Largs KA30 8SN (01475 675881; Fax: 01475 675080). Superb farmhouse accommodation, enormous delicious breakfasts, warm, friendly hospitality. Highly recommended. All rooms en suite. Open all year except Christmas. Packed lunches and special diets. **STB ★★★★ B&B, AA ◆◆◆◆**

Special Diets • Wales

NORTH WALES, BETWS-Y-COED. Jim and Lilian Boughton, Bron Celyn Guest House, Lôn Muriau, Llanrwst Road, Betws-y-Coed LL24 0HD (01690 710333; Fax: 01690 710111). A warm welcome awaits you at this delightful guest house. Ideal centre for touring, walking, climbing, fishing and golf. Car park. Open all year. Evening meals - special diets catered for. Bed and Breakfast from £22 to £30. **WTB ★★★ GUEST HOUSE.**

SOUTH WALES, ST BRIDES WENTLOOG (Near Newport). Mrs C.A. Bushell, Chapel Guest House, Church Road, St Brides Wentloog, Near Newport NP10 8SN (01633 681018; Fax: 01633 681431) Comfortable accommodation in a converted chapel. Guest lounge with TV. Single, double and twin rooms en suite or private bathroom. Beverage trays, TV, shaver points in all rooms. From £25. **WTB ★★★ GUEST HOUSE.**

Disabled • England

CHESHIRE, BALTERLEY. Mrs Joanne Hollins, Balterley Green Farm, Deans Lane, Balterley, Near Crewe CW2 5QJ (01270 820214). One family room en suite, one single and one twin-bedded room on ground floor suitable for disabled guests. Tea-making facilities and TV in all rooms. Children welcome, cot provided. Pets welcome. **ETC** ◆◆◆◆

NORTHUMBERLAND, ALNMOUTH. Janice Edwards, Westlea, 29 Riverside Road, Alnmouth NE66 2SD (01665 830730) All bedrooms are bright, comfortable and en suite with colour TVs, hot drinks facilities, central heating and electric blankets. Two bedrooms on the ground floor. Private parking. No smoking. **ETC** ◆◆◆

SHROPSHIRE, IRONBRIDGE. Jutta and Alan Ward, Linley Crest, Linley Brook, Near Bridgnorth WV16 4SZ (Tel & Fax: 01746 765527). Welcome to our attractive rural retreat. Two of our double bedrooms have ground floor access for guests with restricted mobility, en suite shower, TV, radio/alarm, beverage tray, hair dryer etc. We offer multiple choice breakfasts and cater for special requirements. Euro payment accepted. **ETC** ◆◆◆◆ *SILVER AWARD*

SUSSEX (EAST), HASTINGS. Peter Mann, Grand Hotel, Grand Parade, St Leonards, Hastings TN38 0DD (Tel & Fax: 01424 428510 or 0870 2257025) Seafront family-run hotel; some rooms with colour TV, radio; some en suite. Unrestricted/disabled parking. Non-smoking restaurant. Licensed bar. **ETC** ◆◆◆

NORTH YORKSHIRE, SCARBOROUGH. The Ganton Greyhound, Ganton, Near Scarborough YO12 4NX (01944 710116; FAX: 01944 712705). Good hospitality, good food, and a warm, friendly atmosphere. En suite bedrooms (double, twin, family and disabled). Ideal for exploring this scenic area.

Disabled • Scotland

BORDERS, JEDBURGH. Mrs Susan Forster, Hoolet's Nest, Mount Hooly, Jedburgh TS8 6TJ (Tel & Fax: 01835 850764). Hoolet's Nest is a modern bungalow with a self-contained flat, set in a large garden. One twin and one family room. Half a mile from the A68 north of Jedburgh, on the A698 Kelso road.

ISLE OF SKYE, EDINBANE. Peter & Hilary Prall, Shorefield House, Edinbane, By Portree IV51 9PW (01470 582444; Fax: 01470 582414). A 'family friendly' establishment. Category 1 en suite facilities with easy ramped access to entrance. Traditional Highland breakfast or Continental buffet. **STB** ★★★★ *GUEST HOUSE,* **AA/RAC** ◆◆◆◆

Disabled • Wales

PEMBROKESHIRE, MAENCLOCHOG. Twmpath Guest House, Maenclochog SA66 7RL (01437 532990). In the heart of the Pembrokeshire countryside, offering home comforts, with full facilities for families, elderly and disabled guests. Luxury rooms with full en suite facilities and cuisine of high standard. **WTB** ★★★ *GUEST HOUSE.*

SOUTH WALES, ST BRIDES WENTLOOG (Near Newport). Mrs C.A. Bushell, Chapel Guest House, Church Road, St Brides Wentloog, Near Newport NP10 8SN (01633 681018; Fax: 01633 681431) Comfortable accommodation in a converted chapel. Guest lounge with TV. Single, double and twin rooms en suite or private bathroom. Beverage trays, TV, shaver points in all rooms. From £25. **WTB** ★★★ *GUEST HOUSE.*

Terms quoted in this publication may be subject to increase if rises in costs necessitate

DIRECTORY OF WEBSITE AND E-MAIL ADDRESSES

A quick-reference guide to holiday accommodation with an e-mail address and/or website, conveniently arranged by country and county, with full contact details.

•LONDON

Guesthouse
MacDonald Hotel, 45-46 Argyle Square,
LONDON WC1H 8AL
020 7837 3552
• e-mail: fhg@macdonaldhotel.com
• website: www.macdonaldhotel.com

Hotel
The Elysee Hotel, 20-26 Craven Terrace,
LONDON W2 8EL
020 7402 7633
• e-mail: information@elyseehotel-london.co.uk
• website: www.elyseehotel-london.co.uk

Hotel / B & B
Lincoln House Hotel, 33 Gloucester Place,
LONDON W1V 8HY
020 7486 7630
• e-mail: reservations@lincoln-house-hotel.co.uk
• website: www.lincoln-house-hotel.co.uk

Guesthouse / Hotel
Barry House Hotel, 12 Sussex Place,
Hyde Park, LONDON W2 2TP
020 7723 7340
• e-mail: RSB@barryhouse.co.uk
• website: www.barryhouse.co.uk

Hotel / B & B
Elizabeth Hotel, 37 Eccleston Square,
LONDON SW1V 1PB
020 7828 6812
• e-mail: info@elizabethhotel.com
• website: www.elizabethhotel.com

Hotel
Queens Hotel, 33 Anson Road,
Tufnell Park, LONDON N7
020 7607 4725
• e-mail: queens@stavrouhotels.co.uk
• website: www.stavrouhotels.co.uk

Hotel
Athena Hotel, 110-114 Sussex Gardens,
Hyde Park, LONDON W2 1UA
020 7706 3866
• e-mail: athena@stavrouhotels.co.uk
• website: www.stavrouhotels.co.uk

Hotel
Gower Hotel, 129 Sussex Gardens,
Hyde Park, LONDON W2 2RX
020 7262 2262
• e-mail: gower@stavrouhotels.co.uk
• website: www.stavrouhotels.co.uk

B & B
Sohel & Anne Armanios, 67 Rannoch Road,
Hammersmith, LONDON W6 9SS
020 7385 4904
• website: www.thewaytostay.co.uk

B & B / Hotel / Self-Catering
Windsor House Hotel, 12 Penywern Road,
LONDON SW5 9ST
020 7373 9087
• e-mail: bookings@windsor-house-hotel.com
• website: www.windsor-house-hotel.com

•BERKSHIRE

Hotel
Clarence Hotel, 9 Clarence Road,
WINDSOR, Berkshire SL4 5AE
01753 864436
• website: www.clarence-hotel.co.uk

•CAMBRIDGESHIRE

Guest House
Dykelands Guest House, 157 Mowbray
Road, CAMBRIDGE,
Cambridgeshire CB1 7SP
01223 244300
• e-mail: dykelands@fsbdial.co.uk
• website: www.dykelands.com

Guest House
Victoria Guest House,
57 Arbury Road, CAMBRIDGE,
Cambridgeshire CB4 2JB
01223 350086
• e-mail: victoriahouse@ntlworld.com
• website:
www.SmoothHound.co.uk/hotels/victori3.html

•CHESHIRE

Guest House / Self-Catering
Mrs Joanne Hollins, Balterley Green Farm,
Farm Deans Lane, BALTERLEY, Crewe
Cheshire CW2 5QJ
01270 820 214
• e-mail: greenfarm@balterley.fsnet.co.uk
• website: www.greenfarm.freeserve.co.uk

Guest House / Self-Catering
Mrs Angela Smith, Mill House and Granary,
Higher Wych, MALPAS,
Cheshire SY14 7JR
01948 780362
• e-mail: angela@videoactive.co.uk
• website: www.millhouseandgranary.co.uk

•CORNWALL

Self-Catering
Fiona & Martin Nicolle,
Classy Cottages, Cornwall
07000 423000
• website: www.classycottages.co.uk

Self-Catering
Cornish Traditional Cottages, Blisland,
BODMIN, Cornwall PL30 4HS
01208 821666
• e-mail: info@corncott.com
• website: www.corncott.com

Self-Catering
Tregatherall Farm,
BOSCASTLE, Cornwall PL35 0EQ
01840 250277
• e-mail: tregatherall@ipl.co.uk
• website: www.ipl.co.uk/tregatherall/

Self-Catering
Mr Charles Tippet,
Mineshop Holiday Cottages, Crackington
Haven, BUDE, Cornwall EX23 0NR
01840 230338
• e-mail: tippett@mineshop.freeserve.co.uk
• website: www.crackingtoncottages.co.uk

Self-Catering / Caravan & Camping
Willow Valley Holiday Park,
Bush, BUDE, Cornwall EX23 9LB
01288 353104
• e-mail: willowvalley@talk21.com
• website: www.caravansitecornwall.co.uk

Caravan & Camping
Cornish Coasts Caravan & Camping Park,
Middle Penlean, Poundstock,
Widemouth Bay, BUDE, Cornwall EX23 0EE
01288 361380
• e-mail: info@cornishcoasts.co.uk
• website: www.cornishcoasts.co.uk

Self-Catering
Mr Ian Goodman,
Hilton Farm Holiday Cottages,
Marhamchurch, BUDE, Cornwall EX23 0HE
01288 361521
• e-mail: ian@hiltonfarmhouse.freeserve.co.uk
• website: www.hiltonfarmhouse.co.uk

Caravan & Camping
Widemouth Bay Caravan Park,
Near BUDE, Cornwall
01271 866666
• website:
www.johnfowlerholidays.com/widemouth_bay.asp

Hotel / Self-Catering
Wringford Down Hotel, CAWSAND,
Torpoint, Cornwall PL10 1LE
01752 822287
• e-mail: a.molloy@virgin.net
• website: www.cornwallholidays.co.uk

Hotel
Rosemullion Hotel, Gyllyngvase Hill,
FALMOUTH,
Cornwall TR11 4DF
01326 314690
• e-mail: gail@rosemullionhotel.demon.co.uk
• website:
www.s-h-systems.co.uk/hotels/rosemullion.html

Caravan & Camping
Boscrege Caravan & Camping Park,
Ashton, HELSTON, Cornwall TR13 9TG
01736 762231
• e-mail: enquiries@caravanparkcornwall.com
• website: www.caravanparkcornwall.com

Guest House
Greystones Guest House, 40 West End,
Porthleven, HELSTON TR13 9JL
01326 565583
• e-mail: neilvwoodward@hotmail.com

Self-Catering
Kathryn Broad, Lower Dutson Farm,
LAUNCESTON, Cornwall PL15 9SP
01566 776456
• e-mail: francis.broad@btclick.com
• website:
www.chycor.co.uk/cornish-farmholidays

Self-Catering
Celia Hutchinson,
Caradon Country Cottages, East Taphouse,
LISKEARD, Cornwall PL14 4NH
01579 320355
• e-mail: celia@caradoncottages.freeserve.co.uk
• website: www.caradoncottages.co.uk

Self-Catering
Kaye & Bill Chapman, Well Meadow
Cottage, Coldrinnick Farm, Duloe,
LISKEARD, Cornwall
01503 220251
• e-mail: kaye@coldrinnick.fsnet.co.uk
• website: www.cornishcottage.net

Self-Catering
Sue Jewell, Boturnell Farm Cottages,
St Pinnock, LISKEARD, Cornwall PL14 4QS
01579 320880
• e-mail: boturnell-barns@breathemail.net
• website: www.dogs-holiday.co.uk

Self-Catering
Mrs S. Clemens, Lametton Barton,
St Keyne, LISKEARD, Cornwall PL14 4SQ
01579 343434
• website:
  www.stayincornwall.co.uk/lametton.htm

B & B / Self-Catering
Paul Brumpton, Talehay Holiday Cottages,
Pelynt, near LOOE, Cornwall PL13 2LT
01503 220252
• e-mail: paul@talehay.co.uk
• website: www.talehay.co.uk

B & B
Mrs Dawn Rundle, Lancallan Farm,
MEVAGISSEY, St Austell,
Cornwall PL26 6EW
01726 842284
• e-mail: dawn@lancallan.fsnet.co.uk

Hotel
Golden Bay Hotel, Pentire Avenue,
Pentire, NEWQUAY,
Cornwall TR7 1PD
01637 873318
• e-mail: enquiries@goldenbayhotel.co.uk
• website: www.goldenbayhotel.co.uk

Guest House / Self-Catering
Trewerry Mill Guest House, Trewerry Mill,
Trerice, St Newlyn East, NEWQUAY,
Cornwall TR8 5GS
01872 510345
• e-mail: trewerry.mill@which.net
• website: www.trewerrymill.co.uk

Holiday Park
Treloy Tourist Park, NEWQUAY,
Cornwall TR8 4JN
01637 872063/876279
• e-mail: holidays@treloy.co.uk
• website: www.treloy.co.uk

Hotel
White Lodge Hotel, Mawgan Porth Bay,
Near NEWQUAY, Cornwall TR8 4BN
01637 860512
• e-mail: adogfriendly@aol.com
• website: www.dogfriendlyhotel.co.uk

Guest House
Dewolf Guest House, 100 Henver Road,
NEWQUAY, Cornwall TR7 3BL
01637 874746
• e-mail: holidays@dewolfguesthouse.com
• website: www.dewolfguesthouse.com

B & B / Hotel
Mr Simon Chapman, Camilla House Hotel,
12 Regent Terrace, PENZANCE,
Cornwall TR18 4DW
01736 363771
• e-mail: visitus@camillahouse-hotel.co.uk
• website: www.penzance.co.uk/camilla/

Farmhouse B & B
Rose Farm, Chyannal, Buryas Bridge,
PENZANCE, Cornwall
01736 731808
• e-mail: lally@rosefarmcornwall.co.uk
• website: www.rosefarmcornwall.co.uk

Inn
Crumplehorn Inn, POLPERRO,
Cornwall PL13 2RJ
01503 272348
• e-mail: host@crumplehorn-inn.co.uk
• website: www.crumplehorn-inn.co.uk

Caravan & Camping / Holiday Park
Globe Vale Holiday Park, Radnor,
REDRUTH, Cornwall
01209 891183
• e-mail: globe@ukgo.com
• website: www.globe.ukgo.com

Caravan & Camping / Holiday Park
Chiverton Park, Blackwater, ST AGNES,
Cornwall TR4 8HS
01872 560667
• e-mail: info@chivertonpark.co.uk
• website: www.chivertonpark.co.uk

Hotel / Inn
Mrs J. Treleaven, Driftwood Spars Hotel,
Trevaunance Cove, ST AGNES,
Cornwall TR5 0RT
01872 552428 / 553323
• e-mail: driftwoodspars@hotmail.com
• website: www.driftwoodspars.com

B & B
Mrs Liz Berryman, Polgreen Farm,
London Apprentice, ST AUSTELL,
Cornwall PL26 7AP
01726 75151
• e-mail: polgreen.farm@btclick.com
• website: www.polgreenfarm.co.uk

Holiday Park
St Ives Bay Holiday Park, ST IVES BAY,
Cornwall TR27 5BH
0800 317713 (24hr brochure line)
• e-mail: enquiries@stivesbay.co.uk
• website: www.stivesbay.co.uk

Hotel
Rosevine Hotel, Porthcurnick Beach,
ST MAWES, Cornwall
01872 580206
• e-mail: info@rosevine.co.uk
• website: www.rosevine.co.uk

Hotel
Dalswinton House, ST MAWGAN,
Near Newquay, Cornwall TR8 4EZ
01637 860385
• e-mail: dalswinton@bigwig.net
• website: www.dalswinton.com

Self-Catering
Mr & Mrs C.W. Pestell, Hockadays,
Tregenna, near Blisland, ST TUDY,
Cornwall PL30 4QJ
01208 850146
• e-mail:
  holidays@hockadaysholidaycottages.co.uk
• website: www.hockadaysholidaycottages.co.uk

Hotel & Self-Catering Lodges
St Mellion Hotel, Golf & Country Club,
St Mellion, Near SALTASH, Cornwall
01579 351351
• e-mail: stmellion@americangolf.uk.com
• website: www.st-mellion.co.uk

Caravan & Camping
Wheal Rose Caravan & Camping Park,
Wheal Rose, SCORRIER,
Near Redruth, Cornwall
01209 891496
• e-mail: les@whealrosecaravanpark.co.uk
• website: www.whealrosecaravanpark.co.uk

Hotel
Willapark Manor Hotel, Bossiney,
TINTAGEL, Cornwall PL34 0BA
01840 770782
• e-mail: nick@willapark.co.uk
• website: www.willapark.co.uk

Guest House
Sara Hawkins, Bosayne Guest House,
Atlantic Road, TINTAGEL,
Cornwall PL34 0DE
01840 770514
• e-mail: clark@clarky100.freeserve.co.uk
• website: www.bosayne.co.uk

Self-Catering
Mrs Sandy Wilson, Salutations,
Atlantic Road, TINTAGEL,
Cornwall PL34 0DE
01840 770287
• website: www.salutationstintagel.co.uk

Caravan Park
C.R. Simpkins, Summer Valley Touring Park,
Shortlanesend, TRURO, Cornwall TR4 9DW
01872 277878
• e-mail: res@summervalley.co.uk
• website: www.summervalley.co.uk

Self-Catering
Mrs Sue Zamaria, Colesent Cottages,
St Tudy, WADEBRIDGE, Cornwall PL30 4QX
01208 850112
• e-mail: welcome@colesent.co.uk
• website: www.colesent.co.uk

Please mention this guide when enquiring about accommodation

•CUMBRIA

Hotel
Rothay Manor, Rothay Bridge,
AMBLESIDE, Cumbria LA22 0EH
015394 33605
• e-mail: hotel@rothaymanor.co.uk
• website: www.rothaymanor.co.uk

Caravan Park
Greenhowe Caravan Park, Great Langdale,
AMBLESIDE, Cumbria LA22 9JU
015394 37231
• e-mail: enquiries@greenhowe.com

B & B
Mr Jack Halliday, The Anchorage,
Rydal Road, AMBLESIDE,
Cumbria LA22 9AY
015394 32046
• e-mail: info@anchorageonline.force9.co.uk
• website: www.anchorageonline.force9.co.uk/

Hotel
Appleby Manor Country House Hotel,
Roman Road, APPLEBY-IN-WESTMORLAND,
Cumbria CA16 6JB
017683 51571
• e-mail: reception@applebymanor.co.uk
• website: www.applebymanor.co.uk

Self-Catering / Holiday Homes
Lakelovers, Belmont House, Lake Road,
BOWNESS-ON-WINDERMERE,
Cumbria LA23 3BJ
015394 88855
• e-mail: bookings@lakelovers.co.uk
• website: www.lakelovers.co.uk

B & B
Elaine Packer, The Hill, Gilsland,
BRAMPTON, Cumbria CA8 7SA
016977 47214
• e-mail: info@hadrians-wallbedandbreakfast.com
• website:
www.hadrians-wallbedandbreakfast.com

Hotel
Bridge Hotel, BUTTERMERE,
Cumbria CA13 9UZ
017687 70252
• e-mail: enquiries@bridge-hotel.com
• website: www.bridge-hotel.com

Guest House
Dalegarth Guest House, Hassness Estate,
BUTTERMERE, Cumbria CA13 9XA
017687 70233
• e-mail: dalegarth.buttermere@rdplus.net
• website: www.dalegarthguesthouse.co.uk

Self-Catering
Loweswater Holiday Cottages, Scale Hill,
Loweswater, COCKERMOUTH,
Cumbria CA13 9UX
01900 85232
• website:
www.loweswaterholidaycottages.co.uk

Hotel
Rob Treeby, Ivy House Hotel, Ivy House,
Main Street, HAWKSHEAD, Cumbria
015394 36204
• e-mail: rob@ivyhousehotel.com
• website: www.ivyhousehotel.com

Farm & Self-Catering
Mrs S. Beaty, Garnett House Farm,
Burneside, KENDAL, Cumbria
01539 724542
• e-mail: info@garnetthousefarm.co.uk
• website: www.garnetthousefarm.co.uk

Farmhouse B & B
Mrs Swindlehurst, Tranthwaite Hall,
Underbarrow, near KENDAL,
Cumbria LA8 8HG
015395 68285
• e-mail: tranthwaitehall@aol.com
• website: www.tranthwaitehall.co.uk

Self-Catering
Mrs Val Sunter, "Dora's Cottage",
c/o Higher House Farm, Oxenholme Lane,
Natland, KENDAL, Cumbria LA9 7QH
015395 61177
• website: www.shortbreaks-uk.co.uk/514

Hotel
Derwentwater Hotel, Portinscale, KESWICK,
Cumbria CA12 5RE
017687 72538
• e-mail: info@derwentwater-hotel.co.uk
• website:
www.derwentwater.hotel.dial.pipex.com

B&B
Highside Farm, Bassenthwaite, KESWICK
Cumbria CA12 4QG
017687 76952/76328
• e-mail: deborah@highside.co.uk
• website: www.highside.co.uk

Self-Catering
Brook House Cottage Holidays,
Bassenthwaite Village,
Near KESWICK, Cumbria
017687 76393
• e-mail: a.m.trafford@amserve.net
• website:
www.holiday.cottageslakedistrict.co.uk

Self-Catering
Keswick Cottages, Kentmere, How Lane,
KESWICK, Cumbria CA12 5RS
017687 73895
• **e-mail: info@keswickcottages.co.uk**
• **website: www.keswickcottages.co.uk**

B & B
Mrs S. Park, Langdale, 14 Leonard Street,
KESWICK, Cumbria CA12 4EL
017687 73977
• **website: www.langdaleguesthouse.com**

Self-Catering
16 Hewetson Court, Main Street,
KESWICK, Cumbria
01786 814955
• **e-mail: martyn_d2@hotmail.com**

Caravan & Camping
Mrs L. Lamb, Burns Caravan & Camping
Site, St Johns in the Vale, KESWICK,
Cumbria CA12 4RR
01768 779225
• **e-mail: llamb@callnetuk.com**

B & B
Val Bradley, Rickerby Grange, Portinscale,
KESWICK, Cumbria CA12 5RH
017687 72344
• **e-mail: val@ricor.co.uk**
• **website: www.ricor.co.uk**

Self-Catering
Watendlath Guest House and Barrowside &
Swinside Cottages,
c/o Mrs Walker, 15 Acorn Street, KESWICK,
Cumbria CA12 4EA
01768 774165
• **e-mail: info@watendlathguesthouse.co.uk**
• **website: www.watendlathguesthouse.co.uk**

Guest House
Ian Townsend and Annie Scally, Latrigg
House, St Herbert Street,
KESWICK, Cumbria CA12 4DF
017687 73068
• **e-mail: info@latrigghouse.com**
• **website: www.latrigghouse.com**

Self-Catering
Mrs S.J. Bottom, Crossfield Cottages,
KIRKOSWALD, Penrith, Cumbria CA10 1EU
01768 898711
• **e-mail: info@crossfieldcottages.co.uk**
• **website: www.crossfieldcottages.co.uk**

Hotel & Inn
The Shepherd's Arms Hotel,
Ennerdale Bridge,
LAKE DISTRICT NATIONAL PARK,
Cumbria CA23 3AR
01946 861249
• **e-mail: enquiries@shepherdsarmshotel.co.uk**
• **website: www.sheperdsarmshotel.co.uk**

B & B
Jenny Wickens, Garth Row,
LOWICK GREEN, Ulverston,
Cumbria LA12 8EB
01229 885633
• **e-mail: b&b@garthrow.freeserve.co.uk**
• **website: www.garthrow.co.uk**

Guest House / B & B
Mr & Mrs C. Smith, Mosedale House,
MOSEDALE, Mungrisdale,
Cumbria CA11 0XQ
01768 779371
• **e-mail: mosedale@northlakes.co.uk**
• **website: www.mosedalehouse.co.uk**

Guest House / Self-Catering
Near Howe Country House Hotel,
MUNGRISDALE, Penrith,
Cumbria CA11 0SH
017687 79678
• **e-mail: nearhowe@btopenworld.co.uk**
• **website: www.nearhowe.co.uk**

Caravan & Camping / Self-Catering
Park Foot Caravan & Camping Park,
Howtown Road, Pooley Bridge, PENRITH,
Cumbria CA10 2NA
017684 86309
• **e-mail: park.foot@talk21.com**
• **website: www.parkfootullswater.co.uk**

Guest House
Mrs M. Whittam, Netherdene Guest House,
Troutbeck, Near PENRITH,
Cumbria CA11 0SJ
017684 83475
• **e-mail: netherdene@aol.com**
• **website: www.netherdene.co.uk**

Guest House
Elle Jackson, Albany House,
5 Portland Place, PENRITH,
Cumbria CA11 7NQ
01768 863072
• **e-mail: info@albany-house.org.uk**
• **website: www.albany-house.org.uk**

Self-Catering / Caravan & Camping
Mr & Mrs Burnett, Fell View, Glenridding,
PENRITH, Cumbria CA11 0PJ
01768 482342; Evening: 01768 867420
• e-mail: enquiries@fellviewholidays.com
• website: www.fellviewholidays.com

Self-Catering / Caravan & Camping
Tanglewood Caravan Park, Causewayhead,
SILLOTH, Cumbria CA7 4PE
016973 31253
• e-mail: tanglewoodcaravanpark@hotmail.com
• website: www.tanglewoodcaravanpark.co.uk

Guest House / Self Catering
Mrs Jones, Primrose Cottage, Orton Road,
TEBAY, Cumbria CA10 3TL
01539 624791
• e-mail: info@primrosecottagecumbria.co.uk
• website: www.primrosecottagecumbria.co.uk

Self-Catering
High Dale Park House, Satterthwaite,
ULVERSTON, Cumbria CA12 8LJ
01229 860226
• e-mail: peter@lakesweddingmusic.com
• website: www.lakesweddingmusic.com

Guest House
Mr & Mrs Tyson, Hollywood Guest House,
Holly Road, WINDERMERE,
Cumbria LA23 2AF
015394 42219
• website: www.hollywoodguesthouse.co.uk

Self-Catering
Mr & Mrs Dodsworth, Birthwaite Edge,
Birthwaite Road, WINDERMERE,
Cumbria LA23 1BS
015394 42861
• e-mail: fhg@lakedge.com
• website: www.lakedge.com

Self-Catering
J.R. Benson, High Sett, Sun Hill Lane,
Troutbeck Bridge, WINDERMERE,
Cumbria LA23 1HJ
015394 42731
• e-mail: info@accommodationlakedistrict.com
• website: www.accommodationlakedistrict.com

•DERBYSHIRE

Farmhouse B & B / Self-Catering
Mrs M.A. Richardson, Throwley Hall Farm,
Ilam, ASHBOURNE, Derbyshire DE6 2BB
01538 308202
• e-mail: throwleyhall@talk21.com
• website: www.throwleyhallfarm.co.uk

Guest House
Mr & Mrs Hyde, Braemar Guest House,
10 Compton Road, BUXTON,
Derbyshire SK17 9DN
01298 78050
• e-mail: buxtonbraemar@supanet.com
• website: www.cressbrook.co.uk/buxton/braemar

Self-Catering
R.D. Hollands, Wheeldon Trees Farm,
Earl Sterndale, BUXTON,
Derbyshire SK17 0AA
01298 83219
• e-mail: hollands@earlsterndale.fsnet.co.uk
• website: www.wheeldontreesfarm.co.uk

Hotel
Biggin Hall Hotel, Biggin-by-Hartington,
BUXTON, Derbyshire SK17 0DH
01298 84451
• e-mail: enquiries@bigginhall.co.uk
• website: www.bigginhall.co.uk

Inn
Nick & Fiona Clough, The Devonshire Arms,
Peak Forest, near BUXTON,
Derbyshire SK17 8EJ
01298 23875
• e-mail: fiona.clough@virgin.net
• website: www.devarms.com

Farm / Self-Catering
J. Gibbs, Wolfscote Grange, HARTINGTON,
near Buxton, Derbyshire SK17 0AX
01298 84342
• e-mail: wolfscote@btinternet.com
• website: www.wolfscotegrangecottages.co.uk

FHG PUBLICATIONS

publish a large range of well-known accommodation
guides. We will be happy to send you details or you
can use the order form at the back of this book.

•DEVON

Self-Catering
Toad Hall Cottages,
DEVON
08700 777345
• website: www.toadhallcottages.com

Self-Catering
Waters Reach, West Quay, APPLEDORE,
Devon. C/o Viv and Peter Foley
01707 657644
• e-mail: viv@vfoley.freeserve.co.uk

Holiday Park
Parkers Farm Holiday Park,
Higher Mead Farm, ASHBURTON, Devon
01364 652598
• e-mail: parkersfarm@btconnect.com
• website: www.parkersfarm.co.uk

Self-Catering
North Devon Holiday Homes,
19 Cross Street, BARNSTAPLE,
Devon EX31 1BD
01271 376322
• e-mail: info@northdevonholidays.co.uk
• website: www.northdevonholidays.co.uk

Farm B & B / Self-Catering
Peter Day, Lower Yelland Farm, Fremington,
BARNSTAPLE, Devon EX31 3EN
01271 860101
• e-mail: peterday@loweryellandfarm.co.uk
• website: www.loweryellandfarm.co.uk

Self-Catering
Mr Ridge, Braddon Cottages, Ashwater,
BEAWORTHY, Devon EX21 5EP
01409 211350
• e-mail: holidays@braddoncottages.co.uk
• website: www.braddoncottages.co.uk

Hotel
Sandy Cove Hotel, Combe Martin Bay,
BERRYNARBOR, Devon EX34 9SR
01271 882243 / 882888
• e-mail: rg/4003483@aol.com
• website: www.exmoor-hospitality-inns.co.uk

Self-Catering / Organic Farm
Little Comfort Farm Cottages,
Little Comfort Farm, BRAUNTON,
North Devon EX33 2NJ
01271 812414
• e-mail: jackie.milsom@btclick.com
• website: www.littlecomfortfarm.co.uk

B & B
Mrs Roselyn Bradford, St Merryn,
Higher Park Road, BRAUNTON,
Devon EX33 2LG
01271 813805
• e-mail: ros@st-merryn.co.uk
• website: www.st-merryn.co.uk

Self-Catering
Devoncourt Holiday Flats, Berryhead Road,
BRIXHAM, Devon TQ5 9AB
01803 853748
• e-mail: devoncourt@devoncoast.com

Guest House
Mr John Parry, Woodlands Guest House,
Parkham Road, BRIXHAM,
South Devon TQ5 9BU
01803 852040
• e-mail: Dogfriendly2@aol.com
• website: www.dogfriendlyguesthouse.co.uk

Self-Catering
Wheel Farm Country Cottages, Berry Down,
COMBE MARTIN, Devon EX34 0NG
01271 882106
• e-mail: holidays@wheelfarmcottages.co.uk
• website: www.wheelfarmcottages.co.uk

Self-Catering
Mrs S.R. Ridalls, The Old Bakehouse,
7 Broadstone, DARTMOUTH,
Devon TQ6 9NR
01803 834585
• e-mail: pioneerparker@aol.com
• website: www.oldbakehousedartmouth.co.uk

Farm / B & B
Mrs Karen Williams, Stile Farm, Starcross,
EXETER, Devon EX6 8PD
01626 890268
• e-mail: info@stile-farm.co.uk
• website: www.stile-farm.co.uk

Farmhouse B & B
Mrs J. Bragg, Marianne Pool Farm,
Clyst St George, EXETER, Devon EX3 0NZ
01392 874939
• website:
www.s-h-systems.co.uk/hotels/mariannepool.html

B & B
Mrs Sally Glanville, Rydon Farm, Woodbury,
EXETER, Devon EX5 1LB
01395 232341
• website:
www.hotelon.com/uk/s-w/b&b/rydon-farm.htm

Self-Catering
Christine Duncan, Raleigh Holiday Homes,
24 Raleigh Road, EXMOUTH,
Devon EX8 2SB
01395 266967
• e-mail: c.e.duncan@amserve.net

Farmhouse B&B
Mrs Alison Homa, Mullacott Farm,
Mullacott Cross, ILFRACOMBE,
Devon EX34 8NA
01271 866877
• e-mail: relax@mullacottfarm.co.uk
• website: www.mullacottfarm.co.uk

Farm / Self-Catering
Mrs E. Sansom, Widmouth Farm,
Watermouth, Near ILFRACOMBE,
Devon EX34 9RX
01271 863743
• e-mail: holiday@widmouthfarmcottages.co.uk
• website: www.widmouthfarmcottages.co.uk

Self-Catering
Karen Jackson, Torcross Apartment Hotel,
Torcross, KINGSBRIDGE, Devon
01548 580206
• e-mail: enquiries@torcross.com
• website: www.torcross.com

Hotel
Buckland-Tout-Saints Hotel & Restaurant,
Goveton, KINGSBRIDGE, Devon TQ7 2DS
01548 853055
• e-mail: buckland@tout-saints.co.uk
• website: www.tout-saints.co.uk

Guest House
Tricia & Alan Francis, Glenville House,
2 Tors Road, LYNMOUTH,
North Devon EX35 6ET
01598 752202
• e-mail: tricia@glenvillelynmouth.co.uk
• website: www.glenvillelynmouth.co.uk

Guest House
Mrs J. Parker, Tregonwell, The Olde Sea
Captain's House, 1 Tors Road, LYNMOUTH,
Exmoor National Park, Devon EX35 6ET
01598 753369
• website:
www.SmoothHound.co.uk/hotels/tregonwl.html

Inn
The Exmoor Sandpiper Inn, Countisbury,
LYNMOUTH, Devon EX35 6NE
01598 741263
• e-mail: info@exmoor-sandpiper.co.uk

Farm / B & B
Great Sloncombe Farm,
MORETONHAMPSTEAD,
Newton Abbot, Devon TQ13 8QF
01647 440595
• e-mail: hmerchant@sloncombe.freeserve.co.uk
• website: www.greatsloncombefarm.co.uk

Self-Catering
Mrs Whale, Roselands, Totnes Road,
Ipplepen, NEWTON ABBOT, Devon
01803 812701
• e-mail: enquiries@roselands.net
• website: www.roselands.net

B & B
Mrs Rosemary Ward, Parsonage Farm,
Iddesleigh, OKEHAMPTON,
Devon EX19 8SN
• website:
www.devon-holiday.com/parsonage-farm/

Farm Guest House
Mrs Ann Forth, Fluxton Farm,
OTTERY ST MARY, Devon EX11 1RJ
01404 812818
• website:
www.s-h-systems.co.uk/hotels/fluxtonfarm.html

Guest House
The Lamplighter Hotel, 103 Citadel Road,
The Hoe, PLYMOUTH, Devon PL1 2RN
01752 663855
• e-mail: lamplighterhotel@ukonline.co.uk

Self-Catering / Caravan & Camping
Harford Bridge Holiday Park, Peter Tavy,
TAVISTOCK, Devon PL19 9LS
01822 810349
• e-mail: enquiry@harfordbridge.co.uk
• website: www.harfordbridge.co.uk

Guest House
Mrs Arnold, The Mill, Washfield,
TIVERTON, Devon EX16 9PD
01884 255297
• e-mail: arnold5@washfield.freeserve.co.uk
• website: www.washfield.freeserve.co.uk

Guest House
Aveland Hotel, Aveland Road,
Babbacombe, TORQUAY, Devon TQ1 3PT
01803 326622
• e-mail: avelandhotel@aol.com
• website: www.avelandhotel.co.uk

Self-Catering
Mrs H. Carr, Sunningdale Apartments,
11 Babbacombe Downs Road, TORQUAY,
Devon TQ1 3LF
• website: www.sunningdaleapartments.co.uk

Self-Catering
Mrs J. Ford, Flear Farm Cottages,
East Allington, TOTNES, Devon TQ9 7RF
01548 521227
• e-mail: flearfarm@btinternet.com
• website: www.flearfarm.co.uk

Self-Catering
J. Lincoln-Gordon, Golland Farm,
Burrington, UMBERLEIGH, Devon EX37 9JP
01769 520263
• e-mail: golland@btinternet.com
• website: www.golland.btinternet.co.uk

Self-Catering
Jane Cromey-Hawke, Collacott Farm,
Kings Nympton, UMBERLEIGH,
Devon EX37 9TP
01769 572491
• e-mail: jane@collacott.co.uk
• website: www.collacott.co.uk

Guest House
Sunnymeade Country Hotel, Dean Cross,
West Down, WOOLACOMBE,
Devon EX34 8NT
01271 863668
• e-mail: info@sunnymeade.co.uk
• website: www.sunnymeade.co.uk

Self-Catering/ Camping
Dartmoor Country Holidays,
Magpie Leisure Park, Bedford Bridge,
Horrabridge, YELVERTON, Devon PL20 7RY
01822 852651
• website: www.dartmoorcountryholidays.co.uk

•DORSET

Guest House
Caroline Pielesz, The Walnuts,
2 Prout Bridge, BEAMINSTER, Dorset
01308 862211
• e-mail: caroline@thewalnuts.co.uk

Guest House
S. Barling, Mayfield Guest House,
46 Frances Road, BOURNEMOUTH, Dorset
BH1 3SA
01202 551839
• e-mail: accom@mayfieldguesthouse.com
• website: www.mayfieldguesthouse.com

Hotel / Guest House
Southernhay Hotel, 42 Alum Chine Road,
Westbourne, BOURNEMOUTH,
Dorset BH4 8DX
01202 761251
• e-mail: enquiries@southernhayhotel.co.uk
• website: www.southernhayhotel.co.uk

Hotel
Fircroft Hotel, Owls Road, BOURNEMOUTH,
Dorset BH5 1AE
01202 309771
• e-mail: info@fircrofthotel.co.uk
• website: www.fircrofthotel.co.uk

Hotel / Guest House
Westcotes House Hotel,
9 Southbourne Overcliff Drive,
BOURNEMOUTH, Dorset BH6 3TE
01202 428512
• website: www.westcoteshousehotel.co.uk

Caravan & Camping
Martin Cox, Highlands End Holiday Park,
BRIDPORT, Eype, Dorset DT6 6AR
01308 422139
• e-mail: holidays@wdlh.co.uk
• website: www.wdlh.co.uk

Self-Catering
Westover Farm Cottages,
Wootton Fitzpaine, Near LYME REGIS,
Dorset DT6 6NE
01297 560451
• e-mail: wfcottages@aol.com
• website:
   www.lymeregis.com/westover-farm-cottages/

Guest House / Self-Catering
White Horse Farm, Middlemarsh,
SHERBORNE, Dorset DT9 5QN
01963 210222
• e-mail: enquiries@whitehorsefarm.co.uk
• website: www.whitehorsefarm.co.uk

Hotel
The Knoll House, STUDLAND BAY,
Dorset BH19 3AW
01929 450450
• e-mail: enquiries@knollhouse.co.uk
• website: www.knollhouse.co.uk

**Please mention this guide
when enquiring about
accommodation**

B&B
Mrs Jill Miller, Lower Fifehead Farm,
Fifehead, St Quinton, STURMINSTER
NEWTON, Dorset DT10 2AP
01258 817335
• website: www.ruraldorset.co.uk

Touring Park
Wareham Forest Touring Park, North Trigon,
WAREHAM, Dorset BH20 7NZ
01929 551393
e-mail: holiday@wareham-forest.co.uk
website:
http://freespace.virgin.net/wareham.forest

Self-Catering on Working Farm
Josephine Pearse, Tamarisk Farm Cottages,
WEST BEXINGTON, Dorchester,
Dorset DT2 9DF
01308 897784
• e-mail: tamarisk@eurolink.ltd.net
• website: www.tamariskfarm.co.uk

Self-Catering
Mrs J. Elwood, Lower Farmhouse,
Langton Herring, WEYMOUTH,
Dorset DT3 4JB
01305 871187
• e-mail: jane@mayo.fsbusiness.co.uk
• website: www.characterfarmcottages.co.uk

•DURHAM

Self-Catering
Peter Wilson, East Briscoe Farm,
Baldersdale, BARNARD CASTLE,
Co Durham DL12 9UL
01833 650087
• e-mail: fhg@eastbriscoe.co.uk
• website: www.eastbriscoe.co.uk

Hotel / Golf
Ramside Hall Hotel, Carrville, DURHAM,
Co Durham DH1 1TD
0191 3865282
• e-mail: info@ramsidehallhotel.co.uk
• website: www.ramsidehallhotel.co.uk

Self-Catering
Raby Estates Holiday Cottages,
Upper Teesdale Estate Office,
MIDDLETON-IN-TEESDALE, Barnard Castle,
Co Durham DL12 0QH
01833 640209
• e-mail: teesdaleestate@rabycastle.com
• website: www.rabycastle.com

•GLOUCESTERSHIRE

Lodge
Ian Gibson, Thornbury Golf Lodge, Bristol
Road, Thornbury, BRISTOL, Gloucestershire
01454 281144
• e-mail: info@thornburygc.co.uk
• website: www.thornburygc.co.uk

B & B
Mrs G. Jeffrey, Brymbo, Honeybourne Lane,
Mickleton, CHIPPING CAMPDEN,
Gloucestershire GL55 6PU
01386 438890
• e-mail: enquiries@brymbo.com
• website: www.brymbo.com

Farmhouse B & B
Mrs D. Gwilliam, Dryslade Farm,
English Bicknor, COLEFORD,
Gloucestershire, GL16 7PA
01594 860259
• e-mail: dryslade@agriplus.net
• website: www.drysladefarm.co.uk

Inn
The Wild Duck, EWEN, Gloucestershire
01285 770310
• e-mail: wduckinn@aol.com
• website: www.thewildduck.co.uk

Farmhouse B & B
Suzie Paton, Milton Farm, FAIRFORD,
Gloucestershire GL7 4HZ
01285 712205
• e-mail: milton@farmersweekly.net
• website: www.milton-farm.co.uk

Guest House / Farm
Gunn Mill Guest House, Lower Spout Lane,
MITCHELDEAN, Gloucestershire GL17 0EA
01594 827577
• e-mail: info@gunnmillhouse.co.uk
• website: www.gunnmillhouse.co.uk

B & B
Mrs F.J. Adams, Aston House,
Broadwell, MORETON-IN-MARSH,
Gloucestershire GL56 0TJ
01451 830475
• e-mail: fja@netcomuk.co.uk
• website:
    www.netcomuk.co.uk/~nmfa/aston_house.html

Farmhouse B & B
Robert Smith, Corsham Field Farmhouse,
Bledington Road, STOW-ON-THE-WOLD,
Gloucestershire GL54 1JH
• e-mail: farmhouse@corshamfield.co.uk
• website: www.corshamfield.co.uk

B & B

Mrs Williams, Abbots Court, Church End, Twyning, TEWKESBURY, Gloucestershire GL20 6DA
01684 292515
- e-mail: bernie@abbotscourt.fsbusiness.co.uk
- website:
  www.glosfarmhols.co.uk/abbots-court/

B & B

Mrs Wendy Swait, Inschdene, Atcombe Road, SOUTH WOODCHESTER, Stroud, Gloucestershire GL5 5EW
01453 873254
- e-mail: malcolm.swait@repp.co.uk
- website: www.inschdene.co.uk

•HAMPSHIRE

B & B

Mrs Arnold-Brown, Hilden B&B, Southampton Road, Boldre, BROCKENHURST, Hampshire SO41 8PT
01590 623682
- website: www.newforestbandb-hilden.co.uk

Caravan & Camping

Kingfisher Caravan Park, Browndown Road, Stokes Bay, GOSPORT, Hampshire PO13 9BG
023 9250 2611
- e-mail: info@kingfisher-caravan-park.co.uk
- website: www.kingfisher-caravan-park.co.uk

Caravan & Campsite

Hayling Island Family Campsites, Copse Lane, HAYLING ISLAND, Hampshire
023 9246 2479, 023 9246 4695, 023 9246 3684
- e-mail: lowertye@euphony.net
- website: www.haylingcampsites.co.uk

B & B

Mr & Mrs Farrell, Honeysuckle House, 24 Clinton Road, LYMINGTON, Hampshire SO41 9EA
01590 676635
- e-mail: derekfarrell1@btopenworld.com
- website:
  www.newforest.demon.co.uk/honeysuckle.htm

Hotel

Woodlands Lodge Hotel, Bartley Road, Woodlands, NEW FOREST, Hampshire SO40 7GN
023 8029 2257
- e-mail: reception@woodlands-lodge.co.uk
- website: www.woodlands-lodge.co.uk

B & B

Mr & Mrs T. Jelley, Appledore Cottage, Holmsley Road, Wootton, NEW MILTON, Hampshire, BH25 5TR
01425 629506
- e-mail: info@appledorecottage.co.uk
- website:
  www.newforest-online.co.uk/appledore

•HEREFORDSHIRE

Hotel

The Steppes, Ullingswick, Near HEREFORD, HR1 3JG
01432 820424
- e-mail: info@steppeshotel.co.uk
- website: www.steppeshotel.co.uk

B & B / Farm

Mrs D Sinclair, Holly House Farm, Allensmore, HEREFORD, Herefordshire HR2 9BH
01432 277294
- e-mail: hollyhousefarm@aol.com
- website: www.hollyhousefarm.org.uk

B & B

Mrs Gill Andrews, Webton Court Farmhouse, KINGSTONE, Herefordshire HR2 9NF
01981 250220
- e-mail: gill@webton.fsnet.co.uk

B & B

Mrs S.W. Born, The Coach House, Putley, LEDBURY, Herefordshire HR8 2QP
01531 670684
- e-mail: wendyborn@putley-coachhouse.co.uk
- website: www.putley-coachhouse.co.uk

Self-Catering

Mrs Jane Viner, Docklow Manor, Docklow, LEOMINSTER, Herefordshire HR6 0RX
01568 760668
- e-mail: jane@docklowmanor.freeserve.co.uk
- website: www.docklow-manor.co.uk

B & B

Mrs I. Pritchard, Olchon Cottage Farm, LONGTOWN, Herefordshire HR2 0NS
01873 860233
- website: www.golden-valley.co.uk/olchon/

Guest House / Farm

Mrs Drzymalski, Thatch Close, Llangrove, ROSS-ON-WYE, Herefordshire HR9 6EL
01989 770300
- e-mail: thatch.close@virgin.net
- website: www.thatchclose.com

•ISLE OF WIGHT

Caravan & Camping
Castlehaven Caravan Site, Niton, Near
Ventnor, Isle of Wight, PO38 2ND
01983 855556
• e-mail: caravans@castlehaven.co.uk
• website: www.castlehaven.co.uk

•KENT

Caravan & Camping
Woodlands Park, Tenterden Road,
BIDDENDEN, Kent
01580 291216
• e-mail: woodlandsp@aol.com
• website: www.campingsite.co.uk

Self-Catering
Marion Fuller, Three Chimneys Farm,
Bedgebury Road, GOUDHURST,
Kent TN17 2RA
• e-mail: marionfuller@threechimneysfarm.co.uk
• website: www.threechimneysfarm.co.uk

Farm B & B / Camping
Julia Soyke, Manor Court Farm, Ashurst,
TUNBRIDGE WELLS, Kent TN3 9TB
01892 740279
• e-mail: jsoyke@jsoyke.freeserve.co.uk
• website: www.manorcourtfarm.co.uk

•LEICESTERSHIRE

Guest House
The Highbury Guest House,
146 Leicester Road, LOUGHBOROUGH,
Leicestershire LE11 2AQ
01509 230545
• e-mail: emkhighbury@supanet.com
• website: www.thehighburyguesthouse.co.uk

•LINCOLNSHIRE

B & B
Jenny Dixon, 19 West Street, Kings Cliffe,
PETERBOROUGH, Lincolnshire PE8 6XB
01780 470365
• e-mail: kjhl-dixon@hotmail.com
• website: kingjohnhuntinglodge.com

Hotel
Petwood Hotel, Stixwood Road,
WOODHALL SPA, Lincolnshire
01526 352411
• e-mail: reception@petwood.co.uk
• website: www.petwood.co.uk

•NORFOLK

Self-Catering
Sand Dune Cottages, Tan Lane,
CAISTER-ON-SEA, Great Yarmouth, Norfolk
01493 720352
• e-mail: sand.dune.cottages@amserve.net
• website: www.eastcoastlive.co.uk/sites/
          sandunecottages.php

Farmhouse B & B
Mrs Jenny Bell, Peacock House,
Peacock Lane, Old Beetley, DEREHAM,
Norfolk NR20 4DG
• e-mail: PeackH@aol.com
• website:
www.SmoothHound.co.uk/hotels/peacockh.htm

Self-Catering
Nannette Catchpole, Walcot Green Farm,
DISS, Norfolk IP22 5SU
01379 652806
• e-mail: n.catchpole.wgf@virgin.net
• website: www.walcotgreenfarm.co.uk

Self-Catering
Idyllic Cottages at Vere Lodge,
South Raynham, FAKENHAM,
Norfolk NR21 7HE
01328 838261
• e-mail: major@verelodge.co.uk
• website: www.idylliccottages.co.uk

Self-Catering
Blue Riband Holidays, HEMSBY,
Great Yarmouth, Norfolk NR29 4HA
01493 730445
• website: www.BlueRibandHolidays.co.uk

Farmhouse B & B
Mrs Lynda Mack, Hempstead Hall, HOLT,
Norfolk NR25 6TN
01263 712224
• website: www.broadland.com/hempsteadhall

Guest House B & B
Mrs Christine Lilah Thrower, Whincliff,
Cromer Road, MUNDESLEY-ON-SEA,
Norfolk NR11 8DU
01263 721554
• e-mail: whincliff@freeuk.com
• website: http://whincliff.freeuk.com

Self-Catering
Mr & Mrs Moore, Mangreen Farm Holiday
Cottages, STANFIELD, Dereham,
Norfolk NR20 4HZ
01328 700272
• e-mail: bettymick@compuserve.com
• website: www.mangreen.co.uk

Inn
The Lifeboat Inn and Old Coach House,
Ship Lane, THORNHAM, Norfolk PE36 6LT
01485 512236
• website: www.llifeboatinn.co.uk

•NORTHUMBERLAND

Self-Catering
Village Farm Self-Catering, Town Foot Farm,
Shilbottle, ALNWICK,
Northumberland NE66 2HG
01665 575591
• e-mail: crissy@villagefarmcottages.co.uk
• website: www.villagefarmcottages.co.uk

Self-Catering
Mrs Helen Wyld, New Moor House,
Edlingham, ALNWICK,
Northumberland NE66 2BT
01665 574638
• e-mail: stay@newmoorhouse.co.uk
• website: www.newmoorhouse.co.uk

Hotel
The Cobbled Yard Hotel Ltd, 40 Walkergate,
BERWICK-UPON-TWEED,
Northumberland TD15 1DJ
01289 308407
• e-mail:
  cobbledyardhotel@berwick35.fsnet.co.uk
• website: www.cobbledyardhotel.com

Caravans
D.J. Caravan Holidays (Haggerston Castle),
c/o Mr J. Lane, 11 Wallis Street, Penshaw,
Houghton-le-Spring DH4 7HB
• e-mail: joseph_lane1@hotmail.com
• website: www.djcaravanholidays.com

•OXFORDSHIRE

B & B
Carol Ellis, Wynford House, 79 Main Road,
Long Hanborough, BLADON,
Oxfordshire OX29 8JX
01993 881402
• website:
  www.accommodation.net/wynford.htm

Inn
The Kings Head Inn, The Green,
BLEDINGTON, Oxfordshire
01608 658365
• e-mail: kingshead@orr-ewing.com
• website: www.kingsheadinn.net

Guest House / B & B
Gorselands Hall, Boddington Lane,
North Leigh, WITNEY,
Oxfordshire OX29 6PU
01993 882292
• e-mail: hamilton@gorselandshall.com
• website: www.gorselandshall.com

Guest House
Mrs Elizabeth Simpson, Field View, Wood
Green, WITNEY, Oxfordshire OX28 1DE
01993 705485
• e-mail: bandb@fieldview-witney.co.uk
• website: www.fieldview-witney.co.uk

•SHROPSHIRE

Farm B & B
Mrs M. Jones, Acton Scott Farm,
Acton Scott, CHURCH STRETTON,
Shropshire SY6 6QN
01694 781260
• **e-mail: bandb@actonscottfarm.co.uk**
• **website: www.actonscottfarm.co.uk**

Guest House
Ron & Jenny Repath, Meadowlands,
Lodge Lane, Frodesley, DORRINGTON,
Shropshire SY5 7HD
01694 731350
• **e-mail: meadowlands@talk21.com**
• **website: www.meadowlands.co.uk**

B & B
Ravenscourt Manor, Woofferton,
LUDLOW, Shropshire SY8 4AL
01584 711905
• **e-mail: ravenscourtmanor@amserve.com**
• **website:**
  www.s-h-systems.co.uk/hotels/ravenscourt.html

Self-Catering
Clive & Cynthia Prior, Mocktree Barns
Holiday Cottages, Leintwardine, LUDLOW,
Shropshire SY7 0LY
01547 540441
• **e-mail: mocktreebarns@care4free.net**
• **website: www.mocktreeholidays.co.uk**

Guest House & Self-Catering
Mrs E. Purnell, Ravenscourt Manor,
Woofferton, LUDLOW, Shropshire SY8 6AL
01584 711905
• **e-mail: ravenscourtmanor@amserve.com**
• **website:**
  www.smoothhound.co.uk/ravenscourt

Inn
M.A. Tennant, The Talbot Inn, High Street,
MUCH WENLOCK, Shropshire TF13 6AA
01952 727077
• **e-mail: maggie@talbotinn.idps.co.uk**
• **website: www.the-talbot-inn.co.uk**

B & B
Mrs P. Morrissey, Top Farm House, Knockin,
Near OSWESTRY, Shropshire SY10 2HN
01691 682582
• **e-mail: p.a.m@knockin.freeserve.co.uk**
• **website: www.topfarmknockin.co.uk**

Hotel
Pen-y-Dyffryn Country Hotel, OSWESTRY,
Shropshire SY10 7JD
01691 653700
• **e-mail: stay@peny.co.uk**
• **website: www.peny.co.uk**

B & B
Lythwood Hall Bed & Breakfast,
2 Lythwood Hall, Lythwood, Bayston Hill,
SHREWSBURY, Shropshire SY3 0AD
07074 874747
• **e-mail: lythwoodhall@amserve.net**

Self-Catering
Mrs V. Evans, Church Farm, Rowton,
Near Wellington, TELFORD,
Shropshire TF6 6QY
01952 770381
• **e-mail: church.farm@bigfoot.com**
• **website:**
  www.virtual-shropshire.co.uk/churchfarm

•SOMERSET

Guest House / Farm/ Self-Catering
Jackie & David Bishop, Toghill House Farm,
Wick, BATH, Somerset BS30 5RT
01225 891261
• **website: www.toghillhousefarm.co.uk**

B & B
Mrs C. Bryson, Walton Villa,
3 Newbridge Hill, BATH, Somerset BA1 3PW
01225 482792
• **e-mail: walton.villa@virgin.net**
• **website: www.walton.izest.com**

Self-Catering / Caravan & Camping
T.M. Hicks, Diamond Farm, Weston Road,
BREAN, Near Burnham-on-Sea,
Somerset TA8 2RL
01278 751263
• **e-mail: trevor@diamondfarm42.freeserve.co.uk**
• **website: www.diamondfarm.co.uk**

Caravan & Camping
Beachside Holiday Park, Coast Road,
BREAN SANDS, Burnham-on-Sea,
Somerset TA8 2QZ
01278 751346
• **e-mail: beachside@breansands.fsnet.co.uk**
• **website: www.beachsideholidaypark.co.uk**

Farm B&B / Self-catering
Delia Edwards, Brinsea Green Farm, Brinsea
Lane, Congresbury, Near BRISTOL,
North Somerset BS49 5JN
01934 852278
• **e-mail: delia@brinseagreenfarm.co.uk**
• **website: www.brinseagreenfarm.co.uk**

B & B

Mrs Alexander, Priors Mead,
23 Rectory Road, BURNHAM-ON-SEA,
Somerset TA8 2BZ
01278 782116
• e-mail: priorsmead@aol.com
• website: www.priorsmead.co.uk

B & B / Self-Catering

Butcombe Farm, Aldwick Vale, BUTCOMBE,
Near Blagdon, Somerset BS40 7UW
01761 462380
• e-mail: info@butcombe-farm.demon.co.uk
• website: www.butcombe-farm.demon.co.uk

Caravan & Camping Park

Broadway House Holiday Touring Caravan &
Camping Park, CHEDDAR,
Somerset BS27 3DB
01934 742610
• e-mail: enquiries@broadwayhouse.uk.com
• website: www.broadwayhouse.uk.com

B & B

Mrs C. Bacon, Honeydown Farm,
Seaborough Hill, CREWKERNE,
Somerset TA18 8PL
01460 72665
• e-mail: cb@honeydown.freeserve.co.uk
• website: www.honeydown.freeserve.co.uk

Hotel

Yarn Market Hotel, 25-33 High Street,
DUNSTER, Somerset TA24 6SF
01643 821425
• e-mail: yarnmarket.hotel@virgin.net
• website: www.yarnmarkethotel.co.uk

Inn

Exmoor White Horse Inn, EXFORD,
Somerset TA24 7PY
01643 831229
• website: www.exmoor-hospitality-inns.co.uk

Self-Catering

Mr Hughes, West Withy Farm Holiday
Cottages, Upton, Near Wiveliscombe,
EXMOOR, Somerset TA4 2JH
01398 371258
• e-mail: westwithyfarm@exmoor-cottages.com
• website: www.exmoor-cottages.com

Self-Catering / B & B

Mrs Joan Atkins, 2 Edgcott Cottage,
Exford, EXMOOR, Somerset TA24 7QG
01643 831564
• e-mail: info@stilemoorexmoor.co.uk
• website: www.stilemoorexmoor.co.uk

Farm / Self-Catering

Mrs Styles, Wintershead Farm, Simonsbath,
EXMOOR, Somerset TA24 7LF
01643 831222
• e-mail: info@wintershead.co.uk
• website: www.wintershead.co.uk

Farm Self-Catering & Camping

Westermill Farm, Exford, EXMOOR,
Somerset TA24 7NJ
01643 831238
• e-mail: holidays@westermill-exmoor.co.uk
• website: www.exmoorfarmholidays.co.uk

Self-Catering

Mrs N. Hanson, Woodcombe Lodges,
Bratton, MINEHEAD,
Somerset TA24 8SQ
01643 702789
• e-mail: nicola@woodcombelodge.co.uk
• website: www.woodcombelodge.co.uk

B & B

Mr P.R. Weir, Slipper Cottage,
41 Bishopston, MONTACUTE,
Somerset TA15 6UX
01935 823073
• e-mail: sue.weir@totalise.co.uk
• website: www.slippercottage.co.uk

B & B

Mr & Mrs Painter, Blorenge House,
57 Staplegrove Road, TAUNTON, Somerset
TA1 1DG
01823 283005
• e-mail: enquiries@blorengehouse.co.uk
• website: www.blorengehouse.co.uk

Farm / B & B

Yew Tree Farm, THEALE, Near Wedmore,
Somerset BS28 4SN
01934 712475
• e-mail: enquiries@yewtreefarmbandb.co.uk
• website: www.yewtreefarmbandb.co.uk

Self-Catering
Croft Holiday Cottages, 2 The Croft, Anchor Street, WATCHET, Somerset TA23 0BY
01984 631121
• e-mail: croftcottages@talk21.com
• website: www.cottagessomerset.com

Farm / B & B
Mrs Sheila Stott, 'Lana', Hollow Farm, Westbury-sub-Mendip, WELLS, Somerset
01749 870635
• e-mail: sheila@stott.2366

Hotel
Braeside Hotel, 2 Victoria Park, WESTON-SUPER-MARE, Somerset BS23 2HZ
01934 626642
• e-mail: braeside@tesco.net
• website: www.braesidehotel.co.uk

•STAFFORDSHIRE

Farm B & B / Self-Catering
Mrs M. Hiscoe-James, Offley Grove Farm, Adbaston, ECCLESHALL, Staffordshire ST20 0QB
01785 280205
• e-mail: accom@offleygrovefarm.freeserve.co.uk
• website: www.offleygrovefarm.co.uk

Guest House
Ruth Franks, The Beehive, Churnet View Road, OAKAMOOR, Staffordshire ST10 3AE
01538 702420
• e-mail: thebeehiveoakamoor@btinternet.com
• website: www.thebeehiveguesthouse.co.uk

•SUFFOLK

Guest House
Kay Dewsbury, Manorhouse, The Green, Beyton, BURY ST EDMUNDS, Suffolk IP30 9AF
01359 270960
• e-mail: manorhouse@beyton.com
• website: www.beyton.com

B & B / Self-Catering
Tim & Sarah Kindred, High House Farm, Cransford, FRAMLINGHAM, Woodbridge, Suffolk IP13 9PD
01728 663461
• e-mail: info@highhousefarm.co.uk
• website: www.highhousefarm.co.uk

Farmhouse / Caravan Site
Fiddlers Hall, Cransford, FRAMLINGHAM, Woodbridge, Suffolk IP13 9PQ
• e-mail: johnmann@suffolkonline.com
• website: www.fiddlershall.com

Self-Catering
Kessingland Cottages, Rider Haggard Lane, KESSINGLAND. Contact: S. Mahmood, 156 Bramley Road, Beckenham, Kent BR3 6PG
020 8650 0539
• e-mail: jeeptrek@kjti.freeserve.co.uk
• website: www.k-cottage.co.uk

Self-Catering
Southwold Self-Catering Properties. H.A. Adnams, 98 High Street, SOUTHWOLD, Suffolk IP18 6DP
01502 723292
• e-mail: haadnams_lets@ic24.net
• website: www.haadnams.com

Self-Catering
Mr M. Scott, The Grove, Priory Green, Edwardstone, Lavenham, SUDBURY, Suffolk CO10 5PP
01787 211115
• e-mail: mark@grove-cottages.co.uk
• website: www.grove-cottages.co.uk

Hotel
The Crown & Castle, Orford, WOODBRIDGE, Suffolk IP12 2LJ
01394 450205
• e-mail: info@crownandcastle.co.uk
• website: www.crownandcastle.co.uk

•SURREY

Hotel
Chase Lodge Hotel, 10 Park Road, Hampton Wick, KINGSTON-UPON-THAMES, Surrey KT1 4AS
020 8943 1862
• e-mail: info@chaselodgehotel.com
• website: www.chaselodgehotel.com

Self-Catering
Mrs J.A. Vause, Woodend, High Cotts Lane, WEST CLANDON, Surrey GU4 7XA
01483 222644
• e-mail: deevause@amserve.net
• website: www.hillcrest-mortehue.co.uk

visit the FHG website
www.holidayguides.com

•EAST SUSSEX

Self-Catering
Eva Morris, Pekes, CHIDDINGLY,
East Sussex
020 7352 8088
• e-mail: pekes.afa@virgin.net
• website: www.pekesmanor.com

Hotel
Beauport Park Hotel, Battle Road,
HASTINGS, East Sussex TN38 8EA
01424 851222
• e-mail:
  reservations@beauportprkhotel.demon.co.uk
• website: www.beauportparkhotel.co.uk

Self-Catering
Beach Cottages, Claremont Road,
SEAFORD BN25 2QQ.
Contact: Julia Lewis, 47 Wandle Bank,
London, SW19 1DW
020 8542 5073
• website: www.beachcottages.info

•WEST SUSSEX

Caravan & Camping
Wicks Farm Holiday Park, Redlands Lane,
West Wittering, CHICHESTER,
West Sussex PO20 8QD
01243 513116
• e-mail: wicks.farm@virgin.net
• website: www.wicksfarm.co.uk

B & B
Mrs M.R. Milton, Beacon Lodge B&B,
London Road, WATERSFIELD,
West Sussex RH20 1NH
01798 831026
• e-mail: beaconlodge@hotmail.com
• website: www.beaconlodge.co.uk

•WARWICKSHIRE

Guest House
Linhill Guest House, 35 Evesham Place,
STRATFORD-UPON-AVON,
Warwickshire CV37 6HT
01789 292879
• e-mail: linhill@bigwig.net
• website: www.linhillguesthouse.co.uk

Guest House / B & B
Julia Downie, Holly Tree Cottage,
Pathlow, STRATFORD-UPON-AVON,
Warwickshire CV37 0ES
01789 204461
• e-mail: john@hollytree-cottage.co.uk
• website: www.hollytree-cottage.co.uk

Guest House
Mr & Mrs Learmount,
Green Haven Guest House,
217 Evesham Road,
STRATFORD-UPON-AVON,
Warwickshire CV37 9AS
01789 297874
• e-mail: information@green-haven.co.uk
• website: www.green-haven.co.uk

Self-Catering
Rayford Caravan Park, Riverside,
Tiddington Road,
STRATFORD-UPON-AVON,
Warwickshire CV37 7BE
01789 293964
• e-mail: info@stratfordcaravans.co.uk
• website: www.stratfordcaravans.co.uk

Guest House
Mr & Mrs D. Clapp, The Croft,
Haseley Knob, WARWICK,
Warwickshire CV35 7NL
01926 484447
• e-mail: david@croftguesthouse.co.uk
• website: www.croftguesthouse.co.uk

B & B / Self-Catering
Mrs Elizabeth Draisey, Forth House,
44 High Street, WARWICK,
Warwickshire CV34 4AX
01926 401512
• e-mail: info@forthhouseuk.co.uk
• website: www.forthhouseuk.co.uk

FHG PUBLICATIONS LTD
publish a large range of well-known accommodation guides.
We will be happy to send you details or you can use the
order form at the back of this book.

•WEST MIDLANDS

Hotel

Mr Price, Featherstone Farm Hotel,
New Road, Featherstone, WOLVERHAMPTON,
West Midlands WV10 7NW
01902 725371
• website:
www.featherstonefarm.co.uk/index.html

•WILTSHIRE

Farmhouse / Board

Mrs D. Robinson, Boyds Farm, Gastard,
Near Corsham, BATH, Wiltshire SN13 9PT
01249 713146
• e-mail:
dorothyrobinson@boyds.farm.freeserve.co.uk

Self-Catering

Mrs S. King, Wick Farm, LACOCK,
Chippenham, Wiltshire SN15 2LU
01249 730244
• e-mail: kingsilverlands2@btinternet.com
• website: www.cheeseandcyderhouses.co.uk

Guest House

Alan & Dawn Curnow, Hayburn Wyke Guest
House, 72 Castle Road, SALISBURY,
Wiltshire SP1 3RL
01722 412627
• e-mail: hayburn.wyke@tinyonline.co.uk
• website: www.hayburnwykeguesthouse.co.uk

•WORCESTERSHIRE

Guesthouse / Farm

Mrs S Harrison, Middleton Grange,
Salwarpe, DROITWICH SPA,
Worcestershire WR9 0AH
01905 451678
• e-mail: salli@middletongrange.com
• website: www.middletongrange.com

•EAST YORKSHIRE

B & B

Paws-a-While, KILNWICK PERCY,
East Yorkshire YO42 1UF
01759 301168
• e-mail: paws.a.while@lineone.net
• website: www.pawsawhile.net

•NORTH YORKSHIRE

Self-Catering

Recommended Cottages, North Yorkshire
08700 718 718
• website: www.recommended-cottages.co.uk

B & B / Self-Catering

Mrs E.J. Moorhouse,
The Courtyard at Duke's Place,
Bishop Thornton, HARROGATE,
North Yorkshire HG3 3JY
01765 620229
• e-mail: jakimoorhouse@onetel.net.uk

Caravan & Camping

Bainbridge Ings, Caravan & Camping Site,
HAWES, North Yorkshire DL8 3NU
01969 667354
• e-mail: janet@bainbridge-ings.co.uk
• website: www.bainbridge-ings.co.uk

Farm B & B / Self-Catering

John & Felicity Wiles,
Sinnington Common Farm,
KIRKBYMOORSIDE, York,
North Yorkshire YO62 6NX
01751 431719
• e-mail: felicity@scfarm.demon.co.uk
• website: www.scfarm.demon.co.uk

Farm Self-Catering

A.W. & A. Turnbull, Whitethorn Farm,
Rook Barulth, KIRKBYMOORSIDE,
York, North Yorkshire
01751 431298
• e-mail: turnbull@whitethornfarm.fsnet.co.uk
• website: www.cottageguide.co.uk/oak-lodge

Farmhouse B & B

Mrs Julie Clarke, Middle Farm,
Woodale, Coverdale, LEYBURN,
North Yorkshire DL8 4TY
01969 640271
• e-mail: julie-clarke@amserve.com
• website:
www.yorkshirenet.co.uk/stayat/middlefarm

Self-Catering

Coronation and Forge Valley Cottages,
c/o Mr David Beeley, Barn House, Westgate,
OLD MALTON, North Yorkshire YO17 7HE
01653 698251
• e-mail:
enquiries@coronationfarmcottage.co.uk
• website: www.coronationfarmcottage.co.uk

B & B / Self-Catering
Mrs Sandra Pickering, "Nabgate",
Wilton Road, Thornton-le-Dale, PICKERING,
North Yorkshire YO18 7QP
01751 474279
• website: www.nabgateguesthouse.co.uk

Guest House
Mrs Ella Bowes, Banavie, Roxby Road,
Thornton-Le-Dale, PICKERING, North
Yorkshire YO18 7SX
01751 474616
• e-mail: ella@banavie.fsbusiness.co.uk
• website: www.banavie.uk.com

Hotel
Ganton Greyhound, Main Street, Ganton,
Near SCARBOROUGH,
North Yorkshire YO12 4NX
01944 710116
• e-mail: gantongreyhound@supanet.com
• website: www.gantongreyhound.com

Guest House
Sue & Tony Hewitt,
Harmony Country Lodge,
80 Limestone Road, Burniston,
SCARBOROUGH, North Yorkshire YO13 0DG
0800 2985840
• e-mail: tony@harmonylodge.net
• website: www.harmonylodge.net

Touring Caravan Park
Cayton Village Caravan Park, Mill Lane,
Cayton, SCARBOROUGH,
North Yorkshire YO11 3NN
• e-mail: info@caytontouring.co.uk
• website: www.caytontouring.co.uk

Hotel
Mrs M.M Abbott, Howdale Hotel,
121 Queen's Parade, SCARBOROUGH,
North Yorkshire YO12 7HU
01723 372696
• e-mail: mail@howdalehotel.co.uk
• website: www.howdalehotel.co.uk

Farmhouse B & B / Self-Catering
Mrs Heather Simpson, Low Skibeden
Farmhouse & Cottage, SKIPTON,
North Yorkshire
01756 793849
• website:
www.yorkshirenetco.uk/accgde/lowskibeden

Self-Catering
Mrs Jones, New Close Farm,
Kirkby Malham, SKIPTON,
North Yorkshire BD23 4DP
01729 830240
• e-mail:
brendajones@newclosefarmyorkshire.co.uk
• website: www.newclosefarmyorkshire.co.uk

Self-Catering
Mrs Knowlson, Thrush House,
SUTTON-ON-FOREST, York,
North Yorkshire YO61 1ED
• e-mail: kmkholcottyksuk@aol.com
• website:
www.holidayskmkholcotts-yks.uk.com

Hotel
The Golden Fleece Hotel, Market Place,
THIRSK North Yorkshire
01845 523108
• e-mail: goldenfleece@bestwestern.co.uk
• website: www.goldenfleecehotel.com

Self-Catering
Anne Fawcett,
Mile House Farm Country Cottages,
Mile House Farm, Hawes, WENSLEYDALE,
North Yorkshire DL8 3PT
01969 667481
• e-mail: milehousefarm@hotmail.com
• website: www.wensleydale.uk.com

Self-Catering
Mrs Sue Cooper, St Edmunds, The Green,
Crakehall, Bedale, WENSLEYDALE,
North Yorkshire DL8 1HP
01677 423584
• e-mail:
stedmundscountrycottages@hotmail.com
• website: www.crakehall.org.uk

Self-Catering
Westclose House (Allaker),
WEST SCRAFTON, North Yorkshire
c/o Mr A Cave,
020 8567 4862
• e-mail: ac@adriancave.com
• website: www.adriancave.com/yorks

Self-Catering
White Rose Holiday Cottages,
c/o Mrs Roberts, 5 Brook Park, Sleights,
Near WHITBY, North Yorkshire YO21 1RT
01947 810763
• e-mail: enquiries@whiterosecottages.co.uk
• website: www.whiterosecottages.co.uk

Self-Catering
Mrs N. Pattinson, South House Farm,
Fylingthorpe, WHITBY,
North Yorkshire YO22 4UQ
01947 880243
• e-mail: kmp@bogglehole.fsnet.co.uk
• website: www.southhousefarm.co.uk

B & B / Self-Catering / Holiday Caravans
Mr & Mrs Tyerman, Partridge Nest Farm,
Eskdaleside, Sleights, WHITBY,
North Yorkshire YO22 5ES
01947 810450
• e-mail: barbara@partridgenestfarm.com
• website: www.partridgenestfarm.com

B & B
Mrs Sally Robinson, Valley View Farm,
Old Byland, Helmsley, YORK,
North Yorkshire YO6 5LG
01439 798221
• e-mail: sally@valleyviewfarm.com
• website: www.valleyviewfarm.com

Guest House / Self-Catering
Mr Gary Hudson, Orillia House,
89 The Village, Stockton on Forest,
YORK, North Yorkshire YO3 9UP
01904 400600
• e-mail: orillia@globalnet.co.uk
• website: www.orilliahouse.co.uk

Self-Catering
Mr N. Manasir, York Lakeside Lodges, Moor
Lane, YORK, North Yorkshire YO24 2QU
01904 702346
• e-mail: neil@yorklakesidelodges.co.uk
• website: www.yorklakesidelodges.co.uk

•WEST YORKSHIRE

Self-Catering
Summerwine Cottages, West Royd Farm,
Marsh Lane, Shepley, near HOLMFIRTH,
Huddersfield, West Yorkshire
01484 602147
• e-mail: summerwinecottages@lineone.net
• website: www.summerwinecottages.co.uk

•SCOTLAND

•ABERDEEN, BANFF & MORAY

Guest House
E. Robertson,
Aberdeen Springbank Guesthouse,
6 Springbank Terrace, ABERDEEN,
Aberdeenshire AB11 6LS
01224 592048
• e-mail: betty@springbank6.fsnet.co.uk
• website:
  www.aberdeenspringbankguesthouse.co.uk
  or www.aberdeen-guesthouse.co.uk

B & B
Mrs E. Malim, Invercairn House, BRODIE,
by Forres, Moray IV36 2TD
01309 641261
• e-mail: invercairnhouse@supanet.com
• website: www.invercairnhouse.co.uk

B & B
Mrs H. Massie, Milton of Grange Farm,
FORRES, Morayshire IV36 0TR
01309 676360
• e-mail: hildamassie@aol.com
• website: www.forres-accommodation.co.uk

•ARGYLL & BUTE

Inn
Mr D. Fraser, Cairndow Stagecoach Inn,
CAIRNDOW, Argyll PA26 8BN
01499 600286
• e-mail: cairndowinn@aol.com

B & B
Mrs D. MacCormick, Mains Farm,
CARRADALE, Campbeltown,
Argyll PA28 6QG
01583 431216
• e-mail:
  maccormick@mainsfarm.freeserve.co.uk

Guest House
A.J. Burke, Orchy Bank, DALMALLY,
Argyll PA33 1AS
01838 200370
• e-mail: aj.burke@talk21.com
• website:
  www.loch-awe.com/orchybank/

Self-Catering
Mrs Isabella Crawford, Blarghour Farm
Cottages, Loch Awe-side, By DALMALLY,
Argyll PA33 1BW
01866 833246
• e-mail: **blarghour@btconnect.com**
• website: **www.self-catering-argyll.co.uk**

B & B / Self-Catering
R. Gayre, Minard Castle B&B/Self-Catering,
Minard, INVERARAY, Argyll PA32 8YB
01546 886272
• e-mail: **reinoldgayre@minardcastle.com**
• website: **www.minardcastle.com**

Self-Catering
B & M Phillips, Kilbride Croft, Balvicar,
ISLE OF SEIL, Argyll PA34 4RD
01852 300475
• e-mail: **kilbridecroft@aol.com**
• website: **www.kilbridecroft.fsnet.co.uk**

Self-Catering
Castle Sween Bay (Holidays) Ltd,
Ellery, LOCHGILPHEAD,
Argyll PA31 8PA
01880 770232
• e-mail: **info@ellary.com**
• website: **www.ellary.com**

Self-Catering
Linda Battison, Cologin House,
Lerags Glen, OBAN, Argyll PA3 4SE
01631 564501
• e-mail: **cologin@west-highland-holidays.co.uk**
• website: **www.west-highland-holidays.co.uk**

B & B
Mrs C. MacDonald, Bracker,
Polvinister Road, OBAN, Argyll
01631 564302
• e-mail: **cmacdonald@connectfree.co.uk**
• website: **www.bracker.co.uk**

Hotel
Willowburn Hotel, Clachan Seil,
by OBAN, Argyll PA34 4TJ
01852 300276
• e-mail: **willowburn.hotel@virgin.net**
• website: **www.willowburn.co.uk**

Self-Catering
Isolated Seashore Cottage,
c/o John Rankin, 12 Hamilton Place, Perth,
Tayside
01738 632580
• e-mail: **john@claddie.co.uk**
• website: **www.claddie.co.uk**

•AYRSHIRE & ARRAN

B & B
Mrs Wilcox, Fisherton Farm, Dunure,
AYR, Ayrshire KA7 4LF
01292 500223
• e-mail: **lesleywilcox@hotmail.com**
• website: **www.fishertonfarm.homestead.com**

Self-Catering
Arran Hideaways, Invercloy House,
Brodick, ISLE OF ARRAN
01770 302303
• e-mail: **info@arran-hideways.co.uk**
• website: **www.arran-hideaways.co.uk**

B & B
Mrs Watson, South Whittlieburn Farm,
Brisbane Glen, LARGS, Ayrshire KA30 8SN
01475 675881
• e-mail:
largsbandb@southwhittlieburnfarm.freeserve.co.uk
• website:
www.SmoothHound.co.uk/hotels/whittlie.html

•BORDERS

Self-Catering
Mrs J. Gray, Saughs Farm Cottages,
Saughs Farm, BAILEY, Newcastleton,
Borders TD9 0TT
016977 48346
• e-mail: **skylark@onholiday.co.uk**
• website: **www.skylarkcottages.co.uk**

Self-Catering
Mrs A. Fraser, Overwells, Jedburgh,
ROXBURGH, Roxburghshire
01835 863020
• e-mail: **abfraser@btinternet.com**
• website: **www.overwells.co.uk**

•DUMFRIES & GALLOWAY

Hotel
The Urr Valley Hotel, Ernspie Road,
CASTLE DOUGLAS,
Dumfries & Galloway DG7 3JG
01556 502 188
• e-mail: **info@urrvalleyhotel.co.uk**
• website: **www.urrvalley.demon.co.uk**

Farm
Celia Pickup, Craigadam,
CASTLE DOUGLAS,
Dumfries & Galloway DG7 3HU
01556 650233
- **e-mail: enquiry@craigadam.com**
- **website: www.craigadam.com**

Self-Catering
Mr Ball, Barncrosh Leisure Co Ltd,
Barncrosh, CASTLE DOUGLAS,
Dumfries & Galloway DG7 1TX
01556 680216
- **e-mail: enq@barncrosh.co.uk**
- **website: www.barncrosh.co.uk**

Self-Catering
Catherine McDowall, Shawhill Farmhouse,
DUNDRENNAN,
Dumfries & Galloway DG6 4QT
- **e-mail: mail@shawhill-cottages.co.uk**
- **website: www.shawhill-cottages.co.uk**

Self-Catering
Rusko Holidays,
GATEHOUSE OF FLEET, Castle Douglas,
Dumfries & Galloway DG7 2BS
01557 814215
- **e-mail: gilbey@rusko.demon.co.uk**
- **website: www.ruskoholidays.co.uk**

B & B
June Deakins, Annandale House, MOFFAT,
Dumfriesshire DG10 9SA
01683 221460
- **e-mail: june@annandalehouse.com**
- **website: www.annandalehouse.com**

•DUNDEE & ANGUS

Farmhouse B & B
Rosemary Beatty, Brathinch Farm,
by BRECHIN, Angus DD9 7QX
01356 648292
- **e-mail: adam.brathinch@btinternet.com**

Self-Catering
Jenny Scott, Welton Farm,
The Welton of Kingoldrum, KIRRIEMUIR,
Angus DD8 5HY
01575 574743
- **website: www.cottageguide.co.uk/thewelton**

•EDINBURGH & LOTHIANS

Guest House
Kenneth Harkins, 78 East Main Street,
BLACKBURN, By Bathgate,
West Lothian EH47 7QS
01506 655221
- **e-mail: cruachan.bb@virgin.net**
- **website: www.cruachan.co.uk**

Guest House
Mr & Mrs McWilliams,
Ben Craig Guest House, 3 Craigmillar Park,
EDINBURGH, Lothians EH16 5PG
0131 667 2593
- **e-mail: bencraighouse@dial.pipex.com**
- **website: www.bencraighouse.co.uk**

B & B
McCrae's B&B, 44 East Claremont Street,
EDINBURGH, Lothians EH7 4JR
0131 556 2610
- **e-mail: mccraes.bandb@lineone.net**
- **website:**
  http://website.lineone.net/~mccraes.bandb

Guest House
Mrs Kay, Blossom House, 8 Minto Street,
EDINBURGH EH9 1RG
0131 667 5353
- **e-mail: blossom_house@hotmail.com**
- **website: www.blossomguesthouse.co.uk**

Guest House
D. Green, Ivy Guest House,
7 Mayfield Gardens, Newington,
EDINBURGH, Lothians EH9 2AX
0131 667 3411
- **e-mail: don@ivyguesthouse.com**
- **website: www.ivyguesthouse.com**

Guest House
International Guest House,
37 Mayfield Gardens, EDINBURGH,
Lothians EH9 2BX
0131 667 2511
- **e-mail: intergh@easynet.co.uk**
- **website: www.accommodation-edinburgh.com**

**Please mention this guide
when enquiring about
accommodation**

Hotel
Shirley Mowat, Dunstane House Hotel,
4 West Cootes, Haymarket, EDINBURGH
0131 337 6169
- e-mail:
  reservations@dunstanehousehotel.co.uk
- website: www.dunstanehousehotel.co.uk

B & B
Mr & Mrs R. Inglis, Thornton,
Edinburgh Road, LINLITHGOW,
Lothians EH49 6AA
01506 844693
- e-mail: inglisthornton@hotmail.com
- website: www.thornton-scotland.co.uk

•HIGHLANDS

Self-Catering
A. Simpson, Camusdarach Enterprises,
Camusdarach, ARISAIG,
Inverness-shire PH39 4NT
01687 450221
- e-mail: camdarach@aol.com
- website: www.camusdarach.com

Hotel
The Boat Hotel, BOAT OF GARTEN,
Inverness-shire PH24 3BH
01479 831258
- e-mail: info@boathotel.co.uk
- website: www.boathotel.co.uk

Guest House
Mrs Lynn Benge,
The Pines Country Guest House, Duthil,
CARRBRIDGE, Inverness-shire PH23 3ND
01479 841220
- e-mail: lynn@thepines-duthil.fsnet.co.uk
- website: www.thepines-duthil.fsnet.co.uk

B & B
Mrs Brenda Graham, "Caledonian Cottage",
Station Road, FORT AUGUSTUS,
Inverness-shire PH32 4AY
01320 366401
- e-mail: brenda@ipw.com
- website: www.ipw.com/calcot

Hotel
Allt-Nan-Ros Hotel, Onich, FORT WILLIAM,
Inverness-shire PH33 6RY
01855 821210
- e-mail: fhg@allt-nan-ros.co.uk
- website: www.allt-nan-ros.co.uk

Hotel
Clan Macduff Hotel, Achintore Road,
FORT WILLIAM, Inverness-shire PH33 6RW
01397 702341
- e-mail: reception@clanmacduff.co.uk
- website: www.clanmacduff.co.uk

Self-Catering
Linnhe Lochside Holidays, Corpach,
FORT WILLIAM PH33 7NL
01397 772376
- e-mail: holidays@linnhe.demon.co.uk
- website: www.linnhe-lochside-holidays.co.uk

Guest House
Norma E. McCallum, The Neuk, Corpach,
FORT WILLIAM, Inverness-shire PH33 7LR
01397 772244
- e-mail: theneuk@fortwilliamguesthouse.com
- website: www.theneuk.fsbusiness.co.uk

Self-Catering
Great Glen Holidays, Torlundy, FORT
WILLIAM, Inverness-shire
01397 703015
- e-mail: chris@greatglenchalets.demon.co.uk
- website: www.greatglenchalets.demon.co.uk

Self-Catering
Mr William Murray,
Springwell Holiday Homes, Onich,
FORT WILLIAM, Inverness-shire PH33 6RY
01855 821257
- e-mail: info@springwellholidayhomes.co.uk
- website: www.springwellholidayhomes.co.uk

B & B
Mrs M. MacLean, Innishfree, Lochyside,
FORT WILLIAM, Inverness-shire PH33 7NX
01397 705471
- e-mail: mburnsmaclean@aol.com
- website: www. innishfree.co.uk

Hotels
The Freedom of the Glen Family of Hotels,
Onich, near FORT WILLIAM,
Inverness-shire PH33 6RY
0871 222 3415
- e-mail: reservations@freedomglen.co.uk
- website: www.freedomglen.co.uk

Self-Catering
Miss Jean Ellice, Taigh-an-Lianach,
Aberchalder Farm, INVERGARRY,
Inverness-shire PH35 4HN
01809 501287
- website: www.ipw.com/aberchalder

Guest House / Self-Catering
Nick & Patsy Thompson, Insh House,
KINCRAIG, Kingussie
01540 651377
- **e-mail: inshhouse@btinternet.com**
- **website: www.kincraig.com/inshhouse**

Guest House
Gary Clulow, Sunset Guest House, MORAR,
by Mallaig, Inverness-shire PH40 4PA
01687 462259
- **e-mail: sunsetgh@aol.com**
- **website: www.sunsetguesthouse.co.uk**

Self-Catering Chalets / B & B
D.J. Mordaunt, Mondhuie, NETHY BRIDGE,
Inverness-shire PH25 3DF
01479 821062
- **e-mail: david@mondhuie.com**
- **website: www.mondhuie.com**

Guest House
Mrs J. MacLean, Foresters Bungalow,
Inchree, ONICH, Fort William,
Inverness-shire PH33 6SE
- **website: www.s-h-systems.co.uk/**
         hotels/forestersbungalow.html

Self-Catering
Mr A. Urquhart, Crofters Cottages,
15 Croft, POOLEWE, Ross-shire IV22 2JY
01445 781268
- **e-mail: croftcottages@btopenworld.com**
- **website: www.croftcottages.btinternet.co.uk**

Hotel
Mrs Campbell, Rhiconich Hotel,
RHICONICH, by Lairg, Sutherland IV27 4RN
01971 521224
- **e-mail: rhiconichhotel@aol.com**
- **website: www.rhiconichhotel.co.uk**

Self-Catering
Wildside Highland Lodges, By Loch Ness,
WHITEBRIDGE, Inverness-shire IV2 6UN
01456 486373
- **e-mail: info@wildsidelodges.com**
- **website: www.wildsidelodges.com**

•LANARKSHIRE

Self-Catering
Carmichael Country Cottages,
Carmichael Estate Office, Westmains,
Carmichael, BIGGAR, Lanarkshire ML12 6PG
01899 308336
- **e-mail: chiefcarm@aol.com**
- **website: www.carmichael.co.uk/cottages**

•PERTH & KINROSS

Self-Catering
Loch Tay Lodges, Remony,
ABERFELDY, Perthshire
01887 830209
- **e-mail: remony@btinternet.com**
- **website: www.lochtaylodges.co.uk**

Guest House
Janet Greenfield, "Annfield Guest House",
North Church Street, CALLANDER,
Perthshire
01877 330204
- **e-mail: janet-greenfield@amserve.com**

Guest House
J. Clifford, Merlindale, Perth Road,
CRIEFF, Perthshire
01764 655205
- **e-mail: merlin.dale@virgin.net**
- **website: www.merlindale.co.uk**

Self-Catering
Laighwood Holidays, Laighwood,
Butterstone, By DUNKELD,
Perthshire PH8 0HB
01350 724241
- **e-mail: holidays@laighwood.co.uk**
- **website: www.laighwood.co.uk**

Self Catering
Mrs Hunt, Wester Lix Holiday Cottages,
Wester Lix, KILLIN, Perthshire FK21 8RD
01567 820990
- **e-mail: gill@westerlix.co.uk**
- **website: www.westerlix.co.uk**

B & B
Mrs P. Honeyman, Auld Manse Guest House,
Pitcullen Crescent, PERTH, Perthshire PH2 7HT
01738 629187
- **e-mail: trishaatauldmanse@hotmail.com**
- **website: www.guesthouseperth.com**

Guest House
Jacky Catterall, Tulloch, Enochdhu,
by PITLOCHRY, Perthshire PH10 7PW
01250 881404
- **e-mail: maljac@tulloch83.freeserve.co.uk**
- **website: www.maljac.com**

•STIRLING & TROSSACHS

Caravan & Camping
Riverside Caravan Park, Dollarfield,
DOLLAR, Clackmannanshire FK14 7LX
01259 742896
- **e-mail: info@riverside-caravanpark.co.uk**
- **website: www.riverside-caravanpark.co.uk**

B & B
Mrs Strain, Hawthorndean, Wallacestone
Brae, Reddingmuirhead, FALKIRK,
Stirlingshire FK2 0DQ
- **e-mail: eileenstrain@yahoo.co.uk**

Guest House
Mrs Betty Ward, Ashbank Guest House,
105 Main Street, Redding, FALKIRK,
Stirlingshire FK2 9UQ
01324 716649
- **e-mail: ashbank@guest-house.freeserve.co.uk**
- **website: www.bandbfalkirk.com**

•ISLE OF SKYE

Guest House / B & B
Fiona Scott, Blairdhu House, Old Kyle Farm
Road, KYLEAKIN, Isle of Skye IV41 8PR
01599 534760
- **e-mail: info@blairdhuhouse.co.uk**
- **website: www.blairdhuhouse.co.uk**

•WALES

Self-Catering
Quality Cottages, Cerbid, Solva,
HAVERFORDWEST,
Pembrokeshire SA62 6YE
01348 837871
- **website: www.qualitycottages.co.uk**

•ANGLESEY & GWYNEDD

Country House
Jim and Marion Billingham, Preswylfa,
ABERDOVEY, Gwynedd LL35 0LE
01654 767239
- **e-mail: info@preswylfa.co.uk**
- **website: www.preswylfa.co.uk**

B & B
Mrs Murphy, Ingledene, Ravenspoint Road,
Trearddur Bay, ANGLESEY LL65 2YU
01407 861026
- **e-mail: info@ingledene.co.uk**
- **website: www.ingledene.co.uk**

B & B
Mrs J. Bown, Drws-y-Coed,
Llannerch-y-medd, ANGLESEY LL71 8AD
01248 470473
- **e-mail: drws.ycoed@virgin.net**
- **website:
www.SmoothHound.co.uk/hotels/drwsycoed.html**

Self-Catering within a Castle
Bryn Bras Castle, Llanrug,
near CAERNARFON Gwynedd LL55 4RE
01286 870210
- **e-mail: holidays@brynbrascastle.co.uk**
- **website: www.brynbrascastle.co.uk**

Self-Catering / Caravan
Plas-y-Bryn Chalet Park, Bontnewydd,
CAERNARFON, Gwynedd LL54 7YE
01286 672811
- **e-mail: philplasybryn@aol.com**
- **website:
www.plasybrynholidayscaernarfon.co.uk**

Hotel
Prince of Wales Hotel, Bangor Street,
CAERNARFON, Gwynedd
01286 673367
- **e-mail: info@prince-of-wales-hotel.co.uk**
- **website: www.prince-of-wales-hotel.co.uk**

Guest House
Mrs M.A. Parker, Seaspray Guest House,
4 Marine Terrace, CRICCIETH,
Gwynedd LL52 0EF
- **e-mail: manya.parker@btopenworld.com**
- **website: www.seasprayguesthouse.co.uk**

Self-Catering
Anwen Jones, Rhos Country Cottages,
Betws Bach, Ynys, CRICCIETH,
Gwynedd LL52 0PB
01758 720047
- **e-mail: cottages@rhos.freeserve.co.uk**
- **website: www.rhos-cottages.co.uk**

Guest House
Mrs M. Bamford, Ivy House,
Finsbury Square, DOLGELLAU,
Gwynedd LL40 1RF
01341 422535
- **e-mail: marg.bamford@btconnect.com**
- **website: www.ukworld.net/ivyhouse**

Self-Catering / Caravans
Minffordd Luxury Cottages & Caravans,
Minfford, DULAS, Isle of Anglesey LL70 9HJ
01248 410678
• e-mail: enq@minffordd-holidays.com
• website: www.minffordd-holidays.com

B & B
Mrs G. McCreadie, Deri Isaf,
DULAS BAY, Anglesey LL70 9DX
01248 410536
• e-mail: mccreadie@deriisaf.freeserve.co.uk
• website: www.deriisaf.freeserve.co.uk

Farm B & B
Judy Hutchings, Tal y Foel, DWYRAN,
Anglesey, Gwynedd LL61 6LQ
01248 430377
• e-mail: riding@talyfoel.u-net.com
• website: www.tal-y-foel.co.uk

Self-Catering
Mrs S. Edwards, Dwyfach Cottages,
Pen-y-Bryn, Chwilog, PWLLHELI,
Gwynedd LL53 6SX
01766 810208
• e-mail: llyredwards@ukonline.co.uk
• website: www.dwyfach.co.uk

•NORTH WALES

Hotel
Fairy Glen Hotel, Beaver Bridge,
BETWS-Y-COED, Conwy,
North Wales LL24 0SH
01690 710269
• e-mail: fairyglenhotel@amserve.net
• website: www.fairyglenhotel.co.uk

Guest House
Mr M. Wilkie, Bryn Bella Guest House,
Lôn Muriau, Llanrwst Road,
BETWS-Y-COED, Gwynedd LL24 0HD
01690 710627
• e-mail: welcome@bryn-bella.co.uk
• website: www.bryn-bella.co.uk

Guest House / Self-Catering
Jim & Lilian Boughton,
Bron Celyn Guest House, Lôn Muriau,
Llanrwst Road, BETWS-Y-COED,
North Wales LL24 0HD
01690 710333
• e-mail: welcome@broncelyn.co.uk
• website: www.broncelyn.co.uk

B & B
Christine Whale, Brookside House,
Brookside Lane, Northop Hall,
near CHESTER CH7 4HN
01244 821146
• e-mail: christine@brooksidehouse.fsnet.co.uk
• website: www.brooksidehouse.fsnet.co.uk

Guest House
Sychnant Pass House, Sychnant Pass Road,
CONWY, North Wales LL32 8BJ
01492 596868
• e-mail: bresykes@sychnant-pass-house.co.uk
• website: www.sychnant-pass-house.co.uk

Hotel
Caerlyr Hall Hotel, Conwy Old Road,
Dwygyfylchi, CONWY,
North Wales LL34 6SW
01492 623518
• website: www.caerlyrhallhotel.co.uk

Guest House
Mr & Mrs Watson Jones, Glan Heulog Guest
House, Woodlands, Llanwrst Road, CONWY
01492 593845
• e-mail:
   glanheulog@no1guesthouse.freeserve.co.uk
• website: www.walesbandb.com

Self-Catering
Cottage, CONWAY c/o Mrs G.M. Simpole,
105 Haygreen Road, Terrington-St-Clement,
Kings Lynn, Norfolk PE34 4PU
01553 828897
• e-mail: gsimpole@care4free.net
• website: www.comestaywithus.com/
   wales-hotels/sc-full/brongain.html

Hotel
Moreton Park Lodge, Gledrid, Chirk,
WREXHAM, LL14 5DG
01691 776666
• e-mail: reservations@moretonpark.com
• website: www.moretonpark.com

**Please mention this
guide when enquiring
about accommodation**

•CARMARTHENSHIRE

B & B
Miss S Czerniewicz, Pant y Bas, Pentrefelin,
LLANDEILO, Carmarthenshire, SA19 6SD
01558 822809
• e-mail: anna@pantybas.fsnet.co.uk
• website: www.southwestwalesbandb.co.uk

•CEREDIGION

Self-Catering
Gilfach Holiday Village, Llwyncelyn, Near
ABERAERON, Ceredigion SA46 0HN
01545 580288
• e-mail: info@stratfordcaravans.co.uk
• website: www.stratfordcaravans.co.uk

Self-Catering
Mrs Tucker, Penffynnon, ABERPORTH,
Ceredigion SA43 2DA
01239 810387
• e-mail: jann@aberporth.com
• website: www.aberporth.com

• PEMBROKESHIRE

Self-Catering
John Lloyd, East Llanteg Farm Holiday
Cottages, Llanteg, near AMROTH,
Pembrokeshire SA67 8QA
01834 831336
• e-mail: john@pembrokeshireholiday.co.uk
• website: www.pembrokeshireholiday.co.uk

Farm B & B
Mrs Margaret Williams, Skerryback,
Sandy Haven, St Ishmaels, HAVERFORDWEST,
Pembrokeshire SA62 3DN
01646 636598
• e-mail: skerryback@pfh.co.uk
• website: www.pfh.co.uk/skerryback

Caravan Park
Scamford Caravan Park, Keeston,
HAVERFORDWEST, Pembrokeshire SA62 6HN
01437 710304
• e-mail: holidays@scamford.com
• website: www.scamford.com

Caravan & Camping
Brandy Brook Caravan & Camping Site,
Rhyndaston, Hayscastle,
HAVERFORDWEST, Pembrokeshire
01348 840272
• e-mail: f.m.rowe@btopenworld.com

Self-Catering
T.M. Hardman, High View, Catherine Street,
ST DAVIDS, Pembrokeshire SA62 6RT
01437 720616
• e-mail: enquiries@lowermoorcottages.co.uk
• website: www.lowermoorcottages.co.uk

Farm Guest House
Mrs Morfydd Jones, Lochmeyler Farm
Guest House, Llandeloy, Pen-y-Cwm,
near SOLVA, St David's,
Pembrokeshire SA62 6LL
01348 837724
• e-mail: stay@lochmeyler.co.uk
• website: www.lochmeyler.co.uk

•POWYS

Self-Catering
Mrs Ann Phillips, Tylebrythos Farm, Cantref,
BRECON, Powys LD3 8LR
01874 665329
• e-mail: ann@wernymarchog.co.uk
• website: www.wernymarchog.co.uk

Farm
Gilfach Farm, Sennybridge, BRECON,
Powys LD3 8TY
01874 636818
• e-mail: sm@mip.co.uk
• website: www.breconbeaconsriding.co.uk

Farm Self-Catering
Mrs E. Bally, Lane Farm, Painscastle,
BUILTH WELLS, Powys LD2 3JS
01497 851605
• e-mail: jbally@btclick.com
• website: www.lane-farm.co.uk

Self-Catering
Mrs Jones, Penllwyn Lodges, GARTHMYL,
Powys SY15 6SB
01686 640269
• e-mail: penllwynlodges@supanet.com
• website: www.penllwynlodges.co.uk

Self-Catering
Peter & Jackie Longley, Neuadd Farm,
Penybont, LLANDRINDOD WELLS,
Powys LD1 5SW
01597 851032
- e-mail: jackie@neuaddfarm.fsnet.co.uk
- website: www.neuaddfarm.co.uk

Motel / Caravans
The Park Motel, Crossgates,
LLANDRINDOD WELLS, Powys LD1 6RF
01597 851201
- e-mail: lisa@theparkmotel.freeserve.co.uk
- website: www.theparkmotel.freeserve.co.uk

B & B
Mrs V.J. Madeley, Greenfields, Kerry,
NEWTOWN, Powys SY16 4LH
01686 670596
- e-mail: info@greenfields-bb.co.uk
- website: www.greenfield-bb.co.uk

B & B
Laura Kostoris, Erw yr Danty,
TALYBONT-ON-USK, Brecon,
Powys LD3 7YN
01874 676498
- e-mail: kosto@ukonline.co.uk
- website: wiz.to/lifestyle/

•SOUTH WALES

Guest House / Self-Catering
Mrs Norma James, Wyrloed Lodge,
Manmoel, BLACKWOOD, Caerphilly, Gwent
01495 371198
- e-mail: norma.james@btinternet.com
- website: www.btinternet.com/~norma.james/

Sports Centre / Hotel
Welsh Institute of Sport, Sophia Gardens,
CARDIFF
029 20 300500
- e-mail: wis@scw.co.uk
- website: www.sports-council-wales.co.uk

Hotel
Mr & Mrs J. Llewellyn, Cwrt-y-Gaer,
Wolvesnewton, CHEPSTOW NP16 6PR
01291 650700
- e-mail: john.ll@talk21.com
- website: www.cwrt-y-gaer.co.uk

B & B
Sue Beer, Plas Llanmihangel,
Llanmihangel, near COWBRIDGE,
Vale of Glamorgan CF71 7LQ
01446 774610
- e-mail: plasllanmihangel@ukonline.co.uk

Narrowboat
Castle Narrowboats, Church Road Wharf,
GILWERN, Monmouthshire NP7 0EP
01873 830001
- e-mail: castle.narrowboats@btinternet.com
- website: www.castlenarrowboats.co.uk

Hotel
Culver House Hotel, Port Eynon,
GOWER, Swansea, South Wales SA3 1NN
01792 390755
- e-mail: info@culverhousehotel.co.uk
- website: www.culverhousehotel.co.uk

Guest House
Chapel Guest House, Church Road,
ST BRIDES, Wentloog, near Newport,
Gwent NP10 8SN
01633 681018
- e-mail: chapelguesthouse@hotmail.com
- website: www.SmoothHound.co.uk/

•IRELAND

Co. Clare

Self-catering
Ballyvaughan Village & Country Holiday
Homes, Main Street, BALLYVAUGHAN,
Co. Clare
00 353 65 9051977
- e-mail: vchh@iol.ie
- website: www.ballyvaughan-cottages.com

Co. Dublin

Golf Club
The Royal Dublin Golf Club,
North Bull Island Nature Reserve,
DOLLYMOUNT, Dublin 3
00 353 1 833 6346
- e-mail: info@theroyaldublingolfclub.com
- website: www.theroyaldublingolfclub.com

FHG Diploma Winners 2003

Each year we award a small number of diplomas to holiday proprietors whose services have been specially commended by our readers. The following were our FHG Diploma Winners for 2003.

England

DERBYSHIRE
Mr Tatlow
Ashfield Farm, Calwich
Near Ashbourne
Derbyshire DE6 2EB

DEVON
Mrs Tucker
Lower Luxton Farm, Upottery
Near Honiton
Devon EX14 9PB
◆
Royal Oak
Dunsford Near Exeter
Devon EX6 7DA

GLOUCESTERSHIRE
Mrs Keyte
The Limes, Evesham Road
Stow-on-the-Wold
Gloucestershire GL54 1EN

HAMPSHIRE
Mrs Ellis, Efford Cottage,
Everton, Lymington,
Hampshire SO41 0JD
◆
R. Law
Whitley Ridge Hotel
Beauly Road, Brockenhurst
Hampshire SO42 7QL

HEREFORDSHIRE
Mrs Brown
Ye Hostelrie, Goodrich
Near Ross on Wye
Herefordshire HR9 6HX

NORTH YORKSHIRE
Charles & Gill Richardson
The Coppice, 9 Studley Road
Harrogate
North Yorkshire HG1 5JU
◆
Mr & Mrs Hewitt
Harmony Country Lodge
Limestone Road, Burniston,
Scarborough
North Yorkshire YO13 0DG

Wales

POWYS
Linda Williams
The Old Vicarage
Erwood, Builth Wells
Powys LD2 3SZ

Scotland

ABERDEEN, BANFF & MORAY
Mr Ian Ednie
Spey Bay Hotel
Spey Bay
Fochabers
Moray IV32 7PJ

PERTH & KINROSS
Dunalastair Hotel
Kinloch Rannoch
By Pitlochry
Perthshire PH16 5PW

HELP IMPROVE BRITISH TOURISM STANDARDS

As recommendations are submitted from readers of the FULL RANGE of FHG titles the winners shown above may not necessarily appear in this guide.

Index of towns and counties.
Please also refer to Contents pages 2 and 3.

Aberdeen	ABERDEEN, BANFF & MORAY	Birnam	PERTH & KINROSS
Aberdovey	ANGLESEY & GWYNEDD	Bishop Auckland	DORSET
Aberfoyle	STIRLING & TROSSACHS	Bishop's Castle	SHROPSHIRE
Aberystwyth	CEREDIGION	Bishopsteignton	DEVON
Achnasheen	HIGHLANDS (MID)	Blackburn	LANCASHIRE
Alcester	WARWICKSHIRE	Blackburn	EDINBURGH & LOTHIANS
Alford	LINCOLNSHIRE	Blackpool	LANCASHIRE
Allendale	NORTHUMBERLAND	Bladon	OXFORDSHIRE
Alnmouth	NORTHUMBERLAND	Blairgowrie	PERTH & KINROSS
Alnwick	NORTHUMBERLAND	Boat of Garten	HIGHLANDS (SOUTH)
Alton	STAFFORDSHIRE	Bodmin	CORNWALL
Ambleside	CUMBRIA	Bognor Regis	WEST SUSSEX
Amroth	PEMBROKESHIRE	Boscastle	CORNWALL
Anglesey	ANGLESEY & GWYNEDD	Bournemouth	DORSET
Appleby	CUMBRIA	Bourton-on-the-Water	GLOUCESTERSHIRE
Ardgay	HIGHLANDS (NORTH)	Bowness-on-Windermere	CUMBRIA
Arinagour	ISLE OF COLL	Brae	SHETLAND ISLES
Ardmaddy	ARGYLL & BUTE	Brampton	CUMBRIA
Arundel	WEST SUSSEX	Braunton	DEVON
Ashburton	DEVON	Brayton	CUMBRIA
Ascot	BERKSHIRE	Brechin	DUNDEE & ANGUS
Ashbourne	DERBYSHIRE	Brecon	POWYS
Ashford	KENT	Bridgwater	SOMERSET
Ashkirk	BORDERS	Bridlington	EAST YORKSHIRE
Auchterarder	PERTH & KINROSS	Bridport	DORSET
Axminster	DEVON	Brighton	EAST SUSSEX
Aylsham	NORFOLK	Bristol	GLOUCESTERSHIRE
Ayr	AYRSHIRE & ARRAN	Bristol	SOMERSET
		Brixham	DEVON
Bakewell	DERBYSHIRE	Broadhaven	PEMBROKESHIRE
Bala	ANGLESEY & GWYNEDD	Broadstairs	KENT
Ballachulish	ARGYLL & BUTE	Brockenhurst	HAMPSHIRE
Ballindalloch	ABERDEEN, BANFF & MORAY	Brodie	ABERDEEN, BANFF & MORAY
Balmoral	ABERDEEN, BANFF & MORAY	Broughty Ferry	DUNDEE & ANGUS
Balterley	CHESHIRE	Buckie	ABERDEEN, BANFF & MORAY
Bamford	DERBYSHIRE	Bude	CORNWALL
Banbury	OXFORDSHIRE	Builth Wells	POWYS
Barnstaple	DEVON	Burley	HAMPSHIRE
Barton St David	SOMERSET	Burnham-on-Sea	SOMERSET
Barton-on-Sea	HAMPSHIRE	Burton Joyce	NOTTINGHAMSHIRE
Bath	GLOUCESTERSHIRE	Burwash	EAST SUSSEX
Bath	SOMERSET	Bury St Edmunds	SUFFOLK
Bathgate	EDINBURGH & LOTHIANS	Buttermere	CUMBRIA
Beaminster	DORSET	Buxton	DERBYSHIRE
Beaulieu	HAMPSHIRE		
Bedale	NORTH YORKSHIRE	Cadnam	HAMPSHIRE
Beith	AYRSHIRE & ARRAN	Caldbeck	CUMBRIA
Belton-in-Rutland	LEICESTERSHIRE	Calderbank	LANARKSHIRE
Berwick-upon-Tweed	NORTHUMBERLAND	Callander	PERTH & KINROSS
Betws-y-Coed	NORTH WALES	Callander	STIRLING & TROSSACHS
Beverley	EAST YORKSHIRE	Callington	CORNWALL
Bideford	DEVON	Cambridge	CAMBRIDGESHIRE
Biggar	BORDERS	Canonbie	DUMFRIES & GALLOWAY
Birmingham	WEST MIDLANDS	Canterbury	KENT

Cardiff	SOUTH WALES	Devizes	WILTSHIRE
Carisbrooke	ISLE OF WIGHT	Didmarton	GLOUCESTERSHIRE
Carlisle	CUMBRIA	Diss	NORFOLK
Carmarthen	CARMARTHENSHIRE	Dolgellau	ANGLESEY & GWYNEDD
Carnforth	LANCASHIRE	Dorchester	DORSET
Carradale	ARGYLL & BUTE	Dornoch	HIGHLANDS (NORTH)
Castle Douglas	DUMFRIES & GALLOWAY	Dorrington	SHROPSHIRE
Castleton	DERBYSHIRE	Dover	KENT
Cerne Abbas	DORSET	Driffield	EAST YORKSHIRE
Chale	ISLE OF WIGHT	Droitwich	WORCESTERSHIRE
Chard	SOMERSET	Droitwich Spa	WORCESTERSHIRE
Charmouth	DORSET	Drumnadrochit	HIGHLANDS (SOUTH)
Cheltenham	GLOUCESTERSHIRE	Dulverton	SOMERSET
Chester	CHESHIRE	Dumfries	DUMFRIES & GALLOWAY
Chester	NORTH WALES	Dunlop	AYRSHIRE & ARRAN
Chesterfield	DERBYSHIRE	Dunning	PERTH & KINROSS
Chippenham	WILTSHIRE	Durham	DURHAM
Chipping Campden	GLOUCESTERSHIRE		
Chorley	LANCASHIRE	Eastbourne	EAST SUSSEX
Chudleigh	DEVON	Eccleshall	STAFFORDSHIRE
Church Minshull	CHESHIRE	Edinbane	ISLE OF SKYE
Church Stretton	SHROPSHIRE	Edinburgh	EDINBURGH & LOTHIANS
Churchill	SOMERSET	Edwinstowe	NOTTINGHAMSHIRE
Cilgerran	PEMBROKESHIRE	Edzell	DUNDEE & ANGUS
Clane	CO. KILDARE	Ely	CAMBRIDGESHIRE
Clare	SUFFOLK	Enmore	SOMERSET
Cleethorpes	LINCOLNSHIRE	Exeter	DEVON
Clitheroe	LANCASHIRE	Exford	SOMERSET
Clovelly	DEVON	Exmoor	DEVON
Cockermouth	CUMBRIA	Exmouth	DEVON
Colchester	ESSEX		
Colebrooke	DEVON	Fakenham	NORFOLK
Colwyn Bay	NORTH WALES	Falkirk	STIRLING & TROSSACHS
Colyton	DEVON	Falmouth	CORNWALL
Combe Martin	DEVON	Farnham	SURREY
Compton Abbas	DORSET	Farnsfield	NOTTINGHAMSHIRE
Conwy	NORTH WALES	Felixstowe	SUFFOLK
Corbridge	NORTHUMBERLAND	Filey	NORTH YORKSHIRE
Cornforth	DURHAM	Folkestone	KENT
Corwen	NORTH WALES	Forres	ABERDEEN, BANFF & MORAY
Coventry	WARWICKSHIRE	Fort Augustus	HIGHLANDS (SOUTH)
Coverdale	NORTH YORKSHIRE	Fort William	HIGHLANDS (SOUTH)
Cowbridge	SOUTH WALES	Framlingham	SUFFOLK
Crediton	DEVON	Furzehill	DORSET
Crewkerne	SOMERSET		
Crianlarich	PERTH & KINROSS	Gainsborough	LINCOLNSHIRE
Criccieth	ANGLESEY & GWYNEDD	Gairloch	HIGHLANDS (MID)
Crieff	PERTH & KINROSS	Gatwick	SURREY
Croyde	DEVON	Gilsland	CUMBRIA
Culloden Moor	HIGHLANDS (SOUTH)	Girvan	AYRSHIRE & ARRAN
Cullompton	DEVON	Glasgow	GLASGOW & DISTRICT
Culross	FIFE	Glastonbury	SOMERSET
		Golden Valley	HEREFORDSHIRE
Dalmally	ARGYLL & BUTE	Gower	SOUTH WALES
Dartmouth	DEVON	Grantown-on-Spey	ABERDEEN, BANFF & MORAY
Dawlish	DEVON	Grassington	NORTH YORKSHIRE
Deal	KENT	Great Torrington	DEVON
Delabole	CORNWALL	Great Yarmouth	NORFOLK
Derby	DERBYSHIRE	Gretna	DUMFRIES & GALLOWAY
		Gullane	EDINBURGH & LOTHIANS

Hailsham	EAST SUSSEX	Kirkbymoorside	NORTH YORKSHIRE
Halifax	WEST YORKSHIRE	Kirkcaldy	FIFE
Halland	EAST SUSSEX	Kirkcudbright	DUMFRIES & GALLOWAY
Harlaston	STAFFORDSHIRE	Kirkmichael	PERTH & KINROSS
Harrogate	NORTH YORKSHIRE	Kirkwall	ORKNEY ISLES
Hartfield	EAST SUSSEX	Kyleakin	ISLE OF SKYE
Hartington	DERBYSHIRE		
Hastings	EAST SUSSEX	Lancaster	LANCASHIRE
Hawkshead	CUMBRIA	Langton-by-Wragby	LINCOLNSHIRE
Haworth	WEST YORKSHIRE	Largs	AYRSHIRE & ARRAN
Hayle	CORNWALL	Launceston	CORNWALL
Hayling Island	HAMPSHIRE	Leatherhead	SURREY
Hay-on-Wye	POWYS	Lechlade on Thames	GLOUCESTERSHIRE
Headcorn	KENT	Ledbury	HEREFORDSHIRE
Helmsley	NORTH YORKSHIRE	Leominster	HEREFORDSHIRE
Helston	CORNWALL	Letterkenny	CO. DONEGAL
Henfield	WEST SUSSEX	Leven	FIFE
Henley-on-Thames	OXFORDSHIRE	Leyburn	NORTH YORKSHIRE
Hereford	HEREFORDSHIRE	Lighthorne	WARWICKSHIRE
Hesket Newmarket	CUMBRIA	Lillington	DORSET
Hexham	NORTHUMBERLAND	Lincoln	LINCOLNSHIRE
Honiton	DEVON	Lingfield	SURREY
Hope Valley	DERBYSHIRE	Linlithgow	EDINBURGH & LOTHIANS
Horley	SURREY	Liskeard	CORNWALL
Horley	WEST SUSSEX	Littlehampton	WEST SUSSEX
Horncastle	LINCOLNSHIRE	Llandeilo	CARMARTHENSHIRE
Hyde	CHESHIRE	Llandudno	NORTH WALES
Hythe	HAMPSHIRE	Llanelli	CARMARTHENSHIRE
		Llangollen	NORTH WALES
Ilfracombe	DEVON	Llanidloes	POWYS
Ilminster	SOMERSET	Lochinver	HIGHLANDS (NORTH)
Inveraray	ARGYLL & BUTE	London	LONDON (CENTRAL & GREATER)
Inverness	HIGHLANDS (SOUTH)	Long Buckby	NORTHAMPTONSHIRE
Inverurie	ABERDEEN, BANFF & MORAY	Long Stratton	NORFOLK
Ipswich	SUFFOLK	Looe	CORNWALL
Ireby	CUMBRIA	Loughborough	LEICESTERSHIRE
Ironbridge	SHROPSHIRE	Louth	LINCOLNSHIRE
Isle of Whithorn	DUMFRIES & GALLOWAY	Loweswater	CUMBRIA
		Ludham	NORFOLK
Jedburgh	BORDERS	Ludlow	SHROPSHIRE
		Lulworth Cove	DORSET
Keith	ABERDEEN, BANFF & MORAY	Luss	DUNBARTONSHIRE
Kelvedon	ESSEX	Luton	BEDFORDSHIRE
Kendal	CUMBRIA	Lyme Regis	DORSET
Kenilworth	WARWICKSHIRE	Lymington	HAMPSHIRE
Keswick	CUMBRIA	Lyndhurst	HAMPSHIRE
Kettering	NORTHAMPTONSHIRE	Lynmouth	DEVON
Kew Gardens	LONDON (CENTRAL & GREATER)	Lynton	DEVON
Kilmarnock	AYRSHIRE & ARRAN		
Kilnwick Percy	EAST YORKSHIRE	Macduff	ABERDEEN, BANFF & MORAY
Kimmeridge	DORSET	Machynlleth	POWYS
King's Cross	LONDON (CENTRAL & GREATER	Maenclochog	PEMBROKESHIRE
King's Lynn	NORFOLK	Maentwrog	ANGLESEY & GWYNEDD
Kingsbridge	DEVON	Maidstone	KENT
Kingstone	HEREFORDSHIRE	Malmesbury	WILTSHIRE
Kingston-upon-Thames	SURREY	Malpas	CHESHIRE
Kingussie	HIGHLANDS (SOUTH)	Malton	NORTH YORKSHIRE
Kinlochbervie	HIGHLANDS (NORTH)	Malvern	WORCESTERSHIRE
Kirkby Stephen	CUMBRIA	Malvern Wells	WORCESTERSHIRE

Mansfield	NOTTINGHAMSHIRE
Margate	KENT
Mark	SOMERSET
Market Rasen	LINCOLNSHIRE
Marlborough	WILTSHIRE
Matlock	DERBYSHIRE
Mauchline	AYRSHIRE & ARRAN
Medbourne	LEICESTERSHIRE
Melksham	WILTSHIRE
Mells	SOMERSET
Melrose	BORDERS
Melton Mowbray	LEICESTERSHIRE
Mere	WILTSHIRE
Mevagissey	CORNWALL
Midhurst	WEST SUSSEX
Milford-on-Sea	HAMPSHIRE
Minchinhampton	GLOUCESTERSHIRE
Minehead	SOMERSET
Minster Lovell	OXFORDSHIRE
Moffat	DUMFRIES & GALLOWAY
Monmouth	SOUTH WALES
Montacute	SOMERSET
Montrose	DUNDEE & ANGUS
Morar	HIGHLANDS (SOUTH)
Morecambe	LANCASHIRE
Moretonhampstead	DEVON
Mortehoe	DEVON
Musselburgh	EDINBURGH & LOTHIANS
Nailsworth	GLOUCESTERSHIRE
Near Sawrey	CUMBRIA
New Milton	HAMPSHIRE
Newbiggin on Lune	CUMBRIA
Newcastleton	BORDERS
Newcastle-upon-Tyne	TYNE & WEAR
Newnham Bridge	WORCESTERSHIRE
Newnham-on-Severn	GLOUCESTERSHIRE
Newport	SHROPSHIRE
Newquay	CORNWALL
Newton	POWYS
North Hykeham	LINCOLNSHIRE
North Tawton	DEVON
North Walsham	NORFOLK
Northallerton	NORTH YORKSHIRE
Norwich	NORFOLK
Oakamoor	STAFFORDSHIRE
Oakham	LEICESTERSHIRE
Oban	ARGYLL & BUTE
Okehampton	DEVON
Ombersley	WORCESTERSHIRE
Onich	HIGHLANDS (SOUTH)
Oswestry	SHROPSHIRE
Otterton	DEVON
Ottery St Mary	DEVON
Oxford	OXFORDSHIRE
Oxted	SURREY
Padstow	CORNWALL
Paignton	DEVON
Pathhead	EDINBURGH & LOTHIANS
Peasenhall	SUFFOLK
Peebles	BORDERS
Penrith	CUMBRIA
Penryn	CORNWALL
Penzance	CORNWALL
Perranporth	CORNWALL
Perth	PERTH & KINROSS
Peterborough	LINCOLNSHIRE
Petersfield	HAMPSHIRE
Pickering	NORTH YORKSHIRE
Pilling	LANCASHIRE
Plockton	HIGHLANDS (MID)
Plymouth	DEVON
Polzeath	CORNWALL
Pontefract	WEST YORKSHIRE
Porlock	SOMERSET
Port Isaac	CORNWALL
Portland	DORSET
Portree	ISLE OF SKYE
Portsmouth	HAMPSHIRE
Portsoy	ABERDEEN, BANFF & MORAY
Powerstock	DORSET
Pwllheli	ANGLESEY & GWYNEDD
Quainton	BUCKINGHAMSHIRE
Rackheath	NORFOLK
Raglan	SOUTH WALES
Ravenglass	CUMBRIA
Reading	BERKSHIRE
Redhill	SURREY
Rhos-on-Sea	NORTH WALES
Richmond	NORTH YORKSHIRE
Rickmansworth	HERTFORDSHIRE
Rilla Mill	CORNWALL
Ringwood	HAMPSHIRE
Robin Hood's Bay	NORTH YORKSHIRE
Ropley	HAMPSHIRE
Roseland Peninsula	CORNWALL
Roslin	EDINBURGH & LOTHIANS
Ross-on-Wye	HEREFORDSHIRE
Rye	EAST SUSSEX
St Agnes	CORNWALL
St Andrews	FIFE
St Austell	CORNWALL
St Bride's Wentloog	SOUTH WALES
St Cleer	CORNWALL
St Ives	CORNWALL
St Leonards-on-Sea	EAST SUSSEX
St Neots	CAMBRIDGESHIRE
Salcombe	DEVON
Salisbury	WILTSHIRE
Sandown	ISLE OF WIGHT
Sandy	BEDFORDSHIRE
Saundersfoot	PEMBROKESHIRE
Scarborough	NORTH YORKSHIRE
Scunthorpe	LINCOLNSHIRE

Selsey	WEST SUSSEX	Tolpuddle	DORSET
Sennen	CORNWALL	Tomatin	HIGHLANDS (SOUTH)
Shaldon	DEVON	Torquay	DEVON
Shanklin	ISLE OF WIGHT	Torrington	DEVON
Shap	CUMBRIA	Totland Bay	ISLE OF WIGHT
Shepton Mallet	SOMERSET	Trefriw	NORTH WALES
Sherborne	DORSET	Troutbeck	CUMBRIA
Sheringham	NORFOLK	Tunbridge Wells	KENT
Shillingstone	DORSET		
Shrewsbury	SHROPSHIRE	Uig	ISLE OF SKYE
Sidmouth	DEVON	Ullswater	CUMBRIA
Skipton	NORTH YORKSHIRE	Umberleigh	DEVON
Solihull	WEST MIDLANDS	Uttoxeter	STAFFORDSHIRE
Souldern	OXFORDSHIRE		
South Molton	DEVON	Wadebridge	CORNWALL
Southampton	HAMPSHIRE	Wareham	DORSET
Southport	LANCASHIRE	Warkworth	NORTHUMBERLAND
Spean Bridge	HIGHLANDS (SOUTH)	Warwick	WARWICKSHIRE
Spennymoor	DURHAM	Washford	SOMERSET
Stamfordham	NORTHUMBERLAND	Watford	HERTFORDSHIRE
Stanley	DURHAM	Wells	SOMERSET
Stanley	PERTH & KINROSS	Wells-next-the-Sea	NORFOLK
Stockbridge	HAMPSHIRE	Welshpool	POWYS
Stockport	CHESHIRE	Wensleydale	NORTH YORKSHIRE
Stokesley	NORTH YORKSHIRE	West Down	DEVON
Stonehouse	GLOUCESTERSHIRE	West Runton	NORFOLK
Stornoway	ISLE OF LEWIS	Westcliff-on-Sea	ESSEX
Stow-on-the-Wold	GLOUCESTERSHIRE	Weston-super-Mare	SOMERSET
Stratford-upon-Avon	WARWICKSHIRE	Weymouth	DORSET
Strathpeffer	HIGHLANDS (MID)	Whitby	NORTH YORKSHIRE
Strathyre	PERTH & KINROSS	Whithorn	DUMFRIES & GALLOWAY
Stroud	GLOUCESTERSHIRE	Whitsand Bay	CORNWALL
Sturminster Newton	DORSET	Wicken	CAMBRIDGESHIRE
Surbiton	SURREY	Wickham	HAMPSHIRE
Sutton-in-Ashfield	NOTTINGHAMSHIRE	Winchcombe	GLOUCESTERSHIRE
Swaffham	NORFOLK	Winchelsea	EAST SUSSEX
Swanage	DORSET	Winchester	HAMPSHIRE
Swansea	SOUTH WALES	Windermere	CUMBRIA
Swindon	WILTSHIRE	Windsor	BERKSHIRE
		Winster	DERBYSHIRE
Talgarth	POWYS	Wisbech	CAMBRIDGESHIRE
Talyllyn	ANGLESEY & GWYNEDD	Witney	OXFORDSHIRE
Tamworth	STAFFORDSHIRE	Wiveliscombe	SOMERSET
Tarbert	ARGYLL & BUTE	Wolverhampton	WEST MIDLANDS
Taunton	SOMERSET	Wood Walton	CAMBRIDGESHIRE
Teign Valley	DEVON	Woodbridge	SUFFOLK
Telford	SHROPSHIRE	Woodbury	DEVON
Tenby	PEMBROKESHIRE	Woodchester	GLOUCESTERSHIRE
Tenterden	KENT	Woodhall Spa	LINCOLNSHIRE
Tetsworth	OXFORDSHIRE	Woodstock	OXFORDSHIRE
Tewkesbury	GLOUCESTERSHIRE	Woodton	NORFOLK
Theale	SOMERSET	Worthing	WEST SUSSEX
Thirsk	NORTH YORKSHIRE	Wroxham	NORFOLK
Thornton-le-Dale	NORTH YORKSHIRE	Wyton	CAMBRIDGESHIRE
Thorpe Fendykes	LINCOLNSHIRE		
Tideswell	DERBYSHIRE	Yelverton	DEVON
Tintagel	CORNWALL	York	NORTH YORKSHIRE
Tiverton	DEVON		

THE FHG DIPLOMA

HELP IMPROVE
BRITISH TOURIST STANDARDS

You are choosing holiday accommodation from our very popular FHG Publications.
Whether it be a hotel, guest house, farmhouse or self-catering accommodation, we think you will find it hospitable, comfortable and clean, and your host and hostess friendly and helpful.

Why not write and tell us about it?

As a recognition of the generally well-run and excellent holiday accommodation reviewed in our publications, we at FHG Publications Ltd. present a diploma to proprietors who receive the highest recommendation from their guests who are also readers of our Guides. If you care to write to us praising the holiday you have booked through FHG Publications Ltd. – whether this be board, self-catering accommodation, a sporting or a caravan holiday, what you say will be evaluated and the proprietors who reach our final list will be contacted.

The winning proprietor will receive an attractive framed diploma to display on his premises as recognition of a high standard of comfort, amenity and hospitality. FHG Publications Ltd. offer this diploma as a contribution towards the improvement of standards in tourist accommodation in Britain. Help your excellent host or hostess to win it!

FHG DIPLOMA

We nominate

Because

Name ....

Address...

....

Telephone No..

OTHER FHG TITLES FOR 2004

FHG Publications have a large range of attractive holiday accommodation guides for all kinds of holiday opportunities throughout Britain. They also make useful gifts at any time of year. Our guides are available in most bookshops and larger newsagents but we will be happy to post you a copy direct if you have any difficulty. POST FREE for addresses in the UK. We will also post abroad but have to charge separately for post or freight.

SELF-CATERING HOLIDAYS
in Britain
Over 1000 addresses throughout for self-catering and caravans
in Britain.

The original
Farm Holiday Guide to COAST & COUNTRY HOLIDAYS in England, Scotland, Wales and Channel Islands. Board, Self-catering, Caravans/Camping, Activity Holidays.

BRITAIN'S BEST HOLIDAYS
A quick-reference general guide for all kinds of holidays.

Recommended
WAYSIDE AND COUNTRY INNS of Britain
Pubs, Inns and small hotels.

Recommended
COUNTRY HOTELS
of Britain
Including Country Houses, for the discriminating.

Recommended
SHORT BREAK HOLIDAYS in Britain
"Approved" Accommodation for quality bargain breaks.

CHILDREN WELCOME!
Family Holidays and Days
Out guide.
Family holidays with details of
amenities for children and
babies.

The FHG Guide to
**CARAVAN & CAMPING
HOLIDAYS,**
Caravans for hire, sites and
holiday parks and centres.

PETS WELCOME!
The original and unique guide
for holidays for pet owners and
their pets.

The GOLF GUIDE –
Where to play Where to stay   £9.99
In association with GOLF MONTHLY. Over 2800 golf courses in Britain with convenient
accommodation. Holiday Golf in France, Portugal, Spain, USA, South Africa and Thailand.

Tick your choice and send your order and payment to ....

FHG PUBLICATIONS, ABBEY MILL BUSINESS CENTRE,
SEEDHILL, PAISLEY PA1 1TJ
TEL: 0141- 887 0428; FAX: 0141- 889 7204
e-mail: fhg@ipcmedia.com
Deduct 10% for 2/3 titles or copies; 20% for 4 or more.

FHG

Send to: NAME ....
            ADDRESS ....
            ....
            ....
            POST CODE ....
I enclose Cheque/Postal Order for £ ....
            SIGNATURE...DATE ....

Please complete the following to help us improve the service we provide. How
did you find out about our guides?:

☐ Press   ☐ Magazines   ☐ TV/Radio   ☐ Family/Friend   ☐ Other